THE
"BEST-OF-ALL"
COOK BOOK

THE
"BEST-OF-ALL"
COOK BOOK

Compiled and Edited by
FLORENCE BROBECK

Published by
Kingston House, Chicago
and distributed in association with
J. B. Lippincott Company, Philadelphia and New York

ACKNOWLEDGMENTS

Thanks are due to the following contributors for permission to use the material indicated:

Abelard-Schuman Limited for 3 recipes from Evelyn Patterson's *Gourmet Kitchen;*

Albyn Press for 8 recipes from *Recipes from Scotland,* by F. Marian McNeill;

American Blue Cheese Association for recipe and color photograph;

American Lamb Council for recipe and color photograph;

American Spice Trade Association for 6 recipes from *The A.B.C. of Spice Cookery,* and 5 recipes from *How to Use Spices;*

Angostura-Wuppermann Corp. for 5 recipes from *The Angostura Cook Book,* and 65 recipes from *Professional Mixing Guide;*

Appleton-Century-Crofts for 4 recipes from *Treasures of a Hundred Cooks* by Mary Allen Hulbert, copyright 1949 by Mary Allen Hulbert, reprinted by the permission of the publisher;

Bacardi Imports, Inc. for 2 recipes from *New, Easy Ways to Cook with Rum,* by Clementine Paddleford;

Bantam Books, Inc. for 2 recipes from *The Art of Jewish Cooking,* by Jennie Grossinger;

M. Barrows and Company, Inc., for 7 recipes from *The New Serve It Buffet* by Florence Brobeck, copyright © 1944, 1948 by Florence Brobeck; 8 recipes from *The New Cook It in a Casserole* by Florence Brobeck, copyright © 1955 by Florence Brobeck; 8 recipes from *Kitchens Near and Far* by Herman Smith, copyright 1944 by Herman Smith; 9 recipes from *Good Food from Sweden* by Inga Norberg, copyright 1939 by Inga Norberg; 5 recipes from *Secrets of New England Cooking* by Ella Shannon Bowles and Dorothy S. Towles, copyright 1947 by Ella Shannon Bowles and Dorothy S. Towles; 3 recipes from *A Wine Lover's Cook Book* by Jeanne Owen, copyright 1940 by Jeanne Owen; 13 recipes from *500 Recipes by Request* by Jeanne M. Hall and Belle Anderson Ebner, copyright 1948 by Jeanne M. Hall and Belle Anderson Ebner; 2 recipes from *Cooking with Curry* by Florence Brobeck, copyright 1952 by Florence Brobeck; 10 recipes from *The Home Book of Spanish Cookery* by Marina Pereyra de Azner and Nina Froud, copyright © 1956 by Marina Pereyra de Azner and Nina Froud, copyright

© 1957 by M. Barrows and Company, Inc.; by permission of M. Barrows & Company, Inc.;

The Bobbs-Merrill Company, Inc. for 14 recipes from *The New Joy of Cooking* by Irma S. Rombauer and Marion R. Becker, copyright © 1931, 1953; 9 recipes from *Marian Tracy's Complete Chicken Cookery,* copyright © 1953; used by special permission of the publishers, The Bobbs-Merrill Company, Inc.;

The Bond Wheelwright Company for 8 recipes from *The Book of Good Neighbor Recipes* by Maxine Erickson and Joan M. Rock;

Albert Bonnier, Publishers, for 8 recipes from *The Swedish Princesses Cook Book,* by Jenny Åkerström;

Bob Brown for 8 recipes from *The Vegetable Cook Book,* by Cora, Rose and Bob Brown;

California Strawberry Advisory Board for recipe and color photograph;

Campbell Soup Company for 3 recipes and color photographs;

Chilton Company for 4 recipes from *The Joy of Chinese Cooking* by Doreen Yen Hung Fan; and 10 recipes from *The Gold Cook Book* by Louis P. de Gouy;

P. F. Collier & Son Corporation for 16 recipes from *Woman's Home Companion Cook Book* edited by Dorothy Kirk, copyright 1955 by P. F. Collier & Son Corporation;

Colonial Williamsburg, Inc. for recipe from *The Williamsburg Art of Cookery* by Mrs. Helen Bullock;

Thomas Y. Crowell Company for glossary, 6 recipes, and other material from *How to Cook Well* by Ann Roe Robbins, copyright 1946 by Ann Roe Robbins; 5 recipes from *Delicious Seafood Recipes* by Louis Garrison, copyright 1953 by Louis Garrison; 10 recipes from *501 Easy Cocktail Canapés* by Olga de Leslie Leigh, copyright 1953 by Olga de Leslie Leigh; by permission of Thomas Y. Crowell Company, New York;

Crown Publishers, Inc. for 10 recipes from *The Escoffier Cook Book* by Auguste Escoffier, American edition, copyright 1941 by Crown Publishers, Inc.; 22 recipes from *German Cookery* by Elizabeth Schuler, edited and translated by Joy Gary, copyright 1955 by Crown Publishers, Inc.; 17 recipes from *The Talisman Italian Cook Book* by Ada Boni, translated by Matilde La Rosa, copyright 1950 by Crown Publishers, Inc.; used by permission of the publisher;

Dorothy E. Crozier for 10 recipes and comments from *Egg Cookery* by Lily H. Wallace;

Recipe from *Culinary Arts Institute's Holiday Cookbook,* © Book Production Industries, Inc.;

Diamond Walnut Growers, Inc. for 2 recipes and color photographs;

Doubleday & Company, Inc. for 4 recipes from *The Brown Derby Cook Book,* copyright 1949 by The Brown Derby Service Corporation; 2 recipes from *Trader Vic's Book of Food and Drink,* copyright 1946 by Doubleday & Company, Inc.; 4 recipes from *The Fine Art of Mixing Drinks* by David A. Embury, copyright 1948 by David A. Embury; 10 recipes from *The Complete Book of Home Baking* by Ann Serranne, copyright 1950 by Doubleday & Company, Inc.; 3 recipes from the book *The Glamour Magazine After Five Cook Book* by Beverly Pepper, copyright 1952 by Beverly Pepper, copyright 1951, 1952 by The Condé Nast Publications, Inc.; 6 recipes from *The Art of Fish Cookery* by Milo Miloradovich, copyright 1949 by Milo Miloradovich; 2 recipes from *Foods of Old New England* by Marjorie Mosser, copyright © 1939, 1947, 1957 by Marjorie Mosser; 3 recipes from *The Frances Parkinson Keyes Cookbook,* copyright © 1955 by Frances Parkinson Keyes, copyright 1955 by The Condé Nast Publications; 10 recipes from *Fruit Recipes* by Riley M. Fletcher-Berry, copyright 1907 by Riley M. Fletcher-

Berry; 5 recipes from *The House of Chan Cookbook* by Sou Chan, copyright 1952 by Sou Chan; comments and 8 recipes from *The South American Cook Book,* by Cora, Rose, and Bob Brown, copyright 1939 by Cora, Rose, and Robert Carlton Brown; 4 recipes from *Real French Cooking* by Savarin, copyright © 1956 by Doubleday & Company, Inc.; 5 recipes from *Lüchow's German Cook Book* by Leonard Jan Mitchell, copyright 1952 by Leonard Jan Mitchell; 5 recipes from *The Art of Caribbean Cookery* by Carmen Aboy Valldejuli, copyright © 1957 by Carmen Aboy Valldejuli; 6 recipes from *The Art of Hungarian Cooking,* by Paula Pogany Bennett and Velma R. Clark, copyright 1954 by Doubleday & Company, Inc.; 5 recipes from *The Art of Italian Cooking* by Maria Lo Pinto, copyright 1948 by Doubleday & Company, Inc.; 10 recipes from *The Art of Cheese Cookery* by Nika Standen, copyright 1949 by Nika Standen and Florence Arfmann; by permission of Doubleday & Company, Inc.; 8 recipes from *The Peasant Cookbook* by Marian Tracy, copyright © 1955 by Marian Tracy; 9 recipes from *Carolyn Coggins' Company Cook Book,* copyright 1954 by Carolyn Coggins; by permission of Doubleday & Company, Inc. (Hanover House) ;

E. P. Dutton & Co., Inc. for 8 recipes from *French Home Cooking* by Claire de Pratz, revised by Georgia Lingafelt, copyright 1925, 1953, 1956 by E. P. Dutton & Co., Inc., reprinted by permission of the publishers;

Marion W. Flexner for 2 recipes from her book *Dixie Dishes;*

The Florence Crittenton League, Inc. for 2 recipes from *Specialty of the House;*

Ford Motor Company for 8 recipes from the *Ford Treasury of Favorite Recipes from Famous Eating Places,* Volume 2, compiled by Nancy Kennedy;

Katherine B. Gruelle for 19 recipes from her book *Hawaiian and Pacific Foods;*

Harper & Brothers for 4 recipes from *The Alice B. Toklas Cook Book,* copyright 1954 by Alice B. Toklas; 3 recipes from *Around the World in Eighty Dishes* by Lesley Blanch, copyright 1955 by Lesley Blanch Gary;

Hastings House, Publishers, Inc. for 7 recipes from *Clementine in the Kitchen* by Phineas Beck;

Hawthorn Books, Inc. for 3 recipes from *The Cape Cod Cook Book* by Peter Hunt, copyright © 1954 by Hawthorn Books, Inc., by permission of Hawthorn Books, Inc., 70 Fifth Avenue, New York, N.Y.;

Hill and Wang, Inc. for 13 recipes from *The Viennese Cookbook* by Irma Rhode;

Houghton Mifflin Company for 7 recipes and the Meal Planning Section from *The New Basic Cook Book* by Marjorie Heseltine and Ula M. Dow, copyright 1933 and 1936 by Marjorie Heseltine and Ula M. Dow, copyright 1947 and 1956 by Marjorie Heseltine and Ula Dow Keezer; 8 recipes from *Helen Corbitt's Cook Book,* copyright 1957 by Helen L. Corbitt; 7 recipes from *Thoughts for Food,* copyright 1938, 1946 by Institute Publishing Company; 11 recipes from *Thoughts for Buffets,* copyright 1958 by Institute Publishing Company; 4 recipes from *Choice Receipts* by Mrs. Thomas Bailey Aldrich; by permission of and arrangement with Houghton Mifflin Company, the authorized publishers;

Hutchinson & Co. (Publishers) Ltd. for 10 recipes from *Mme. Prunier's Fish Cookery Book,* edited by Ambrose Heath;

Institute Publishing Company for 8 recipes from *More Thoughts for Food;*

Junior League of Dallas for 4 recipes from *The Junior League of Dallas Cook Book;*

Alfred A. Knopf, Inc. for 3 recipes from *The Perfect Hostess Cook Book* by Mildred O. Knopf, copyright 1950 by Mildred O. Knopf, by permission of Alfred A. Knopf, Inc.;

Kraft Foods Company for 5 recipes from *The Cheese Cook Book* by Marye Dahnke;

The Estate of Mrs. C. F. Leyel for 8 recipes from *The Gentle Art of Cookery* by Mrs. C. F. Leyel and Miss Olga Hartley;

J. B. Lippincott Company for 6 recipes from *The Bed-Book of Eating and Drinking* by Richardson Wright, copyright 1943 by Richardson Wright; 6 recipes from *French Cooking for Americans* by Louis Diat, copyright 1946 by Louis Diat; published by J. B. Lippincott Company;

Little, Brown & Company for 16 recipes and notes from *Helen Brown's West Coast Cook Book,* copyright 1952 by Helen Evans Brown; 14 recipes from *American Regional Cookery* by Sheila Hibben, copyright 1932, 1946 by Sheila Hibben; 27 recipes from *The New Fannie Farmer Cook Book* by the Boston Cooking School; 8 recipes from *Toll House Cook Book* by Ruth Wakefield, copyright 1930, 1936, 1937, 1938, 1940, 1948, 1953 by Ruth Graves Wakefield; 6 recipes from *Herbs for the Kitchen,* by Irma Goodrich Mazza, copyright 1939 by Irma Goodrich Mazza; 13 recipes and comments from *The Cordon Bleu Cook Book* by Dione Lucas, copyright 1947 by Dione Lucas; 6 recipes from *The Book of Entrées* by Janet M. Hill, copyright 1931 by Janet McKenzie Hill, copyright 1937, 1940, 1948, 1951 by Robert B. Hill; 3 recipes from *The Holiday Candy Book* by Virginia Pasley, copyright 1952, by Virginia Pasley; 20 recipes and comments from *Smörgåsbord and Scandinavian Cookery* by Florence Brobeck and Monika Kjellberg, copyright 1948 by Little, Brown & Company; 4 recipes from *André Simon's French Cook Book,* copyright 1938 by André L. Simon, copyright 1948 by André L. Simon and Crosby Gaige; by permission of Little, Brown & Company;

London Wine and Food Society for section on how to serve wine from *Let Mine Be Wine* by André L. Simon;

George Mardikian for 9 recipes from his book, *Dinner at Omar Khayyam's;*

Meredith Publishing Company for 9 recipes and comments from *Better Homes and Gardens Cook Book;*

Julian Messner, Inc. for 20 recipes from *The New World Wide Cook Book* by Madame Metzelthin, copyright date December 1939 by Pearl V. Metzelthin, copyright assigned to Julian Messner, Inc., 1952;

Metropolitan Life Insurance Company for 5 recipes from *Metropolitan Cook Book;*

Frederick Muller, Ltd. for 11 recipes from *The Wine and Food Menu Book* by André L. Simon;

Nabisco (National Biscuit Company) for 2 recipes and color photographs;

National Macaroni Institute for recipe and color photograph;

National Pickle Packers Association for color photograph;

Oxford University Press for 6 recipes from *Tante Marie's French Pastry,* translated and adapted by Charlotte Turgeon, copyright 1954 by Oxford University Press, reprinted by permission of the publisher;

Pan-American Coffee Bureau for 16 recipes and information from *Fun with Coffee;*

Peter Pauper Press for 2 recipes from *Holiday Candies* by Edna Beilenson;

Pioneer Press for 2 recipes from *Tennessee Cook Book* by Martin Rywell; 4 recipes from *Wild Game Cook Book* by Martin Rywell;

Prentice-Hall, Inc. for 5 recipes from *Elena's Secrets of Mexican Cooking* by Elena Zelayata, copyright © 1958 by Prentice-Hall, Inc., Englewood Cliffs, N.J. Published by Prentice-Hall, Inc.;

G. P. Putnam's Sons for 10 recipes from *How to Cook and Eat in Russian,* by Alexandra Kropotkin; 20 recipes from *Edith Barber's Cook Book,* copyright 1940 by Edith Barber, by permission of G. P. Putnam's Sons;

Rand McNally & Company for 6 recipes from *European Cooking* by Herman Dedichen, reprinted by permission of Rand McNally & Company;

Anna Wetherill Reed for 7 recipes from her book, *The Philadelphia Cook Book of Town and Country;*

Rinehart & Company, Inc. for 9 recipes from *Wonderful Ways to Cook* by Edith Key Haines, copyright 1951 by Edith Key Haines, reprinted by permission of Rinehart & Company, Inc., New York, Publishers;

Roy Publishers for 9 recipes from *Old Warsaw Cook Book* by Rysia;

Settlement Cook Book Company for 30 recipes from *The Settlement Cook Book* by Mrs. Simon Kander;

Simon and Schuster, Inc. for 3 recipes from *Alexandre Dumas' Dictionary of Cuisine,* edited by Louis Colman, copyright © 1958 by Louis Colman; 3 recipes from *House and Garden's Cook Book,* copyright © 1956, 1957, 1958 by Condé Nast Publications, Inc.; reprinted by permission of Simon and Schuster, Inc.;

Spencer Press, Inc. for 4 recipes, comments, and 2 color photographs from *The American Peoples Cookbook,* copyright © 1956 by Spencer Press, Inc.;

Stephen Greene Press for 3 recipes from *The Venison Book* by Audrey A. Gorton;

Tabasco, McIlhenny and Company, for color photograph;

Tea Council of the U.S.A., Inc. for 8 tea recipes, comments and color photograph from *What You Should Know About Tea;*

Time, Inc. for 5 recipes from *Picture Cook Book,* by the Editors of *Life;*

Times-Picayune Publishing Company for 2 recipes from *The Picayune Creole Cook Book;*

Charles E. Tuttle Company for 6 recipes from *Rice and Spice* by Phyllis Jervey; 4 recipes from *The Art of Chinese Cooking* by the Benedictine Sisters of Peking; 3 recipes from *Recipes from the East* by Irma Walker Ross; 16 recipes and suggestions from *Hibachi Cooking in the American Manner* by George E. Engler;

United Rum Merchants Ltd. for 3 recipes from *Rum in the Kitchen* by Iris Styrett;

United States Committee for the United Nations for 4 recipes from *Favorite Recipes from the United Nations,* edited and tested by the American Home Economics Association;

May B. Van Ardsdale for 5 recipes and 2 charts from *Our Candy Recipes, and Other Confections,* by May B. Van Ardsdale and Ruth Parrish Casa Emellos;

The White Turkeys for 4 recipes from *Let's Talk Turkey* by F. Meredith Dietz;

Women's National Press Club for 3 recipes from *Who Says We Can't Cook!* by members of the Women's National Press Club.

FOREWORD

AN ANTHOLOGY of cook books is something like a big Christmas pudding. The best of everything in the kitchen goes into the pudding. And the best of more than a hundred cook books has gone into this anthology. Some are old books, treasured for the cookery of the South or the Midwest, or for great dinners given by long-ago hostesses. Such books are no longer available unless you can hunt them down in second-hand shops or find them at auctions. Other books in this anthology are very new, sparkling with modern ideas on diet as well as on home entertaining.

Some of the more than a hundred books come from Europe, Mexico, South America, and Asia, their savory dishes fragrant on the printed page; and triumphs of subtle flavoring and inspired cookery when tried in our kitchens. There are books in this anthology written by home economists and nutritionists, by food columnists and newspaper cookery editors. Books by women's magazine food editors, by great chefs, by famous hosts and hostesses and party specialists. Books by the owners of restaurants, inns, club dining-rooms in America and from many other places around the world. Books by travelers who have journeyed around the world in quest of unusual dishes. And, of course, some of the great books of European gastronomy are included.

From the book written by two well-known nutritionists, this anthology includes all the information needed by young home-makers on planning day-by-day meals and providing adequate nutrition for their families. For these young cooks as well as for the more experienced homemakers the selections from the one hundred and twenty-four cook books include such basic method-instruction as how to bake breads and cakes, prepare poultry and sea food, meats and game. Superb cheese dishes, pastas, unusual soups and salads are selections from the best of all Italian and Spanish cook books. There are appetizers and first-course dishes from French, Italian, Russian, Scandinavian, and Spanish books as well as from fabulous American hostess cook books.

The desserts are truly international, culled from books published in Austria, England, France, Hawaii, Hungary, and Italy as well as from South America, and masterpieces from recent American cook books. There are more than one thousand recipes. Over three hundred of these recipes are marked with a star for beginner cooks of all ages and especially for teen-age chefs. Page after page, there are answers to questions which arise in home-meal planning and cookery. These pages contain treasures of time-tested recipes, from very simple basic dishes to elaborate concoctions from the carefully selected old and new books.

From an English cook book in this anthology, this definition of cookery, by the nineteenth-century author, art critic, and social reformer—John Ruskin—"Cookery means carefulness and inventiveness, willingness, and readiness of appliances. It means the economy of your grandmothers and the science of the modern chemist; it means much tasting and no wasting; it means English thoroughness and French art and Arabian hospitality."

And from a nineteenth-century cook book published in Minnesota, this caution to homemakers of that day: "Bad dinners go hand in hand with total depravity, while a properly fed man is already half saved."

FLORENCE BROBECK,
New York, January, 1960

CONTENTS

Glossary

Absorbent Paper. Any paper that is porous and will therefore absorb moisture. Used mostly in cooking to drain grease from such foods as bacon and sausage. Plain brown wrapping paper or paper toweling are the simplest ones to use in the kitchen; paper with a smooth or glazed surface is not absorbent.

A La King. Food served in a rich cream sauce, usually seasoned with mushrooms, green pepper, and pimiento, and often flavored with sherry.

Anchovy. A tiny fish, with a distinctive flavor, member of the herring family. It is smoked and then either packed in fillets or whole in oil, or made into a paste.

Antipasto. Italian appetizers or hors d'oeuvre. An assortment of small portions of several foods, such as salami, tomato, deviled eggs, sardines, anchovies, and spiced beets. A diversity of fish, meats, and vegetables is used, all cold and spicy.

Arrowroot. A finely powdered starch, used for thickening in the same way cornstarch and flour are used. It comes from the root of a tropical plant and, since it is not so easy to obtain as ordinary thickeners, its use is not prevalent. However, it is easily digested and, so, is good for preparing food for invalids and infants.

Aspic. Jelly made from concentrated meat stock which is strong enough to stiffen when it is cold. The jelly is well seasoned, transparent, and used to give a shiny coat to meat and other foods. The word is also used for seasoned stock such as tomato juice, fish broth, and fruit juice which has been thickened with gelatin.

Au Gratin. Most of us think of any food that is cooked *au gratin* as a scalloped dish (meat, fish, or vegetables in a cream sauce), with cheese topping, and that it is the cheese which gives it the name *au gratin*. Actually the word is based on the French *gratiner,* which means to brown, and it applies to any dish which is topped with bread crumbs (usually buttered and often mixed with grated cheese), and browned either in the oven or under the broiler.

Bake. To bake is to cook food in the oven, at an even temperature, with dry heat. The term applies to all foods except meat; cooking all meat (except ham) in the oven is called *roasting* rather than *baking.*

Bar-le-Duc. A well-flavored jelly

which is often served with cream cheese or cottage cheese and crackers for dessert. Originally it was made from white currants, but now various fruits such as gooseberries, strawberries, and other berries are used.

Baste. To keep food moistened by spooning liquid or fat over the surface while it is cooking. The basting liquid may be melted fat, meat drippings, or a special sauce.

Batter. A mixture of flour, liquid, and other ingredients to be baked, such as pancakes, muffins, cakes and cookies. Generally speaking, a batter is thin enough to be mixed with a spoon, in contrast to dough mixed by hand.

Beat. To stir food well, which can be done in several ways. A spoon can be used, in a regular movement in which the spoon makes a circular path, continually bringing the under part to the surface. A rotary beater or electric mixer can do the work with less muscular strain and more efficiency.

Bind. To thicken various liquids such as soup, gravy, sauce, and stew. This is done to prevent separating, or to make the liquid more palatable. The thickening agents may be flour, cornstarch, or eggs (either whole eggs or yolks only).

Bisque. A thick cream soup usually made with a shellfish base. Or a frozen cream dessert with macaroon crumbs or chopped nuts added.

Blanch. This word comes from the French *blanche,* which means white; and to blanch is to whiten. In cooking it means to pour boiling water over food, after which the food is sometimes drained and plunged into cold water. This is done to nuts to facilitate the removal of the skins. Foods such as sweetbreads and calves' brains are put first into boiling water, then into ice water to firm and whiten them.

Blend. To combine two or more ingredients so that they are well mixed and intermingled. Blending is usually a quick process, done in a few seconds with a mixing spoon.

Boil. To cook in a liquid which is boiling. At sea level, the boiling point is 212 degrees F. It decreases about 1 degree F. for every 500 feet of elevation, so that at 1000 feet it is 210 degrees F., and so forth. When liquid boils, it is full of bubbles which break on the surface. Slow boiling is just as effective as rapid boiling.

Bouquet Garni. A bunch of mixed herbs used for seasoning. They may be tied together or put into a small cheesecloth bag for easy removal.

Braise. To cook food, usually meat, by first browning on all sides in a small amount of fat, then adding a little liquid and cooking at low temperature in a tightly covered utensil either in the oven or on top of the stove.

Bread. To bread is to cover food with a bread coating before cooking. The coating can be just dry bread crumbs, or the food may be dipped first in beaten egg and then in crumbs, corn meal, or flour.

Brine. A solution of water and salt, with sufficient salt to saturate or strongly impregnate the water.

Brochette. Brochette is the French word for skewer, and any food *en* *brochette* is cooked on a skewer. This same type of food is called a shish kebab, also shashlik.

Broiling. Broiling is cooking food with the heat applied directly on it. This means that it is cooked either under the heat of a broiler or over hot coals. In most ranges there is a broiling oven, with the heat overhead; the food is placed a few inches below the heat and the top surface is cooked by direct heat. Broiling is also done out-of-doors, or over an open fire, with the food placed in a special broiling rack which leaves all sides open so that the heat can be applied directly to the surface.

Broth. Clear stock which results from boiling meat, chicken, shellfish, mushrooms, and vegetables.

Brush. To cover lightly with a liquid such as melted butter, milk, cream and egg whites. This is best done with a pastry brush, although a small piece of crushed paper or a cloth can be used.

Café Au Lait. Coffee mixed half and half with hot milk.

Canapé. Literally, the French word for couch or sofa; used for small appetizers to be served with cocktails; consists of small pieces of fried or toasted bread covered with various toppings.

Canard. The French word for duck.

Candy. "To candy" is used in two ways. Candied fruits are cooked in a heavy sugar syrup, drained, dried and usually rolled in sugar. Candied or glazed vegetables are cooked over slow heat with sugar and butter until a dark syrup coating is formed.

Capon. A male chicken that was castrated when young. Capons grow larger than the average chicken. Their weight runs from 7 to 10 pounds, but they still have tender, well-flavored meat.

Caramel. The brown syrup which forms when sugar is cooked very slowly in a heavy pan. It melts and develops the characteristic caramel flavor and golden-brown color.

Casserole. Originally, this word meant a French copper saucepan or glazed earthenware dish in which food was cooked and then served. Now it refers to any baking dish made of glass, earthenware pottery, china, copper, or aluminum in which food can be both cooked and served. It also refers to the actual food cooked in such a dish.

Caviar. The roe (eggs) of sturgeon or other fish. The most famous and best caviar comes from Russian sturgeon, which have large black eggs. There is also a red caviar which is salmon roe. Caviar is eaten as a canapé with cocktails, or as a first course, usually served with chopped hard-cooked egg, chopped onion, and lemon juice. Also used to garnish stuffed hard-cooked egg salads.

Chantilly. A castle north of Paris. The name was originally given to cakes that were scooped out, filled with preserved fruit, and topped with whipped cream. Now the name applies to any dish that has whipped cream as one of the ingredients, usually on the top.

Cheese. A protein food which is made from the curd of whole, partly skimmed, or skimmed milk. It is salted, and sometimes cured by the use of bacteria or molds. Formerly, many cheeses came only from foreign countries such as France, Switzerland, and Holland, but now many excellent varieties are made in this country.

The standard cheese found almost everywhere is known by various names: Cheddar, American, store, or "rat" (because it is used to bait mouse traps). It is solid yellow, well flavored, and useful in many ways. It does have a very pronounced flavor. Milder cheese, such as Swiss, is better with some of the delicately flavored foods. There is a wide variety of cheeses from various countries, and here are some of the better known ones: American or Cheddar, bleu, Brie, Camembert, Cheshire, cottage, pot cheese (this is not cured), cream (also not cured), Edam, Gorgonzola, Gouda, Gruyère, Liederkranz, Limburger, mysost, Neufchâtel, Parmesan, pineapple (Cheddar in the shape of a pineapple), Roquefort, sage, stilton, and Swiss.

Chill. To leave food in the refrigerator or any other cold place for several hours, or until it is thoroughly cold.

Chop. To cut food up into small pieces. This should be done with a sharp knife or with a food chopper in a regular chopping bowl.

Chowder. A thick unstrained soup, usually with salt pork, potatoes, and onions as a base. Generally made with shellfish such as clams, although sometimes made with vegetables.

Cider. Juice pressed from apples and variously processed. Used as a beverage and for making vinegar.

Clarify. To clarify is a term used in connection with fat, and means to make it pure and clear. Butter is occasionally clarified when it is used as a sauce. Cooking fat that is used for deep-fat frying several times should be clarified to remove sediment. Add some boiling water to the fat when it is almost cold, stir well, and then let cool. The fat will collect in a cake on the top, which you can lift out. Scrape off the sediment which has collected on the bottom of the cake. Reheat as needed.

Coat. To completely cover a surface with a specified mixture. The term is often used in connection with food prepared for frying.

Cobbler. A form of deep-dish fruit pie, made with a thick layer of fruit, topped with rich biscuit dough instead of pie crust.

Cocktail. (1) A drink made with mixed alcoholic beverages, or liquor and fruit juice. (2) An appetizer or first course made with fruit or vegetable juice. (3) A first course consisting of mixed fruits, or shellfish served with a tart sauce.

Coddle. To cook in water which is below the boiling point. The use of the term is confined to eggs primarily, but sometimes refers to fruits.

Combine. To mix or blend two or more ingredients together. Combining is a short affair, taking only a few seconds as a rule.

Compote. Stewed fruit, usually more than one kind, cooked in heavy sugar syrup to retain the shape of the fruit. The word is also used for dishes in which fruit, candy, or preserves are served.

Condiment. A general term for substances that are used to season and add flavor to food. They can either be added directly, such as salt, pepper, spices and herbs, or served with it, such as bottled sauces, relishes, and pickles.

Consommé. A clear, light-colored soup, usually made with chicken and beef, and well seasoned.

Cordon Bleu. Originally this was a rosette of dark blue ribbon awarded to highly skilled cooks during the days of the French kings, Charles II and Louis XV. Today it is the name of a famous cooking school in Paris, and people who can boast of a *cordon bleu* have attended it.

Corn meal. Corn meal is a preparation made from ground corn, used for making cornbread and other baked goods.

Corn Syrup. A sweet syrup, made from cornstarch, which is used for various desserts. It is not as sweet as sugar, molasses, and maple syrup, but both the light and dark varieties are widely used because of their thick, smooth consistency.

Court Bouillon. This is a highly seasoned liquid used for cooking fish and shellfish. The base is water, and the seasonings are many and varied, and they impart their flavor to the fish.

Cracklings. The crisp brown bits of pork left when the fat has been rendered from diced salt pork. Also the crisp top crust of a roast of pork.

Cream (noun). The rich part of milk, containing a high percentage of butter fat, which rises to the top when milk is left standing. It is sold as heavy cream when the butter-fat content is 30 to 40 percent and will whip; as light (or coffee) cream, when the butter-fat content is 18 to 22 percent and will not whip.

Cream (verb). This term is always used in cooking in connection with fat. Fat is "creamed" for cake batter and various baked dishes, used either alone or with sugar. Creaming actually means mixing and softening. Use a large mixing spoon or wooden spoon, mash the fat against the side of the bowl with the back of a spoon until it is soft enough to stir. Then stir the fat until it is of a soft, creamy, fluffy consistency. The fat is easier to cream if it stands at room temperature until softened, but it must not be melted over heat. An electric mixer may be used.

Cream Sauce. A white sauce made with butter (or other fat), flour, milk or cream, and salt and pepper.

Creole. Most of the Creoles in this country live in Louisiana. They are descendants of the early French and Spanish settlers. They developed a distinctive regional cuisine, characterized by seasonings that are high and varied, but subtle. A Creole sauce is a mixture of tomatoes, onions, green peppers, and other seasonings.

Crisp. To restore crispness to wilted or soggy food, either by soaking the food in cold water (vegetables), or warming it in a slow oven to dry out moisture (cereals, crackers, melba toast).

Croquettes. The word comes from a French verb meaning to crunch. Croquettes should always have a crisp crust. They consist of a mixture of cooked chopped food (meat, eggs, fish, cheese, vegetables or chicken), blended with very thick cream sauce, shaped into cones or small balls or rolls, coated with egg and bread crumbs, and fried golden brown.

Croustade. A toasted bread case used as a container for foods like creamed chicken, creamed oysters, and creamed dried beef.

Crouton. The French word for crust. Croutons are small cubes of bread which are either toasted or fried in butter.

Cube. To cut various meats, vegetables, and bread into small squares.

Curdle. Curdling is a physical change which sometimes takes place when an acid is mixed with eggs or milk; the mixture coagulates and becomes a combination of some thick and some watery-looking portions. The complaint with curdling is the appearance of the food. It is still edible but the food looks unappetizing. Sometimes beating the mixture with a rotary beater restores the smooth appearance. Curdling can be usually avoided if foods likely to curdle are brought just to boiling and then removed from heat.

Curry. A highly flavored condiment of Indian origin, made by grinding several spices together.

Custard. A mixture of eggs and milk, usually sweetened, and flavored with vanilla, almond extract, or other flavorings. There are two kinds of custard: soft, or *boiled*, custard, which is stirred while it is cooked, such as a custard sauce; and firm, *baked* custard, which is cooked without stirring.

Cut. To cut into small slices, dice or bits with a sharp knife or kitchen scissors.

Cut and Fold. This is a gentle motion used to incorporate egg whites into another mixture without breaking the air bubbles. Use a spoon or wire whisk. Cut straight down, then turn the spoon to a horizontal position and slide it across the bottom of the dish and up at one side, turning the mixture over as you do so. You actually fold the mixture over itself rather than beat or stir it.

Cut in Shortening. This term is used for a step in making biscuits, pie crust, and other pastry. Cold solid shortening is added to the flour and then mixed with it so that the shortening is separated into small particles about the size of a pea bean. This is done with two knives or a pastry blender.

Cutlet. (1) A thinly sliced piece of meat, usually veal, cooked until it is covered with a brown crust. (2) Chopped meat, fish or poultry, combined with a thick cream sauce, shaped into cutlet form breaded, then fried or grilled.

Demitasse. The French for "half cup." Small after-dinner cups of black coffee which hold about 4 ounces in contrast to the 6 to 8 ounces of tea and coffee cups.

Deviled. Food cooked with hot seasonings such as mustard and pepper. Sometimes there is a special sauce, either combined with the food or used as a basting liquid.

Dice. The words *dice* and *cube* are used interchangeably. Both mean to cut into small cubes, usually with a sharp knife.

Dissolve. To melt completely, so

that the solid food to be dissolved vanishes entirely in the liquid.

Dot. To cover the surface of food with small bits of fat, usually butter then, as the fat melts in cooking, it spreads over the entire top.

Dough. A mixture of flour, liquid, and other ingredients, used for breads, cakes, and cookies. A soft dough can sometimes be stirred, but some doughs are too heavy to be beaten with a spoon and must be manipulated with the hands (kneaded).

Dredge. To cover a surface completely with dry ingredients, such as flour and sugar. Either sprinkle the dry ingredient over the surface with a spoon, or (if it is flour) roll the solid substance thoroughly in flour, then shake off any excess.

Drippings. Drippings are pan gravy, the fat and juices rendered from meat and poultry when they are cooked.

Dumplings. Dumplings are a form of bread, made with flour, baking powder, liquid and other ingredients. They are either steamed in stew gravy or soups (stew dumplings) or in sweet syrup (dessert dumplings).

Dust. To cover a surface very lightly, usually with flour or sugar. A dusting is the merest sprinkling, so that the top surface is still visible. This is in contrast to dredging, when the entire surface is covered with an even thick crust.

Eclair. An oblong pastry made with popover and cream-puff type batter which produces a shell, hollow in the center. The hollow is filled with whipped cream or custard, a second shell inverted over it, and the top iced with chocolate, coffee, vanilla or mocha icing.

Emulsion. Small globules of one liquid suspended within another, forming a homogeneous whole; such as French dressing, mayonnaise and similar dressings.

Entrée. In most meals today, the entrée is just another name for the main-course dish. In a formal dinner, the entrée is a light savory course served between the fish and the main course or roast.

Fats. This is a general term for the various fats used on the table and in cooking. It includes butter, lard, bacon fat, vegetable shortenings, drippings, oils, and margarine.

Fillet. A boneless and usually skinless piece of meat or fish; usually a choice cut.

Flake. To break apart lightly into small pieces; usually done with a fork. The term is generally used in connection with fish. Any odd bits of skin and bone are removed at the same time.

Flavoring Extract. Products used to add flavor to various dishes, generally desserts. Among the most useful extracts are vanilla, almond, orange, lemon, and maple.

Florentine. The name given to a dish, one of the ingredients being spinach.

Fold. See CUT AND FOLD.

Fondue. A dish made with eggs, cheese, and milk. Sometimes bread crumbs are added; sometimes the dish is baked.

Fowl. A large chicken, and also usually an ancient one, which is well flavored but must be cooked with long, slow, moist cooking to be tender.

Frappé. A frozen or iced mixture or drink. Either sweet fruit juices frozen until mushy and served in glasses or drinks like crème de menthe, filled with shaved ice.

Fricassee. The word comes from the French *fricasser,* meaning to fry. It applies usually to chicken, although lamb, veal, and rabbit are also fricasseed. The meat is cut into pieces, usually browned, and then stewed and combined with a rich, thick gravy; sometimes the browning is done after the meat is stewed.

Fritters. Various foods combined with a batter, and fried in deep or shallow fat until the crust is crisp and brown.

Fry. To cook in fat, on the top of the stove. If the food is cooked in a small amount of fat, the method is often called sautéing or pan-frying. If the fat is hot and deep enough to cover the food entirely, it is called deep-fat or French frying.

Game. Wild birds or animals used for food: wild duck, wild turkey, grouse, partridge, woodcock, pheasant, venison, wild goose, and quail.

Garnish. To decorate food to make it more attractive; parsley and water cress are familiar garnishes which add both color and flavor.

Gelatin. A substance used to thicken various foods. It is sold in powdered form, usually in packages each holding 1 tablespoon of gelatin, which will solidify about 1 pint of liquid.

Giblets. The liver, heart, and gizzard of poultry.

Glacé. A term applied to any food that has a shiny, clear, hard coating. Glacé nuts are cooked in a thin sugar syrup to the crack stage (when a little dropped into a cup of cold water hardens instantly and breaks); glacé pastries have a shiny frosting.

Goulash. The Hungarian name for a thick meat stew, made with beef or veal and seasoned with vegetables and paprika.

Grate. To break up food into small particles by rubbing it across a grater.

Gravy. A liquid mixture of fat, flour, liquid, and seasonings.

Grill. To broil food (usually meat) over an open fire or under a broiling unit in a range.

Grind. To break food into small bits by running it through a meat grinder equipped with either a fine or coarse cutting blade.

Guava. A fruit grown in semitropical countries, which in the United States is seldom seen fresh. It is, however, available canned and in delicious jelly.

Gumbo. A thick, well-seasoned stew or main-course dish, made with various combinations of ingredients. Always contains either okra or filé powder (dried sassafras) or both.

Herb. Culinary herbs are plants which have aromatic leaves or seeds used for seasoning food. There are also medicinal herbs and sweet herbs (such as lavender and lemon verbena) used for their fragrance.

Hors D'Oeuvre. A French term meaning literally "entirely outside the mark"; it refers to: (1) various appetizers, other than canapés, served with cocktails before a meal, such as celery, olives, small smoked sausages; (2) a first course consisting of a variety of salty, tart, and crisp foods such as smoked fish, eggs, spiced vegetables, served in separate dishes. Each person selects a little of whatever appeals to him.

Infusion. A liquid extract obtained by pouring boiling water over the material (tea, coffee, herbs), and letting it steep until the flavor is extracted.

Junket. A milk dessert, used to a great extent for infants and children, which is thickened by rennet, an easily digested enzyme extract.

Kirsch. This is also called kirschwasser and literally means cherry water. It is a cherry cordial, made from morello cherries, used to flavor fruit desserts and other dishes.

Kisses. Meringue-like cookies and candies of which the chief ingredients are well-beaten egg whites and sugar.

Kitchen Bouquet. A commerical product useful in gravy making. It is a dark brown liquid and adds both color and flavor to the gravy.

Knead. To work dough with your hands.

Lard. (1) The fat rendered from a slaughtered hog. The finest kind is "leaf lard," made from fat surrounding the kidneys. (2) To add fat to lean meat, either by laying strips of salt pork or bacon over the top, or by inserting small pieces of fat (salt pork or bacon) right into the meat, by slipping them into gashes with a knife or special larding needle.

Leaven. To make a dough or batter porous and light. There are various leavening agents: yeast, baking powder, baking soda, and eggs.

Macédoine. A French word meaning medley, or hodgepodge of cut-up vegetables or fruits.

Maître D'Hôtel. A French term meaning head steward or cook. In culinary phrases the term applies to a sauce containing butter, lemon juice, and minced parsley, usually served on fish or vegetables.

Marinade. A well-seasoned liquid mixture, usually made with oil and an acid mixture (vinegar, wine, or fruit juices) in which food is marinated.

Marinate. To soak for a period of time in a marinade, often French dressing or a wine mixture. Use enough liquid to cover the food entirely, leaving it to soak for a period ranging from a few hours to several days. The food absorbs flavor from the marinade. It is also claimed that the acid in most marinades helps tenderize the meat.

Mask. To coat or completely cover one food with a layer of mayonnaise, whipped cream, a thick sauce, or a jelly, or aspic.

Meat Extract. Concentrated meat essence (usually beef), sold in solid form in small jars. It does not have much food value but does have excellent flavor and is useful for seasoning.

Meringue. A mixture of stiffly beaten egg whites and sugar (and a pinch of cream of tartar added for a good stiff meringue), used as a topping for pies, cakes, and various desserts. Also a cakelike mixture made of well-beaten egg whites and sugar, flavored with vanilla or almond extract, and baked until firm. Used as a shell or tart for ice cream, fruit, and custards.

Mince. To cut up or chop very fine.

Mocha. A flavoring made with coffee infusion. Often chocolate is added. Also a variety of coffee from Arabia.

Mousse. Desserts made with sweetened whipped cream and other ingredients, frozen without stirring. Also gelatin dishes made with cream and finely chopped vegetables, fish, chicken, and other ingredients.

Pan-broil. To cook foods in a hot pan, with no additional fat or just enough to keep the food from sticking, so that the cooking somewhat resembles broiling. The pan should be hot, the fat poured off as it accumulates, so cooking is more like broiling than frying.

Parboil. Parboiling is a preliminary cooking. It means to boil for a short time, not long enough to cook the food completely.

Pare. To cut off the outside covering as thinly as possible; usually done with a small sharp knife called a paring knife.

Pasta. An Italian word meaning paste. It refers to such foods as spaghetti, noodles, and macaroni, made with a flour-and-water dough.

Pastry Bag. A cone-shaped bag made of a firm fabric, so tubes may be inserted in the tip. Such mixtures as whipped cream and cake frosting can be piped through to decorate cakes and desserts. Mashed potatoes can be piped around meat dishes and planked foods.

Petit Fours. Little fancy cakes, made in special forms (squares, diamonds, rounds), and usually iced in various colors.

Piccalilli. A relish made of various ingredients, some of which may be cabbage, tomatoes, peppers, onions, celery, cucumbers, and spices.

Pilaf. A Turkish way of cooking rice or cracked processed wheat which also is used in several Central European countries.

Pilau. A Southern way of cooking rice, usually with tomatoes and various seasonings, and sometimes with meat such as ham or chicken. Term also used interchangeably with *pilaf* in America.

Poach. To cook in liquid which is below the boiling point. It is really the same as simmering, except that poached is usually applied to solid foods such as eggs, fish, and fruit which are cooked gently to keep the shape intact; *simmering* is a more general term.

Purée. The word means strained, and refers to food which is cooked until soft and pressed through a strainer, usually a fine one, so that the mixture is very smooth. The name is also given to soup which is made with strained food (usually vegetables) and thinned with cream or stock.

Quahaug. An Indian name for hard-shell clams.

Ragout. The French word for thick, well-seasoned stew.

Ramekin. A small individual baking dish, usually round and shallow, which can be used for both oven cooking and table service.

Ravigote. A French term meaning shallot sauce. The base is mayonnaise, and it is well seaoned with shallots and various herbs such as tarragon and chives; it is generally served with cold crab.

Render. To remove fat from meat by cooking slowly in a heavy pan or double boiler until the fat melts and can be drained off.

Risotto. The Italian word for rice. The term is applied to a special way of cooking rice with onion and stock, usually served with grated cheese.

Roast. Originally, to roast was to cook meat on a turning spit before or over an open fire. Now it means to cook in the oven, and the term is usually applied to meat, poultry, and game (other oven cooking is called *baking*). There are, however, a few other oven-cooked foods, such as corn, which are also roasted.

Roe. The eggs of fish, which are clustered together and encased in a very thin transparent skin. The roe which is most commonly eaten is that of sturgeon, shad, cod, carp, and mullet. Salted roe is called caviar.

Roll. To roll is a term used mainly in baking for preparing such doughs for use as pie crust, cookies, and biscuits which are rolled with a rolling pin, usually on a pastry board. It also applies to foods that are coated with flour or bread crumbs, being rolled in a large mass of the dry material.

Roux. A blended mixture of cooked fat and flour, usually in equal proportions, used to thicken liquids such as stews and soup. A white roux is cooked gently for a short time, just until the raw taste is gone from the flour but not long enough for the flour to change color. A pale roux is cooked until the flour just begins to turn color; a dark roux, long enough to brown the flour.

Saddle. A very good cut of lamb. The long saddle is loin and rump, the short saddle, loin only.

Sauté. Sauté is a French word meaning tossed in a pan or lightly fried. It is really synonymous with frying, but sautéing is gentle frying in a small amount of fat.

Savory. An English term for a course served after dessert. It is a small portion of a piquant, salty, sharp-tasting food such as anchovies on toast, cheese and mustard on toast, a hot cheese tart, which is intended to cut the dead sweet of the dessert. Also as an adjective, meaning good flavor with tang.

Scald. To heat a liquid until it is just below the boiling point. It will be hot enough so that bubbles start to appear around the sides. When scalding milk, it is best to use a double boiler because boiling milk foams up and boils over. Scalding also means to immerse a solid food in boiling liquid for a short time.

Scallop. To cook food in a casserole or baking dish. The food may be meat, fish, or vegetables, and is usually mixed with cream sauce topped with buttered bread crumbs or grated cheese or both.

Score. To cut gashes or narrow grooves along the surface of food, usually in the fat surrounding meat, to prevent the meat from curling up.

Sear. To brown the surface of meat at high temperature, either in the oven or on top of the stove in very little fat. This is supposed to seal the outside surface and keep the juices in; this theory is in some disfavor now, but it does give certain meats a good color and flavor.

Shortening. Shortening is fat used in baking. The fat makes the product tender, or "short," that is, easily broken, with a soft crumb. Any fat, either animal or vegetable, may be used for shortening.

Shred. To cut or tear food into thin strips; often done on a special cutter on the grater.

Shuck. To shuck is to remove the shells from shellfish such as oysters and clams. A shuck is the shell itself.

Sift. To put dry ingredients such as flour and sugar through a flour sifter or sieve.

Simmer. To cook in liquid which is below the boiling point. It is not actually bubbling, but the bubbles form slowly and break just below the surface, and the liquid is barely trembling.

Sliver. To cut up into very thin slices, usually lengthwise or at a slant; usually applied to nuts.

Soufflé. From the French meaning "to blow." A soufflé is a light puffy dish made with meat, vegetable, fish, fruit, and with sweet purées. it is made light, either with stiffly beaten egg whites, or for a cold dessert with whipped cream.

Spit. A device for roasting meat over an open fire. It is a pointed iron bar which holds the meat suspended over the fire, and slowly rotated so that the meat cooks evenly.

Steam. To cook food either over or surrounded by steam. This is done in a regular steamer with a perforated container placed over boiling water, also in a double boiler, or in a pressure cooker.

Steep. To extract flavor, color, and other qualities from a substance by adding boiling water and then letting the mixture stand.

Stew. To cook solid food in a small amount of liquid, usually at a gentle heat, often below the actual boiling point. A stew is a well-seasoned mixture of meat or fish with vegetables, cooked together in a small amount of liquid.

Stir. To blend ingredients together by using a circular motion. It is done either to combine two or more ingredients or to get a smooth consistency as in sauce making.

Stock. The broth in which food has been cooked; it may be meat, poultry, fish, vegetables or a combination of foods.

Suet. The hard white fat which surrounds the loin and kidney of meat animals such as beef and lamb. For most cooking purposes, beef suet is considered best.

Tapioca. A starch made from cassava. The entire supply comes from Java. Used in making desserts.

Timbale. The word literally means "kettledrum." It is a mixture of minced food such as fish, poultry, meat, or vegetables with cream sauce; usually baked in individual portions in timbale molds or custard cups. Also refers to decorative irons used in making deep-fat fried waffles and small crisp desserts.

Truffles. A type of black fungi, something like mushrooms, with an exceptionally good flavor. They grow mostly in France, under oak trees in clusters beneath the ground. Those from Pèrigord are considered among the finest.

Truss. To tie up a fowl or any other meat so that it will keep its shape while it is cooked.

Try Out. This has the same meaning as *render*.

Turbans. Fillets of fish, either

rolled up and secured with skewers or wrapped into muffin tins, filled with stuffing, and baked.
Whip. To beat various ingredients rapidly to incorporate air and increase volume. This is usually done with a rotary beater, electric mixer, fork, or wire whisk.
Vegetable Shortenings. *See* FATS.
The Glossary taken from HOW TO COOK WELL, *by Ann Roe Robbins*

Calories in Non-Alcoholic Beverages

	CALORIES
6 ounces (average table cup) tea or coffee with 1 teaspoon sugar, 1 tablespoon light cream	70
6 ounces tea, 2 teaspoons sugar, slice lemon	35
6 ounces cocoa, made with milk	220
6 ounces orange juice, fresh, frozen, or canned	85
6 ounces pineapple juice, canned	120
6 ounces lemonade, 2 teaspoons sugar	40
6 ounces (1 bottle) cola beverage	85
6 ounces whole milk	125
6 ounces buttermilk	70
6 ounces skim milk	70

Calories in Alcoholic Beverages

	QUANTITY	APPROXIMATE CALORIES
Beer (depending on alcoholic content)	12 ounces	130–189
Wines:		
Dry, red or white	4-ounce glass	111
Sweet, red or white	4-ounce glass	125
Dry sherry	3-ounce glass	124
Dry champagne	3-ounce glass	75
Whiskey	2 tablespoons, 1-ounce pony	72–84
Gin	2 tablespoons, 1-ounce pony	76–79
Rum	2 tablespoons, 1-ounce pony	96
Cordials	2 tablespoons, 1-ounce pony	97
D.O.M., chartreuse, kirsch	2 tablespoons, 1-ounce pony	101–102
Green chartreuse	2 tablespoons, 1-ounce pony	122
Martini cocktail	3 ounces	166
Manhattan cocktail	3 ounces	157

TEMPERATURE DEFINITIONS

DEGREES FAHRENHEIT

180 DEGREES F.—simmering point of water and clear liquids

212 DEGREES F.—boiling point of water

220 DEGREES F.—jellying point for jams and jellies

234 DEGREES TO 240 DEGREES F.—soft-ball stage for syrups (*a little dropped in cup of cold water forms soft ball*)

255 DEGREES F.—hard-cracked stage for syrups (*a little dropped in cup of cold water instantly hardens and can be broken or cracked*)

320 DEGREES F.—caramel stage for syrups (*a little dropped in cup of cold water hardens to caramel firmness*)

(*See also* syrup temperatures in Candy section.)

OVEN TEMPERATURES

Slow or low oven	250 DEGREES TO 300 DEGREES F.
Moderately slow oven	300 DEGREES F.
Moderate oven	325 DEGREES TO 375 DEGREES F.
Moderately hot oven	400 DEGREES F.
Hot oven	425 DEGREES TO 450 DEGREES F.
Very hot oven	450 DEGREES TO 500 DEGREES F.

BREAD-BAKING TEMPERATURES

Yeast loaf	400 TO 425 DEGREES F. OVEN	*40 to 45 minutes*
Yeast rolls	400 TO 450 DEGREES F. OVEN	*15 to 20 minutes*
Yeast rolls, sweet	350 TO 375 DEGREES F. OVEN	*15 to 20 minutes*
Biscuits	450 DEGREES F. OVEN	*12 to 15 minutes*
Muffins	400 TO 425 DEGREES F. OVEN	*20 to 25 minutes*
Popovers, start at	450 DEGREES F. OVEN	*20 minutes*
then reduce heat to	350 DEGREES F. OVEN FOR	*15 to 20 minutes*
Cornbread	400 TO 425 DEGREES F. OVEN	*20 to 30 minutes*
Nut bread	350 DEGREES F. OVEN	*50 to 75 minutes*
Gingerbread	350 DEGREES F. OVEN	*40 to 50 minutes*

CAKE-BAKING TEMPERATURES

For ready-mix cakes, follow directions on package. In general, follow recipe directions on temperatures.

Angel cake	325 DEGREES F. OVEN	*60 to 75 minutes*
Sponge cake	325 DEGREES F. OVEN	*60 to 75 minutes*
Cakes with shortening:		
Cupcakes	350 DEGREES TO 375 DEGREES F. OVEN	*20 to 25 minutes*
Layers	350 DEGREES TO 375 DEGREES F. OVEN	*25 to 35 minutes*
Loaf cake	350 DEGREES F. OVEN	*50 to 60 minutes*
Sheet cake	375 DEGREES TO 400 DEGREES F. OVEN	*20 to 30 minutes*
Fruit cake	250 DEGREES TO 275 DEGREES F. OVEN	*2 to 4 hours*

MEASUREMENTS

"Few grains" *equal* less than 1/8 teaspoon
3 teaspoons *equal* 1 tablespoon
4 tablespoons *equal* 1/4 cup
8 tablespoons *equal* 1/2 cup
16 tablespoons *equal* 1 cup
2 cups *equal* 1 pint
2 pints *equal* 1 quart
4 quarts *equal* 1 gallon

DEEP-FAT FRYING CHART

Time and temperatures vary with kind of fat. In general, follow recipes.

Croquettes of		
cooked food	375 DEGREES TO 385 DEGREES F.	*2 to 4 minutes*
uncooked food	370 DEGREES F.	*5 to 6 minutes*
Doughnuts	375 DEGREES F.	*2 to 3 minutes*
Fritters	365 DEGREES TO 375 DEGREES F.	*2 to 5 minutes*
French-fried		
potatoes	370 DEGREES F.	*5 to 7 minutes*
then		
increase heat to	390 DEGREES F.	*1½ minutes*
Oysters	375 DEGREES F.	*1 to 2 minutes*

PIE-BAKING CHART

Pastry shell	450 DEGREES F. OVEN for	*12 to 15 minutes*
Custard pie, starts at	450 DEGREES F. OVEN for	*10 minutes*
then reduce heat to	325 DEGREES F. OVEN for	*25 minutes*
Two-crust pie with cooked filling	425 DEGREES TO 450 DEGREES F. OVEN	*25 to 35 minutes*
Two-crust pie with uncooked filling start at	450 DEGREES F. OVEN for	*10 minutes*
then reduce heat to	350 DEGREES F. OVEN and bake	*30 to 40 minutes*

COOKIE-BAKING CHART

Bars, strips, squares	350 DEGREES F. OVEN	*25 to 30 minutes*
Drop cookies	350 DEGREES TO 400 DEGREES F. OVEN	*10 to 15 minutes*
Rolled, cut with cookie cutter	375 DEGREES TO 400 DEGREES F. OVEN	*8 to 12 minutes*
Refrigerator cookies, thinly sliced	375 DEGREES TO 400 DEGREES F. OVEN	*7 to 10 minutes*

CANS AND THEIR CONTENTS

The labels of cans or jars of identical size may show a net weight for one product that differs slightly from the net weight on the label of another product, due to the difference in the density of the food. For example, pork-and-beans (1 pound), blueberries (14 ounces), in the same size can.

APPROXIMATE NET WEIGHT	APPROXIMATE CUPS
8 ounces	1
10½ ounces (also called Picnic)	1¼
12 ounces	1½
1 pound (also called No. 300)	1¾
16 to 17 ounces (also called No. 303)	2
1 pound, 4 ounces (also called No. 2)	2½
1 pound, 13 ounces (also called No. 2½)	3½
3 pounds, 3 ounces (also called No. 3 cylinder)	5¾
6½ pounds to 6¾ pounds (also called No. 10)	12 to 13

Strained and homogenized foods for babies and chopped junior foods come in small jars and cans, weight given on label. Many specialties, such as caviar, fish paste, smoked turkey, sardines, anchovies, pimientos, foreign foods such as tomato paste, pickled peppers, Mexican and Italian pastas, and sauces, Chinese foods, French vegetables, *pâté*, and other products are sold in cans of many shapes and sizes, but weight is given on label. Recipes usually call for such ingredients by the can, specifying weights.

EQUIVALENTS

FOOD	EQUIVALENTS
Dairy Products and Eggs	
Butter or margarine	¼-pound stick equals ½ cup
	1 pound equals 2 cups, 1 ounce equals 2 tablespoons
Eggs, large	5 whole eggs equal 1 cup
	8 to 10 whites equal 1 cup
	12 to 14 yolks equal 1 cup
Milk, evaporated	1 (14½-ounce) can holds 1⅔ cups
dry skim	1 cup weighs 4 ounces
	¾ to 1 cup plus 4 cups of water make about 1 quart skim milk
Fats	
Hydrogenated	1 cup weighs 6⅔ ounces
Lard	1 cup weighs 8 ounces, 1 pound equals 2 cups
	1 ounce equals 2 tablespoons
Flour, meal, cereals	
Corn meal	1 cup weighs 3 to 4 ounces
Macaroni	1 cup (4 ounces) measures 2¼ cups cooked
Noodles	1 cup (2⅔ ounces) measures 2¼ cups cooked
Oats, rolled	1 cup weighs 5 ounces
Rice	1 cup (7½ ounces) measures 4 cups cooked
	1 pound raw equals 2⅓ cups
Spaghetti	1 cup (3⅓ ounces) measures 2⅛ cups cooked
White flour	
sifted all-purpose or bread	1 cup weighs 4 ounces, 1 pound equals 3¼ to 4 cups
Cake flour	1 cup weighs 3½ ounces, 1 pound equals 4¼ cups
Whole-wheat flour, stirred	1 cup weighs 4¼ ounces, 1 pound equals 3¾ cups
Sugar	
Brown, packed	1 cup weighs 7 ounces, 1 pound equals 2¼ cups
Granulated	1 cup weighs 7 ounces, 1 pound equals 2¼ cups
Confectioners' (powdered)	1 cup weighs 4 ounces, 1 pound equals 3¼ cups

MEAL PLANNING

Cooking for the family, day after day, for the health and pleasure of youngsters as well as older members, calls for understanding of the fundamentals of nutrition, and care, skill, and imagination in meal planning. One of the soundest books on the subject of family nutrition, meal planning, and cookery is *The New Basic Cook Book,* by Marjorie Heseltine and Ula M. Dow. With this book in the kitchen any culinary question is quickly answered with the authority of two long-experienced and famous home economists. Heseltine and Dow wrote the book over twenty years ago and have recently revised it, adding new discoveries in nutrition and modern developments in cookery techniques. Here is what they say about meal planning:

> The day's meals must be both nourishing and satisfying. The foods served must be those the family can afford to buy and those that the cook has time and energy to prepare. The person who plans the meals, cooks the food, and presides at the table has a lot to do with the health and happiness of the family. The secret of enjoying this biggest of all household tasks is to do it well.
>
> Each day every member of the family should eat enough of the various kinds of food that he needs to keep him in good condition. A bowing acquaintance with the fundamentals of nutrition adds interest and dignity to food preparation.
>
> The chart which follows shows what each of the principal groups of foods contributes to the body's needs.
>
> **Checking the Day's Foods.** It is one thing to know what common foods contribute to the diet. It is equally important to know how much of each of the essential foods we should eat each day. As a check in measuring the adequacy of the day's meals, nutritionists have set up the simple guide which follows in *The Basic 7 Food Groups.* Eating these foods will furnish the proteins, the minerals, and the vitamins that the average healthy individual needs; other foods not in the list may also be eaten to satisfy the appetite.

SOME COMMON FOODS
AND THEIR MOST IMPORTANT CONTRIBUTIONS
TO BODY'S NEEDS

MILK AND CHEESE

Fresh whole milk (or its equivalent in unsweetened evaporated or dried whole milk).

Is main source of calcium and riboflavin. Supplies also protein, phosphorus, vitamin A, and thiamine.

Fresh skim milk and buttermilk (or equivalent in dried skim milk or dried buttermilk).

Makes same contributions as whole milk, except vitamin A.

Cream

Contributes more vitamin A than whole milk does and less of the other vitamins and minerals.

Cheese made from whole milk.

A generous serving supplies equivalent of 1 cup whole milk in protein, calcium, phosphorus, and vitamin A.

Cottage cheese

Is good source of protein and phosphorus; is low in the other minerals and in vitamins.

EGGS, LEAN MEAT, FISH

Eggs
Lean muscle meat, including poultry.
Liver, kidneys, and other organs.
Fish
Shellfish, such as oysters

Are most important for protein, iron, thiamine, riboflavin, and niacin. These foods supply phosphorus also. Eggs and liver supply vitamin A. Salt-water fish and shellfish supply iodine.

VEGETABLES

Vegetables in general

Are important sources of various minerals and vitamins, some more than others, as shown below.

Chard, kale, spinach, turnip greens, water cress, and other thin, dark-green leaves.

Thin dark-green leaves eaten raw or properly cooked are an important source of iron, vitamin A, thiamine, and riboflavin. Generous servings of such raw greens, supply liberal amounts of vitamin C. Many of these greens help fulfill the body's needs for calcium.

FOOD	Most important contributions to body's needs
Broccoli, peas, string beans, sweet potatoes, carrots, and other green or yellow vegetables.	*Other green vegetables and yellow ones are valuable chiefly for vitamin A. Sweet potatoes are economical energy foods.*
Cabbage	*A good source of vitamin C if eaten raw.*
Tomatoes—raw, cooked, or commercially canned.	*Are an excellent source of vitamin C and a good source of vitamin A.*
Potatoes, white (Irish)	*Baked or boiled in skins, potatoes, especially new potatoes, are a good source of vitamin C, and provide appreciable amounts of iron and thiamine. They are also economical energy foods.*
Mature beans, peas, and other legumes, such as peanuts and lentils.	*Are good sources of protein, iron, thiamine, and riboflavin. Help meets the body's needs for calcium and phosphorus. Are economical energy foods.*

FRUITS

Fruits in general	*All fruits help in meeting the body's needs for iron, thiamine, and riboflavin. Some fruits make special contributions, as shown below.*
Oranges, grapefruit, strawberries, and cantaloupe.	*These fruits are the best source of vitamin C. One average serving will supply a day's need for vitamin C.*
Apples, bananas, peaches, pears, and most of the common fresh fruits, raw.	*These fruits, eaten raw in generous quantities, provide significant amounts of vitamin C, although much less of it than the fruits listed above.*
Peaches, apricots, and prunes, and other yellow-fleshed fruits.	*Yellow-fleshed fruits supply important amounts of vitamin A.*
Dried apricots, dates, figs, prunes, and raisins.	*These dried fruits are better-than-average sources of iron.*

GRAIN PRODUCTS

Grain products in general	*Are economical energy foods that furnish significant amounts of protein.*

FOOD	*Most important contributions to body's needs*
Dark or whole-grain or enriched bread, flour, and breakfast cereals.	*Are important sources of iron, thiamine, and riboflavin.*
Macaroni, grits, white rice	*Are refined grain products; they cannot take the place of potatoes or other vegetables.*
NUTS **Nuts in general***	*Are concentrated sources of energy and protein and fairly good sources of phosphorus and thiamine.*
SUGAR AND SYRUPS **Refined sugar** **Corn syrup** **Honey** **Molasses** **Sorghum syrup**	*Are concentrated energy foods. Dark molasses and sorghum syrup contribute also calcium and iron.*
FATS AND OILS **Butter** **Margarine** **Lard and hardened vegetable fats** **Olive oil and other salad oils** **Bacon** **Salt pork** **Cod-liver oil**	*Are concentrated energy foods. Butter, cod-liver oil, and margarine to which vitamin A has been added are important sources of vitamin A. Cod-liver oil is also very rich in vitamin D.*

* This does not include the peanut, which is a legume, and is therefore listed with the vegetables.

THE BASIC FOOD GROUPS

Meals that measure up. How the foods needed during the day shall be combined into meals is a matter for each family to decide. Most individuals, active or sedentary, do better if they start the day with a substantial breakfast. Those who sit at a desk all day may prefer a light lunch at noon so that they will not be drowsy by midafternoon. Families that eat the noon meal together may find that it works best to have the main meal of the day then, especially if the children are young. The three plans for a day's meals given below merely illustrate how the same foods can be combined into quite different types of meals.

PLAN I
Full Breakfast
Fruit (or juice)
Cereal (preferably dark) and milk
Egg (with bacon if desired)
Toast and butter
Beverage (of choice)

PLAN II
Light Breakfast
Fruit (or juice)
Cereal and milk
OR
Egg on toast
Beverage

PLAN III
Very Light Breakfast
Fruit (or juice)
Toast and butter
Beverage

PLAN I
Light Lunch
Cheese or salad sandwich
Milk

PLAN II
Medium Lunch
Cream soup or egg dish
Bread and butter
Dessert
Beverage

PLAN III
Noonday Dinner
Meat (or substitute)
Potato
Cooked vegetable
Bread and butter
Dessert (of fruit or milk if otherwise lacking)
Beverage

PLAN I
Dinner
Soup or fruit juice
Meat (or substitute)
Potato
Cooked vegetable
Salad (or second cooked vegetable)
Bread and butter (if needed)
Dessert (of fruit or milk if otherwise lacking)
Beverage

PLAN II
Dinner
Meat (or substitute)
Potato
Cooked vegetable
Salad (or second cooked vegetable)
Bread and butter
Dessert (of fruit or milk if otherwise lacking)
Beverage

PLAN III
Light Supper
Cream soup or chowder
Salad or egg dish
Bread and butter
Beverage

All nutrition information and menus above from THE NEW BASIC COOK BOOK, *by Marjorie Heseltine and Ula M. Dow*

THE "BEST-OF-ALL"

APPETIZERS

THE RECIPES THAT FOLLOW HAVE BEEN SELECTED FROM THESE DISTINGUISHED BOOKS:

The Bed-Book of Eating and Drinking	*Richardson Wright*
The Brown Derby Cook Book	*Staff of Brown Derby Restaurants*
Carolyn Coggins' Company Cook Book	*Carolyn Coggins*
Delicious Seafood Recipes	*Louis Garrison*
501 Easy Cocktail Canapés	*Olga de Leslie Leigh*
Good Food From Sweden	*Inga Norberg*
Helen Corbitt's Cook Book	*Helen Corbitt*
House and Garden's Cook Book	
Junior League of Dallas Cook Book	
Rum In The Kitchen	*Iris Syrett*
Thoughts for Food	
Trader Vic's Book of Food and Drink	*Trader Vic*
Wonderful Ways to Cook	*Edith Key Haines*

APPETIZERS

More than thirty years ago a little cook book called *Tried Temptations* was published by a woman who liked to cook and to feed friends around the table in her charming home the best from her kitchen, the best of her imagination and skill in meal preparation. *Tried Temptations,* by Edith Key Haines, was a revelation in that day of few gourmet cook books. Superb dishes! A new (for America) approach to home cookery. There had to be more such recipes available to home cooks, and so eventually her larger book, *Wonderful Ways to Cook* (from which these five appetizers are taken), appeared; it has been making culinary history in many homes ever since.

★ANCHOVIES ANTOLINI

1 (3½-ounce) can or jar boneless anchovy fillets
Flour
1 beaten egg
3 tablespoons olive oil

DRAIN fillets; dip in flour, then in egg, and roll again in flour. Using a small skillet, brown lightly on both sides in hot olive oil. Serve hot on cocktail picks. Makes 12 or more servings.

CHEESE CIGARETTES LA CREMAILLERE

20 slices fresh sandwich bread cut ¼-inch thick
2 tablespoons butter
2 tablespoons flour
½ cup milk
½ teaspoon salt
⅛ teaspoon black pepper
⅓ cup grated Parmesan cheese
1 egg yolk
1 pound shortening melted for deep frying (360 degrees F.)

BUY bread at a grocer's or delicatessen where it can be cut with an automatic slicer. If you cut it yourself, heat the knife blade first by running hot water over it.

Make a cream sauce in the top of a double boiler, using the butter, flour, milk, and seasoning. Stir until smooth. Add cheese. Stir until melted and blended. Remove from heat, briskly stir egg yolk in, and then continue cooking and stirring over low heat for about 3 minutes. Set aside until cold and thick.

Remove crusts from bread and cut each slice in half. Spread with cheese mixture and roll up tightly like a cigarette.

Heat the shortening in a heavy saucepan to 360 degrees F. If you do not have a deep-fat thermometer, test the fat with a piece of bread; it should brown quickly. Drop the "cigarettes" in and let them brown lightly, turning them as necessary. When browned, drain a few minutes on thick paper toweling.

These are easy to make and very little trouble to fry. They can be made ahead of time (but not fried) and kept wrapped in waxed paper in the refrigerator, or frozen, until frying time. Serve hot. Makes 40 "cigarettes."

★OLIVE AND TOMATO MADY

2 hard-cooked eggs
4 tablespoons olive oil
12 large ripe olives, chopped fine
15 small cocktail olives, chopped fine
¼ teaspoon dried crushed marjoram
½ teaspoon dried crushed bay leaves
1 teaspoon dill seeds or finely chopped fresh dill
¼ teaspoon black pepper
2 tablespoons finely chopped parsley
3 medium-size tomatoes
Mayonnaise

MASH egg yolks, add olive oil a little at a time, and mix to a paste. Chop egg whites very fine. Mix together all ingredients except tomatoes. Chill in covered bowl.

Dip tomatoes in scalding water and remove skins. Chill. Before serving, cut in halves and spread with olive mixture. Top with dab of mayonnaise. Makes 6 servings.

SHAD ROE RING

1 (7¾-oz.) can shad roe
½ cup cold water
1½ tablespoons gelatin (2 tablespoons if weather is hot)
1 (10½-oz.) can consommé
¾ cup water or celery or other vegetable stock
1 teaspoon salt
2 teaspoons lemon juice
½ cup mayonnaise
1-quart ring mold

DRAIN shad roe, remove and discard skin, separate the little beadlike eggs with a fork. Pour ½ cup cold water into a large bowl, sprinkle gelatin on water, let stand. Combine consommé, ¾ cup water or vegetable stock, and salt and bring to boiling point. Pour into the soaked gelatin, and stir until gelatin is dissolved. Set aside until cool but not thickened. Add lemon juice. Pour mayonnaise in, beating as you pour. Add roe, mix lightly together, and let stand, stirring occasionally, until thick enough to keep roe from settling to the bottom. Finely diced drained cucumber makes a good addition if it is not used in the sauce; mix it in when the roe is added. Turn into the mold rinsed with cold water, and chill 5 to 6 hours. Unmold and garnish with sliced tomato and water cress. Good for bridge salad surrounded with shrimp and slices of tomato. Serve with mayonnaise with diced cucumber added. Makes 6 to 8 servings.

★STUFFED DILL PICKLES

2 large dill pickles
1 (3-oz.) jar or can deviled tongue
2 teaspoons mayonnaise

½ teaspoon A-1 (or Diablo) sauce
1 tablespoon finely-chopped celery or celery leaves

REMOVE the ends of the pickles, scrape out inside, and wipe as dry as possible. Make a paste of the remaining ingredients and pack tightly into the hollow pickles. Chill for 3 hours or until stuffing is firm. Cut into thin slices and serve on round toasted crackers.

Five recipes above from WONDERFUL WAYS TO COOK, *by Edith Key Haines*

Say "Brown Derby" to an old New Yorker, and he thinks of Al Smith and his hat. Say "Brown Derby" to Californians and to thousands of hungry travelers who have sampled the fare in the restaurants by that name in Los Angeles and Beverly Hills, and you will hear praise and enthusiastic reminiscing of the succulent dishes served there. In the *Brown Derby Cook Book,* many of these recipes have been put together for you by the restaurants' staff. Here are four first-course delicacies from its pages.

★BROWN DERBY CHEESE MIX

1 pound Cheddar cheese, ground fine
1½ tablespoons English mustard
2 tablespoons Worcestershire sauce

1 tablespoon salt
1 cup milk

LET cheese stand at room temperature until warm and soft. Put in electric mixer, add mustard, Worcestershire, and salt. Turn mixer to low speed until mixture is smooth. Increase speed and add milk slowly. Keep mixing until cheese is fluffy. Store in refrigerator and use as needed on crackers, in sandwiches, on toast strips, on English muffins, in pizza combinations and wherever a tangy, delicious cheese mixture is needed. Number of servings depends on how the cheese mix is used.

MEDALLIONS OF LOBSTER PARISIENNE

1 (1-pound) lobster
1 tablespoon gelatin
2 tablespoons broth

1 cup mayonnaise
1 medium-size dill pickle, sliced

PLUNGE lobster into boiling water. When shell is red (after about 10 minutes of boiling), remove from water, drain, let cool. Cut shell; remove meat and cut it into slivers about the size of a crab leg. Chill thoroughly. Dissolve gelatin in heated broth; pour into bowl and set in crushed ice. Add mayonnaise, stirring constantly until mixture begins to thicken. Dip lobster slivers in this glaze. Then lay them on draining rack and place in refrigerator until coating is set. Arrange on slices of dill pickle, or on toast or croutons garnished with dill pickle. Makes 4 servings.

MELON SUPREME AU VIN

4 balls each, watermelon, cantaloupe, Persian, and honeydew
  melon

½ cup sweet white wine
4 frosted mint leaves

POUR wine over melon balls in a bowl; let stand covered in refrigerator 1 hour. Frost mint leaves by dipping them first in egg white, then in fine granulated sugar. Let dry before using. Arrange melon balls in ice-cold fruit-cocktail glass. Pour any juice from bowl over balls. Garnish with mint leaves. Makes 1 serving.

★STUFFED SALAMI HORNS EN CHEESE

12 slices Italian salami (sliced paper thin)
1 (2½-oz.) package cream cheese

1 tablespoon minced chives
2 tablespoons sour cream
36 capers

FOLD salami slices around your finger to form cornucopias. To make sure they hold their shape, brush with egg white, or use small wooden pick. Chill in refrigerator about ½ hour. Blend cheese, chives, and sour cream until smooth. Use a pastry bag to fill horns with this mixture. Garnish with capers. Makes 12 servings.

The four recipes above from THE BROWN DERBY COOK BOOK *by the Staff of Brown Derby Restaurants*

To open *Carolyn Coggins' Company Cook Book,* is to feel a warm glow of pleasure and anticipation. Her "Grace Before Meals" and her opening chapter on the hospitable habit of drop-in-for-coffee stimulate the reader to turn page after page, enjoying the good flavor of the printed recipes and, later, in the kitchen, the dishes themselves. Here are three of her appetizers.

★LIVERWURST SPREAD

½ pound liverwurst
1 teaspoon lemon juice
½ teaspoon Worcestershire sauce
¼ teaspoon crumbled dried sage
¼ teaspoon paprika

COMBINE all ingredients, mixing until softened and smooth. Makes 1 generous cup. Spread on toast, crackers, or thick chunks crusty French bread; or fill salami rolls or ham cornucopias.

★PEANUT-STUFFED CELERY

4 ounces cream cheese
1 tablespoon onion juice
½ teaspoon curry powder
2 tablespoons heavy cream
12 stalks celery cut in 24 4-inch lengths
½ cup chopped peanuts

MIX cheese, onion juice, curry powder, and cream until thin enough to spread easily when filling the celery. Dip filled top of each stick into the nuts and arrange on platter. Cover and chill. Makes 24 pieces.

SOFT-CENTER CHEESE BALLS

4 ounces (1¼ cups) grated Swiss cheese
1 tablespoon flour
¼ teaspoon salt
½ teaspoon Worcestershire sauce
3 stiffly-beaten egg whites
Bread crumbs
Deep fat for frying

MIX cheese with flour and seasonings. Add stiffly-beaten egg whites. Shape mixture into walnut-size balls. Roll in crumbs. Fry in deep hot fat (375 degrees F.) until golden brown. Drain on thick paper towels. Serve hot or reheated. These can be prepared several hours before serving, and reheated in a chafing dish or electric skillet at the table. Makes 12 to 14 balls.

The three recipes above from CAROLYN COGGINS' COMPANY COOK BOOK

You will want to give a party just to have an excuse for serving some of the good sea-food dishes from Louis Garrison's book on good eating from the briny. Here are two first-course favorites from that book, *Delicious Seafood Recipes*.

CRAB CANAPES

1 cup cooked, canned, or quick-frozen crab flakes	2 teaspoons mayonnaise
2 teaspoons chopped chives	Salt and cayenne
1 teaspoon Worcestershire sauce	12 toast strips

LOOK over crab flakes, remove any fibers. Combine crab with chives, Worcestershire, and mayonnaise. Season with salt and a little cayenne. Spread mixture on toast strips and place in broiler (500 degrees F.) 3 inches below heat. Broil 2 minutes. Serve hot. Makes 12 canapés.

This author suggests preparing toast for canapés with any of these basic butters. Slice bread 1/4 inch thick. Toast lightly on one side and butter other side while hot with one of the special butters. Cut into desired shapes: squares, diamonds, rounds, or strips. Then heap canapé mixture on top, and broil as directed.

CANAPE BUTTERS

Anchovy: Blend 2 tablespoons anchovy paste with 6 tablespoons butter.

Lobster: Blend 1 tablespoon lobster coral with 2 tablespoons butter.

Shrimp: Mash 6 cleaned cooked shrimp, blend with 2 tablespoons butter.

Horse-radish: Blend 1 tablespoon freshly-ground horse-radish with 1 tablespoon butter.

★SHRIMP DIP

10 cooked shrimp	1/2 teaspoon prepared mustard
1 tablespoon lemon juice	2 tablespoons pearl onions
1 teaspoon prepared horse-radish	Salt and cayenne
4 tablespoons mayonnaise	

REMOVE dark line from shrimp, wash and dry. Chop fine; sprinkle with lemon juice. Mix together the horse-radish, mayonnaise, mustard, and onions. Season to taste with salt and a little cayenne. Add shrimp; blend thoroughly.

Serve in chilled bowl, set in larger bowl of cracked ice. Thin toasted crackers or potato chips are dipped or spread with the mixture. Makes 20 servings.

The two recipes and other information above from DELICIOUS SEAFOOD RECIPES, *by Louis Garrison*

One of the best first-course dishes is an oyster-and-herb dish in the handsome *House and Garden's Cook Book,* prepared by various staff writers and contributors to that magazine. Here it is:

★OYSTERS BROILED WITH HERBS

12 osyters on half shell	¼ cup chopped chervil
8 tablespoons (¼ pound) butter	1 teaspoon freshly-ground black
½ cup chopped parsley	pepper
¼ cup chopped chives	Salt

DRAIN oysters, look over for bits of shell; return oysters to their half shells. Blend butter, herbs, pepper and a little salt to taste. Top each oyster with a heaping teaspoon of herb mixture. Arrange shells in flameproof pan and run under broiler heat 2 or 3 minutes, or just until edges of oysters curl. Serve hot. Makes 3 or 4 servings as first course; on a buffet table as an appetizer it makes 12 servings.

The recipe above from HOUSE AND GARDEN'S COOK BOOK, *by that magazine's staff contributors and editors*

❦

A is for anchovy and a great many other delicious tidbits in a small, lively book, *501 Easy Cocktail Canapés,* by Olga de Leslie Leigh, devoted to the hostess who has drop-in guests and planned parties dotting her calendar month after month. These mouthwatering bites are just a few examples.

ANCHOVY CHEESE TARTS

2 tablespoons anchovy paste	2 tablespoons chili sauce
1 cup (¼ pound) grated Cheddar cheese	12 miniature rich-pastry tart shells

BLEND anchovy paste, cheese, and chili sauce. Fill prebaked shells. Heat in moderate oven (375 degrees F.) until mixture is bubbly. Serve hot. Makes 12 tarts.

★BOLOGNA PINWHEELS

½ cup Roquefort or blue cheese	2 tablespoons finely-chopped
2 tablespoons sherry	parsley
1½ tablespoons thick commercial sour cream	12 to 15 thin slices bologna, skin removed

BLEND cheese, sherry, sour cream, and parsley. Spread slices of bologna with mixture. Roll each slice and wrap rolls in waxed paper. Chill 1 hour or longer. When ready to serve, slice each roll in bite-size pin-wheels. Spear each pinwheel with wooden cocktail pick. Makes about 60 wheels.

★CUCUMBER TIDBITS

1 or 2 medium-size cucumbers
1 (3-oz.) package cream cheese
Mayonnaise

Salt and cayenne
4 tablespoons finely-chopped parsley

PEEL cucumbers and cut into ½-inch slices. Mash cheese and thin slightly with mayonnaise for good spreading consistency. Season to taste with salt and a little cayenne. Spread cheese mixture on both sides of each slice of cucumber, then roll slices in chopped parsley on all sides. Place on platter, cover, and chill 1 hour or longer. Makes 20 or more slices.

★HAM AND CHEESE SPREAD

1 cup ground cooked ham
½ cup grated Cheddar cheese
1 small dill pickle, finely diced

½ cup chopped raw bacon or 1 (5-oz.) jar snappy cheese-spread

COMBINE all ingredients. Mix well. Spread on crackers, toast, or use as sandwich filling. Makes 1¼ cups, about 36 canapé servings.

LOBSTER AND LETTUCE ROLLS

1 (6-oz.) can or package quick-
   frozen lobster meat
1 (3-oz.) package cream cheese
2 tablespoons grated onion

2 tablespoons finely-chopped parsley
1 tablespoon sherry
Lettuce

MASH lobster meat with cheese, onion, parsley, and sherry. Add salt and pepper if necessary. Cover and chill in refrigerator. To serve, roll small amounts of lobster mixture in 2- by 3-inch strips of crisp cold lettuce. Secure each roll with wooden pick. Makes 24 rolls.

★SMOKED-TURKEY BALLS

1 cup ground smoked-turkey
   meat
1 (3-oz.) package cream cheese

3 tablespoons thick sour cream
Grated Parmesan cheese

BLEND smoked turkey and cheese, adding enough sour cream to make a smooth mixture. Shape in bite-size balls. Roll balls in grated Parmesan cheese. Chill 1 hour or longer. Makes 32 balls.

PASTRY PINWHEELS

Piecrust mix

1 pound ground beef, well seasoned

½ cup chopped raw bacon or 1
(5-oz.) jar snappy cheese-spread

USE your favorite pastry mix. Follow directions on package for mixing
dough. Roll out on lightly floured board to ⅛-inch thickness. Cut in
squares 5 by 5 inches and spread with meat mixed with bacon or cheese-
spread. Roll up each pastry square. Place rolls on platter, cover with
waxed paper and chill 1 hour or longer. When ready to use, slice rolls in
½-inch pinwheels. Bake on cookie sheet in hot (450 degrees F.) oven
about 12 minutes, or until pastry is done and golden. Makes about 25
pinwheels. Serve hot.

PASTRY STRAWS

2 or 3 cloves garlic

⅛ pound (4 tablespoons) butter
or margarine

1 package piecrust mix

Salt or garlic salt

PEEL and mash garlic, blend with butter or margarine. Prepare piecrust
mix as directed on package. Combine dough with garlic and butter or
margarine. Work smoothly into ball of dough. Roll out on lightly
floured board ⅛ to ¼ inch thick. Cut strips of dough ½ inch wide and
6 inches long. Give each strip several twists and lay it on a greased cookie
sheet. Bake in hot oven (450 degrees F.) for about 10 minutes, or
until golden. Sprinkle liberally with salt or garlic salt before serving.
Makes about 68 straws.

PUFF SHELLS, MINIATURE

1 cup water

½ cup margarine

1 cup all-purpose flour, sifted

4 eggs

Various fillings (below)

START oven at moderately hot (400 degrees F.) .

Combine water and margarine in upper part of double boiler, stir
until fat is melted. Stir in flour until batter is well blended. Remove
from heat and let cool. Beat eggs until thick; blend into batter until
smoothly mixed. Drop ½ teaspoonfuls of batter on greased cookie sheet.
Bake about 15 minutes, or until puffs are golden.

Split warm puffs open. Fill with one of the following mixtures:

A mixture of 1 (3-oz.) package cream cheese with 1 (5-oz.) jar
Roquefort spread. Moisten mixture with a little sherry, milk, or cream;
Chicken salad (chopped fine) ; Deviled ham mixed with mustard mayonnaise; Liver paste mixed with anchovy butter; Crab meat mixed with
herb mayonnaise. Makes 20 or more puffs.

SHRIMP IN ASPIC

1 tablespoon gelatin	¼ teaspoon salt
½ cup cold water	⅛ teaspoon paprika
¼ cup boiling shrimp juice from can or kettle	Tabasco sauce
¾ cup boiling consommé	32 canned, cooked, or quick-frozen cleaned shrimp
2 tablespoons lemon juice	

SOAK gelatin in cold water to soften. Add boiling shrimp liquid or consommé and stir until gelatin is dissolved. Add lemon juice, salt, paprika, and 3 or 4 drops of Tabasco. Pour into square cake pan which has been rubbed with cooking oil. Chill until mixture begins to set. Then lay shrimp in aspic, row after row, in such a way that when aspic is firm, it can be cut into squares with a shrimp in the center of each. Chill aspic until firm. Double aspic recipe if greater depth is desired. Makes 32 servings using small to medium shrimp.

The ten recipes above from 501 EASY COCKTAIL CANAPÉS, *by Olga de Leslie Leigh*

❦

Gourmets who get about swear that the batter-fried shrimp at Trader Vic's are the best. Here is the recipe from *Trader Vic's Book of Food and Drink*. Trader Vic uses large raw shrimp, shelled, dark vein removed, tails left on for appearance and also as handles for people who like to eat shrimp with their fingers.

BATTER-FRIED SHRIMP

Trader Vic says, "The secret lies in the batter. Mix these ingredients but don't work or stir too much, and don't get too much batter on the shrimp or prawns, whichever you use."

2 cups all-purpose flour, sifted	2¼ cups water
½ cup cornstarch	½ cup milk
¼ cup white corn meal	2 pounds fresh shrimp
½ teaspoon baking powder	Oil for deep frying
1 slightly-beaten egg	

SIFT flour, cornstarch, corn meal, and baking powder together. Combine egg, water, and milk. Beat into dry ingredients lightly, just enough to blend.

Place batter in a small bowl, a small amount at a time, and mix in plenty of large shrimp so that not too much batter encases them. Have oil very hot, about 400 degrees F. on frying-thermometer. Lower a few shrimp at a time in frying basket. As soon as they are golden, about 2 or 3 minutes, lift out, drain on absorbent paper. Serve immediately. Makes 12 servings of about 4 shrimp per person (jumbo shrimp) or 15 servings of 4 shrimp per person using smaller shrimp.

The recipe above from TRADER VIC'S BOOK OF FOOD AND DRINK, *by Trader Vic*

There is plenty of evidence that people live well in Dallas, Texas. One of the most convincing proofs is the cook book compiled by the Junior League of Dallas, and called *The Junior League of Dallas Cook Book*. The League parties get off to a good start with such canapés as these.

★BACON AND TOMATO CANAPE

Finely chopped, crisp cooked
  bacon
Mayonnaise
Rounds of buttered toast

Thin slices onion
Thin slices peeled tomato
Chopped parsley
Sliced stuffed olives

COMBINE bacon with just enough mayonnaise to make a spreading consistency. Spread on toast rounds. Place slice of onion, then slice of tomato on each, sprinkle with chopped parsley, and garnish with olive slice. Serve at once. Allow 2 teaspoons finely chopped bacon to each toast-round.

HAM CANAPE

½ pound baked ham, ground
4 tablespoons finely-chopped
  chutney
⅔ cup chili sauce

Cayenne and black pepper to taste
6 rounds buttered toast
6 tablespoons grated Cheddar
  cheese

COMBINE ham, chutney, chili sauce, and light seasoning of cayenne and pepper. Spread on toast-rounds. Sprinkle with cheese. Place under low broiler heat until cheese is melted. Serve at once. Makes 6 servings.

★SALAMI ROLLS

24 paper-thin slices salami
2 (3-oz.) packages cream cheese
2 tablespoons prepared horse-
  radish

2 tablespoons onion juice
1 teaspoon Worcestershire sauce
Salt and pepper

PULL off any skin or edge from the salami. Blend the remaining ingredients, seasoning lightly with salt and pepper to taste. Spoon the mixture into center of each slice, roll up tightly, cover with waxed paper and chill. Fasten rolls with small wooden picks if necessary. Can be made a day in advance and kept well wrapped in refrigerator. Makes 24 rolls.

★VEGETABLE HORS D'OEUVRE

1 firm head red cabbage	½ cup thick sour cream
2 or 3 (3-oz.) packages cream cheese	3 tablespoons onion juice
	1 tablespoon Worcestershire sauce
¼ pound Roquefort or blue cheese	Crisp raw cauliflowerettes, small tender celery stalks, carrot sticks

WASH and trim cabbage, cut off stem so cabbage rests firmly on its base. Hollow out center, leaving decorative curly edge of outer cabbage leaves uncut. Blend cheese with cream and onion juice, increasing amount of cream if necessary to give consistency of a dip. Season with Worcestershire. Fill center of cabbage with cheese dip. Surround cabbage on its platter with cauliflowerettes, celery, and carrot sticks. If desired, garnish of olives and parsley may be added. Dip vegetables into cheese mixture. Makes enough for 30 or more servings.

The four recipes above from THE JUNIOR LEAGUE OF DALLAS COOK BOOK

❦

More Texas food. The world-famous Zodiac Room of the Neiman-Marcus specialty store in Dallas owes its renown for superb dishes to Helen Corbitt, who was described by one well-fed patron as the greatest cook in Texas. We add to our collection of appetizers some from her cook book, *Helen Corbitt's Cook Book.*

CHIPPED BEEF AND HORSE-RADISH

2 (3-oz.) packages cream cheese	2 (2½-oz.) jars dried or chipped beef, finely chopped
2 teaspoons horse-radish	
1 teaspoon prepared mustard	2 tablespoons butter

SOFTEN cream cheese with horse-radish and mustard. Sauté finely chopped dried beef in the butter until well frizzled. Form cheese mixture into a ball or log, and roll in the dried-beef mixture. Wrap in waxed paper and chill. Slice and serve with toasted buttery crackers. Makes 40 or more servings. (Continued on following page.)

Or you may use cream cheese and divide it into as many different-flavored parts as you wish. For instance, crushed garlic or garlic powder in one part, chopped anchovies in another, chopped black and green olives in another, curry powder in another. Combine all the flavors into a ball or loaf, keeping each as separate from the others as possible. Then roll the whole mixture in chopped parsley or nuts, wrap in waxed paper, and chill. When the guests knife into it, they cannot tell what they are getting and it causes a furor. Any kind of crackers or thin bread keeps your guests coming back for more.

★FROZEN LOG

½ pound sharp Cheddar cheese
8 slices uncooked lean bacon
½ teaspoon Worcestershire sauce
2 small onions, peeled

1 teaspoon dry mustard
2 teaspoons mayonnaise
Toasted bread rounds, crackers, or
    split English muffins

PUT all ingredients except bread or crackers through food chopper, mix, and roll into a log with diameter the size of a half dollar. Wrap in waxed paper. Freeze or chill several hours. To serve, slice, place on toast rounds, crackers, or English muffins, and brown under low broiler heat until bacon bits are cooked and mixture is bubbly. Serve at once. Makes 30 or more servings.

LOBSTER AND CUCUMBER DIP

1 cup cooked, canned, or quick-
    frozen lobster meat
2 tablespoons butter
1 medium-size cucumber, chopped
    fine

Mayonnaise
Salt and pepper
Whole-wheat toast or thin strips
    of bread

PUT lobster meat through grinder. Sauté in butter 2 or 3 minutes; let cool. Combine with cucumber and enough chilled mayonnaise to make about 1½ to 1¾ cups. Season lightly with salt and pepper. Place in bowl and set in larger bowl of cracked ice. Spread on toast points or strips of bread. Makes 20 or more servings.

SHRIMP CANAPE

1 pound large shrimp, 20 to 25 to
    the pound
1 clove garlic, peeled
½ lemon, sliced
½ cup mayonnaise
½ teaspoon curry powder

¼ cup Major Grey's chutney
White bread
Caviar
Strips canned pimiento
Finely-chopped parsley

COVER shrimp with boiling salted water, add garlic clove, and lemon slices, and cook 15 to 20 minutes, or until shrimp turn pink. Drain, let cool. Using kitchen scissors, cut shell along black line; remove shell, tail, and black line. Rinse shrimp, drain, and chill.

Combine mayonnaise, curry powder, and chopped chutney. Cut sliced bread with round cutter or half-moon shape. If round cutter is used, cut rounds of bread in half. Spread with mayonnaise mixture. Cut shrimp in half lengthwise, placing one piece on each half-moon of bread and fitting shrimp to shape of bread. Place dot of caviar for the eye and circle shrimp with thin strip of pimiento. Sprinkle finely chopped parsley on the inner curve of the shrimp on the bread. Makes a nice tea sandwich also. Must be served immediately. Makes 40 or more canapés or sandwiches.

The four recipes above from HELEN CORBITT'S COOK BOOK

❦

Rum is a subtle flavor in cookery and with fruit. These first-course delicacies are exceptional mostly because the fragrance of rum and its tone and accent set them apart. They are from the kitchen of a Cordon Bleu (Paris) graduate, Iris Syrett, who prepared a rum booklet for Americans, *Rum In The Kitchen*.

CANTALOUPE AU RHUM

1 cantaloupe   ¼ cup Demerara rum
4 tablespoons sugar

CUT slice off top of melon; use silver spoon to scoop out all seeds. Combine sugar and rum, pour into melon, cover with top slice. Chill 2 or 3 hours. Slice in bowl to catch juices. Makes 2 or 4 servings.

PAMPLEMOUSSE AU RHUM

3 grapefruit   1 cup golden Jamaica rum
2 or 3 tablespoons sugar

CUT grapefruit in half, remove seeds, cut fruit out without damaging shells. Remove membrane from fruit, place in bowl with enough sugar to sweeten and pour in rum. Cover and let stand for 2 hours. Just before serving, heat fruit in enamel or glass saucepan, pour back into grapefruit shells, and serve very hot. May be garnished with mint or candied cherry. Makes 6 servings.

PERLES DE MELON AU RHUM

1 cantaloupe	Juice 2 oranges
4 tablespoons sugar	1 cup light Hart rum

CHILL melon; scoop out melon balls and place in dessert or fruit-cocktail glasses which have been packed in crushed ice. Sprinkle in sugar and pour mixed orange juice and rum over the melon balls. Serve at once. Makes 4 or more servings.

The three recipes above from RUM IN THE KITCHEN, *by Iris Syrett*

❦

Gleanings from that delectable *Bed-Book of Eating and Drinking* pleasurably reveal Richardson Wright's ideas on canapés. This long-time editor of *House and Garden Magazine* says:

Cold leftover finnan haddie into which is mixed mayonnaise and a touch of horse-radish makes desirable hors d'oeuvres.

Smoked salmon may be enjoyed in its innocence, but for flavors, lay the paper-thin slices on well-buttered brown bread, squeeze on lemon juice, and grind coarse pepper over them.

The *spécialité de la maison,* which appears unheralded on party occasions at the Wright home, is a *pâté.* How to make it? Simmer chicken livers in chicken stock and then chop fine with crisp bacon and a hard-cooked egg, seasoning with a minced onion, salt, and pepper, after which add a slight amount of mayonnaise. [The author did not say so, but he probably served this with toasted crusty French bread, or thin, thin toast.]

Savory rice—everyone has his own version—is sometimes placed in grape leaves, which are rolled and steamed. Then chill and serve with French dressing.

The above four ideas from THE BED-BOOK OF EATING AND DRINKING, *by Richardson Wright*

❦

The cold buffet, or smörgåsbord, has become so popular in America that our cuisine has been enriched by many Scandinavian dishes. These favorites come from *Good Food From Sweden,* by Inga Norberg.

ANCHOVY SAVORY (HOT)

2 (2¾-oz.) bottles or cans anchovy
  fillets
3 medium-size potatoes
½ tablespoon chopped peeled
  onion

3½ tablespoons butter
3 tablespoons bread crumbs

DRAIN 18 fillets, pat dry. Wash, pare, and slice potatoes. Use 1 table-spoon butter to grease shallow 1-quart baking dish. Sprinkle 1 tablespoon crumbs in bottom and around sides of dish. Make alternate layers of potatoes, anchovies, and dabs of onion. Cover with remaining dabs of butter and crumbs. Bake 30 minutes, or until potatoes are tender and browned, in hot (425 degrees F.) oven. Place hot baking dish on table warmer so guests can help themselves. Makes 4 to 6 appetizer servings.

HERRING SAVORY (HOT)

2 salt herrings
⅓ cup bread crumbs
2 tablespoons butter

4 tablespoons heavy cream
2 teaspoons chopped chives

SOAK herring in cold water overnight. Drain, skin, fillet, and remove all bones. (Or buy 4 herring fillets.) Roll fillets in bread crumbs, and ar-range in greased shallow baking dish, with 1 tablespoon of butter. Sprinkle herring with remaining crumbs, dot with butter. Bake in moderately hot (400 degrees F.) oven 5 to 10 minutes. Pour cream over, return to oven, and bake 15 minutes longer, or until herring is done. Sprinkle with chopped chives. Serve as warm appetizer from a table warmer. Makes 6 or more appetizer servings.

SMORGASBORD PLATTERS
(also see Scandinavian chapters)

For cold smörgåsbord platters, very thin slices cold roast lamb, veal, or beef, decorated with sliced gherkins or cucumber and cubes of aspic.

Sliced cold boiled potatoes marinated in French dressing, drained and sprinkled with finely chopped parsley. Garnish with rolled anchovies.

Herring salad. Potato salad. Stuffed celery. Mixed cooked-vegetable salad with mayonnaise mounded on serving dish and garnished with quartered tomatoes.

Deviled eggs. Tomatoes filled with cooked vegetable salads and mayonnaise. Drained pigs' knuckles in their own jelly, gar-nished with pickled beets.

(Continued on following page.)

Liver *pâté*, platter garnished with sliced hard-cooked eggs, olives, lettuce cups filled with beet salad.

Mounds of lobster in aspic. Shrimp coated with mayonnaise. Cold baked stuffed mussels. Smoked salmon with mustard sauce.

The three recipes above from GOOD FOOD FROM SWEDEN, *by Inga Norberg*

❧

When *Thoughts for Food* first appeared—a book, strangely, without an author's name on it—Rex Stout, as famous for his gourmet cookery as for his Nero Wolfe stories and many others, said, "A godsend for the woman who would like to have a reputation as an exceptional table hostess. . . . Gets 4 stars." Those stars still twinkle over this book and a second one, called *More Thoughts for Food,* because they are filled with imaginative menus, superb cookery, and delicious dishes. Here are 7 appetizers from *Thoughts for Food.*

APPETIZER PIE

Large round-loaf rye bread
Softened butter
Small jar caviar
Lemon juice
Onion juice
Small can red salmon, drained and flaked
Mayonnaise
Small jar sardellen paste
1 (3-oz.) package cream cheese
Small can boneless, skinless sardines
Worcestershire sauce
¾ cup finely-minced cooked ham
½ green pepper, finely chopped
Riced whites and yolks 6 hard-cooked eggs
1 cup ground olives and nuts mixed with mayonnaise

CUT a slice of bread crosswise from the center of the loaf. Remove crust from slice, butter generously. Place on round platter. In the center of the slice fill a circle 2 inches across with caviar seasoned with lemon and onion juice. Around this central circle, in rings, place or pipe mixtures of (1) salmon combined with mayonnaise (2) sardellen paste blended with cream cheese (3) mashed sardines blended with cream cheese and seasoned with Worcestershire sauce (4) ham, green pepper, and mayonnaise blended together (5) a ring of riced hard-cooked eggs (6) ring of olive-nut mayonnaise. Bring platter to table at once; cut into pie-shaped wedges. Makes 6 servings.

The number of savory mixtures around the "pie" depend on the size of the loaf. Various other mixtures may be piped around this "pie," keeping assorted and contrasting colors and flavors in the combination.

CANAPE HONORE

Red-ripe tomatoes
Rounds thinly-sliced bread
Caviar
Hard-cooked egg
Onion juice
Salt and paprika

Worcestershire sauce
Ketchup
Olive oil
Fillets, boneless anchovies
Finely chopped parsley

SKIN tomatoes. Cut into as many thin slices as canapés desired. Cut thin slices of bread into rounds the same size as tomato slices. Toast bread on one side; spread untoasted side with caviar. Place tomato slice on top. Blend mashed or riced hard-cooked egg with a little onion juice, salt, paprika, Worcestershire sauce, ketchup, and olive oil. Mix smoothly and spread on tomato. Crisscross anchovy fillets to form a latticework on top; sprinkle lightly with parsley. Serve canapé as first course with stuffed celery or black olives as garnish.

HOT CANAPE OF SARDINES AND TOMATO

Rounds thinly-sliced bread
Boned skinless sardines
Salt
Lemon juice
Worcestershire sauce
Cayenne

Finely-minced parsley
Creamed butter
Tomato slices
Grated Cheddar or Parmesan
   cheese

TOAST rounds of bread on one side. Make paste of mashed sardines blended with a little salt, lemon juice, Worcestershire, a few grains cayenne, minced parsley, and enough creamed butter so that it spreads easily. Spread untoasted side of bread rounds. Top with slice of peeled tomato. Sprinkle thickly with cheese. Brown under moderate broiler heat until cheese melts. Serve hot.

CELERY PARISIENNE

12 celery hearts
1½ cups stock or bouillon
12 whole black peppers or peppercorns

French dressing
Anchovy paste

CUT leaves from celery hearts. Cover celery with stock or bouillon (size of celery determines amount of stock), add peppercorns, simmer until tender. Drain. Flavor French dressing with a little anchovy paste. Pour over celery. Cover, chill several hours. Drain and serve as part of antipasto or hors d'oeuvres assortment. Makes 12 servings.

CELERY-ROOT APPETIZER

3 celery roots	Mayonnaise
Salt and pepper	6 or more rolled anchovies
1 tablespoon onion juice	Riced hard-cooked egg yolk
1 teaspoon English mustard	Shredded lettuce

BOIL celery roots until tender; drain, peel, and mash. Season lightly with salt and pepper. Blend onion juice, mustard, and mayonnaise into mashed roots until the mixture has the consistency of mashed potatoes. Shape into 2-inch cones and place on rest of lettuce. Make indentation on top and place rolled anchovy in it. Surround each cone with a border of riced egg. Makes 6 or more servings. Serve with hors d'oeuvres or garnish of small open-face sandwiches of smoked salmon, ham, cheese, or smoked turkey.

FILLED CANTALOUPE

2 cantaloupes	2 tablespoons sloe gin
2 cups red raspberries	2 teaspoons lemon juice
2 cups blueberries	1½ tablespoons powdered sugar

CHILL melons and fruits. Cut melons in half, remove seeds and stringy portion; drain. With sharp paring knife cut sawtooth edge around each half. Combine raspberries and blueberries, add sloe gin, lemon juice, and sugar. Fill melon halves. Serve on cracked ice. Makes 4 servings.

Adjust amount of fruit and flavoring to the size of the melons. The berries should just fill each melon half. Makes 4 servings.

FILLED HONEYDEW MELON

1 honeydew melon	¼ cup sherry
½ cup watermelon balls	¼ cup apricot brandy
½ cup cantaloupe balls	½ cup orange juice
½ cup pitted black cherries	

CUT honeydew melon in quarters. With ball cutter carefully scoop out balls of all edible melon down to the shell. Retain shells. Combine honeydew balls with watermelon and cantaloupe balls and cherries. Pour over them the combined sherry, apricot brandy, and orange juice. Chill. Drain balls. Refill melon shells. Makes 4 servings.

The seven appetizer recipes above from THOUGHTS FOR FOOD

THE "BEST-OF-ALL"

BEVERAGES

THE RECIPES THAT FOLLOW HAVE BEEN SELECTED FROM THESE DISTINGUISHED BOOKS:

The A.B.C. of Spice Cookery	*American Spice Trade Association*
The Angostura Cook Book	*Angostura-Wuppermann Corporation*
The Bed-Book of Eating and Drinking	*Richardson Wright*
Buckeye Cookery	
The Fine Art of Mixing Drinks	*David A. Embury*
Fun With Coffee	*Pan-American Coffee Bureau*
Let Mine Be Wine	*André L. Simon*
Trader Vic's Book of Food and Drink	*Trader Vic*
What You Should Know About Tea	*Tea Council of the U.S.A., Inc.*
Woman's Home Companion Cook Book	*Dorothy Kirk, ed.*

BEVERAGES

Coffee and tea are so important in the American way of life that each of these ancient, delicious potations is represented in the modern food world by its own bureau of information, maintained by the growers or by the importers and distributors. Long research, the trying out of every kind of coffeemaker, every tea method, have been the objectives of these organizations; the recipes they have developed are the source to which cook book writers turn when they want to pass along the newest, the best, to their readers.

From *Fun With Coffee,* here is what the Pan-American Coffee Bureau says about making its favorite brew.

Coffee

Always start with a thoroughly clean coffeemaker, of whatever style and method you use. Rinse coffeemaker with hot water before using. Wash thoroughly after each use and rinse with hot water.

Fresh coffee is best. Buy coffee in the size of can or package which will be entirely consumed within a week after opening.

Fresh water is important, too. Start with freshly drawn cold water.

For best results, use the full capacity of your coffeemaker. Never brew less than ¾ of its capacity.

Consistent timing is important. After you find the exact timing to obtain results desired in your coffeemaker, stick to it in order to get uniform results.

Coffee should never be boiled; when boiled, an undesirable flavor change takes place.

Serve coffee as soon as possible after brewing. Freshly brewed coffee tastes best. But if coffee must be kept any length of time before serving, hold it at serving temperature by placing the pot in a pan of near-boiling water or set the pot over very low heat.

Follow directions which come with your favorite coffeemaker, using 1 standard coffee measure—or its equivalent of 2 level measuring tablespoons—of coffee to each ¾ measuring cup (6 fluid ounces) of water for each serving. These proportions apply to all methods and all coffeemaking utensils, except the *ibrik* for Oriental coffee, the *macchinetta* for Italian drip coffee, and the various *espresso* pots available for home use. For these special devices, follow recipes given below or the manufacturer's instructions which come with the pots.

Various Hot Coffee Recipes

CAFE BRULOT DIABOLIQUE

This is a favorite in New Orleans, and a spectacular *spécialité de la maison* at Antoine's of that Louisiana city.

6 pieces lump sugar
8 whole cloves
1 (1-inch) stick cinnamon
1 lemon peel, cut in small pieces

4 jiggers (¾ cup) cognac
4 demitasses hot freshly-brewed
coffee

PLACE all ingredients, except hot coffee, in silver chafing dish. Ignite the cognac with a match. Stir the mixture. After a minute or two, slowly pour in the hot black coffee and continue to stir. Ladle at once into *brûlot* cups or demitasses. Makes 4 servings.

★CAFE AU LAIT

Café au lait is the breakfast drink of France and many Latin countries. To make it, brew 1½ measuring cups strong hot coffee and heat 1½ measuring cups rich milk. Using 2 pots, pour coffee from one and milk from the other into each cup. Makes 4 servings. (Many versions of *café au lait* are found in Austria, Germany, and elsewhere in Europe. Hot chocolate, hot milk, hot coffee are sometimes combined; sometimes hot cream is served into a warmed cup, then steaming coffee poured in with a little hot milk.)

CAFE CAPPUCCINO

Follow directions below for Italian coffee. Combine steaming coffee with equal amount of hot milk. Pour into tall cups and sprinkle with cinnamon or nutmeg. Sometimes served with whipped cream and a little grated orange peel.

★HOT MOCHA JAVA

4½ measuring cups hot coffee   Whipped cream or marshmallows
4½ measuring cups hot cocoa or
    chocolate

COMBINE these hot beverages. Serve hot, but do not boil. Pour into cups or mugs and top with dab of whipped cream or a marshmallow. Makes 10 to 12 servings.

IRISH COFFEE

Fine granulated sugar   Irish whisky
Strong black coffee   Slightly-whipped cream

PLACE 2 teaspoons sugar in a warmed wine glass. Fill glass about ⅔ full with hot coffee. Mix. Add about 2 tablespoons Irish whisky. Top with softly whipped cream. Makes 1 serving.

★ITALIAN COFFEE
Espresso

4 standard coffee measures (8 level   1½ measuring cups water
    tablespoons) French or Italian-
    roast pulverized coffee

A DRIP pot may be used, but a *macchinetta* is best. This consists of a pair of cylinders of nickel, tin, or aluminum; each has a handle, and one has a spout. These cylinders fit together to form the pot, and there is a coffee sieve between them. Measure the coffee into the sieve. Pour measured water into the cylinder without the spout and put pots together, the empty one on top. Place on heat and wait for small opening in the lower cylinder to steam. Then remove from heat and turn the *macchinetta* upside down until all the brew has dripped through to the lower part of the pot. Then pour. This coffee is usually served in demitasses or 4-ounce glasses with a twist of lemon peel and sugar, never with cream. Makes 4 demitasses.

The same roast of coffee is used in making *espresso* coffee. Follow manufacturer's instructions on *espresso* machine.

★TURKISH COFFEE

In the Near East this special coffee is served very hot in very small cups about the size of half an eggshell. It is important that each guest get his share of the creamy foam formed on the coffee.

1½ measuring cups water	4 tablespoons finely-pulverized
4 teaspoons sugar	coffee

MEASURE water into heavy saucepan. Add sugar and bring to boil. Stir coffee in. Bring to boil again. Let brew froth 3 times, then remove from heat. Add few drops cold water. Spoon some of the foam into each small cup and pour the coffee in to fill. Makes 4 or 5 demitasses.

★VIENNESE COFFEE

Brew extra-strength coffee. Sweeten to taste and top with whipped cream. Some versions include a little spice and hot milk.

COFFEE AND LIQUEURS

Fill a demitasse ¾ full of hot coffee. Then add a dash of any one of these: white crème de menthe, curaçao, kümmel, anisette, or Cointreau.

Cognac or bourbon in a demitasse of coffee is called Coffee Royale.

Various Iced Coffee Beverages

★COFFEE NECTAR

2¼ measuring cups strong cold coffee	1 tablespoon Angostura bitters
	1 pint coffee ice cream

PLACE all ingredients in bowl or electric blender. Beat until smooth and creamy. Pour into tall chilled glasses. Serve straws with this. Makes 4 servings.

★COFFEE TROPICALE

This is the favorite way of serving iced coffee in El Salvador and other Latin American countries.

Cracked ice	1 tablespoon granulated sugar
1½ measuring cups strong cold coffee	

FILL electric blender container half full of chopped ice. Add coffee and sugar. Blend until foamy. Pour into 4 tall chilled glasses. Makes 4 servings.

★FROSTED COFFEE HAWAII

2 measuring cups strong cold   1 cup chilled pineapple juice
  coffee   1 pint soft coffee ice cream

COMBINE ingredients and beat thoroughly with rotary beater or in blender until mixture is smooth and foamy. Pour into tall chilled glasses. Serve straws with this. Makes 4 to 5 servings.

★ICED COFFEE

Make hot coffee double-strength by using half the amount of water to the usual amount of coffee. Pour hot over ice cubes in tall glasses. The coffee's extra strength allows for the dilution caused by the ice.

Another version of iced coffee: Make regular-strength coffee and chill in nonmetallic container in refrigerator no more than 3 hours. Pour over ice in tall glasses.

Or make coffee as usual. Freeze in cubes in refrigerator trays. To serve, pour regular-strength hot coffee over coffee ice cubes.

Iced instant coffee: Mix twice the usual amount of instant coffee with a little water (hot or cold, according to package directions) in each glass. Add ice cubes, water, and stir thoroughly.

★MOCHA FROSTED

2½ measuring cups strong cold   5 tablespoons chocolate syrup
  coffee   1 pint coffee ice cream

COMBINE ingredients and mix with rotary beater or with blender until smooth. Pour into tall chilled glasses. Serve straws with this. Makes 4 or more servings.

★SPICY ICED COFFEE

3 measuring cups hot double-   4 allspice berries
  strength coffee   Cream or whipped cream
2 cinnamon sticks   Sugar
4 whole cloves

POUR double-strength coffee over all the spices in a glass or nonmetallic bowl. Let stand 1 hour. Strain, pour over ice cubes in tall glasses. Serve with cream and sugar or dab of whipped cream. Serve straws with this. Makes 3 or 4 servings.

Coffee information and recipes above from booklet FUN WITH COFFEE, *by Pan-American Coffee Bureau*

Tea

From *What You Should Know About Tea,* by the Tea Council of the U.S.A., Inc.,

The first suggestion is to make tea in a preheated pot; rinse pot with boiling water, or let pot stand full of hot water, then empty; add tea and boiling water according to recipes which follow. The covered pot helps keep the mixture hot while it brews.

Bring fresh cold tap water to a full rolling boil. Place 1 teaspoon of tea, or 1 tea bag, per person, or for each cup of tea in warmed pot. Pour boiling water over tea in warmed pot, allowing 1 measuring cup of water for each teaspoon or bag of tea.

Brew (that is, let stand) by the clock, 3 to 5 minutes, depend-on the strength desired. Stir the tea before pouring to make sure it is uniformly strong. If you like weak tea, simply add a little hot water to the cup. Some tea experts suggest milk, not cream, served with tea. Fresh lemon or orange slices point up the flavor of some teas. Some teas brew light, some dark. Learn to brew the tea you prefer by the clock, to the strength you like best.

HOT TEA CONCENTRATE

To serve tea to a crowd, prepare tea concentrate ahead of time:

1½ quarts cold fresh water	¼ pound loose tea

BRING water to a full rolling boil. Remove from heat and immediately add loose tea. Stir to immerse leaves. Cover. Let stand 5 minutes. Strain into large teapot until ready to use. When ready to serve, bring a large pot of freshly boiled piping hot water to the table, pour about 2 tablespoons tea concentrate into a cup, then fill about ⅘ full with hot water. Stir. Vary the amount of concentrate as desired. Makes 40 to 45 teacups.

★HOT SPICED AFTERNOON TEA

4 quarts water	1¼ cups sugar
1 teaspoon whole cloves	1 cup strained orange juice
1 stick cinnamon	¾ cup strained fresh lemon juice
5 level tablespoons tea leaves or	
15 tea bags	

ADD spices to water. Bring water to full rolling boil in large enamel kettle. Remove from heat. Immediately add tea or tea bags. Let stand 4 minutes. Stir and strain. Add sugar, stir until dissolved. Add fruit juices. To reheat for serving, place over low heat; do not boil. Makes 25 to 30 teacups.

SKI BALL

This famous hot drink is not only popular with outdoor winter-sports fans, but it makes a good winter-night party beverage.

Boiling water
Tea bags or loose tea
1½ teaspoons sugar for each glass
1 cinnamon stick muddler per
  glass

1 thick lemon slice studded with
  3 to 6 cloves for each glass
Tea glasses with handles, or
  glasses in holders

BRING water to full rolling boil. Place tea in preheated teapot, using 1 teaspoon tea or 1 tea bag for each serving. Pour boiling water over tea. Let stand 3 to 5 minutes. Place sugar, cinnamon stick, and lemon slice in each ski-ball glass. Stir tea and strain into glasses. Serve immediately. (Add cognac or rum to taste, if desired.)

Various Iced Tea Beverages

★ICED TEA

Follow the rules for making hot tea, but use 50 percent more tea to allow for the dilution caused by the melting ice. (You use 1 quart water and 4 tea bags to make 4 cups hot tea.) Use 1 quart water and 6 tea bags or 6 teaspoons tea leaves to make 4 tall glasses iced tea. Pour strained hot tea over ice cubes in glass. Decorate with thin slice of lemon or orange or sprig of fresh mint.

To make a 2-quart pitcher of iced tea use:

1 quart freshly-drawn cold water
⅓ cup loose tea or 15 tea bags

Sliced lemon
Sugar

BRING water to full rolling boil in 1½-quart saucepan. Remove from the heat, and while still bubbling, add all the tea at once. Stir. Let stand 5 minutes uncovered. Stir. Strain into glass pitcher in which there is an additional 1 quart of freshly drawn cold water. *Do not refrigerate.* Serve in ice-filled tall glasses with slice of lemon and sugar to taste. Makes 2 quarts, 8 to 10 or more glasses.

★TEA LEMONADE

2 quarts water
5 level tablespoons tea or 15 tea
  bags

¾ cup cold water
¾ cup sugar
¾ cup strained fresh lemon juice

BRING 2 quarts freshly drawn cold water to full rolling boil in large saucepan. Remove from heat. Immediately add tea. Brew 4 minutes. Stir and strain. Make a syrup by combining cold water and sugar in saucepan and simmering 10 minutes. Add this syrup and fresh lemon juice to tea. To serve, pour over ice cubes in tall chilled glasses. Makes about 12 glasses.

★TEA PUNCH

2 quarts water

5 level tablespoons tea or 15 tea
  bags

2 cups stained fresh lemon juice

4 cups strained fresh orange juice

1½ quarts grape juice

2 cups sugar

2 quarts water

1 quart ginger ale

BRING 2 quarts freshly drawn cold water to full rolling boil in large saucepan. Remove from heat. Add tea immediately. Brew 4 minutes. Stir and strain into glass pitcher holding all the remaining ingredients except ginger ale. Mix. Just before serving, pour mixture into punch bowl over block of ice. Stir in ginger ale. Makes about 50 punch cups.

Tea information and recipes above from WHAT YOU SHOULD KNOW ABOUT TEA, *by Tea Council of the U.S.A., Inc.*

❦

The *Woman's Home Companion Cook Book*, compiled by its staff food editors and edited by Dorothy Kirk, is fragrant with such good home beverages as:

★HOT CHOCOLATE

2½ (1-oz.) squares unsweetened
  chocolate

⅓ cup sugar

Salt

½ cup boiling water

4 cups milk

Whipped cream or marshmallows

MELT chocolate in top of 1½- or 2-quart double boiler over boiling water, add sugar and few grains salt. Add boiling water, stirring until well blended. Place pan directly over low heat, boil about 3 minutes. Add milk gradually, heat to boiling point. Beat until frothy. Pour into warmed cups. Top each with whipped cream or marshmallow if desired. Makes about 6 servings.

Hot Chocolate Made with Chocolate Syrup: Scald desired amount of milk, add 2 tablespoons Chocolate Syrup (*see* recipe on page 64) for each cup scalded milk. Stir until syrup is dissolved. Serve as above.

Rich Chocolate: Whip ½ cup heavy cream. Fold into 1 cup Chocolate Syrup (*see* recipe below). Place heaping tablespoon or more in each serving cup. Fill cups with scalded milk. Makes about 8 servings.

★CHOCOLATE SYRUP

5 (1-oz.) squares unsweetned
   chocolate
1½ cups sugar

⅛ teaspoon salt
1¼ cups boiling water

MELT chocolate in top of 1-quart double boiler over boiling water. Add sugar and salt. Add boiling water, stirring until well blended. Place pan directly over very low heat. Boil about 5 minutes, without stirring. Add 1 teaspoon vanilla if desired. Cool. Pour into glass jar and cover. Keep in refrigerator. Makes about 2¼ cups syrup.

★HOT COCOA

6 tablespoons cocoa
4 to 6 tablespoons sugar
⅛ teaspoon salt

½ cup water
5 cups milk
Whipped cream or marshmallows

COMBINE cocoa, sugar, and salt in 1½- or 2-quart saucepan; add water, place over low heat, stir until sugar is dissolved; boil 3 minutes. Add milk, stir; heat to boiling point. Beat until frothy. Add ½ teaspoon vanilla if desired. Top each cup of hot cocoa with whipped cream or a marshmallow. Makes 6 to 8 servings.

SPICED TEA IN MUGS   →

6 cups boiling water
6 tea bags
2 teaspoons grated lemon peel
2 teaspoons grated orange peel
½ cup fresh orange juice

¼ cup lemon juice
½ cup pineapple juice
Sugar to taste
8 to 10 thin slices lemon stuck
   with 3 or 4 cloves each
8 to 10 long cinnamon sticks

Pour boiling water over tea bags in large teapot. Brew 5 minutes. Remove tea bags. In enamel, agate or glass saucepan combine peel, and fruit juices, adding sugar to taste. Simmer gently 5 minutes. Pour mixture into teapot. Serve hot in mugs with clove-studded lemon slices with a cinnamon stick in each mug. Makes 8 to 10 mugs. Serve with hot apple fritters or other favorite fruit fritters.

Recipe and color photograph, courtesy Tea Council of the U.S.A., Inc.

Various Cold Chocolate Drinks

★CHOCOLATE MILK SHAKE

2 tablespoons chocolate syrup   Whipped cream if desired
1 cup cold milk

BLEND syrup and milk well, or beat with rotary beater. Serve in tall chilled glass. Top with whipped cream if desired. Serve with straws. Makes 1 tall glass.

Frosted Chocolate: Make Chocolate Milk Shake as described above. Float small dip of chocolate or vanilla ice cream on top of each serving. Also called Chocolate Float. Serve with straws and long-handled spoon.

Minted Chocolate: Add 2 or 3 drops peppermint extract to each cup of milk used in making Chocolate Milk Shake. Garnish with whipped cream topping with sprig of mint.

← POTATO CHOCOLATE CAKE

1 cup hot unseasoned mashed potatoes
2 cups sugar
⅔ cup shortening
4 eggs
1 teaspoon vanilla extract
2 cups all-purpose flour, sifted
1 cup cocoa powder
3 teaspoons baking powder
1 teaspoon each powdered cinnamon and nutmeg
½ teaspoon salt
¼ cup milk
1 cup chopped walnuts

Prepare mashed potatoes. An easy way is to follow directions for two servings on package mashed potatoes. Measure, set aside. Start oven at moderate (350 degrees F.). Line bottoms of two 9-inch layer pans, or oblong pan 13 × 9 × 2 inches with waxed paper cut to fit, grease paper lightly. Gradually beat sugar into shortening until fluffy. Add eggs, one at a time, beating well. Add vanilla and potatoes. Sift all dry ingredients together 3 times; add about ¼ of dry ingredients to egg mixture, beat, add ¼ of milk, beat well; continue adding dry ingredients and milk alternately until all are used. Stir walnuts in. Pour into pans. Bake layers in moderate oven 40 to 45 minutes, or loaf cake 50 minutes, or until done when tested. Let stand 5 minutes in pans. Turn out on racks, peel off paper. Let cool. Frost with Butter Cream or other favorite frosting and sprinkle thickly with chopped walnuts. Makes 8 or more servings.

Recipe and color photograph, courtesy Diamond Walnut Growers, Inc.

Fruit Juice Beverages

★LEMONADE

1 cup sugar
1 cup water

Peel of 2 lemons, grated or cut in pieces
1 cup lemon juice

COMBINE sugar, water, and lemon peel in 2-quart glass or enamel saucepan; stir over low heat until sugar is dissolved; boil about 7 minutes. Cool. Add lemon juice and 4 cups water. If sweeter lemonade is preferred, use less lemon juice. Pour over ice in pitcher or tall glasses. Serve straws with these. Makes 6 to 8 servings.

Minted Lemonade: Bruise some mint leaves with a spoon and place in the bottom of the pitcher before adding lemonade. Garnish each glass with sprig of mint.
Pink Lemonade: Add a little grenadine to the lemonade.
Raspberry Lemonade: Add 1 pint crushed raspberries to boiled sugar-water mixture. Strain. Add lemon juice and continue recipe as directed.
Limeade: Substitute lime juice for lemon juice in Lemonade recipe above. Add a very little green pure food coloring if desired.
Orangeade: Substitute 2 cups orange juice for lemon juice called for in Lemonade recipe above; add ¼ cup lemon juice.

★GRAPE COOLER

½ cup sugar
2 cups water
1 cup grape juice

1 cup orange juice
½ cup lemon juice

MAKE a syrup of the sugar and water; cool. Add fruit juices. Mix well. Pour over ice in pitcher or tall glasses, adding some ginger ale if desired. Serve straws with these. Makes 6 to 8 servings.

★PINEAPPLE MINT JULEP

6 sprigs fresh mint
¾ cup sugar
¾ cup lemon juice

3 cups unsweetened pineapple juice
3 cups ginger ale
Sprigs of mint for garnish

WASH mint leaves; bruise with spoon; cover with sugar. Add lemon juice; let stand about 15 minutes; add pineapple juice. Pour over ice in pitcher or tall glasses; add ginger ale. Garnish with sprigs of mint. Serve straws with these. Makes about 8 servings.

Fruit Punches (Non-alcoholic)

★GRAPE CIDER PUNCH

4 sticks cinnamon

24 whole cloves or 1 teaspoon
allspice

5 cups sweet cider or apple juice

4 cups grape juice

½ cup lemon juice

1 teaspoon grated lemon peel

1 teaspoon grated orange peel

2 quarts ginger ale

6 very thin orange slices

COMBINE spices and 2 cups cider in 1½- or 2-quart glass or enamel sauce-pan; place over low heat, bring to boiling point, and simmer about 5 minutes. Remove from heat; let stand ½ hour; strain. Combine with remaining cider, grape juice, lemon juice, lemon and orange peels in large enamel kettle. Pour into glass jars or pitchers to chill.

When ready to serve, pour over ice in punch bowl and add ginger ale. Garnish with orange slices. Makes 35 to 40 punch-cup servings.

★SPICED PINEAPPLE PUNCH

1 cup sugar

1½ cups water

2 sticks cinnamon

8 whole cloves

4 cups unsweetened pineapple
juice

1 cup orange juice

½ cup lemon juice

COMBINE sugar, water, and spices in 2-quart glass or enamel saucepan; place over low heat; boil 3 to 5 minutes. Strain, and let cool. Add fruit juices, pour over ice in pitcher or punch bowl. Makes 8 to 10 punch-cup servings.

All chocolate, cocoa, and fruit drinks above from WOMAN'S HOME COM-PANION COOK BOOK, *edited by Dorothy Kirk*

This good fruit punch comes from *The A.B.C. of Spice Cookery,* by the American Spice Trade Association.

★SPICED FRUIT PUNCH

2 cups boiling water
2 teaspoons tea
2 cups light corn syrup or 1½
  cups honey
Salt
¼ teaspoon ground cloves
1 quart loganberry or any tart
  fruit juice

¾ cup lemon juice
2 quarts ginger ale
Sprig fresh mint
6 thin orange slices
6 whole cloves

ADD tea to boiling water; cover; steep for 5 minutes. Strain, combine with syrup or honey, few grains salt, ground cloves in 1½-gallon enamel kettle. Mix, let cool. Add fruit juice, lemon juice, and ginger ale. Mix, pour over ice in punch bowl. Garnish with fresh mint. Add the orange slices studded with cloves. Makes about 4 quarts, 16 cups, or 24 punch cups.

The recipe above from THE A.B.C. OF SPICE COOKERY, *by the American Spice Trade Association*

❧

These hot drinks are recommended by the staff writers of *The Angostura Cook Book.*

★HOT CALYPSO CIDER

2 quarts cider or apple juice
¼ cup brown sugar, packed, or
  maple sugar

3 orange slices
3 lemon slices
2 tablespoons Angostura bitters

HEAT cider or juice with sugar added, in large enamel saucepan or soup marmite. Stir until sugar is dissolved. Add orange and lemon slices; simmer 10 minutes. Add bitters, stir, and serve. Makes about 2 quarts, 8 or more mugs.

★TEENERS' HOT TOM-AND-JERRY

6 egg yolks
¾ cup sugar
⅛ teaspoon salt
1 tablespoon Angostura bitters

6 stiffly-beaten egg whites
4 cups scalded milk
Grated nutmeg

In medium-size glass or ceramic punch bowl beat egg yolks with ½ cup sugar, salt, and bitters until fluffy. Add remaining sugar to stiffly beaten egg whites, beating in until smooth, and fold into first mixture. Beat scalded milk with rotary beater and stir gradually into the egg mixture. Ladle at once from bowl into mugs. Sprinkle top of each mug with a few grains of nutmeg. Makes 8 to 10 servings.

The two recipes above from THE ANGOSTURA COOK BOOK, *by the Angostura-Wuppermann Corporation*

❀

There is no author's name on *Buckeye Cookery,* a favorite Ohio cook book of the nineteenth century. But many Middle Western cooks supplied its recipes, one of which follows.

A mulled drink is a hot drink, usually cider, wine, or a mixture of fruit juices with spice added—a favorite for winter holiday parties. (*See* Alcoholic Beverages section for additional mulled beverages.)

★MULLED CIDER

2 quarts cider　　　　　　　6 whole allspice
½ cup brown sugar, packed　2 or 3 cinnamon sticks
4 whole cloves

COMBINE all ingredients in 2½-quart glass or enamel saucepan. Heat slowly to boiling point; do not boil; simmer for 5 minutes. Ladle into warmed mugs or cups. Makes 10 servings.

In the nineteenth-century Middle West, warm gingerbread was the favorite food served with this hot drink.

This recipe from an old Ohio cook book, BUCKEYE COOKERY, *published in 1881*

Alcoholic Beverages

Since bar drinks are a part of entertaining in many homes, the favorites are given here, professional recipes of established reputation. An excellent source is *The Professional Mixing Guide,* by

The Angostura-Wuppermann Corporation. Correctly mixed, such drinks deserve to be served in the right glass, not only because they fit into that particular glass, but because tradition and custom, only slightly influenced by changing styles in glassware, call for a certain glass for each bar drink.

Bar drinks also call for bar accessories. The right glasses, a good bottle opener, corkscrew, stirring spoon, strainer, a shaker and mixer, small lemon cutting board, insulated bowl for ice cubes, an ice scraper for frappéd drinks, sharp fruit-slicing knife, bar measures such as jigger (holds 1½ ounces, or 3 tablespoons liquid), a pony (holds 1 ounce, or 2 tablespoons liquid), straight wineglass (holds 4 ounces, or ½ cup) and a teaspoon and table-spoon are essentials.

In addition, some mixers like to use simple syrup as a sweet-ener. This is made by combining 1 pound sugar and 2 cups water in a saucepan. Bring slowly to boiling point. Remove from heat. Cool. Keep in covered glass jar in refrigerator. Reheat if sugar settles out. Makes about 3 cups syrup. Use as called for in recipes.

ABSINTHE COCKTAIL

2 dashes Angostura bitters
1 jigger absinthe substitute

1 jigger simple syrup
Lemon peel

SHAKE well with cracked ice. Strain into cocktail glass containing a twist of lemon peel. Makes 1 cocktail.

ABSINTHE FRAPPE

3 dashes Angostura bitters
1 jigger absinthe substitute

½ pony anisette
Shaved ice

SHAKE thoroughly with shaved ice until frosted. Strain into cocktail glass. Makes 1 drink.

ADONIS COCKTAIL

2 dashes orange bitters
¾ pony sweet vermouth

1 jigger dry sherry

STIR well in cracked ice. Strain into cocktail glass. Makes 1 cocktail.

ALEXANDER COCKTAIL

1 pony dry gin
¾ pony heavy cream

¾ pony crème de cacao

SHAKE vigorously with cracked ice. Strain into a large cocktail glass. Makes 1 cocktail. (Use brandy in place of gin for a Brandy Alexander.)

AMER PICON COCKTAIL

1 pony Amer Picon
1 pony dry gin

¾ pony sweet vermouth
Dash curaçao

STIR well in cracked ice. Strain into cocktail glass. Makes 1 cocktail.

AMERICAN BEAUTY COCKTAIL

1 dash white crème de menthe
½ pony orange juice
½ pony grenadine

½ pony dry vermouth
½ pony brandy
Port wine

SHAKE first five ingredients well with cracked ice. Strain into cocktail glass. Top with port. Makes 1 cocktail.

ANGEL'S KISS

¼ crème de cacao
¼ crème yvette

¼ heavy cream
¼ brandy

POUR ingredients into a liqueur glass very carefully in order listed, so as to produce a layer-upon-layer *pousse-café* effect. Makes 1 cocktail.

ANISETTE COCKTAIL

1 dash Angostura bitters
1 jigger Pernod

1 teaspoon Benedictine

SHAKE well with cracked ice and serve in frosted cocktail glass. Makes 1 cocktail.

APPETIZER COCKTAIL

3 dashes Angostura bitters
1 jigger dry gin

1 jigger Dubonnet
Juice ½ orange

STIR well in cracked ice. Strain into large cocktail glass. Makes 1 cocktail.

BACARDI COCKTAIL

Juice ½ lime
½ teaspoon sugar

Dash grenadine
1 jigger Bacardi rum

SHAKE well in finely chipped ice. Strain into cocktail glass. Makes 1 cocktail. (Called Bacardi Flyer when made by same formula and strained into a glass which is then filled with dry champagne.)

BALTIMORE BRACER

½ anisette
½ brandy

1 egg white

SHAKE thoroughly with cracked ice. Strain into cocktail glass. Makes 1 cocktail.

BAMBOO COCKTAIL

2 dashes Angostura bitters   1 jigger dry vermouth
1 jigger sherry

STIR well in cracked ice. Strain into cocktail glass. Makes 1 cocktail.

BENEDICTINE FRAPPE

FILL a cocktail glass with shaved (snow) ice. Pour in Benedictine. Serve
with 2 short straws. Makes 1 cocktail.

BLOODY MARY

1 jigger vodka   2 jiggers tomato juice
2 dashes A-1 Sauce or Worcester-
    shire

SHAKE well. Serve in tall glass. Makes 1 cocktail.

BRANDY COCKTAIL

2 dashes Angostura bitters   ½ pony curaçao
½ teaspoon simple syrup   Twist of lemon peel
1 jigger brandy

STIR well in cracked ice. Strain into cocktail glass. Add twist of lemon
peel. Makes 1 cocktail.

BRANDY FLOAT

FILL an Old Fashioned glass nearly full with chilled carbonated water.
Rest the bowl of a teaspoon on top, and slowly pour into it 1 pony of
brandy, allowing the brandy to overflow. Then carefully slide the spoon
out from under the brandy, and the liquor will float. Makes 1 cocktail.

BRANDY SMASH

4 sprigs fresh mint   Seltzer
1 teaspoon sugar   1 jigger brandy

MUDDLE the mint and sugar lightly in an Old Fashioned glass. Add
splash of seltzer. Add ice and brandy. Garnish with mint. Stir slightly and
serve with stir rod. Makes 1 cocktail.

BRONX COCKTAIL

½ dry gin   ¼ sweet vermouth
¼ dry vermouth   Juice ½ orange

SHAKE well with cracked ice. Strain into cocktail glass. Makes 1 cocktail.

CANADIAN COCKTAIL

2 dashes Angostura bitters   1 dash curaçao
1 jigger Canadian whisky   1 teaspoon sugar

SHAKE well with ice. Strain into cocktail glass. Makes 1 cocktail.

CHAMPAGNE COCKTAIL

PLACE 1 lump sugar in a "saucer" champagne glass. Saturate sugar with Angostura bitters. Add twist of orange or lemon peel, or both. Fill with chilled champagne. Makes 1 cocktail. (Sometimes made by adding 1 pony Southern Comfort and a dash of Angostura to champagne glass, then filling with chilled champagne.)

CLOVER CLUB COCKTAIL

½ teaspoon sugar   1 egg white
½ pony fresh lime or lemon juice   ½ pony grenadine
1 jigger dry gin

SHAKE thoroughly with ice. Strain into a large cocktail glass. Makes 1 cocktail.

COGNAC SOUR

3 dashes Angostura bitters   ¾ pony lemon juice
1 jigger cognac   1 teaspoon sugar

SHAKE well with ice. Strain into Delmonico glass. Makes 1 sour.

CRÈME DE MENTHE FRAPPE

FILL cocktail glass with fine ice. Add green or white crème de menthe. Serve with short straws. Makes 1 frappé.

DAQUIRI COCKTAIL

Juice ½ lime   1 teaspoon sugar
1 jigger Puerto Rican or Cuban
   rum

SHAKE well with finely shaved ice. Strain into cocktail glass. Makes 1 cocktail. (Shake strenuously with cracked ice or use electric mixer. Serve unstrained, with short straws, in "saucer" champagne glass and it's a Frozen Daquiri.)

DUBONNET COCKTAIL

½ Dubonnet   Lemon peel
½ dry gin

STIR in ice, strain into cocktail glass. Twist of lemon peel optional. Makes 1 cocktail.

EL PRESIDENTE

1 jigger (Gold Label) rum   ½ pony dry vermouth
½ pony curaçao   Dash grenadine

SHAKE well in ice. Strain into cocktail glass. Twist of orange peel sometimes added. Makes 1 cocktail.

GIBSON COCKTAIL

⅔ dry gin   3 small pearl onions
⅓ dry vermouth   Twist lemon peel

STIR gin and vermouth well in cracked ice. Strain into cocktail glass prepared with 3 small onions. Twist lemon peel over cocktail for the oil. Makes 1 cocktail.

GIMLET

3 parts London dry gin   Thin slice lime
1 part sweetened lime juice   Green minted cherry

STIR gin and lime juice in ice in pitcher. Serve in cocktail glass. Hollywood version, garnish with slice of lime and green minted cherry. Makes 1 cocktail.

GIN 'N' BITTERS

5 generous dashes Angostura   1 jigger dry gin
  bitters   Cube of ice

PUT bitters in Old Fashioned glass with large cube of ice. Pour gin over all. Stir. Serve with stir rod. Makes 1 cocktail. (It's a Gin 'n' It when a jigger of sweet vermouth and ½ pony dry gin are served in the same way.)

JACK ROSE COCKTAIL

1 jigger applejack   Juice ½ lemon
½ pony grenadine

SHAKE with cracked ice. Strain into cocktail glass. Makes 1 cocktail.

MANHATTAN COCKTAIL

Dash Angostura bitters   ⅓ sweet vermouth
⅔ whisky

STIR slightly in ice in mixing glass. Strain and serve in cocktail glass. Makes 1 cocktail.

MARTINI COCKTAIL

⅔ dry gin   Olive or pearl onion
⅓ dry vermouth

STIR in cracked ice, strain into cocktail glass dressed with olive or onion. Makes 1 cocktail.

MARTINI COCKTAIL (SWEET)

Dash orange bitters   **⅓ sweet vermouth**
⅔ dry gin

STIR in cracked ice. Strain into cocktail glass. Makes 1 cocktail.

OLD FASHIONED COCKTAIL

2 or 3 dashes Angostura bitters   **1 maraschino cherry, if desired**
Seltzer   **1 jigger favorite liquor (rye, bour-**
1 lump sugar   **bon, Scotch, rum, applejack,**
2 cubes ice   **brandy, Irish whisky, vermouth)**
Twist of lemon peel

DASH of bitters, then a splash of seltzer on lump of sugar in Old Fashioned glass. Muddle, add 2 cubes ice, twist of peel, and cherry. Pour in liquid, stir well, and serve. Makes 1 cocktail.

ORANGE BLOSSOM COCKTAIL

1 jigger dry gin   **1 teaspoon sugar**
1 pony orange juice

SHAKE well with cracked ice. Strain into cocktail glass. Makes 1 cocktail.

PINK LADY COCKTAIL

¾ pony dry gin   **½ pony grenadine**
¼ pony applejack   **1 egg white**
½ pony fresh lemon juice

SHAKE with cracked ice very strenuously. Strain into cocktail glass. Makes 1 cocktail.

ROB ROY COCKTAIL

1 or 2 dashes Angostura bitters   **⅓ sweet vermouth**
⅔ Scotch

STIR in mixing glass with cracked ice until thoroughly mixed. Strain into cocktail glass. Makes 1 cocktail.

SIDECAR COCKTAIL

⅓ lemon juice   **⅓ brandy**
⅓ Cointreau

SHAKE well with ice. Strain into cocktail glass. Makes 1 cocktail.

STINGER COCKTAIL

1 pony white crème de menthe   1¼ ponies brandy

SHAKE well with ice. Strain into cocktail glass. Makes 1 cocktail.

VERMOUTH COCKTAIL

3 dashes Angostura bitters   ¼ thin slice lemon
1 jigger sweet vermouth

STIR bitters and vermouth in cracked ice. Strain into cocktail glass. Decorate with lemon. Makes 1 cocktail.

VODKA COCKTAIL

Juice ½ fresh lime   1 jigger vodka
½ pony cherry brandy

SHAKE well with cracked ice. Strain into cocktail glass. Makes 1 cocktail.

WHISKY COCKTAIL

2 dashes Angostura bitters   1 jigger whisky

STIR well with ice. Strain and serve in cocktail glass. Makes 1 cocktail.

WHISKY SOUR

3 generous dashes Angostura   1 teaspoon sugar
  bitters   Slice orange
1 jigger rye or bourbon whisky   Maraschino cherry
¾ pony lemon juice

SHAKE with ice. Strain into Delmonico glass prepared with slice of orange and cherry. Makes 1 cocktail.

Tall Drinks

BLACK VELVET

½ chilled champagne   ½ ice-cold stout

POUR together, simultaneously and slowly into 14-ounce collins glass. Makes 1 serving.

BOURBON AND SODA

1 jigger bourbon   Soda

POUR bourbon into an 8-ounce highball glass. Add ice. Fill with soda, stir slightly, and serve. Makes 1 serving. (Can be made with rye, Scotch, Canadian or Irish whisky, applejack, or rum.)

BRANDY DAISY

2 ponies brandy
½ pony grenadine
Juice 1 lemon

Sliced orange, or lemon, or
maraschino cherry

POUR brandy, grenadine, and lemon juice into a mix glass; fill with finely cracked ice. Shake well, pour unstrained into 8-ounce highball glass. Decorate with fruit. Serve with straws. Makes 1 serving.

BUCKAROO

4 or 5 dashes Angostura bitters
1 jigger bourbon or rye

1 bottle cola

DASH Angostura into 10-ounce highball glass, add ice, whisky, then cola to fill. Stir slightly. Makes 1 serving.

CLARET LEMONADE

Juice 1 lemon
2 teaspoons sugar

3 ponies claret
3 ponies water

SQUEEZE lemon into mixing glass; add sugar, claret, water, and ice. Shake well. Serve in 10-ounce collins glass with straws. Makes 1 serving.

CUBA LIBRE

Juice ½ lime
3 cubes ice

1 jigger Puerto Rican or Cuban
   rum
Cola

SQUEEZE lime juice into 10-ounce collins glass and drop in lime shell. Add 3 cubes ice and the rum. Fill glass with cola. Serve with stir rod. Makes 1 serving.

FRENCH '75

Juice 1 lemon
1 teaspoon sugar

2 ponies dry gin or brandy
Chilled champagne

SHAKE lemon juice, sugar, and gin or brandy with cracked ice. Pour into 8-ounce highball glass. Fill with champagne. Stir. Makes 1 serving.

GIN BUCK

Juice ½ lime
1 jigger dry gin

Ginger ale

SQUEEZE lime into a 10-ounce highball glass and drop lime shell in. Add ice, then gin, and fill glass with ginger ale. Stir slightly. Makes 1 serving.

GIN AND TONIC

Fresh lime or lemon peel

1 jigger dry gin

Thin slice lime or lemon

Indian quinine water

RUB peel of fresh lime or lemon around inside edge of 8-ounce glass. Pour gin in, add 2 cubes ice and slice of lime or lemon. Fill glass with quinine water. Stir slightly. Makes 1 serving. Can also be made with rum or vodka.

GIN FIZZ

1 pony fresh lemon juice

1 teaspooon sugar

1 jigger dry gin

Carbonated water

SHAKE lemon juice, sugar, and gin with cracked ice. Strain into 10-ounce highball glass. Fill with carbonated water. Stir slightly. Makes 1 serving. With 1 egg yolk added, this is a Golden Fizz. Shake well and pour into 8-ounce highball glass, fill with carbonated water.

GIN RICKEY

½ lime

1 jigger dry gin

Carbonated water

SQUEEZE lime into 10-ounce highball glass, drop lime shell in. Add ice cubes and gin. Fill with carbonated water. Serve with stir rod. Makes 1 serving.

GIN SLING

3 dashes Angostura bitters

1 jigger dry gin

Twist lemon peel

Carbonated water

ADD cracked ice to 8-ounce highball glass, Angostura, gin, and twist of lemon peel. Fill with carbonated water. Stir slightly. Makes 1 serving.

HORSE'S NECK

1 lemon

1 jigger gin or whisky

Ginger ale

PEEL lemon spiral fashion in 1 piece. Place 1 edge of peel over lip of 10-ounce collins glass, let remainder curl inside the glass. Add cubes of ice. Pour in gin or whisky, fill with ginger ale. Makes 1 serving.

MINT JULEP

4 sprigs fresh mint

1 teaspoon sugar

Seltzer

2 jiggers bourbon

Rum

FILL a 10-ounce collins glass with finely crushed ice and place to one side. Strip leaves from 2 sprigs fresh mint, place them in mixing glass, and sprinkle with 1 teaspoon sugar. Macerate with muddler until mint flavor is released from leaves. Add splash of seltzer and the bourbon. Stir gently, then strain into the prepared collins glass over the ice. Work a bar spoon up and down in the mixture until the outside of the glass begins to frost. Top with a splash of rum, garnish with 2 sprigs mint, and serve with straws. Do not touch the glass with hands; use towel while handling to facilitate frosting. Makes 1 serving.

RUM COLLINS

Juice 1 lemon
1 teaspoon sugar

1 jigger rum
Carbonated water

SHAKE lemon juice, sugar, and rum with ice and pour unstrained into 10-ounce collins glass. Fill with carbonated water. Stir slightly and serve with straws. Makes 1 serving.

SCREW DRIVER

POUR jigger of vodka into highball glass with ice. Fill with orange juice and stir. Makes 1 serving.

SHERRY COBBLER

3 ponies medium-sweet sherry
1 teaspoon sugar

Carbonated water
Fruits, if desired

MIX sherry and sugar in 10-ounce collins glass. Add finely shaved ice and carbonated water to fill. Stir slightly. Decorate with fruits if desired. Serve with straws. Makes 1 serving.

SILVER FIZZ

1 pony lemon juice
1 jigger dry gin
1 teaspoon sugar

1 egg white
Carbonated water

COMBINE juice, gin, sugar, and egg white. Shake vigorously with cracked ice. Strain into 8-ounce highball glass. Fill with carbonated water. Stir slightly. Makes 1 serving.

SPRITZER

⅓ Rhine wine

⅔ seltzer

POUR chilled wine into highball glass. Add chilled seltzer. Stir slightly. Makes 1 serving.

TOM COLLINS

Juice 1 lemon
1 teaspoon sugar or simple syrup

1 jigger dry gin
Carbonated water

SHAKE juice, sugar or syrup, and gin with cracked ice. Pour unstrained into 10-ounce collins glass. Fill with carbonated water. Stir and serve with straws. Makes 1 serving.

VERMOUTH CASSIS

2 jiggers dry vermouth
½ pony crème de cassis

Carbonated water

STIR vermouth and crème de cassis in 8-ounce highball glass with ice cubes. Fill with carbonated water. Stir slightly and serve. Makes 1 serving.

ZOMBIE
(Original Carioca recipe)

1 pony tropical heavy-bodied rum
2 ponies Puerto Rican or Cuban
  Gold Label rum
1 pony White Label rum
2 teaspoons apricot brandy
¾ pony unsweetened pineapple
  juice
¾ pony papaya juice
1 teaspoon sugar

Juice 1 lime
Splash of 151-proof tropical heavy-
  bodied rum
1 green cherry
½-inch pineapple cube
1 red cherry
Sprig mint
Powdered sugar

COMBINE the tropical rum, Puerto Rican and White Label rums, apricot brandy, pineapple juice, papaya juice, sugar, and lime juice with ice and shake well. Pour unstrained into 14-ounce zombie glass. Float a splash of 151-proof tropical heavy-bodied rum on top. Spike on a wooden cocktail pick, in the order named, the green cherry, the pineapple cube, and the red cherry. Decorate the glass with this and a sprig of mint. Sprinkle powdered sugar over all and serve with straws. Makes 1 serving.

Punches and Cups

FISH HOUSE PUNCH

¾ pound sugar
1 quart lemon juice
2 quarts Jamaica rum

1 quart brandy
2 quarts water
¼ cup peach brandy

COMBINE all ingredients in large glass punch bowl, mix, and let stand 2 hours at room temperature, stirring occasionally. To serve, add large block clear ice to bowl, stirring and spooning mixture over it. Makes 30 to 45 punch glasses.

PLANTER'S PUNCH

5 dashes Angostura bitters
1 pony fresh lime juice
1 pony simple syrup or 2
  teaspoons sugar

2 jiggers heavy-bodied rum
Chilled carbonated water
1 thin slice lemon
Grated nutmeg

PLACE bitters, juice, syrup or sugar, and rum in mixing glass with finely shaved ice and shake vigorously. Pour unstrained into a 10-ounce collins glass. Fill with chilled carbonated water. Stir slightly. Garnish with slice of lemon and dust with nutmeg. Serve with straws. Makes 1 serving.

WEDDING RECEPTION PUNCH

3 ripe fresh peaches, unpeeled
1 bottle (⅘) sauterne
1 teaspoon Angostura bitters

2 bottles (⅘ each) dry champagne
Fresh strawberries

WASH peaches, rub with damp cloth, then pierce deeply and thoroughly with tines of fork. Place in bottom of punch bowl. Place ice-block in punch bowl on peaches. To serve, combine sauterne and bitters, pour into punch bowl. Add champagne. Garnish punch and individual servings with unhulled strawberries. Makes about 25 punch-cup servings.

CHAMPAGNE CUP

2-quart glass pitcher
Cracked ice
2 oranges, thinly sliced
6 thin slices pineapple
Lemon peel

1 jigger maraschino liqueur
1 jigger chartreuse
1 jigger brandy
1 bottle chilled champagne

PLACE 1-inch layer of cracked ice in bottom of pitcher. Garnish with few orange slices, 1 or 2 slices of pineapple, and few small pieces of lemon peel. Add maraschino liqueur, chartreuse, and brandy. Make a second layer of ice, garnish with orange, pineapple, and lemon peel. Repeat layers of ice and garnishes until pitcher is half full. Place long bar spoon in the ice, fill pitcher with chilled champagne. Stir and serve. Makes 12 or more punch-cup servings.

CLARET CUP

2-quart glass pitcher
1 lemon, thinly sliced
1 orange, thinly sliced
5 thin slices fresh pineapple
1 jigger curaçao
1 jigger brandy

1 jigger simple syrup or 3 tablespoons sugar
1 dash maraschino syrup
1 pony lemon juice
8 maraschino cherries
1 quart claret, chilled
1 pint chilled carbonated water

COMBINE all ingredients except claret and carbonated water in pitcher. Pour in claret and let stand a few minutes. Add carbonated water, stirring with the claret, but not disturbing fruit in bottom. Makes 10 to 12 punch-cup servings.

Hot Drinks (Alcoholic)

GLOGG

2 ponies Angostura bitters
¾ cup granulated sugar
1 pint claret
1 pint sherry

½ pint brandy
Large seedless raisins and unsalted
  almonds

COMBINE bitters, sugar, wines, and brandy in a marmite or casserole which can be placed directly over heat. When steaming hot, serve in mugs, adding 1 raisin and 1 almond to each serving. Makes 10 punch-glass servings.

HOT BUTTERED RUM

2 dashes Angostura bitters
2 jiggers Puerto Rican or Cuban
  rum

1 teaspoon butter
Hot water
3 or 4 whole cloves

DASH the bitters into a mug. Add rum; place teaspoon with the butter in the rum. Pour hot water into mug to ¾ full. Add cloves. Stir; let steep few minutes. Inhale; then sip! Makes 1 serving. (Less rum may be used for less hearty drinkers.)

MULLED CLARET

2 jiggers claret
1 cup water
2 dashes Angostura bitters
1 teaspoon sugar
½ teaspoon ground cinnamon

¼ teaspoon ground cloves
½ teaspoon ground allspice
1 teaspoon or little more lemon
  juice

HEAT all together a few minutes in a glass or enamel saucepan. Strain into mug or 2 small mugs. Makes 1 or 2 servings. (Other wines, especially red wines, may be substituted for claret in this recipe.)

TODDY

1 teaspoon sugar	1 lemon slice
1 jigger whisky	4 whole cloves
Small stick cinnamon	Boiling water
Dash lemon bitters or piece lemon peel	

COMBINE all ingredients except boiling water in mug or heatproof glass. Add boiling water until ⅔ full. Stir mixture a little. Serve with spoon. Also serve a small pitcher of hot water on side. Makes 1 serving. (Any whisky may be used, also rum, applejack, or gin.)

TOM AND JERRY

1 egg	¾ pony rye whisky or brandy
1 tablespoon sugar	Hot milk or water
¾ pony Jamaica rum	Grated nutmeg

BEAT egg yolk and white separately, the white until light but not quite stiff. Then combine them in an 8-ounce goblet or china mug. Add sugar and liquor; fill glass or mug with hot milk or water. Stir well. Add few grains grated nutmeg to top. Serve at once. Makes 1 serving.

All drinks above from PROFESSIONAL MIXING GUIDE, *by the Angostura-Wuppermann Corporation*

❧

Old English names appear on the hot drinks in *The Fine Art of Mixing Drinks,* by David A. Embury, as in the recipes which follow.

POSSETS

According to Mr. Embury, a posset consists of sweetened spiced milk curdled with hot ale or wine. Eggs are frequently added to the mixture, and sometimes, when eggs are used, the milk is omitted and the mixture is called Egg Posset.

ALE POSSET

10 egg yolks	1 quart heavy cream
5 egg whites	1 pint ale
1 tablespoon sugar	Spices as desired

BEAT yolks and whites with sugar and cream, and when thoroughly blended, stir in ale. Sprinkle liberally with nutmeg and, if desired, add ground cinnamon, cloves, or other spices. Warm over low heat, stirring until mixture thickens. Serve in mugs or punch cups. Makes about 12 or more servings.

EGG POSSET

12 egg yolks	2 quarts dry white wine
½ cup sugar	
1 teaspoon mixed ground spices	
(nutmeg, cinnamon, cloves)	

BEAT yolks to froth, adding sugar and spices. Heat wine to boiling point, remove from heat, stir slowly into egg mixture. Serve at once. Makes about 20 or more mugs or punch cups.

WINE POSSET

1 quart milk	1 teaspoon grated lemon peel
½ pint dry white wine	Spices as desired
1 tablespoon sugar	

BOIL milk and wine together until milk curdles. Strain off whey and dissolve sugar and grated lemon in it. Press curdled milk through sieve, sprinkle with grated nutmeg and any other spices desired. Beat into sweetened whey, serve piping hot. Makes from 4 to 6 servings.

NEGUS

The negus is a sweetened spiced wine (usually port) served with hot water. It is quite similar to mulled drinks, but traditionally differs from them in that the wine is heated by the addition of hot water instead of by the hot-poker or saucepan method. The drink is said to have been invented by Colonel Francis Negus during Queen Anne's reign.

1 quart port	Spices as desired
1 tablespoon sugar	Juice 2 lemons
Grated peel 1 lemon	1 quart boiling water

WARM the wine but do not let boil. Pour into heated jug with sugar, peel, spices, and lemon juice; let stand in warm place 15 minutes. Add boiling water, stir well, serve piping hot. Makes from 8 to 10 mugs.

The four recipes above from THE FINE ART OF MIXING DRINKS, *by David A. Embury*

Holiday Drinks

Here are two famous holiday recipes of Richardson Wright, author of *The Bed-Book of Eating and Drinking*.

EGGNOG

6 eggs
2 tablespoons sugar
1 cup rye whisky
1 pint milk

2 jiggers brandy or rum
1 pint heavy cream, lightly
  whipped
Grated nutmeg

COMBINE egg yolks and sugar in serving bowl and beat until smooth. Slowly add whisky, then milk, stirring steadily. Add brandy or rum, stirring; then add cream. Beat egg whites stiff, fold into mixture. Chill in refrigerator at least 3 hours. Serve in punch cups with a little grated nutmeg on each serving. Makes about 12 punch cups.

PUNCH FOR NEW YEAR'S DAY

1 quart brandy
⅓ cup Jamaica rum
⅓ cup curaçao
5 cups water
Juice 2 lemons

1 orange, thinly sliced
⅓ fresh pineapple, pared and
  cut up
⅔ cup raspberries (quick-frozen,
  fresh, or drained canned)

MIX brandy, rum, and curaçao. Add water, lemon juice and fruit. Let stand in large glass punch bowl or pitcher for about 1 hour. Add block of ice to bowl. Stir punch around and over it. Serve very cold. Makes 12 or more punch-cup servings.

The two above recipes from THE BED-BOOK OF EATING AND DRINKING, *by Richardson Wright*

This unusual hot Thanksgiving punch is from *Trader Vic's Book of Food and Drink*.

THANKSGIVING PUNCH (HOT)

1 quart Jamaica rum	3 sticks cinnamon
2 teaspoons ground allspice	3 teaspoons butter
1 quart apple cider	

COMBINE all ingredients in large chafing dish or marmite and heat to steaming. Serve in heated mugs. Makes 10 or more punch-cup servings.

Trader Vic says, "If I were going to serve this to friends on Thanksgiving Day, I'd rig myself up a chafing-dish setup on the buffet or side table, bank it with fruit and fall berries and candles, and set the mugs around the base while the mixture keeps warm on an alcohol lamp or electric plate."

This recipe from TRADER VIC'S BOOK OF FOOD AND DRINK, *by Trader Vic.*

THE SERVICE OF WINE

André L. Simon, who has been known to the world's gastronomes for many years as the President of the London Wine and Food Society, is the author of several books on good dining (more of these later, in our foreign cookery pages) and on wines. From his small paper-bound book *Let Mine Be Wine*, here is his basic information for homemaker and host on how to serve wine:

The service of wine should be such that any and every wine has every chance to show how good it can be, which means, chiefly, served in good condition, at the right temperature, in the right glasses, and at the right time.

Decanting. Most red wines and some white ones, those which have been made without chemists and chemicals, neither pasteurized, filtered, nor sterilized, throw a sediment in the bottle as they grow old, and it is important that such sediment be left in the bottle when the wine is served. The best way is to decant any such old wine, that is to say, pour it out with the greatest care possible into a clear glass decanter.

Make sure that the decanter is beautifully clean, polished outside and quite free from the faintest imaginable taint inside. Glass decanters which are not used frequently are liable to acquire a mustiness which would ruin any wine, and they must be well rinsed and dried before use. Having made sure that the decanter is all that it should be and holds a quart of wine, one should proceed as follows:

Lift the bottle from its bin very gently and place it tenderly in a wine cradle (or basket holder). Carry the bottle in its cradle to the nearest convenient place where there is a table that is firm on its four legs and where there is a good light. Place the bottle in its cradle on the table; remove the capsule or wax protecting the cork; wipe the neck of the bottle thoroughly.

Introduce the point of the corkscrew in the center of the cork; drive it steadily and fully with the right hand while the left hand steadies the bottle. Hold the bottle down firmly with the left hand, while the right pulls the cork with all the strength it may require, but without jerks.

Once the cork is out, wipe the inside of the neck of the bottle with a clean cloth, allowing a little wine to come over the cloth. Lift the bottle out of the cradle with the right hand, hold it at eye level, and pour the wine slowly into the decanter, which is being held in the left hand up near the lip of the bottle.

Watch the wine as it flows from the bottle into the decanter through the neck of the bottle until you perceive dust, or slime, or any solid matter arriving in the neck of the bottle. Stand the bottle up at once and leave in it whatever wine may remain, with the sediment, crust, or lees.

Some people decant old wines through a funnel packed with muslin or litmus paper; this is wrong, as the wine will never be as brilliant again after it has been filtered thus. It may save time and trouble, but it is not fair to any fine wine, and even less fair to any wine-loving guest.

Young wines, both the red and the white, quite clear and free from all sediment, may also be decanted, or merely poured from the bottle into a decanter, just for its appearance. A bottle upon a well-appointed dinner table never looks in keeping with the silver and flowers. But a nice decanter of wine does, and the wine in it can be seen and adds its color and sparkle to the setting.

Temperature. The temperature of the wine at the time of drinking does not matter very much. One must always, of course, allow for personal likes and dislikes, and one person may like white wines colder than another; but this does not in any way alter the rule that all white wines are best served cold, and the sweeter they are, the colder they should be.

Red wines, on the contrary, have everything to lose and nothing to gain by being chilled, still less iced. The ideal temperature for red wines is that of the dining room, providing that the room is not overheated. No red wine should ever be served warm; it should strike the palate as fresh, not cold, but almost cool. [Today's popular rosé wines are usually chilled. Ed.]

Glasses. The shape, size, and color of wine glasses can help or mar the enjoyment of wine. A good wine deserves a good glass, and a good glass should be clear crystal, unadorned, and not only perfectly clean but well polished. Glass captures and retains odors of all sorts; many a good bottle of wine has been condemned as bad simply because it was served in glasses which seemed perfectly clean, but had been wiped with an unclean cloth or had been kept wrapped in paper.

The wine glass should be large enough to hold a fair measure of wine when only half full; sufficiently curved in at the top to collect the bouquet of the wine, yet open enough to allow any nose a free entry. The thinner and finer the glass, the better it is for the wine.

The order of wines. The order in which different wines should be served is a matter of taste and common sense, taste being more uncertain than common sense. It is only common sense, for instance, to serve a dry wine before rather than after a sweet one; a younger wine before an older one; a white wine with fish and white meats; a red wine with red meats and venison. These are the main rules of the order of service of wines, and like all rules, they have many exceptions.

The following main divisions of these rules have long proved acceptable to most people:

Before meals, a glass of dry slightly chilled sherry or on festive occasions a glass of chilled and really dry champagne.

With hors d'oeuvres, fish, and white meats, a light, young, inexpensive white wine, slightly chilled, or on special occasions a better wine.

With soup, a fuller sherry and not chilled, or a glass of Madeira.

With red meat and game any of the many red wines at hand, fair, fine, or great, according to the occasion and the guests.

With cheese and dessert, a port, sherry, or Madeira, or any other fortified wine, fuller or lighter, according to weather.

With curry, beer is best; curry will ruin any fine wine.

The advice above from LET MINE BE WINE, *by André L. Simon*

THE
"BEST-OF-ALL"

BREADS

THE RECIPES THAT FOLLOW HAVE BEEN
SELECTED FROM THESE DISTINGUISHED
BOOKS:

The A.B.C. of Spice Cookery	*American Spice Trade Association*
American Regional Cookery	*Sheila Hibben*
The Cheese Cook Book	*Marye Dahnke*
The Complete Book of Home Baking	*Ann Seranne*
Good Neighbor Recipes	*Maxine Erickson and Joan M. Rock*
Helen Corbitt's Cook Book	*Helen Corbitt*
The Philadelphia Cook Book	*Anna Wetherill Reed*
Secrets of New England Cooking	*Ella Shannon Bowles and Dorothy S. Towle*
Woman's Home Companion Cook Book	*Dorothy Kirk, ed.*

BREADS

The fragrance of freshly baked bread, quite apart from the nostalgic pleasure it gives those of us who grew up in bread-baking homes, is both inviting and assuring to the visitor who catches a whiff of this special perfume at your open door. Inviting, because freshly baked bread is a symbol of a happy kitchen, and assuring because, if no other viands were offered, hunger could be satisfied with a cutting from a new loaf.

This fragrance, this sense of a happy kitchen and well-fed household, pervades Ann Seranne's *The Complete Book of Home Baking*. Here are some of her comments and recipes.

WHAT CONSTITUTES A GOOD LOAF OF BREAD?

Some insist on a thick, crisp crust, others want a crust that is soft and delicate. Some prefer a loose, open-textured inner bread, while still others like it fine-grained.

Let us settle for the standards set by the Wheat Flour Institute, of Chicago, a wise and noble arbiter of all problems in home-baking. The Institute says: "A good loaf is symmetrical in shape, good in volume and rich golden-brown in color. The entire loaf is brown, although the top may be somewhat deeper in color than the sides and bottom. The crumb is silky in appearance, uniformly creamy white in color, and reasonably fine and even in grain. Good bread *tastes* good. It has a somewhat bland flavor, yet at the same time the delicious, indescribable flavor of wheat."

BASIC RECIPE FOR PLAIN BREAD DOUGH

There are a thousand and one recipes for plain bread dough. Almost every good "old-fashioned" housewife has her favorite which has been handed down in her family through the generations. It is always successful, and she swears by it as the only recipe. But just in case your great-grandmother did not pass her bread recipe along, here is a modern recipe, easy and as foolproof for the home kitchen as any in existence.

2 cakes or packages yeast	4 teaspoons salt
2 cups lukewarm water	4 tablespoons shortening
2 cups milk	12 cups all-purpose flour, sifted
4 tablespoons sugar	

(For 2 loaves, *divide ingredients in half*. For 6 loaves, *add ½ the recipe, except for yeast, since 2 cakes are sufficient*. For 8 loaves, *use twice recipe, except for yeast, since 2 cakes are sufficient*.)

One loaf equals 1 dozen rolls, or 1 coffee ring.

METHOD

Soften yeast in ½ cup lukewarm water.

Scald the milk and pour it into a large mixing bowl. Add sugar, salt, shortening, and the rest of the warm water (1½ cups). Let cool to lukewarm (80 degrees to 85 degrees F.).

Add 2 cups sifted flour, stirring well, then add the softened yeast. Add 4 more cups flour and beat with a wooden spoon until almost smooth and elastic. The batter should sheet from the spoon.

Add the remaining flour (6 cups) to make a dough that is light but does not stick to the hands. More or less flour than is called for in the ingredients may be necessary to arrive at the exact dough, as flours vary a great deal in moisture and gluten content.

Turn dough out on lightly floured board, cover with folded cloth or towel, and allow to rest 10 minutes. Then knead dough until smooth and elastic.

Shape dough into a ball and place in a lightly greased bowl. Brush surface of the dough lightly with melted shortening, cover, and allow it to rise in a warm place (80 degrees to 85 degrees F.) until doubled in bulk (about 2 hours).

Punch dough down, cover, and allow to rise again, until doubled in bulk (about 1 hour). If preferred, shape dough into loaves after the first rising.

Divide the dough into 4 equal portions. Shape each part into a smooth ball, cover, and allow to rest 10 minutes.

Shape each portion into a loaf. Place loaves in greased bread pans, 3½ × 7½ × 2¾ inches. The dough should fill the pans ⅔ full. Cover with a damp cloth and allow loaves to rise until doubled in bulk (about 1½ hours). The sides of the raised dough should reach the top of the pan, and the center should be well rounded above it.

Bake in a moderately hot oven (400 degrees F.) 50 minutes.

COOLING

Bread and rolls should be removed from the pans as soon as taken from the oven, and placed on wire cooling racks or across the edges of the baking pans, so air can reach them on all sides.

This prevents moisture from condensing and spoiling the crispness of the crust and the lightness of the inner bread.

For a shiny, tender crust, brush the loaves with warm water while still hot and cover them with a clean towel for a few minutes to allow them to steam slightly.

STORING

When thoroughly cooled, bread and rolls may be stored in a clean breadbox or tin. Sterilize the breadbox at least once a week by washing it in hot sudsy water, scalding it with boiling water, and drying it well—if possible in the sunshine. Wrapping individual loaves in waxed paper preserves the freshness for a longer time. Highly spiced, fruit, or nut breads should be tightly wrapped in waxed paper to prevent the flavors from penetrating plain loaves. Remove stale bread from the box, as it will take the moisture away from fresh loaves.

Keeping bread in the refrigerator in plastic refrigerator bags retains the fresh quality for the longest possible time.

To Freshen Bread and Rolls. *Sprinkle with water and warm in a moderate oven, or place in a dampened brown-paper bag and heat in a moderate oven until the bag is dry.*

TO MAKE SWEET DOUGH OR COFFEE RINGS FROM PLAIN BREAD DOUGH

AFTER the first rising of the Plain Bread Dough (as described in bread recipe) work into the dough with the hands

2 eggs, well beaten	½ cup sugar
¼ cup melted shortening	¾ to 1 cup sifted all-purpose flour

or enough flour to make a dough that no longer sticks to your hands or to the mixing bowl. Then knead and allow it to rise at proper temperature until doubled in bulk (1½ hours). Punch down, divide into rolls, coffeecakes or rings, and allow to rise again before baking. Makes 4 dozen sweet rolls, or 2 dozen sweet rolls and 2 coffeecakes.

For a combination of plain bread and sweet rolls, make a quantity of dough sufficient for 4 loaves of bread. After the first rising, divide dough in half. Proceed with one half as for bread, shaping it into 2 loaves. To the other half add ½ the ingredients listed above in recipe for sweet dough and follow the directions for a sweet dough. Makes 2 dozen sweet rolls, or 1 dozen sweet rolls and 1 coffeecake, plus 2 loaves plain bread. (While coffeecake is still warm it may be iced with boiled icing and sprinkled with chopped nuts and raisins.)

VIENNA BREAD

Make Plain Bread Dough according to directions and shape it into 4 long thin loaves. With kitchen scissors make gashes on tops of loaves about 3 inches apart and 1½ inches deep. Place loaves several inches apart on a greased baking sheet and let them rise until doubled in bulk. Brush tops with slightly beaten egg white and bake in a hot oven (425 degrees F.) 50 minutes. Remove from oven, brush tops again with egg white, and sprinkle with salt and poppy or sesame seeds. Return loaves to oven for 10 minutes longer, or until seeds are browned.

BUTTER BRAIDS

Divide enough Plain Bread Dough to make 1 large loaf into 6 ropes, make 2 braids of these, one a little smaller than the other. Place the smaller braid on top of the large braid, tapering both at the ends. Press ends together. Brush top with beaten egg, sprinkle with poppy seeds. Let rise, and bake according to directions for plain bread.

BREAD STICKS

Roll out Plain Bread Dough ½-inch thick and cut it into strips ½-inch wide. Roll the cut pieces between palms of hands into small pencil-like strips and place on a greased baking sheet. Cover and allow the sticks to rise in a warm place until doubled in bulk. Brush with beaten egg white, sprinkle with poppy seeds, if desired, and bake 10 minutes in hot oven (425 degrees F.).

CRUSTY PLAIN WATER ROLLS OR BREAD

1 cake or package yeast
1 cup lukewarm water
1 tablespoon sugar
1 teaspoon salt
2 tablespoons melted shortening

4 cups enriched flour, sifted
2 lightly-beaten egg whites
Extra shortening
Extra egg white

SOFTEN yeast in ¼ cup lukewarm water. To the rest of the water in a mixing bowl add the sugar, salt, and shortening. Add 1 cup of the flour and beat well. Add the softened yeast and the beaten egg whites and mix thoroughly. Add sufficient flour to make a soft dough.

Turn the dough out on a lightly floured board and knead until it is smooth and elastic (about 8 minutes). Shape into a smooth ball and place in a lightly greased bowl. Brush the surface lightly with melted shortening, cover, and allow it to rise in a warm place until doubled in bulk (about 2 hours). Punch down, cover, and allow to rise again until doubled in bulk (about 1 hour). Punch down and divide into small portions for rolls, or in half for 2 loaves.

Let dough rest 10 minutes. Shape into round rolls and place 2 inches apart on a greased baking sheet; or shape into loaves and place in greased baking pans. Cover lightly with folded cloth or towel and allow to rise in a warm place until doubled in bulk (about 1½ hours).

Place a large flat pan filled with boiling water in the bottom of the oven a few minutes before putting in the rolls or bread. Bake rolls in a hot oven (450 degrees F.) 20 minutes. Bake loaves in moderate oven (375 degrees F.) 50 minutes. Ten minutes before the baking time is complete, brush the tops with lightly beaten egg white. Makes 2 dozen rolls.

BREAD VARIATIONS FROM BASIC RECIPE

After all the flour is mixed in, add the special ingredients and mix thoroughly. Then knead and proceed as for plain bread. You may wish to divide the dough into loaves and make different breads with each loaf.

Cracked-Wheat Bread: To each loaf add 2 tablespoons honey and 1 cup cracked wheat.

Whole-Wheat Bread: To each loaf add 4 tablespoons molasses and ¾ cup graham flour.

Rye-Molasses Bread: To each loaf add 2 tablespoons molasses, 2 tablespoons dark corn syrup, and ¾ cup rye flour. Bake in moderately hot oven (400 degrees F.) 40 minutes. One cup seedless raisins may also be added, as well as ½ cup chopped nuts.

Bran Bread: Substitute 4 cups bran for 4 cups of the wheat flour. Additional wheat flour may be necessary to bring the dough to the correct consistency for kneading.

Buttermilk Bread: Use ½ cup buttermilk or sour milk and ½ cup water for the liquid. Sift 1 teaspoon soda with the first addition of flour.

BASIC SWEET DOUGH

2 cakes or packages yeast	1 teaspoon salt
¼ cup lukewarm water	½ cup shortening (part butter)
1 cup milk	5 cups all-purpose flour, sifted
½ cup sugar	2 beaten eggs

SOFTEN yeast in lukewarm water. Scald milk, add sugar, salt, and shortening, let cool to lukewarm (80 degrees to 85 degrees F.) . Add part of flour to make thick batter and mix well. Add softened yeast and eggs and beat thoroughly. Add enough additional flour to make dough which is soft but does not stick to hands. Turn out on lightly floured board and knead until smooth and satiny. Place in greased bowl, cover, and allow to rise in warm place until doubled in bulk (about 1½ hours) . Punch down and allow to rest 10 minutes. Then shape into rolls, tea rings, or coffeecakes. Allow to rise until doubled (about 1 hour) . Bake in moderate oven (350 degrees F.) , 30 minutes for coffeecakes, 20 to 25 minutes for rolls. Makes 3 dozen rolls, or 3 coffeecakes, or 3 medium-size loaves.

HOT CROSS BUNS

½ recipe for Basic Sweet Dough	1 cup currants
1 teaspoon ground cinnamon	Confectioners' Sugar Icing
½ teaspoon ground allspice	

To ½ the recipe for Basic Sweet Dough add the cinnamon, allspice, and currants. Follow recipe. When dough is light and doubled in bulk, punch it down and let it rest 10 minutes. Divide into 18 parts and shape each part into a ball. Place balls ½ inch apart on a greased baking sheet and allow to rise in a warm place until doubled in bulk (about 1 hour). Bake in moderate oven (350 degrees F.) 20 minutes. Remove at once from pans and make a cross of Confectioners' Sugar Icing on each roll. Makes 18 rolls.

CONFECTIONERS' SUGAR ICING

Combine ¾ cup confectioners' sugar and 2 tablespoons hot milk. Beat until smooth and flavor with a little vanilla. Use at once on buns.

SCHNECKEN
Sour-Cream Dough Snails

1 cake or package yeast
¼ cup lukewarm water
½ cup shortening (part butter)
2½ cups all-purpose flour, sifted
2 beaten eggs

½ cup sugar
1 teaspoon salt
1 cup sour cream
Sugar, cinnamon, chopped nuts, and seedless raisins

SOFTEN yeast in the lukewarm water. Cut shortening into flour, add yeast, eggs, sugar, salt, and sour cream. Beat very thoroughly and place in greased bowl. Cover and place in the refrigerator overnight. The next day remove bowl from refrigerator to a warm place and allow dough to rise until doubled in bulk. Punch down, place on a lightly floured board, and knead, adding more flour to make a dough that is not sticky. Roll out into a thin sheet. Sprinkle the surface thickly with sugar, cinnamon, chopped nuts, and raisins, and roll up like a jelly roll. Cut in ½-inch slices and place on greased baking sheet. Allow to rise in a warm place until doubled in bulk. Bake in moderate oven (350 degrees F.) about 30 minutes. Makes 12 or more *schnecken*.

All baking recipes above from THE COMPLETE BOOK OF HOME BAKING, *by Ann Seranne*

❧

Good Neighbor Recipes is the source of another baking-day treasure which most homemakers will welcome, a basic sour-cream dough from which many delicious rolls, coffeecakes, and other breads are made. This friendly book, a collaboration of two American culinary personalities, Maxine Erickson and Joan M. Rock, is rich in superb cookery. Here is one of their delicious and adaptable recipes.

BASIC SOUR-CREAM DOUGH
FOR ROLLS AND COFFEECAKES

¼ cup butter, margarine, or shortening

½ cup sugar

1 teaspoon salt

2 cups sour cream scalded

2 packages or cakes yeast

¼ cup lukewarm water

3 well-beaten eggs

6 cups all-purpose flour, sifted

COMBINE butter, margarine, or shortening, sugar, and salt in mixing bowl. Add scalded sour cream; stir until fat is melted and sugar and salt dissolved. Let cool to lukewarm. Soften yeast in lukewarm water; stir until smooth. Add to cooled sour-cream mixture, with beaten eggs. Add 2 cups sifted flour; beat well. Add 2 more cups flour; beat again. Stir in remaining flour to make a smooth, soft dough.

Turn dough without kneading into a well-greased bowl; turn dough over to grease all surfaces. Cover lightly with folded cloth or towel. Let rise in warm place until doubled in bulk. Punch down dough in bowl. Turn out on lightly floured board. Knead gently until smooth and elastic and slightly blistered on the surface. Use for rolls, coffeecakes, or coffee rings. Makes 24 to 36 rolls, or 2 coffeecakes or rings. Bake rolls in moderate oven (375 degrees F.) about 50 minutes or until risen and browned. Bake coffeecakes and rings at same temperature about 35 minutes, or until done.

The recipe above from GOOD NEIGHBOR RECIPES, *by Maxine Erickson and Joan M. Rock*

BANANA WALNUT BREAD →

¾ cup sugar

¼ cup shortening

2 eggs

1 cup mashed ripe bananas

2 cups all-purpose flour, sifted

2 teaspoons baking powder

½ teaspoon salt

¼ teaspoon soda

1 cup chopped walnuts

Start oven at moderate (350 degrees F.). Grease a loaf pan, 9 × 5 × 3 inches. Combine sugar and shortening in mixing bowl, beat well, add eggs, one at a time, beating after each addition. Beat batter until light. Add mashed bananas, beat well. Sift dry ingredients together 3 times, stir into batter, beating smooth. Add walnuts. Pour into prepared pan. Bake in moderate oven 60 to 70 minutes. Let cool in pan 5 minutes, turn out on rack and let cool. Slices nicely even when warm. Makes 18 slices ½ inch thick. Wrap any unsliced remaining loaf in foil or freezer-wrap and store in freezer or refrigerator. Slices neatly when frozen.

Recipe and color photograph, courtesy Diamond Walnut Growers, Inc.

American cook books are full of delicious breads; some are regional favorites which have become popular all over the country. One of these is Boston Brown Bread. And for an authentic recipe we turn the pages of that neighborly book called *Secrets of New England Cooking,* by Ella Shannon Bowles and Dorothy S. Towle.

STEAMED BOSTON BROWN BREAD

1 cup corn meal	Hot water
1 cup rye flour	½ cup molasses
1 cup graham flour	2 cups sour milk
1 teaspoon salt	1 cup seedless raising
1 teaspoon soda	Extra flour

COMBINE meal, flours, and salt in mixing bowl. Dissolve soda in about 2 tablespoons hot water and stir at once into the molasses. Combine with sour milk, then mix into the dry ingredients. Lightly flour raisins and add to mixture. Blend batter smoothly. Pour into 3 well-greased 1-quart molds with tight covers, filling ⅔ full.

Steam 3 hours in kettle of boiling water. Uncover molds, place in a very slow oven (250 degrees F.) 20 minutes to dry and crust the tops of the loaves, and let loaves recede a little from molds. Makes 3 loaves.

The recipe above from SECRETS OF NEW ENGLAND COOKING, *by Ella Shannon Bowles and Dorothy S. Towle*

← STRAWBERRY-RHUBARB CRUMB PIE

1 quart fresh California strawberries	2 tablespoons lemon juice
2 cups diced rhubarb	2 tablespoons butter or margarine, softened
2 cups sugar	2 tablespoons brown sugar
½ cup all-purpose flour, sifted	¼ teaspoon powdered cinnamon
10-inch unbaked pastry shell	Flour

Wash berries, hull, and drain. Combine in bowl with rhubarb, granulated sugar, and ½ cup flour; mix lightly. Let stand 30 minutes. Start oven at hot (425 degrees F.). Turn fruit mixture into pastry-lined pan. Sprinkle with lemon juice. Combine butter or margarine, brown sugar, and cinnamon, and blend; add ½ cup flour and mix well. Sprinkle mixture over strawberry mixture. Bake in hot oven 1 hour, or until crust is lightly browned. Makes 5 or 6 servings.

Recipe and color photograph, courtesy California Strawberry Advisory Board

EASY-EASY BRIOCHES

A dough as rich and soft as this is not kneaded. Thorough mixing is essential, as well as a long cold "repose" in the refrigerator to properly ripen the delicate dough. In fact, you cannot knead it, so once you start working it into shape, work quickly before the dough warms up.

1 cup milk, scalded	¼ cup lukewarm water
¼ cup butter	4 well-beaten egg yolks
⅓ cup sugar	Grated peel 1 lemon
1 teaspoon salt	4½ cups all-purpose flour, sifted
1 package or cake yeast	

POUR scalded milk over butter, sugar, and salt in mixing bowl. Stir to melt butter and dissolve sugar. Let cool to lukewarm. Soften yeast in lukewarm water; stir and add to lukewarm milk mixture; stir in beaten egg yolks and lemon peel. Add about ⅓ of the sifted flour; beat well to make smooth stiff batter. Stir in remaining flour to make soft smooth dough. Cover; let rise in warm place until light and bubbly.

Turn out on lightly floured board. Toss dough back and forth between palms of hands, then pat on board until smooth. Place in greased bowl; brush top with melted butter. Cover tightly and store overnight in refrigerator.

Shape small pieces of cold dough quickly with the fingers; place in greased muffin pans. Cover; let rise until dough fills pan ¾ full. Bake in hot oven (425 degrees F.) about 15 to 20 minutes. Makes about 3 dozen brioches.

OATEN BREAD

2 teaspoons salt	1 teaspoon sugar
2 cups boiling water	¼ cup lukewarm water
1 cup rolled oats	½ cup brown sugar (packed)
1 tablespoon shortening	½ cup lukewarm water
1 package or cake yeast	5 cups all-purpose flour, sifted

ADD salt to boiling water; stir in oats and shortening. Let cool to lukewarm. Put yeast in large mixing bowl; add the 1 tablespoon sugar and the ¼ cup lukewarm water. Let stand until feathery, about 1 hour. Add brown sugar dissolved in the ½ cup lukewarm water to yeast mixture. Stir ½ of the sifted flour into yeast mixture; beat until smooth. Add remaining flour and cooled-oats mixture to make moderately stiff dough.

Knead dough lightly on floured board until smooth; place in greased bowl; cover and let rise until doubled in bulk. Punch dough down; divide into 2 parts. Let stand, covered, on lightly floured board for about 15 minutes. Form each portion into a loaf; place in greased bread pans. Cover and let rise until doubled in bulk. Bake in moderate oven (375 degrees F.) about 45 minutes. Makes 2 medium loaves.

The two recipes above from GOOD NEIGHBOR RECIPES, *by Maxine Erickson and Joan M. Rock*

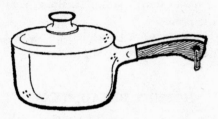

Readers of Sheila Hibben's carefully documented reports on foods and other matters in *The New Yorker* admire her integrity and respect her wide experience, good taste, and restrained enthusiasm. In her book, *American Regional Cookery,* are traditional long-famous recipes for American breads. Here are some of them.

SALT RISING BREAD, OKLAHOMA

1 cup milk, scalded
1½ teaspoons salt
2½ tablespoons sugar
¼ cup white corn meal

1 cup lukewarm water
2 tablespoons lard
Flour
Extra milk

LET scalded milk cool to lukewarm. Add salt, half the sugar, and the corn meal. Pour mixture into a stone crock or jar, cover, and set the bowl in a kettle of hot water. Keep in warm place about 6 hours, or until it ferments. When gasses escape freely, pour in 1 cup lukewarm water, mix, add lard, remaining sugar, and 2 cups sifted flour, beating well. Put jar back into kettle of hot water in warm place. Let rise until batter is light and bubbly. Turn batter into a mixing bowl (which has been warmed by rinsing with hot water) and gradually stir in enough more flour to make rather stiff dough.

Turn out onto a lightly floured board and knead for about 12 minutes. Divide dough, shape into loaves in 2 greased bread pans, brush with milk, cover with a clean cloth, and let rise in a warm place until 2½ times original bulk. Bake in moderate oven (375 degrees F.) 10 minutes. Lower heat to 350 degrees F. and bake 25 minutes longer. Makes 2 loaves.

CRACKLING BREAD, GEORGIA

2 cups white corn meal
½ teaspoon salt
2 cups milk, scalded

1½ cups freshly-rendered cracklings

START oven at moderately hot (400 degrees F.). Sift the meal and salt together into a mixing bowl. Pour in enough scalded milk to make a stiff dough. Add the cracklings, cut in small pieces. Mix well with the meal, and mold into 4 oblong cakes or pones. Place in a hot greased baking pan. Flatten out the pones with the hands. Bake in moderately hot oven 20 minutes. Makes 4 pones.

Cracklings are the crisp pork tissue left after the lard is tried out, or rendered. They must be eaten very fresh, preferably a few hours after the fat is rendered.

HOMINY BREAD, TEXAS

2 cups hot boiled grits
1 tablespoon butter
3 eggs
½ cup white corn meal

½ teaspoon salt
2 teaspoons baking powder
Milk

START oven at moderate (350 degrees F.). Stir the butter into the hot grits, add well-beaten egg yolks, and sift in corn meal, salt, and baking powder. Pour in enough milk to make the consistency of thin custard (the amount will depnd upon the consistency of the grits), and fold in the stiffly beaten egg whites. Turn into a buttered 1-quart baking dish. Bake in moderate oven about 1 hour. Makes 6 servings.

SPOON BREAD, VIRGINIA

1 pint milk, scalded
½ cup water-ground white corn
    meal
¾ teaspoon salt

1 tablespoon butter
2 eggs
½ teaspoon baking powder

FILL 1-quart baking dish with hot water to heat the dish. Let stand. Start oven at moderate (350 degrees F.).

Pour the milk into the corn meal and salt gradually, beating hard to avoid lumps; add the butter. Add beaten egg yolks and baking powder and mix well. Fold in the stiffly-beaten egg whites. Drain hot baking dish, grease quickly, and turn batter into dish. Bake in moderate oven 45 minutes. Serve at once. Makes 4 servings.

The four recipes above from AMERICAN REGIONAL COOKERY, *by Sheila Hibben*

Baking-Powder Breads

Texans must like fruit-flavored breads. *Helen Corbitt's Cook Book,* of the dishes popular in that state, includes so many recipes for these breads that it is difficult to keep our selection to the four which follow.

APRICOT NUT BREAD

½ cup diced dried apricots
1 egg
1 cup sugar
2 tablespoons melted butter
2 cups all-purpose flour, sifted
3 teaspoons baking powder

¼ teaspoon soda
¾ teaspoon salt
½ cup strained orange juice
¼ cup water
1 cup sliced Brazil nuts or
  almonds

SOAK apricots ½ hour. Drain and grind. Start oven at moderate (350 degrees F.). Beat eggs until light, stir in sugar, and mix well. Stir in butter. Sift flour with baking powder, soda, and salt; add alternately to butter mixture with orange juice and water. Add nuts and apricots, mix well. Pour into greased loaf pan. Bake in moderate oven 1½ hours. Makes 1 loaf.

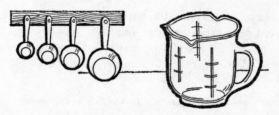

BANANA BREAD

1¾ cups all-purpose flour, sifted
2¾ teaspoons baking powder
½ teaspoon salt
⅓ cup shortening

⅔ cup sugar
2 eggs
1 pound (3 or 4) ripe bananas

START oven at moderate (350 degrees F.). Sift together flour, baking powder, and salt. Beat shortening with electric mixer until creamy. Add sugar and eggs. Continue beating at medium speed 1 minute. Peel bananas, cut into mixing bowl with egg mixture, and mix until blended. Add flour mixture, beating at low speed about 30 seconds or only until blended. Do not over-beat. Scrape bowl and beater once or twice. Turn batter into buttered loaf pan. Bake in moderate oven about 1 hour and 10 minutes, or until done. Makes 1 loaf. (Keeps well in refrigerator.)

ORANGE, DATE, AND PECAN BREAD

1 orange
½ cup boiling water
1 cup pitted dates
1 cup sugar
2 tablespoons melted butter
1 beaten egg

2 cups all-purpose flour, sifted
1 teaspoon baking powder
¼ teaspoon salt
1 teaspoon soda
½ cup chopped pecans

START oven at moderate (350 degrees F.). Squeeze juice from orange and add boiling water to make 1 cup liquid. Remove pulp from orange and put peel through chopper. Combine peel and dates. Add juice-water mixture, sugar, butter, and egg. Sift flour, baking powder, salt, and soda together and add to date mixture. Mix and add chopped nuts. Bake in greased loaf pan in moderate oven about 50 minutes. Let cool in pan. Makes 1 loaf.

PEANUT BUTTER AND BACON BREAD

1 cup sugar
1 tablespoon melted shortening
1 cup milk
1 well-beaten egg
1 cup smooth peanut butter

½ teaspoon salt
2 cups all-purpose flour, sifted
3 teaspoons baking powder
1 cup chopped unsalted peanuts
1 cup chopped crisp bacon

MIX sugar, shortening, and milk with beaten egg. Add peanut butter. Sift salt, flour, and baking powder together into the egg mixture. Add nuts and bacon and let stand in greased loaf pan 20 minutes. Bake in moderate oven (350 degrees F.) 1 hour, or until done. Makes 1 loaf.

The four recipes above from HELEN CORBITT'S COOK BOOK

A little spice cook book, *The A.B.C. of Spice Cookery*, by the American Spice Trade Association, gives us this gingerbread:

PLANTATION GINGERBREAD

2¾ cups all-purpose flour, sifted
2 teaspoons baking powder
2 teaspoons ground ginger
2 teaspoons ground cinnamon or
    ½ teaspoon ground allspice
¼ teaspoon ground cloves
½ teaspoon baking soda

4 tablespoons cocoa
½ teaspoon salt
1 cup shortening
1 cup molasses
2 eggs
1 cup milk

START oven at moderate (350 degrees F.). Sift flour, baking powder, spices, soda, cocoa, and salt together twice. Cream shortening well, add sugar gradually, beating steadily. Add molasses and beat smooth. Add beaten eggs, then sifted dry ingredients alternately with the milk. Pour into greased 10-inch square pan lined with waxed paper which also has been greased. Bake in moderate oven 50 minutes, or until done. Makes 12 to 16 pieces.

Gingerbread recipe from THE A.B.C. OF SPICE COOKERY, *by American Spice Trade Association*

Biscuits and Muffins

These are among the sound, many-times-tested recipes of the *Woman's Home Companion Cook Book,* edited by Dorothy Kirk.

BAKING-POWDER BISCUITS

Ready-mixes and heat-and-serve biscuits, muffins, and almost everything the home cook wants to bake are available in food stores all over America. But if you want to mix your own biscuits, here is a classic recipe.

2 cups all-purpose flour, sifted	4 tablespoons shortening
3 teaspoons baking powder	¾ cup milk
1 teaspoon salt	

START oven at hot (425 degrees F.). Sift flour; measure; add baking powder and salt; sift again. Cut shortening into flour with pastry blender or 2 knives, blending it until the mixture resembles coarse corn meal. Stirring with a fork, add enough milk to make soft dough, or until flour leaves sides of bowl and follows fork. Continue stirring until all flour disappears. Turn dough out on lightly floured board; knead lightly about ½ minute. Turn smooth side up and pat dough or roll out ½-inch thick. Cut with floured biscuit cutter.

Transfer biscuits to ungreased baking sheet. Place 1 inch apart if crusty biscuits are desired or close together for softer biscuits with less crust. Bake in hot oven 12 to 15 minutes. Makes 14 to 16 (2-inch) biscuits.

Chef's Specialty Biscuits: To flour-fat mixture add 2 tablespoons chopped chives or 1 tablespoon green pepper and 1 tablespoon chopped pimiento; stir milk in and proceed as directed for biscuits.

Orange Tea Biscuits: To flour-fat mixture add 1 tablespoon grated orange peel; stir in milk and proceed as directed. Press a small cube sugar dipped in orange juice into top of each biscuit before baking.

Sour-Milk Biscuits: Substitute sour milk or buttermilk for milk called for in recipe. Add ½ teaspoon soda and decrease baking powder to 1 teaspoon; sift soda with other dry ingredients.

The biscuit recipe and variations from WOMAN'S HOME COMPANION COOK BOOK, *edited by Dorothy Kirk*

❦

From that useful volume, *Good Neighbor Recipes,* by Maxine Erickson and Joan M. Rock, here are muffins you will enjoy.

FEATHERY MUFFINS

2 cups all-purpose flour, sifted	1 beaten egg
½ teaspoon salt	1 cup milk
3 teaspoons baking powder	4 tablespoons melted shortening
2 tablespoons sugar	

START oven at hot (425 degrees F.). Grease 14 muffin pans. Sift flour, salt, baking powder, and sugar together. Combine beaten egg, milk, and melted shortening. Make a well in center of flour mixture; add liquid all at once. Mix only until flour is dampened. Batter will be lumpy. Spoon quickly into greased muffin pans, filling ⅔ full. Bake in hot oven until delicately browned and top springs back under light finger pressure, about 15 minutes. Makes 14 (2½-inch) muffins. (If muffin pans are not all filled, put a little water in empty compartments.)

Rice Muffins: Use recipe for Feathery Muffins. Stir 1 cup cold cooked rice into egg-and-milk mixture before adding to dry ingredients. Be sure all rice grains are soft. Bake as described.

Corn-and-Bacon Muffins: Substitute melted bacon fat for other shortening in recipe for Feathery Muffins. Stir into dry mixture before adding liquid, ¼ cup drained, canned kernel corn and ¼ cup crumbled crisp bacon. Bake as described.

The muffin recipes above from GOOD NEIGHBOR RECIPES, *by Maxine Erickson and Joan M. Rock*

Cheese Biscuits, Muffins and Bread

The cheese recipes which follow are from *The Cheese Cook Book* by Marye Dahnke. America owes its best cheese cookery to this home economist who came north from her Tennessee birthplace more than twenty years ago to create and develop a home-recipe kitchen for the Kraft Foods Company. Our present-day cheese products, easy to use, foolproof, and delicious, as well as most of the golden recipes found in every modern American cook book and women's magazines, were first developed in Marye Dahnke's kitchens.

CHEESE BISCUITS

2 cups all-purpose flour, sifted
½ cup packaged dehydrated
　grated American Cheddar
　cheese
½ teaspoon salt
4 teaspoons baking powder
¼ cup shortening
1 cup milk

START oven at hot (425 degrees F.). Grease baking sheet. Sift flour, cheese, salt, and baking powder together. Cut in shortening. Add milk to make a soft dough. Toss onto floured board and knead lightly about ½ minute. Roll dough to ¾-inch thickness, cut with floured biscuit cutter, and place on greased baking sheet. Bake in hot oven, 12 to 15 minutes. Makes 20 to 24 small biscuits.

CHEESE BREAD

1¼ cups milk
1 tablespoon sugar
1 teaspoon salt
½ tablespoon butter or margarine
½ cake or package yeast
1 tablespoon lukewarm water
2¾ cups all-purpose flour, sifted
1½ cups shredded American
　Cheddar cheese
Melted butter or margarine

SCALD milk; add sugar, salt, and ½ tablespoon of butter or margarine. Let cool to lukewarm. Crumble yeast into 1 tablespoon of lukewarm water, let soften a few minutes, and add to the milk mixture. Add 2 cups flour and mix well. Add cheese and remaining flour, and mix again. Turn out and knead on a lightly floured board for 10 minutes. Place dough in a greased bowl, brush with melted butter or margarine; cover, and let rise in warm place until double in bulk.

　　Knead bread, shape into loaf, place in greased 4-×-8-inch loaf pan, and brush with melted butter or margarine. Cover with a fresh towel and let rise until double in bulk. Bake in moderate oven (375 degrees F.) 50 minutes. Makes 1 loaf.

CHEESE MUFFINS

½ pound American Cheddar
  cheese, shredded
2 cups all-purpose flour, sifted
4 teaspoons baking powder
1 tablespoon sugar

½ teaspoon salt
1 beaten egg
1 cup milk
3 tablespoons melted butter or
  margarine

START oven at hot (425 degrees F.). Grease 12 muffin tins. Blend shredded
cheese with sifted dry ingredients. Combine beaten egg and milk, and add
to flour-and-cheese mixture, beating only enough to blend all ingredients.
Fold the melted butter or margarine in. Bake in greased muffin tins in hot
oven, 20 minutes, or until done. Makes 12 muffins.

The cheese recipes above from THE CHEESE COOK BOOK, *by Marye Dahnke*

❦

For your file of good doughnuts and various fritters, we turn
once more to the *Woman's Home Companion Cook Book,*
edited by Dorothy Kirk.

Doughnuts, Fritters, Pancakes, Waffles

DOUGHNUTS

4½ cups all-purpose flour, sifted
4½ teaspoons baking powder
1 teaspoon salt
¼ teaspoon ground nutmeg
½ teaspoon ground cinnamon
2 tablespoons shortening

1 cup sugar
2 eggs, or 4 egg yolks
1 cup milk
Deep fat for frying
Confectioners' sugar

SIFT flour, measure, add baking powder, salt, nutmeg, and cinnamon and
sift again. Cream shortening; add sugar gradually, continue beating until
light and fluffy. Add eggs or egg yolks, one at a time, beating after each
addition. Add milk and flour mixture alternately, stirring until blended.
Chill dough ½ hour. Roll out on lightly floured board to about ¼-inch
thick. Cut with floured doughnut cutter, cover, and let stand 20 to 30
minutes.

Drop into deep hot fat (365 degrees to 375 degrees F.) and fry
3 to 5 minutes, or until golden brown. Turn doughnuts as they rise to the
surface. Drain on absorbent paper. Fry only a few at a time.

Sprinkle with confectioners' sugar if desired. Makes about 3½ dozen
doughnuts.

RAISED DOUGHNUTS

1 package yeast

1/4 cup warm water

3/4 cup milk

4 cups all-purpose flour, sifted

3/4 cup sugar

2 well-beaten eggs

2 teaspoons grated lemon peel

1/2 cup melted, cooled shortening,
  or salad oil

3/4 teaspoon grated nutmeg

1/2 teaspoon salt

Fat for deep frying

Powdered sugar

SPRINKLE yeast over warm water. Let stand 5 minutes. Stir. Bring milk to
a boil. Remove at once from heat and let cool until only warm. Add
yeast, 1/2 sifted flour, and 2 tablespoons sugar. Beat until smooth. Cover
and let rise in a warm place (80 degrees to 85 degrees F.) about 1/2 hour.
Then stir beaten eggs in with lemon peel, shortening, and remaining
flour sifted with remaining sugar, nutmeg, and salt. Beat 10 to 15 minutes
by hand or 4 to 5 minutes in electric mixer, or until bubbles appear on
surface. Cover and let rise about 1 hour. Turn out on lightly floured
board and roll out 1-inch thick. Cut with floured doughnut cutter; cover
and let rise about 1 hour or until doubled in bulk.

Drop doughnuts, raised side down, into deep hot fat (365 degrees to
375 degrees F.) and fry about 2 to 3 minutes, turning doughnuts to
brown on both sides. Drain on absorbent paper; brush while still warm
with Confectioners' Frosting or sprinkle with powdered sugar. Makes
2 1/2 to 3 dozen doughnuts.

FRITTER-COVER BATTER

1 cup all-purpose flour, sifted

1/2 teaspoon salt

1 tablespoon sugar (for fruit
  fritters only)

1 slightly-beaten egg

1 cup milk

1 tablespoon melted shortening

SIFT flour; measure; add salt and sugar (if batter is to be used for fruit
fritters) and sift again. Combine beaten egg, milk, and melted shortening;
pour into flour mixture and stir until smooth.

Dip sea food, slices of fish, vegetables, or fruit into the batter. Drop
into deep hot fat (365 degrees to 375 degrees F.) and fry until well
browned on all sides, turning fritters as they rise to the surface. Or fry
them in a small amount of fat in a skillet. Drain on absorbent paper.
Makes about 6 servings.

Note: If thicker coating is desired, decrease milk to 2/3 cup and add
1 teaspoon baking powder to the flour with the salt and sugar. For a more
delicate, puffy coating, use 2 eggs instead of one: separate eggs and combine beaten yolks with milk and melted shortening and pour into the
flour mixture, beating until smooth; beat whites until stiff but not dry,
and fold into batter.

Griddlecakes

★PANCAKES

1½ cups all-purpose flour, sifted
2½ teaspoons baking powder
¾ teaspoon salt
3 tablespoons sugar

1 well-beaten egg
¾ cup to 1¼ cups milk
3 tablespoons shortening, melted

SIFT flour, measure; add baking powder, salt, and sugar and sift again. Combine egg, milk, and melted shortening (slightly cooled) ; the amount of milk to use will depend upon thickness of pancakes desired; ¾ cup milk gives thick cakes, 1¼ cups milk makes them quite thin. Pour into flour mixture, stirring just enough to moisten dry ingredients. Do not beat.

Bake on a hot griddle, greased or not, according to the kind you use. (Follow manufacturer's instructions about greasing.) Serve hot with butter and syrup, honey, or sweet preserves. Makes 1 to 1½ dozen cakes.

Apple Pancakes: Increase sugar to ¼ cup; add 2 tablespoons of the sugar to 1 cup chopped apples; let stand a few minutes. Sift remaining sugar and ⅛ teaspoon cinnamon with dry ingredients. Fold sweetened chopped apples into batter before baking. Serve with honey.

Blueberry Pancakes: Increase sugar to ¼ cup; add 2 tablespoons of the sugar to 1 cup blueberries; let stand a few minutes. Sift remaining sugar with dry ingredients. Fold sweetened berries into batter before baking.

Corn Pancakes: Add 1 cup drained canned or cooked corn to liquid ingredients; serve with grilled ham and pineapple.

★WAFFLES

1⅓ cups all-purpose flour, sifted
2 teaspoons baking powder
½ teaspoon salt
1 tablespoon sugar

1 egg
1 cup milk
4 tablespoons melted shortening
   or salad oil

SIFT flour, measure; add baking powder, salt, and sugar. Sift again. Beat egg yolk; add milk and melted shortening; pour into flour mixture and stir just enough to moisten dry ingredients. Fold in egg white, which has been beaten stiff but not dry. Bake 4 to 5 minutes in moderately hot waffle baker. Makes 3 to 4 waffles.

De Luxe Waffles: Increase sugar in waffle recipe to 2 tablespoons; use 2 eggs instead of 1; increase shortening to 6 tablespoons.

Pecan Waffles: Add ½ cup chopped pecans to waffle recipe. Serve with ice cream and butterscotch sauce.

★CHOCOLATE WAFFLES

2 cups all-purpose flour, sifted	2 eggs
3 teaspoons baking powder	1½ cups milk
½ teaspoon salt	4 tablespoons shortening
6 tablespoons sugar	2 (1-oz.) squares chocolate

SIFT flour; measure it, add baking powder, salt, and sugar; sift again. Beat egg yolks; add milk; pour into flour mixture. Melt shortening and chocolate together and add to batter. Stir just enough to moisten dry ingredients. Fold in egg whites which have been beaten until stiff but not dry. Bake 5 to 6 minutes in a waffle baker not quite so hot as for plain waffles. Serve hot with whipped cream or ice cream. Makes 5 to 6 waffles.

The doughnut, fritter, pancake, and waffle recipes above from WOMAN'S HOME COMPANION COOK BOOK, *edited by Dorothy Kirk*

❧

Before leaving the good fragrance of griddlecakes stirred up in this chapter, two special recipes from a very special book must be added as a finale. The book is *The Philadelphia Cook Book,* by Anna Wetherill Reed, a treasury of old-time dishes, luxurious, delectable, long-ago favorites in Quaker state homes and in some of its restaurants and inns. Here is the recipe for buckwheat cakes used by the Valley Forge Tea Room.

OLD FASHIONED BUCKWHEAT CAKES

⅓ cup yellow corn meal	1¼ cups buckwheat flour
2 cups scalded milk	1 tablespoon dark, or Barbados,
⅓ teaspoon salt	molasses
¼ yeast cake softened in ½	¼ teaspoon soda dissolved in ¼
cup lukewarm water	cup lukewarm water

POUR milk over corn meal and let stand ½ hour. Add salt, dissolved yeast cake, and buckwheat to make the batter the right consistency for pouring. Cover bowl. Let rise (at moderately warm kitchen temperature) overnight. In the morning, stir thoroughly, adding the molasses, soda, and water. Pour onto a hot griddle, 1 tablespoon at a time. Turn cakes when bottom is browned and top is bubbly. Serve hot with butter and syrup or light molasses. Makes 20 or more cakes.

★BUTTERMILK GRIDDLECAKES

2 cups all-purpose flour, sifted   2 well-beaten eggs
1 teaspoon baking soda   2 cups buttermilk
1 teaspoon salt   2 tablespoons butter, melted
1 tablespoon sugar

SIFT flour, measure, and sift all dry ingredients together. Combine beaten eggs and buttermilk; add flour mixture and beat until smooth. Add butter. Bake on hot griddle. Makes about 24 small cakes.

★CORN-MEAL GRIDDLE CAKES

½ cup coarse yellow corn meal   1½ teaspoons salt
1½ cups boiling water   ⅓ cup brown sugar
1¼ cups milk   1 well-beaten egg
2 cups whole-wheat flour   1 tablespoon butter, melted
1½ teaspoons baking powder

ADD the meal to the boiling water and boil 5 minutes; turn into a bowl and add the milk. Mix flour, baking powder, salt, and sugar and add to corn meal. Add egg and melted butter. Mix. Bake on hot griddle. Makes 20 to 24 cakes.

The three recipes above from THE PHILADELPHIA COOK BOOK, *by Anna Wetherill Reed*

THE "BEST-OF-ALL"

CAKES AND COOKIES

THE RECIPES THAT FOLLOW HAVE BEEN SELECTED FROM THESE DISTINGUISHED BOOKS:

Better Homes and Gardens Cook Book	*Foods Editors of* Better Homes and Gardens
The Cheese Cook Book	*Marye Dahnke*
Edith Barber's Cook Book	*Edith Barber*
New, Easy Ways to Cook with Rum	*Clementine Paddleford*
Who Says We Can't Cook!	*Members of the Women's National Press Club*

CAKES AND COOKIES

Cake mixes, some packaged with the pan in which to bake them, some packaged with icing and filling, for every kind of cake—dark and light, large and small, filled with fruit or downy with egg whites—have made cake-bakers out of even the timid cooks who used to claim they had no "hand" for baking. And having made the glamorous creations which are easily concocted because of modern food-manufacturers' magic, these same cooks welcome the challenge of home-kitchen cake recipes.

One of the great magazine test kitchens in this country is in Iowa, at *Better Homes and Gardens,* where the food editors test recipes, create new dishes, and have compiled one of the best cook books available to American homemakers. Their cakes are superb. These general instructions for cakemaking and recipes which follow are taken from that book, *The Better Homes and Gardens Cook Book.*

Excellent cake, even-grained, tender, light, and delicately flavored, may easily be achieved by anyone who carefully follows a few proved rules. Contrary to the belief of some, success in cakemaking is not due to good luck or to a knack for baking. It is due to accurate measurements, a complete understanding of the method of mixing, using a technique that's best for the kinds and amounts of ingredients, and to correct baking.

Cakes may be divided into two classifications: those containing shortening and those without shortening (angel and sponge cakes). The two kinds are very different in the way they are mixed and in their appearance and texture, but many of the same rules for cakemaking apply to both. Cakes may be baked as layers, loaves, sheets, or cupcakes—but many recipes cannot be used interchangeably.

The quality of a finished cake can be only as good as the ingredients that go into its making. Fine granulated sugar is essential for delicate texture. Vegetable fats, butter, or lard may be used as shortening. All should be at room temperature when they are used. Cake flour made from soft-wheat flour has a more tender gluten and is best for delicate cakes made with shortening and for angel and sponge cakes. If a recipe calls for cake flour and you substitute all-purpose flour, the texture will not be as fine; when substituting for cake flour, use 2 tablespoons less per cup of all-purpose flour. Eggs should have thick whites and yolks that do not spread when eggs are broken. (They beat to best volume after they are three days old.)

Mixing Cakes with Shortening. Read recipe carefully to understand method. Assemble all ingredients and utensils. Measure accurately, using standard measuring cups and spoons. Preheat oven to specified temperature, and prepare pans. Cakes are more easily removed from pans if waxed paper, cut to fit bottom of pans, is used. Sides of pan should not be greased.

All ingredients should be room temperature. Sift flour once, measure—pile lightly in measuring cup and level off with spatula. Then sift with other dry ingredients 3 times. Cream shortening until slightly soft; add sugar and continue creaming until mixture is light and fluffy. It makes little difference if shortening is first thoroughly creamed and sugar added gradually; but since thorough creaming is important, it is easier if shortening is softened and sugar added slowly. Sufficient time should be given to this step to allow sugar to dissolve; this helps to insure a fine even grain and a moist velvety cake. In measuring brown sugar, pack firmly in cup. Wash eggs; separate yolks from whites. Yolks may be added to mixture, one at a time, and beaten vigorously after each addition, or beaten separately until thick and lemon-colored. In white cakes this step is omitted.

Add flavoring extracts to creamed mixture or with liquid. Add dry ingredients in four portions, alternately with liquid in three portions, starting and ending with flour. Stirring around the bowl in same direction after each addition of flour and liquid tends to give cake a finer texture than when batter is beaten across bowl. The average number of strokes in stirring dry and liquid ingredients is 225 strokes for master recipe. Counting strokes is not necessary for veteran cooks, but it helps a beginner. Cakes containing a higher proportion of sugar or fat should be stirred more than this. Undermixed cakes are coarse and become dry in a short time. Overmixing results in compact, solid texture.

Beat egg whites until stiff but not dry. Fold into cake batter lightly but quickly with a down-under-up-and-over stroke. Pour batter into pans and spread to sides. Place pans in the oven so they do not touch each other or the sides of the oven. Do not place pans directly over another pan. If necessary, stagger the pans on 2 shelves. During the first quarter (of baking), cake begins to rise; second quarter, rising continues and surface begins to brown; third quarter, rising is completed and browning continues; fourth quarter, cake finishes baking. When done, cake shrinks slightly from sides of pan; top springs back when pressed lightly with finger, and a cake tester or wooden pick inserted into center of cake comes out clean. Regardless of time given in recipe, test cake for doneness.

Warm cake is fragile; if allowed to stand in pan 5 minutes it becomes rigid enough to withstand handling. Loosen edge with knife; turn out on wire rack to cool. Pull off paper immediately. Let layers cool before frosting. Brush off loose crumbs and place bottom of layers together with frosting or filling. In frosting cake, cover sides first, then top, spreading frosting out to edge with a light swirling motion.

Mixing Cakes with Electric Mixer. Electric mixers are time-and-labor savers in cakemaking. In using them, it is necessary to alter the mixing technique. Even at low or medium speeds, electric mixers beat twice as powerfully as by hand.

First, cream shortening at low speed; then at same speed add sugar and increase to medium speed as mixture becomes creamy. Turn to high speed and add unbeaten eggs or egg yolks, according to recipe, one at a time, beating about one minute after each addition. Turn to low speed and add sifted ingredients alternately with liquids, stopping immediately when flour disappears. When egg whites are added last, beat them first at high speed with 1/4 cup sugar. Then proceed with cake without washing beaters. Scrape down batter with rubber spatula as bowl revolves.

★FLUFFY YELLOW CAKE
MARTHA WASHINGTON CAKE

1 cup shortening
2 cups sugar
4 egg yolks
1 teaspoon vanilla extract
3 cups all-purpose flour, sifted

1/4 teaspoon salt
3 teaspoons baking powder
1 cup milk
4 stiffly beaten egg whites

START oven at moderate (350 degrees F.). Grease three 8-inch layer-cake pans, line with waxed paper and grease the paper.

Cream shortening and sugar thoroughly. Add egg yolks and vanilla; beat well. Sift dry ingredients together; add alternately with milk. Fold in egg whites. Bake in prepared pans in moderate oven, 30 minutes. Follow directions for baking and cooling. Put together with favorite filling; frost with favorite icing. Makes 3-layer cake; 8 or more servings.

DELICATE WHITE CAKE

⅔ cup shortening	2 teaspoons baking powder
2 cups sugar	1 cup water
1 teaspoon vanilla extract	4 stiffly-beaten egg whites
3 cups cake flour	1 teaspoon baking powder
¼ teaspoon salt	

START oven at moderate (350 degrees F.). Grease two 9-inch cake pans, line with waxed paper and grease the paper.

Thoroughly cream shortening and sugar; add vanilla. Sift flour with salt and 2 teaspoons baking powder, add to shortening alternately with water, beating well after each addition. Fold in egg whites, beaten with remaining teaspoon baking powder. Bake in two prepared pans in moderate oven, 30 minutes. Follow directions for baking and cooling. Put together and frost with Seven-Minute Frosting. Makes 2-layer cake, 8 or more servings.

LADY BALTIMORE CAKE

¾ cup shortening	½ cup milk
2 cups sugar	½ cup water
3 cups cake flour	½ teaspoon vanilla extract
¾ teaspoon salt	½ teaspoon lemon extract
3 teaspoons baking powder	6 stiffly-beaten egg whites

START oven at moderate (350 degrees F.). Grease two 9-inch square layer-cake pans, line with waxed paper and grease the paper.

Thoroughly cream shortening and sugar. Sift dry ingredients together and add to shortening alternately with milk and water; beat smooth after each addition. Add extracts. Fold in egg whites. Bake in prepared pans in moderate oven, 30 minutes. Follow directions for baking and cooling. Put layers together with Lady Baltimore Filling and frost with ⅔ recipe for Seven-Minute Frosting tinted delicate pink. May be decorated with leaves and flowers of butter-frosting and with tiny center nosegay of real flowers. Makes 2-layer cake, 8 or more servings.

Lady Baltimore Filling: To remaining ⅓ of Seven-Minute Frosting, add ¼ cup each chopped figs, seedless raisins, candied cherries, and chopped pecans.

LORD BALTIMORE CAKE

1 cup shortening	1 teaspoon soda
1¾ cups sugar	2 teaspoons cream of tartar
7 egg yolks	½ teaspoon ground nutmeg
3¼ cups all-purpose flour, sifted	1 cup milk
¼ teaspoon salt	½ teaspoon lemon extract

START oven at moderate (350 degrees F.). Grease two 9-inch cake pans, line with waxed paper and grease the paper.

Thoroughly cream the shortening and sugar. Add egg yolks, one at a time, mixing smooth after each addition. Sift dry ingredients and add alternately with milk and lemon extract. Bake in prepared pans in moderate oven 35 to 40 minutes. Follow directions for baking and cooling. Put layers together with Lady Baltimore Filling (*see* above). Frost with Seven-Minute Frosting. Decorate sides with additional chopped fruits and top with small candy hearts. Makes 2-layer cake, 8 or more servings.

POUND CAKE

1 cup shortening	10 stiffly-beaten egg whites
1 cup butter	4½ cups cake flour
2 cups sugar	½ teaspoon salt
10 well beaten egg yolks	1 teaspoon baking powder
¼ cup lemon juice	2 teaspoons ground nutmeg

START oven at moderate (325 degrees F.). Grease loaf pan (5½-×-10½-inch size), line with waxed paper and grease the paper.

Cream the shortenings and sugar; add yolks and lemon juice, beat thoroughly. Fold egg whites into shortening, then sifted dry ingredients. Bake in prepared pan in moderate oven 1½ hours. Makes 1 loaf, 12 or more servings. For small Pound Cake, cut ingredients in half; bake in pan 4½-×-9-inch size, 1 hour and 15 minutes. Follow directions for baking and cooling.

BRIDE'S CAKE
WEDDING CAKE

¾ cup shortening	1 cup milk
2 cups sugar	6 stiffly-beaten egg whites
1 teaspoon vanilla extract	½ cup chopped blanched almonds
3 cups cake flour	¼ cup chopped citron
½ teaspoon salt	¼ cup chopped candied cherries
4 teaspoons baking powder	

START oven at moderate (350 degrees F.). Grease two 10-inch layer cake pans, line with waxed paper and grease the paper.

Cream the shortening and sugar thoroughly; add vanilla. Sift flour with salt and baking powder, add to shortening alternately with milk. Fold egg whites in, then nuts and fruits. Bake in prepared pans in moderate oven 30 minutes. Follow directions for baking and cooling cake. Frost with double recipe for Boiled Frosting. Makes large 2-layer cake. Makes 8 to 10 servings. For very large 3-tiered cake, increase recipe one-half. May be decorated with butter-frosting flowers, all white, and topped with small bride and groom dolls.

GROOM'S CAKE
WHITE FRUIT CAKE

1 cup shortening
1 cup sugar
5 eggs
2 cups all-purpose flour, sifted
1 teaspoon salt
1½ teaspoons baking powder
¼ cup unsweetened pineapple juice
¼ pound citron chopped fine
¼ pound each orange peel and lemon peel chopped fine

½ cup chopped candied cherries
1¼ cups chopped candied pineapple
½ cup chopped pitted dates
½ cup chopped dried apricots
½ cup chopped figs
½ pound white raisins
2 (4-oz.) cans moist shredded coconut
2 cups sliced blanched almonds

START oven at slow (275 degrees F.) . Grease five 1-pound loaf pans, line with waxed paper and grease the paper.

Cream the shortening and sugar thoroughly. Add eggs, one at a time, beating well after each addition. Reserve ½ cup flour for fruits. Sift remaining flour with salt and baking powder, add alternately with pineapple juice to shortening and sugar. Add floured fruits, coconut, and nuts; stir only until well blended. Pour into prepared pans. Bake in slow oven 1½ hours. Decorate with additional candied pineapple, almonds, cherries, or citron. Continue baking another hour. Let cool in pans. Then place cakes in tins or jars with tight cover. Slice and place in small boxes, as wedding-cake gifts for guests at a bridal breakfast or other party. Or slice and serve with bride's cake. Can be baked in round layer pans and frosted with Boiled Frosting. Makes 50 or more servings.

Angel and Sponge Cakes

Success in making angel cake depends on the degree to which the egg whites are beaten, the lightness with which the sugar and flour mixtures are incorporated, and the temperature at which the cake is baked. Measure all ingredients; sift half the sugar with the flour 4 times. It's easier to separate whites from yolks if eggs are cold. But egg whites will yield a larger volume if allowed to stand until they reach room temperature before beating.

Both angel and sponge cakes are cooled in the inverted pan. If cake falls from pan, it may be due to pan having been greased at some time, or to insufficient baking. If a brown crust is desired, remove cake from pan just as soon as it is cool. The longer the sponge cakes remain in the pan, the more the crust will adhere to pan.

ANGEL CAKE

1 cup cake flour	1½ teaspoons cream of tartar
¾ cup sugar	¾ cup sugar
1¾ cups egg whites	1 teaspoon vanilla extract
¾ teaspoon salt	

START oven at moderate (325 degrees F.). Sift flour with ¾ cup sugar 4 times. Beat egg whites with salt until frothy; add cream of tartar and beat until stiff but not dry. Add remaining ¾ cup sugar to egg whites, 1 tablespoon at a time, folding in thoroughly. Add vanilla with last addition of sugar. Sift flour mixture over top, a little at a time, and fold in lightly with down-under-up-over motion. Bake in 10-inch ungreased angel-cake pan in moderate oven 1 hour and 15 minutes. Invert pan over an upside-down funnel, funnel of cake pan over funnel end. Let cake cool thoroughly. Loosen with spatula. Turn pan upside down again. Hit pan sharply on edge of table, cake drops out; turn it over onto a serving platter; frost and decorate as desired. Makes 10 or more servings.

HOT-WATER SPONGE CAKE

4 egg yolks	1 teaspoon baking powder
1½ cups sugar	1 teaspoon lemon or vanilla
½ cup boiling water	extract
1½ cups cake flour	4 stiffly-beaten egg whites
¼ teaspoon salt	

START oven at moderate (325 degrees F.). Beat egg yolks until very thick;

gradually add sugar and continue beating. Add boiling water, mix well, and add sifted dry ingredients. Mix until smooth, and add extract. Fold in egg whites.

Bake in ungreased 10-inch angel-cake pan in moderate oven 1 hour. Invert pan (as for angel cake) to cool. Serve plain or frosted. Makes 10 servings.

General cakebaking information and all cake recipes above from BETTER HOMES AND GARDENS COOK BOOK, *by The Foods Editors of* Better Homes and Gardens

Good Cakes from All Over

Not so long ago the Women's National Press Club, of Washington, D.C., published a cook book of its members' favorite recipes. These are unusual recipes, each with a story—a story about the origin of the dish. Here is one of the best cakes in that book, *Who Says We Can't Cook!*

CHOCOLATE CAKE

The recipe was contributed by Gertrude Dieken, who said, "Whenever I want a really splurgy dessert I serve this 6-to-7-inch-high chocolate lusciousness. The cake recipe came from a ranch wife in Montana and was tested in our *Farm Journal* kitchens. Its popularity spread like wildfire over the western range. We had more comments on it than any cake recipe we printed. It is one of the most superior chocolate cakes in existence."

¾ cup butter	3 cups cake flour
2¼ cups sugar	1½ teaspoons soda
1½ teaspoons vanilla extract	¾ teaspoon salt
3 eggs	1½ cups ice water
3 (1-oz.) squares unsweetened chocolate, melted	

START oven at moderate (350 degrees F.). Grease three 8-inch layer-cake pans, line with waxed paper and grease the paper.

Cream the butter and sugar together smoothly, add vanilla; beat. Add eggs. Beat until light and fluffy. Add melted chocolate; beat. Sift cake flour, soda, and salt together. Add sifted dry ingredients to creamed mixture alternately with ice water. Pour into prepared pans. Bake in moderate oven 30 to 35 minutes. Let cool 5 minutes in pans; loosen edges with spatula, and turn layers out onto cooling rack. When completely cool, put together with Date Cream Filling, and frost the top and sides with Special Frosting. Makes one 3-layer cake; 8 or more servings.

DATE CREAM FILLING

1 cup milk
½ cup chopped pitted dates
¼ cup sugar
1 tablespoon flour

1 beaten egg
½ cup chopped nuts
1 teaspoon vanilla extract

Heat milk in top of double boiler with dates. Combine sugar and flour; add egg, beat smooth. Add slowly to hot milk-and-date mixture. Cook, stirring, until thick. Let cool. Stir in nuts and vanilla. Makes enough filling for 3 layers.

SPECIAL FROSTING

2 cups sugar
1 cup cream

2 (1-oz.) squares unsweetened chocolate, grated

Boil sugar, cream, and chocolate together over high heat 3 minutes without stirring. Reduce heat, continue cooking until syrup reaches soft ball stage (238 degrees F. on candy thermometer). Wipe any crystals from sides of pan (with fork wound with damp cheesecloth) but do not stir or frosting will be sugary. Let cool. Beat until creamy and of spreading consistency. If frosting becomes too thick, add small amount of cream and beat smooth. Makes enough frosting for top and sides of this 3-layer cake.

WELLESLEY FUDGE CAKE

Gladys Montgomery, who gave this recipe to the Women's National Press Club cook book says, "This cake originated in a small tea room in Wellesley, Mass. It is not as expensive to make as it appears because it is a large cake."

2⅔ cups brown sugar (packed)
⅔ cup butter
3 egg yolks and 1 whole egg
4 (1-oz.) cakes unsweetened chocolate
⅔ cup boiling water

2⅔ cups all-purpose flour, sifted
1½ teaspoons baking powder
⅛ teaspoon salt
⅔ cup thick sour milk
1¼ teaspoons soda
1 teaspoon vanilla extract

START oven at moderate (350 degrees F.). Grease two 9-inch square cake pans, line with waxed paper and grease the paper.

Cream the sugar and butter together until light and fluffy. Add yolks and extra egg, one at a time, beating thoroughly. Melt chocolate in double boiler, add hot water, and stir until the consistency of thick paste. Mix with butter, sugar, and egg mixture. Dissolve soda in sour milk. Sift flour 3 times, measure, add baking powder and salt, and sift together into mixing bowl which contains the butter, sugar, and egg mixture, alternating with sour milk. Add vanilla. Bake in prepared pans, in moderate oven 30 to 35 minutes. Let cool 5 minutes in pans; loosen with spatula and turn out to cool completely on cake rack. Spread Fudge Cake Frosting between layers and on top of cake. Makes one 2-layer cake; 8 or more servings.

FUDGE CAKE FROSTING

4 (1-oz.) squares unsweetened chocolate
Powdered sugar
2 tablespoons butter

½ teaspoon vanilla extract
¼ cup coarsely-chopped walnuts or pecans

Melt chocolate in upper part of double boiler over hot water. Stir just enough powdered sugar into it to make correct consistency for spreading on cake. Add butter and vanilla. Remove from heat. Let cool slightly. Spread between layers of cake and on top.

SPECIAL FRUIT CAKE

Violet Faulkner, food editor of *The Washington Evening Star,* contributed this recipe to the Press Club book.

½ pound citron
½ pound each candied orange and lemon peel
½ pound candied pineapple
½ pound candied cherries
2 pounds seedless raisins
2 pounds pitted dates
1 pound walnut meats
3 cups all-purpose flour, sifted
1 teaspoon salt

1 teaspoon baking powder
1 teaspoon ground nutmeg
1 teaspoon ground cloves
2 teaspoons ground cinnamon
2 teaspoons ground allspice
7 eggs
2 cups brown sugar (packed)
1 cup wine, brandy, or fruit juice
1 cup butter, melted

START oven at slow (250 degrees F.). Grease 1 or 2 large tube cake pans; line with waxed paper and grease the paper.

Cut or chop fruit and nuts fine and dredge with 2 cups flour. Sift salt, baking powder, spices, and remaining 1 cup flour. Beat eggs until light; add sugar; beat until fluffy; sift dry ingredients into egg and sugar. Mix well; add floured fruit and nuts. Mix; add wine, brandy, or fruit juice. Stir in melted butter and mix thoroughly. Mixture is very heavy; use wooden spoon or your hands. Pour into prepared pans. Place shallow pan of water in bottom of oven during baking. Bake in slow oven, 4 hours. Remove from oven. Let cool in pans on rack several hours, or overnight.

Remove from cake pans; wrap in brandy-soaked cloth (trickle a little extra brandy over cake from time to time). Store in tightly covered tin containers and keep in cool place. Keeps well for as long as 2 years; improves with age. Makes 50 or more servings.

The three cakes above from WHO SAYS WE CAN'T COOK!, *by Members of the Women's National Press Club*

Two Cheesecakes

Until only a few years ago cheesecake was a specialty of professional bakers. But home economists have simplified, improved, varied the old European recipes. From Marye Dahnke's cheese kitchen, these 2 luscious cakes are chosen from four cheesecake recipes featured in her cook book, *The Cheese Cook Book*.

HOLLYWOOD CHEESECAKE

18 zwieback, rolled (or 1½ cups zwieback crumbs)
3 tablespoons butter or margarine
2 tablespoons sugar
1 pound cream cheese
½ cup sugar
⅛ teaspoon ground cinnamon
½ teaspoon vanilla extract
1 teaspoon grated lemon peel
1 tablespoon lemon juice
2 eggs
1 cup thick sour cream
1 tablespoon sugar
1 teaspoon vanilla extract

START oven at moderately slow (300 degrees F.). Blend zwieback crumbs with butter or margarine and 2 tablespoons sugar; press into the bottom of a 9-inch spring-form pan. (A spring-form pan is a round baking tin from which the side can be removed; it allows serving the cake from the bottom of the pan. It is impossible to move cheesecake onto a plate without this base.) Bake this bottom crust in slow oven 5 minutes. Let cool.

Blend cheese, softened at room temperature, with the ½ cup sugar, cinnamon, ½ teaspoon vanilla, lemon peel, and juice. Add egg yolks, one at a time, mixing well after each yolk is added. Beat egg whites until stiff; fold into cheese mixture, then pour on top of crumb crust in prepared pan. Bake in moderately slow oven 45 minutes.

Blend sour cream with the 1 tablespoon sugar and 1 teaspoon vanilla. Spread this mixture over the top of the cake. Return to oven for an additional 10 minutes. Let cool before removing the side of the pan. Do not invert. Makes 8 to 10 servings.

DEVIL'S FOOD CHEESECAKE

3 (1-oz.) squares unsweetened chocolate
2 (3-oz.) packages cream cheese
½ teaspoon red food coloring
1 cup sugar
2 eggs
2 cups cake flour
1 teaspoon soda
¼ teaspoon salt
1 cup water
1 teaspoon vanilla extract
Orange or Chocolate Cream-Cheese Frosting

START oven at moderate (350 degrees F.). Grease two 8-inch layer-cake pans. Line with waxed paper and grease the paper.

Melt chocolate and let cool slightly. Cream the cheese thoroughly; add chocolate and red coloring. Add sugar gradually. Add eggs, one at a time, blending well. Sift flour, soda, and salt together. Add alternately with water to chocolate-cheese mixture. Blend in vanilla. Pour into prepared pans. Bake in moderate oven 30 minutes. When cool, frost with Orange or Chocolate Cream-Cheese Frosting. Makes 6 to 8 servings.

ORANGE CREAM-CHEESE FROSTING

2 (3-oz.) packages cream cheese	2 teaspoons orange juice
4 cups confectioners' sugar	1 teaspoon grated orange peel

Blend cheese and sifted sugar. Add orange juice and peel and beat smooth. Spread on cake.

CHOCOLATE CREAM-CHEESE FROSTING

2 (3-oz.) packages cream cheese	4 (1-oz.) squares unsweetened
4 tablespoons milk	chocolate, melted
4 cups confectioners' sugar	1/8 teaspoon salt

Soften cheese with milk, beating smooth. Add sifted sugar, one cup at a time, blending after each addition. Add chocolate and salt and blend well. Spread on cake.

The cheesecake and frosting recipes from THE CHEESE COOK BOOK, *by Marye Dahnke*

Fillings and Frostings

Edith Barber, a food writer, newspaper columnist, home economist who has pioneered in experimental and creative cookery for American food manufacturers, has also compiled her own cook book, *Edith Barber's Cook Book.* Using the dishes she had served to discriminating guests through the years, and supplementing her own hostess cookery with many other recipes, this book is one of the soundest and best. Use her fillings and frostings with cake recipes given in preceding pages. Or buy un-iced cakes and give them the glamour frosting treatment.

★BUTTER FROSTING

4 tablespoons butter	1 teaspoon vanilla extract
¼ teaspoon salt	1 egg yolk
2½ cups sifted confectioners' sugar	3 tablespoons milk

CREAM the butter. Stir in salt and half the sugar gradually, blending well after each addition. Add vanilla. Beat in unbeaten egg yolk. Stir in milk alternately with remaining sugar. This makes frosting for two 9-inch layers, or 2 dozen cupcakes.

Almond Butter Frosting: Sprinkle toasted blanched almonds over the frosting after it has been spread on cake.

Orange Butter Frosting: Substitute 3 tablespoons orange juice for milk, and 2 teaspoons grated orange peel for vanilla extract.

Chocolate Butter Frosting: Reduce milk to 1½ tablespoons and add 2 (1-oz.) squares chocolate (melted) with vanilla extract.

★MOCHA FROSTING

⅓ cup butter	¾ teaspoon salt
4 cups sifted confectioners' sugar	1 (1oz.) square chocolate melted
½ teaspoon vanilla extract	⅓ cup strong coffee

CREAM butter, stir in half the sugar gradually, blending well after each addition. Add vanilla, salt, and chocolate, and mix well. Stir in remaining sugar alternately with the coffee, beating well after each addition. Add more coffee if frosting is too thick. Makes frosting for two 9-inch layers or 2 dozen cupcakes.

★CARAMEL FROSTING
BUTTERSCOTCH FROSTING

1½ cups brown sugar (packed)	1½ cups milk
1½ cups granulated sugar	2 tablespoons butter

COOK sugars and milk over low heat, stirring until sugars are dissolved. Then cook without stirring until a small amount will form a very soft ball when tried in cold water (232 degrees F.) on candy thermometer. Remove from heat and add butter. Let cool to lukewarm. Beat until creamy and thick enough to spread. Makes frosting for two 9-inch layers or 2 dozen cupcakes. If necessary, place frosting over hot water to keep soft while spreading.

★BOILED FROSTING

1½ cups sugar
1 tablespoon light corn syrup
½ cup water

2 stiffly-beaten egg whites
1 teaspoon vanilla extract

STIR sugar, corn syrup, and water over low heat until sugar is dissolved. Bring to boiling, cover for 2 minutes, then cook uncovered, without stirring, until a small amount will form a soft ball when tried in cold water, (238 degrees F.) on candy thermometer. Remove from heat. Beat syrup slowly into stiffly-beaten egg whites. Add vanilla. Place bowl of frosting in pan of boiling water and continue beating until thick enough to spread. Makes frosting for two 9-inch layers or 2 dozen cupcakes.

Coconut Frosting: Sprinkle 2 cups grated or shredded coconut over Boiled Frosting after it has been spread on cake.

★SIX-MINUTE FROSTING
SEVEN-MINUTE FROSTING

2 egg whites
1½ cups sugar
5 tablespoons water

2 teaspoons light corn syrup
1 teaspoon vanilla extract

MIX unbeaten egg whites, sugar, water, and corn syrup in top of double boiler. Beat with rotary beater until sugar is dissolved. Place over boiling water and cook, beating constantly, for 6 minutes (or 7 minutes according to some cooks), or until frosting will stand in peaks. If an electric beater is used, the beating time will be about 4 minutes. Remove from heat. Add vanilla and beat until thick enough to spread. Makes frosting for two 9-inch layers or 2 dozen cupcakes.

Marshmallow Frosting: Add 8 marshmallows, cut in small pieces, as soon as above frosting is removed from heat.

★CREAM FILLING
CUSTARD FILLING

⅔ cup sugar
½ cup flour
⅛ teaspoon salt
2 cups scalded milk

2 slightly-beaten egg yolks
1 teaspoon vanilla extract
½ cup heavy cream, whipped

MIX sugar, flour, and salt in top of double boiler. Stir in scalded milk gradually. Stir over hot water until mixture thickens, cover, and cook 10 minutes. Stir some of hot mixture into slightly-beaten egg yolks, pour back into remaining hot mixture. Stir 2 minutes longer over hot water. Let cool. Fold in vanilla and whipped cream. Makes filling for three 9-inch layers.

Coconut Cream Filling: Add ½ cup shredded coconut to Cream Filling.

Butterscotch Filling: Substitute brown sugar, firmly packed, for granulated sugar in Cream Filling recipe.

★ORANGE FILLING

½ cup sugar

5 tablespoons flour

⅛ teaspoon salt

½ cup orange juice

1 tablespoon lemon juice

½ cup water

1 slightly-beaten egg

1 tablespoon butter

1½ teaspoons grated orange peel

Mix sugar, flour, and salt in top of double boiler. Stir in fruit juices, water, and slightly-beaten egg and cook over hot water 10 minutes, or until thick, stirring constantly. Remove from hot water. Stir butter and orange peel in. Makes filling for two 9-inch layers.

Cookies and Small Cakes

Almost any cake recipe may be baked in cupcake form. Use muffin pans, lining with pleated paper cup; or grease pan, line with waxed paper and grease the paper. Fill ⅔ full. When baked, cupcakes should fill pan and have rounded top. Bake in moderately hot oven (400 degrees F.) 18 to 20 minutes. Let cool 5 minutes in pans, then remove to cake rack to cool. Use any frosting recipe. Decorate frosted cupcakes with nuts, grated chocolate, coconut, small candies, flowers of butter frosting, or for special occasions, decorate with tiny candles or insert a fresh flower in each just before serving. Any cake recipe calling for 2¼ to 2½ cups flour makes 1½ to 2 dozen cupcakes.

★BUTTERSCOTCH WAFERS

1¼ cups all-purpose flour, sifted

1½ teaspoons baking powder

½ teaspoon salt

½ cup shortening

2 cups brown sugar (packed)

2 well-beaten eggs

1½ cups chopped nuts

Start oven at moderate (325 degrees F.). Mix and sift flour, baking powder, and salt. Melt shortening, stir in sugar, and mix well. Remove from heat and stir in well-beaten eggs. Stir in sifted dry ingredients to which nuts have been added. Drop by ½ teaspoonfuls on greased baking sheet and bake in moderate oven about 15 minutes. Let cool slightly, then remove carefully with thin knife or spatula. If cookies harden on sheet, return to the oven a few minutes. Makes 9 dozen wafers, 1½ to 2 inches in diameter.

★CHOCOLATE CRISPS

1¼ cups all-purpose flour, sifted
¼ teaspoon baking soda
½ teaspoon salt
½ cup shortening
½ cup brown sugar (packed)
½ cup granulated sugar

1 egg
½ teaspoon vanilla extract
½ cup broken nuts
½-pound cake of sweet baking
    chocolate

START oven at moderately hot (400 degrees F.). Mix and sift flour, soda, and salt. Cream shortening, add sugars gradually, blend well. Stir unbeaten egg and vanilla into shortening mixture. Add sifted dry ingredients. Stir in nuts. Break chocolate into small pieces, stir them in, and mix. Drop by teaspoonful about 2 inches apart on ungreased baking sheet. Bake in moderately hot oven from 7 to 9 minutes. Makes about 4 dozen cookies.

★CHOCOLATE PECAN COOKIES

¾ cup sifted flour
½ teaspoon salt
½ cup shortening
1 cup sugar

2 well-beaten eggs
3 (1-oz.) squares chocolate, melted
1 teaspoon vanilla extract
¾ cup chopped pecans

START oven at moderate (325 degrees F.). Mix and sift flour with salt. Cream shortening, add sugar slowly, and cream until fluffy. Stir well-beaten eggs into shortening. Add chocolate and vanilla and mix well. Stir in sifted dry ingredients and pecans; mix. Drop by teaspoonful on greased baking sheet and let stand a few minutes. Flatten dough by pressing with the bottom of a tumbler covered with a damp cloth. Bake in moderate oven 12 to 15 minutes. Makes 2½ dozen cookies.

★NUT MACAROON WAFERS

2 egg whites
½ cup sugar
¼ teaspoon salt

½ teaspoon almond extract
1 cup ground nuts

START oven at moderate (350 degrees F.). Beat egg whites until dry and stiff enough to hold shape. Fold sugar and salt in carefully. Add almond extract and nuts. Drop by teaspoonful on ungreased baking sheet. Bake in moderate oven about 15 to 20 minutes. Remove from pans at once. Makes 1½ dozen wafers.

★MERINGUES

3 egg whites   ⅛ teaspoon salt
¾ cup sugar   ½ teaspoon vanilla extract

START oven at slow (275 degrees F.). Beat egg whites until stiff and dry. Gradually beat in ½ cup sugar and salt. Fold in remaining sugar and vanilla. Drop by tablespoonful on ungreased baking sheet, piling mixture high in center of each meringue. Bake in slow oven about 40 to 45 minutes, until meringues are dry on the surface and will slip off the sheet easily. Remove from sheet with wet knife or spatula. If meringues are to be served with ice cream, press in bottom crust. Makes 10 medium-size or 18 small meringues or kisses.

★OLD-FASHIONED SOFT MOLASSES COOKIES

4 teaspoons baking soda   1 cup shortening
¼ cup hot water   1 cup sugar
4½ cups all-purpose flour, sifted   1 egg
2 teaspoons ground ginger   1 cup molasses
2 teaspoons ground cinnamon   ¾ cup coffee or water
½ teaspoon salt

START oven at hot (425 degrees F.). Dissolve soda in hot water and set aside to cool. Mix and sift flour, spices, and salt. Cream the shortening, add sugar slowly, and beat until fluffy. Stir unbeaten egg into shortening and mix well. Stir in molasses. Add sifted dry ingredients alternately with coffee or water, beating well after each addition. Stir in cooled soda-and-water mixture. Drop by teaspoonful on greased baking sheets and bake in hot oven about 10 minutes. These cookies should be stored in a tightly covered cookie jar and a few slices of bread added to keep them soft. Makes 4 to 5 dozen cookies.

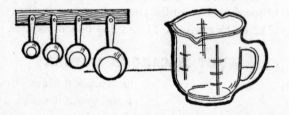

★REFRIGERATOR BUTTERSCOTCH COOKIES

2 cups all-purpose flour, sifted   1¼ cups brown sugar (packed)
2 teaspoons baking powder   1 well-beaten egg
⅛ teaspoon salt   ½ cup chopped nuts
½ cup shortening   1½ teaspoons vanilla extract

Mix and sift flour, baking powder, and salt. Cream the shortening, add sugar slowly and beat until fluffy. Stir well-beaten egg, nuts, and vanilla into shortening. Add sifted dry ingredients. Shape into rolls 1½ inches in diameter. Wrap in waxed paper and chill in refrigerator. When hard enough to cut, slice very thin. Start oven at hot (425 degrees F.). Bake slices on ungreased baking sheet for about 10 minutes. Makes about 4 dozen cookies.

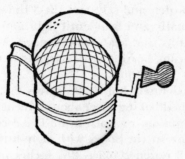

★SUGAR COOKIES

3 cups all-purpose flour, sifted	1 cup sugar
2 teaspoons baking powder	2 well-beaten eggs
½ teaspoon salt	½ teaspoon vanilla extract
⅔ cup shortening	¼ cup milk

Mix and sift flour, baking powder, and salt. Cream the shortening, add sugar slowly, and beat until fluffy. Stir in well-beaten eggs and vanilla into shortening. Add sifted dry ingredients alternately with the milk. Blend well and chill.

Start oven at moderate, 375 degrees F. Roll dough ¼ inch thick on lightly floured board. Cut with floured cookie cutter in round or fancy shapes. The cookies may be brushed with unbeaten egg white, decorated with sliced nuts, and sprinkled with sugar. Bake on ungreased baking sheet in moderate oven 10 to 12 minutes. Makes about 3½ dozen 3-inch cookies.

The fifteen recipes for fillings, frosting, and cookies, above, from EDITH BARBER'S COOK BOOK, *by Edith Barber*

❧

Clementine Paddleford's widely syndicated articles and columns on food contain many good recipes. Her cook book *New, Easy Ways to Cook with Rum,* prepared for Bacardi rum importers, includes these two superior cookie recipes.

GOLDEN RUM COOKIES

2 cups all-purpose flour, sifted	1 cup sugar
2 teaspoons baking powder	3 well-beaten eggs
½ teaspoon salt	1 teaspoon vanilla extract
1 cup butter	½ cup light rum

Mix flour, baking powder, and salt, and sift 3 times. Cream butter until soft. Add sugar gradually and beat until light and fluffy. Add eggs and vanilla to butter mixture and beat until blended. Add sifted dry ingredients alternately with rum, beating until smooth after each addition. Chill dough in refrigerator for 1 hour.

Start oven at moderately hot (400 degrees F.). Drop dough by teaspoonful onto ungreased baking sheet about 2 inches apart. Bake in moderately hot oven 8 minutes, or until firm. These cookies do not brown deeply. Let cool. Store in tin boxes with tight-fitting covers, or tightly covered jars. Makes 8 dozen cookies, 2½ inches in diameter.

BACARDI RUM BALLS

2 (4¾-oz.) packages vanilla wafers, crushed (about 52 wafers)	½ cup strained honey
6 tablespoons golden rum	1 pound ground walnuts
	Confectioners' sugar

Thoroughly blend all ingredients except sugar. Using a level tablespoonful of mixture for each ball, form spoonful into ball. Roll each in sugar. Store in tightly covered container to "ripen" a few days. Makes 4½ dozen balls. These balls keep moist and fragrant as long as 6 weeks.

The two recipes above from NEW, EASY WAYS TO COOK WITH RUM, *by Clementine Paddleford*

THE
"BEST-OF-ALL"

CHEESE DISHES

THE RECIPES THAT FOLLOW HAVE BEEN SELECTED FROM THESE DISTINGUISHED BOOKS:

The Art of Cheese Cookery *Nika Standen*
Ford Treasury of Favorite Recipes, Vol. 2 *Nancy Kennedy*
The Glamour Magazine After Five Cook
Book *Beverly Pepper*

CHEESE

Good cheese plays so many roles in American menus that it appears, in this book, in one form or another in almost every section, including the foreign-recipe pages. Some of the best cheese cookery does not fit into any other group of recipes, and so this golden food—so good, nourishing, and adaptable in the kitchen —rightly enjoys a few pages of its own.

In the second volume of the *Ford Treasury of Favorite Recipes,* compiled by Nancy Kennedy, is a cheese mixture which can grace a fruit-and-cheese tray after dinner, or be served with drinks, or go into lunchboxes and picnic baskets as a sandwich filler. It is a favorite at the Lindsey Tavern, Lincoln, Rhode Island.

★LINDSEY CLUB CHEESE

2 tablespoons small stuffed olives	1 pound cream cheese
1 green pepper	1 teaspoon paprika
2 tablespoons finely-chopped parsley	2 drops Tabasco sauce
½ pound Roquefort cheese	1 teaspoon Worcestershire sauce
½ pound sweet butter	

PUT olives and green pepper through fine meat grinder or blender. Press excess moisture from mixture. Put Roquefort through grinder. Melt butter; combine all ingredients in bowl and blend. Serve in loaf form with crackers. Makes 12 generous servings.

FRIED CAMEMBERT CHEESE

A California restaurant, in the Danville Hotel, Oakland, is famous for this cheese dish.

Camembert cheese	Fat for deep frying
Beaten egg	Currant jelly or Bar-le-Duc
Bread crumbs	Crackers or melba toast

CUT rind from firm Camembert cheese. Cut into desired portions, about the size of small croquettes. Dip each in beaten egg, roll in crumbs, place on platter and chill in refrigerator until coating is firm and cheese hardened. To serve, fry these crumbed portions quickly in deep, hot fat, using frying basket. Serve hot, with jelly and crackers as snack; or omit jelly and serve hot with salad. Or serve hot as first course, with crisp toast strips.

CHEESE BLINTZES

Traveling on (by Ford of course, or Lincoln or Mercury) the researching gourmet who compiled this book found unusual blintzes in a Hollywood restaurant, Rand's Round-Up.

Blintzes are good in any language; at Russian restaurants they are slightly different than this recipe.

2 eggs
2 cups water
⅛ teaspoon vanilla extract
2 cups all-purpose flour, sifted
⅛ teaspoon ground nutmeg
4 tablespoons sugar
¾ teaspoon baking powder
⅛ teaspoon salt

Cooking oil
½ pound cottage cheese (use dry or pot cheese)
½ pound cream cheese
Butter for frying
Powdered sugar
Sour cream

BEAT eggs in bowl, add water and vanilla and mix well. Sift flour, nutmeg, sugar, baking powder, and salt together, then sift into egg mixture, combining with a few strokes. Heat a 5-inch skillet and grease with a few drops oil. When hot add small amount of batter and tip skillet to spread batter over bottom. Brown blintz on 1 side only, turn it out on a warmed plate, brown side up. Cook all blintzes as quickly as possible.

Combine cheeses, mixing smoothly. Place spoonful of mixture on each blintz. Fold blintz edges toward middle so they lap over filling. Add a little butter to skillet; return folded blintzes to skillet and sauté in hot butter on both sides until lightly browned. Serve at once with powdered sugar and sour cream. Makes 15 blintzes.

The three recipes above from the FORD TREASURY OF FAVORITE RECIPES, VOL. 2, *compiled by Nancy Kennedy*

One cook-book writer likes cheese so much, she has studied its origins, its varieties, and devoted many hours—and a whole book—to cheese cookery. She is Nika Standen, and here are some of the usable, enjoyable dishes from her book, *The Art of Cheese Cookery.*

AMERICAN FONDUE

This old favorite derives from a famous Swiss dish (which you will find in the Swiss section).

2 cups milk
2 cups dry bread cubes
1 teaspoon salt
½ teaspoon dry mustard

⅛ teaspoon pepper
2 cups (½ pound) grated Cheddar or Swiss cheese
4 eggs

SCALD milk. Add bread cubes, seasonings, and cheese. Cook over low heat, stirring constantly, until cheese is melted.

Slowly pour the cheese mixture over well-beaten egg yolks. Stir until well blended. Let cool.

Start oven at moderate (325 degrees F.). Butter 1½-quart baking dish. Beat egg whites until stiff but not dry. Fold into cooled cheese mixture. Pour into prepared baking dish. Baking in moderate oven, 50 minutes, or until set. Makes 4 to 6 servings.

CHEESE FRITTERS

1 cup all-purpose flour, sifted
1 cup (¼ pound) grated sharp cheese
½ teaspoon salt
Pepper
½ teaspoon dry mustard

½ teaspoon finely-chopped parsley
1 egg
2 tablespoons melted butter
½ cup lukewarm water
Fat for deep frying

SIFT flour, add cheese, seasonings, and parsley, mix well. Combine well-beaten egg yolk, butter, and water. Add to cheese-and-flour mixture. Beat egg white until stiff but not dry. Fold into mixture. Drop by tablespoonful into deep hot fat (365 degrees F.) Fry until browned. Drain on thick paper toweling. Makes 8 fritters. Serve hot with tomato or chili sauce, or ketchup.

★CHEESE POPOVERS

1 cup all-purpose flour, sifted
½ teaspoon salt
1 cup milk

2 slightly-beaten eggs
1 cup (¼ pound) finely grated Cheddar cheese

SIFT flour and salt together. Add milk, eggs, and cheese. Beat with rotary beater until well blended and bubbly. Butter cold custard cups or muffin or popover pans. Fill half full of batter. Place in cold oven. Start heat at hot (425 degrees F.) for 20 minutes, then reduce heat to moderate (350 degrees F.) and bake 20 to 25 minutes longer. Makes 12 to 16 popovers. Serve as soon as they come out of oven.

CHEESE SOUFFLE

4 tablespoons butter
4 tablespoons flour
1 teaspoon salt
Cayenne

1½ cups milk
½ pound Old English process
    cheese, thinly sliced or grated
6 eggs

MELT butter in top of double boiler placed over boiling water. Remove from boiling water and blend in flour, adding salt and a few grains of cayenne. Add milk gradually, blending well. Return pan to boiling water and cook, stirring constantly until the sauce is thick and smooth. Add sliced cheese and continue cooking, stirring frequently, until cheese is melted. Remove from heat and slowly add beaten egg yolks, blending them in well. Let mixture cool slightly.

Start oven at slow (300 degrees F.). Pour slightly cooled cheese mixture into stiffly-beaten egg whites, cutting and folding thoroughly together. Pour at once into ungreased 2-quart casserole. Run tip of a teaspoon around the mixture 1 inch from edge of casserole, making a slight track, or depression. This forms the "top hat" on the soufflé as it bakes and puffs up. Bake in slow oven 1 hour and 15 minutes. Carry soufflé in baking dish to table and serve immediately. Makes 4 servings.

BLUE CHEESE FANTANS

2 cups all-purpose flour, sifted
3 teaspoons baking powder
1 teaspoon salt
4 tablespoons shortening
¾ cup milk

1 cup (¼ pound) blue cheese,
    at room temperature
2 tablespoons butter, softened
Heavy cream

SIFT flour, measure, and sift again with baking powder and salt. Cut shortening in with 2 knives or pastry blender until mixture seems coarse and crumbly. Stir in milk, mixing gently with a fork until soft dough is formed. Toss on lightly floured board.

Start oven at hot (450 degrees F.). Turn and knead dough on board gently 10 times. Roll into rectangle 8 × 12 inches. Cut lengthwise into 6 strips and cut strips in half crosswise. Mix cheese and butter together until soft and creamy. Spread 3 strips of dough with mixture. Cover with 3 more strips, spread with cheese mixture, repeat until all are put together sandwich fashion. Cut crosswise into 12 pieces. Spread each "sandwich" slightly into a fan, place in greased muffin pan. Or, do not spread layers, and place sandwiches on greased baking sheet, or in shallow pan. Brush tops with cream. Bake in hot oven 15 to 18 minutes, or until done. Makes 12 fantans.

CHEESE POTATO PUFFS

6 medium-size potatoes	2 eggs
4 tablespoons butter	1 cup (¼ pound) grated Cheddar
½ cup hot light cream or top	cheese
milk	Melted butter

PARE potatoes, cook in boiling salted water until tender. Drain; shake over heat until dry. Start oven at moderate (350 degrees F.). Mash potatoes, beat in butter and cream until fluffy. Add well-beaten egg yolks and cheese; mix well. Fold in stiffly-beaten egg whites. Place mounds of potatoes on greased baking sheet. Brush with melted butter. Bake in moderate oven 15 to 20 minutes, or until lightly browned. Makes 4 to 6 servings, as garnish around platter of ham, steak, or other meat.

This mixture also may be heaped in a greased baking dish and baked in a moderate oven until puffy and brown on top.

CHEESE SPOON BREAD

1 cup corn meal	3 cups milk, scalded
1½ teaspoons salt	1 cup (¼ pound) grated sharp
½ teaspoon dry mustard	Cheddar cheese
Cayenne	3 well-beaten eggs

START oven at moderate (350 degrees F.). Butter 2-quart baking dish. Mix corn meal, salt, mustard, and a few grains cayenne. Stir corn-meal mixture gradually into scalded milk, stirring constantly to avoid lumps. Cook until mixture thickens. Remove from heat, add cheese, and stir until cheese melts. Add eggs. Pour into prepared baking dish. Bake in moderate oven 35 to 40 minutes. Makes 4 to 6 servings.

COTTAGE-CHEESE DESSERT SOUFFLE

2 tablespoons butter	2 teaspoons grated orange or
3 tablespoons flour	lemon peel
½ teaspoon salt	½ cup toasted chopped almonds
1 cup milk	½ cup seedless raisins
3 eggs	1 cup (½ pound) cottage cheese
½ cup sugar	Fine dry bread crumbs

START oven at moderate (350 degrees F.). Butter 1½-quart baking dish generously and sprinkle thickly with crumbs.

Melt butter, remove from heat, and blend in flour and salt. Return to low heat, add milk gradually, mixing until well blended. Cook, stirring constantly until thick and smooth. Beat egg yolks until light and lemon colored. Beat sugar and orange or lemon peel into eggs; add nuts, raisins, cheese, and white sauce. Blend well. Beat egg whites until stiff but not dry. Fold into cheese mixture. Pour into prepared baking dish. Place baking dish in shallow pan of hot water. Bake in moderate oven, 50 minutes to 1 hour, or until top is brown and soufflé is set. Carry dish immediately to table and serve, with any preferred fruit sauce. Makes 6 to 8 servings.

WELSH RABBIT I

2 tablespoons butter	3 cups (¾ pound) sharp Cheddar
¾ teaspoon salt	cheese, grated or slivered fine
½ teaspoon dry mustard	¾ cup beer or ale
⅛ teaspoon pepper	1 well-beaten egg

MELT butter in chafing dish or saucepan. Add seasonings and cheese. Cook over low heat, stirring all the time until cheese is melted. Stir in beer or ale. Mix well. Just before serving, stir egg in quickly. Serve on toast or crackers. Makes 4 servings.

WELSH RABBIT II

4 tablespoons butter	½ teaspoon prepared mustard
4 tablespoons flour	2 cups milk
1 bouillon cube, broken into pieces	2 cups (½ pound) sharp Cheddar cheese, grated or slivered fine
1 teaspoon salt	2 tablespoons sherry, if desired

MELT butter in chafing dish or saucepan. Remove from heat and blend in flour; add bouillon cube and seasonings. Return to low heat, add milk slowly, blending well. Cook, stirring constantly until thick and smooth. Add cheese and cook until melted and well blended. Just before serving stir in sherry. Serve at once on hot toast or crackers, toasted soft rolls, or toasted English muffins. Makes 4 to 6 servings.

The ten recipes above from THE ART OF CHEESE COOKERY, *by Nika Standen*

O ne of the best of the small cook books designed for busy home-makers is *The Glamour Magazine After Five Cook Book,* by Beverly Pepper. It is lively and full of menus and suggestions for quick—but delicious—meals and simple recipes for parties and after-work dinners. Originally planned "as a chart to aid the working girl who comes home, tired and spent from her office day, only to face the insurmountable problem of preparing an original meal for her husband or guests." Three of her cheese recipes:

CHEESE AND EGGS ITALIAN

¼ cup olive oil
8 eggs
Salt and pepper
1 teaspoon dried rosemary

¼ cup ketchup
Tabasco sauce
8 small thin slices Cheddar cheese
8 crisp slices bacon

USE 4 individual cup-size casseroles or 1½-quart baking dish. Start oven at moderate (350 degrees F.) .

Pour 1 tablespoon oil into each small casserole, or 4 tablespoons into larger baking dish. Set casseroles in oven a few minutes to warm. Break eggs, one at a time, into a saucer; slip 2 whole eggs into each individual casserole, or slip 8 eggs into larger baking dish. Sprinkle eggs lightly with salt, pepper, and a pinch of rosemary. Add to each small casserole 1 tablespoon ketchup, dash Tabasco, and 2 slices cheese. Season larger casserole the same way, but cover with sliced cheese. Place in oven until cheese is melted and browning. Just before serving, garnish tops of small baking dishes or larger casserole with crumbled bacon. Makes 4 servings.

CHEESE LASAGNE

4 ounces wide lasagne noodles
1 (10-½-oz.) can condensed mushroom soup
1 cup (½ pound) cottage cheese
¼ teaspoon curry powder

¼ pound Swiss cheese, thinly
   sliced
¼ cup buttered crumbs
2 tablespoons grated Parmesan
   cheese

COOK noodles until tender in boiling salted water; drain. Combine soup and cottage cheese, add curry powder, blend well.

Start oven at moderate (375 degrees F.) . Butter 1½-quart casserole. Make alternate layers of noodles, Swiss cheese, and soup mixture in casserole. Combine crumbs and Parmesan cheese and sprinkle over top. Bake in moderate oven 25 minutes. Makes 4 servings.

★GRILLED CHEESE ROLLS

This is quick and easy; a good idea for salad, or with soup. Or it makes a hot snack for a cold night when freshly made coffee and a big bowl of apples decorate the fireside bridge table.

Split hard rolls (or thick slices crusty French bread). Dip in milk, then in grated Parmesan cheese. Dot with butter. Broil under moderate heat until lightly browned.

The three cheese recipes above from THE GLAMOUR MAGAZINE AFTER FIVE COOK BOOK, *by Beverly Pepper*

THE "BEST-OF-ALL"

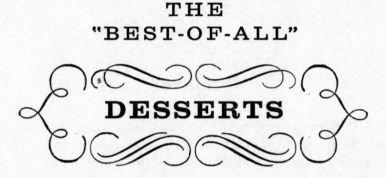

DESSERTS

THE RECIPES THAT FOLLOW HAVE BEEN SELECTED FROM THESE DISTINGUISHED BOOKS:

DESSERTS

Custards

Irma Rombauer, author of that cook book with the inspiring title, *The Joy of Cooking,* said in the introduction to her book, "Although I have been modernized by life and my children, my roots are Victorian."

Who better than a true Victorian can tell modern cooks how to make a custard? The following recipes are from *The New Joy of Cooking.*

CUP CUSTARD

2 cups milk
¼ cup sugar
⅛ teaspoon salt
3 beaten egg yolks or 2 whole
    eggs

½ teaspoon vanilla extract
⅛ teaspoon ground nutmeg

START oven at moderate (325 degrees F.). Scald milk with sugar and salt. When steaming hot, pour slowly over beaten yolks or eggs, stirring continuously. Add vanilla, continue stirring. Beat until well blended. Pour into 1-quart baking dish or 4 or 5 individual custard cups or molds. Sprinkle top lightly with nutmeg. Place casserole or cups in shallow pan of hot water. Place in moderate oven. Bake about 45 minutes, or until custard is set. To test, insert a silver knife or spoon. If the custard does not adhere to the knife or spoon, it is ready to be removed from the oven. Let cool; then chill in refrigerator. Serve with caramel syrup or fruit sauce. Makes 4 or 5 servings.

CARAMEL CUSTARD

½ cup sugar
1 tablespoon hot water
2 cups milk

3 beaten egg yolks
½ teaspoon vanilla or almond
    extract

START oven at moderate (325 degrees F.). Stir sugar in small iron skillet over high heat until it melts; add hot water, stirring until sugar is dissolved. Scald milk, add melted sugar, mix. Pour slowly into beaten egg yolks, stirring continuously. Add flavoring. Beat until well blended. Pour into a 1-quart mold or 4 individual custard cups. Place mold or cups in shallow pan of hot water. Place pan in moderate oven and bake about 45 minutes, or until firm (*see* Cup Custard recipe above). Remove from oven; let cool; then chill. Makes 4 servings.

COFFEE CUSTARD

1 cup strong, freshly made coffee	⅛ teaspoon salt
1 cup top milk	2 beaten eggs or 3 egg yolks
4 tablespoons sugar	Cream or whipped cream

START oven at moderate (325 degrees F.). Combine coffee, milk, sugar, and salt; heat to scalding. Pour slowly over beaten eggs or yolks. Beat until well blended. Pour into 1-quart mold or casserole, or into 4 individual custard cups. Set mold, baking dish, or custard cups in shallow pan of hot water. Place pan in moderate oven and bake about 45 minutes, or until custard is set (*see* Cup Custard recipe above). Remove from oven; let cool; then chill. Serve cold with cream or whipped cream. Makes 4 servings.

MAPLE CUSTARD

4 eggs	½ cup chopped nuts
¾ cup maple syrup	⅛ teaspoon salt
3 cups milk	

START oven at moderate (325 degrees F.). Beat egg yolks with maple syrup. Add milk and nuts and blend. Whip egg whites with salt until stiff. Fold yolk mixture into stiffly-beaten whites. Pour into 4 to 6 individual custard cups. Place cups in shallow pan of hot water. Bake in moderate oven about 45 minutes, or until custard is set. See Cup Custard recipe. Remove from oven; let cool; chill. Makes 4 to 6 servings.

FLOATING ISLAND

"Boiled" Custard (recipe flavored with lemon peel)	3 tablespoons sugar
3 egg whites	½ teaspoon vanilla extract or few drops almond extract
⅛ teaspoon salt	

PREPARE custard as in following recipe. Chill, pour into 1½-quart baking dish lightly buttered. Start oven at very hot (500 degrees F.).

Whip egg whites with salt until stiff. Add the sugar and vanilla or almond extract very slowly, whipping constantly. Heap egg whites on top of the custard. Place dish in very hot oven about 2 minutes, just long enough to brown the tips of the meringue. Remove at once from oven. Let cool and serve. Makes 5 servings.

"BOILED" CUSTARD

The author says this custard is badly named, since "it must not be permitted to boil at any time."

3 to 4 egg yolks
¼ cup sugar
⅛ teaspoon salt
2 cups milk

1 teaspoon vanilla extract, or rum,
  sherry, or a little grated
  lemon peel

BEAT egg yolks slightly in 1-quart saucepan; add sugar and salt, and beat to combine. Scald milk and stir slowly into egg mixture. Place over low heat; stir constantly. Do not let boil. Some cooks prefer to cook this in a double boiler over boiling water. Either way, as soon as thickened, remove from heat. Let cool. Add flavoring, chill thoroughly. This makes about 2½ cups custard sauce. Also called *Soft Custard* and *Custard Sauce*.

CREME BRULEE

2 cups heavy cream (40-percent
  cream)

4 well-beaten egg yolks
Brown sugar or maple sugar

STIR cream in a saucepan over low heat, bring to boiling point, and boil exactly 1 minute. Remove from heat. Pour in a slow stream into the well-beaten egg yolks. Beat constantly. Stir and cook over very low heat until mixture is nearly boiling, or stir and cook 5 minutes in upper part of double boiler over boiling water. Pour cream-egg mixture into a well-buttered 1-quart baking dish. Let cool. Chill well.

Cover custard in baking dish with ⅓-inch layer of brown or maple sugar. Place dish under broiler heat, keeping broiler door open. Sugar forms a crust in a few minutes. Remove dish. Let cool. Chill. Serve cold. Makes 4 servings.

ZABAGLIONE

Sabayon Sauce

The American version of a famous Italian dessert.

8 egg yolks
1 cup confectioners' sugar
½ cup Madeira or sherry

8 stiffly-beaten egg whites
⅛ teaspoon salt

BEAT egg yolks until very light in the top of a double boiler; gradually add sugar, beating well. Place over boiling water; do not let water touch bottom of the double-boiler top-pan. Beat mixture constantly with whisk or wire beater. When it is foamy, gradually add wine; continue to beat custard until it doubles in bulk and begins to thicken. Remove from heat. Fold stiffly-beaten egg whites (salt having been added during beating) into custard. Serve at once, as sauce on a dessert or as the dessert itself, piled in tall parfait or wine glasses, or sherbet glasses. Makes 4 servings.

The eight custard recipes above from THE NEW JOY OF COOKING, *by Irma S. Rombauer*

❦

More information and good recipes for custards come from *The New Basic Cook Book,* by Marjorie Heseltine and Ula M. Dow.

VARIATIONS ON PLAIN CUSTARD

If the custard is cooked too long, the egg will separate in distinct particles. The custard may be made smooth by beating rapidly with a rotary egg beater.

Here are some variations on plain custard.

Fruit Custard: Slice peaches, bananas, or oranges; add sugar; chill thoroughly. Arrange fruit in serving dishes; pour chilled Soft Custard, or "Boiled" Custard, over fruit. Serve with crisp cookies.

Trifle: Cut day-old sponge cake or other plain cake to fit bottom of individual dessert dishes. Pour thoroughly chilled "Boiled" Custard over cake. Top with whipped cream and garnish with cube of red jelly or halved red cherry.

Tipsy Pudding: Use 2 tablespoons sherry in place of vanilla extract in recipe for "Boiled" Custard. Proceed as in the recipe for Trifle.

Tipsy Trifle: Slice 4 small cupcakes or the equivalent in sponge cake or plain cake into a serving dish. Pour over cake 1 cup strong freshly made (but cooled) black sweetened coffee or 1 cup sherry. Let stand 15 minutes. Pour hot "Boiled" Custard over all; chill. Makes 4 servings.

Baked Coconut Custard: Follow recipe for Cup Custard. Place 1 tablespoon shredded coconut in each mold, or 4 to 6 tablespoons coconut in bottom of larger baking dish, before pouring in custard. Additional coconut may also be sprinkled over the custard after the mixture is partially set.

Baked Chocolate Custard: Follow recipe for Cup Custard with either one of the following changes. (1) Place one 1-oz. square of chocolate and the cold milk in the top of the double boiler, heat over boiling water until chocolate has melted; beat with rotary egg beater until smooth; complete the recipe. Or (2) mix ¼ cup cocoa with the sugar, and complete recipe as given.

★RICE CUSTARD

¼ cup sugar or honey	¾ cup cooked rice
¼ teaspoon salt	¼ cup seedless raisins
2 slightly-beaten eggs	1 teaspoon lemon juice
2 cups milk, scalded	½ teaspoon vanilla extract

START oven at moderate (350 degrees F.). Butter shallow 1½-quart baking dish.

Combine sugar or honey, salt, and eggs; beat enough to mix. Add hot milk slowly, mix, then add rice, raisins, lemon juice, and vanilla. Pour mixture into prepared baking dish. Bake in moderate oven about 45 minutes. Let cool. Cut out in squares; serve alone or with cream. Makes 4 to 6 servings.

The seven recipes and suggestions above from THE NEW BASIC COOK BOOK, *by Marjorie Heseltine and Ula M. Dow*

Frozen Desserts

Another great name in American cookery is Fannie Farmer. Her early books educated several generations of homemakers. More recent editions of the book which bears her name are an inspiration to present-day home cooks. Here are the instructions from *The New Fannie Farmer Cook Book* for making the all-American favorite, ice cream.

HOMEMADE ICE CREAM IN A FREEZER

A 2-quart ice-cream freezer is a practical size for a small family. If your freezer is too large, you will need a wasteful amount of ice. Use a canvas bag and a heavy wooden mallet for crushing ice, unless you buy crushed ice from a dealer. Measure ice with a large scoop or cup. Use coarse rock salt for freezing.

Prepare mixture to be frozen, and chill it thoroughly (an hour or more). Scald freezer can and rinse with cold water. Crush ice and measure out 3 to 6 parts ice to 1 part rock salt. The less salt in proportion to ice, the finer the grain of the ice cream, but the longer it takes to freeze.

To freeze. Put can in tub (of freezer) and fit dasher into place. Fill can no more than ⅔ full of mixture (to allow for expansion during freezing), cover, and adjust top and crank. Turn once or twice to be sure all is in place. Fill tub ⅓ full of crushed ice. Put in remaining ice and salt in alternate layers until slightly above level of mixture in can. Pack solidly, forcing down with handle of mallet or heavy wooden spoon. Let stand 5 minutes, then begin turning crank slowly and steadily to insure smooth fine-grained cream. Add more ice and salt from time to time, using the same proportions. After the ice cream is frozen to a mush (5 to 10 minutes), turn crank more rapidly until it turns with difficulty, showing that mixture is sufficiently frozen.

To pack. Drain off water, wipe lid of can, remove lid, and lift out dasher. Pack mixture down solidly with spoon, cover top of can with heavy waxed paper. Put cork (wrapped in waxed paper) in opening of lid and replace on can, or put a solid cover on the can. Repack freezer, using 4 parts ice to 1 part salt. Cover freezer with newspapers or heavy cloth. If you prefer, pack frozen cream in refrigerator tray. Let ice cream stand at least 30 minutes before serving, 2 hours if possible.

To serve. Serve from can with large spoon or ice cream scoop. Or remove can from freezer, wipe it carefully, and let stand 1 minute in cool water. Remove cover, run knife around edge of cream, and invert on large serving dish. For convenience in serving, cut slices. If frozen mixture does not slip out easily, wipe can with cloth wrung out of hot water.

To serve commercial ice cream. Let bulk ice cream soften slightly so you can spoon it into a deep serving bowl as if it were fresh from a home freezer. When serving commercial mold of ice cream, place it on serving dish and add touch of decoration such as a sprinkling of chopped toasted nuts or toasted coconut, glazed fruit, or spun sugar.

To pack in refrigerator. Pack homemade or commercial ice cream in individual molds or paper cups and decorate with fruit, nuts, or whipped cream garnished on with pastry bag and tube. Place in freezing compartment. Set temperature low enough to keep ice cream firm.

For a more elaborate dessert, line freezing tray or mold with ice cream and fill center with whipped cream, sweetened and flavored.

REFRIGERATOR ICE CREAMS

Ice-cream mixes are well adapted to refrigerator freezing. Vary flavoring as you like. Fruit sherbet and cream sherbet are also successful in refrigerator freezing. See the recipes for these and for mousses and parfaits, which are especially suitable, since they are frozen without stirring.

Set temperature of refrigerator according to manufacturer's directions. Prepare mixture to be frozen and pour it into an ice-cube tray with racks removed. Put tray into place and freeze until mixture is mushy.

Spoon into chilled bowl and beat with rotary or electric beater until well blended. If mixture is rich with cream, avoid overbeating. Spoon back into freezing tray and freeze until firm, about 3 hours.

Set temperature at normal and leave cream an hour or more to "ripen," which improves the flavor.

To adapt a recipe for refrigerator freezing, keep the proportion of sugar low, not more than 1 to 4, or substitute corn syrup for ⅓ of the sugar. Beaten egg whites help make a light mixture. One teaspoon gelatin to each cup makes a smoother ice cream.

ICES AND SHERBETS

Ices are made of sweetened fruit juices, usually diluted with water. They are often called *sherbets* as well, but a milk or cream sherbet is made with milk or cream, not water. *Frappés* and *sorbets* are frozen only to a mush.

Freeze in crank freezer or in refrigerator.

Serve plain or in a mound surrounded by prepared fruit. Lemon ice is delicious with preserved cherries or with orange sections and strips of fresh pineapple. Another way to serve lemon ice or other ice or sherbet is to top individual servings with whipped cream decorated with chopped pistachio nuts. Or pour rum over the ice.

★LEMON ICE

2 cups sugar	¾ cup lemon juice
4 cups boiling water	1 tablespoon grated lemon peel

DISSOLVE sugar in water. Let cool. Add lemon juice and peel. Freeze as described. Makes 3 pints, 9 servings.

Orange: 3 cups orange juice, ¼ cup lemon juice, grated peel 2 oranges, sugar to taste.

Fruit Juice: 1½ cups grapefruit juice, ½ cup lemon juice, 1½ cups orange juice, sugar to taste.

Mint: Flavor Lemon Ice above with oil of peppermint and color delicately with green vegetable coloring.

Raspberry and Currant: ⅔ cup raspberry juice, 1⅓ cups currant juice, 2 cups sugar, or to taste.

★MILK SHERBET

Juice 3 lemons, or 2 oranges   Few grains salt
  and 2 lemons   1 quart milk
1½ cups sugar

MIX sugar, juice, and salt. Add gradually to milk (curdled appearance will disappear in freezing). Freeze. Makes 3 pints, 9 servings.

★ORANGE CREAM SHERBET

1¼ cups sugar   2 cups milk
1½ cups orange juice   ½ pint light cream
Few grains salt

MIX sugar, juice, and salt. Add gradually to milk and cream. Freeze. Makes 3 pints, 9 servings.

★FRUIT SHERBET (WITH GELATIN)

3 cups puréed fruit, fresh or   2 tablespoons lemon juice
  canned   1½ tablespoons gelatin in 2
Few grains salt   tablespoons water
Sugar

ADD salt, sugar, and lemon juice to fruit purée. Dissolve soaked gelatin over hot water and add to fruit. Mix well, put in freezing tray. When nearly firm, spoon into chilled bowl and beat well. (For richer dessert, fold in ½-pint heavy cream, whipped). Return to tray and finish freezing. Makes 1 quart, 6 or more servings.

To prepare purée, drain canned fruit, or wash and peel fresh fruit and remove pits or seeds. Put through coarse sieve, ricer, or food mill. To keep peaches from darkening, sprinkle with lemon juice or simmer 5 minutes in thin sugar syrup (¼ cup sugar and 2½ cups water boiled together 3 minutes). Drain. Use as described.

Ice Creams

Ice creams are made of all cream (Philadelphia type) or of cream or milk thickened with eggs or other thickening. Commercial ice cream mixes are very satisfactory. Vary any of them by suggestions which follow.

★PHILADELPHIA ICE CREAM

1 quart light cream   Few grains salt
¾ cup sugar   1½ tablespoons vanilla extract

SCALD cream. Add sugar and salt, let cool. Add flavoring. Freeze. Makes 3 pints, 9 servings.

★CUSTARD ICE CREAM

2 cups milk
1 tablespoon flour or cornstarch
¾ cup sugar
1 slightly-beaten egg, or 2
  slightly-beaten egg yolks

¼ teaspoon salt
1 pint heavy cream
1 tablespoon vanilla extract

SCALD 1½ cups milk. Add remaining ½ cup cold milk to flour or corn-starch and sugar, mixed together in upper part of double boiler. Add scalded milk slowly and cook and stir over hot water 8 minutes. Add egg or egg yolks; cook 2 minutes. Let cool. Add salt, cream, and flavoring. Freeze. Makes 3 pints, 9 servings.

★FRENCH VANILLA ICE CREAM

½ cup sugar
⅛ teaspoon salt
4 to 6 slightly-beaten egg yolks

2 cups scalded milk
1 pint heavy cream
1 tablespoon vanilla extract

MIX sugar, salt, and egg yolks in upper part of double boiler. Pour in milk, stirring constantly. Cook in double boiler over boiling water until mixture coats spoon. Remove from heat. Let cool; strain, add cream and vanilla. Freeze. Makes 3 pints, 9 servings.

ICE CREAM VARIATIONS

Bisque: Add 1 cup finely-chopped nuts to Philadelphia Ice Cream mixture. Toasted (not salted) almonds and hazelnuts are especially good for this.

Burnt Almond: Add 1 cup finely-chopped blanched toasted almonds to Caramel Ice Cream mixture (below).

Butterscotch: Cook sugar of Philadelphia Ice-Cream recipe with 2 tablespoons butter until melted and well browned. Dissolve in hot milk or cream of the recipe. Then complete recipe.

Caramel: Caramelize half the sugar of the Philadelphia Ice-Cream recipe. Add slowly to hot mixture.

Chocolate: Make Custard Ice Cream (above), melting two 1-oz. squares chocolate with the milk as it is scalded. Increase sugar to 1¼ cups.

Coffee: Flavor Philadelphia Ice-Cream mixture to taste with powdered coffee or coffee essence.

Coffee-Brandy: Add brandy to taste (3 to 4 tablespoons) to Coffee Ice Cream before freezing.

Frozen Tom and Jerry: Freeze French Vanilla Ice Cream (above) to a mush. Add 2 tablespoons rum and 1 tablespoon brandy, and finish freezing. Serve in frappé glasses.

Ginger. Add ½ cup Canton (preserved) ginger cut in small pieces and 3 tablespoons ginger syrup to Philadelphia Ice-Cream mixture; then add 2 tablespoons sherry.

Maple: Use maple syrup or maple sugar in place of sugar called for in Philadelphia recipe. If desired, add 1 cup chopped nuts, stirring them into cream when nearly frozen.

Marron: Add 1 cup canned marrons, forced through a sieve. Reduce sugar of Philadelphia recipe by ½. Flavor to taste with sherry.

Peppermint Candy: Omit sugar of Philadelphia recipe. Crush ½ pound peppermint-stick candy and add to hot milk or cream. Complete recipe as described.

Pistachio: Add 1 teaspoon almond extract and ½ cup pistachio nuts, chopped fine, to French Ice-Cream mixture. Color very light green.

Praline: Add 1 cup chopped blanched and toasted almonds. Caramelize half the sugar of the Philadelphia recipe and add slowly to scalded milk or cream.

★FRESH FRUIT ICE CREAMS

Banana: Omit vanilla of Philadelphia recipe. Put 2 peeled ripe bananas through sieve or blender. Sprinkle with lemon juice. Stir into partly frozen ice cream and add sugar to taste. Complete the freezing as described in recipe.

Blueberry: Stew 1 quart blueberries until soft, with 1 cup sugar. Mash, strain, let cool. Combine with Philadelphia Ice-Cream mixture when half frozen. Mix well and complete freezing as described in recipe.

Peach: Peel, slice, and crush fruit to make 2 cups. Sprinkle with ½ cup sugar. Combine with half-frozen Philadelphia mixture. Complete freezing as described.

Raspberry or Strawberry. Mash 1 quart berries, sprinkle with ½ cup sugar, cover, let stand 2 hours. Mash and strain. Combine with half-frozen Philadelphia Ice Cream. Complete freezing.

All ice cream information and recipes above from THE NEW FANNIE FARMER COOK BOOK, *by the Boston Cooking-School*

Various Ice Cream Desserts

The good food and gracious hospitality at Toll House Inn, Whitman, Massachusetts, made many thousands of friends for Ruth Wakefield, who has long presided over this Cape Cod oasis for hungry travelers and summer residents. Just to mention the names of some of the desserts served at the colorful Toll House tables is to ignite a great appetite. Here are some of the long-time favorites which are included in her book, *Toll House Cook Book*.

★ANGEL PARFAIT

½ teaspoon gelatin softened in 1 tablespoon cold water 5 minutes
1 cup sugar
½ cup water

3 stiffly-beaten egg whites
1 pint heavy cream, whipped
1 teaspoon vanilla extract

ADD gelatin to cold water. Boil sugar and ½ cup water to soft ball stage (238 degrees F. on candy thermometer). Pour this hot syrup slowly over stiffly-beaten egg whites. Add gelatin. Beat until cool. Fold in whipped cream and vanilla. Pour mixture into freezing tray of refrigerator and freeze without stirring until mixture is firm, about 3 hours. Makes 2 pints, 6 or more parfait servings.

Golden Parfait: Substitute well-beaten egg yolks for egg whites in recipe above.

★FROZEN ORANGE-PRUNE WHIP

1 stiffly-beaten egg white
½ cup sugar
½ cup puréed prunes
1 cup heavy cream, whipped

½ cup orange juice
½ teaspoon grated orange peel
1 tablespoon lemon juice

BEAT sugar into stiffly-beaten egg white. Add prune purée. Combine whipped cream, orange juice, peel, and lemon juice. Blend with prune mixture. Freeze in deep-freezing tray of refrigerator 3 hours, or until firm. Makes 6 servings.

★ICE CREAM TARTS OR PIE

3 stiffly-beaten egg whites
½ cup sugar
1 teaspoon vanilla extract

1 pint ice cream, chocolate or coffee preferred
6 pastry tart shells or an 8-inch pie shell (baked and cooled)

BEAT sugar into stiffly-beaten egg whites. Add vanilla. Fill tart shells or pie shell with ice cream. Cover with the meringue. Brown quickly under broiler until meringue is set and golden. Serve at once. Makes 6 servings.

★LIME MOUSSE

1 cup heavy cream, whipped
¼ cup powdered sugar

4 drops oil of lime or 2 table-
    spoons grated fresh lime peel
Green food coloring

COMBINE cream, sugar, and lime oil or peel. Add very small amount of green food coloring to make delicate pale green. Freeze in refrigerator tray, or fill mold, pack in ice and salt and chill until firm, 3 to 4 hours. Makes 1 pint, 3 or 4 servings.

★PEACH MOUSSE

1 cup mashed or puréed ripe or
    canned peaches
⅓ cup sugar
3 tablespoons light corn syrup

Few grains salt
½ teaspoon almond extract
½ pint heavy cream, whipped

COMBINE peach purée, sugar, corn syrup, salt, and flavoring. Chill in refrigerator tray 1 or 2 hours or until firm. Turn out into chilled bowl, beat to break up, then beat whipped cream in smoothly. Freeze without stirring, 1 hour or until firm. Makes 1½ pints, 4 to 6 servings.

★WILD ROSE MOUSSE

2 cups pineapple juice
¼ cup lemon juice
⅓ cup sugar
Pink food coloring

½ pint heavy cream, whipped
¼ cup confectioners' sugar
1 teaspoon vanilla extract

COMBINE fruit juices with ⅓ cup sugar. Color delicate pink. Pour into large refrigerator freezing tray. Combine whipped cream, confectioners' sugar, and vanilla. Pour over fruit-juice mixture. Freeze 4 hours. Makes 1 quart, 6 servings. (If desired, ½ cup chopped nuts may be added to cream mixture before freezing.)

★MANHATTAN (FROZEN) PUDDING

1½ cups orange juice
¼ cup lemon juice
⅓ cup sugar (or to taste)
½ pint heavy cream, whipped

¼ cup confectioners' sugar
1 teaspoon vanilla extract
⅔ cup chopped walnuts or finely-
    crushed macaroon crumbs

COMBINE fruit juices and ⅓ cup sugar. Pour into deep refrigerator freezing tray. Combine whipped cream, confectioners' sugar, vanilla, and nuts. Pour whipped cream mixture over fruit juices to fill tray. Freeze 4 to 5 hours. Makes 8 servings.

★MAPLE FANGO

¾ cup maple syrup
3 stiffly-beaten egg whites

1 to 2 cups heavy cream, whipped, depending on strength of maple flavor desired

COOK maple syrup over low heat until it boils and threads from spoon. Pour slowly over stiffly-beaten egg whites. Beat until cold. Fold in whipped cream. Pour into freezing tray and freeze without stirring 2 hours or longer. Makes 6 to 8 servings.

The nine recipes above from TOLL HOUSE COOK BOOK, *by Ruth Wakefield*

❧

A companion volume to those inspiring menu and cookery books, *Thoughts for Food,* and *More Thoughts for Food* has been published as *Thoughts for Buffets.* It is as rich in superb dishes as the original volumes, both without an author's name. A publisher's note on the buffet book admits that it is "the product of the loving care, patience, and great imagination of a group of Chicago hostesses." Every cook, west and east of Chicago, should wave her apron in salute. Here are six frozen desserts from *Thoughts for Buffets.*

BAKED ALASKA AFLAME

2 pints packaged ice cream
Sponge cake, baked in single-layer oblong pan, 13 × 9 × 2 inches, or 10-inch round layer pan
¼ teaspoon salt
4 egg whites

½ cup sugar
1 teaspoon vanilla extract
4 empty half eggshells
Brandy
2 (10-oz.) packages quick-frozen berries, thawed, or 1 cup chocolate syrup

IN advance, spread ice cream on sponge cake (on serving plank or oven-proof platter); place in freezer. Add salt to egg whites and beat until stiff. Add sugar gradually, beating until stiff; fold in vanilla.

Start oven at hot (450 degrees F.). Remove cake from freezer; cover with meringue. Be certain that the ice cream is completely sealed by meringue. Quickly place 4 empty eggshells in meringue, hollow side up, so as to form 4 cups, and space them evenly. Bake in hot oven 4 or 5 minutes, or until meringue is slightly brown. Remove, fill eggshells at once with brandy, ignite each with match and bring the Alaska to the table flaming. Serve immediately onto dessert plates, with crushed berries or chocolate syrup. Makes 6 to 8 servings.

★BLACK RASPBERRY MOUSSE

12 ladyfingers
2 packages black raspberry gelatin
1 cup boiling water
2 cups cold water

3 teaspoons lemon juice
1 quart vanilla ice cream
1 cup heavy cream
½ cup sliced strawberries

LINE 10-inch pie plate with ladyfingers split and cut in half, round end up. Pour 1 cup boiling water over raspberry gelatin. Stir until dissolved. Add 2 cups cold water, the lemon juice, and ice cream. Stir until smoothly blended. Pour into prepared pie plate. Place in coldest part of refrigerator and chill until set. To serve, cover with whipped cream and berries. Makes 8 servings.

★BROWNIE ALASKA PIE

1 (16-oz.) package brownie mix
1 quart vanilla ice cream

Raspberry sauce

MAKE up brownie batter according to directions on package. Spread in two 9-inch pie pans as pie shells and bake one of them in a moderate oven (350 degrees F.) for about 25 minutes, or until done. Let cool. (Freeze other pan, unbaked, for next party.)

Fill cooled baked brownie shell with scoops of ice cream. Serve with raspberry sauce. Makes 6 servings.

COCONUT ICE-CREAM BALLS

2 quarts vanilla ice cream
2 cups grated coconut (or
   slightly more)

Kahlua (a crème de café made
   in Mexico) or use Mocha sauce

MAKE ice-cream balls in advance, using scoop. Roll each in coconut, place on platter in freezer ready to serve. (Balls hold shape perfectly when wrapped individually in waxed paper.) To serve, unwrap frozen balls (first warming each slightly with hands) and place in low wide sherbet or dessert glasses. Pour Kahlua or Mocha sauce over. Makes 8 to 12 balls.

★BAYOU SAUCE

1 cup heavy cream
4 tablespoons sugar

¼ cup lemon juice
Grated peel of 1 lemon

Whip cream; fold in sugar, juice, and peel. Chill. Makes 1¾ cups fluffy sauce. Serve with Lemon Sherbet Mousse, page 154.

★ICE CREAM BALLS WITH FRUIT
En Coquille

9- or 10-inch meringue shell

12 ice-cream balls of various flavors (coffee, pistachio, chocolate,
strawberry) about 3 pints in all

2 or more cups grated coconut

2 cups fruit cut in pieces, ripe
peaches, berries, or canned
fruits

MAKE ice-cream balls in advance, roll in coconut. Wrap individually in waxed paper, place on platter, and set in freezer.

To serve, unwrap balls (first warming each slightly with hands), place in meringue shell, cover with fruit. Makes 6 or more servings.

★LEMON SHERBET MOUSSE

1 package lemon gelatin

1 cup boiling water

½ cup cold water

1½ tablespoons lemon juice

1½ pints lemon sherbet

Fresh strawberries, sliced or left
whole

DISSOLVE gelatin in boiling water. Add cold water and lemon juice. Beat or blend lemon sherbet in. Pour into individual molds. Chill in refrigerator until firm. Unmold on dessert dishes. Garnish with strawberries. Serve with Bayou Sauce. Makes 6 to 8 servings.

The six recipes above from THOUGHTS FOR BUFFETS

Fruit Desserts

In the nineteen-forties plenty of people bought *Clémentine in the Kitchen* just for the famous, bold, beautiful etchings in it by Samuel Chamberlain. Mr. Chamberlain called himself Phineas Beck for the purpose of writing this unusual cookbook about a French cook from Burgundy who fed an American family so well that their whole concept of foods was enlarged, enriched, and wondrously benefited. Here are seven of their favorite fruit desserts, from that book.

BANANAS FLAMBE

Ripe bananas

Butter

Sugar

Kirsch, brandy, or applejack

Whipped cream, flavored with
vanilla

START oven at moderate (325 degrees F.). Peel bananas and remove strings. Place fruit in shallow baking dish in which about 1 tablespoon of butter for each banana is melting. Sprinkle bananas generously with sugar. Place dish in moderate oven; turn bananas once or twice in baking period, which should be about 25 to 35 minutes, or until fruit is browned and soft. Warm some kirsch, brandy, or applejack and pour over bananas just before bringing the dish to the table. Ignite liqueur with a match, shake the dish gently until the flame dies down, and serve. Whipped cream, chilled and flavored with a little vanilla, makes a contrasting accompaniment. "We like the plump red bananas best for this dish," says Mr. Chamberlain. Allow 1 banana per serving.

BLUEBERRY TART

Rich pastry shells, 7-inch square, ¾-inch high edge

Raspberry syrup made by melting raspberry jam or jelly, or cooked fresh berries

BAKE the most delectable flaky pastry shells possible; let them cool. To serve, fill each with a layer of large fresh blueberries. Pour raspberry syrup over the blueberries, place tarts in a very hot oven (575 degrees F.) just long enough to make them hot. Bring to the table at once. Make one tart for each person.

APPLE CHARLOTTE MONSEIGNEUR

4 or 5 apples
Butter
4 tablespoons sugar
Few drops vanilla extract

Cooked dried apricots, puréed
1 or 2 brioches
1 cup Sabayon Sauce

START oven at moderate (350 degrees F.). Wash, pare, and core apples; cut in small pieces and cook slowly in 1 or 2 tablespoons butter until golden brown. Add sugar and vanilla, and stir. Now add to the apples ⅓ as much apricot purée. Mix lightly. Line buttered 1½-quart charlotte mold with slices of brioche buttered on both sides. Fill center with fruit mixture. Place in moderate oven until crusty brown. Let cool slightly. Unmold on round serving dish and serve with "Boiled" Custard, or Sabayon Sauce. Makes 6 servings.

APPLE CHARLOTTE HERVINE

5 or 6 thin slices bread buttered on both sides
2 cups thick applesauce

1 cup thick stewed pitted cherries
½ pound dried apricots
Kirsch or port

START oven at moderate (350 degrees F.). Butter 1-quart charlotte mold. Cut crusts from bread and cut slices in narrow strips. Line bottom and sides of mold with bread strips, allowing them to overlap. Mix applesauce and cherries together, and pour into mold. Bake in moderate oven 25 minutes, or until bread is crusty brown. Let cool slightly. Unmold on a round dish. Serve with cold Apricot Sauce. Makes 4 to 6 servings.

APRICOT SAUCE

½ pound dried apricots
1½ cups water

1 tablespoon kirsch or port

Put apricots in saucepan with 1½ cups water; cover and cook slowly until fruit is tender. Let cool. Put through sieve with juice from saucepan. Stir in kirsch or port. Chill and serve on warm charlotte.

PEARS ROSEMONDE

6 firm pears
¾ cup sugar
2 cups water
1 cup preserved black cherries

1 cup apricot jam
¼ cup finely-diced candied pine-
    apple, soaked in ½ cup rum
Sabayon Sauce

WASH and peel pears. Combine sugar and water in saucepan; bring to a boil. Cook pears in this syrup until tender; let cool in the syrup. Carefully cut each pear through from stem to bottom and remove core. Arrange pear halves on serving dish in circle around preserved cherries. Fill pear cavities with apricot jam mixed with diced pineapple which has soaked in rum. Spoon Sabayon Sauce (custard sauce) on pears and serve. Makes 6 servings. (A finger of sponge cake with each serving adds just the right contrast and flavor to this dessert).

SECKEL PEARS IN RED WINE

1 cup sugar
1 cup water
12 small Seckel pears

1 cup red wine
4 whole cloves

COMBINE sugar and water in large saucepan; bring to a boil and cook 2 or 3 minutes. Wash and peel pears, but leave whole and with stems on. Add pears to syrup, lower heat, and cook gently; add wine and cloves; continue cooking until pears are tender. Let cool in syrup. Chill. Serve cold with some of their syrup spooned over them. Makes 6 servings.

STRAWBERRIES CHANTILLY

2 cups ripe strawberries
1½ cups heavy cream, whipped

3 or 4 tablespoons powdered
    sugar
Few drops vanilla extract

WASH and hull berries, and slice in half. Stir lightly through whipped cream which has been sweetened and flavored with sugar and vanilla. Let cream mixture chill in refrigerator in serving dish. Serve at table into chilled dessert dishes. Makes 6 or more servings.

The seven recipes above from CLEMENTINE IN THE KITCHEN, *by Phineas Beck*

T*he Settlement Cook Book* has been for many years the one complete authentic source of all cookery information and guidance for thousands of American families. In one edition after another, the sound recipes of the book tested in Settlement cooking classes, in school home-economics classes, and in the homes of famous cooks have been tried by young homemakers (with success) and used by older hostesses with affectionate gratitude to Mrs. Simon Kander, the woman who was responsible for editing and compiling this large conclusive volume.

Here are some of the popular fruit desserts from its pages.

BLACKBERRY ROLL

Biscuit dough   1 cup sugar
2 tablespoons butter, melted   **Cinnamon**
1½ quarts blackberries, washed,
drained, cleaned

MAKE biscuit dough, using favorite mix, or use the following recipe:

BISCUIT DOUGH FOR FRUIT ROLL, SHORTCAKE, ETC.

2 cups all-purpose flour, sifted   2 tablespoons sugar
4 teaspoons baking powder   ½ cup butter or shortening
½ teaspoon salt   ¾ cup milk

Start oven at hot (450 degrees F.). Sift dry ingredients together 3 times; work butter or shortening in with tips of fingers, add milk quickly. Toss on floured board; pat, roll out to ¼-inch thickness, cut with large biscuit cutter, or roll as described in various recipes which follow. Bake in hot oven 12 to 15 minutes, for biscuits for shortcake. Makes 6 large biscuits for 6 shortcake servings.

For Blackberry Roll, toss dough on lightly-floured board, roll ½-inch thick, spread with melted butter, and strew half the berries over all. Sprinkle with half the sugar, and dust lightly with ground cinnamon. Fold dough inward on the ends (to hold berries in), then roll up like a jelly roll. Place roll in large greased baking pan, surround with the rest of the berries sprinkled with sugar. Bake 20 minutes in hot oven, or until dough is done and lightly browned. Cut in slices and serve warm, with sauce from the pan. Makes 6 or more servings.

Cherry Roll. Use recipe above, substituting stewed fresh or canned pitted cherries, drained and sweetened. Sweeten to taste.

FRUIT DESSERT WITH WINE AND MACAROONS

1 pint raspberries or sliced ripe peaches	1 cup white wine
½ cup sugar	1 pound macaroons, crushed
6 eggs	2 tablespoons powdered sugar

SWEETEN fruit with 2 or 3 tablespoons sugar and set it aside. Beat egg yolks in upper part of double boiler until light, adding remaining granulated sugar gradually. Stir in wine slowly. Place pan over boiling water, stir continuously, cooking a few minutes until mixture coats spoon. Remove from heat, let cool. Butter 1½-quart heatproof dish; make layer of macaroon crumbs in dish, cover with fruit, pour on some of the cooled custard mixture; repeat layers until everything is used. Whip egg whites stiff, gradually adding powdered sugar. Heap on filled dish. Place under low broiler heat to brown the meringue delicately. Serve at once. Makes 6 servings.

GINGERED FIGS

1 pound dried figs	Sugar
Juice and grated peel ½ lemon	1 tablespoon lemon juice
Large piece ginger root	1 cup heavy cream, whipped

WASH figs, remove stems. Drain; cover with cold water in enamel or glass saucepan, add peel and juice ½ lemon and ginger root. Bring to a boil, lower heat and cook slowly until figs are puffed and soft. Remove figs to serving dish. Measure syrup in saucepan, add ½ as much sugar; simmer until thick and add the tablespoon of lemon juice. Pour over figs. Serve with whipped cream. Makes 6 servings.

PEACH COBBLER

1 egg	2 tablespoons butter
⅔ cup sugar	Biscuit dough
2 cups sliced ripe or canned peaches	Hard Sauce

START oven at hot (450 degrees F.). Beat egg lightly, add sugar and peaches, pour into buttered 1½-quart baking dish. Dot top of mixture with butter. Cover with Biscuit Dough (see Blackberry Roll) rolled and cut in strips or biscuits. Bake in hot oven 20 minutes, or until lightly browned. Serve with Hard Sauce. Makes 6 servings.

Rhubarb Cobbler. Follow directions above, substituting diced fresh rhubarb for peaches and using slightly more sugar.
Cherry Cobbler. Use same recipe, substituting pitted fresh or canned cherries for peaches. Sweeten to taste.

★SCALLOPED APPLES
BROWN BETTY

2 tablespoons butter	Juice and grated peel 1 lemon
2 cups soft bread crumbs	3 cups apples, pared and cut fine
½ cup sugar	¼ cup water
¼ teaspoon ground cinnamon	Cream
¼ teaspoon ground nutmeg	

START oven at moderate (350 degrees F.). Melt butter, add crumbs, mix. Combine sugar, spice, and lemon peel. Pour ¼ of the buttered crumbs into the bottom of a buttered 1½-quart baking dish. Then add ½ of the apples. Sprinkle with ½ of the sugar-spice mixture; add another ¼ of the crumbs, the remainder of the apples, and the sugar and spices. Sprinkle lemon juice and water over all, and add rest of crumbs to top of dish. Cover dish; bake 45 minutes in moderate oven. Uncover, turn heat up to very hot to brown top of dish quickly. Serve with plain or whipped cream. Makes 6 servings.

★STRAWBERRY SHORTCAKE

Biscuit Dough	1 to 1½ quarts strawberries
Butter	Heavy cream

MAKE Biscuit Dough according to recipe for Blackberry Roll. Cut large biscuits and bake as described. Split, butter quickly, fill with sweetened crushed berries; add spoonful of berries to top of each, then a spoonful of whipped cream. Makes 6 or more servings.

Gelatin Desserts

In general, follow directions on package of gelatin. Or 1 tablespoon granulated gelatin makes 1 pint jelly; ½ cup sweetened and flavored jelly powder makes 1 pint jelly. Granulated gelatin must be soaked in cold water first, then dissolved in hot water, or fruit juice, or over hot water. Flavored jelly powder is dissolved in 2 cups hot water, or in 1 cup hot water and 1 cup cold water, or other liquid or according to directions on package.

To mold jelly. Rinse mold in cold water before pouring mixture in.

To unmold jelly. Dip mold for a second in warm (not hot) water, loosen edges slightly with thin knife or spatula; or wrap mold in cloth wrung out of hot water. Then turn serving dish over mold, invert mold and dish, and carefully remove mold.

To make jellies into layers, let first layer begin to harden but not quite set before adding next layer.

★COFFEE JELLY

2 tablespoons gelatin	⅔ cup sugar
1 cup cold water	4 tablespoons lemon juice
2½ cups clear strong hot coffee	Whipped cream

SOAK gelatin in cold water 5 minutes or longer. Stir into hot coffee until dissolved. Add sugar and lemon juice, stir well. Pour into wet 1-quart mold or 4 individual cup molds. Let chill 2 hours, or until firm. Serve with whipped cream. Makes 4 servings.

★LEMON SPONGE
SNOW PUDDING

1 tablespoon gelatin	1 cup sugar
¼ cup cold water	¼ cup lemon juice
1 cup boiling water	3 egg whites

SOAK gelatin in cold water 5 minutes, add boiling water, sugar, and lemon juice; stir until dissolved; strain. When mixture begins to thicken, beat egg whites stiff and fold in, beat thoroughly, and pour into wet 1-quart or 5-cup mold. Serve with "Boiled" Custard. Makes 4 or more servings.

★ORANGE JELLY

2 tablespoons gelatin	1 cup sugar
1 cup cold water	1½ cups orange juice
1 cup boiling water	3 tablespoons lemon juice

SOAK gelatin in cold water 5 minutes; dissolve in boiling water. Add sugar, stir well; add fruit juice. Strain into wet 4 or 5-cup mold. Let chill. Makes 4 to 5 servings.

WINE JELLY

2 tablespoons gelatin	1 cup claret, Madeira, sherry,
½ cup cold water	or port
2 cups boiling water	3 tablespoons lemon juice
1 cup sugar	

ADD cold water to gelatin and let stand 5 minutes to soften. Add boiling water, stirring until dissolved; strain. Add sugar, and when cool, add wine and lemon juice. Pour into 4 or 5 wet individual molds, or 1 larger mold. Let chill. Serve plain or with cream. Makes 4 or 5 servings.

For stronger wine flavor, add 1 tablespoon brandy to wine and use 1 tablespoon less water; or use only 1 cup boiling water and increase wine to 2 cups.

CHOCOLATE CHARLOTTE RUSSE

2 tablespoons gelatin
¼ cup cold water
2 (1-oz.) squares chocolate, grated
1 pint milk
1 cup sugar
1 teaspoon vanilla extract

1 pint heavy cream
1 dozen ladyfingers
Extra whipped cream
Candied cherries and pistachio
nuts

SOAK gelatin in cold water 5 minutes. Melt chocolate in upper part of double boiler over hot water; add milk and sugar, stirring; cook 5 minutes, or until smooth. Add softened gelatin and stir until dissolved. Let cool; add vanilla. Whip cream until stiff; add chocolate-gelatin mixture gradually and stir gently until it begins to thicken.

Line a 1½-quart buttered mold with ladyfingers. When the cream is so thick that it will just pour, turn it gently into the lined mold. Chill 1 hour or longer. At serving time turn out on a dessert platter. Surround with rosettes or whirls of whipped cream, and garnish with bits of candied cherries and chopped pistachio nuts. Makes 6 to 8 servings. Also can be made in individual molds or custard cups.

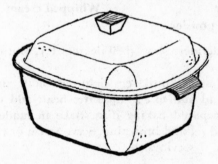

NESSELRODE PUDDING

5 eggs
½ cup sugar
2 cups hot milk
2 tablespoons gelatin
½ cup cold water

3 tablespoons chopped almonds
⅔ cup seedless raisins
1 tablespoon finely-diced citron
Few grains salt
1 teaspoon vanilla extract

BEAT egg yolks with sugar in saucepan, stir in hot milk; cook few minutes, stirring constantly, until mixture coats spoon. Soften gelatin in cold water. Add to hot milk mixture and stir until gelatin is dissolved. Add nuts, raisins, citron, and salt; mix. Let cool, then chill. When cold, add stiffly-beaten egg whites flavored with vanilla. Pour into wet 6-cup mold. Chill until stiff. Serve with plain or whipped cream. Makes 6 to 8 servings.

Favorite Puddings

★BERRY PUDDINGS

1 quart blueberries, raspberries,
    or blackberries
¼ cup flour
1 quart hot milk
2 cups bread crumbs

¼ cup sugar
Few grains salt
2 tablespoons butter
Hard Sauce

WASH berries, look over, drain. Sprinkle flour over berries and let stand ½ hour. Start oven at moderate (350 degrees F.). Pour milk over crumbs, add sugar, salt, and floured berries, mix. Pour into greased 2½-quart baking dish. Dot with butter. Bake 45 minutes in moderate oven. Serve warm with Hard Sauce. Makes 6 servings.

★GRANT THOMAS PUDDING

2 eggs
1 cup sugar
3 tablespoons flour
1 teaspoon baking powder

1 cup chopped walnuts
1 cup chopped dried figs
Whipped cream

START oven at moderately slow (300 degrees F.). Butter shallow 1-quart baking dish.

Beat eggs and sugar until very light. Sift flour and baking powder together 3 times and add to egg mixture; beat; add nuts and figs. Stir well. Pour into prepared baking dish. Bake in moderately slow oven, 25 minutes, or until set and browning. Serve warm or cold with whipped cream. Makes 5 or 6 servings.

★RICE PUDDING

3 tablespoons bread crumbs
3 cups cooked rice
2 cups milk
⅛ teaspoon salt
⅓ cup sugar

1 tablespoon butter, melted
1 well-beaten egg
Grated peel 1 lemon
¼ cup seedless raisins

START oven at moderate (350 degrees F.). Butter 1½-quart baking dish; sprinkle bottom of dish with bread crumbs; reserve few crumbs for top of pudding.

Combine cooked rice and remaining ingredients; mix well. Pour into prepared baking dish. Sprinkle crumbs over top of mixture. Bake 20 minutes, or until top is browning. Makes 6 servings.

If desired, fruit may be added in layers to the rice.

★CHOCOLATE BREAD PUDDING

¾ cup dry bread crumbs	⅛ teaspoon salt
2 cups scalded milk	½ teaspoon vanilla extract
1 (1-oz.) square bitter chocolate	1 slightly-beaten egg
⅓ cup sugar	Cream or Vanilla Sauce

SOAK crumbs in 1¾ cups scalded milk for ½ hour. Start oven at moderate (325 degrees F.). Melt chocolate over hot water, then add sugar and remaining ¼ cup milk; stir to make smooth paste. Add to crumbs with salt, vanilla, and beaten egg, mix. Pour into well-buttered 1-quart baking dish. Bake in moderate oven ½ hour, or until set and top is browning. Serve warm with cream or Vanilla Sauce. Makes 4 or 6 servings.

★COCONUT PUDDING

1 cup bread crumbs	2 slightly-beaten eggs
1 quart hot milk	¼ cup sugar
1 cup grated coconut	Few grains salt
2 tablespoons melted butter	Grated peel ½ lemon

SOAK crumbs few minutes in 1 cup hot milk; mash well. Soak coconut in remaining hot milk 1 hour. Start oven at moderately slow (300 degrees F.). Combine all ingredients, mixing well. Pour into buttered 2-quart baking dish. Bake in moderately slow oven ½ hour, or until set and top is browning. Serve slightly warm, with or without cream. Makes 6 servings.

The seventeen recipes above from THE SETTLEMENT COOK BOOK, *by Mrs. Simon Kander*

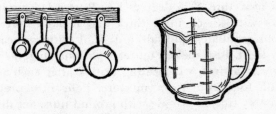

Soufflé Desserts

One of the best of the chef-written cook books, called a classic by discriminating food editors and writers, is *The Gold Cook Book* by Louis P. De Gouy. It is a giant of a book, one of the most complete and satisfying, full of inspiration for home meals and parties. Here are four of Chef De Gouy's soufflé desserts, the recipes stepped down to home size.

ALMOND SOUFFLE

2¼ cups powdered sugar
1 cup all-purpose flour, sifted
¼ teaspoon salt
2 cups milk
¾ teaspoon almond extract

6 slightly-beaten egg yolks
8 stiffly-beaten egg whites
Powdered sugar
Sliced toasted almonds

START oven at moderate (375 degrees F.). Butter 2-quart soufflé dish generously; sprinkle bottom and sides with ¼ cup powdered sugar.

Mix and sift remaining 2 cups powdered sugar, flour, and salt together into saucepan. Stir in milk gradually and add flavoring; stir constantly over low heat to boiling point. Remove from heat; stir in beaten yolks; then fold in stiffly-beaten egg whites. Pour into prepared soufflé dish. Quickly decorate top with almonds; sprinkle with powdered sugar. Place dish at once in shallow pan of hot (not boiling) water and set in moderate oven. Bake 20 to 25 minutes, or until soufflé is risen to almost double its original size and is delicately browned. Do not open oven door while soufflé is baking. Serve at once. A soufflé cannot wait, as it will fall almost immediately. No sauce of any kind should be served with an almond soufflé. Makes 8 servings.

HONEY SOUFFLE

4 eggs
1 tablespoon kirsch
1 cup sugar, sifted with
   1 tablespoon pastry flour
¼ teaspoon salt

Ground nutmeg
¼ cup melted butter
¼ cup honey
1 teaspoon ground pistachio nuts
Raspberry Sauce

START oven at moderate (375 degrees F.). Butter 1½-quart soufflé dish. Beat egg yolks with kirsch until thick and lemon-colored. Add sugar sifted with flour gradually, add salt, a dash of nutmeg, beating continually until very light. Beat melted butter and honey together, add to yolk mixture a little at a time, still beating briskly after each addition. Beat egg whites stiff, fold into honey mixture. Pour into prepared baking dish (should be ⅔ full). Sprinkle with ground nuts. Set dish in shallow pan of warm water. Bake 35 to 40 minutes in moderate oven. Serve at once with Raspberry Sauce. Makes 4 to 6 servings.

BLUEBERRY SOUFFLE

2 cups blueberries
1 teaspoon lime or lemon juice
1 cup sugar
3 tablespoons water
7 egg whites

Few drops almond extract
½ teaspoon grated lemon peel
3 or 4 tablespoons shredded
   toasted almonds

Wash and drain blueberries. When dry, put through fine strainer. Sprinkle lime or lemon juice over the puréed berries. Boil sugar and 3 tablespoons water together until syrup spins a thread (280 degrees F. on candy thermometer); stir puréed blueberries in and blend well. Remove from heat, set aside to cool.

Start oven at moderately hot (400 degrees F.). Butter 1½-quart soufflé dish generously.

Beat egg whites until stiff, adding few drops of flavoring and grated lemon peel, beating continuously. Fold into the cooled blueberry mixture. Turn into the prepared soufflé dish at once. Place dish in shallow pan of hot (not boiling) water; bake in moderately hot oven 20 minutes. Sprinkle almonds lightly over soufflé and bake 5 minutes longer. Serve at once. Makes 6 servings.

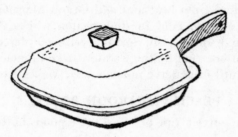

CHOCOLATE SOUFFLE, FRENCH STYLE

3 tablespoons butter, creamed (not melted)
3 or 4 tablespoons sugar
1 cup milk
½ cup all-purpose flour, sifted
4 eggs
½ cup sugar
2 (1-oz.) squares chocolate, melted

Start oven at moderate (375 degrees F.). Spread 1½-quart soufflé dish generously with creamed butter, then sprinkle heavy coating of granulated sugar in dish.

Heat ½ cup milk to boiling point. In the upper part of a double boiler, blend ½ cup cold milk into the flour until smooth, then add hot milk, stirring continually. Cook over hot water, stirring until thickened. Remove from heat and beat until smooth. Add unbeaten egg yolks, one at a time, beating them in thoroughly. Add ¼ cup sugar and melted chocolate, beating well. Beat egg whites stiff with remaining ¼ cup sugar. Combine the two mixtures lightly. Pour into prepared baking dish. Set dish in shallow pan of hot (but not boiling) water. Bake in moderate oven, 25 minutes. Serve at once. Makes 6 servings.

The four recipes above from THE GOLD COOK BOOK, *by Louis P. De Gouy*

Soufflés Flavored with Liqueurs

Soufflés from Jeanne Owen's *A Wine Lover's Cook Book*.

SOUFFLE GRAND MARNIER

4 tablespoons butter	2 tablespoons Grand Marnier
3 tablespoons flour	2 egg yolks
⅔ cup rich milk, heated	3 stiffly-beaten egg whites
2 tablespoons sugar	Powdered sugar

START oven at moderate (350 degrees F.). Butter 1½-quart soufflé dish.
Melt butter in saucepan, blend flour slowly into it, add hot milk slowly, stirring continually. Add sugar, and continue to stir and cook until thick. Remove from heat and add Grand Marnier; mix. Beat egg yolks in one at a time. Fold in stiffly-beaten whites. Pour mixture at once into prepared soufflé dish. Sprinkle with powdered sugar; set dish in shallow pan of hot (not boiling) water. Bake in moderate oven about 40 minutes, or until firm. Serve immediately. Makes 4 to 6 servings.

PEACH MACAROON SOUFFLE

1 cup mashed, or puréed, ripe or canned peaches	6 tablespoons butter
½ cup macaroon crumbs soaked in 2 tablespoons brandy	6 tablespoons sugar
	3 eggs

START oven at moderate (350 degrees F.). Butter 1-quart deep soufflé dish. Combine peaches and brandy-soaked crumbs. Cream butter and sugar together until light. Beat in one egg yolk at a time. Combine with fruit mixture. Beat egg whites stiff and fold into yolk mixture. Pour at once into prepared baking dish. Set dish in shallow pan of hot (not boiling) water. Bake in moderate oven 35 to 40 minutes, or until firm. Makes 4 servings.

APRICOT SOUFFLE

1 cup puréed apricots	2 tablespoons kirsch
1 or 2 teaspoons sugar	4 stiffly-beaten egg whites

START oven at moderate (350 degrees F.). Butter 1-quart deep soufflé dish. Use cooked dried apricots or canned or fresh fruit; mash through sieve to make 1 cup purée. Heat with sugar, stirring until sugar is dissolved; add kirsch, mix well. Fold egg whites beaten stiff with few grains salt into fruit mixture. Pour at once into prepared baking dish. Set dish in shallow pan of hot (not boiling) water. Bake in moderate oven 35 to 40 minutes. Serve at once. Makes 4 servings.

The recipes above from A WINE LOVER'S COOK BOOK, *by Jeanne Owen*

THE "BEST-OF-ALL"

EGG DISHES

THE RECIPES THAT FOLLOW HAVE BEEN SELECTED FROM THESE DISTINGUISHED BOOKS:

The Book of Entrées	Janet M. Hill
The Cordon Bleu Cook Book	Dione Lucas
Egg Cookery	Lily Haxworth Wallace
Herbs for The Kitchen	Irma Goodrich Mazza
The Williamsburg Art of Cookery	Mrs. Helen Bullock

EGGS

There is a special language concerning eggs, according to Lily Haxworth Wallace's book, *Egg Cookery*. Eggs are "fresh" or "cold storage." *Fresh* means new-laid eggs bought at a farmer's road-side stand or from his back door, or brought in to your kitchen from your own poultry house—eggs which have never been in storage. Since most food stores sell only storage eggs, "Fancy" or "Grade A" eggs are the freshest, largest, and finest from the storage crates. They are the "fresh" eggs most housekeepers buy. The best rule for purchasing eggs is to buy the best grade available and to use them promptly. The color of the shell does not in any way influence the flavor of the egg, this cookery author points out.

Eggs vary in size, the average being 8 eggs to the pound. Some recipes call for egg whites by cup measurement; there are 8 to 10 whites or 12 to 14 yolks in 1 measuring cup.

Always place eggs in the refrigerator as promptly as possible after they come in from the grocer's or farmer's; eggs kept at room temperature lose quality quickly. In the refrigerator they should be in a covered container, away from strong-flavored foods; uncovered, eggs absorb odors and lose moisture rapidly. A fresh egg has a dull rather than shiny shell. Do not wash eggs until just before using them; badly soiled surfaces may be lightly wiped with damp cloth before putting in refrigerator container.

When eggs are to be used in a recipe, break each separately into a cup or saucer before adding it to other ingredients.

Fresh eggs have no odor. The white is clear, heavy, and elastic. The yolk has a good even color and it stands up from the white; in less-fresh eggs the yolk seems flattened. If an egg has any odor or discoloration, don't hesitate to discard it.

★CODDLED EGGS

Place eggs in saucepan containing enough cold water to cover well. Bring to a boil, cover pan, reduce heat, and cook 3 minutes, keeping water just below boiling point. Serve in shell, in egg cup; 1 or 2 eggs make 1 serving. Eggs taken from refrigerator just before cooking require about one additional minute cooking time.

★HARD-COOKED EGGS

Allow 2½ cups water for each egg. Place eggs gently in water; cover saucepan; bring gradually to a boil. When boiling, turn heat off. Let pan stand where it will not cool too quickly. Let eggs remain 30 to 45 minutes in the gradually cooling water. Drain, cover with cold water. When eggs are cold, drain and place in refrigerator until needed.

★SCRAMBLED EGGS

4 eggs
Salt and pepper

4 tablespoons milk
2 tablespoons butter

BEAT eggs, season, add milk. Use heavy frying pan; melt butter, pour in egg mixture, and cook over moderate heat until thick and creamy, stirring constantly. Lift the cooked portion of egg from bottom of pan, and allow uncooked portion to take its place. Serve on toast, or with frizzled dried beef, broiled ham, crisp bacon or sausages. Makes 2 servings.

Scrambled eggs may be cooked in upper part of double boiler or chafing dish over boiling water. May be varied by using canned or stewed tomatoes in place of milk. Or when eggs are almost done, stir in 1 teaspoon finely-minced parsley with few drops onion juice. Or stir in ⅓ cup grated cheese, or ½ cup minced cooked chicken, ham, tongue, or cooked chicken livers.

★SHIRRED EGGS

4 tablespoons butter
4 eggs

Salt and pepper
Paprika

START oven at moderate (350 to 375 degrees F.). Melt butter in shallow 1-quart baking dish, or 2 individual baking dishes. Break eggs one at a time into a saucer, then slip into baking dish, sprinkle with salt and pepper. Bake in moderate oven until set, about 15 minutes. Dust lightly with paprika. Serve eggs in the dish in which they were cooked. Makes 2 to 4 servings.

Shirred Eggs au Gratin: Follow recipe for Shirred Eggs. Sprinkle eggs generously before baking with equal amounts of buttered crumbs and grated cheese, to which ¼ teaspoon dry mustard has been added.

Shirred Eggs Mornay: Follow recipe for Shirred Eggs. Top eggs before baking with a cheese-flavored cream sauce; sprinkle with buttered crumbs. Bake until lightly browned.

★EGGS BENEDICT

2 English muffins   4 poached eggs
4 thin slices broiled ham   Hollandaise Sauce

SPLIT, toast, and butter muffins. Trim ham to fit shape of muffin; cover each portion of muffin with slice of ham. Top with carefully trimmed poached egg. Spoon Hollandaise Sauce over the egg and serve at once. Usually 1 poached egg makes 1 serving, but for a brunch or luncheon dish, this favorite is sometimes made by using both halves of the English muffin, placed in a shallow serving dish or on a plate, topped with 2 poached eggs and Hollandaise Sauce, and served to each guest.

★POACHED EGGS

Have salted water at boiling point in a shallow wide saucepan or deep frying pan. Break eggs one at a time into a saucer, slip eggs carefully but quickly into the water, which should barely cover the eggs. The water must just simmer; cover; let cook 3 to 5 minutes, until whites are just set and a thin film has formed over the yolks. Using perforated spoon, lift eggs carefully from water onto buttered toast or anchovy toast, sprinkle each egg with pepper and salt, and serve. One or 2 eggs make 1 serving.

Eggs also may be poached in milk. When ready to serve, place eggs on toast on a warmed platter, set platter in warm oven with oven door open. Quickly make sauce; thicken hot milk with creamed butter and flour (1½ tablespoons to each cup milk), stir constantly until boiling and slightly thickened, season and pour over eggs on toast. Serve at once.

Egg poachers or muffin rings may be used to confine and shape eggs during poaching. Butter the poachers or rings, place in water in saucepan or skillet and slip each egg from saucer into poacher. *Poached Eggs Opera Style:* Place hot poached eggs on rounds of buttered toast. Pour spoonful of hot Shrimp Sauce over each egg, sprinkle with finely-minced parsley, and garnish with cooked asparagus tips. One or 2 eggs make 1 serving.

Poached Eggs with Mushroom Sauce: Place hot poached eggs on split, toasted and buttered English muffins, or buttered toast. Pour spoonful of Mushroom Sauce over each. Allow 2 tablespoons hot sauce for each egg. One or 2 eggs make 1 serving.

Poached Eggs with Cheese Sauce, Poached Eggs with Tomato Sauce, Poached Eggs with Lobster Sauce are good brunch dishes.

Comments and eleven recipes above from EGG COOKERY, *by Lily Haxworth Wallace*

Omelets

To TV fans and many New Yorkers who have attended her gourmet cookery classes, the name of Dione Lucas means superb cookery and omelets, wonderfully made, quick, easy, and delicious. Mrs. Lucas put her theories about omelets and much else of gourmet cookery into her *Cordon Bleu Cook Book*. She states, "For omelets it is necessary to have a cast-iron or aluminum pan. The metal must be of a porous nature; so copper, tin-lined, or stainless steel pans are not recommended for this purpose.

"When the pan is new, rub over the cooking surface with a piece of dry steel wool, then clean pan thoroughly with cooking oil. Never touch the pan with water at any time. When it is thoroughly clean, fill with cooking oil and let stand for about 48 hours. Pour off the oil (which, of course, can be used again) and wipe the pan thoroughly. Make it very hot, and the pan is then seasoned for use."

To make an omelet:

1 teaspoon butter	1 teaspoon cold water
3 eggs	Salt and pepper

Test the heat of the pan by trying it with a small piece of butter. If the butter sizzles briskly without browning when it dissolves, the pan has reached the right temperature. Drop in at once the 1 teaspoon butter, and the eggs beaten only a little with the teaspoon of water and a little seasoning. Stir egg mixture in omelet pan quickly with a fork and shake pan until eggs begin to set. Then stir more slowly on the top of the set eggs for 1 or 2 minutes. Leave for a second. Fold omelet over to the edge of the pan. Turn out at once onto a hot serving dish. Makes 1 or 2 servings.

Herb Omelet: Follow Omelet recipe above. Mix a small amount of fresh herbs (parsley, chives, tarragon, thyme) to make 1 tablespoon; add ½ teaspoon chopped onion, a small fragment of garlic. Add all to hot butter just before adding eggs. Complete recipe as described for plain omelet. Small croutons of fried bread may be added to the herbs if desired. Makes 1 or 2 servings.

Potato Omelet: Sauté ½ thinly sliced potato; combine with 1 tablespoon crisply fried onions. Mix into egg mixture just before pouring into the omelet pan. Makes 2 servings.

Spinach Omelet: Wash about 1 cup of spinach; drain; cook in a little butter. Drain and chop coarsely. Mix with a little thick sour cream and seasoning. Spoon onto omelet just before folding over. Serve with additional sour cream and a little paprika on top of the omelet. Makes 2 servings.

Information and four omelet recipes above from THE CORDON BLEU COOK BOOK, *by Dione Lucas*

Ideas on omelets vary from kitchen to kitchen. Visiting Irma Goodrich Mazza's kitchen in the flavorful, pungent, aromatic book which she calls simply *Herbs for the Kitchen,* some interesting omelet variations and ideas are discovered. This author asks: "Are you one of that great group of people that thinks an omelet something to be served only at breakfast? Then you are missing a lot of fun. For omelets, properly and rightly considered are one-dish meals of high degree.

"There are various sorts of omelets. The French kind, in a thousand guises; the Italian frittata, changefully packed with tender vegetables; and our own housewives' pride, the "puffy" or soufflé omelet. All are dinner and supper dishes of the first order."

ITALIAN OMELET WITH ZUCCHINI

Frittata of Zucchini

3 tablespoons olive oil
1 peeled onion
1 peeled clove garlic
5 washed and sliced small zucchini
1 large fresh or canned tomato
Salt and pepper
1 teaspoon sweet marjoram or thyme
9 eggs

HEAT oil in large iron skillet; thinly slice onion and garlic into hot oil. Cook slowly 10 minutes, then add zucchini. Add peeled, cut-up tomato, salt, pepper, and herbs. Stir well, cover, and cook slowly until vegetables are tender. Remove from heat, let cool. Beat eggs lightly in a bowl, adding light seasoning of salt and pepper. Stir into the cooled vegetable mixture. Mix well. Cover and cook over low heat until the sides of the frittata shrink away from the pan. If the middle puffs up, puncture it several times with the point of a paring knife. Place skillet under low broiler heat to finish cooking. Cut into pieces like a pie, and serve at once. Makes 6 servings.

SPANISH SOUFFLE OMELET

A soufflé or puffy omelet is just what the name suggests. In this type, the egg whites and yolks are separated. The whites are stiffly beaten, the yolks beaten to a cream. Combined, they cook into a fluffy affair that melts in the mouth. Make it so it will stand up full and proud when served. The secret of preserving the shape of a soufflé omelet is slow cooking.

3 tablespoons butter	Dash pepper
4 eggs	Spanish Sauce
3 tablespoons hot water	1 tablespoon grated Romano
1 teaspoon salt	cheese

HEAT 8-inch iron skillet, add butter, let it melt, tilting skillet so butter runs well up on sides. Beat egg whites until stiff. Beat yolks until creamy, then add hot water, salt, and pepper; mix well, fold in beaten whites and pour mixture into skillet. Leave over low heat until omelet is brown on bottom, then set skillet under low broiler heat to lightly brown top of omelet. Test with cake tester, and if it does not come out clean, place skillet in a hot oven until done. Remove, and with sharp knife carefully cut omelet across, lift out one half to a warm platter, cover with Spanish Sauce, top with other half of omelet and add remainder of sauce. Sprinkle with cheese and serve at once. Makes 4 servings.

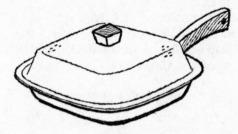

SPANISH SAUCE

1 clove garlic	Dash pepper
2 tablespoons olive oil	½ bay leaf
1 peeled onion	½ teaspoon wild marjoram
1 (8-oz.) can tomato sauce	½ teaspoon chili powder (or
½ teaspoon ground cumin seed	½ Japanese chili without
⅓ teaspoon salt	seeds)

Peel garlic, split lengthwise, and run wooden pick through each piece. Brown slowly in oil, then mince onion into the hot oil and cook slowly 10 minutes. Add sauce and seasonings, stir; cook 15 minutes. Remove garlic and discard it. Add more salt to taste. Makes about 1⅛ cups.

EGGS IN HELL

4 tablespoons olive oil	1 teaspoon minced parsley
1 peeled clove garlic	Salt and pepper
1 peeled onion	8 eggs
2 (8-oz.) cans tomato sauce	4 or 8 thin slices French bread,
½ teaspoon minced thyme	dry-toasted in oven
½ teaspoon minced sweet basil	

HEAT oil in large skillet which has a tight cover. Split garlic and run wooden pick through each piece. Brown slowly in oil, mince onion into skillet, cook slowly 10 minutes, or until yellow. Add tomato sauce and all seasonings and herbs. Cook 15 minutes, stirring often. When done, remove garlic and discard it. Break eggs one at a time into a saucer, then slip each egg into the hot sauce, spacing them as evenly as possible. Spoon sauce over them. Cover skillet, cook slowly 20 minutes, or until eggs are cooked through. Serve hot over toast slices on warmed plates. Makes 4 servings.

★STUFFED EGGS DE LUXE

6 hard-cooked eggs	1½ teaspoons finely cut chives
4 tablespoons crumbled Roque-	1½ teaspoons thyme
fort cheese	Salt, pepper, paprika
1½ teaspoons horse-radish mustard	

PEEL cooled eggs; cut lengthwise in halves, remove yolks. Mash or sieve yolks with remaining ingredients, seasoning with a little salt and pepper. Refill halves, sprinkle top lightly with paprika. Use as garnish on salads, appetizer trays, for picnics. Makes 6 or 12 servings.

The four recipes above from HERBS FOR THE KITCHEN, *by Irma Goodrich Mazza*

❦

The entrée, that delicious, usually luxurious, appetizing dish which old-time hostesses served between the first course of luncheon or dinner and the main course has moved up into the main-dish class in today's meals. The modern menu is streamlined, unless the occasion is a formal dinner in a servant-staffed home. *The Book of Entrées,* by Janet M. Hill, a rich source of superb recipes which may be served as main dishes, was published early in this century. Its cookery is sound as well as inspired, and it is one of the most useful books any hostess can own. Here are some egg recipes from its pages.

FRIED STUFFED EGGS

6 hard-cooked eggs	Cream
4 drained and mashed anchovies	2 tablespoons water
¼ cup soft bread crumbs	1 egg
2 tablespoons melted butter	Soft white crumbs
Salt and pepper	Fat for deep frying

SHELL eggs, cut in halves lengthwise. Press yolks through a sieve, add anchovies, the ¼ cup of crumbs, butter, seasonings, and enough cream to make it the right consistency for stuffing egg whites. Fill the white halves, press the filled halves together. Beat water and the uncooked egg together. Dip stuffed eggs in beaten egg, then crumbs. Fry in deep hot fat. Drain on thick paper toweling. Serve with tartare sauce. Makes 6 hot appetizer servings; or 3 servings as summer luncheon main dish.

EGG TIMBALES

6 eggs	1½ cups top milk
1 teaspoon salt	24 cooked, drained asparagus tips,
⅛ teaspoon pepper	or 3 cups cooked peas, or
1 teaspoon finely-minced parsley	1 cup tomato sauce
2 teaspoons onion juice	

START oven at moderate (325 degrees F.). Butter 6 individual custard cups. Beat eggs, adding salt, pepper, parsley, onion juice, and milk. Pour into prepared cups. Set cups in shallow pan of hot water. Bake in moderate oven until centers are firm, about 45 minutes. Test as for baked custard with silver knife; knife tip, inserted about 1 inch, comes out clean when custard is done. Unmold onto warmed serving platter. Surround with hot asparagus tips, or peas, or cover with tomato sauce. Makes 6 servings. If asparagus is served, add spoonful Hollandaise or Cheese Sauce to each serving of 4 short stalks.

Egg Timbales in Pimiento Cases: Butter 8 individual custard cups. Line each with drained canned pimiento. Trim top of pimiento with kitchen scissors to match edge of cup. Pour egg mixture (above recipe) into pimiento cups. Mixture should come to edge of pimiento. Cook as described. Unmold hot onto squares of buttered toast. Serve with hot well-seasoned Cream Sauce. Makes 6 to 8 servings.

The three recipes above from THE BOOK OF ENTRÉES, *by Janet M. Hill*

From the collection of old Virginia recipes in *The Williamsburg Art of Cookery* comes one more way to prepare and serve stuffed eggs.

★WILLIAMSBURG STUFFED EGGS

12 hard-cooked eggs	⅛ teaspoon savory
3 large mushrooms	1 teaspoon prepared mustard
2 tablespoons butter	1 tablespoon lemon juice
1 tablespoon minced onion	Salt and pepper
1 tablespoon finely minced parsley	About 3 cups finely-ground cooked chicken or veal, moistened with
1 tablespoon fine bread crumbs	cream sauce or gravy

SHELL eggs, cut in halves. Wash and peel mushrooms, mince into hot butter in saucepan; add onion, stirring. Cook 2 or 3 minutes. Add parsley, crumbs, herb, mustard, lemon juice, and season lightly with salt and pepper. Mix well and add to mashed egg yolks; stuff white halves with this mixture.

Start oven at moderate (325 degrees F.). Grease shallow, wide baking dish or pan. Spread chicken or veal forcemeat in bottom, arrange stuffed egg halves on top of meat mixture. If meat seems dry, add a small amount cream sauce or gravy over eggs and forcemeat. Bake about 20 minutes, in moderate oven or until tops are browning. Serve hot with Mushroom Sauce or Cream Sauce made with white wine as part of the liquid of the recipe. Makes 8 to 12 servings. A good dish to be kept hot on buffet-table warmer, and to serve with a salad as a supper dish.

The recipe above from THE WILLIAMSBURG ART OF COOKERY, *by Mrs. Helen Bullock*

THE
"BEST-OF-ALL"

FISH AND SHELLFISH

THE RECIPES THAT FOLLOW HAVE BEEN SELECTED FROM THESE DISTINGUISHED BOOKS:

The Art of Fish Cookery	Milo Miloradovich
The Art of Jewish Cooking	Jennie Grossinger
The Book of Entrées	Janet M. Hill
Choice Receipts	Mrs. Thomas Bailey Aldrich
Delicious Seafood Recipes	Louis Garrison
Dixie Dishes	Marion W. Flexner
Ford Treasury of Favorite Recipes, Vol. 2	Nancy Kennedy, ed.
Helen Brown's West Coast Cook Book	Helen Evans Brown
Herbs for the Kitchen	Irma Goodrich Mazza
Let's Talk Turkey	F. Meredith Dietz
The Philadelphia Cook Book	Anna Wetherill Reed
The Picayune Creole Cook Book	The New Orleans Times-Picayune
Secrets of New England Cooking	Ella Shannon Bowles and Dorothy S. Towle

FISH AND SHELLFISH

Fish and shellfish cookery need not appear only in the foreign cook-book section of this anthology; American cooks, from settler days to the present, have developed their own dishes, using fresh fish from the oceans, lakes and inland streams, and the superior frozen and canned sea food available everywhere in the country.

One of the best books on the subject is *Delicious Seafood Recipes,* by Louis Garrison. Here are some of the favorites from that author's kitchen.

BAKED SHAD

4-pound shad with roe	1 teaspoon grated onion
Salt and pepper	1½ teaspoons flour
2 egg yolks	1 tablespoon lemon juice
½ cup light cream	1 cup bread crumbs
4 tablespoons butter	

ASK the fish dealer to clean and bone shad. Rinse quickly in cold salted water; wipe dry, rub fish inside and out with salt and pepper. Parboil roe, drain, and mash. Beat egg yolks, combine with cream. Melt 2 tablespoons butter in saucepan, add onion and flour, blend; stir in egg yolks and cream slowly, mix, add mashed roe. Cook slowly, stirring continually until sauce thickens. Season with lemon juice, salt, and pepper.

Start oven at moderately hot (400 degrees F.). Butter long shallow baking dish. Place shad in dish, pour sauce over; cover with crumbs and dot with remaining 2 tablespoons butter. Bake in moderately hot oven 35 to 40 minutes, or until fish flakes easily when tested with a fork. Serve garnished with fried parsley. Makes 6 servings.

To bake in foil: Place ready fish on large piece of foil; season with salt, pepper, lemon juice. Bring foil up over fish and press all edges tightly together. Bake in moderately hot oven (400 degrees F.) about 20 minutes to the pound. When almost done, open the foil, pour sauce in, cover with crumbs and finish cooking with foil open.

FRESH COD WITH OYSTERS

3 pounds codfish steaks

3 tablespoons finely-chopped
peeled onion

1 dozen oysters in their liquor

½ cup white wine

3 tablespoons butter

2 tablespoons flour

Salt and pepper

1 tablespoon lemon juice

1 tablespoon chopped parsley

RINSE steaks in cold salted water; wipe dry. Place in well-buttered large shallow casserole. Cover with onion. Cook oysters in their own liquor until edges curl; drain; reserve liquor.

Start oven at moderate (350 degrees F.). Pour wine and liquor from oysters over fish in baking dish. Bake 15 minutes, or until fish flakes when tested with fork. Remove fish to hot serving dish and keep warm.

Reserve sauce from dish. Melt butter in large saucepan; add flour, stir well to blend. Add sauce from baking dish, salt and pepper. Cook, stirring until smooth. Add oysters, and when hot, pour over fish in serving dish. Sprinkle with lemon juice and parsley. Makes 4 to 6 servings.

POMPANO WITH CRAB SAUCE

2 pounds pompano fillets

Salt and pepper

1 tablespoon lemon juice

9 tablespoons butter

1 egg yolk

1 tablespoon water

2 cups cleaned crab meat

¼ cup white wine

4 tablespoons chopped onion

4 large mushrooms, chopped

2 tablespoons flour

1 cup fish stock

2 tablespoons chopped parsley

Lemon slices

RINSE fillets in cold water; wipe dry. Sprinkle with a little salt, pepper, and the lemon juice. Melt 4 tablespoons butter in heavy iron skillet; sauté fillets 5 minutes. Beat egg yolk slightly with 1 tablespoon water. Sauté crab meat in 2 tablespoons butter 5 minutes; stir wine, egg yolk, and water into crab meat; cook, stirring constantly, until thick.

Sauté onion and mushrooms in remaining 3 tablespoons butter; add flour, blend, and brown lightly. Add fish stock slowly, stirring continually. Cook, stirring until smooth. Add seasoning if needed.

Start oven at hot (425 degrees F.). Line shallow baking dish with aluminum foil, leaving ends long enough to fold back over the dish when it is filled. Place half the fillets in the dish on the foil; cover with crab sauce. Place remaining fillets on top, cover with mushroom-and-onion sauce. Fold foil over fillets, fasten tightly. Bake 10 minutes, or until fish flakes when tested. Unwrap; place fillets and sauce in hot serving dish. Sprinkle with chopped parsley. Serve with lemon slices. Makes 6 servings.

The three recipes above from DELICIOUS SEAFOOD RECIPES, *by Louis Garrison*

Mrs. Thomas Bailey Aldrich must have been a good cook because *Choice Receipts,* the cook book she wrote in 1925, is full of delicious dishes. Her fish recipes, which follow, have been adapted to modern cooking equipment.

★CREAMED SHAD ROE

4 to 6 baked patty shells
2 or 3 shad roes, parboiled and
  cut in small pieces
2 tablespoons butter
2 tablespoons flour

½ teaspoon salt
½ teaspoon lemon juice
1½ cups light cream or top milk
⅛ teaspoon paprika

USE pastry mix or your favorite pastry recipe and make patty shells. Start oven at hot (450 degrees F.).

Melt butter in saucepan; stir in flour smoothly; add salt, lemon juice, and cream or milk, stirring slowly; cook, stirring until thickened. Add parboiled roe, stir only until very hot. Spoon into baked pastry shells, add few grains paprika as garnish. Makes 4 to 6 servings.

FINNAN HADDIE DELMONICO

1 finnan haddie
½ cup heavy cream
4 hard-cooked eggs, sliced
2 tablespoons butter

2 tablespoons finely-chopped
  parsley
2 tablespoons grated cheese

CUT fish in strips, cover with cold water in saucepan and heat to boiling; let stand 10 minutes. Drain; rinse well. Flake the fish. Start oven at moderate (350 degrees F.). Combine flaked fish with cream and sliced eggs in shallow baking dish. Add dabs of butter, and sprinkle with parsley and cheese. Bake few minutes until top is browned. Makes 2 to 4 servings.

FRESH CODFISH POINT SHERLEY STYLE

2-pound codfish, cleaned and
  split
Salt and pepper

¼ cup melted butter
1 tablespoon grated cheese

START oven at moderate (350 degrees F.). Butter shallow baking dish with cover. Lay fish, skin side up, in prepared dish. Season with salt and pepper. Brush generously with melted butter combined with grated cheese. Cover dish. Bake in moderate oven about 30 minutes, or until fish flakes easily with fork. Remove cover, baste with butter mixed with cheese. Let brown 5 to 10 minutes. Remove to hot serving dish. Makes 3 or 4 servings.

PERFECT CODFISH BALLS

6 medium-size potatoes
½ pound (1 cup) salt codfish bits
  or fillets
Boiling water
1 tablespoon butter
1 teaspoon onion juice

⅛ teaspoon pepper
Hot milk
1 beaten egg yolk
1 tablespoon water
½ cup fine cracker crumbs
Fat for deep frying

WASH and pare potatoes, cut in chunks. Soak codfish in cold water 30 minutes, or scald twice, and drain; cut into small pieces. Combine fish with potatoes in kettle with boiling water to cover. Cook until potatoes are tender, 10 to 15 minutes. Drain well, shake over heat a minute, then beat and mash with wooden potato masher, adding butter, onion juice, pepper, and just enough hot milk to make mixture right consistency to form into balls. Roll balls in egg yolk mixed with water, then in crumbs. Chill crumbed balls 15 minutes. Then fry, using frying basket, in deep hot fat (375 degrees F.) 3 to 5 minutes, or until golden brown. Drain on thick paper towels. Makes 4 to 6 servings. Serve with tomato sauce.

The four recipes above from CHOICE RECEIPTS, *by Mrs. Thomas Bailey Aldrich*

❧

Once more this anthology relies on the superb cookery of Janet M. Hill, with the following recipes from *The Book of Entrées*.

FILLETS OF HALIBUT ST. GERMAIN

8 halibut fillets
Juice 1 lemon
Salt and pepper
Melted butter
1 beaten egg
2 tablespoons water

½ cup bread crumbs
Deep fat for frying
8 thin slices lemon
Thick Béarnaise Sauce
Hot fried potato balls

RINSE fillets, wipe dry. Sprinkle with lemon juice, a little salt, and pepper. Roll, fasten each with wooden pick dipped in melted butter (for easy removal). Mix beaten egg with 2 tablespoons water. Dip rolled fillets in egg-and-water mixture, then in crumbs. Let stand a few minutes to dry. Fry in deep hot fat (375 degrees F.) for about 6 minutes. Drain on thick paper towels. Arrange lemon slices on serving platter; remove wooden picks and place rolled fillets on lemon slices. Add spoonful thick Béarnaise Sauce to top of each. Garnish platter at ends with hot fried potato balls. Makes 4 to 8 servings.

FILLETS EN COCOTTE

8 fillets striped bass, whitefish, or   Melted butter
    halibut   1¼ cups Mornay Sauce
Salt and pepper   ½ cup grated Parmesan cheese

START oven at moderate (325 degrees F.). Butter 8 small individual baking dishes. Rinse fillets, wipe dry. Trim fillets to same shape and size. Roll each and fasten with wooden pick dipped in melted butter. Place 1 fillet in each prepared baking dish. Pour Sauce over each, and sprinkle top generously with cheese. Bake in moderate oven for about 12 minutes or until fish flakes. Serve in baking dishes. Makes 8 servings.

The two recipes above from THE BOOK OF ENTRÉES, *by Janet M. Hill*

❦

A hungry reader would expect to find savory fish dishes in *Herbs for the Kitchen,* by Irma Goodrich Mazza. Here are two favorites.

BAKED HALIBUT WITH BUTTER PASTE

2-pound halibut steak   3 tablespoons flour
6 thin slices fat salt pork   ½ teaspoon salt
2 peeled and sliced onions   Cayenne
½ bay leaf   ½ cup cracker crumbs
Pepper   3 strips bacon
4 tablespoons butter

START oven at slow (300 degrees F.). Butter shallow baking dish. Lay salt-pork slices in baking dish, cover with onions. Sprinkle lightly with pepper and broken bay leaf. Place rinsed and dried halibut on this. Cream the butter and flour, salt, and few grains cayenne together; spread this paste over fish. Sprinkle with cracker crumbs, then lay bacon slices on top. Cover dish with buttered waxed paper. Bake in slow oven 1 hour. Remove paper for last 15 minutes of cooking. Makes 6 servings.

★FISH STEAK WITH DRESSING

1 small fish steak for each serving   1 teaspoon mixed herbs, such as
Cooking oil   thyme, chervil, and parsley
Salt and pepper   Salt and pepper
2 teaspoons bread crumbs   1 egg
1 tablespoon butter   Sliced bacon
1 chopped shallot

RINSE and dry steaks; oil surface, rub with salt and pepper. Make dressing: ingredients listed make sufficient dressing for one steak.

    Start oven at moderate (325 degrees F.). Mix crumbs, butter, shallot, herbs, and a little salt and pepper; bind with slightly-beaten egg (1 egg is enough regardless of amount of dressing). Spread dressing on steaks in shallow pan or baking dish. Lay strip of bacon on each. Bake in moderate oven 30 minutes. Serve garnished with minced parsley and lemon quarters.

The two recipes from HERBS FOR THE KITCHEN, *by Irma Goodrich Mazza*

❧

A question sure to be asked the traveler who returns from New Orleans is, "Did you eat any pompano?" And the answer most likely will be "Yes," because this favorite fish is so well worth the praise local cooks and visitors give it. Here is a popular way of preparing this fish and others, according to *The Picayune Creole Cook Book,* the famous culinary collection prepared long ago by the staff of the famous Southern newspaper, the *Times-Picayune.*

POMPANO A LA MAITRE D'HOTEL

3-pound pompano or 2 smaller fish	Juice 1 lemon
	Parsley
Salt and pepper	Thin slices lemon
Olive oil	Maître d'Hôtel Butter
3 tablespoons butter	

HAVE pompano split down the back and cleaned. Rinse, wipe dry. Rub well with salt, pepper, and a little olive oil. Broil under moderate heat until tender and done, turning fish once during broiling. When done, place on warmed serving dish, add dabs of butter and lemon juice. Garnish with parsley and lemon slices. Serve with Maître d'Hôtel Butter. Makes 4 servings.

FLOUNDER A LA ORLY
Fillets of Sole A la Orly

6 fillets flounder or sole	Salt and pepper
1 egg	3 tablespoons butter
1 cup milk	Parsley
½ cup bread crumbs	Tomato Sauce

RINSE fillets, wipe dry. See that all bones are removed. Beat egg with milk; dip fillets in egg-milk mixture, then into crumbs seasoned with a little salt and pepper. Let dry a few minutes. Heat butter in skillet, sauté crumbed fillets until lightly browned on all sides; test for doneness; fish should flake easily. Serve on hot platter garnished with parsley and accompanied by a hot Tomato Sauce. Makes 3 to 6 servings.

The two recipes above from THE PICAYUNE CREOLE COOK BOOK, *by the staff of the New Orleans* Times-Picayune

Up the East Coast at Philadelphia, that traditional cook book for hostesses of the area, *The Philadelphia Cook Book*, by Anna Wetherill Reed, feat⁓es some unusual fish cookery.

BAKED SHAD WITH ROE

2-pound shad	Soft bread crumbs
1 pair roe	1 cup chopped mushrooms
1 tablespoon chopped parsley	½ cup dry white wine
Salt and pepper	Thin slices lemon dipped in
1 tablespoon butter	chopped parsley

HAVE the fish dealer split and bone shad. Rinse fish, wipe dry. Scald roe, drain, split, and scrape eggs out. Add chopped parsley, a little salt and pepper, the butter, and 2 or 3 tablespoons crumbs. Stuff shad and tie up or sew with needle and string.

Start oven at slow (275 degrees F.). Grease shallow baking dish. Place stuffed shad in dish, dot with butter. Bake 35 to 40 minutes, basting frequently with own juices. Sauté mushrooms 5 minutes in 2 tablespoons juice from baking pan; pour wine over mushrooms, stir, heat, and pour over fish. Garnish with lemon slices and serve from baking dish. Makes 4 servings.

CRAB MEAT LUMPS SOUFFLE

2 cups crab-meat lumps	Cayenne
2 cups thick well-seasoned cream	3 eggs
sauce	½ cup grated Swiss cheese

START oven at moderately hot (400 degrees F.). Butter 2-quart soufflé dish. Look over crab meat, removing all bones and fibers. Heat lumps in oven; when warm, season with a little salt and pepper. Add dash of cayenne to cream sauce, combine with beaten yolks and cheese; beat well. Mix carefully with warm crab lumps. Whip egg whites until stiff. Fold into crab mixture. Pour into prepared soufflé dish. Set dish in shallow pan of warm water. Bake in moderately hot oven 20 minutes, or until top is lightly browned. Serve at once. Makes 4 to 6 servings.

HALIBUT MOUSSE

2 pounds halibut fillets	Celery salt
4 slices white bread	4 egg whites
1 pint light cream, warmed	Lobster Sauce or mayonnaise
Salt and pepper	

Rinse fillets, pat dry. Put through grinder, using finest knife. Cut crusts from bread, and soften bread in bowl with 1 cup warm cream; let stand 10 minutes. Combine with ground fish; add remaining 1 cup cream, a little salt, pepper, and celery salt, beat all together until very smooth. (Electric beater, 8 minutes).

Start oven at moderately hot (400 degrees F.). Butter 2-quart mold. Whip egg whites until stiff and fold into fish mixture, until smooth. Pour into prepared mold, cover with buttered paper. Set mold in shallow pan of hot water and bake in moderately hot oven 45 minutes. Serve at once with Lobster Sauce. Or let cool, chill, and serve with mayonnaise. Makes 4 to 6 servings.

OYSTERS BELLEVUE

½ cup butter	2 dozen (bulk) oysters
1 teaspoon English mustard	2 tablespoons sherry or Madeira
Salt, pepper, celery salt	Parsley
1½ cups finely-chopped celery	Toast points
3 cups light cream	

Melt butter in top of 2-quart double boiler or chafing-dish pan over hot water. Stir in mustard, add a little salt, pepper, and celery salt to taste; stir, add celery and cook 5 minutes, or until tender, stirring frequently. Then stir cream in slowly and bring to boiling point. Add drained oysters and cook about 5 minutes, to heat oysters and let edges curl; add sherry or Madeira, stir, and serve at once on hot toast with parsley garnish. Makes 6 servings.

The four recipes above from THE PHILADELPHIA COOK BOOK, *by Anna Wetherill Reed*

❧

Moving up to New York and New England from Philadelphia, the cook book of the White Turkey Restaurants, *Let's Talk Turkey,* by F. Meredith Dietz, includes fish and shellfish hints and recipes every cook will enjoy reading and trying in her kitchen.

BROILED FISH WITH TOASTED ALMONDS

When broiling any fish, such as halibut, swordfish, flounder, sole, fresh mackerel, or any fillets, have ready 1 tablespoon blanched (unsalted) almonds, and 2 or 3 tablespoons butter per serving. Brown almonds lightly in moderate oven. Broil fish as usual. When ready to serve, melt butter, mix at last minute with almonds so they will remain crisp, and pour over fish on warmed serving platter.

BROILED FLOUNDER WITH ANCHOVY BUTTER

3 pounds flounder fillets or split whole fish	Paprika
	2 tablespoons anchovy paste
Salt and pepper	2 tablespoons unsalted butter

IF whole fish is used (in place of fillets) have fish dealer remove head and scales and clean fish thoroughly inside and out. Rinse fillets or whole fish, pat dry. Place flounder or fillets in pan, season lightly with salt, pepper, and paprika. Blend anchovy paste and butter over heat until melted. Pour about half over fish. Broil under moderate heat. When browned, turn fish, pour remaining anchovy butter over it, and baste with butter in pan. Broil until second side is browned and fish flakes easily. Place on warmed serving dish and serve at once. Makes 4 servings.

BALTIMORE CRAB CAKES

1½ pounds crab meat	2 cups thick cream sauce
1 strip celery, minced	1 teaspoon salt
1 green pepper, minced	2 drops Tabasco sauce
2 tablespoons butter	½ teaspoon Worcestershire sauce
½ peeled onion, grated	½ cup bread crumbs
1 tablespoon lemon juice	Fat for deep frying
2 eggs	

LOOK over crab meat carefully and remove all bones and fibers, but do not break up lumps. Sauté celery and green pepper in butter until tender, about 5 minutes. Combine with crab meat. Add onion and lemon juice. Beat eggs slightly, combine with cream sauce, add salt, Tabasco, and Worcestershire. Combine with crab-meat mixture. Form into 6 cakes. Roll cakes in crumbs. Fry in deep hot fat (375 degrees F.). Serve with Caper or Tartare Sauce. Makes 6 servings.

DEVILED CRAB

1 pound crab meat	Salt and pepper
8 hard-cooked eggs	6 crab shells
1 green pepper	6 saltine crackers
1 cup mayonnaise	4 tablespoons butter
½ cup thick cream sauce	Parsley
½ teaspoon dry English mustard	Tartare Sauce
¼ teaspoon Tabasco sauce	

LOOK over crab meat, removing all shells, bones, and fibers. Chop eggs and green pepper fine; combine mayonnaise with cream sauce, adding mustard, Tabasco, and a little salt and pepper. Combine with crab meat. Fill cleaned crab shells.

Start oven at moderate (350 degrees F.). Arrange filled crab shells in shallow baking pan. Top shells with crushed crackers and dabs of butter. Bake until tops are lightly browned. Serve hot, with garnish of parsley, and with Tartare Sauce. Makes 6 servings.

The four recipes above from LET'S TALK TURKEY, *by F. Meredith Dietz*

❦

One of the best fish cook books written in America is the complete, well-edited *The Art of Fish Cookery,* by Milo Miloradovich. Of course this author included recipes for frogs' legs, recipes which vary greatly from the European way of cooking this delicacy.

FROGS' LEGS BROILED MAITRE D'HOTEL

16 frogs' legs	Maître d'Hôtel Butter
½ cup (¼ pound) butter	Salt and pepper

WIPE frogs' legs with damp cloth. Join every two legs by passing joint of one leg through muscle of other. Melt butter in small saucepan; brush frogs' legs with about half the melted butter, season lightly with salt and pepper. Arrange pieces on broiler rack. Broil 5 minutes under moderate broiler heat. Turn frogs' legs, brush with remaining melted butter, broil 5 minutes more, or until golden brown and tender. Place on warmed serving platter and pour Maître d'Hôtel Butter over them. Serve immediately while very hot. Makes 4 servings.

MAITRE D'HOTEL BUTTER

4 tablespoons butter	2 teaspoons lemon juice
⅛ teaspoon pepper	1 sprig fresh tarragon, chopped
1 teaspoon chopped parsley	1 sprig fresh chervil, chopped

Melt butter in saucepan over low heat, add pepper, parsley, lemon juice, and herbs; mix. Pour over broiled frogs' legs and serve at once. Makes a little more than ¼ cup sauce.

If fresh herbs are not available, use 1 teaspoon each, dried.

FROGS' LEGS DEEP FRIED

16 frogs' legs	1½ cups peanut oil
1 well-beaten egg	Tartare Sauce
2 tablespoons water	Salt and pepper
1 cup cracker crumbs	

WIPE frogs' legs with damp cloth. Join two legs by passing joint of one leg through muscle of the other; dip in egg mixed with water, then in crumbs. Pour oil in large heavy skillet or frying kettle. Heat, but do not allow to smoke. (About 375 to 390 degrees F. on frying-thermometer; bread browns in 40 seconds.) Fry legs 10 minutes, or until golden brown and tender. Serve piping hot, with Tartare Sauce. Serves 4.

LOBSTER BORDELAISE

1½ pounds fresh lobster meat
4 tablespoons butter
2 tablespoons flour
¼ teaspoon salt
⅛ teaspoon cayenne
⅛ teaspoon ground nutmeg
1 cup rich milk
1 small onion, peeled and
  minced

½ small carrot, scraped and
  minced
¼ teaspoon orégano
¼ cup claret
4 or 5 slices buttered toast
12 stuffed olives, chopped
Water cress

USE quick-frozen or cooked lobster meat if available from fish dealer. If not available, buy one live 2-pound lobster; boil and prepare as for chilled fresh lobster, below. Melt butter in upper part of double boiler over boiling water. Gradually add flour, stirring smoothly; add salt, cayenne, and nutmeg. Pour milk into small saucepan over medium heat, add onion, carrot, and orégano; sauté gently 5 minutes. Slowly pour milk and vegetables into butter-flour mixture in double boiler, stir continually until very smooth and sauce begins to thicken, about 6 minutes. Cook 5 minutes more, add lobster meat, mix well; heat 3 minutes; add claret, heat 2 minutes more. Serve piping hot over buttered toast on warm plates. Garnish each serving with chopped olives and water cress. Makes 4 to 6 servings.

LOBSTER BRANDY BLAZED

2 lobsters (1½ pounds each)
½ cup (¼ pound) butter
4 scallions, or 2 tablespoons
  cut chives
1 tablespoon curry powder

1 cup heavy cream
Salt
⅜ cup (3 jiggers) brandy
Water cress

BOIL lobster as usual. Let cool. Remove meat from claws and tail; cut into large cubes and set aside. Melt 4 tablespoons butter in saucepan over low heat, add scallions or chives, cook 2 minutes; add curry powder, stirring constantly. Gradually add cream, continue stirring; season lightly with salt, let heat thoroughly, stirring constantly; do not boil. Set sauce aside and keep hot over low heat. Melt remaining 4 tablespoons butter in separate pan; add lobster meat and heat, stirring 5 minutes. When hot, pour brandy over lobster, remove from heat. Quickly set brandied lobster meat ablaze with lighted match; let blaze only ½ minute. Arrange lobster on warmed serving platter, pour steaming hot cream sauce over it, and garnish with water cress. Serve at once. Makes 4 servings.

Can be made with defrosted quick-frozen lobster meat, or canned or cooked fresh lobster bought at fish dealers. Amount of curry powder may be increased or decreased according to taste.

LOBSTER BOILED IN COURT BOUILLON

4 live lobsters (2 pounds each)	2 cloves
6 quarts water	6 peppercorns
2 tablespoons salt	¼ cup red-wine vinegar
2 large carrots, washed and	1 large onion, peeled and sliced
scraped	2 stalks celery, with tops
2 bay leaves	

POUR water into 3-gallon kettle; add salt, carrots, bay leaves, cloves, peppercorns, vinegar, onion, and celery. Cover, bring to boiling over high heat. Lower heat slightly and boil 10 minutes. Place lobsters in boiling broth. When broth begins to boil again, cook 10 minutes (if lobsters are less than 2 pounds each, boil only 7 minutes). Remove lobsters from bouillon, serve immediately or let cool at room temperature before placing in refrigerator.

To serve chilled boiled lobster, remove from refrigerator. Place lobsters on back, split from head to tail, spread open. Remove dark vein running length of lobster; remove small sac back of head. Do not discard edible green and coral. Crack large claws. Serve whole on chilled platter garnished with lemon quarters and mayonnaise or Tartare Sauce. Makes 4 servings.

MUSSELS BAKED IN RHINE WINE

4 dozen mussels in shells	½ cup Rhine wine
1 teaspoon salt	1 tablespoon grated Parmesan
¼ teaspoon paprika	cheese
½ teaspoon crumbled dill	4 slices lean bacon
1 teaspoon minced peeled onion	

SELECT large, fresh mussels with shells closed; scrub shells well, rinse thoroughly under running water. (If time allows, after scrubbing mussels let them soak 2 hours in large kettle of water. Discard any mussels that float.)

Pour 1 inch water into large kettle, add 1 teaspoon salt and the mussels; cover, bring to boiling and let mussels steam 3 minutes, or until shells begin to open. Remove mussels, drain. Take mussels from shells, remove dark, hairy beard. (Strain broth from kettle through sieve, set broth aside and use like clam broth, if desired.)

Start oven at moderate (350 degrees F.). Butter large casserole. Place mussels in casserole, season lightly with salt, paprika, dill, and minced onion. Pour wine over, sprinkle grated cheese on top. Arrange bacon slices over all. Bake in moderate oven 15 minutes, or until bacon is crisp. Serve piping hot from casserole. Makes 6 or more servings.

Shrimp Baked in Rhine Wine: Cooked shrimp and prawns are delicious prepared by the same recipe. Any preferred green herb garnish may be arranged over top before bringing casserole to table.

The six recipes above from THE ART OF FISH COOKERY, *by Milo Miloradovich*

❧

West Coast fish cookery is another important, delectable aspect of the American cuisine. One of the best books of inspired, home-tested recipes, using the sea food available along the Pacific shore, is *Helen Brown's West Coast Cook Book.* Some of her fish and shellfish recipes follow.

BAKED ALBACORE

4-pound piece albacore (a tuna)	1 herb bouquet
2 cups white wine	Thin lemon slices
½ teaspoon salt	3 tablespoons flour
2 grinds fresh pepper	3 tablespoons butter
1 cup chopped peeled onion	¼ cup minced parsley

COVER cleaned ready-to-cook albacore with 2 cups white wine and marinate several hours in refrigerator. Start oven at moderately hot (400 degrees F.). Place fish and wine in large casserole, season with salt and pepper. Add onion and herb bouquet. Cover with very thin slices lemon. Bake, basting occasionally with juice in the casserole, in moderately hot oven 45 minutes, or until fish is tender and flakes easily when poked with fork. When done, pour off juices, thicken with the flour and butter, stirring until smooth; correct seasoning, pour back into baking dish to heat, add parsley. Serve very hot. Makes 8 servings.

BROILED KING CRAB LEGS

There are several kinds of crabs on the West Coast. The most renowned is the Dungeness crab; the most spectacular, the gargantuan King crab; and the most ubiquitous, the smaller but delicious rock crab. The Dungeness crab is large compared with its Eastern cousin, producing about 6 times as much meat from each shell; but the mighty Dungeness becomes a midget when compared with the King crabs of northern waters. These enormous creatures sometimes measure 10 feet from claw to claw. They live in Alaska, but are flown south to our fancier restaurants and markets.

The recipe for broiled King crab legs should be numbered among the world's cookery classics. When purchased, the crab legs will undoubtedly be precooked. Use the large middle section of the leg, allowing one for each serving. Split shell with heavy pointed knife (a boning knife) the length of the leg. The shell is tough, not brittle, rather like heavy celluloid. Make a cross cut in the middle. Lay back the shell just enough to allow the entrance of the sauce, which is a simple one: equal parts melted butter and lemon juice. Broil the sauced crab legs over glowing charcoal, cut side up, and baste several times with the sauce while cooking. (Can be cooked in a kitchen-range broiler, too.) Allow only time enough for the bottom side to become nut brown. Serve hot in shell. The dish has been served flambé, but why try to improve perfection?

★CLAM HASH

A Seattle favorite which was originated by Yankee settlers.

2 cups chopped clams	Salt and pepper
2 cups chopped baked potatoes	½ cup cream
¼ cup minced peeled onion	Parsley
5 tablespoons butter	Lemon quarters

COMBINE drained clams and potatoes. Sauté onion in 3 tablespoons butter about 5 minutes; mix with clams and potatoes, season with a little salt and freshly-ground pepper. Melt remaining 2 tablespoons butter in frying pan. Pour clam mixture in, spread evenly, and let bottom brown. Turn heat low, and after about 10 minutes, pour cream over mixture. Continue to cook for about 15 to 20 minutes, a half hour's cooking all together. Fold like an omelet and serve on hot platter garnished with parsley and lemon. As good for dinner as it is at breakfast. Makes 4 to 6 servings.

★COOS BAY CLAM CAKES

2 cups ground clams	¼ teaspoon dried thyme
2 beaten eggs	2 tablespoons grated peeled onion
½ cup dry bread crumbs	Extra crumbs
½ teaspoon salt	3 tablespoons butter

COMBINE drained clams, eggs, crumbs, salt, thyme, and onion. Form into 6 small cakes, or 12 appetizer balls. Dust lightly with crumbs. Fry quickly in hot butter. Serve hot as luncheon dish or as appetizers. Makes 6 or 12 servings.

COPALIS CLAM PIE

Pastry for 2-crust 8-inch pie

2 tablespoons minced parsley

¼ cup chopped peeled onions

3 tablespoons butter

3 tablespoons flour

1½ cups milk or light cream

Salt and pepper

1½ cups chopped drained clams

START oven at hot (425 degrees F.). Line an 8-inch pie dish with pastry and sprinkle it with 1 tablespoon minced parsley. Sauté onions in butter in saucepan until tender; add flour, and cook 2 minutes, stirring well. Then add milk or cream (part clam juice may be used) and cook until thick. Stir continually. Season lightly. Make alternate layers of chopped, drained clams and the cream sauce in lined pie dish. Sprinkle top with remaining tablespoon of parsley. Cover with top layer of pastry, perforate pastry with fork tines in several places, crimp edge as for any pie. Bake in hot oven 25 minutes, or until pastry is browned. Makes 6 servings.

CREOLE-STYLE SHRIMP　　→

1½ lbs. fresh or frozen large shrimp

3 cups water

3 tablespoons lemon juice

1 teaspoon salt

1 teaspoon Aćcent

3 or 4 sprigs parsley

1 clove garlic, peeled and split

1 bay leaf

Small piece celery with leaves

Wash shrimp and drop them into the boiling mixture of water, lemon juice, salt, Aćcent, parsley, garlic, bay leaf, and celery. Cover tightly and simmer 5 minutes, or until shrimp are pink and tender. Drain shrimp and cover with cold water to chill. Drain, peel, and remove dark vein down the back. Place shrimp in a casserole and add Creole Sauce. Mix to distribute shrimp evenly. Heat in a moderate oven (350 degrees F.) for 30 minutes. Serve shrimp mixture over hot rice. Makes 6 servings.

CREOLE SAUCE

¼ cup butter or margarine

1 cup diced celery

⅔ cup chopped onion

½ cup finely-chopped green pepper

1 cup water

1 (6-oz.) can tomato paste

1 tablespoon minced parsley

½ teaspoon salt

¼ teaspoon Aćcent

4 or 5 drops Tabasco sauce

Melt butter in a skillet, and add celery, onion, and green pepper. Cook over low heat until onion becomes transparent. Blend in remaining ingredients.

Recipes and color photograph, from The American Peoples Cookbook © *Spencer Press, Inc.*

PORTLAND OYSTER RABBIT

1 cup small oysters
(West Coast oysters are very
small; better chop larger
varieties)
1 tablespoon butter

½ pound (Oregon) Cheddar
cheese, grated
Salt and pepper
2 eggs, beaten
4 slices buttered toast

COOK oysters in their own liquor until edges curl, about 3 minutes on moderate heat. Pour off liquor and reserve it. In the top part of a double boiler or chafing-dish pan over hot water melt the butter, add cheese and a little salt and pepper. Cook slowly while cheese melts. Then slowly stir oyster liquor in, and the eggs. When smooth, stir in oysters, and serve at once on toast. Don't forget some ice-cold beer. Makes 4 servings.

← **SWEET-SOUR SALMON STEAKS**

1½ cups water
1 medium-size onion, sliced
1 carrot, sliced
1 lemon, thinly sliced
1 teaspoon Aćent
½ teaspoon salt
3 or 4 peppercorns
4 (½-lb.) salmon steaks

2 tablespoons butter or margarine
1 cup brown sugar, packed
14 gingersnaps, crushed (about
1 cup)
1 cup vinegar
¼ cup dark, seedless raisins

In a Dutch oven or in a deep kettle with a tight cover, combine the water, onion, carrot, lemon, Aćent, salt, and peppercorns. Bring the mixture to boiling. Meanwhile, pat dry the salmon steaks. (If using frozen steaks, follow package directions for thawing.) Arrange the steaks on a large square of cheesecloth, pull up the corners of the cheesecloth, and tie together. Lower the salmon into the hot liquid, cover, and simmer 10 minutes.

Melt the butter or margarine in a small saucepan. Add the brown sugar and cook, stirring frequently, until the sugar is melted. Remove from heat. Combine the gingersnap crumbs and the vinegar, and gradually add this mixture to the butter-and-sugar mixture. Stir until smooth; set aside. Remove kettle from heat, take out the salmon, and carefully remove the cloth. Strain the liquid and return it to the kettle. Add raisins and the vinegar mixture; return kettle to heat, and stir constantly until it reaches boiling. Carefully lower salmon steaks into the liquid, cover tightly and simmer 5 minutes. Let salmon cool in the liquid. Serve warm or chill in the refrigerator. (Chilling overnight produces a stronger sweet-sour flavor.) Remove steaks to serving dish. Makes 4 servings.

Recipe and color photograph, from **The American Peoples Cookbook** © *Spencer Press, Inc.*

OYSTER NOTES

Oysters Meunière: Dip cleaned, rinsed, and dried fresh oysters into seasoned flour. Brown quickly but gently in butter. Serve at once on buttered toast with hot melted butter and lemon juice poured over. One, two, or more oysters, depending on size, make 1 serving.

Oyster Balls: An early Puget Sound recipe. Cook oysters in butter or their own liquor about 3 minutes, or until edges curl. Let cool slightly, chop, mix with equal amount of mashed potatoes, with little chopped parsley, and 1 or 2 beaten egg yolks. Form in balls, dip in flour, fry in deep hot fat. (The original recipe said bear grease.) One or more fried balls make 1 serving.

Oyster Shortcake: Just what you'd guess. Hot biscuits split, hot creamed oysters, plenty of them, and a sprinkling of parsley for color.

Oysters Maréchale are glorified fried oysters, popular with the smart set of San Francisco in the Nineties. A thick sauce is made with oyster liquor cooked with cream, chopped truffles, and mushrooms, thickened with egg yolk, and made piquant with lime juice. The oysters are dipped (masked) into this, then into crumbs, then into beaten egg, and then crumbs again. Then fried in butter! Two or more of these make 1 serving.

The six recipes, comments, and oyster notes above from HELEN BROWN'S WEST COAST COOK BOOK

❧

Visiting Florida gourmet inns with the travelers in the *Ford Treasury of Favorite Recipes,* we meet a Key West specialty.

KEY WEST SHRIMP SAUTE

A favorite at the Tradewinds Restaurant, Key West, Florida.

32 raw jumbo shrimp	1 cup sherry
4 tablespoons garlic butter	¼ cup finely-chopped parsley

WASH, peel, and devein shrimp. Sauté in 2 tablespoons garlic butter over moderate heat about 5 minutes, until just barely cooked. Remove shrimp to hot serving dish. Turn heat high under frying pan, add 1 or 2 tablespoons additional garlic butter, parsley, and sherry, cook and stir about 30 seconds until sauce is hot again. Pour sauce over shrimp. Serve at once. Makes 4 or more servings.

LOBSTER THERMIDOR

A favorite at Captain Tom's Seafood Restaurant, Miami, Florida.

1½-pound lobster, freshly boiled
¼ cup melted butter
6 stuffed olives, chopped fine
6 tablespoons finely chopped
  mushrooms
Salt and pepper

2 tablespoons (1 jigger) sherry
5 tablespoons rich cream sauce
2 tablespoons grated Parmesan or
  Cheddar cheese
Paprika

REMOVE all lobster meat and dice it; reserve shell. Moisten meat with 3 tablespoons melted butter; add olives, mushrooms, salt and pepper to taste. Cook gently 5 minutes, or just until hot. Add wine, stirring. Stir cream sauce and half the cheese in, mix, remove from heat. Start oven at moderate (350 degrees F.). Fill empty lobster shell with mixture, and top with remaining cheese, the remaining 1 tablespoon melted butter, and a dash of paprika. Bake in moderate oven until top is lightly browned. Serve hot. Makes 1 serving.

OYSTERS CASINO

Known wherever good oysters are served, this dish is a specialty of Lighthouse Inn and Keepers' Lodge, at Ocean Beach, New London, Connecticut.

6 oysters
Small shallow baking dish full of
  rock salt
1 onion, peeled and chopped
½ green pepper, chopped
½ canned pimiento, chopped
¼ clove garlic, peeled and
  chopped
½ stalk celery, chopped

Sprig parsley, cut fine
¾ cup bread crumbs
2 strips half-cooked bacon
½ cup melted butter
2 tablespoons lemon juice
⅛ tablespoon Worcestershire
  sauce
Tabasco sauce

OPEN oysters, drain, place lower shells holding oysters on salt-filled baking dish. Start oven at slow (275 degrees F.). Mix onion, green pepper, pimiento, garlic, celery, parsley, and crumbs. Spoon half of crumb mixture onto oysters. Cut bacon into 6 equal pieces and place a piece on top of each crumbed oyster. Cover bacon with remaining crumb mixture. Add spoonful of melted butter to each. Bake in slow oven 15 minutes, or until browned. Before serving, add spoonful of melted butter combined with lemon juice and Worcestershire sauce; add quick small dash Tabasco and serve at once. Makes 1 or 2 servings.

FLORIDA STONE CRABS WITH SAUCE FIESTA

Claws of 6 large Florida stone
  crabs
¼ cup chopped peeled onions
¼ cup chopped green pepper
½ cup chopped celery

2 tablespoons oil or butter
¼ teaspoon dry mustard
1 teaspoon Worcestershire sauce
1 cup ketchup
⅓ cup prepared horse-radish

BOIL the claws of the crabs in very salty water 10 to 12 minutes. Drain, crack claws under a napkin. Chill meat in bottom half of shells.

To make sauce, simmer onions, green pepper, and celery in oil or butter 6 to 8 minutes. Add remaining ingredients, mix and bring gently to boiling, stirring constantly. Sauce should be piping hot and crabs, very cold. Sauce also good with other seafood. Makes 6 servings. About 2 cups sauce.

SHRIMP AU GRATIN

We're back in New Orleans for a good supper of shrimp, at the Court of Two Sisters, on Royal Street.

2 pounds shrimp
Juice ½ lemon
½ cup butter
1 cup all-purpose flour, sifted
1 teaspoon salt

¼ teaspoon pepper
3 beaten egg yolks
2 tablespoons sherry
¼ cup grated Parmesan cheese
¼ cup bread crumbs

WASH shrimp, place in 2-quart saucepan with 1 quart water and juice of half lemon. Bring to boil, and boil gently 10 minutes. Drain, reserving the stock. Peel and devein shrimp. Melt butter in a saucepan, stir flour in smoothly and slowly, adding 4 cups shrimp stock, stirring constantly. Stir in seasonings, egg yolks, wine, and 2 tablespoons cheese. Add shrimp. Start oven at moderate (375 degrees F.) . Butter 2½-quart casserole. Pour shrimp mixture in. Top with crumbs and remaining 2 tablespoons cheese. Bake in moderate oven for about 15 minutes, or until top is browned. Makes 6 to 8 servings.

The five recipes above from FORD TREASURY OF FAVORITE RECIPES, *Vol. II, compiled by Nancy Kennedy*

❦

W ho else could tell us how to make gefilte fish? Jennie Grossinger, of course, in her interesting, richly personal book, *The Art of Jewish Cooking.* (More about this book appears in sections which follow.)

BAKED GEFILTE FISH

3 pounds halibut or pike fillets	1 beaten egg
1 peeled onion	2 tablespoons salad oil
2 slices white bread soaked in	2 onions, peeled and sliced
½ cup water	1 green pepper, diced
2 teaspoons salt	1 cup canned tomato sauce
½ teaspoon pepper	

GRIND the fish and onion together. Transfer to chopping bowl and add soaked bread squeezed dry, 1½ teaspoons salt, ¼ teaspoon pepper, and egg. Chop until fine and smooth. Shape into 12 balls.

Start oven at moderate (325 degrees F.) . Combine oil, sliced onions, green pepper, tomato sauce, and remaining salt and pepper in a 2-quart baking dish. Arrange fish balls in sauce. Bake in moderate oven about 45 minutes. Baste frequently with sauce in dish. Makes 6 servings.

The recipe above from THE ART OF JEWISH COOKING, *by Jennie Grossinger*

❦

Whaen cooks think about Southern dishes which can be adapted to kitchens anywhere in America, they turn to Marion Flexner's books. These good recipes are from her book *Dixie Dishes*.

★JAMBALAYA

This Creole specialty is usually made in a deep heavy skillet with lid or in a Dutch-oven type of pot.

2 tablespoons butter	1 tablespoon chopped parsley
2 onions, peeled and chopped	Salt and pepper
1 tablespoon flour	1 cup uncooked rice
2 cups water	¼ teaspoon thyme
1 (No. 1) can tomatoes	1 bay leaf
1 green pepper, chopped	2 cups cleaned and cooked shrimp
1 bud garlic, peeled and chopped	2 cups oysters

MELT butter in skillet or pot, add onions, and cook gently until browned; stir in flour slowly and let brown lightly. Stir in water, let mixture cook; stir continually until smooth paste is formed. Add tomatoes and their juice, green pepper, garlic, parsley, a little salt and pepper, rice, and herbs. Mix, put lid on pot, place over low to moderate heat and simmer 30 to 45 minutes, until rice has taken up nearly all the liquid and is quite done. Add shrimp and oysters with oyster liquid. Cover pot, let all heat thoroughly (until edges of oysters are curled) and the Jambalaya is ready to serve. Any other cooked fish or shellfish may be added. Serves 6.

SCALLOPED OYSTERS AND SPAGHETTI

1 pint oysters and their liquor	Salt and pepper
2 tablespoons flour	2 cups cooked spaghetti
1 cup milk	(one 5-oz. package)
1 cup light cream	¼ cup bread crumbs
3 tablespoons butter	½ cup grated Parmesan cheese
¼ cup chopped celery	Extra butter for casserole top

REMOVE any bits of shell from oysters. Blend flour with a little milk to make a paste, add rest of milk and cream, stirring smoothly. Cook celery in butter in a saucepan until softened, add thickened milk and cream slowly, stirring continually, blending to make a smooth sauce. Add oysters and their liquor, salt and pepper. Start oven at moderate (375 degrees F.). Butter 2-quart baking dish. Pour layer of spaghetti in dish, cover with oysters and sauce, repeat layers until dish is full. Sprinkle bread crumbs on top, and grated cheese over the crumbs. Dot with about 2 tablespoons butter. Bake in moderate oven 25 to 30 minutes, until crumbs and cheese form brown crust. Serve at once. Makes 6 servings.

The two recipes above from DIXIE DISHES, *by Marion W. Flexner*

❧

New England cooks claim they are the best when it comes to cooking the small sweet scallops their husbands and sons bring in from the sea or buy at the wharf. Here are some recipes using this succulent sea food from *Secrets of New England Cooking,* by Ella Shannon Bowles and Dorothy S. Towle.

FRIED SCALLOPS

1 pint small scallops	2 tablespoons water
Flour	¼ cup cracker crumbs
Salt and pepper	Fat for deep frying
1 beaten egg	

WASH and drain scallops. Cut in half, if large, or cut into ¾-inch cubes. Mix flour and a little salt and pepper together; roll scallops in seasoned flour. Dip in beaten egg mixed with water, then in cracker crumbs. Let stand a few minutes to dry. Fry in deep hot fat (375 degrees F.) 3 to 4 minutes, until golden brown. Drain on thick paper towels. Serve on hot platter, with Tartare or chili sauce in small lettuce cups as garnish. Makes 4 servings.

Broiled Scallops: Prepare scallops as you would for frying (above), arrange on ovenproof platter or in shallow pan. Dot with butter or bacon fat. Broil 10 minutes under moderate heat, turning scallops once during cooking. Should be browned and tender. Serve with crisp bacon and quarters of lemon.

HUNTINGTON SCALLOPS

3 tablespoons lemon juice	2 tablespoons water
1 tablespoon olive oil	¼ cup bread crumbs
1 teaspoon salt	2 tablespoons grated cheese
½ teaspoon pepper	3 tablespoons minced ham
½ teaspoon minced parsley	1 teaspoon minced chives
1 quart small scallops	Fat for deep frying
1 beaten egg	

Mix lemon juice, olive oil, salt, pepper, and parsley. Pour over washed and drained scallops. Let stand 30 minutes. Drain, dip scallops in beaten egg mixed with water, then roll in crumbs mixed with the cheese, ham, and chives. Let stand a few minutes. Fry in deep hot fat (375 degrees F.). Drain on thick paper towels. Serve hot with Tartare Sauce. Makes 6 servings.

SCALLOP CASSEROLE

1½ pints small scallops	½ teaspoon pepper
½ onion peeled and sliced	½ teaspoon dry mustard
4 tablespoons butter	1 tablespoon lemon juice
4 tablespoons flour	2 teaspoons parsley
2 cups milk	Buttered crumbs
1 teaspoon salt	

START oven at moderate (350 degrees F.). Butter 2-quart baking dish. Wash and drain scallops; cut any large ones in half. Sauté onion in butter until brown. Stir in flour smoothly, until lightly browned; add milk, stirring constantly, add seasonings and lemon juice. Cook and stir until smooth. Add scallops, pour into prepared baking dish. Cover with buttered crumbs. Bake in moderate oven 30 minutes. Makes 6 servings.

CLAMBAKE FOR TWENTY

For a seashore clambake, dig a pit about 18 inches deep, 4 to 6 feet long, and 2 feet wide. Line cavity with round stones. Make a hot fire on the stones, and keep it burning 2 hours or longer so stones are thoroughly heated. When foods are ready to go in, rake fire off. Cover hot stones with rockweed and a layer of seaweed, pour in bushel or more of washed, drained clams, add 20 small live lobsters, 20 washed potatoes, 20 or more ears of sweet corn (cleaned and rewrapped in husks) . Cover thickly with rockweed, then a layer of seaweed, a tarpaulin, and then with a few hot stones to keep tarpaulin down at all sides. Let foods steam 2 hours or longer. (Some clambake specialists spray foods with water before covering pit.)

Experienced timing, if the stones have been very hot, produces a wonderful feast, usually at the end of about 2 hours of steaming. Clambake cooks make a butter-and-lemon-juice sauce seasoned with grated onion for clams and lobsters. Add Worcestershire sauce, ketchup, Tabasco if desired. Some hosts also provide hot clam chowder as a first course at such a fiesta. Hot coffee and rolls are usually part of the menu.

The four recipes and information above from SECRETS OF NEW ENGLAND COOKING, *by Ella Shannon Bowles and Dorothy S. Towle*

THE
"BEST-OF-ALL"

MEATS AND GAME

THE RECIPES THAT FOLLOW HAVE BEEN SELECTED FROM THESE DISTINGUISHED BOOKS:

The American Peoples Cook Book	*Melanie De Proft, ed.*
Cooking with Curry	*Florence Brobeck*
The Gold Cook Book	*Louis P. De Gouy*
500 Recipes by Request	*Jeanne M. Hall and Belle Anderson Ebner*
Foods of Old New England	*Marjorie Mosser*
House and Garden's Cook Book	
Specialty of The House	*The Florence Crittenton League, Inc.*
Tennessee Cook Book	*Martin Rywell*
Treasures of a Hundred Cooks	*Mary Allen Hulbert*
The Venison Book	*Audrey Alley Gorton*

MEATS AND GAME

One of the most interesting of the large, complete family-size cook books of this country is *The American Peoples Cook Book*, prepared in the Culinary Arts Institute, Chicago, Illinois. Its editor, the director of the Institute, is Melanie De Proft, whose warm, friendly pages in *The Family Weekly* newspaper magazine make important additions to American culinary history because she invites recipes from her readers all over America and publishes them. Many of these reader recipes are included in her book, and they give a special home quality to its pages, wonderful dishes which feed families to their utmost satisfaction.

For general information on the selection of meat, *The American Peoples Cook Book* provides trustworthy guidance to all cooks.

Inspection stamp. All meats processed by packers who ship their products across state lines must pass Federal inspection. The round purple Federal inspection stamp (U.S. INSP'D & P'S'D) guarantees that the meat is from healthy animals slaughtered under sanitary conditions and that it is wholesome. Meats handled by packers who market locally must pass city and state inspections. These inspections guarantee wholesomeness, not quality.

Grade stamp. Quality grading is a separate operation and may be done according to government grade standards or according to packers' own standards, which are usually closely in line with government grades. Grade and brand names are stamped on the meat with a roller stamp which leaves its mark along the full length of the carcass. The purple ink used for both inspection and grade stamps is a harmless vegetable dye which need not be cut away before cooking.

Official U.S. quality grades are "Prime," the absolutely top quality, found in meat from prize animals, and seldom seen in retail shops; "Choice," the highest quality usually available for home use; "Good," "Commercial," and "Utility." These grades are applied to beef, veal, and (with the exception of the "Commercial" grade) to lamb. Pork is not officially graded, except by the packer. Where grade stamps are in evidence, the homemaker can rely on them as indexes to the quality of the meat. But in many cases, as in selecting precut and prepackaged meats, her own knowledge of the appearance of quality is a valuable guide.

What to look for in beef. Beef of good to prime quality, whatever the cut, is thick-fleshed and compact, implying a plump, stocky animal; in lower grades the flesh is thinner, indicating that the animal was rangy and angular. There is a good covering of fat, which becomes thinner and patchier in lower grades, and a generous marbling or flecking of fat throughout the lean (almost absent in the lowest grades). Color in all grades varies from light to dark red. Bones of young beef are red and porous; as the animal matures they become harder and white.

What to look for in veal. Veal, which always comes from a young animal (calves three months to one year old), is very different in appearance from beef. The lean is a light grayish-pink in color, has no marbling and very little covering fat. The bones are red and porous; in the youngest veal the ends may still be pliable. Veal is fine-grained and less firm than beef of comparable grade; because the animal is young, veal is likely to be tender.

What to look for in lamb. Of the sheep in this country, 93 percent are marketed as lambs and yearlings; only 7 percent as mutton (lamb more than one year old). The bones, fat, and color of lean meat are all indications of the age of lamb. Young lamb has red bones, which become white as the animal matures. The lean is light to dark pink in lambs, darkening to light red in yearlings and light to dark red in mutton. Lamb fat is rather soft and creamy or pinkish in color; with maturity it becomes white and much harder, even brittle.

What to look for in pork. Pork usually comes from animals under a year old and is almost always tender; the quality of American pork is quite uniform, with fewer grades than other meats. The color of young pork is grayish-pink, which becomes pinker in older animals. The flesh is firm, fine in grain, well marbled (flecked) with fat and covered with a layer of firm white fat.

Prepackaged meats. For shoppers' self-service, meats are cut, weighed, packaged, and priced by the meat dealer, and are placed in refrigerated open cases for selection. Because they are wrapped in transparent material, the shopper can see the exact number of pieces she is buying, judge the quality, and quickly compare prices and values.

Storage. Meat should be placed in the home refrigerator as soon as possible after purchase. Remove fresh meat from the market wrappings and rewrap loosely in waxed or parchment paper.

Ground meat, chops, and mechanically tenderized (pounded) steaks should not be stored for more than one to three days. Due to the spicing, fresh pork sausage keeps better than other ground meats, usually up to a week. Beef roasts, legs of lamb, and similar large cuts will keep in good condition for as long as one week. Variety meats such as heart, kidneys, and liver are highly perishable and should be used within two days. Prepackaged table-ready sliced meats and frankfurters are exceptions to the loose-wrapping rule; they will keep from two to three weeks if left in their original moistureproof wrappings, or if snugly rewrapped at home in moistureproof material.

Longer storage periods are possible in the freezer compartment of the refrigerator, which has a temperature of 25 degrees F. or lower. For freezing in this compartment, meats should be closely wrapped in a freezer-wrapper material. Even the most perishable meats and ground beef will keep for two or three weeks under these conditions. Fresh meats can be stored in home deep-freezers at a temperature of 0 degrees F. or below for much longer periods. They should first be wrapped in freezer-wrapping material which is moisture-vaporproof. Maximum frozen-storage periods recommended are: for ground meat and sausage, 1 to 3 months; fresh pork, 3 to 6 months; veal and lamb, 6 to 9 months; beef, 6 to 12 months.

★STANDING RIB ROAST OF BEEF

3-rib (6 to 8 pounds) standing roast of beef
1½ teaspoons salt
1 teaspoon Accent
⅛ teaspoon pepper

HAVE meat dealer loosen chine bone to make carving easier. Start oven at moderately slow (300 degrees F.). Wipe meat with clean damp cloth. Place roast, fat side up, in shallow roasting pan. Season with mixed salt, Accent, and pepper. Insert roast-meat thermometer in center of thickest part of lean; be sure bulb does not rest on bone or in fat. Roast in moderately slow oven, allowing 18 to 20 minutes per pound for rare; 22 to 25 minutes per pound for medium; and 27 to 30 minutes per pound for well-done meat. Roast is done when thermometer registers 140 degrees F. for rare; 160 degrees F. for medium; and 170 degrees F. for well done. Meat drippings may be used for gravy or Yorkshire Pudding (below). Makes 12 servings.

*YORKSHIRE PUDDING

½ cup hot drippings from roast beef
4 eggs
2 cups milk
2 cups all-purpose flour, sifted
1 teaspoon salt

Turn oven up to moderately hot (400 degrees F.). Pour hot drippings from beef into baking pan 11 × 7 × 1½ inches; keep pan hot. Beat eggs with rotary beater, gradually beating in milk and the flour sifted with the salt; continue to beat until smooth. Pour into baking pan over hot drippings. Place in moderately hot oven at once; bake 30 to 40 minutes, or until puffed and golden brown. Cut into squares and serve immediately with the standing rib roast. Makes 12 servings.

ROLLED POT ROAST OF BEEF WITH SOUR CREAM GRAVY

3 tablespoons fat

4-pound rolled pot roast of beef

1 medium-size onion, peeled and quartered

1 teaspoon salt

1 teaspoon Accent

⅛ teaspoon pepper

¼ cup hot water

1 bay leaf

4 cups (about 5-oz. package) noodles

4 tablespoons butter

HEAT fat in Dutch oven. Wipe roast with clean damp cloth. Add meat to hot fat and brown well on all sides over medium heat. Season meat with salt, Accent, and pepper; add onion, hot water, and bay leaf. Cover pot tightly. Simmer (do not boil) for about 3 hours. Add more water during cooking period if necessary. About 15 minutes before meat is done, cook noodles; drain; dress with melted butter and serve with roast. Makes 8 to 12 servings.

SOUR CREAM GRAVY

Liquid from roasting pot

½ cup water

1 tablespoon flour

1½ cups thick sour cream

1½ tablespoons lemon juice

1½ tablespoons grated lemon peel

¾ teaspoon sugar

When meat is tender, remove from cooking pot and keep it warm on serving platter in hot oven with oven door left open. Strain liquid, return it to the pot, and place over medium heat. Put ½ cup water into 1-pint screw-top jar, sprinkle the 1 tablespoon flour onto the water; cover jar tightly and shake until mixture is well blended. Slowly stir flour mixture into pot liquid. Cook and stir constantly, 3 to 5 minutes. Remove from heat. Stirring vigorously with a French whip, whisk beater, or fork; add in very small amounts the blended cream, lemon juice, peel, and sugar. Place over low heat and stir constantly until hot, 3 to 5 minutes, and ready to boil. Do not let sauce boil. Serve at once with pot roast and noodles. Makes 12 servings.

The above information about meats and recipes from THE AMERICAN PEOPLES COOK BOOK, *by The Culinary Arts Institute, Melanie De Proft, editor*

In Wabasha, Minnesota, a few years ago the Hotel Anderson's recipes for some of its world-famous cookery were combined in a cook book by Jeanne M. Hall and Belle Anderson Ebner. They called their book *500 Recipes by Request,* and in its foreword paid tribute to the wonderful cookery of Grandmother Anderson, who founded the hotel and whose meals enticed travelers from afar as well as local gourmands. Some of their special recipes follow.

LUXURY SIRLOIN STEAK

4-pound sirloin steak
1 clove garlic, peeled
6 medium-size onions, peeled and
　sliced

½ pound butter, melted
2 cups ketchup

WIPE steak with clean damp cloth. Cut tiny slits all over it and insert slivers of garlic. Place on broiler pan and sear under high broiler heat until lightly browned on both sides. Start oven at moderate (375 degrees F.). Pour onions into shallow roasting pan; lay seared steak on onions; combine melted butter and ketchup and pour over steak. Bake in moderate oven for about 1 hour, occasionally spooning sauce in pan over meat. Makes 6 to 8 servings.

PAN-FRIED T-BONE STEAK

2-pound T-bone steak
½ clove garlic, peeled

4 tablespoons butter

WIPE steak with clean damp cloth. Rub meat with cut garlic. Place butter in heavy skillet. When butter turns light brown, place steak in skillet and cook quickly on one side until lightly browned. Lift steak with long-handled fork, hold above skillet until butter darkens slightly, return meat to skillet and cook other side quickly. Remove steak again until the butter is still darker, replace steak and cook to taste. Serve on hot platter and pour any remaining browned butter from the pan over the meat. Makes 3 to 4 servings.

★LAMB LOAF

1½ pounds lamb shoulder, ground
½ cup milk
2 beaten eggs
2 cups rice flakes

Salt and pepper
1 cup cooked or canned peas,
　drained

START oven at moderate (350 degrees F.). Combine meat, milk, eggs, rice flakes, and seasonings and mix well. Stir in peas, shape into loaf in baking pan. Bake in moderate oven for about 1 hour. Serve hot or cold. Makes 8 or more servings.

★BEST-EVER MEAT LOAF

2 pounds round steak, ground	1 (No. 2) can tomatoes
1 pound salt pork, ground	1 teaspoon salt
2 beaten eggs	Pepper
1 cup bread crumbs	

COMBINE meats with eggs and crumbs, mix smoothly. Form into loaf in baking dish. Pour tomato juice seasoned with salt and a little pepper over mixture and let stand for about ½ hour. Start oven at moderate (350 degrees F.). Cover loaf with mashed tomato pulp. Bake in moderate oven for 1¾ hours, basting frequently with tomato juice. Serve hot or cold. Makes 8 or more servings.

VEAL CHOPS BAKED IN CREAM

4 medium-size veal chops	1 cup light cream
1 clove garlic, peeled and sliced	½ cup chopped peeled onions
Flour	Salt and pepper
4 tablespoons butter	

START oven at moderate (350 degrees F.). Wipe chops with clean damp cloth. Make small slit in center of each chop and insert small piece of garlic. Dip chops in flour; brown in butter in heavy skillet. Remove chops to baking dish. Remove bits of garlic and discard. Stir cream and onions into fat in skillet, cook and stir 1 minute, then pour over chops in baking dish. Bake in moderate oven 30 minutes. Makes 4 servings.

BARBECUED PORK CHOPS WITH PRUNES

¼ cup chili sauce	Pepper
2 tablespoons lemon juice	6 pork chops, 1-inch thick
1 tablespoon grated onion	2 tablespoons fat
½ teaspoon dry mustard	½ cup hot water
1 tablespoon Worcestershire sauce	24 whole cloves
½ teaspoon salt	24 parboiled or stewed prunes
	6 pared sweet potato halves

COMBINE and mix chili sauce, lemon juice, onion, mustard, Worcestershire, salt, and a little pepper. Pour over chops in shallow dish; let chops stand for one hour, turning them occasionally. Drain chops, reserving marinade; brown chops in fat over low heat. Add hot water and the seasoning mixture in which chops marinated. Insert 1 clove in each prune and place prunes and sweet potatoes on top of chops. Cover skillet, cook at high heat until steaming vigorously; then lower heat and cook 40 minutes or more, until meat and potatoes are done. Arrange meat in center of hot platter with prunes and potatoes. Makes 6 servings.

SOUR CREAM VEAL

2 pounds veal shoulder	2 tablespoons flour
2 large onions, peeled and sliced	1 cup sour cream
	Paprika
2 tablespoons fat	Salt and pepper

HAVE meat dealer cut veal into 2-inch cubes. Brown onions in fat, push to one side; dredge veal with flour, and brown in same fat. Add a little hot water if necessary to prevent burning. Cover pan and cook slowly for about 30 minutes. Add cream and seasonings and continue to cook over low heat 10 minutes longer or until meat is tender. Makes 4 servings.

The seven recipes above from 500 RECIPES BY REQUEST, *by Jeanne M. Hall and Belle Anderson Ebner*

It is a pleasure to look at *House and Garden's Cook Book,* by its staff editors and contributors, and rewarding to read. Here are some of the best veal recipes from its handsome pages.

TERRINE OF VEAL

2 pounds veal scallops, pounded very thin	20 strips lean bacon
	½ teaspoon dried thyme
2 pounds cooked ham, or cooked Canadian bacon	1 crumbled bay leaf
	Black pepper
12 to 15 young green onions	½ cup dry white wine
2 or 3 sprigs parsley	

POUND veal scallops paper-thin even if meat dealer has pounded them. Slice cooked ham or Canadian bacon very thin. Chop green onions and parsley together to make about ¾ cup. Line a loaf mold or bread pan with about 12 strips of bacon; place layer of veal scallops on bottom; sprinkle meat with some of the chopped onion and parsley, add few grains thyme, a bit of bay leaf, a brief grind of black pepper. Top with layer of ham or Canadian bacon. Then add another layer of veal, seasonings, and ham or Canadian bacon. Repeat layers until mold is full and all meat used. Top with remaining 8 strips of bacon; pour the wine over all. Start oven at moderately slow (300 degrees F.). Cover mold or pan; bake for 2 hours, or until meat is thoroughly cooked.

Remove pan from oven; remove cover, weight down terrine while it cools. To do this, cover with layers of heavy foil, place a plate on top and heavy weights on this. When the terrine has cooled to room temperature, place it, weights and all, in refrigerator to chill several hours. The juices form a rich jelly around the meat. To serve, remove weights, plate, and foil and turn the loaf with the jellied juices out onto a chilled decorative platter. Cut into thin slices and serve a bit of jelly with each slice. Makes 12 or more servings.

VEAL SCALLOPS PIQUANT

1 cup toasted bread crumbs
1 tablespoon finely-chopped peeled garlic
2 tablespoons chopped parsley
1 teaspoon dry mustard
¼ cup grated Parmesan cheese
Dash cayenne pepper

12 paper-thin small scallops veal
Flour
1 cup dry white wine
2 tablespoons butter
¼ cup olive oil
Worcestershire sauce
Tabasco sauce

COMBINE crumbs, garlic, parsley, mustard, cheese, and cayennne. Mix lightly but as evenly as possible. Veal should be cut thin to start with and pounded paper-thin either by meat dealer or in your kitchen. Dip veal scallops in flour, then in ½ cup wine (poured in bowl) ; then press into crumb mixture to coat both sides of meat. When all pieces are ready to cook, heat mixture of a little butter and oil in frying pan; sauté veal, turning each piece carefully with spatula. Add more butter and oil to frying pan as needed during cooking. When all scallops are browned and tender, remove to hot platter. Add remaining ½ cup wine, a dash of Worcestershire and Tabasco to pan, cook and blend for 1 minute. Pour over scallops and serve. Makes 4 or more servings. (Usually 3 small scallops make 1 serving.)

The two recipes above from HOUSE AND GARDEN'S CQOK BOOK, *by staff editors and contributors*

Corned Beef

An authentic New England recipe for corned beef is important to most homemakers. And Marjorie Mosser gives us that recipe, and much else of culinary merit, in her *Foods of Old New England*.

In New England, many families corn their own beef. They buy rump, flank, or thick rib, rub the meat with coarse salt; then cover the meat with water. The water is salted with the same coarse salt until an egg or potato will float in it. A platter weighted with a brick or rock is usually kept on top of the meat so it will stay submerged. Many New Englanders leave the meat in pickle only overnight. Others allow it to stay in pickle from a week to a month. Still others put fresh meat in heavily salted water, cook it until tender (usually about 2 hours), allow it to cool in salted water, and serve it cold.

If you buy corned beef, buy the fattest piece obtainable, put it on to cook in cold water to cover, and simmer until tender, usually from 1½ to 4 hours, depending on the meat. Let it stand in its own liquor until cool. Then take from liquor, place in deep loaf pan with meat fibers running the long way of the pan. Pull up layers of the meat with a fork, and press pieces of fat into the openings from the outer edge. When whole loaf has been larded this way, cover it with foil or waxed paper, a plate, and heavy weight. Chill thoroughly. Serve cold the following day. Allow ¼ to ⅓ pound as 1 serving.

★CORNED BEEF HASH

6 medium-size potatoes
1 peeled onion
4 cups chopped cooked corned beef

Salt and pepper
4 tablespoons butter
½ cup boiling water

SCRUB potatoes, drain, cover with water and boil in jackets until done. Let cool, peel, and place in chopping bowl with onion and corned beef from which all gristle has been removed. Chop, chop, chop very fine. (Coarsely chopped hash is an abomination.) Add seasoning as needed. Melt butter in hot frying pan, add boiling water, stir, add hash, stirring lightly until heated through. Cook over low heat press down with spatula from time to time until crust forms on bottom. Fold over like an omelet, serve hot with ketchup or stewed tomatoes. Makes 8 servings.

★RED FLANNEL HASH

1½ cups chopped cooked corned beef
1½ cups chopped boiled potatoes
1½ cups chopped boiled beets
1 onion, peeled and minced

¼ cup milk
1 teaspoon Worcestershire sauce
Salt and pepper
2 tablespoons butter

COMBINE beef, potatoes, beets, onion, milk, Worcestershire, and season to taste. Add mixture to butter in hot frying pan. Stir occasionally until thoroughly heated. Cook slowly pressing down with spatula from time to time, until hash is browned and crusty underneath. Fold over as for an omelet and garnish with parsley. Makes 6 servings.

The two recipes and comments above from FOODS OF OLD NEW ENGLAND, *by Marjorie Mosser*

O ne of the favorite older books in many American kitchen libraries is *Treasures of a Hundred Cooks,* a collection of family recipes, all good dishes, from many sources, compiled by Mary

Allen Hulbert. One of her recipes for boiled-beef tongue merits a place among the best.

BEEF TONGUE

1 beef tongue, smoked or fresh (4 to 5 pounds)	1 quart water
Boiling water	4 slices peeled onion
Salt	Sprig parsley and thyme
Flour	Salt and pepper
3 tablespoons butter	¼ cup sherry
1 (No. 2) can tomatoes	6 whole cloves

SCRUB and rinse beef tongue. Cover with boiling water lightly seasoned with salt. Bring to boiling, reduce heat, cover pot and cook gently, just barely simmering, about 3 hours. Remove from liquid, drain, let cool enough to remove skin and fat. Dredge with flour, brown lightly in hot butter. Combine tomatoes, water, onion, herbs, and a little salt and pepper in a 3-quart kettle. Bring to boiling and boil gently for about ½ hour. Add browned beef tongue, lower heat and cook gently for 1 hour. Just before serving add sherry and cloves, spoon sauce over tongue. Drain tongue, serve on hot platter. Makes 8 to 10 servings.

ROAST LAMB

4- to 6-pound leg of lamb	1 teaspoon Worcestershire sauce
1 clove garlic, peeled and sliced	1 teaspoon paprika
Few fresh mint or rosemary leaves	½ teaspoon salt
3 tablespoons olive oil	Pepper
1 tablespoon vinegar or lemon juice	2 teaspoons sugar
	Flour

RINSE meat; pat dry. Pierce in several places with skewer and insert small bits of garlic with crushed mint or rosemary leaves. Make a thick paste by combining the olive oil, vinegar or lemon juice, Worcestershire, paprika, salt, a grind of fresh pepper, and the sugar; add enough flour to thicken. Rub meat thoroughly with this, then dredge flour on to crust it entirely.

Start oven at hot (500 degrees F.). Heat roasting pan with a few pieces of lamb fat or suet in it. Place roast in hot pan and into the oven immediately. Sear 15 to 20 minutes, until crust has hardened and lightly browned. Then reduce heat to moderate (350 degrees F.) and continue roasting. Baste occasionally with juices in roasting pan. For medium-well done (as Europeans like lamb), allow 25 minutes per pound for roasts under 6 pounds, and 22 minutes per pound for roasts over 6 pounds; for well done, as most Americans like this meat, allow 30 to 35 minutes per pound roasting time. Makes 10 or more servings.

BAKED VEAL CHOPS OR CUTLETS

6 veal chops	1 cup hot bouillon or water
Salt and pepper	Flour
¾ cup dry bread crumbs	1 cup light cream
3 tablespoons butter	Grated nutmeg
Paprika	

START oven at moderate (325 degrees F.). Trim chops, wipe with clean damp cloth, and season lightly with salt and pepper. Place in shallow (metal base) baking dish or pan, cover with crumbs, dot with butter, and sprinkle lightly with paprika. Pour bouillon or hot water carefully in around chops, but not over them. Cover and bake in moderate oven for about 45 minutes to 1 hour, depending on thickness of chops. Uncover dish or pan for last 20 minutes of cooking. When done, remove cutlets to hot serving dish, and keep dish warm in oven, with oven door open. Add to liquid in baking pan 1 tablespoon sifted flour, stirring until smooth; pour hot cream in slowly, stirring continually. Add little salt if needed and dash of ground nutmeg, bring to boiling and boil 2 or 3 minutes, stirring continually. Pour around cutlets and serve. Makes 6 servings.

The three recipes above from TREASURES OF A HUNDRED COOKS, *by Mary Allen Hulbert*

❦

Blanquette de Veau is the French name for a very simple veal dish which has long been popular in America. It is one of the recommended recipes in an unusual book, *Specialty of The House,* published by The Florence Crittenton League, Inc. (to raise funds for this welfare organization). Famous editors and food writers contributed their favorite dishes to the collection.

BLANQUETTE DE VEAU

This recipe for Blanquette de Veau is by Charlotte Adams, author of cook books, writer, and radio commentator.

1½ pounds leg of veal, cut in chunks	2 tablespoons butter
	2 tablespoons flour
Boiling water	2 egg yolks
1 teaspoon salt	3 tablespoons lemon juice
Freshly-ground pepper	½ cup light cream
12 small white onions, peeled	3 or 4 cups hot cooked rice

COVER veal with boiling water and boil 2 minutes. Drain, and rinse with

cold water. Cover again with boiling water in large saucepan, add seasonings and onions, and cook at low boil for 1 hour. Melt butter, blend in
flour, add cup of broth from veal saucepan (strained) and blend in
smoothly. Beat egg yolks and mix with lemon juice. Add a little of the
veal sauce to the eggs and blend, then stir back into veal sauce. Add
cream, heat but do not boil. Place veal in hot serving dish. Pour sauce
over it. Surround with hot cooked rice. Makes 4 servings.

POTTED BREAST OF VEAL WITH GINGER

Another contributor to *Specialty Of The House* is famous food
photographer George Lazarnick. Here is his best veal dish:

4-pound piece breast of veal	2 medium-size onions, peeled and
4 teaspoons salt	diced
2 teaspoons pepper	3 tablespoons hot water
2 teaspoons ground ginger	½ tablespoon flour
2 tablespoons fat	3 or 4 cups hot noodles

WIPE veal with clean damp cloth. Mix salt, pepper, and ginger and rub
well into meat. Let meat stand, preferably overnight (in covered bowl
in refrigerator). Sear veal in hot fat in Dutch oven or heavy pot; turn
meat, add onions and lightly brown other side of meat in onions and
the fat. Add the 3 tablespoons hot water, cover pot, and cook over low
heat from 1½ to 1¾ hours, adding a little hot water from time to time if
necessary. When meat is done, remove to a hot serving dish. Stir ½ tablespoon flour in a little water until smooth, then stir into pot. Cook 2 to 3
minutes, stirring. Use pot sauce as gravy around roast with hot noodles.
Makes 4 to 6 servings.

The two recipes above from SPECIALTY OF THE HOUSE, *by The Florence
Crittenton League, Inc.*

❧

Small regional cook books usually contain the best local dishes of
the community in which they are published and are of special in-
terest to cooks who live elsewhere. Such is the case with the *Tennessee Cook Book,* compiled by Martin Rywell. It is not for beginners however, since many of the recipes assume that all cooks
know temperatures and cooking time and other techniques of
preparation. But with one of the large general cook books of our
country at hand, any of the Tennessee recipes which seem too general or casual can be completed according to kitchen-tested home-
economics rules. Tennessee cooks undoubtedly achieve the same
good results with native skill and long experience.

Here are two recipes from that book, newly edited for cooks who do not like to guess.

BAKED HAM

1 boiled or precooked smoked
   ham (10 to 12 pounds)
2 cups brown sugar, packed
1 tablespoon dry mustard
1 tablespoon vinegar

1 teaspoon celery seed
2 or 3 tablespoons finely-rolled
   cracker crumbs
Ginger ale

START oven at hot (450 degrees F.). Place ham, from which skin has been removed, fat side up in roasting pan. Score fat surface with ice pick or heavy kitchen fork. Mix sugar, mustard, vinegar, celery seed, and cracker crumbs to a paste, using a little more vinegar if needed. Spread paste over scored surface. Pour ginger ale around (not over) ham in pan about ½ inch deep. Bake uncovered in hot oven 30 minutes, basting frequently with juices from bottom of pan. Makes 20 to 25 servings.

[Ham Dixie, which is not included in the Tennessee book, originated in that state, in spite of its title. Use thick slice ham for broiling; spread with peanut butter, cover with drained, soaked raisins, and finely chopped pared apples. Place in baking pan. Bake in moderately hot oven, (400 degrees F.) about 20 minutes. Lower heat to moderate, (325 degrees F.) and bake 25 minutes longer. Baste occasionally with juices in pan. Serve hot, with baked yams and hot turnip greens. Ed.]

ROAST PORK AND SWEET POTATOES

4 to 6 pounds fresh pork loin
Salt and pepper

5 ginger wafers (snaps) crushed
8 sweet potatoes

START oven at moderate (325 degrees F.). Wipe meat with clean damp cloth. Rub with salt and pepper. Place fat side up in roaster. If meat thermometer is used, make a hole with skewer through fat side of roast and insert thermometer so that bulb will be in center of roast, but not touching bone. Roast uncovered. Allow 40 to 45 minutes per pound roasting time. Baste occasionally with juices from pan. Turn roast once.

Scrub potatoes, drain, pare. Cut in halves or quarters, if large, and place around roast about 45 minutes before meat is done. Baste potatoes with juices in pan, turn several times. Sprinkle ginger wafer crumbs over roast after it is about half-cooked and baste with pan juices. Serve meat on hot platter surrounded by potatoes. Makes 8 to 12 servings.

The two recipes above from TENNESSEE COOK BOOK, *by Martin Rywell*

❧

From the first book on curries published in America, *Cooking with Curry*, by Florence Brobeck, comes this Cantonese style beef curry. Exceptionally good!

BEEF CURRY WITH ONIONS

2 tablespoons curry powder

½ clove garlic, peeled and chopped

2 tablespoons olive or peanut oil

1 teaspoon salt

½ teaspoon pepper

1 thin slice green ginger root, or preserved ginger, mashed

2 pounds beef, cubed

4 small onions, peeled and cut in thin strips

3 tablespoons soy sauce

1 cup beef or chicken bouillon, or hot water

2 tablespoons cornstarch

¼ cup cold water

6 cups hot cooked rice

STIR curry powder in the center of a large, heavy frying pan over heat. When very hot, add garlic; mash it and stir oil in a little at a time; add salt, pepper, and ginger, mix well. Add meat, stirring well. Add onions; stir and cook until onions are tender. Add soy sauce and bouillon or hot water. Cover pan, bring mixture to boiling, cook 5 minutes, or until meat is tender. Mix cornstarch and water together, stir into meat mixture; cook and stir until sauce thickens. Serve hot on mound of hot rice. Makes 6 servings.

CURRIED LAMB KATMANDU STYLE

3 pounds breast or leg of lamb, cut in serving pieces

¼ cup flour

½ cup fat

2 large onions, peeled and sliced

1 clove garlic, peeled and minced

1 medium-size tart apple, pared, cored and chopped

¾ teaspoon dry mustard

¼ teaspoon powdered ginger

2 tablespoons curry powder

1 tablespoon brown sugar

3 cups meat stock or bouillon

2 tablespoons tomato purée or condensed tomato soup

1 teaspoon salt

¼ teaspoon pepper

6 cups hot cooked rice or saffron rice

Dash cayenne

Bombay chutney and curry condiments

REMOVE all fat from meat. Dredge meat with flour. Heat fat in large, deep frying pan or Dutch oven. Sauté onions and garlic in fat until onions are transparent. Add meat, apple, seasonings, sugar, stock or bouillon, and tomato purée or soup. Cover; simmer 1 to 2 hours, or until meat is tender. If necessary, add more stock. Skim off excess fat. Remove meat to warmed platter; season sauce with salt and pepper and thicken, if desired, by adding about 1 tablespoon flour mixed with 1 tablespoon water. Stir; let boil 2 or 3 minutes, stirring constantly; pour over meat. Surround with spoonfuls of hot rice or saffron rice. Add light sprinkling of paprika or cayenne. Serve chutney and curry condiments with this dish. Serves 6.

The recipes above from COOKING WITH CURRY, *by Florence Brobeck*

Variety Meats

For superb cookery and easy-to-follow recipes, the huge cook book by Louis P. De Gouy is outstanding. Called *The Gold Cook Book,* it is the source of hundreds of delicious dishes. The succulent variety meats, so well understood by chefs and especially by French and Italian cooks, are well represented in his book. A few of his suggestions follow.

DRIED BEEF AMANDINE

2 cups hot cream sauce
1 cup split, toasted almonds
1 (4-oz.) jar dried beef
Boiling water

6 slices toast
Anchovy Butter
Parsley

COMBINE almonds and hot cream sauce. Pour boiling water over dried beef, drain, shake and drain again. Stir into almond sauce; heat to boiling point. Serve at once on toast spread with Anchovy Butter. Garnish with parsley. Makes 6 servings.

The author also suggests serving creamed dried beef in a hot Noodle Ring, or as a shortcake, using your best baking-powder biscuits split and buttered.

BEEF HEART LOAF PARISIAN STYLE

3-pound piece beef heart
½ pound pork shoulder
2 eggs
2 slices bread, crumbled
Sherry
1 teaspoon crumbled sage
1½ teaspoons salt

¼ teaspoon freshly-ground pepper
⅛ teaspoon each, ground nutmeg, thyme, mace, and marjoram
1 tablespoon each grated onion, chopped parsley, chives, and green pepper
Butter, garlic

START oven at moderate (325 to 350 degrees F.). Wash heart thoroughly, remove all gristle and membrane, put through food chopper with the pork. Beat eggs, add to meat mixture; add the bread soaked in enough sherry to make it very wet; add sage, salt, pepper, spices, herbs, onion, parsley, chives, and green pepper. Mix thoroughly. Rub bread pan with garlic and grease with butter. Pour heart mixture into pan and shape as loaf. Bake in moderate oven from 1½ to 1¾ hours. Unmold on hot serving platter. Garnish with water cress, pickle fans, and olives. Serve sliced, preferably with hot brown gravy. Makes 8 to 12 servings.

★FRANKFURTERS IN GOLDEN JACKETS

Plain pastry

Prepared mustard

Chopped raw bacon

Chopped parsley, onion, or chives

Small frankfurters

ROLL pastry very thin. Brush with prepared mustard, then sprinkle with mixture of chopped raw bacon, parsley, or onion, or chives. Cut into rectangles to fit frankfurters. Cut ends from frankfurters; enclose each in rectangle of pastry, folding it over evenly; seal edges by wetting pastry, then pinching firmly together. Start oven at moderately hot (400 degrees F.). Grease baking sheet, lay pastry-wrapped franks on baking sheet, prick pastry in several places with sharp tines of fork. Bake for about 12 minutes, or until pastry is golden. Serve sizzling hot.

BAKED LIVER AND ONIONS DELMONICO

2 large Bermuda onions, peeled
    and sliced

3 tablespoons butter

⅓ cup hot water

6 slices calves' liver

Flour

Salt and pepper

1 large bay leaf

1 sprig thyme

8 sprigs parsley

Butter

START oven at moderate (350 degrees F.). Arrange onion slices in a generously greased baking dish. Melt the 3 tablespoons butter in ⅓ cup hot water and pour over the onions. Cover dish and bake in moderate oven for about 30 minutes, turning onion slices once with a spatula, and taking care to keep them in shape.

Rinse liver, drain, remove tubes and skin. Dredge slices with flour seasoned with salt and pepper. Arrange over onions, add herbs (tied together with thread). Dot liver with butter (using about 2 tablespoons). Cover dish. Bake for about 25 to 30 minutes. Uncover and continue baking until liver is brown and cooked. Remove herb bouquet and discard it. Serve from baking dish with Delmonico potatoes. Serves 8.

DELMONICO POTATOES

1 cup hot medium white sauce

½ cup grated cheese

3 hard-cooked eggs, coarsely
    chopped

1 quart cold sliced boiled potatoes

½ cup buttered crumbs

Start oven at moderate (350 degrees F.). Stir cheese into sauce, add chopped eggs. Make a layer of potatoes in generously buttered shallow 2-quart baking dish. Cover with layer of sauce. Repeat layers. Cover top layer of sauce with crumbs. Bake in moderate oven 25 minutes or until top is well browned. Serve right from baking dish. Makes 8 servings.

VEAL KIDNEYS ARDENNAISE

8 veal kidneys
⅓ cup sweet butter
1 tablespoon each finely-chopped
    green pepper, mushrooms, and
    onion
Salt and pepper

3 tablespoons brandy
1 cup boiling bouillon or veal
    stock
4 to 8 pieces toast
Parsley

WASH kidneys, drain, split. Remove fat, membranes, and skin. Cut into
½-inch slices. Heat butter in saucepan, stir in green pepper, mushrooms,
and onion; cook and stir over low heat just until mixture begins to color.
Season sliced kidneys with salt and pepper, add to mixture in pan, blending well. Continue cooking and stirring 4 minutes longer. Pour the
brandy into a large soup ladle, set it aflame, and let the flaming brandy
drop over the kidney mixture, stirring meanwhile. When flame dies out,
add the boiling-hot bouillon or stock, and stir from the bottom of the
pan. Cover and simmer gently for 10 minutes. Serve on freshly-made
toast; thicken sauce in pan with ½ tablespoon flour, let boil 1 or 2
minutes, strain over the kidney mixture. Garnish with parsley. Makes
4 to 8 servings.

The six recipes above from THE GOLD COOK BOOK, *by Louis P. De Gouy*

Three Venison Recipes

A refreshingly new approach to the cooking of game meats is
given in *The Venison Book,* by Audrey Alley Gorton. When
this huntsman-cook-writer first sought venison recipes to try, he
was puzzled to find that most cook books, whether general or devoted to game cookery, implied that the meat itself was indifferent
and palatable only after long hanging followed by prolonged soaking in a spicy marinade. "My own experience," he said, "and that
of my deer-hunting friends, indicates that one may expect venison to be not inferior to beef in eating quality. I suspect that the
tradition of disguising the flavor of venison with spices and herbs
dates from Medieval times, and was originated by necessity."

He does give spicy marinades in his book, but this recipe for a
simple roast of venison is quite different and gratifying simple.

ROAST VENISON

Neck roast of venison
Buttermilk for marinating

Sliced bacon for larding
Salt and pepper

COVER meat with buttermilk and let stand in refrigerator overnight. Drain, wipe meat with clean damp cloth. Place in roasting pan. Start oven at moderate (350 degrees F.). Lard meat with strips of bacon threaded into a larding needle. The lardoons are drawn through the meat about 1 inch apart. Or simply lay strips of bacon on the meat, about 1 inch apart; bind them to the meat by wrapping with thread. Season roast all over with salt and pepper.

Roast in moderate oven as for beef. If you use a meat thermometer, the reading should be 140 degrees F., which is the temperature for rare beef. Without thermometer, for *rare,* allow 25 minutes per pound for roasts under 5 pounds, 21 minutes per pound for roasts over 5 pounds. For *medium* roast, allow 35 minutes per pound for roasts under 5 pounds, and 27 minutes per pound for roasts over 5 pounds. For *well done,* allow 40 minutes per pound for roasts under 5 pounds, and 33 minutes per pound for roasts over 5 pounds. When ready to serve, remove strings, place roast on hot platter. A 5-pound roast makes 8 or more servings.

VENISON STROGANOFF

The author of the book on venison says that some people insist this stew is better when made in advance and reheated at serving time. The trick, he adds, is to use the very best and tenderest venison steak, as the meat should not be overcooked.

1½ pounds venison steak	1 cup sour cream
4 tablespoons butter	Salt, paprika
½ pound mushrooms, cleaned, peeled, and broken	Hot rice, noodles, or baking-powder biscuits
1 tablespoon flour	

CUT steak into thin strips about ¼-inch wide and 1 inch long. The meat should be cut across the grain; this makes it more tender. Melt 3 tablespoons butter in heavy frying pan or skillet, with cover. When butter is bubbling, add meat, cover, and cook slowly, stirring occasionally. At end of 15 minutes, add mushrooms broken into small pieces. Cover, cook for 10 minutes longer, stirring occasionally.

Pour meat-and-mushroom mixture into top of double boiler or chafing dish over hot water. Melt remaining 1 tablespoon butter in the frying pan, stir flour in smoothly, add sour cream and stir over low heat 3 or 4 minutes. Pour over meat and mushrooms and simmer over boiling water 10 to 15 minutes. Season to taste with salt, adding a little paprika for color on top.

Serve hot in ring of hot rice or noodles, or on split baking-powder biscuits. Biscuits should be larger than usual, about 3-inches in diameter. Makes 6 servings.

VENISON POT ROAST WITH VEGETABLES

Here is another of the venison author's favorites. He says: "I can't think of a more satisfying dinner for a closed-in winter evening than one of venison pot roast; serve in a ring of its own vegetables with plenty of crusty French bread. It can hold its own as a company dish and has an added attraction in that it doesn't require intense last-minute attention."

3- to 4-pound boneless venison
   roast
½ cup cubed salt pork
2 tablespoons butter
1½ cups hot water
1 cup dry white wine
6 carrots, scraped
6 small onions, peeled

1 stalk celery, chopped
1 teaspoon parsley flakes, or
   chopped fresh parsley
½ teaspoon dried thyme
Salt and pepper
6 small potatoes, pared and
   halved

WIPE meat with clean damp cloth, lard well by inserting cubes of salt pork into cuts made in the meat. Heat butter in Dutch oven or deep top-of-the-stove casserole and brown meat on all sides. Add hot water, wine, all vegetables except potatoes; add herbs and a little salt and pepper. Cover, cook gently for 3 hours on top of the stove, or in a moderately slow oven, until meat is tender. Cook at simmering temperature, rather than lively boiling, to keep meat tender and juicy, and to prevent vegetables from cooking to pieces. If liquid gets too low, add hot water or mixture of hot water and white wine. About 30 minutes before meal is to be served, correct the seasoning, since potatoes tend to draw saltiness from the liquid. When potatoes are done, remove meat and vegetables to a hot platter. If necessary, reduce liquid rapidly over high heat, keeping meat and vegetable platter hot in oven with oven door left open. Pour a little hot pot-liquor over meat; serve the rest in a warmed gravy boat. Makes 6 to 8 servings.

The three recipes above from THE VENISON BOOK, *by Audrey Alley Gorton*

THE
"BEST-OF-ALL"

PASTAS AND RICE

THE RECIPES THAT FOLLOW HAVE BEEN SELECTED FROM THESE DISTINGUISHED BOOKS:

Edith Barber's Cook Book	*Edith Barber*
The Frances Parkinson Keyes Cookbook	*Mrs. Frances Parkinson Keyes*
Rice and Spice	*Phyllis Jervey*

PASTAS AND RICE

If you are looking for exotic, delicious Italian and Sicilian pasta dishes, you will find them in the section of this book devoted to the best-of-all foreign cook books. But equally good, and among the most popular dishes in American cookery today, are the macaroni, spaghetti, noodle, and rice recipes which have been developed by this country's home economists in magazine and food manufacturers' test kitchens and by countless home cooks. These dishes, in general, are economical, replace potatoes in the diet, and are such good eating that they are favorites with teen-age members of the family as well as the grownups.

Edith Barber, whose sound, informative, and always reliable recipes in her syndicated columns are used by thousands of readers, has included scrumptious pastas in her book, which, logically enough, is called, *Edith Barber's Cook Book*. Her recipes use only those products which are available in general grocery stores all over the country.

There are many new pastas in grocery stores today. Both macaroni and spaghetti have emerged in the fancy shapes and varieties which once were available only in bulk at Italian shops. Pasta packages (bags, boxes) vary in size. Weight of contents is stated on the label, Miss Barber reminds her readers, and the 8-ounce package is one of the most useful for average family cookery.

These macaronis and spaghettis should be boiled in a large amount of salted water, 1 teaspoon of salt to each quart of water. Macaroni, if bought in stick form, is usually broken into pieces before it is cooked. The long, thin sticks of spaghetti need not be broken, for they soften immediately in the boiling salted water. The time of cooking depends on the brand of macaroni or spaghetti, varying from 9 to 20 minutes.

Noodles cook in approximately 7 minutes. But follow directions on package. None of these products should be overcooked; when tender, drain macaroni, spaghetti, and noodles at once in a colander or strainer and rinse with hot water. They may then be dressed with butter, or a sauce, or with browned buttered crumbs and seasoned with salt and pepper. Or use them as called for in various recipes. An 8-ounce package supplies about 4 cups cooked macaroni, spaghetti, or noodles.

★SPAGHETTI AND MUSHROOM SAUCE

¼ pound salt pork	¼ cup minced parsley
1 tablespoon olive oil	1 (4-oz.) can tomato paste
1 clove garlic, peeled	1 cup mushroom stock
¼ cup minced peeled onions	Salt and pepper
½ pound (2 cups) sliced mush-rooms	2 teaspoons sugar
	1 (8-oz.) package spaghetti

CUT salt pork into small cubes. Heat oil in heavy saucepan, add pork and garlic, and sauté over medium heat 5 minutes, or until pork is light brown. Remove garlic and discard it. Add onions, mushrooms, and parsley and cook for 3 minutes. Add tomato paste and mushroom stock (made by cooking stems and tough portions of mushrooms in 1½ cups water about 10 minutes). Add salt and pepper to taste; add sugar, cook for 5 minutes. Cook spaghetti as directed on package, rinse and drain. Arrange on hot platter. Pour sauce around spaghetti. Makes 6 servings.

★BAKED MACARONI AND CHEESE

8-ounce package macaroni	½ teaspoon dry mustard
4 tablespoons butter	½ teaspoon paprika
4 tablespoons flour	2½ cups milk
1½ teaspoons salt	1 cup (¼ pound) grated cheese
¼ teaspoon pepper	1 teaspoon Worcestershire sauce

COOK macaroni as directed on package, rinse and drain. Start oven at moderately hot (400 degrees F.). Butter 2-quart baking dish. Melt butter in large saucepan, stir flour in smoothly, adding salt, pepper, mustard, and paprika. When well blended, add milk slowly, stirring constantly over low heat until mixture thickens and boils. Add cheese and Worcestershire sauce, and stir until cheese has melted. Add drained macaroni and pour into prepared baking dish. Bake in moderately hot oven 20 minutes or until top is browned. Makes 6 generous servings.

For crusty top, sprinkle macaroni lightly with paprika and 1 cup buttered crumbs before baking.

Baked Macaroni with Meat. Add 1 cup chopped cooked ham, corned beef, or smoked tongue to casserole. Reduce salt to ½ teaspoon.

Baked Macaroni with Shrimp. Substitute 1 cup cooked or canned (deveined) shrimp for cheese. Add ¼ cup minced green pepper or ½ cup diced celery.

Baked Macaroni with Tuna Fish. Add 1 cup canned, flaked, and drained tuna fish.

Baked Macaroni with Vegetables. Add 1 cup cooked vegetables to macaroni before baking. (Peas are especially good; so are green beans cut into small pieces.)

NOODLE RING

8-ounce package noodles	¼ teaspoon pepper
2 tablespoons butter	½ cup rich milk
1 teaspoon salt	3 eggs

Cook noodles as directed on package, rinse and drain. Start oven at moderate (375 degrees F.). Grease 1½-quart ring mold. Stir butter, salt, pepper, milk, and well-beaten egg yolks into noodles. Whip egg whites stiff, and fold in. Pour into prepared ring mold, set in shallow pan of hot water. Bake in moderate oven for about 30 minutes, until set. Turn out on warmed round platter, and fill center with creamed fish, chicken, vegetables, or a curry of meat, chicken, or shrimp. Makes 6 servings.

★NOODLES WITH POPPY SEEDS AND ALMONDS

8-ounce package noodles	¼ cup sliced blanched almonds
4 tablespoons butter	2 teaspoons poppy seeds

Cook noodles as directed on package, rinse, and drain. Melt 1 tablespoon butter, add nuts and cook over low heat until almonds are lightly browned. Add remaining butter and poppy seeds, mix well and combine with hot noodles. Serve at once. Makes 6 servings.

MIX-AHEAD MEAT LOAF ⟶

2 pounds ground beef	2 eggs
1 cup tomato juice or milk	1½ teaspoons salt
1 cup dry bread crumbs	¼ teaspoon pepper
½ cup chopped onions	½ teaspoon orégano
¼ cup chopped green pepper	Green pepper rings for garnish

Start oven at moderate (350 degrees F.). Combine all ingredients, mixing well. Pack into loaf pan 9 × 5 × 3 inches. Bake in moderate oven 1 hour. Turn out on warmed serving platter, garnish with green pepper rings. Makes 8 servings.

Serve with it scalloped mixed vegetables. Menu includes mugs of old-fashioned pea soup, the meat loaf and vegetables, an upside-down cake, green salad, and beverage.

Recipe for Mix-Ahead Loaf and color photograph, courtesy Campbell Soup Company

FRIED NOODLES

Cook contents of 8-ounce package of noodles as directed on package. Rinse, drain. Dry on towel. When dry, fry in deep hot fat (390 degrees F.) about 1 minute, until brown. Drain on thick paper towels. Sprinkle with salt. Makes 6 servings.

The five basta recipes and variations above from EDITH BARBER'S COOK BOOK

←——— CHICKEN MARENGO WITH EGG NOODLES

2 (2½-lb.) frying chickens, cut in serving pieces
½ cup seasoned flour
⅓ cup salad oil
¼ cup butter or margarine
12 small white onions, peeled and boiled
12 medium-sized mushrooms
1 clove garlic, peeled and finely chopped

2 tablespoons flour
½ cup water
3 tablespoons sherry
4 medium-sized tomatoes, peeled and quartered
Salt
8-ounce package medium egg noodles, freshly cooked and hot
Parsley for garnish

Place pieces of chicken and the seasoned flour into a clean paper bag, close bag tightly, and shake vigorously so that all pieces of chicken are well coated with flour. Cook chicken in hot salad oil in heavy skillet over medium heat until browned on all sides. Cover and cook over low heat 40 minutes, or until tender. Melt butter or margarine in saucepan, add onions, mushrooms, and garlic; cover and cook 10 minutes, stirring frequently. Sprinkle 2 tablespoons flour over mixture, blend in. Gradually add ½ cup water mixed with the sherry, cook over low heat, stirring constantly until thickened. Add tomatoes and about 1 teaspoon salt. Cover and cook 10 minutes, stirring frequently.

Arrange hot noodles on warmed serving platter, place chicken in center, pour vegetable sauce over and around chicken. Garnish platter with parsley. Makes 6 servings.

Recipe for Chicken Marengo and color photograph, courtesy National Macaroni Institute

Warm, generous hospitality echoes from every page of *The Frances Parkinson Keyes Cookbook*. This celebrated writer has enjoyed visiting in many parts of the world, and from her hosts everywhere she acquired recipes for the best of that country's cookery. At home her reputation for the good cookery served at her parties brought her many recipes from interested friends. When she had accumulated a rich horde of such cookery rules, she put them together in her diverting cook book. Her best spaghetti dish comes from a friend in Maine. Here it is:

★SPAGHETTI WITH MEAT SAUCE

2 cloves garlic, peeled and
   crushed
2 tablespoons olive oil
1 small onion, peeled and
   chopped
½ green pepper, seeded and
   chopped
½ pound ground beef

1 (No. 2½) can tomatoes
1 (4-oz.) can tomato paste
Water
1 teaspoon salt
½ teaspoon pepper
½ teaspoon sugar
¾ pound spaghetti

BROWN garlic in oil in large saucepan, and discard garlic. Add onion and green pepper and sauté until golden brown. Remove onion and green pepper and set them aside; to the oil remaining in the pan add beef and cook, stirring, until meat is browned. Add tomatoes and tomato paste. Fill tomato paste can with water and add, along with the reserved cooked onion and green pepper. Season with salt, pepper, sugar, and cook over very low heat for about 2 hours, stirring occasionally.

Cook spaghetti as directed on package, until just tender. Drain, rinse well with hot water, drain again. Pour spaghetti into warmed serving dish, pour sauce over it. Serve with Parmesan cheese. Serves 6.

★HAM A LA BRECK (MACARONI DISH)

8-ounce package macaroni
1 cup chopped cooked ham
1½ cups milk
4 slightly-beaten eggs

½ teaspoon salt
⅛ teaspoon pepper
1 tablespoon prepared mustard
1 teaspoon onion juice

COOK macaroni as described on package. Drain, pour into 2-quart buttered baking dish. Start oven at moderate (350 degrees F.). Sprinkle ham over macaroni. Combine remaining ingredients, mix well, and pour over the ham and macaroni. Bake uncovered in moderate oven about 30 minutes. Makes 6 servings.

The two recipes above from THE FRANCES PARKINSON KEYES COOKBOOK

What well-flavored reading there is for the armchair traveler, and the armchair cook, in Phyllis Jervey's *Rice and Spice*. As the daughter of a diplomat, then wife of an army officer, the Texas-born author traveled East and West, and wherever she went, she collected interesting dishes. She found rice and flavorful rice cookery almost everywhere, and added the new dishes to her repertoire of recipes for family and friends. In her general basic cookery instructions for this versatile food, the author says:

It is not necessary to wash packaged rice. Modern rice is machine-milled and comes ready to be cooked. Cook rice in as little water as possible. It will retain more flavor and will have a better texture than if a large quantity of water is used. For converted minute rice, brown, and wild rice, follow directions on package.

FEATHERED RICE

1 cup long-grain rice	Salt
2 cups chicken broth, or vegetable juice, consommé, or soup stock	1 clove garlic, peeled and mashed

START oven at moderate (375 degrees F.). Spread rice on baking sheet, or in shallow pan, brown in oven, stirring with long-handled fork. When browned, pour into greased 2-quart baking dish. Add boiling chicken stock or other liquid, salt to taste, stir garlic evenly through mixture. Lower oven heat to 350 degrees F. Bake rice mixture 30 minutes. To this savory rice add about 1 cup hot cubed cooked meat, shellfish, ham, or game, 2 sliced hard-cooked eggs, or ¾ cup grated cheese. The rice without additions makes 2 or 3 servings. With any of the additions stirred through the baked rice, the casserole makes 4 servings.

HERBED WILD RICE

1 cup wild rice	½ teaspoon poultry seasoning
4 tablespoons butter	⅛ teaspoon dried thyme
¼ cup chopped peeled onions	¼ cup chopped chives
¼ cup chopped celery	4 cups chicken broth
1 teaspoon salt	

WASH rice thoroughly, drain. Melt butter, sauté onions and celery until golden. Add rice, salt, poultry seasoning, herbs, and broth. Simmer slowly about 20 minutes, or until tender and rice has absorbed liquid. Delicious as stuffing for fowl, duck, or game birds and to serve with cold meats. Makes 2 or more servings.

RED RICE, CAROLINA

1 cup raw Carolina rice

Ham bone with little meat on it

2 fresh or canned tomatoes

Salt and pepper

COMBINE rice and ham bone in kettle with cover. Add just enough water to cover, add cut up tomatoes and season to taste. Cover tightly. Cook gently (simmer, not boil) until rice is dry. Remove ham bone; mince the ham from the bone and add to rice, mix through. Serve hot. Excellent with roast chicken or game. Makes 4 servings.

★RICE PIE

2 cups boiled rice

2 tablespoons melted butter

1 beaten egg

2 cups well-seasoned leftover
  beef stew or any stew

2 hard-cooked eggs, sliced

2 tablespoons butter

2 tablespoons chopped parsley

START oven at moderate (350 degrees F.). Mix cooked rice with melted butter and beaten egg. Line 1½-quart deep baking dish with a little more than ½ of the rice mixture. Pour stew or meat mixture into center with sliced eggs. Cover with remaining rice. Dot with butter and sprinkle top with parsley. Bake in moderate oven about 20 minutes, or until top is light brown and bubbly. Makes 6 servings.

WILD RICE

The author of the rice book says it is impossible to give a hard and fast rule for the cooking of wild rice. The kernels vary as to length, thickness, and hardness.

The quick method of cooking wild rice is to wash it thoroughly with cold water, drain, place in a large saucepan, add 4 cups salted water per cup of rice. Cover and allow to simmer 20 minutes or longer. Do not overcook. It is at its best when cooked slowly so it will retain its nutty flavor.

FRIED WILD RICE WITH ALMONDS

½ cup salad oil

1 clove garlic, peeled and minced

½ cup chopped green pepper

½ cup chopped peeled onions

3 cups cooked wild rice

Salt, pepper, paprika

1 cup sliced blanched almonds

SAUTÉ garlic and vegetables in oil until softened. Add rice, seasonings, and almonds, stirring. Mix well, fry slowly, stirring constantly for about 7 minutes. Serve with veal stew. Or as a main dish. Makes 6 servings.

The six recipes above from RICE AND SPICE, *by Phyllis Jervey*

THE
"BEST-OF-ALL"

PIES AND TARTS

THE RECIPES THAT FOLLOW HAVE BEEN SELECTED FROM THESE DISTINGUISHED BOOKS:

Carolyn Coggins' Cookbook	*Carolyn Coggins*
500 Recipes by Request	*Jeanne M. Hall and*
	Belle Anderson Ebner
Good Neighbor Recipes	*Maxine Erickson and*
	Joan M. Rock
The New Joy of Cooking	*Irma S. Rombauer*
Wonderful Ways to Cook	*Edith Key Haines*

PIES AND TARTS

When making pie pastry, says Irma Rombauer in *The New Joy of Cooking,* all materials used should be as cold as possible. The water should be iced. Pie dough should be handled lightly and as little as possible. Here are some of her pastry recipes, starting with pastry for a 2-crust pie, or 2 single crusts.

PIE CRUST PASTRY

1¾ cups cake flour or 1½ cups all-purpose flour, sifted
½ teaspoon salt
1 teaspoon baking powder

4 tablespoons lard
2 tablespoons butter
¼ cup ice water

SIFT flour with salt and baking powder. Divide shortening into 2 parts. Cut half of shortening into flour mixture with two knives or a pastry blender until it looks like corn meal. Cut in remaining shortening coarsely until mixture is in lumps about the size of peas. Sprinkle 3 tablespoons ice water over mixture. Blend in lightly. If the dough will hold together so that it may be gathered up in a ball, stop handling it. If not, use a little additional water. Add last of ice water where ingredients are driest. Some cooks make fine pie crust with a fork, lifting the ingredients to permit the moisture to spread. Others use a spoon deftly, or touch the dough lightly with fingertips. If possible, chill dough 12 hours; if not, chill it for at least 10 minutes.

As soon as the dough will hold together, stop handling it. Divide into 2 parts, one slightly larger than the other. Keep smaller part for top crust. Chill it. Roll out larger part for bottom crust about ⅛ inch thick, using as little flour as possible on the board and on roller (or roll dough between sheets of waxed paper). Roll dough in one direction only. Lift roller, do not push to and fro. Do not stretch dough. Cut it 1 inch larger than the pan to allow for shrinkage in baking.

To lift pastry from board, fold it in half, lay the fold across the center of the pie pan, and unfold it, or roll dough around the rolling pin and unroll it onto the pan. Prick it with tines of fork in several places. Do not grease pan.

For 1-crust pie make a fluted edge around pan with dough that laps over, or build up a rim with a narrow strip of pastry. "Full" this strip on, pressing with fingers, or press with fork.

If pie is to be filled with juicy mixture, brush bottom pastry lightly with white of egg or melted butter. Fill pie (according to recipe), moisten edge of pastry rim with water. Roll dough for top crust, cut it 1 inch larger than pan, prick with tines of fork in several places, or fold over and make decorative gashes with knife (stem with leaves is the old-time favorite gash) to allow steam to escape. Place top crust on filled pie. "Full" in the surplus dough and crimp to edge of bottom pastry or press it around edge with fork, or cut lower crust ½ inch larger than upper crust and fold it over upper-crust edge, like hem.

Top may be brushed with milk or with 1 beaten egg mixed with 1 tablespoon water. This makes a glossy top.

If pie is filled with juicy fruit or custard, fasten a piece of parchment tape around it, which is removed, of course, before serving.

For lattice top. Cut pastry for top crust into ½-inch-wide strips with a knife or pastry jagger. Place strips across top of pie, making lattice effect, moisten rim of lower crust slightly with water where strips meet edge of pie, press end of strip gently to lower pastry rim.

To bake empty shell. Consult pie recipes. Or bake pie pastry on bottom of pie pan, that is, invert pan and fit dough over pan. Prick in several places with tines of fork, press down lightly around edge. Cut a round of pastry for top crust. Prick it, and bake on baking sheet.

Use same procedure for tarts, using muffin pans. Cut dough into rounds 4½ to 5½ inches across, fit into or over back of muffin pans, prick with fork. Bake large shell, or tart shells in very hot oven (500 degrees F.) 10 minutes, or until slightly browned.

Pie dough may be made in advance, wrapped in waxed paper and placed in refrigerator. It will keep for 3 or 4 days.

CHEESE PIE CRUST

Add ⅓ cup grated American cheese to regular pastry or Hot Water Pie Crust.

HOT WATER PIE CRUST

½ cup lard
¼ cup boiling water
1½ cups cake flour

½ teaspoon baking powder
½ teaspoon salt

PLACE lard in bowl, pour boiling water over it. Beat until cold and creamy. Chill a few minutes or longer. Sift cake flour and measure, sift again with baking powder and salt. Combine lard mixture with dry ingredients and stir until they form a smooth ball. Cover dough and chill until firm. Roll. Makes pastry for 2-crust pie, or 2 single pie shells.

Dough will keep for 1 week in refrigerator; age improves it.

APPLE PIE

Pastry for 2-crust pie
6 medium-size apples
½ to ⅔ cup granulated or
  brown sugar, packed
¼ teaspoon ground cinnamon
⅛ teaspoon ground nutmeg

⅛ teaspoon salt
1 tablespoon cornstarch
1½ tablespoons butter
1 tablespoon lemon juice
½ teaspoon grated lemon peel
2 tablespoons water or cream

LINE 9-inch pie pan with Pie Crust Pastry or Cheese Pie Crust. Pare, core, and cut apples into very thin pieces. Combine sugar, spices, salt, and cornstarch, sift over apples, stir apples gently until pieces are well coated. Place in layers in pastry-lined pie pan. Dot with butter. Sprinkle with lemon juice and peel. Add water or cream.

Start oven at very hot (450 degrees F.). Cover filled pie pan with top layer of pastry, crimp edge or press with fork. Prick top with tines of fork. Bake for 10 minutes at very hot temperature, then reduce oven to moderate (350 degrees F.). Bake for about 45 minutes to 1 hour. Crust should be well browned. Serve warm or cold. Makes 1 pie, 6 servings.

Very juicy apples require 1½ tablespoons cornstarch; spices may be omitted, and if apples are a flavorful variety, omit lemon juice and peel.

Cheese Apple Pie. Bake pie without upper crust in very hot oven (450 degrees F.) for 20 minutes. Then sprinkle over top 1 cup grated cheese. Place pie under broiler heat to melt and brown cheese. Serve warm.

Sour Cream Apple Pie. Make 1-crust apple pie, use the larger amount of sugar, brown sugar preferred. Omit butter. After filling pie shell with apples, pour 1 cup thick sour cream over the apples. Bake as described for Apple Pie.

The pie pastry information and six recipes above from THE NEW JOY OF COOKING, *by Irma S. Rombauer*

Sometimes a fancy pie shell adds a delectable flavor, a gourmet surprise touch to a familiar pie. Carolyn Coggins is well known for the unusual, the especially good variations of familiar cookery themes which she gives in her book, *Carolyn Coggins' Company Cookbook*. Here are some of her special pie crusts.

GRAHAM-CRACKER CRUST

1¼ cups graham-cracker crumbs   ¼ cup sugar
  (about 16 crackers)   ½ cup butter or margarine

MIX crumbs and sugar together. Melt butter or margarine and combine smoothly and evenly with crumbs and sugar. Press mixture against sides and in bottom of a 9-inch pie plate. (Removal will be easier if pan is first lined with aluminum foil.) Chill shell until firm. Or start oven at moderate (375 degrees F.) and bake 8 minutes. Let cool or chill before using. Makes one 9-inch pie shell.

SCALLOPED VANILLA-WAFER SHELL

30 vanilla wafers, rolled   3 tablespoons softened butter or
  (1 cup crumbs)   margarine
          10 additional vanilla wafers

ROLL or grind about 30 wafers to make 1 cup crumbs. Mix with softened butter or margarine, blend thoroughly. Press mixture evenly and firmly in bottom and along sides of 9-inch pie pan. To form scalloped edge, cut 10 wafers in half and place cut side down around the crumb shell. Chill about ½ hour. Or start oven at moderate (375 degrees F.), and bake 8 minutes. Chill before using. Makes one 9-inch pie shell.

MERINGUE SHELL

4 egg whites   ¼ teaspoon salt
¼ teaspoon cream of tartar   1 cup sugar

START oven at slow (250 degrees F.). Beat egg whites until foamy, add cream of tartar and salt, continue beating the mixture until it is stiff but not dry. Add sugar gradually, beating until meringue is stiff. Arrange meringue in a large circle about 9 inches in diameter and from about ½ to ¾-inch thick on several thicknesses of paper towels on a baking sheet. Build up sides with remaining meringue to height of 1½ inches. Bake in slow oven 2 hours, or until meringue shell is dry and lightly browned. Let cool. Makes one 9-inch shell.

BAKED COCONUT CRUST

⅓ cup butter
3 tablespoons sugar
1 egg yolk

1 cup all-purpose flour, sifted
1 cup shredded coconut

COMBINE butter and sugar and blend well. Add egg yolk, mix thoroughly. Add flour and mix well; add coconut, blend evenly. Pat coconut mixture into greased 9-inch pie pan or plate, shaping evenly into pie shell. Chill ½ hour. Start oven at moderate (350 degrees F.). Bake pie shell until brown, about 25 minutes. Let cool. Makes one 9-inch pie shell.

★CHOCOLATE COCONUT CRUST, UNBAKED

2 tablespoons butter
2 (1-oz.) squares unsweetened chocolate

⅔ cup sifted confectioners' sugar
2 tablespoons hot milk or water
1½ cups shredded coconut

COMBINE butter and chocolate in top of double boiler over hot water, stir until chocolate is melted. Combine sugar and milk or water, stir, add to chocolate mixture. Add coconut and stir well. Spread and press in bottom and sides of greased 9-inch pie pan. Chill until firm. Makes one 9-inch pie shell.

GINGERSNAP CRUST

1½ cups crushed gingersnap crumbs
2 tablespoons sugar

¼ cup butter, softened but not melted

START oven at moderate (350 degrees F.). Combine crumbs and sugar. Blend butter in with pastry cutter or fingers very thoroughly. Line 8-inch pie pan with crumbs mixture, press against side and in bottom of pan to fit smoothly. Bake in moderate oven 10 to 15 minutes. Let cool. Makes one 8-inch pie shell.

The six recipes above from CAROLYN COGGINS' COMPANY COOKBOOK

❦

And here are answers to a hostess's prayers, four of the many excellent pies Edith Key Haines gives in her book, *Wonderful Ways To Cook,* perfect for the best of all parties.

CHOCOLATE PIE CORONET

Unbaked 10-inch pie shell
½ cup cocoa powder
3 cups rich milk
5 eggs

1 teaspoon salt
¼ cup sugar
2 teaspoons vanilla extract
Meringue or whipped cream

MAKE your best pie pastry, using favorite recipe or a mix. Start oven at moderate (350 degrees F.). Place cocoa in saucepan, stir in 1 cup milk gradually, stir and cook over low heat until scalded and blended. Beat eggs with salt added until light-colored and creamy. Add sugar and continue beating until thick and fluffy. Add remaining milk to the cocoa and gradually stir cocoa mixture into egg mixture. Add vanilla and beat. Pour into unbaked pie shell. Bake in center of moderate oven for 1 hour and 15 minutes, or until silver knife blade inserted in center comes out clean. Let cool, cover with meringue, and brown lightly in oven or under broiler. Or cover with whipped cream, using pastry bag. Makes 6 to 8 servings.

PRUNE PECAN PIE

Baked 8-inch pie shell
12 prunes
2 tablespoons cornstarch
¾ cup corn syrup
⅛ teaspoon salt
Grated peel 1 lemon

3 egg yolks
1 tablespoon butter
½ cup coarsely-chopped pecans
2 tablespoons vanilla extract, or
   1 tablespoon sherry
Brown Sugar Meringue

PREPARE and bake pastry shell. Cook prunes and cut up, removing pits. Mix cornstarch with a little of the syrup in top of double boiler over hot water, stir until smooth. Add remaining syrup, salt, lemon peel, and egg yolks, beat well. Add butter, cook over boiling water 10 minutes, or until thickened, stirring constantly. Remove from heat, add prunes, nuts, vanilla or sherry, and let cool slightly. Fill pie shell and set it aside until it is cold and stiffened. Cover with meringue and brown slightly in oven or under broiler. Makes 5 to 6 servings.

BROWN SUGAR MERINGUE

½ cup medium-brown sugar,
  packed
3 egg whites

⅛ teaspoon salt
1 teaspoon vanilla extract

Start oven at moderate (350 degrees F.). Rub sugar through a medium strainer or sieve. Beat egg whites, salt, and vanilla in large bowl until rounded peaks are formed when beater is removed. Add sugar gradually and continue beating until stiff-pointed peaks are formed and the texture is fine, smooth, and shiny. (Use large bowl, egg whites need plenty of room to expand; use electric beater if possible.)

Arrange on top of pie, and if you like, sprinkle lightly with granulated sugar. Brown slightly in moderate oven or under broiler heat. A brown-sugar meringue is slightly coarser than a white-sugar meringue, but has greater volume and is delicious. Makes right amount for one pie.

DEEP PEACH PIE

4½ pounds fresh peaches   1 tablespoon butter
½ cup sugar   Puff pastry, or rich pie pastry to
¼ cup strawberry jam   cover 8-inch pan

WASH, peel, stone, and slice peaches. Start oven at hot (425 degrees F.) . Arrange sliced peaches in buttered glass baking dish 10½ × 6½ inches or in 8-inch round baking dish. Sprinkle first 2 layers of peaches with sugar, dot with jam and butter, sprinkle top layer with sugar only. Cover with pastry, crimp to edge of dish, and gash with decorative cuts to let steam out. Bake in center of hot oven 45 to 50 minutes, or until crust is delicately browned. Serve slightly warm or cold. Makes 6 servings.

SOUR CREAM COCONUT PIE

Pastry for 1-crust 8-inch pie   1 cup commercial sour cream
3 egg yolks   2 teaspoons vanilla extract
½ cup sugar   1 (4-oz.) can moist coconut finely
¼ teaspoon salt   chopped
1 tablespoon flour   3 egg whites for meringue
¼ teaspoon ground cinnamon

MAKE pastry by favorite recipe or use mix. Line 8-inch pie pan, flute edge. Start oven at very hot (450 degrees F.) . Beat yolks, sugar, and salt together with rotary beater for 5 minutes. Sift flour and cinnamon together into yolks and beat. Stir in sour cream and add vanilla and coconut. Mix, and pour into pastry-lined pie plate. Bake on rack placed in lowest groove in very hot oven 15 minutes, then reduce heat to very slow oven (280 degrees F.) , place pan on middle rack of oven, and continue baking 20 to 25 minutes, or until filling shrinks a little from crust and is puffed and lightly browned. Remove from oven. Overbaking will cause pie to crack. Make Brown Sugar Meringue (above) , using the 3 egg whites; spoon onto pie and brown lightly. Makes 5 servings.

The four recipes above from WONDERFUL WAYS TO COOK, *by Edith Key Haines*

❧

In the introduction to the pie and pastry pages of *500 Recipes by Request,* the authors Jeanne M. Hall and Belle Anderson Ebner say, "We discovered long ago that Pecan Pie had to be on our menu [at Hotel Anderson] every single meal—including breakfast—and so it is. We suggest you cut smaller pieces of this pie and our Black Walnut Pie than you do with other pies!"
Here are some of their best (all are best) pies.

AMBASSADOR BLACK BOTTOM PIE

1 tablespoon gelatin
¼ cup cold water
4 eggs
2 cups rich milk, scalded
1 cup sugar
1¼ tablespoons cornstarch
1½ (1-oz.) squares chocolate, melted

1 teaspoon vanilla extract
Baked Gingersnap Crust
¼ teaspoon cream of tartar
1 teaspoon rum flavoring, or 1 tablespoon rum
1 cup heavy cream
2 tablespoons powdered sugar
½ (1-oz.) square chocolate, shaved

Soak gelatin in the cold water. Beat egg yolks in top of double boiler; slowly add milk. Combine ½ cup sugar and the cornstarch and stir into egg mixture. Cook over hot water, stirring occasionally, 20 minutes, or until custard heavily coats spoon. Remove from heat and pour 1 cup of the custard into a bowl. Add melted chocolate to this, beat well with rotary beater. When cool, blend in vanilla. Pour into cooled Gingersnap Pastry Shell. Chill thoroughly.

While remaining custard is still hot, blend in gelatin and stir until dissolved. Let cool, but do not let stiffen. Beat egg whites until frothy, add cream of tartar and beat, gradually adding the remaining ½ cup sugar; beat until stiff. While gelatin-and-custard mixture is smooth and soft, fold in egg whites and blend in rum or rum flavoring.

As soon as the chocolate custard in pie shell has stiffened, cover with fluffy rum-custard mixture. Chill few minutes until firm. Then spread top with whipped cream which has been mixed with powdered sugar. Sprinkle shaved chocolate over top. Makes 6 servings.

BANANA-CURRANT PIE

¾ cup sugar
⅓ cup all-purpose flour, sifted
2 cups milk, scalded
2 eggs
1 teaspoon butter

1 teaspoon vanilla extract
Baked 9-inch pastry shell
1 (6-oz.) glass currant jelly
3 ripe bananas, sliced
4 tablespoons sugar

Mix sugar and flour and combine with milk in top of double boiler over hot water. Cook, stirring constantly, until thickened. Slowly add beaten yolks, continue cooking 2 or 3 minutes. Remove from heat, add butter and vanilla. (If custard curdles, beat with rotary beater before chilling.) Set aside to cool. Line sides and bottom of baked, cooled pastry shell with a thin layer of jelly. Cut bananas into small pieces and fold into custard. Pour custard into prepared pastry shell. Beat egg whites stiff, gradually adding the 4 tablespoons sugar. Spread this meringue over custard filling. Start oven at moderate (350 degrees F.) . Place meringue-covered pie in oven and brown lightly, about 15 minutes. Makes 6 servings.

BLACK WALNUT PIE

1 cup finely-chopped black walnuts
1 cup brown sugar, packed
¾ cup light molasses
2 tablespoons flour

½ teaspoon salt
1 cup water
1 beaten egg
Pastry-lined 9-inch pan

START oven at moderate (350 degrees F.). Combine nuts, sugar, and molasses. Mix flour, salt, and water, stirring smoothly; add egg and mix. Combine nut mixture with egg mixture, pour into pastry-lined pan. Bake in moderate oven 50 minutes, or until light brown. Makes 6 servings.

COFFEE PIE

30 marshmallows
1 cup very strong hot coffee
1 tablespoon butter

1 cup heavy cream
½ cup finely-chopped nuts
Baked 9-inch pastry shell

CUT marshmallows in quarters. Dissolve butter in coffee and pour over marshmallows; let cool. Whip cream and fold into coffee mixture, sprinkle with nuts. Pour into baked, cooled pie shell, chill in refrigerator. Makes 6 servings.

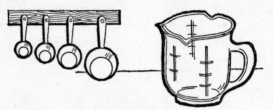

PECAN PIE

4 slightly-beaten eggs
1 cup dark corn syrup
2 teaspoons vanilla extract
1 cup sugar
½ teaspoon salt

3 tablespoons melted butter
Pastry for 9-inch pie shell
½ tablespoon flour
1 cup coarsely-chopped pecans

BEAT eggs, syrup, vanilla, sugar, and salt together. Add melted butter. Start oven at very hot (450 degrees F.). Line 9-inch pie pan with pastry, crimp edge; sprinkle flour over pastry. Arrange pecans evenly in shell. Pour filling in slowly. Place in very hot oven and bake 10 minutes. Reduce heat to moderate (350 degrees F.) and continue baking 50 minutes more. Pecan pies are particularly dependent on proper baking: remove from heat when filling still quivers a little; do not bake until the filling is completely firm. Let cool. Makes 6 servings.

PUMPKIN CHIFFON PIE

3 eggs	1 teaspoon ground ginger
1¼ cups strained cooked pumpkin	⅛ teaspoon ground cloves
2 tablespoons melted butter	1 tablespoon gelatin
½ cup brown sugar, packed	¼ cup cold water
½ teaspoon salt	6 tablespoons sugar
1 teaspoon ground cinnamon	Baked 9-inch pastry shell
½ teaspoon ground nutmeg	1 cup heavy cream

BEAT egg yolks slightly in top of double boiler; add pumpkin, butter, brown sugar, salt, and spices. Cook over hot water, stirring occasionally until mixture thickens. Remove from heat; add gelatin, which has been softened in the cold water. Stir until smooth, let cool. Beat egg whites stiff, slowly adding 6 tablespoons sugar. Fold into pumpkin mixture, pour into cooled pastry shell. Top with whipped cream. Makes 6 servings.

The six recipes above from 500 RECIPES BY REQUEST, *by Jeanne M. Hall and Belle Anderson Ebner*

In *Good Neighbor Recipes* the authors, Maxine Erickson and Joan M. Rock, offer the homemaker some very practical, helpful advice as well as delicious recipes.

"When baking a pie, we look to the future and some time-saving by shaping and baking 6 or 8 tart shells. Rounds of pastry, fitted over the backs of muffin pans or in patty pans, well pricked (with fork) before baking, produce pastry shells which can be converted quickly into desserts.

"Let baked tart shells cool completely. Carefully store in covered tin box, with crumpled waxed paper in and around each shell to prevent chipping or breaking.

"In addition to packaged puddings which may be cooked and used to fill tart shells, almost any pie mixture can be baked in tart shells."

★GLAZED WALNUT MINCE TARTS

Here is a quickie using baked tart shells. It always brings compliments far in excess of the time and work involved. Spoon canned moist mincemeat into baked tart shells. Top with coarsely broken walnut meats. Drizzle a little honey over nuts. Place under broiler heat a few minutes to glaze. Serve warm or cold.

★JIG-TIME BANANA BUTTERSCOTCH PIE OR TARTS

Baked and cooled 8- or 9-inch
pastry shell, or
6 baked and cooled tart shells

1 package butterscotch pie filling
Sliced ripe bananas
Whipped cream

HAVE pastry shells baked and cooled. Have butterscotch filling cooked, cooled but not "set." Slice bananas directly into pastry shells. Pour cooled filling over bananas at once. Spread whipped cream on top. Chill thoroughly. Just before serving, garnish with banana slices. Makes 6 servings.

RUM-WHIPPED CREAM PIE OR TARTS

Baked, cooled 9-inch pie shell,
crumb crust, or 6 tart shells
1 tablespoon gelatin
¼ cup cold water
1 cup milk, scalded
6 tablespoons sugar

⅛ teaspoon salt
2 egg whites
3 tablespoons rum
1 cup heavy cream
Grated sweet chocolate

SOFTEN gelatin in cold water, then stir into scalded milk until dissolved. Add sugar; stir until both sugar and gelatin are completely dissolved. Chill until mixture is just ready to set. Add salt to egg whites, beat until stiff but not dry. With same egg beater, whip thickened gelatin until light and spongy. Fold beaten egg whites and rum into gelatin mixture. Whip cream and fold in lightly. Pour into pie shell or tart shells, sprinkle grated chocolate on top. Chill until firm.

The three recipes above from GOOD NEIGHBOR RECIPES, *by Maxine Erickson and Joan M. Rock*

Additional tart recipes, also puff paste, in Foreign section. *See* Index.

THE "BEST-OF-ALL"

POULTRY AND GAME BIRD DISHES

THE RECIPES THAT FOLLOW HAVE BEEN SELECTED FROM THESE DISTINGUISHED BOOKS:

Evelyn Patterson's Gourmet Kitchen	*Evelyn Patterson*
Kitchens Near and Far	*Herman Smith*
Marian Tracy's Complete Chicken Cookery	*Marian Tracy*
The New Cook It in a Casserole	*Florence Brobeck*
The New Serve It Buffet	*Florence Brobeck*
Wild Game (Wild Fowl) Cook Book	*Martin Rywell*

POULTRY AND
GAME BIRDS

When buying dressed, ready-to-cook chicken or other poultry for the table, count on about ¾ pound, as purchased, for each person. A 5-pound fowl will give about 3 cups diced cooked meat for creamed dishes, pies, salads, and aspics. A 4½-pound roasting chicken makes about 6 servings, sometimes more. A duckling, braised or roasted, serves 1 to 4 (usually breast meat only) depending on size; cold roast duck slices economically and serves 4 easily. A guinea hen is usually cooked like chicken, and makes the same number of servings. Squab and squab-chickens (the latter are small, compact, usually cooked whole—but see recipes) make 1 serving each. Most game birds make 1 to 2 servings each, depending on the bird and the way it is cooked. A 15-pound turkey will serve 20 people, 1 serving each, slightly more when cold and carefully cut for buffet service.

The basic ways of cooking chicken and other poultry are broiled, fried, roasted, stewed (boiled, poached, fricasseed), and prepared variously in casseroles. Cooks all over the world have created variations on these simple themes, and the result is a richly diversified and seemingly endless harvest of good chicken recipes.

To broil chicken or turkey (small broiler turkey), use young birds only, under moderate broiler heat, the broiler pan with halved birds or smaller pieces, skin-side down, brushed with melted butter and seasoned with salt and pepper or with other seasonings such as herbs, onion juice, or a marinade according to recipes. The birds should be about 5 to 6 inches from the heat. Turn pieces from time to time, broil until tender and well browned, about 30 minutes, or according to some special recipe variation.

To roast chicken, guinea hen, turkey, use moderate (325 to 350 degrees F.) oven. A small roasting bird (2½ to 4 pounds) will need about 1-hour cooking time, a 4- to 5-pound bird from about

1½ to 2 hours. Brush bird with butter, or whatever recipe suggests; use open pan; count on more roasting time when bird is stuffed. The bird is done when flesh is slightly shrunken beneath crisp skin and the thick portion of breast and thighs is tender and does not drip pink juice when speared carefully with fork or skewer, and when joints are not stiff when worked gently with fingers (fingers in cooking mit, or protected with foil and a folded towel!)

The best roasting turkeys weigh from 10 to 16 pounds. Follow directions for roasting stuffed chicken (above). For 12-pound turkey, allow 25 to 35 minutes per pound roasting time, depending on plumpness of bird. Details of selection, preparations, stuffings, and cooking time are given in the recipes.

The quest for the best-of-all chicken recipes for this book led first to *Marian Tracy's Complete Chicken Cookery,* the thorough, interesting and abundantly varied volume Marian Tracy put together after long research and months of special test cookery. A well seasoned chicken fricassee is first in her collection.

CHICKEN FRICASSEE

1 ready-to-cook stewing chicken (about 3 pounds) cut for frying	3 tablespoons chicken fat
Boiling water	About ½ cup flour
1 medium-size onion, peeled and chopped	3 cups chicken broth
4 peppercorns, 2 whole cloves, 1 piece bay leaf	½ teaspoon grated lemon peel
	¼ teaspoon black pepper
	2 to 3 tablespoons white wine
1 tablespoon salt	1 egg yolk
	¼ cup light cream

RINSE chicken, drain. Place in large pot and barely cover with boiling water. Add onion, peppercorns, cloves, bay leaf, and salt. Simmer until meat is tender, about 2½ to 3 hours. Take chicken out, strain broth. Make fricassee gravy: mix chicken fat and flour in large saucepan over heat, add 3 cups broth slowly, stirring; cook and stir constantly until thickened. Add lemon peel, pepper, and white wine.

Add more seasoning if needed. Let simmer about 5 minutes. Add chicken to gravy and heat. Beat egg yolk and cream together and add a little of the hot gravy, stirring until blended. Pour into the gravy-and-chicken mixture and cook 2 to 3 minutes, stirring all the time. Serve at once. Makes 5 to 6 servings.

Usually served with hot rice, or on mashed potatoes, or on split and toasted biscuits.

★BRUNSWICK STEW

4-pound chicken, disjointed
¼ cup butter or bacon drippings
½ cup chopped peeled onions
5 tomatoes, peeled and quartered,
　or No. 2½ can
1 cup boiling water
6 whole cloves

Pepper and salt
2 or 3 cups fresh, or 2 packages
　quick-frozen lima beans
2 or 3 cups corn cut from cob, or
　canned whole-kernel corn
2 teaspoons Worcestershire sauce
1 cup toasted bread crumbs

RINSE chicken, pat dry. Brown chicken in the fat in a large heavy pan or Dutch oven. Add onions, tomatoes, 1 cup boiling water, cloves, and pepper. Simmer together until chicken is nearly tender, about 40 minutes. Add lima beans and corn. Cover, simmer until chicken is done and vegetables tender, about 20 minutes longer. Season with salt, pepper, and Worchestershire. Stir in crumbs. Makes 8 servings.

CHICKEN AND CLAM SOUFFLE

3 tablespoons butter
3 tablespoons flour
1 (7-oz.) can minced clams
1 cup juice from clams, or add
　milk to clam juice to fill cup

Salt, pepper
1 (8-oz.) can boned chicken,
　chopped fine
3 eggs
⅓ cup finely-chopped parsley

START oven at moderate (350 degrees F.). Grease 2-quart deep soufflé dish. Melt butter in large saucepan, blend flour in smoothly, add clam liquid, salt, and pepper, stirring constantly until smooth and thick. Stir in drained clams and chicken, mix well. Remove from heat, blend in beaten yolks. Whip egg whites stiff and fold in with parsley. Pour at once into prepared baking dish; set dish in shallow pan of hot water. Bake in moderate oven 45 to 50 minutes, or until top is golden brown and springs back when lightly touched. Serve at once. Makes 4 servings.

CHICKEN BREASTS WITH
WHITE WINE AND WHITE GRAPES

4 plump chicken breasts, split
4 tablespoons butter
Salt and pepper

½ cup dry white wine
¾ cup white seedless grapes

START oven at moderate (350 degrees F.). Rinse chicken, pat dry. Spread pieces with butter, bake in moderate oven ½ hour. Add wine and baste chicken with wine and butter from the pan. Continue cooking, basting frequently, another 20 minutes, or until chicken is browned and tender. Just before breasts are done, add the grapes, spooning over chicken and into pan sauce. Serve on warmed platter. Makes 4 servings.

CHICKEN PIE WITH SWEET POTATO CRUST

2 cups diced or sliced cooked
  chicken
2 green peppers, sliced thin
1 (No. 2) can small boiled onions
  (drained, save juice)
⅓ cup finely-chopped parsley

2 tablespoons butter
2 tablespoons flour
2 cups chicken broth
1 teaspoon grated lemon peel
Salt and pepper

PUT a layer of chicken in 2-quart baking dish, a layer of green pepper, then a layer of onions. Sprinkle generously with parsley. Repeat until all ingredients are used. Make a thin sauce by melting butter over moderate heat, blending in flour, and adding chicken broth slowly, stirring until thickened and smooth; add lemon peel, a little salt and pepper, mix. Pour over chicken in baking dish. Then top with Sweet Potato Crust and bake in moderate oven about 40 minutes. Makes 6 servings.

SWEET POTATO CRUST

1 cup mashed cooked sweet potatoes (canned may be used,
  just mash with fork)
¼ cup melted butter
1 beaten egg
1 tablespoon grated orange peel

1 tablespoon orange juice (2 tablespoons undiluted frozen
  concentrate)
1 cup all-purpose flour, sifted
1 teaspoon baking powder
½ teaspoon salt

Start oven at moderate (350 degrees F.). Mix sweet potato with butter, egg, orange peel, and juice. Sift flour with baking powder, combine with potato mixture, beating until smooth. Roll out on lightly-floured board to about ¼-inch thickness and shape to fit top of casserole. Place on top, crimp on as for pie crust, and bake in moderate oven about 40 minutes.

CHICKEN SMOTHERED IN ONION RINGS

2 chicken breasts, split
1 large onion, peeled and sliced
  very thin
3 tablespoons butter

1 tablespoon lemon juice
Salt and pepper
1 teaspoon Worcestershire sauce

START oven at moderate (350 degrees F.). Butter shallow baking dish. Rinse chicken, drain. Place in casserole, cover with onion rings, dot with butter, sprinkle with lemon juice, a little salt and pepper, and the Worcestershire sauce. Cover, and bake in moderate oven 45 minutes; uncover dish and bake until tender and done, about 15 minutes longer. Makes 4 servings.

HAM AND CHICKEN PIE WITH OYSTERS

2 cups sliced cooked chicken
½ pound sliced cooked ham, slices cut in quarters
1 pint bulk oysters

3 cups chicken gravy made with the oyster liquor as part of the liquid
Pastry for 1-crust pie
2 tablespoons milk

START oven at very hot (450 degrees F.). Make layer of chicken in casserole, add layer of ham and layer of oysters, repeat until all ingredients are used. Pour gravy over all. Place pastry on top, and crimp to edge of dish as for any pie. Pierce with tines of fork. Brush crust with milk. Bake in very hot oven 20 to 30 minutes, or until crust is well browned. Makes 4 servings.

SIMPLE AND SAVORY BARBECUED CHICKEN

2½ to 3½ pound broiler-fryer chicken, cut as for frying
2 tablespoons fat
1 medium-size onion, peeled and chopped
1 (8-oz.) can tomato sauce

½ tablespoon prepared mustard
1 teaspoon salt
1 tablespoon vinegar
2 tablespoons brown sugar
1 tablespoon Worcestershire sauce
½ cup hot water

RINSE chicken and pat dry. Brown chicken 15 to 20 minutes in fat in frying pan, turning pieces occasionally. Remove chicken to roasting pan. Start oven at moderate (350 degrees F.). Cook onion in pan in which chicken browned; when tender, add remaining ingredients and ½ cup hot water. Stir to mix; simmer 10 minutes, stirring well. Pour over chicken in baking pan. Bake in moderate oven about 1 hour, basting frequently with sauce in pan. If sauce cooks down too much, add little hot water or tomato juice. Makes 4 to 5 servings.

STEWED CHICKEN WITH DUMPLINGS

3½-pound chicken, cut in pieces
3 tablespoons fat from under skin

⅓ cup chopped peeled onions
Salt and pepper

RINSE chicken and drain. Brown in chicken fat in kettle, adding onions and seasoning. Add 1 quart hot water, cover, bring to boiling, then reduce to simmering temperature and let simmer about 2 hours; top with Dumplings. Makes 4 servings.

DUMPLINGS

1 cup all-purpose flour, sifted
2 teaspoons baking powder
½ teaspoon salt

½ cup milk
Cornstarch

Sift flour, baking powder and salt together into bowl, stir milk in gradually, mixing to a batter. Increase heat under chicken kettle; when liquid is boiling rapidly, drop spoonfuls of batter in. Cover kettle and cook 5 to 8 minutes, or until dumplings are puffy and light. Remove chicken and dumplings to warmed serving dish; keep them warm while thickening sauce in kettle with 1 tablespoon cornstarch. Stir, and boil sauce 2 or 3 minutes. Pour over chicken and dumplings. Serve at once.

The nine recipes above from MARIAN TRACY'S COMPLETE CHICKEN COOKERY

🌿

The author of *Evelyn Patterson's Gourmet Kitchen,* is the youngest of nine children of a Dutch family. She gathered recipes in Europe and the Middle East, and now, settled in New Jersey, has taught gourmet and advanced cookery in an adult school in Princeton, does catering, sells her own packaged frozen crêpes Suzette, and is a mother and hostess in a busy household. Her book is small, but a rich source of the delectable, unusual dishes which make guests sigh with pleasure and beg for the recipes.

Here are some of Evelyn Patterson's favorite chicken recipes.

CHICKEN CITRON

The author comments on this dish: "A most elegant way to serve chicken and most simple to prepare."

6 pounds frying chicken, or 4 or 5 pounds chicken legs and split breasts
½ cup butter
2 tablespoons sherry
2 tablespoons white wine
Grated peel 1 medium orange
Grated peel 1 large lemon
3 teaspoons lemon juice
Salt and pepper
1½ cups light cream
4 tablespoons grated Parmesan cheese
3 to 5 cups hot boiled rice

RINSE chicken, pat dry. Remove skin. Sauté chicken in heavy skillet in foaming butter until golden brown all over. Cover and continue to cook over low heat until tender, about 20 minutes longer. Remove chicken from pan. Stir sherry and white wine into pan drippings; add orange and lemon peel, lemon juice, and a little salt and pepper. Mix, stir cream in slowly. Return chicken to skillet and shake pan over low heat about 5 minutes. Arrange chicken on warmed serving platter, pour pan sauce over, sprinkle with cheese and serve at once. Fluffy boiled rice makes a perfect accompaniment. The sauce will be thin. Makes 6 servings.

CHICKEN BREASTS IN CREAM AND BRANDY

6 small chicken breasts, split
Salt and pepper
½ cup butter
½ pound mushrooms, sliced

3 tablespoons (2 jiggers) brandy, warmed
1 tablespoon flour
1½ cups heavy cream, heated
1½ teaspoons tomato paste

RINSE chicken, pat dry. Season pieces with salt and pepper, and cook in butter in heavy skillet over moderate heat about 30 minutes. Turn them often. When chicken is brown and tender, add mushrooms and cook another 5 minutes. Pour warm brandy over, and touch with lighted match to blaze it. When flame dies down, remove chicken and mushrooms to warmed serving dish, and keep it warm in hot oven with oven door left open. Blend flour into juices in pan, stirring smoothly; stir hot cream in slowly, mixing well, and stir in tomato paste. When very hot, pour over chicken and mushrooms. Serve at once. Makes 6 servings.

GARLIC FRIED CHICKEN

2 small frying chickens, cut in
  serving pieces
1 cup sour cream
2 tablespoons lemon juice
¼ teaspoon Worcestershire sauce
1 large clove garlic, peeled and
  mashed

½ teaspoon salt
¼ teaspoon pepper
¼ teaspoon celery salt
⅛ teaspoon paprika
Flour for dredging
Butter for frying

RINSE chicken, pat dry. Place in bowl which has tight-fitting cover. Mix all ingredients except flour and butter and pour over chicken, taking care that all pieces are covered. Cover bowl and let stand in refrigerator 12 hours. When ready to fry, lift pieces out of sauce and dredge with flour. Fry in about 1 inch of hot butter in heavy skillet over low heat, turning pieces frequently to prevent burning. Or deep-fry pieces. Makes 6 or more servings.

The three recipes above from EVELYN PATTERSON'S GOURMET KITCHEN

❀

One of my own books, *The New Cook It in a Casserole,* is a good source of wonderful chicken recipes given me by friends, chefs, and gastronomes I've met here and there. I serve this one often; it is simple and guests always ask for the recipe.

BAKED DEVILED CHICKEN

4-pound chicken, boiled or roasted
Prepared mustard (mild)
2 tablespoons finely-chopped
  parsley
1 cup medium white sauce

1 teaspoon Worcestershire sauce
¼ cup heavy cream
Salt
Paprika

SLICE all meat from bones. Start oven at moderate (350 degrees F.), and butter 1-quart wide baking dish. Spread chicken in dish, spoon mustard generously over all. Sprinkle with parsley. Combine white sauce, Worcestershire, and cream, add salt if needed. Pour over chicken, sprinkle lightly with paprika. Bake in moderate oven 25 minutes, until bubbly, and top is browning. Makes 6 servings.

CHICKEN MARSALA

Small roasting chicken, quartered
4 tablespoons butter or margarine
1 pint Marsala
½ clove garlic, peeled and
  chopped
1 teaspoon mixed dried herbs,
  marjoram, basil, rosemary

3 whole cloves
1½ teaspoons salt
½ teaspoon pepper
½ teaspoon paprika
4 tablespoons grated Gruyère
  cheese

START oven at moderate (325 degrees F.). Rinse chicken, pat dry. Brown chicken in butter or margarine in flameproof (metal-base) casserole. Add wine, garlic, herbs, cloves, salt, and pepper. Cover, bake in moderate oven 1 hour. Baste frequently during baking with liquid in baking dish. Uncover at end of hour, and let chicken bake and brown 20 to 30 minutes longer. Sprinkle top with paprika and generously with cheese, continue to bake until cheese is melted and browning. Makes 4 servings.

GOOBER CHICKEN CASSEROLE

2 chicken breasts, halved, or 1
  small frying chicken, cut in
  serving pieces
Poultry seasoning, or salt, pepper,
  paprika and celery salt

4 tablespoons butter or margarine
½ cup bouillon
1 cup chopped peanuts
1 cup light cream
½ cup sour cream

RINSE chicken, pat dry. Sprinkle pieces with poultry seasoning (or mixture of salt, pepper, paprika, and celery salt). Brown chicken in butter or margarine in flameproof (metal-base) casserole. Pour bouillon around chicken. Start oven at moderate (350 degrees F.). Bake chicken 45 minutes. Mix peanuts, cream, and sour cream and pour over chicken. Add light sprinkling of poultry seasoning, and continue baking 15 minutes or longer, until chicken is tender and done. Makes 4 servings.

HERBED OVEN CHICKEN

3 plump chicken breasts, halved
5 tablespoons olive oil
Juice 2 lemons
½ teaspoon each dried thyme,
  basil, marjoram

1 tablespoon cut fresh chives
Flour, salt, pepper
1 cup hot water
1 tablespoon minced parsley
Paprika

RINSE chicken, pat dry. Place in bowl and pour 3 tablespoons oil over chicken, squeeze juice of 1 lemon over pieces, and sprinkle with mixed herbs and chives. Cover dish, let stand in refrigerator 3 or 4 hours. Start oven at moderate (375 degrees F.). Drain chicken, saving marinade. Sprinkle pieces lightly with flour, salt and pepper. Brown in remaining 2 tablespoons hot oil in large flameproof (metal-base) casserole about 20 minutes. Mix marinade with about 1 cup hot water, the parsley, and the remaining lemon juice. Pour into baking dish around chicken. Sprinkle chicken lightly with paprika. Cover dish, bake in moderate oven about 30 minutes. Uncover dish, bake about 20 minutes more, or until chicken is done. Baste frequently with sauce in dish. Makes 6 servings.

SAFFRON-BASTED CHICKEN

Plump frying chicken, cut in serving pieces
2 teaspoons salt
½ teaspoon pepper
½ cup flour
4 tablespoons butter or margarine
½ teaspoon saffron, stirred into
  ¼ cup warm water

¼ cup lemon juice
Melted butter or margarine
¼ cup seedless raisins, soaked and
  drained
¼ teaspoon each dried thyme and
  orégano
½ teaspoon dried rosemary

RINSE chicken, pat dry. Place in paper bag with salt, pepper, and flour. Close bag tightly and shake to thoroughly coat chicken. Brown chicken in hot butter or margarine in flameproof (metal-base) casserole 20 minutes. Start oven at moderate (375 degrees F.). Spoon extra fat from dish, mix with saffron and hot water, add lemon juice, melted butter or margarine and baste chicken. Add raisins. Place casserole in moderate oven, bake 25 minutes, or until chicken is done. Baste 3 or 4 times during baking period with the mixture of saffron, water, lemon juice, and melted butter. Sprinkle with mixed herbs. Serve at once. Makes 6 servings.

The five recipes above from THE NEW COOK IT IN A CASSEROLE, *by Florence Brobeck*

After chicken comes duck in the order of the poultry cookery world. Some of the best duck recipes are designed for buffet service. These dishes, which can be served at buffet suppers or any dinner party, come from *The New Serve It Buffet,* by Florence Brobeck.

DUCK WITH SPICE

4-pound duckling
½ pound fresh fat pork, chopped
1 onion, peeled and chopped
1 clove garlic, peeled and chopped
2 stalks celery, chopped
Grated peel 1 lemon
¼ teaspoon each ground cloves,
   cinnamon, allspice, and nutmeg
   mixed

2 tablespoons soy sauce
1 cup hot water
12 mushrooms
2 tablespoons flour
1 tablespoon finely-chopped
   parsley
3 cups hot rice

RINSE duck, pat dry. Cut into pieces for serving. Heat pork in deep hot frying pan, add onion, garlic, celery, lemon peel, mixed spices, soy sauce, and hot water; stir. Add duck. Cover pan, let simmer on low heat about 2 hours. Stir occasionally and baste pieces of duck. Add cleaned sliced mushrooms, and sprinkle mixture with flour. Cook, stirring frequently, about 10 minutes longer. Add parsley and serve with hot rice. Makes 6 servings.

ROAST DUCK

2 ducklings, about 6 pounds each
1 lemon
2 or 3 apples
1½ cups apple juice

2 sweet Spanish onions, peeled
   and chopped
1½ teaspoons salt
Pepper

START oven at moderate (350 degrees F.). Wash and drain the cleaned ducks. Dry cavities, rub all over and inside with cut lemon. Fill each bird with large pieces unpared apples. Set birds on rack in large roasting pan and roast uncovered in moderate oven about 1 hour.

Then remove rack, pour off all fat from pan; combine apple juice, onions, salt, a little pepper and pour over ducks. Continue roasting 40 minutes to 1 hour longer. Time depends on thickness of flesh. Baste 2 to 3 times with juices in pan. When birds are done, lift them to warm serving platter, discard cooked apple from interiors; pour gravy from pan over birds and serve at once. Makes 6 to 8 servings.

If thickened gravy is preferred, add 1 tablespoon flour, stir and boil 2 to 3 minutes.

ROAST DUCK WITH RAISINS

1 duckling, about 6 pounds
2 or 3 onions
1 tablespoon butter
½ cup uncooked rice

½ cup seedless raisins
Salt and pepper
Chicken giblets or duck liver
1 lemon

SELECT a medium-to-small duck ready for cooking. Rinse, pat dry; drain thoroughly. Peel and chop onions, and cook in butter. When tender and beginning to brown, add washed, drained rice, raisins, a little salt and pepper, chopped chicken giblets or duck liver, continue cooking and stirring about 15 minutes. Stuff duck, sew or skewer vent. Start oven at moderate (350 degrees F.). Place duck in uncovered roasting pan, and roast in moderate oven 25 to 30 minutes for each pound. About 30 minutes before end of cooking time, turn bird breast-side down. Baste with lemon juice frequently while cooking. Serve hot or cold. Makes 6 servings.

ROAST TURKEY

Stuff and roast a turkey like chicken or duck. Use moderate (350 degrees F.) oven and 25 to 30 minutes per pound roasting time. Buy ready-to-cook fowl. If quick-frozen poultry is bought, follow directions on package for defrosting and roasting. Make stuffing and stuff bird just before it goes in oven. Do not stuff bird and hold in refrigerator; stuffings spoil quickly and are unsafe.

BASIC STUFFING

1 loaf day-old bread, or 12 to 14 cups crumbs (3 to 3½ quarts)
2 teaspoons salt
¾ teaspoon pepper
1½ teaspoons poultry seasoning

1 cup finely-chopped celery and celery tops
1 slightly-beaten egg
½ pound butter or margarine, melted
½ cup finely-minced peeled onions

Break dry bread into pieces, add seasonings and celery and the slightly-beaten egg. Melt butter or margarine in skillet, add onions and cook until tender. Stir this into crumb mixture and blend thoroughly. Stuff turkey, sew up vent or use skewers. Will stuff a 10-pound bird.

Olive Stuffing. Add 1 cup green or ripe olives chopped fine to above recipe.

Oyster Dressing or Stuffing. Add 1 cup small drained oysters to the the basic dressing; omit olives.

PEANUT STUFFING FOR TURKEY

4 cups finely-diced celery
4 cups boiling water
½ cup minced onion
¾ cup butter or margarine
3 quarts lightly-packed bread
  crumbs or cubes

½ teaspoon finely-minced fresh
  basil, or orégano, or ¼ teaspoon dried basil
1 tablespoon salt
1 teaspoon pepper
1 cup chopped roasted unsalted
  peanuts

Simmer celery in boiling water in covered 2-quart saucepan 15 to 20 minutes, or until tender; drain, reserving 1 cup of the liquid for the dressing. Cook onion in butter or margarine until tender but not brown. Mix crumbs and seasonings, add celery, cup of celery liquor, onion, butter or margarine, and chopped nuts. Mix thoroughly with fork. Makes stuffing for 10-pound turkey.

The six recipes from THE NEW SERVE IT BUFFET, *by Florence Brobeck*

Game Birds

Stina is a name well known to collectors of cook books. Herman Smith wrote *Stina, The Story of a Cook* about the family cook of his childhood home, his friend, substitute mother, and inspired teacher of all things gustatory. Later he wrote *Kitchens Near and Far,* about dishes he discovered in his travels such as:

BREAST OF WILD OR DOMESTIC DUCKS

4 stalks celery
2 chicken bouillon cubes in
  2 cups hot water
2 duck breasts, halved
3 tablespoons butter

1 small onion, peeled and sliced
1 teaspoon grated orange peel
Salt and pepper
Brandy

CUT celery into 1-inch pieces; dissolve bouillon cubes in 2 cups hot water, pour over celery, and cook uncovered over low heat until liquid is reduced to 2 or 3 tablespoons. Rinse duck breasts, pat dry, cook in butter until nicely browned, turning pieces a few times. Remove from fat, cook onion in same pan until soft and yellow. Add celery, orange peel, and a light seasoning of salt and pepper.

Start oven at moderately slow (300 degrees F.). Butter casserole, add cooked duck breasts, pour over them the celery and onion mixture, cover dish. Bake in moderately slow oven about 20 minutes, or until meat is tender and done. Just before serving, pour brandy over, ignite with match, and blaze the duck. Makes 2 to 4 servings. Serve with Spoonbread and Apple Butter Croquettes.

APPLE BUTTER CROQUETTES

2 cups apple butter (thick, dark)

1 cup soft bread crumbs

1 well-beaten egg

Cracker crumbs

Fat for deep frying

Combine apple butter and enough bread crumbs to make mixture which can be shaped into croquettes. Add 1 or 2 tablespoons water to beaten egg, mix. Dip croquettes in egg, then in cracker crumbs. Let dry about 15 minutes. Use frying basket and fry in deep hot fat (390 degrees F.) 2 to 3 minutes. Drain on thick paper towels. Serve hot with duck. Makes 8 to 12 croquettes.

PARTRIDGE OR SQUABS CASSEROLE

2 partridges, or squabs, cleaned and ready to cook

4 carrots, scraped and sliced thin

4 small onions, peeled and each stuck with clove

2 bay leaves

1 tablespoon minced parsley

1/8 teaspoon each dried thyme and rosemary

4 slices lean bacon, cut in inch squares

12 small pork sausages

1 medium-size green cabbage, chopped

2 chicken bouillon cubes

1 cup boiling water

1/2 teaspoon salt

Butter and flour

PLACE carrots, cloved onions, bay leaves, parsley, and herbs in bottom of greased 3-quart casserole. Cook bacon squares until lightly browned. Remove bacon and reserve; cook sausages in same fat until they brown. Remove and reserve sausages. Cook partridges or squabs on all sides in the same fat. Put them in the casserole on the vegetables and herbs. Surround with bacon and sausages. Cover with chopped cabbage. Dissolve bouillon cubes in 1 cup boiling water, add salt, pour over contents of dish. Cover. Start oven at moderately slow (300 degrees F.). Cook birds 1½ hours, or until tender and done. Remove to warmed serving dish, thicken juices in dish with a small piece of butter rolled in flour. Pour over birds. Serve hot with wild or brown rice and a tart jelly. Makes 2 or 4 servings.

DUCK WITH PEANUT CROQUETTES

2 small ducks, quartered

1/2 cup sherry

1/4 cup soy sauce

Vegetable oil

1 cup chopped roasted unsalted peanuts

2 cups hot mashed potatoes

1 teaspoon minced peeled onion

2 teaspoons chopped parsley

3 eggs

Salt and pepper

Bread crumbs or crushed corn-flakes

Fat for deep frying

RINSE duck pieces, drain. Marinate in combined wine and soy sauce 2 or 3 hours in covered dish in refrigerator, turning pieces a few times. Drain, reserve marinade. Coat ducks with vegetable oil and broil under moderate heat. Place pan about 5 inches from heat, cook slowly, basting with oil and any remaining marinade or a little sherry and soy sauce several times during cooking period. Young ducks should broil tender and well-browned in about 30 minutes. (Older birds should be sautéed in a little oil instead of broiled.) Serve at once with croquettes. Add garnish of heated orange marmalade or kumquats. Makes 4 or 8 servings.

PEANUT CROQUETTES

Mix nuts, potatoes (which have been mashed with milk and butter), onion, parsley, and 2 beaten eggs. Season lightly with salt and pepper and shape into croquettes. Let stand few minutes. Dip in remaining egg, beaten and mixed with 2 tablespoons cold water; then into crumbs or corn flakes. Fry in deep hot fat (390 degrees F.) 3 to 5 minutes, or until browned. Drain on thick paper towels. Serve hot with duck. Makes 8 to 12 croquettes.

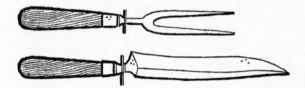

ROAST PHEASANT (OR ROAST CHICKEN)

1 pheasant, cleaned and ready to cook, or small roasting chicken
½ lemon
½ pound liver sausage in 1 piece
1 cup croutons, or small toasted bread cubes
1 small onion, peeled and minced
¼ teaspoon each ground nutmeg and thyme
Salt and pepper
1 tablespoon minced parsley
½ cup sliced black olives
3 slices bacon or thin salt pork
4 juniper berries, crushed
½ cup melted butter

RINSE bird, pat dry. Rub inside and out with lemon. Mash liver sausage and beat smoothly, mix with croutons, onion, seasonings, parsley, and olives and stuff bird with mixture. Start oven at moderate (350 degrees F.). Place stuffed bird in baking pan or casserole, lay bacon or salt pork over breast. Roast 20 to 25 minutes to the pound, or until done, basting often with melted butter mixed with crushed juniper berries. Makes 2 servings. If small chicken is roasted by this recipe, it makes 4 or 5 servings.

There is no substitute for juniper berries; the pungent flavor and fragrance add much to a dish of game. But if none is available, use a little currant jam and grated orange peel with melted butter for basting.

SQUABS WITH GREENGAGE PLUMS

4 squabs, or squab-chickens
1 cup minced peeled onions
1 cup diced celery
3 tablespoons melted butter or
  margarine
1 tablespoon grated orange peel
½ teaspoon salt
¼ teaspoon black pepper

1 cup coarse toasted bread crumbs
Flour and butter
Juice 1 orange
1 cup boiling water
½ teaspoon paprika
8 canned greengage plums and
  their syrup

RINSE squabs or small chickens, pat dry. Start oven at moderately hot (400 degrees F.). Cook onions and celery in butter or margarine until tender and yellow. Add orange peel and seasonings, stir in bread crumbs, mix well. Stuff birds with this mixture, sew up opening or skewer. Mix equal amounts of flour and butter to a paste and spread on birds. Roast in moderately hot oven 15 minutes, reduce heat to moderate (350 degrees F.), and cook 45 minutes longer, or until squabs are tender. Baste with a mixture of the orange juice, boiling water, and paprika. Serve hot, garnished with greengage plums which have been heated in their syrup. Makes 4 servings.

The five recipes above from KITCHENS NEAR AND FAR, *by Herman Smith*

❦

A cook book from Tennessee, again by Martin Rywell, is the *Wild Game Wild Fowl Cook Book,* teeming with information and recipes for every kind of game the huntsmen of the area have ever brought in to their kitchens. Here are four selections from that book.

BRAISED WILD DUCK

Wild duck
Juice 1 lemon
½ teaspoon salt
¼ teaspoon pepper
3 slices bacon
1 onion, peeled and sliced

1 carrot, scraped and sliced
½ tablespoon parsley
⅛ teaspoon dried thyme
2 tablespoons brown sugar
1 tablespoon orange juice
½ teaspoon grated lemon peel

DISJOINT the cleaned and ready-to-cook duck. Rinse, pat dry. Rub pieces with lemon juice, season with salt and pepper. Place in large skillet with bacon, onion, carrot, parsley, and thyme. Cook at high heat until bird is browning, reduce heat, cook and stir. Drain most of fat off. Sprinkle duck with brown sugar, orange juice, and grated lemon peel. Cover; cook slowly 30 minutes, or until duck is tender and done. Add more fruit juice from time to time if necessary. Makes 2 to 4 servings.

BROILED GROUSE

Grouse, cleaned and ready to cook
Peanut butter
3 tablespoons butter

⅛ teaspoon dried basil
1 tablespoon Worcestershire sauce
1 tablespoon tarragon vinegar

RINSE bird, pat dry. Split down back. Spread peanut butter all over both sides. Mix basting sauce by combining remaining ingredients. Broil 5 or 6 inches from moderate broiler heat, basting several times during 15 minutes' cooking time. Cook longer if necessary. Should be browned and tender. Makes 2 servings.

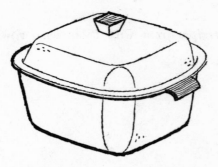

PHEASANT IN SOUR CREAM

Pheasant, cleaned and ready to cook
1 tablespoon butter
½ cup chopped ham
1 carrot, scraped and sliced

Salt and pepper
2 stalks celery, chopped
½ cup stock or bouillon
½ cup orange juice
1 cup sour cream

RINSE bird, pat dry, disjoint. Brown in butter in flameproof (metal-base) casserole. Add ham, carrot, seasoning, celery, pour stock and orange juice over all, cover. Start oven at moderately slow (300 degrees F.). Cook pheasant 2 hours, just simmering. Test for doneness; increase heat if necessary and cook until tender and done. Just before serving, add sour cream, stirring around bird with juices in bottom of casserole. If gravy needs thickening, remove bird to warmed serving dish and stir about 1 tablespoon flour and 1 tablespoon hot water into dish, boil, and stir on top of range over high heat 2 to 3 minutes. Pour over bird and serve. Makes 2 or more servings.

ROAST QUAIL

Quail, cleaned and ready to cook	Liver of bird, mashed with fork
Ground allspice	1 tablespoon melted butter
Salt and pepper	½ teaspoon ground pistachio nuts
½ cup bread crumbs soaked in apple cider	Sliced salt pork
	Boiling water

START oven at hot (450 degrees F.). Rinse bird, pat dry, rub well with allspice, salt, and pepper, inside and out. Mix stuffing of cider-soaked crumbs, mashed quail liver, butter, and nuts. Stuff bird. Sew up or use skewers. Place on rack in roasting pan, cover breast of bird with thin slices fat salt pork, add ½ cup boiling water to pan. Bake in hot oven 15 minutes. Reduce heat to moderate (375 degrees F.) and bake 20 minutes longer, or until bird is tender and done. One small bird makes 1 serving.

The above four recipes from WILD GAME WILD FOWL COOK BOOK, *by Martin Rywell*

THE "BEST-OF-ALL"

SALADS AND SALAD DRESSINGS

THE RECIPES THAT FOLLOW HAVE BEEN SELECTED FROM THESE DISTINGUISHED BOOKS:

The Alice B. Toklas Cook Book	*Alice B. Toklas*
American Regional Cookery	*Sheila Hibben*
Fruit Recipes	*Riley M. Fletcher-Berry*
Helen Brown's West Coast Cook Book	*Helen Evans Brown*
The Vegetable Cook Book	*Cora, Rose, and Bob Brown*

SALADS AND
SALAD DRESSINGS

Salads are increasingly popular in American menus, not only because the benefits of adding raw fruit, greens, and vegetables to the diet have been stressed by nutritionists and widely publicized as aids toward better health, but because patio and outdoor dining and simple informal meals indoors and out have become a national habit. Also the variety possible in salads, and the numerous imaginative, succulent, eye-filling, and appetite-satisfying salads which appeal to readers of the home magazines have influenced the national menu. A salad may be served as part of a large meal, or it may be the main dish.

Wherever fruits and vegetables grow abundantly, salads are especially important in home and restaurant menus. California, Florida, and Texas, as well as the great apple-orchard areas, have given the country a colorful and flavorful incentive for varying its salads, and eating them often.

Turning to *Helen Brown's West Coast Cook Book,* in which there is an amusing history of salads in early California, Mrs. Brown relates: "Today everyone on the Coast likes salads, even the children, and most of them eat at least one a day. We make the ordinary ones just as they are made elsewhere, but our own salads —the salads we have created or improved upon—are those in which we take pride."

Here are some of her favorite salads, starting with Avocado Salad and its dressing.

★AVOCADO SALAD

4 avocados
½ cup wine vinegar
½ cup olive oil
2 tablespoons minced parsley
2 tablespoons minced green
  pepper

2 tablespoons minced green
  onions
Crisp lettuce

WASH avocados, cut in halves from top to bottom, remove the large round seed. Mix dressing by combining all ingredients, except lettuce, in bottle and shaking well. Place each avocado-half on lettuce on chilled plate, spoon the dressing into the cavity. Makes 8 servings.

CAESAR SALAD

"And now," says this California author, "we come to it—the most talked-of salad of a decade, perhaps of the century. Like all recipes that have become widely known, several chefs and restaurants have claimed to have originated this salad. Actually many of them have had a hand in promoting it, though not necessarily as a Caesar. As for its origin, the best guess seems to be that the whole thing started in Tia Juana during prohibition, but whether it was actually created by one named 'Caesar,' or just named for him, is a matter of considerable discussion. The salad is at its best when kept simple, but sometimes, when made by show-offs, it occasionally contains too many ingredients. This is a simple version:"

1 clove garlic, peeled and crushed	½ teaspoon salt
¾ cup olive oil	2 eggs
2 cups croutons	Juice 1 large lemon
2 to 3 heads romaine	6 to 8 fillets anchovies (optional)
Pepper	½ cup grated Parmesan cheese

ADD garlic to olive oil, let stand overnight. Brown 2 cups croutons, made from stale sourdough French bread if possible, in ¼ cup of this garlic oil, stirring carefully so that all sides are colored. Drain on thick paper towels. Break the washed and drained romaine into a large bowl, grind on a generous amount of fresh black pepper, add ½ teaspoon salt, then dress the greens with remaining ½ cup garlic oil. Turn salad with fork and spoon until every leaf is glossy with oil. Cook eggs 1 minute in shell, in boiling water, then break each from its shell into middle of salad. Squeeze lemon juice directly over eggs (if lemons are small, use 1½ or 2) and mix so there is a creamy look to the lettuce. Add anchovy fillets snipped into bits (and some Caesar addicts say you must add them).

Now taste it, and don't hesitate to use your fingers. More salt? More lemon? Add them, or vinegar if you wish, plenty of experts do. (Others insist on a slug of Worcestershire!) The seasoning is now as you want it, so a good ½ cup of Parmesan is tossed in, the salad mixed some more, and finally the croutons are added, and the salad served at once before the croutons become limp and soggy. Like any salad of this kind, the artist adds or subtracts as he goes along, so Caesar salad, as *you* make it, is all your own. This recipe makes servings for 12, more or less.

CELERY VICTOR

"Here's a world-famous salad originated by Chef Victor Hirtzler of the superb St. Francis Hotel, of San Francisco. This is the recipe as given to me, and as they now serve it at the hotel."

1 bunch hearts of celery	1 teaspoon each chopped chervil
1 to 1½ cups seasoned chicken	and parsley
bouillon	Tarragon French Dressing
2 onions, peeled and sliced	Sliced tomato
2 small carrots, scraped and sliced	Sliced hard-cooked egg
Herb bouquet	Anchovy fillets
Pepper	Pimiento strips

WASH and drain celery, cut bunch in half from top to bottom, trim root end, remove all but the tiniest leaves. Lay celery flat in saucepan, cover with chicken bouillon or stock, add onions, carrots, and herb bouquet. Cook slowly. When celery is tender, let cool in stock. (Drain off stock later for soup.) Press any excess stock from celery, arrange on salad plates, sprinkle with coarsely-ground black pepper, chervil, and parsley. Cover with French dressing (made with tarragon vinegar). Chill. Serve garnished with tomato and egg slices, or with cooked chilled crab legs. Or cross anchovy or pimiento strips over celery. A small celery heart makes 2 or more servings.

POTATO SALAD WITH WHITE WINE

5 large potatoes	¼ cup minced green onions
⅔ cup white wine	2 tablespoons minced parsley
⅓ cup salad oil	Salt and pepper
1 tablespoon white-wine vinegar	¼ cup melted butter

SCRUB potatoes, rinse, drain. Boil in water until just tender. Peel, slice or dice, and dress while warm with combined remaining ingredients. Let stand in refrigerator several hours before serving. Makes 8 servings.

WHITE CUCUMBER SALAD

Helen Brown claims that this is one of the world's best salads —particularly good served with fish, but also a fine "extra" salad on a buffet table.

For each large cucumber:	Salt
1 tablespoon grated onion	Sliced onions, optional
½ cup mayonnaise	

WASH cucumbers, slice very thin. For each cucumber, mix 1 tablespoon grated onion with ½ cup mayonnaise. Arrange layer of cucumbers in shallow bowl, sprinkle with salt, and spread with mayonnaise. Combine until all is used, ending with mayonnaise on top. Cover and place in refrigerator 12 to 24 hours before serving. The dressing will thin and turn white in the standing, the flavors will mingle, and the cucumbers will wilt. But don't let that stop you, that's the reason the salad is so good. Cucumbers may be alternated with paper-thin slices of onion. One cucumber makes 2 or more servings.

The five recipes above and comments from HELEN BROWN'S WEST COAST COOK BOOK

❦

American *Regional Cookery,* that carefully compiled book by Sheila Hibben, includes some of the country's most delicious salads.

★CHICKEN SALAD, VIRGINIA
TURKEY SALAD, VIRGINIA

2⅔ cups cubed cooked chicken or turkey

1 cup coarsely-cut celery

¾ cup mayonnaise

Crisp lettuce

USE steamed chicken or turkey if making salad in large quantities, although leftover roast fowl can also be used. Cut white meat and tender portion of the upper joint into pieces about the size of a large hazelnut, being careful to discard all sinews, bits of gristle, and fat. Mix with mayonnaise and season to taste with salt and freshly-ground pepper. Cover and chill in refrigerator at least 1 hour. Add celery and mix thoroughly. Serve garnished with crisp hearts of lettuce. Makes 6 servings.

NEW ENGLAND COLESLAW

1 medium-size cabbage

¾ teaspoon (scant) dry mustard

1 tablespoon sugar

1½ teaspoons salt

3 well-beaten egg yolks

1 cup milk, scalded

⅓ cup cider vinegar

WASH and drain cabbage, remove wilted leaves and stems, cut firm cabbage into quarters, then shred fine and let stand in ice water in china bowl. Drain and dry carefully on clean towels. Combine mustard, sugar, salt, and egg yolks in the top of an enamel or glass double boiler, stir hot milk in gradually and cook and stir over boiling water until thick. Remove from heat, stir in vinegar, and pour over drained, dried cabbage. Let cool, then chill. Allow ½ cup slaw per portion. Makes 4 or more servings.

POTATO SALAD, WISCONSIN

1 small cucumber
¼ cup wine vinegar
2 tablespoons sugar
1 teaspoon salt
½ cup ice water
2 cups sliced freshly-boiled
    potatoes
1 cup chopped celery

4 scallions, chopped
2 tablespoons chopped green
    pepper
½ cup mayonnaise
Pepper
3 stuffed hard-cooked eggs
2 boiled beets, sliced
Hearts of lettuce

PEEL cucumber, slice very thin, rinse in several waters, and let stand 1 hour in mixture of vinegar, sugar, 1 teaspoon salt, and the ice water. Combine potatoes, celery, scallions, green pepper, and mayonnaise; season well with salt and a coarse grinding of pepper, toss with fork until well mixed. Chill thoroughly. Drain all liquid from cucumber, combine with potato mixture, and turn onto bed of lettuce hearts on chilled platter. Add stuffed-egg halves and beet slices. Makes 6 to 8 servings.

VEGETABLE SALAD, COLORADO

⅓ cup navy beans
Salt and pepper
½ pound string beans
2 small beets
½ peeled clove garlic
1 cup finely-diced celery

¼ cup chopped green pepper
4 scallions, sliced
1 bunch water cress, washed and
    dried
Hard-Boiled Egg Dressing

SOAK navy beans overnight in cold water to cover. Drain, cover with fresh cold water and simmer 2 or 3 hours or until tender. Drain, season with a little salt and pepper. Cook string beans as usual, and boil the beets. Combine navy beans and drained string beans in bowl lightly rubbed with garlic, add celery, green pepper, scallions, and water cress. pour Hard-Boiled Egg Dressing over, toss, turn into chilled salad bowl. Garnish with peeled, sliced, chilled beets and extra whole scallions. Makes 4 or more servings.

★WALDORF SALAD, MANHATTAN

2 cups diced pared apples
1 cup cubed celery hearts
⅓ cup coarsely chopped walnuts
¾ cup mayonnaise

Salt and pepper
Lettuce hearts
Walnut halves

COMBINE apples, celery, and chopped walnuts, add mayonnaise and mix lightly. Season lightly with salt and pepper. Turn onto bed of lettuce hearts, garnish with walnut halves. Makes about 4 servings.

WILTED SALAD, INDIANA

2 heads garden or Boston lettuce	2 teaspoons vinegar
4 slices bacon	Sugar, optional
Salt and pepper	

SEPARATE lettuce leaves, wash carefully, and dry. Cook bacon in skillet, remove bacon. Place lettuce in warmed serving bowl, sprinkle with salt and pepper, and pour warm fat from skillet over lettuce. Heat vinegar in same skillet and pour over greens. Toss until thoroughly mixed. Eat at once. In Indiana a little sugar is sometimes added to this, but outsiders will probably like it better without. Makes 4 to 6 servings.

The six recipes above from AMERICAN REGIONAL COOKERY, *by Sheila Hibben*

❧

One of the many cook books by Cora, Rose, and Bob Brown is *The Vegetable Cook Book* (which we dip into again in the chapter on vegetable cookery). Here and there in the Browns' book are such good salad ideas that they must be included here.

BEET SALAD

2 cups cubed cooked beets	Sugar
2 cups chopped raw cabbage	Salt
½ cup freshly-grated horse-radish	Lettuce hearts
Vinegar	

COMBINE beets and cabbage, dress with a mixture of horse-radish and sweetened vinegar, touched up with a little salt. Serve cold, on lettuce hearts, with or without mayonnaise. Makes 6 servings.

The Browns add: "Whole cooked beets, hollowed out, make fine containers for a combination of chopped cabbage, chopped hard-cooked eggs, chopped sweet pickle, and French dressing. You might like them better stuffed with cream cheese and Roquefort mashed together, or with plain cottage cheese. Serve each filled beet on lettuce, with or without mayonnaise as garnish. One good-sized beet or 2 small ones make 1 salad serving."

LENTIL SALAD

This specialty of Near Eastern cooks belongs on all tables, according to the authors of this vegetable book. Combine cold cooked lentils with finely chopped cooked meat, mix with little French dressing spiked with mustard. And serve in lettuce cup as salad, ¾ cup mixture as 1 serving.

HOT CELERIAC SALAD

3 or 4 celeriacs
Boiling water
2 tablespoons lemon juice
1 onion, peeled and minced

1 teaspoon minced parsley
1 tablespoon tarragon vinegar
1 teaspoon prepared mustard
2 to 3 tablespoons olive oil

Wash trim and pare celeriacs, cut into quarters, drop into rapidly boiling water to cover; add lemon juice to water. Cook 20 to 30 minutes, or until tender. Drain, mix onion, parsley, vinegar, and mustard and pour over celeriac in bowl, mix gently but thoroughly, add a little olive oil and mix again. Eat while warm with roast meat. Makes 3 or 4 servings.

Or let cooked, drained celeriac cool. Cut into cubes and combine with potato salad. Or mix with mayonnaise and heap in hollowed-out beets or tomatoes and serve as individual salads.

★MIAMI SEAFOOD AVOCADO

3 ripe avocados
1½ cups cooked mixed sea food
such as crab meat and small
shrimp or chunks of lobster

Russian Dressing
Hard-cooked egg
1 tablespoon chopped parsley
12 anchovy fillets

Wash avocados, wipe dry. Cut into halves from top to bottom, remove seed. Fill centers with any preferred mixture of chilled cooked sea food combined with Russian dressing. Chop egg fine, combine with parsley, garnish top of each stuffed avocado and cross pair of anchovy fillets on top of each. Serve on bed of cracked ice. Makes 6 servings.

The four recipes above from THE VEGETABLE COOK BOOK, *by Cora, Rose, and Bob Brown*

❧

Alice B. Toklas, famous companion of Gertrude Stein, put Miss Stein into *The Alice B. Toklas Cook Book,* along with countless other writers, painters, and characters of their days together in France and in the United States. From one of their friends in London, she includes an international salad, which Miss Toklas says is ideal for poets with delicate digestions. And so good, too, for the rest of us.

APHRODITE SALAD

Apples
Celery
Yoghurt

Black pepper
Salt
Crisp lettuce

THE beauty of this salad, says the author, depends on how quickly the apples are peeled and stirred with finely chopped celery into the bowl of yoghurt. (Speed prevents the apples from turning brown.) Season with a grind of fresh black pepper and salt to taste. Eat with crisp lettuce. No quantities are given by the author: But about 1 apple, ¼ cup chopped celery, 1 cup yoghurt, all cold, all fresh, make 1 serving of this poets' salad. It is, with Boston brown bread or toasted brioche, a good luncheon for a warm day.

NICOISE SALAD

2 cups diced pared potatoes
2 cups diced string beans
2 tablespoons olive oil
1 tablespoon lemon juice
Salt and pepper

8 anchovy fillets
16 stoned black olives
1 tablespoon capers
2 quartered, peeled tomatoes
Chopped fresh or dried basil

COVER potatoes with cold salted water, bring to boiling, and cook until just tender; do not overcook. Cook string beans in boiling salted water about 20 minutes or until tender, but not overcooked. Drain vegetables, let cool. When cold, combine and mix with oil and lemon juice, using more of both if needed to coat vegetables lightly. Season with grind of pepper and little salt. Place in mound in salad dish, garnish with anchovies, olives, capers, tomatoes, and a sprinkling of basil. Makes 4 generous servings, or 6 smaller ones.

★PORT ROYAL SALAD

1 cup sliced boiled potatoes
1 cup French-cut cooked string
  beans
1 cup shredded pared apples
Salt and pepper

Mayonnaise
Few cubed cooked string beans
Quartered lettuce hearts
Quartered hard-cooked eggs

COMBINE cold cooked vegetables and freshly-shredded apples; season lightly. Coat with mayonnaise, toss to mix lightly. Turn into salad bowl, garnish top with added mayonnaise, decorate with cubed beans, surround with lettuce and eggs. Makes 4 servings.

★WINTER SALAD

2 tablespoons French mustard
1 teaspoon salt
¼ teaspoon pepper

1 tablespoon paprika
1 cup heavy cream
2 or 3 large sweet Spanish onions

PREPARE dressing by combining all ingredients except onions. Mix smoothly. Just before serving, peel and slice onions, separating slices into rings. Pour dressing over rings, and serve. Makes 3 or 4 servings.

The four recipes above from THE ALICE B. TOKLAS COOK BOOK

Fruit Salads

At the turn of this century a fine, serious, and delightful book on fruit was written by Riley M. Fletcher-Berry. Called *Fruit Recipes*, it contained photographs, histories, and nutritional charts on all the fruits known to the Western world, and some scarcely heard of, and "nine hundred different ways of using them." Among these ways is a salad, or salad suggestion for most of the fruits. Here are some of them to adapt to modern menus.

APPLE SALAD

Green, red, or yellow eating apples may be scooped out and filled with nuts, chopped celery, and some fruit other than apple, mixed with the cubed apple pulp, all bound with mayonnaise. Serve with mayonnaise as top garnish, place on nasturtium or grape leaves on salad plates. One stuffed apple makes 1 serving.

CHERRY SALAD

Stone ripe sweet cherries. Place in the heart of each a nut, preferably hazelnut. Serve generous spoonful on crisp lettuce with mayonnaise, or with a cream or other dressing flavored with maraschino. One-half to ¾ cup stuffed cherries with mayonnaise makes 1 serving.

GRAPEFRUIT SALAD

Skinned sections of grapefruit dressed with French dressing or mayonnaise are served on crisp lettuce. Add chopped celery or nuts, or stoned black cherries, or clusters of fresh ripe currants. A light sprinkling of sugar makes some grapefruit more palatable. About ½ cup grapefruit sections makes 1 serving.

GUAVA SALAD

Peel and slice guava as far outside the seed center as possible, removing seeds remaining on inner side. Use either the large pale-yellow pear guava, mild in flavor, or the vermilion-tinted red, tart fruit (the original apple guava). Serve on lettuce or tender cabbage heart with French dressing. Mayonnaise, however is preferred by some. As with other fruits, variety almost without end may be made by adding celery or nuts, or other fruits.

KUMQUAT SALAD

For a fruit salad, few fruits give greater piquancy than thinly sliced or quartered kumquats as garnish to any fruit mixture. Or they may form the body of the salad, with celery, sliced or cubed banana, pineapple, pear, orange or cherries, added. Nuts make a good addition. Combine lightly with mayonnaise. Or combine all additions with the salad dressing, leaving the kumquat free for its pungent flavor and its dramatic color when used as garnish.

MELON SALAD

Fully ripe melon is delicious for salads, cut in cubes or balls served alone or with other fruits, such as peaches and bananas. Serve with mayonnaise plain, or flavored with a liqueur-French dressing to which has been added a suspicion of maraschino. Or serve with whipped cream.

ORANGE SALAD

Peeled sections of orange on lettuce, tender cabbage leaves, or sorrel with a simple French dressing seasoned with a little salt, paprika, or Tabasco. The dressing may be omitted and the salad varied by substituting sherry with a little paprika as finish. Or combine orange sections with chopped celery, apples and nuts; or with sliced banana alone with mayonnaise.

PEACH SALAD

Sliced ripe peaches combined with the same amount of thin sections of banana and almonds; or with celery, walnuts, and finely cut apple or pear; all with French dressing, or liqueur-flavored French dressing.

PINEAPPLE SALAD

Cut the fruit of 1 small ripe pineapple in small cubes, combine with 1 cup grapefruit sections, and ½ cup nuts or chopped celery. Add candied cherries or drained preserved cherries. Serve on lettuce with mayonnaise. Makes about 4 servings.

PLUM SALAD

Greengages make one of the prettiest of fruit salads. They may be used with bananas, halved or cubed, with good effect. Sprinkle powdered sugar over halved plums in a bowl, let stand 1 hour. Or marinate in liqueur-flavored French dressing. Serve with liqueur-flavored whipped cream.

GARNISHES

The author of this old book, which has been an inspiration for countless home economists, home cooks, and chefs in the half-century since it was published, has this to say about garnishes for fruit salads.

"The garnishing appeals to the eye, but even the gaily graceful nasturtium (blossom and leaf) has a spicily stimulating mission stomachward. Cress may be either a garnish or the body of the salad, as also may be lettuce. But sprigs of fresh ripe currants, white or red, may be used; parsley (a stimulant in disguise), sprays of cherries or kumquats, or figs and dates softly ripe or the dried variety freshened by steaming. Or there may be a base of fruit-flavored gelatin."

The ten recipes and comments above from FRUIT RECIPES, *by Riley M. Fletcher-Berry*

Gelatin Salads

At the beginning of this chapter some especially good salads appear from the pages of *Helen Brown's West Coast Cook Book.* This California cook-author believes that: "Aspics do, of course, fit into the salad category in two ways, one being that they are usually garnished with lettuce or other greens, the other that a salad dressing of sorts is served with them. Some of them, those in which meat or fish predominate, can often constitute the main dish of a summer meal." Here are some of her aspic salads.

ALTIVO AVOCADO ASPIC

1 envelope (1 tablespoon) gelatin
1/4 cup cold water
1/2 cup boiling chicken stock
1 1/4 cups sieved avocado
1/2 cup sour cream or mayonnaise

1/2 teaspoon salt
2 teaspoons lemon juice
Cayenne
Water cress or lettuce
Mayonnaise or sour cream

SOAK gelatin in cold water, then dissolve in boiling chicken stock. Let set until consistency of egg white, then mix with sieved avocado, sour cream or mayonnaise, salt, lemon juice, and few grains cayenne. (If sour cream is used, increase seasoning a little.) Pour into small mold and allow to set. Unmold on salad greens. Serve with mayonnaise or sour cream. Double this for more servings. Makes 4 servings.

★TOMATO ASPIC WITH DILL

2 envelopes (2 tablespoons) gelatin
½ cup cold water
2 (8-oz.) cans tomato sauce
2 cups water

½ teaspoon dill seeds
2 tablespoons lemon juice
2 teaspoons sugar

Soak gelatin in ½ cup cold water. Heat tomato sauce with 2 cups water and crushed dill seeds, simmer 3 or 4 minutes, add lemon juice and sugar. Strain over gelatin, stir until dissolved and pour into 5-cup mold. Basil may be used instead of dill, if desired. Chill until set. Cut into cubes as garnish for green salad. Or if chilled in ring mold, fill center with green salad. Makes 8 servings.

TOMATO MOUSSE

Make Tomato Aspic in above recipe. But reduce water cooked with tomato sauce to ½ cup and lemon juice to 2 teaspoons. When partially set, fold in 1½ cups heavy cream whipped until quite stiff. Chill until set. Can be served with salad—as described for aspic—or broken lightly with fork and served as jellied soup with sour cream and chives. Makes about 8 servings.

WINE ASPIC FOR COLD
GAME, FISH, MEAT, POULTRY

2 envelopes (2 tablespoons) gela-
     tin
½ cup cold water
2¾ cups stock
½ cup wine

Herbs
Salt and pepper
1 tablespoon lemon juice
2 pounds cold sliced meat or fish

This all-purpose aspic base is varied according to the meat used: with beef, use beef stock; with fish, make a stock of fish trimmings; with vension, a venison stock; with chicken, duck, turkey, stock from the pot in which the bird was cooked. White wine is better with fish and poultry aspics; red wine, with meat and game.

Soak gelatin in cold water, then dissolve in boiling stock, add wine, and season highly with herbs (orégano, basil, thyme, and marjoram, about ⅟₁₆ teaspoon each), add salt, pepper, and lemon juice. Partially chill, then fold in about 2 pounds (more or less) cooked fish, game, or meat, cooked tender and either sliced or cut into good-sized pieces. Pour into shallow pan or dish or large decorative mold. Chill. Makes 8 servings.

Salad Dressings

CALIFORNIA GREEN GODDESS SALAD DRESSING

Mrs. Brown says of this recipe: "There have been innumerable imitations and variations of this famous salad dressing since it was first created at the Palace Hotel, in honor of George Arliss, who was opening in William Archer's play *The Green Goddess*. This recipe is one given me by the Palace Hotel, and who should know better than they how it is prepared?"

8 to 10 anchovy fillets	3 cups mayonnaise
1 green onion	¼ cup tarragon vinegar
¼ cup minced parsley	¼ cup finely-cut chives
2 tablespoons minced tarragon	

IN A garlic-rubbed bowl, mince anchovies with onion, add parsley, minced tarragon, mayonnaise, vinegar, and chives. Combine and serve on vegetable and green salads. Makes about 3¾ cups dressing.

★CARTE MADERA SOUR CREAM SALAD DRESSING

2 hard-cooked egg yolks	1 cup sour cream
2 tablespoons lemon juice	Salt and pepper

MASH yolks, work in lemon juice, and combine with sour cream. Add a little salt and pepper, beat until thoroughly mixed. Makes about 1¼ cups dressing.

★DILL SOUR CREAM DRESSING

Add chopped fresh dill to Sour Cream Dressing, for cucumbers, shrimp, string beans, or lobster.

★MAYONNAISE AND SOUR CREAM DRESSING

Just combine mayonnaise and sour cream in equal parts. Good for fruit salads.

★QUICK SOUR CREAM DRESSING

Add lemon juice or vinegar, salt and pepper to taste, to sour cream.

WINE FRENCH DRESSING

½ cup red wine
¼ cup red-wine vinegar
¾ cup salad oil

1 teaspoon salt
Freshly-ground pepper
Garlic (optional)

MIX wine, wine vinegar, and salad oil. Season, and if you want garlic in it, add a sliver, or mix in a bowl rubbed with a cut bud of garlic. Makes about 1½ cups dressing.

The ten recipes above from HELEN BROWN'S WEST COAST COOK BOOK

❧

A_nd among the excellent salad dressings in *American Regional Cookery,* by Sheila Hibben, are:

★FRENCH DRESSING

4 tablespoons olive oil
1 tablespoon wine vinegar

1 teaspoon salt
Generous grinding black pepper

IN dressing lettuce and other greens, rubbing the bowl with a cut bud of garlic and then mixing oil and vinegar in it is always an improvement. But note that for grapefruit, orange, and other fruit salads the flavor of garlic is disaster. Also French dressing should always be made fresh; bottled garlic-flavored dressing can go far to ruining a salad. This recipe makes 5 tablespoons dressing.

★FRUIT SALAD DRESSING, CALIFORNIA

2 egg yolks
¼ cup sugar
1 teaspoon salt
Few grains cayenne

1 teaspoon butter
4 tablespoons vinegar
¾ cup heavy cream

BEAT egg yolks in top of glass or enamel double boiler, add sugar, salt, and cayenne and continue beating until very light. Add butter and vinegar, and cook over boiling water, stirring constantly until quite thick. Let cool, chill in refrigerator. Whip cream stiff. Fold into egg mixture, correct seasoning if necessary. Makes about 2 cups dressing.

★HARD-BOILED EGG DRESSING, COLORADO

3 hard-cooked egg yolks
1 teaspoon tarragon mustard
5 tablespoons olive oil

2 tablespoons wine vinegar
Freshly-ground pepper
Salt

PRESS yolks through fine sieve, add mustard, olive oil, and wine vinegar. Season highly with freshly-ground pepper and salt to taste. Beat until smooth. Toss with vegetable salad. Makes about ¾ to 1 cup dressing.

★WHOLE EGG MAYONNAISE, BOSTON

1 egg
1 teaspoon salt
½ teaspoon dry mustard
¾ cup olive oil

⅓ cup corn oil
2½ tablespoons wine vinegar
Freshly-ground black pepper
Tabasco

BEAT egg hard 5 minutes, add dry ingredients and beat well. Pour in ¼ cup combined oils, beat hard, and add 1 tablespoon vinegar. Add half of remaining oil and beat until mixture thickens. Beat in remaining vinegar and remaining oil, season with freshly-ground black pepper and Tabasco. Continue beating until thick and well blended. Makes about 1½ cups dressing.

The four recipes above from AMERICAN REGIONAL COOKERY, *by Sheila Hibben*

For the cook who prefers to make her own salad dressings, the recipe for *Mayonnaise* given above is a joy to use. The usual recipe, found in most cook books calls for only one kind of oil, and a cider vinegar. *Russian Dressing,* a variation of mayonnaise, is made by combining ½ cup mayonnaise, ½ cup chili sauce, 1 tablespoon each chopped green pepper and chopped young onion or chives. Makes about 1 cup dressing.

THE
"BEST-OF-ALL"

SAUCES

THE RECIPES THAT FOLLOW HAVE BEEN
SELECTED FROM THESE DISTINGUISHED
BOOKS:

The A.B.C. of Spice Cookery	*American Spice Trade Association*
How To Cook Well	*Ann Roe Robbins*
How To Use Spices	*American Spice Trade Association*
The Settlement Cook Book	*Mrs. Simon Kandor*
Thoughts for Buffets	

SAUCES

A cook must know how to make White Sauce for countless dishes she serves her family in the course of a year. This basic sauce is one of the first lessons in domestic science classes, and it is the first essential of beginner cooks in their homes. That wise, thorough, and well-edited *The Settlement Cook Book* starts its sauce chapter with the White Sauce recipe and variations which follow.

★STANDARD RECIPES FOR WHITE SAUCE
For Soups
(Very Thin)

1 tablespoon butter   ⅛ teaspoon pepper
1 tablespoon flour   1 cup hot milk
¼ teaspoon salt

For Fish, Meats, and Vegetables
(Thin)

2 tablespoons butter   ¼ teaspoon salt
2 tablespoons flour   1 cup hot milk or cream
⅛ teaspoon pepper

For Soufflés
(Medium)

3 tablespoons butter   ⅛ teaspoon pepper
3 tablespoons flour   1 cup hot milk
¼ teaspoons salt

For Croquettes and Cutlets
(Thick)

4 tablespoons butter   ⅛ teaspoon pepper
⅓ cup flour   1 cup hot milk
¼ teaspoon salt

METHOD of cookery is the same for all: melt butter in saucepan, remove from heat, stir flour in smoothly. Return to heat, cook and stir until it bubbles, then add ⅔ of the hot milk at once, stir and cook; add rest of milk gradually and stir until boiling. Let boil, stirring constantly, until thickened; add seasonings. Use as called for in recipes. Makes about 1 cup sauce.

Cream Sauce or Yellow Sauce. Use 1 cup thin White Sauce and 2 beaten egg yolks. Pour a few spoonfuls of sauce gradually into beaten yolks, mix well, then stir into remaining White Sauce and cook slowly, stirring constantly until thick. Serve at once, over cooked asparagus, boiled fish, meat, or poultry. Makes about 1½ cups sauce.

★BEARNAISE SAUCE

2 green onions
2 tablespoons tarragon vinegar
4 egg yolks
1 teaspoon finely-chopped parsley
4 tablespoons butter
1 tablespoon soup stock or bouillon
½ teaspoon salt
⅛ teaspoon paprika

CHOP onions, combine with vinegar in enamel or glass saucepan, bring to boiling point, lower heat and let simmer until reduced ½; strain, let cool. Beat yolks into cooled onion vinegar one at a time, return to low heat and cook slowly until smooth, stirring constantly. Add butter gradually, stir, add stock or bouillon and seasoning. Serve hot with broiled meat or fish. Makes about ¾ cup sauce.

★BROWN SAUCE

2 tablespoons butter or fat
2 tablespoons flour
½ teaspoon salt
⅛ teaspoon pepper
1 cup water, meat, fish, or vegetable stock, or use bouillon cube

BROWN butter or fat in saucepan, stir in flour smoothly, and let brown lightly; add seasonings and ⅔ cup water or stock, stirring and cooking. Gradually add remaining ⅓ cup water or stock, stir, let cook 5 minutes. Serve hot over vegetables, dumplings, pastas, and various meat dishes. Makes about 1 cup sauce.

Anchovy Sauce: Season Brown Sauce with a little anchovy essence. Or mash 3 or 4 anchovy fillets until smooth, add to Brown Sauce with about 1 teaspoon lemon juice, heat and stir a moment. Serve hot. Makes about 1 cup sauce.

Caper Sauce: Add ¼ cup drained capers to Brown Sauce. Serve hot with boiled mutton or fish. Makes about 1¼ cups sauce.

Mushroom Sauce: Drain very small can sliced or chopped mushrooms; use liquor from can as part of liquid with beef stock in making Brown Sauce. Add mushrooms, stir and heat. Serve hot over meat, chicken, and as called for in various recipes. Makes about 1½ cups sauce.

★BARBECUE SAUCE

1 cup diced peeled onions
2 tablespoon fat
1 cup chopped tomatoes
1 cup diced green peppers
1 cup diced celery
2 tablespoons brown sugar

½ tablespoon dry mustard
2 cups stock from roast or soup,
   or use meat cube or canned
   bouillon
Salt and pepper
1 cup ketchup

Cook onions slightly in fat in 2-quart saucepan; add remaining ingredients, stir, mix well. Cook over low heat about 1 hour. Sauce should be reduced about ½ by this time, and well blended. Serve with any meat but not with fowl. Makes about 3½ cups sauce.

★CHEESE SAUCE

Add 3 tablespoons grated Cheddar cheese to 1 cup hot thin or medium White Sauce, or to Cream Sauce. Stir and heat until cheese melts. Makes about 1 cup, using White Sauce, 1½ cups using Cream Sauce.

Mornay Sauce: Add ¼ cup each grated Parmesan and Swiss cheese to 1 cup hot thin White Sauce. Stir until melted. Use for au gratin sliced chicken, and as called for in recipes. Makes 1½ cups sauce.

CREOLE SAUCE

1½ cups Brown Sauce
2 tablespoons butter
2 tablespoons chopped peeled
   onion
2 tablespoons chopped green
   pepper
¼ cup sliced or chopped mushrooms

3 tablespoons sieved canned
   tomato
½ teaspoon salt
½ teaspoon paprika
1 teaspoon ketchup
1 teaspoon Kitchen Bouquet

Make Brown Sauce. Then cook onion in butter lightly, add green pepper, mushrooms, and tomato, stir and cook 2 or 3 minutes. Combine with Brown Sauce, season with remaining ingredients, and cook together over low heat about 20 minutes. Serve hot over thick broiled steak, sweetbreads, or pastas. Makes about 2 cups sauce.

EGG SAUCE

1 cup Brown Sauce made with
  fish stock

2 beaten egg yolks

1 tablespoon vinegar or lemon
  juice

MAKE Brown Sauce, stir while hot into beaten yolks, let cook a moment, stirring constantly until thick. Remove from heat, stir in vinegar or lemon juice, mix. Serve hot on boiled fish. Makes about 1¼ cups sauce.

HOLLANDAISE SAUCE

½ cup butter

2 or 3 egg yolks

1 tablespoon lemon juice

Few grains cayenne

¼ teaspoon salt

½ cup boiling water

BEAT butter until creamy in top of glass or enamel double boiler. Add yolks one at a time, beating well. Add lemon juice, cayenne, and salt, beating. About 5 minutes before serving, place over boiling water and stir the ½ cup boiling water rapidly into egg mixture, stirring and cooking until thickened. Serve at once. Makes about 1¾ cups sauce.

★HORSE-RADISH SAUCE (COLD)

1 cup heavy cream

Salt and white pepper

¾ cup grated horse-radish root, or
  drained prepared horse-radish

1 tablespoon sugar

1 tablespoon vinegar or lemon
  juice

WHIP cream until stiff, gradually beat in remaining ingredients. Wonderful with cold meats, aspics, hot roast meat. Makes about 2 cups sauce.

★APPLE HORSE-RADISH SAUCE

Combine 3 grated, pared apples and few chopped almonds with an equal amount of prepared horse-radish. Makes about 1¾ cups sauce.

★MAYONNAISE HORSE-RADISH SAUCE

Combine ¼ cup prepared horse-radish with 1 cup mayonnaise. Makes 1¼ cups sauce.

★HORSE-RADISH SAUCE (HOT)

Make Brown Sauce, add 3 tablespoons prepared horse-radish. Or make thin White Sauce or Hollandaise Sauce, remove from heat, add 3 or 4 tablespoons prepared horse-radish and ½ cup ketchup. So good with hot or cold meats and aspics. Makes about 1¾ to 2 cups sauce.

★TARTARE SAUCE

1 cup mayonnaise	1 tablespoon chopped olives
1 tablespoon chopped capers	1 tablespoon chopped cucumber
1 tablespoon tarragon vinegar	pickle

HAVE all ingredients cold. Combine, serve cold with fish, aspics, and seafood cocktails, and as suggested in recipes. Sometimes 1 tablespoon chopped chives or green onion is added. Makes about 1¼ cups sauce.

★TOMATO SAUCE

1¾ cups stewed or canned	3 cloves
tomatoes	2 tablespoons butter or other fat
2 slices peeled onion	2 tablespoons flour
8 peppercorns	1 tablespoon sugar
1 bay leaf	¼ teaspoon salt

COOK tomatoes 15 minutes with onion and spices, strain. Heat butter or fat in saucepan, stir flour in smoothly, add ⅔ of the hot strained tomatoes, stirring continually; add remaining ⅓ of the tomatoes. Cook and stir until thick. Season to taste. Serve hot over chops, fish, meat loaf, macaroni, and other pastas. Makes about 1½ cups sauce.

The fourteen recipes above from THE SETTLEMENT COOK BOOK, *by Mrs. Simon Kandor*

❧

The little cook book, *How To Use Spices,* published by The American Spice Trade Association, contains many recipes for tangy, flavorful sauces. Here are some of the best.

MUSTARD RAISIN SAUCE

3 tablespoons butter or margarine	½ cup seedless raisins
2 tablespoons flour	6 whole peppercorns
1½ cups stock from ham, tongue,	3 whole cloves
or beef	1 teaspoon dry mustard
½ cup brown sugar, packed	½ teaspoon salt
2 tablespoons lemon juice	¼ teaspoon grated lemon peel
1 tablespoon cider vinegar	

MELT butter or margarine in saucepan, stir flour in smoothly; remove from heat, stir in stock, cook and mix, adding remaining ingredients. Cook, stirring until slightly thickened. Serve hot over sliced beef tongue, aspic of meat, or with boiled or baked ham or barbecued meats. Makes about 3 cups sauce.

★CUCUMBER SAUCE FOR FISH

1 cup finely chopped, peeled
  cucumbers
½ teaspoon salt
1 tablespoon sugar

1 tablespoon cider vinegar
⅛ teaspoon white pepper
½ cup heavy cream

SPRINKLE cucumbers lightly with salt, let stand in covered glass jar or china bowl in refrigerator about 1 hour. Drain; combine with sugar, vinegar, and pepper. Whip cream, fold cucumbers in. Serve with broiled salmon steaks, cold boiled salmon, broiled fillets of haddock, swordfish steak, and other fish. Makes about 2 cups.

★MUSHROOM CELERY SAUCE

¼ pound (5 large) fresh mushrooms
2 tablespoons butter or margarine
1 (10½-oz.) can condensed cream
  of celery soup

¼ cup chicken or beef stock or
  bouillon
¼ teaspoon poultry seasoning
¼ teaspoon salt
¹⁄₁₆ teaspoon ground black pepper

WASH mushrooms, peel, slice tops and stems. Sauté in butter or margarine 4 or 5 minutes, until tender. Add remaining ingredients and cook until mixture is smooth and hot. Use slightly more bouillon if needed. Serve over vegetable soufflés, omelets, or croquettes. Makes about 1¾ cups sauce.

★SPICY SEAFOOD COCKTAIL SAUCE

1 cup canned Italian or Spanish
  tomato sauce
½ cup chili sauce
1 teaspoon minced onion
⅛ teaspoon garlic powder

1 teaspoon mixed pickling spice
  (tied in cheesecloth bag)
1 tablespoon prepared horseradish
1 tablespoon cider vinegar
1 tablespoon lemon juice

COMBINE all ingredients in enamel or glass saucepan. Cook, stirring until hot. Remove spice bag. Chill sauce. Serve with seafood cocktail. Makes about 1½ cups sauce.

★VINAIGRETTE SAUCE

½ cup French Dressing
1 tablespoon finely-cut parsley
1 tablespoon finely-chopped
  green pepper

2 tablespoon chopped pickle
1 teaspoon chopped chives
½ teaspoon paprika

COMBINE all ingredients; beat well with rotary beater. Serve cold over cooked hot green beans, or chilled cooked asparagus, or sliced boiled potatoes. Makes about ¾ cup sauce.

The five recipes above from HOW TO USE SPICES, *by The American Spice Trade Association*

❦

And from another small cook book, *The A.B.C. of Spice Cookery,* also published by the same American Spice Trade Association, here are four more sauces you will find yourself using often because they are so good.

★MINT SAUCE

¼ cup vinegar
¾ cup water
¼ cup flaked dried or finely-cut
  fresh mint leaves

1 tablespoon lemon juice
1 to 2 tablespoons sugar
¼ teaspoon salt

SIMMER vinegar in enamel or glass saucepan with half the water and half the mint until mixture reduces about half, about 4 to 5 minutes. Strain, add remaining water, lemon juice, sugar, and salt and remaining mint. Bring to boiling. Remove from heat, let cool. Chill. Serve with hot or cold lamb. Makes about ⅔ cup sauce. Reduce amount of sugar to make a tart sauce.

★PAPRIKA BUTTER SAUCE

½ cup butter
½ teaspoon salt
⅛ teaspoon pepper

¾ teaspoon paprika
1 tablespoon lemon juice

CREAM butter until fluffy. Beat in gradually the seasonings and lemon juice. Add to hot broiled fish, vegetables, steak. Makes about ½ cup sauce.

★POPPY SEED SAUCE

¼ to ½ cup butter
Juice ½ lemon

1 teaspoon poppy seeds
Dash cayenne

MELT butter, add remaining ingredients. Serve this dressing hot on hot or cold cooked asparagus, broccoli, cauliflower, and other vegetables. Makes about ⅓ to ⅝ cup sauce.

★SAVORY SAUCE FOR POTATOES

¼ cup butter
¼ teaspoon each onion, garlic and
   celery salt
½ teaspoon paprika

1 teaspoon parsley flakes or finely-
   chopped fresh parsley
¹⁄₁₆ teaspoon ground mace

MELT butter, add remaining ingredients. Serve hot over boiled new potatoes, or sliced boiled large potatoes. Makes about ¼ cup sauce.

The four recipes above from THE A.B.C. OF SPICE COOKERY, *by The American Spice Trade Association*

Dessert Sauces

Hᴏᴡ *To Cook Well* is the name of one of the best cook books in the huge library of America's food writers. Ann Roe Robbins, who wrote it, cooks superbly, and has put her recipes and ideas, help for beginners, and inspiration for gourmets into this volume. Here are some of her dessert sauces.

HARD SAUCE

⅓ cup butter
1 cup sifted confectioners' sugar

1 teaspoon vanilla extract or 1
   tablespoon brandy
Nutmeg

LET butter stand in medium-sized mixing bowl at room temperature about ½ hour to soften a little. Add sugar, about 1 tablespoon at a time, stirring well with spoon. Add vanilla or brandy last. Excellent on many kinds of dessert such as plum pudding, brown Betty, fruit pie. A little grated nutmeg may be sprinkled on top. Makes 10 or more servings.

Brown-Sugar Hard Sauce: Follow recipe above. Use ⅓ cup butter, 1 cup brown sugar firmly packed, then sifted, 1½ teaspoons vanilla or 2 tablespoons brandy or sherry. Fold in ½ cup heavy cream which has been whipped until stiff. The whipped cream makes a lighter sauce and stretches the number of servings to 15 or more.

Strawberry Hard Sauce: Follow recipe for Hard Sauce, omitting flavorings. Mash 1 pint hulled ripe or quick-frozen berries and sweeten with ¼ cup sugar. Drain juice, add juice slowly to hard sauce, stirring in smoothly. Then add berries, folding them in. Chill before serving. This sauce will separate a little, but it tastes wonderful. Serve either on warm cottage pudding or over toasted angel food or sponge cake. Makes 20 or more servings.

★BUTTERSCOTCH SAUCE

1 cup brown sugar, packed	1 tablespoon butter
3 tablespoons flour	½ teaspoon vanilla extract
1 cup boiling water	⅛ teaspoon salt
¼ cup cream or top milk	

COMBINE sugar and flour in saucepan, add water slowly, stirring and cooking until thickened; then lower heat and simmer gently 3 to 4 minutes longer, stirring continually. The mixture will be thick and must be stirred to avoid scorching. Just before serving, remove from heat, add cream or milk, butter, salt, and vanilla, and mix. If too thick, add little more cream. Should be served hot or warm on coffee or vanilla ice cream, cake, cottage pudding, toasted angel food, or sponge cake. Makes 6 to 7 servings.

★CHOCOLATE SAUCE

½ cup cocoa powder	¾ cup milk
1 cup granulated sugar	1 tablespoon butter
⅛ teaspoon salt	¼ teaspoon vanilla extract
2 tablespoons corn syrup	

COMBINE cocoa, sugar, salt, corn syrup, and cold milk in saucepan. Mix well, stir over low heat until mixture is smooth and sugar melted. Let cook on very low heat without stirring until a little dropped into cup of cold water forms soft lump (220 degrees F. on candy thermometer). Remove from heat, add butter and vanilla. Serve warm or cold on various desserts and ice cream. Also makes good base for chocolate-milk drinks. Makes 6 to 7 servings.

★COFFEE CREAM SAUCE

2 egg yolks	½ cup double-strength brewed
¼ cup sugar	coffee
⅛ teaspoon salt	1 cup heavy cream, whipped

BEAT yolks until thick and lemon-colored in top of double boiler, about 3 to 4 minutes with rotary beater. Add sugar, salt, and coffee and stir until well blended. Cook over boiling water, stirring constantly until thickened. Remove from heat, let cool. Fold in whipped cream. Serve with chocolate desserts, especially soufflés, steamed puddings, chocolate bread pudding, custard, or blancmange. Makes 7 to 8 servings.

★FUDGE SAUCE

1¼ cups cocoa powder	½ cup milk
¾ cup sugar	½ cup light corn syrup
½ teaspoon salt	2 tablespoons butter
1 tablespoon cornstarch	2 tablespoons vanilla extract

SIFT cocoa, sugar, salt, and cornstarch together in the top of a double boiler. Add milk and corn syrup and mix well. Cook over boiling water 15 to 20 minutes, stirring constantly, until thickened. Remove from heat, and stir in butter. Let sauce cool a little and add vanilla. Serve warm or cold on ice cream or cake. Makes 7 to 8 servings.

★LEMON SAUCE

1 tablespoon cornstarch	½ teaspoon grated lemon peel
½ cup sugar	2 tablespoons lemon juice
1 cup water	⅛ teaspoon salt
2 tablespoons butter	

COMBINE cornstarch and sugar in enamel or glass saucepan, slowly stir in cold water; cook over low heat, stirring constantly until sauce thickens. (A cornstarch sauce thickens before it reaches the boiling point, so this will take only a few minutes.) Remove from heat, stir in butter, lemon peel, juice, and salt. Serve at once. Good on cottage pudding, soufflés, fruit pudding, apple desserts, leftover cake, tapioca, peach cobbler, and many other desserts. Makes 5 to 6 servings.

The six recipes above from HOW TO COOK WELL, *by Ann Roe Robbins*

❧

A few more dessert sauces will round out your collection, especially since they are from *Thoughts for Buffets,* that helpful book which a group of Chicago hostesses put together from their favorite party and home menus.

CARAMEL SAUCE

1 pound wrapped caramels	½ cup miniature marshmallows
¾ cup light cream	1 tablespoon rum (optional)

UNWRAP caramels, place in top of double boiler with cream, over boiling water. Heat until melted, add marshmallows, let melt slightly, beat to mix, add rum. Serve at once, or let cool; reheat for later use. Makes 3 cups sauce.

MARRON SAUCE

¼ cup syrup from bottled preserved marrons
½ cup water

1 tablespoon cornstarch
⅛ teaspoon salt
2 tablespoons sherry

COMBINE syrup and ¼ cup water in saucepan, heat to boiling. Mix cornstarch with remaining ¼ cup water and add to boiling syrup, stirring constantly until thickened. Add salt and sherry. Serve warm or cold over ice cream and other desserts. Makes 6 to 8 servings.

★RASPBERRY SAUCE

¼ cup sugar
2 teaspoons cornstarch

1 (10-oz.) package quick-frozen
   raspberries, thawed

COMBINE sugar and cornstarch, stir in berries. Cook over moderate heat, stirring constantly, until mixture thickens and is clear. Let cool before serving. Delicious on ice cream, fruit soufflés, baked Alaska. Makes 6 to 8 or more servings.

RUM SAUCE

2 cups milk
4 egg yolks
½ cup sugar

⅜ cup rum
½ cup heavy cream

SCALD milk in top of double boiler. Beat yolks with sugar, add to milk slowly, stirring continually. Cook over boiling water until thickened and mixture coats spoon. Let cool. Stir in rum, whip cream and fold in. Chill. Serve cold on warm desserts such as puddings and apple cakes. Makes 8 to 12 or more servings.

VANILLA SAUCE

2 cups light cream or milk
½ cup sugar
4 beaten egg yolks

1 teaspoon vanilla extract
½ cup heavy cream
¼ cup liqueur or cordial

HEAT light cream or milk in top of double boiler; bring to boiling over direct heat; remove. Mix sugar with egg yolks and stir into hot cream. Cook over boiling water, stirring constantly until mixture thickens and coats spoon. Add vanilla. Let cool. Just before serving, fold in whipped cream and liqueur. Makes 8 to 10 servings.

The five recipes above from THOUGHTS FOR BUFFETS

THE
"BEST-OF-ALL"

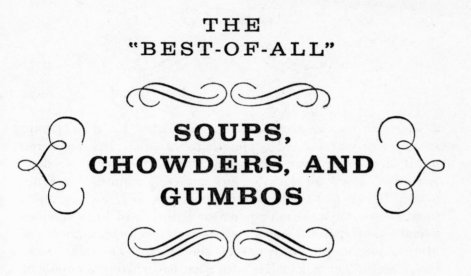

SOUPS,
CHOWDERS, AND
GUMBOS

THE RECIPES THAT FOLLOW HAVE BEEN SELECTED FROM THESE DISTINGUISHED BOOKS:

The Angostura Cook Book	*Angostura-Wuppermann Corporation*
The Frances Parkinson Keyes Cookbook	*Mrs. Frances Parkinson Keyes*
Kitchens Near and Far	*Herman Smith*
Metropolitan Cook Book	*Metropolitan Life Insurance Co.*
More Thoughts for Food	
The Perfect Hostess Cook Book	*Mildred O. Knopf*
Peter Hunt's Cape Cod Cookbook	*Peter Hunt*

SOUPS, CHOWDERS, AND GUMBOS

American homemakers can have available on their pantry shelves excellent canned soups, soups in dried and powdered forms, and soups, even richly delicious bisques, in their deep freezers, all ready for the table in a matter of minutes. But many women like to make a big family soup, especially for a winter's night supper, or a refreshing iced or jellied soup for a summer noonday porch party. Some of the best-of-all recipes for soups are in *More Thoughts for Food*, one of those three "Thoughts" cook books, each filled to its edges with good flavor. Here are some of their recipes for clear soups.

CLEAR MUSHROOM SOUP

Stems from 1 pound mushrooms, or ½ pound whole mushrooms   7 cups well-seasoned bouillon   Sherry

Wash mushrooms, chop fine, add to hot bouillon, simmer 30 minutes. Strain through cheesecloth. Reheat, flavor with 1 or 2 tablespoons sherry. Makes 8 or more servings.

HERB TOMATO SOUP   ⟶

Mix 1 (10½-oz.) can condensed tomato soup, ⅓ teaspoon rubbed savory, ⅛ teaspoon sweet basil and 1 soup can of water in saucepan. Simmer few minutes. Serve hot; top each serving with a pat of butter and a sprinkling of chopped parsley. Makes 2 to 3 servings.

Also shown in this menu-photograph, vegetable-medley platter containing asparagus, carrots Julienne, lima beans, garnished with stuffed eggs and stuffed mushrooms; Danish blue-cheese sauce is served over the stuffed mushrooms. For dessert, mint-gelatin mold, served with custard sauce.

Recipe for Herb Tomato Soup and color photograph, courtesy Campbell Soup Company

BOUILLON

5 pounds beef shank, cut in pieces
3 quarts cold water
Beef bones
¼ pound beef liver
2 tablespoons diced lean raw ham
1 No. 2 can tomatoes
1 teaspoon peppercorns
2 bay leaves
2 cloves

1 tablespoon salt
3 carrots, scraped and sliced
2 stalks celery, diced
2 large onions, peeled and left whole
1 turnip, pared
6 sprigs parsley
Paprika

PLACE about ⅔ of the meat in 1-gallon soup kettle, cover with the 3 quarts cold water, let stand ½ hour. Brown remainder of beef in hot frying pan with marrow from bones; add browned meat and bones to kettle, heat to boiling. Skim thoroughly, reduce heat, cover kettle and let simmer 2 hours. Add remaining ingredients and continue to cook slowly 3 hours longer. Strain, let cool. Skim fat from top. Clarify bouillon. Makes about 1½ quarts bouillon.

To clarify bouillon. Use white and shell of 1 egg for each quart stock. Break shell into small pieces and add with slightly-beaten egg white to stock. Place over low heat, stir constantly until it begins to boil. Boil 2 minutes. Remove from heat, add 1 tablespoon ice water, and set aside 10 minutes. Strain through double cheesecloth placed over a fine-mesh strainer.

BOUILLON FIGARO

To rapidly boiling clarified bouillon add dash Maggi seasoning and finely-cut cooked noodles. Use about 1 tablespoon noodles for each cup bouillon.

←   **BLUE CHEESE CHILI SALAD DRESSING**

¾ cup crumbled American blue cheese (about 4 ounces)
⅔ cup wine vinegar

¼ cup salad oil
⅛ teaspoon chili powder

Mix your favorite Chef's Salad. Then combine the cheese, vinegar, oil, and chili powder; mix, and pour over a large salad (to serve 6 or 8) toss and serve at once. Makes about 2 cups dressing.

Recipe for Blue Cheese Chili Salad Dressing and color photograph, courtesy American Blue Cheese Association

BOUILLON WITH EGG BARLEY

1½ quarts Bouillon
Egg barley

Dash Maggi seasoning

HEAT clarified bouillon (above) to boiling point, add egg barley gradually and boil 10 minutes. Add dash Maggi seasoning. Serve at once. Makes 6 or more servings.

EGG BARLEY

Beat 1 egg, add about ⅞ cup sifted all-purpose flour, or enough to make a dough, knead it into a hard ball. Break into small pieces. Let dry. Grate into small crumbs and dry in slow (250 degrees F.) oven a few minutes. Use in soup as described.

BOUILLON WITH VEGETABLE DUMPLINGS

1 bunch parsley
1 stalk celery
½ green pepper
½ peeled onion
2 tablespoons poultry fat
1 slice bread

Salt and pepper
Ground ginger
Noodle dough
1 egg white
1½ quarts bouillon

WASH and drain vegetables, chop fine or grind together, using fine blade. Cook in hot fat 10 minutes, stirring. Add to bread which has been soaked in water and then squeezed dry. Season lightly with salt, pepper, and ginger. Roll noodle dough thin and cut into 2-inch squares. Place small amount of vegetable-bread mixture on each square, dampen edges with egg white, fold over and press firmly together with fork. Let dumplings stand on breadboard several hours to dry. Drop into 1½ quarts boiling bouillon, add dash of Maggi seasoning, boil 10 minutes. Makes 6 or more servings.

★CONSOMME A L'ORANGE

Place wafer-thin slice of unpeeled orange and ½ teaspoon minced parsley in each warmed soup cup or plate. Add hot, well-seasoned consommé or bouillon.

★CONSOMME WITH EGG PUFFS

3 tablespoons flour
2 tablespoons poultry fat
Water
2 eggs

Salt and pepper
1 cup peas
2 quarts bouillon
1 tablespoon minced parsley

Brown flour in fat, add enough water to form thick paste; remove from heat, add eggs, one at a time, beating thoroughly after each addition; season lightly. Add peas to hot bouillon, bring bouillon to boiling, drop very small spoonfuls of batter into boiling soup. Cook until puffs rise to top. Serve in warmed soup plates, sprinkle parsley on puffs. Makes 8 or more servings.

★CLEAR TOMATO SOUP

1 (No. 2½) can tomatoes
1 teaspoon sugar
1 stalk celery, diced
1 large onion, peeled and chopped

1 tablespoon butter
2 tablespoons flour
1 quart boiling-hot bouillon
Croutons

Combine tomatoes, sugar, and celery. Sauté onion in butter until brown, stir in flour smoothly and let cook 2 minutes. Stir into bouillon. Add tomato mixture, bring to boiling point again, lower heat, and let simmer 2 hours. Strain. Reheat and serve with croutons. Makes 5 or more servings.

JELLIED MADRILENE

1 quart chicken stock
1 quart cooked or canned
  tomatoes
1 cup diced celery
½ cup diced scraped carrots
½ cup sliced peeled onions
6 sprigs parsley
4 cloves
2 bay leaves

2 teaspoons salt
½ teaspoon peppercorns
1/16 teaspoon cayenne
3 tablespoons gelatin
1/3 cup cold water
2 tablespoons sherry
1 teaspoon sugar
½ teaspoon lemon juice

Combine stock, tomatoes, vegetables, cloves, bay leaves, salt, peppercorns, and cayenne in 3-quart soup kettle. Bring to boiling, lower heat, and let simmer 45 minutes. Strain, cool, and clarify. There should be 3 pints. Reheat. Soften gelatin in 1/3 cup cold water. Stir into hot soup, add sherry, sugar, and lemon juice. Fill 6 or more bouillon cups and chill in refrigerator. Or chill in large bowl until jellied, break with fork, and spoon into chilled cups at serving time. Garnish with very thin slice lemon, finely-minced parsley on the lemon. Makes 6 or more servings.

The ten recipes above from MORE THOUGHTS FOR FOOD

Thousands of young homemakers have found it easier to plan and serve meals just because they own the small, lively, well-edited, authentic *Metropolitan Cook Book,* which is published by the Metropolitan Life Insurance Company. Its editors drew upon the latest findings of the home economists of the American Institute of Baking, American Meat Institute, Poultry and Egg National Board, and other large test kitchens. Here are some of the soups from its pages.

SOUP STOCK

2 to 3 pounds bone and meat
3 quarts water
Few sprigs parsley
1 onion, peeled and sliced
Celery stalk and leaves cut fine

1 or 2 carrots, scraped and sliced
1 bay leaf
4 cloves
6 peppercorns
Salt to taste

LESS expensive cuts of meat—shin, neck, oxtail—and small scraps of meat such as flank end of steak, or leftovers and bones of roast or poultry, may be used for soups. Cut meat into small pieces. Pour cold water over meat in large soup kettle, 1 quart water for each pound meat. Let stand ½ hour. Then bring to boiling slowly, add remaining ingredients, cover kettle, let simmer over low heat about 3 hours. Skim off froth which rises during first part of cooking. At end of 3 hours remove from heat, let cool. Then strain and place in refrigerator in covered jar until used. Fat will rise to top and form a protective covering. If part of stock is used, fat should be removed and heated with remaining stock then let cool, and returned to refrigerator. Will keep a week. Makes 1 to 2 quarts stock.

★ONION SOUP

2 tablespoons butter or margarine
2 medium-size onions, peeled and thinly sliced
2 cups beef or chicken stock or canned bouillon

Salt and pepper
French bread
Grated Parmesan cheese

MELT butter or margarine in 1-quart saucepan, add onions, and cook gently until lightly browned. Add stock, and salt and pepper if needed; simmer about 15 minutes. Toast slices of French bread, sprinkle generously with cheese, brown lightly under broiler heat. Place 1 slice cheese toast in each soup bowl, pour hot soup over it. Makes 2 servings.

★SPLIT-PEA SOUP

1 cup dried green or yellow split peas	Ham bone or end of ham (optional)
1 small onion, peeled and quartered	4 cups stock, water, or milk Salt

WASH peas, look over, cover with 3 cups cold water and soak overnight. (Quick-cooking varieties need no soaking.) To cook, add onion and a little salt to soaked peas. If ham is used, omit salt. Cover and bring to boiling, then lower heat and let cook slowly until peas are soft, 1 hour or longer for most dried peas. Remove ham bone. Put peas through food mill or sieve, return to liquid they have cooked in, add stock, water, or milk. Bring to boiling again, reduce heat, stir well. Makes 4 to 6 servings.

Bean Soup: Use dried white beans, red kidney beans, or leftover baked beans in recipe above. With baked beans omit first step. Sieve cooked beans (white, red, baked) or leave whole. Complete the recipe as given above. Add crisp bits of cooked bacon or small cubes ham before serving. Makes 4 servings.

Lentil Soup: Follow recipe for Split-Pea Soup, using washed and drained lentils. Add diced, scraped carrot, few sprigs parsley, and 1 cut-up tomato or ¼ cup ketchup. Cooked lentils may be put through sieve or left whole. About 15 minutes before serving, add 1½ frankfurters, thinly sliced. Makes 4 servings.

The five recipes above from METROPOLITAN COOK BOOK, *by The Metropolitan Life Insurance Co.*

❦

A winter soup made with cabbage, from Herman Smith's *Kitchens Near and Far,* is filling enough for a one-dish supper.

CABBAGE SOUP

2 large onions, peeled and minced	Salt and pepper
3 tablespoons butter or margarine	½ pint sour cream
2 quarts beef stock	2 tablespoons minced parsley
1½ pounds green cabbage, chopped fine	1 teaspoon caraway seeds

COOK onions in butter or margarine until soft and yellow, add to boiling stock with cabbage and seasoning. Cook rapidly 10 minutes. Into each warmed soup bowl or plate put a dessert spoonful of sour cream which has been combined with the parsley and caraway seeds. Pour soup over and serve. Makes 8 or more servings.

GARLIC SOUP

2 to 4 cloves garlic, peeled and minced fine

2 tablespoons oil or butter

3 pints beef or chicken stock, or use bouillon cubes

6 (4-inch) squares toasted bread

2 hard-cooked eggs, sliced

6 tablespoons grated cheese

2 tablespoons minced parsley

Cook garlic in butter or oil in 2-quart kettle until soft but not browned. Add stock, bring to boiling, reduce heat, and let simmer 20 minutes. Place toast in 6 warmed soup bowls or plates, cover with thin egg slices, pour soup over all. Sprinkle each serving with combined cheese and parsley. Makes 6 servings.

JOHN'S WATER CRESS SOUP

2 bunches water cress

1 quart veal or chicken stock, or use bouillon cubes

½ pound lean pork

White corn meal

2 tablespoons butter

1 small onion, peeled and minced

Salt, pepper, nutmeg

1 cup light cream

About ¼ cup fried noodles

Wash and drain the water cress, chop fine. Cook it in the stock 20 minutes on low heat. Cut pork into tiny cubes, coat with corn meal, cook over low heat in butter with onion until light brown. Add pork to water cress and stock, let simmer about ½ hour. Add seasonings and cream, stir, and serve in warmed soup bowls. Add spoonful of crisp fried noodles to each serving. Makes 4 servings.

The three recipes above from KITCHENS NEAR AND FAR, *by Herman Smith*

❦

Around Cape Cod many families have Portuguese cooks. The artist Peter Hunt, almost as famous as the Cape, has lived in that area for many years. His cook, a Portuguese, always wears her hat in the kitchen, which may or may not have some bearing on the quality of her cooking. In any case, here are two of the Portuguese soups long established as favorites in the Hunt household.

KALE SOUP

1 cup dried pea beans

1 large onion, peeled and sliced

1 pound choriços (high spiced sausages), browned on all sides

1 pound kale, washed, drained, trimmed

1 tablespoon salt

½ teaspoon pepper

1 tablespoon vinegar

2½ quarts water

2 cups diced, pared potatoes

SOAK beans overnight in cold water to cover. In the morning, drain, pour into 3-quart soup kettle, add onion, sausages cut in pieces, kale broken in pieces, salt, pepper, vinegar, and the 2½ quarts water. Bring to boiling, reduce heat, let simmer on low heat 2 to 3 hours. Add potatoes and one additional cup water if needed. Continue cooking 10 minutes or until potatoes are tender. Makes 6 large servings.

★FISH CHOWDER

½ cup salt pork cubes
1 cup chopped, peeled onions
6 cups cold water
3 cups diced potatoes
1 teaspoon salt
¼ teaspoon pepper

½ teaspoon saffron
1 tablespoon vinegar
2 pounds lean fish (haddock, whiting, or flounder) cut in chunks

IN deep, heavy kettle, try out pork cubes slowly, turning them frequently until only crisp bits remain. Remove these crisp bits to use later. Cook onions in the hot fat until soft and golden. Add water, potatoes, seasoning, and vinegar. Let boil about 10 minutes or until potatoes are half done. Add fish, continue cooking gently 15 minutes or until fish is tender. Add browned pork bits and serve. Makes 6 servings.

The two recipes above from PETER HUNT'S CAPE COD COOKBOOK

❧

If you are still in the mood for seacoast soups, *The Angostura Cook Book,* prepared for the Angostura-Wuppermann Corporation, is the source of several soups which will feed your family and guests with satisfaction.

ELAINE'S CRAB SOUP

2 hard-cooked eggs
1 tablespoon butter, melted
1 tablespoon flour
Grated peel 1 lemon
Salt and pepper
1 quart milk

½ pound canned or cooked crab meat, flaked
½ cup cream
1 teaspoon Angostura bitters
Sherry (optional)

MASH eggs in 2-quart saucepan, add butter, stir flour in smoothly, add lemon peel and dash of pepper. Bring milk to boiling, pour slowly into egg mixture, stirring constantly. Add flaked crab meat, cook stirring over low heat 5 minutes. Add cream and again bring to boiling point. Remove from heat, add a little salt, the bitters, and 1 tablespoon sherry. Serve at once in warmed bowls. Makes 4 or more servings.

LOBSTER CHOWDER

2 (6½-oz.) cans lobster, or 2 (8-oz.)
rock lobster tails
2 cups diced pared potatoes
Boiling water
¼ cup butter or margarine
½ cup minced peeled onions

½ cup minced celery
¼ cup minced green pepper
3 pints milk
2 teaspoons Angostura bitters
Pilot crackers

DRAIN lobster, cut into small cubes. If deep-frozen lobster tails are used, thaw, pull meat from shell, and cut into small cubes. Cook potatoes in salted boiling water to cover until tender, drain. Melt butter or margarine in 2-quart kettle, add onions, celery, green pepper, and diced rock-lobster meat. Cook 3 minutes over low heat until lobster is tender and has lost its transparency. Add potatoes and milk and bring slowly almost to boiling point. (If canned lobster is used, add with the milk.) Correct seasoning and add bitters. Serve in warmed bowls, with pilot crackers. Makes 6 servings.

VICHYSSOISE CONTINENTAL

1½ cups sliced, peeled onions or 6
leeks, sliced
3 cups sliced, pared potatoes
4 cups water
5 chicken bouillon cubes
1 cup milk

1 cup cream
2 teaspoons bitters
Salt and pepper
Paprika
Minced chives or parsley

COMBINE onions or leeks and potatoes in 2½-quart kettle. Add 4 cups water, bring to boiling, add bouillon cubes. Stir and heat, cook over moderate heat until vegetables are very soft. Press through sieve. Reheat soup, add milk, cream, and bitters. Correct seasoning by adding a little salt, pepper, and paprika. Chill. To serve, beat thoroughly. Pour into chilled cream-soup cups, add chives or parsley. Makes 6 servings.

The three recipes above from THE ANGOSTURA COOK BOOK, *by The Angostura-Wuppermann Corporation*

❧

W hen Frances Parkinson Keyes was writing in Louisiana, she gathered many local recipes for the collection she had accumulated from many parts of the world. Her gumbo recipes, from famous hostesses in and near New Orleans, are among the best in her varied and interesting book, *The Frances Parkinson Keyes Cookbook*. Here is one of her recipes for gumbo.

SEAFOOD AND OKRA GUMBO

12 small hard-shell crabs, or 2
    pounds crab meat
2 pounds shrimp
2½ pounds small tender okra
3 tablespoons shortening
1 large onion, peeled and sliced
1 green pepper, minced
3 cloves garlic, peeled and minced
3 cups cooked or canned tomatoes

2½ quarts shrimp stock and oyster
    liquor combined
3 sprigs parsley
3 sprigs fresh thyme, or 1 tea-
    spoon dried thyme
1 bay leaf
Salt and pepper
3 dozen bulk oysters
Hot freshly-cooked dry rice

SCALD crabs in boiling water and clean, removing the spongy substance and sand bag. Remove claws and crack them, and cut bodies into quarters. Wash shrimp thoroughly, remove heads and shells. Remove dark vein that runs along back. Cook shrimp heads 30 minutes in 2½ quarts salted water; strain, reserving liquid, and discarding shrimp trimmings.

Wash okra, slice ⅛-inch thick. In large (at least 1-gallon) kettle melt shortening and sauté okra, onion, green pepper, and garlic over low heat about 1 hour, or until okra ceases to "rope." Stir frequently. Stir in tomatoes gradually, and add the combined shrimp stock and oyster liquid. Add parsley, thyme, bay leaf, crabs and shrimp; simmer over low heat about 45 minutes. Add oysters and simmer 15 minutes longer. Serve over hot freshly cooked dry rice in large soup plates. Makes servings for large buffet party, 12 or more plates.

The recipe above from THE FRANCES PARKINSON KEYES COOKBOOK

❧

U nusual soups, as tempting as they are different, are among the collector's recipes of the *The Perfect Hostess Cook Book,* by Mildred O. Knopf. One of the best is a cold soup, to highlight a summer luncheon party.

★RED CAVIAR MADRILENE

3½ (12½-oz.) cans tomato
    madrilène
2 ounces (4 tablespoons) red
    caviar

½ pint sour cream
¼ cup chopped chives

POUR tomato madrilène into 6 individual bouillon cups. Stir a heaping teaspoon red caviar into each cup. Place cups on tray, cover lightly with waxed paper, chill in refrigerator until set. Just before serving, top each with teaspoon sour cream and sprinkle with chives. Makes 6 servings.

APPLE AND BANANA SOUP WITH CURRY

1 pint chicken stock or consommé
1 apple
1 banana
1 potato, pared and diced fine

1 onion, peeled and diced
1 pint light cream
1 tablespoon curry powder
3 tablespoons finely-cut chives

HEAT chicken stock or consommé in 1-quart saucepan. Pare apple and cut small pieces into the stock, slice banana and add potato and onion. Cook over moderate heat until vegetables and fruit are soft. Press through a strainer. Add cream and curry powder, mix smoothly. Chill in refrigerator in covered bowl. When thoroughly chilled, serve in chilled soup cups, sprinkled with chives. Makes 6 servings.

TOMATO-SURPRISE SOUP

1 onion, peeled and diced
¼ cup diced celery
6 tablespoons butter
5 tablespoons flour
1 quart milk
1 pint light cream

3 cups cooked or canned tomatoes
1/16 teaspoon soda
Salt and pepper
About 1 cup flaked crab meat
½ cup best sherry

COMBINE onion and celery in 2-quart enamel or glass saucepan with butter; cook until soft. Remove from heat, stir in flour smoothly. (No lumps, please.) Return pan to heat, stir in milk a little at a time, stirring and cooking until it thickens. Add cream, a little at a time, stirring. Bring to boil, and boil 3 minutes, stirring constantly. Strain tomatoes through sieve into bowl, add soda, mix, stir into cream sauce, season with salt and pepper to taste. Add flaked and carefully cleaned crab meat. Reheat slowly, stirring, adding sherry. Serve at once in warmed cream-soup bowls. Makes 8 servings. [The author says, "Add as much flaked crab as preferred."]

The three recipes above from THE PERFECT HOSTESS COOK BOOK, *by Mildred O. Knopf*

THE
"BEST-OF-ALL"

VEGETABLE DISHES

THE RECIPES THAT FOLLOW HAVE BEEN SELECTED FROM THESE DISTINGUISHED BOOKS:

The Art of Jewish Cooking	*Jennie Grossinger*
The Cordon Bleu Cook Book	*Dione Lucas*
Hibachi Cookery In The American Manner	*George E. Engler*
Peter Hunt's Cape Cod Cookbook	*Peter Hunt*
The Vegetable Cook Book	*Cora, Rose, and Bob Brown*

VEGETABLES

In the last few years Japanese restaurants have become popular in American cities and the thousands of young homemakers who have enjoyed the simple, well-flavored, delicious foods served around the low tables in these restaurants have acquired a new concept of cookery. Many of them have adapted the Japanese recipes in their homes, using, at least for barbecues and other outdoor entertaining, the hibachi stoves—small charcoal-fueled affairs.

George E. Engler, an American in Japan, put together a lively, informative cook book for his Japanese and American friends, on how to use the hibachi for American dishes. His way with vegetables (learned from Japanese cooks as well as from American methods) as described in *Hibachi Cookery In The American Manner,* is timely and is in accord with nutritional trends to preserve garden-fresh flavor and original vitamin and mineral content. His recipes are, of course, as usable in our kitchens as on hibachi stoves in the patio or in the back yard. They are simple, practical, and result in the best of vegetable dishes.

Here are George Engler's general instructions for vegetable cookery.

PREPARATION AND COOKING METHODS

All vegetables should be thoroughly washed in warm water before cooking. Do not soak fresh vegetables which are to be cooked in water, as this weakens tissues. Dried beans and peas should be soaked in cold water for at least 3 hours. Navy beans (other dried legumes according to package directions) should be soaked overnight.

Vegetables should not be overcooked; too much boiling will result in loss of food values, and the vegetables will become soft and mushy and spoil the appearance of the finished dish. Most vegetables should be cooked in the least amount of water possible, in a covered pot so that steam does the cooking. In all cases, the water should be boiling before vegetables are added.

Strong-flavored vegetables, such as cabbage, cauliflower,

sprouts, and turnips are cooked in deep water, uncovered, to allow the strong odors to escape and to preserve the color of the vegetables.

Vegetables should be seasoned after water has been drained off; make use of this liquid by adding it to stock pot, or in making Cream Sauce, except with strong-flavored vegetables, in which case discard the cooking liquid. Canned vegetables are already cooked; heat them, but do not boil. Unless vegetables are to be served immediately, keep them hot in double boiler until serving time. Cook quick-frozen vegetables by directions on the package.

★ASPARAGUS

Wash thoroughly to remove sand, drain. Cut off tough lower ends of stalks, tie in bundles. Use tall asparagus cooker, stand bundles in boiling water with tips above water, cover and boil gently until lower ends are tender, 15 to 25 minutes. Serve with seasoning of salt, pepper, and melted butter.

Or serve with hot Cheese Sauce, Hollandaise, or White Sauce.

Or bread the stalks and fry in deep hot fat.

Or chill and use in salads, or serve with Vinaigrette Sauce.

Average serving is 4 to 6 stalks, depending on size of asparagus and way it is served. As bought, about ¼ pound makes 1 serving.

★GREEN BEANS

Wash thoroughly, remove tips and strings running along outer edge. Cook in boiling water to cover, 15 to 20 minutes. Drain. Season and serve with melted butter.

Or sauté with chopped bacon and sliced onions.

Or serve with Cheese Sauce, Hollandaise, or White Sauce.

Or chill, and use in salads.

As bought, about ¼ pound makes 1 serving.

Wax beans: Prepare and serve like green beans.

★GREEN LIMA BEANS

Wash pods, drain, and shell. Boil limas in small amount of water, 20 to 30 minutes. Add salt and pepper, just as they finish cooking. Serve like green beans with melted butter.

Or serve with Cheese Sauce, Hollandaise, or White Sauce.

Or combine with stewed tomatoes and onions and serve hot.

Or chill, and serve in salads.

As bought, 1 pound shelled beans (3 pounds in pods) makes 6 servings.

★BEETS

Remove leaves, wash leaves thoroughly and save. Scrub beets, rinse, and drain. Cook uncovered in boiling water, 30 to 60 minutes. Drain, and pull skins off. If beets are small, leave whole. Slice larger beets. Season and serve with melted butter.

Creamed Beets: Add beets to medium White Sauce.

Harvard Beets: Combine ½ cup sugar, ½ tablespoon cornstarch, ¼ cup water, ¼ cup vinegar in large enamel or glass saucepan, stir and heat to boiling; boil 5 minutes. Add about 1½ cups sliced cooked beets and 2 tablespoons butter, and serve hot.

As bought, 1 pound beets yields about 2 cups sliced or small whole beets, 3 to 4 servings.

Beet Greens: Follow directions for cooking and serving spinach.

★BROCCOLI

Remove tough outer leaves and root ends. Look over carefully for insects. Wash carefully, drain, cook uncovered in boiling water, 15 to 20 minutes. Drain, serve like asparagus. As bought, about ½ pound makes 1 serving.

★BRUSSELS SPROUTS

Cut off stems and remove wilted leaves. Clean, wash, and drain. Cook uncovered in boiling water, 10 to 15 minutes. Drain and serve like asparagus, except for deep frying. As bought, 1 quart sprouts makes 6 servings.

★CABBAGE

Remove outer leaves. Shred or cut into quarters or eighths. Cook uncovered in boiling salted water, about 20 minutes. Drain. Serve with melted butter, Cheese Sauce, or White Sauce.

Or sauté with chopped bacon and onion.

Or serve with melted butter seasoned with soy sauce.

Or combine and heat with stewed tomatoes.

As bought, about ¼ pound makes 1 serving.

★CARROTS

Wash and scrape. Leave whole, or dice, slice, or cut julienne, depending on the size and shape of carrots. Cook in boiling water until tender, about 15 to 20 minutes. Drain. Season and serve with melted butter.

Or combine with cooked peas or celery, or both, season and serve with melted butter.

Or serve with White Sauce.

Or bread larger pieces of carrot and deep fry.

Or glaze cooked carrots by sautéeing few minutes in butter and sugar in frying pan.

Or chill and serve in salads.

As bought, ⅓ pound makes 1 serving.

★CAULIFLOWER

Remove leaves and stalk. Wash and cook uncovered in boiling water, 20 minutes if left whole, about 8 minutes if separated into flowerettes. Season and serve like asparagus.

As bought, ⅓ to ½ pound makes 1 serving.

★CORN ON THE COB

Remove husks and silk. Cook in boiling water 8 to 15 minutes. Serve at once with melted butter, salt, and pepper. Count 2 medium-sized ears as 1 serving. Garden-fresh corn, pulled and brought into the kitchen in a matter of minutes after leaving the stalk, cooks in 3 to 5 minutes, especially the small-grain tender white varieties and some small-grain yellow varieties.

★GREEN PEAS

Wash, drain, and shell. Cook peas in boiling water until tender. If pods are very young (or for Chinese snow peas) shelling is not necessary. Remove string and ends and cook whole, 10 to 15 minutes. Season peas with salt and pepper and serve with melted butter. Add cooked snow peas to various Chinese dishes (as given in Foreign Cookery section. *See* Index.).

Cooked peas may be served with White Sauce.

Or combined with cooked carrots and other vegetables.

Or, cold, added to vegetable salads and aspics.

As bought, ½ pound peas in pods makes 1 serving; 1 pound peas in pods makes about 1 cup shelled peas.

★OKRA

Wash thoroughly, cut off stems. If pods are large, slice. Cook in boiling water, 20 to 30 minutes, or until tender and no longer ropy. Drain. Combine with stewed tomatoes, reheat, season with salt and pepper.

Or sauté cooked okra with onion and green pepper.

Or bread large pieces cooked okra and deep fry.

As bought, ¼ pound makes 1 serving.

★ONIONS

Peel, cook whole if small. If large, slice or quarter. Cook uncovered in boiling water, 8 to 10 minutes. Drain. Season, combine with melted butter or Cream Sauce or White Sauce.

Or sauté raw onion and green pepper in butter with cooked green beans and bacon.

Or combine with other cooked vegetables.

Or bread slices raw onion and deep fry.

As bought, ¼ pound makes 1 serving.

★SPINACH

Remove roots and all spoiled leaves; wash carefully through several cold waters to remove all sand and insects. Drain slightly; place in top of double boiler and steam in its own moisture; do not add water. Cook about 8 minutes. Season with salt, pepper, and melted butter; garnish with hard-cooked egg slices and lemon wedges.

Or combine with Cheese Sauce or White Sauce.

Or chop and add to scrambled eggs.

Or chill and use in cooked-vegetable aspic or salads.

As bought, about ⅓ pound spinach makes 1 serving.

★SQUASH

Wash, drain, pare, and remove seeds from small yellow summer squash. Cut into pieces, steam in double boiler 20 to 30 minutes, or until very soft. Mash, season with salt, pepper, and butter or cream; whip to lightness. A good flavor variation is made with sieved cooked onions beaten into mashed squash.

Or parboil sticks or pieces of squash, drain, and wipe dry. Bread them and deep fry. Or bake, seasoned with salt, pepper, and butter.

As bought, ⅓ to ½ pound makes 1 serving.

Zucchini Squash: Scrub, rinse, and drain. Slice and cook in small amount of oil 4 or 5 minutes, or until tender. Season with salt and pepper.

Or bread quartered zucchini and deep fry.

As bought, 1 small zucchini makes 1 serving.

★TURNIPS

Wash, pare, cut into cubes. Cook, uncovered, in boiling water 15 to 30 minutes. Season with salt and pepper and add melted butter.

Or combine with White Sauce.

Or drain and sauté with onions in butter.

As bought, ⅓ pound makes 1 serving.

The suggestions and seventeen recipes above from HIBACHI COOKERY IN THE AMERICAN MANNER, *by George E. Engler*

❧

Much the same type of simple cookery is sponsored by the Browns (Cora, Rose, and Bob) in *The Vegetable Cook Book*. But they also include many more elaborate dishes which are such good eating they deserve to be added to every kitchen library. Such a one is this dish of Brussels sprouts:

★STUFFED BRUSSELS SPROUTS

1 quart Brussels sprouts	Salt and pepper
1 cup minced cooked lamb	1 beaten egg
½ cup crumbs	Brown Sauce, or browned butter

WASH, drain sprouts, and remove wilted or damaged leaves. Remove centers with short, sharp knife. Fill with mixture of lamb, crumbs, seasoning, and beaten egg. Tie each small stuffed sprout with thread. Steam in upper part of double boiler, or cook uncovered in a little fast-boiling water, 20 to 25 minutes. Drain, remove strings, dress with small amount hot Brown Sauce or browned butter. Makes 6 servings.

★SCALLOPED CAULIFLOWER

1 medium-sized head cauliflower	1 beaten egg
1 cup fine bread crumbs	Salt and pepper
2 tablespoons melted butter	Ground nutmeg
Light cream or top milk	1 tablespoon onion juice

TRIM cauliflower, wash, drain, and separate into flowerettes. Cook uncovered in boiling water until almost tender, 6 to 8 minutes. Drain, place in greased 2-quart baking dish. Start oven at moderate (375 degrees F.). Combine crumbs, butter, enough cream or milk to moisten; add beaten egg, about ½ teaspoon salt, ⅛ teaspoon pepper, few grains nutmeg, and the onion juice. Blend, spread over cauliflower. Cover dish. Bake 10 minutes in moderate oven. Uncover, let bake until top is lightly browned. Makes 4 to 6 servings.

★YAMS

Although many people consider yams and sweet potatoes as one and the same vegetable, the yam belongs to a different tuber family. It is cooked in the many ways in which we cook sweet potatoes, and since yams are deeper in color, more moist or tender, and sweeter than sweet potatoes, they make excellent combinations with game. It is with game dishes they are most highly esteemed in the Southern part of the U.S. Here is one recipe:

★GEORGIA YAMS WITH DUCK OR GAME

Wash, scrub, and drain medium-sized or small yams. Cover with cold water, bring to boiling, and boil until tender, 15 to 25 minutes. Drain, peel, slice. Start oven at moderate (350 degrees F.). Grease 2-quart baking dish.

For each 2 cups sliced yams, use:

2 tablespoons butter
½ cup brown sugar, packed
Ground nutmeg

1 cup pared and sliced apples
½ cup chopped nuts
Extra butter

MAKE layer of sliced cooked yams in bottom of prepared dish, add dabs of butter, sprinkle with little sugar and few grains nutmeg; make layer of apples on yam slices, add butter, little sugar, nutmeg; cover with remaining yam slices, add remaining butter, sugar and nutmeg. Sprinkle top with nuts and extra dabs of butter. Bake uncovered in moderate oven, 30 to 40 minutes, or until top is well browned. Makes 6 servings.

The four recipes above from THE VEGETABLE COOK BOOK, *by Cora, Rose, and Bob Brown*

❧

Much more sophisticated and Continental-influenced vegetable cookery appears in that treasury of many luxurious recipes, *The Cordon Bleu Cook Book,* by Dione Lucas. For instance, this artichoke recipe:

ARTICHOKES WITH VINAIGRETTE SAUCE

6 artichokes
½ lemon
2 tablespoons vinegar

1 tablespoon lemon juice
½ teaspoon salt
Vinaigrette Sauce

To boil artichokes, strip off larger outside leaves, cut off stalks and trim bases neatly. Rub with lemon to prevent their turning black. Snip off the top of each leaf with kitchen scissors within a couple of inches of the base. Remove the inner choke; tie thread around the largest circumference of each artichoke. Blanch head-down in fast-boiling water to which is added vinegar, lemon juice, and salt. Turn heat down, let simmer 15 minutes. If leaves come off easily, the artichoke is fully cooked. Drain and cool. Serve cold with a Vinaigrette Sauce. Makes 6 servings.

BROCCOLI SOUFFLE

3 tablespoons fat
3 tablespoons flour
Salt
Cayenne pepper
¾ cup milk
2 tablespoons grated Parmesan
  cheese

1 teaspoon dry mustard
3 beaten egg yolks
1 cup sieved cooked broccoli
4 egg whites
Sweet butter

MELT fat in saucepan, stir in flour smoothly, add salt, few grains cayenne, and when well blended, stir in milk slowly. Cook, and stir until thickened; add cheese, mustard, egg yolks, and broccoli, blend well. Start oven at moderately hot (400 degrees F.). Grease soufflé dish and tie wide band of waxed paper around the outside; it should be several inches higher than the dish. Whip egg whites until stiff. Fold into broccoli mixture. Pour at once into prepared soufflé dish. Bake 30 minutes in moderately hot oven. Remove dish from oven, quickly remove paper, add few curls sweet butter to top of soufflé. Serve at once. Makes 6 servings.

MUSHROOM SOUFFLE

2 tablespoons fat
3 tablespoons flour
Salt
Cayenne pepper
¾ cup milk

½ cup sautéed sliced mushrooms
3 or 4 beaten egg yolks
2 tablespoons grated cheese
5 egg whites

MELT fat in saucepan, remove from heat, stir in flour smoothly, add salt, and cayenne. When well blended, return to heat, stir in milk, cook and stir until thickened. Start oven at moderately hot (400 degrees F.). Grease soufflé dish and tie wide band of waxed paper around the outside; it should be several inches higher than dish. Add mushrooms, egg yolks, and cheese to sauce. Whip egg whites until stiff, fold into mushroom mixture, and pour into prepared dish. Bake 30 minutes in moderately hot oven. Remove dish, discard paper band and serve at once. Makes 6 servings.

MUSHROOMS WITH SHERRY

2 cups mushrooms
2 or 3 tablespoons butter
Salt and pepper

1 tablespoon sherry
1 tablespoon finely-chopped dill

WASH and drain mushrooms; slice very thin into hot butter in saucepan. Season with salt and pepper, cook briskly 2 or 3 minutes, stirring once or twice. Pour sherry over and sprinkle with dill. Serve hot with any chicken dish. Makes 4 servings.

PEAS JOHN SCOVILLE

1 cup small pearl onions
2 cups shelled peas
½ pound small white mushrooms

Juice 1 lemon
¼ cup olive oil
Salt and pepper

WASH and skin onions, drain, cover with cold water and bring to boiling. Remove from heat and drain. Cover peas with cold water, bring to a boil, and drain. Wash mushrooms in water and lemon juice; drain. Cut into thick slices, sauté in hot oil in flameproof (metal-base) casserole 2 or 3 minutes. Add onions, peas, a little salt and pepper, cover casserole with lid, and shake over low heat 10 to 15 minutes or until peas are just soft but not mushy. Serve in casserole. Makes 4 to 6 servings.

★POTATOES BOULANGERE

1 pound potatoes, pared and
   sliced
¼ pound Gruyère cheese, sliced
   thin
1 pound onions, peeled and
   sliced thin

Salt and pepper
½ cup stock or bouillon
½ cup bread crumbs
¼ cup graded cheese
4 tablespoons butter, melted
French mustard

START oven at moderate (350 degrees F.). Grease 2-quart casserole. Arrange a layer of sliced potatoes in casserole, add thin slices cheese, and layer of onion slices. Sprinkle with salt and pepper; repeat layers until dish is full. Press down well, pour stock or bouillon over all.

Sprinkle with bread crumbs and a little grated cheese. Pour melted butter over. Cover with piece of buttered waxed paper. Bake in moderate oven 20 minutes, remove paper, continue baking 10 to 15 minutes longer, or until potatoes are done and browned. Serve at once. Makes 6 servings.

★POTATOES ANNA

2 pounds potatoes
Salt and pepper

¾ cup butter, melted
French mustard

START oven at hot (425 degrees F.). Butter a shallow pan, such as round layer-cake pan. Scrub, rinse, pare potatoes, cut into thin slices. Arrange slices in pan, slightly overlapping. Sprinkle with salt, pepper, little melted butter, and about ⅛ teaspoon French mustard. Repeat layers, seasoning each same way, until pan is full. Pour remaining melted butter over all. Press slices down well. Bake in hot oven 40 to 50 minutes, or until potatoes begin to come away from side of pan. Remove from oven, slide knife carefully around side of pan and give it a knock on the edge of the stove. Turn out on hot serving platter and serve at once. Makes 6 servings.

★POTATOES MONTROUGE

4 potatoes
4 carrots
1 egg
3 tablespoons grated cheese
2 tablespoons fat

2 tablespoons sour cream
Salt and pepper
½ teaspoon dry mustard
Additional grated cheese and
   butter

SCRUB, rinse, and pare potatoes in long slices. Wash and scrape carrots, and cut in long slices. Cover both vegetables with water and cook until very soft. Drain, rub through sieve or strainer. Beat egg, grated cheese, the fat, sour cream, salt, pepper, and mustard together, then into potato-carrot mixture. Arrange on heatproof serving dish, sprinkle with cheese, dot with butter. Brown under moderate broiler heat. Makes 6 or more servings.

★POTATOES SAUTEE

2 pounds potatoes
5 tablespoons butter
Salt and pepper

1 tablespoon chopped fresh
   rosemary or other herb

SCRUB potatoes, rinse, pare. Cover with water, bring to a boil. Remove from heat, drain, and dry well with towel. Cut into thick slices. Melt butter in heavy skillet, add potatoes, season with salt and pepper. Shake over heat until they begin to brown, add herb, and continue cooking until done. Heap on hot serving dish, sprinkle lightly with additional rosemary or other herb. Serve at once. Makes 6 servings.

The nine recipes above from THE CORDON BLEU COOK BOOK, *by Dione Lucas*

A traditional family potato dish from *The Art of Jewish Cooking*, that amazingly good book by Jennie Grossinger, is:

POTATO KUGEL

3 eggs
3 cups grated, drained potatoes
1/3 cup potato flour
1/2 teaspoon baking powder
1 1/2 teaspoons salt

1/8 teaspoon pepper
3 tablespoons grated onion
4 tablespoons melted butter or
  fat

START oven at moderate (350 degrees F.). Grease 1 1/2-quart baking dish. Beat eggs until thick, stir potatoes, potato flour, baking powder, salt, pepper, onion, and butter or fat into eggs, mix well. Turn into prepared baking dish. Bake in moderate oven about 1 hour, or until top is well browned. Serve hot. Makes 6 to 8 servings.

The recipe above from THE ART OF JEWISH COOKING, *by Jennie Grossinger*

❧

The potato pancakes in Peter Hunt's kitchen are Polish, according to his amusingly decorated and informative cook book, *Peter Hunt's Cape Cod Cookbook*. Here is the recipe given him by two friends who feature the pancakes at an annual breakfast party.

★POTATO PANCAKES

1 1/2 pounds potatoes
1 pint milk
3 eggs
2 tablespoons butter

Powdered cinnamon
Sugar
Sour cream

SCRUB, rinse, and pare potatoes. Boil until tender, drain. Rub through sieve or strainer into mixing bowl. Add beaten egg yolks, butter, and light sprinkling of cinnamon and sugar. Whip egg whites stiff and fold into batter. Cook as you would thin pancakes, on a hot griddle. Serve with sour cream. Makes 6 to 8 servings.

The recipe above from PETER HUNT'S CAPE COD COOKBOOK

THE
"BEST-OF-ALL"

HOSTESS HELPERS

THE RECIPES THAT FOLLOW HAVE BEEN SELECTED FROM THESE DISTINGUISHED BOOKS:

Our Candy Recipes, and Other Confections   *May B. Van Arsdale and Ruth Parrish Casa Emellos*

The Holiday Candy Book   *Virginia Pasley*

Holiday Candies   *Compiled by Edna Beilenson*

Picture Cook Book   *Editors of LIFE*

HOSTESS HELPERS

No cook book is really complete without these good candies, special preserves, and a word or two about sandwiches.

Candies and Confections

For Christmas kitchen parties, teenage cookery sessions, and many other occasions, recipes for fine homemade candies and other sweets should be in the kitchen file of the best of all good things to eat. To answer candymaking questions, there is one authoritative book, *Our Candy Recipes, and Other Confections,* by May B. Van Arsdale and Ruth P. Casa Emellos. It is professional enough to please chefs and commercial confectioners, yet simple enough to provide any home candymaking session with whatever is most wanted. For tea table, gift box, the after-dinner coffee tray, here are five recipes from these authors:

★CANDIED ORANGE PEEL

4 medium-sized oranges	1 cup water in which orange
Cold water	peel cooked
2 cups sugar	Extra sugar

WITH point of sharp knife, cut through peel of each orange so it can be removed in quarters. Cover peel with cold water, bring to boiling point, reduce heat and cook slowly until soft. Drain, saving water for making syrup.

Scrape out white inner portion of cooked peel with teaspoon. With scissors cut yellow skin into thin strips. Combine sugar and 1 cup water in which peel cooked. Should there be less than 1 cup of this liquid, add water to make up the measure. Boil to 238 degrees F. on candy thermometer (soft ball is formed when a little is dropped in a cup of cold water). Add orange peel, cook slowly 10 minutes or longer, until most of water has evaporated. Drain in coarse sieve. Drop peel, few pieces at a time, in a pan containing granulated sugar. Separate pieces with forks, roll each piece until completely covered with sugar. Shake off excess. Makes about 70 pieces candied peel.

Candied Grapefruit or Lemon Peel: Candied grapefruit peel can be prepared in same way as orange. Because of size of grapefruit, peel should be removed in 6 sections. Use fresh water for syrup instead of water in which peel cooked. In cooking syrup for lemon peel, use fresh water and add 6 or 7 whole cloves.

★HONEY CARAMELS

2 cups sugar	½ cup milk
1 cup light corn syrup	½ cup strained honey
1 cup condensed milk	¼ cup butter
½ cup light cream	2 teaspoons vanilla extract

COMBINE all ingredients except vanilla in 1½-quart saucepan. Cook over low heat, stirring slowly but constantly, until mixture reaches 248 degrees F. on candy thermometer (firm ball is formed when a little is dropped in a cup of cold water). Remove from heat, add vanilla, turn at once into lightly-greased square or oblong pan. When almost cold, mark lines for cutting with pointed knife. When cold, turn block of candy out of pan onto waxed paper. Cut into squares at once with sharp knife. Wrap each caramel in waxed paper or colored foil. Makes 72 caramels, about 2¼ pounds.

★PENUCHI

3 cups brown sugar, packed	1½ teaspoons vanilla extract
1 cup light cream	⅔ cup broken black-walnut
1 tablespoon butter	kernels

COMBINE sugar and cream in 1½-quart saucepan, cook over low heat, stirring slowly but constantly until temperature of 236 degrees F. is reached on candy thermometer (soft ball is formed when a little is dropped in a cup of cold water). Remove from heat, add butter, and set aside to cool without stirring.

When lukewarm (110 degrees F.), beat until thick and creamy. Add vanilla and nuts and mix. Pour into lightly-greased square or oblong pan. When cold, cut into squares. Makes 18 pieces, 1¼ pounds.

★STUFFED PRUNES

15 prunes	¼ cup blanched almonds
6 candied apricots	Orange juice, optional

WASH prunes, drain. Steam about 5 minutes. Remove seeds. Put candied apricots and nuts through food chopper, knead well together. If apricots are dry, add a little orange juice to moisten. Stuff prunes. Do not roll prunes in sugar because it detracts from the black shiny appearance and does not improve flavor. Makes 15 stuffed prunes.

★SPICED NUTS

½ pound blanched almonds, pecans, or walnuts
2 cups confectioners' sugar
½ cup cornstarch
2 teaspoons salt
½ cup ground cinnamon

2 teaspoons ground ginger
1 tablespoon ground cloves
1 teaspoon ground nutmeg
1 egg white
1½ tablespoons cold water

ALMONDS may be used alone or combined with pecans or walnuts or both. Heat nuts in slow oven 10 minutes. Sift sugar, cornstarch, salt, and spices together 3 times to mix thoroughly. Combine egg white and water in bowl and beat slightly so egg will not be stringy. Put a few nuts at a time into a coarse strainer and dip up and down in egg white until each nut is well coated with egg. Drain. Roll drained nuts in small amount of spice mixture on sheet of waxed paper. When all are coated with spice, pour layer of the spice mixture into a shallow pan, scatter spiced nuts over this, leaving spaces between nuts. Cover with remaining spice mixture. Start oven at very slow (200 degrees F.). Bake nuts 3 hours. The long baking gives spices opportunity to penetrate the nuts and also makes nuts crisp. Finished nuts should be completely covered with a thin, brittle coating of the spiced sugar mixture. Remove pan from oven, sift sugar from nuts. Keep sugar-spice mixture in covered glass jar for future use. Makes ½ pound spiced nuts.

★TABLE FOR CANDYMAKERS
To be used as guide in purchasing materials

Almonds	1 cup weighs 4	ounces;	4	cups to pound
Butter	" " " 8	"	2	" " "
Cherries, candied	" " " 8	"	2	" " "
Cocoa	" " " 4½	"	3½	" " "
Corn Syrup	" " " 12	"	1⅓	" " "
Dates	" " " 5¾	"	2⅘	" " "
English wal- nuts, shelled	" " " 3¾	"	4¼	" " "
Peanuts, shelled	" " " 6¼	"	2½	" " "
Pecans, shelled	" " " 3¾	"	4¼	" " "
Pistachio nuts	" " " 4	"	4	" " "
Raisins	" " " 5	"	3⅓	" " "

(*See* Equivalent Tables, Index, for other products.)

CANDY TEMPERATURE CHART

Fudge, penuchi, operas, maple cream, etc.	234 or 238 degrees F.	soft	ball	cold	water
Fondant	238 or 240 degrees F.	"	"	"	"
Caramels	246 or 248 degrees F.	firm	"	"	"
Taffies	265 to 270 degrees F.	hard	"	"	"
Butterscotch, toffee, etc.	290 to 300 degrees F.	crack	"	"	"
Brittles	300 to 310 degrees F.	hard crack	"	"	
Clear hard candies	310 degrees F.	"	"	"	"

The two charts and five recipes above from OUR CANDY RECIPES, AND OTHER CONFECTIONS, *by May B. Van Arsdale and Ruth Parrish Casa Emellos*

Ready-mix fudges and other candy mixes available today seem to have encouraged youngsters as well as grownups to make more candy at home, and candy-recipe books are in demand the year round. A second such book in your kitchen might be *The Holiday Candy Book,* by Virginia Pasley. The recipes are easy to follow. Here are three of the best:

★HAZELNUT TRUFFLES

1 cup finely-ground hazelnuts	½ cup water
½ cup sugar	2 tablespoons confectioners'
2 (1-oz.) squares bitter chocolate, grated	sugar
	2 teaspoons cocoa

MIX nuts with sugar and chocolate in 1-quart suacepan. Blend in water gradually. Place over low heat, stirring constantly until chocolate is melted and sugar dissolved. Mixture will be thick and hard to handle. Let cool. Form into balls, using about 2 teaspoons of mixture for each. Roll balls in combined confectioners' sugar and cocoa. Makes 24 to 36 truffles.

★HONEY NOUGAT

2 cups sugar

2 cups light corn syrup

½ cup water

¼ cup egg whites

5 tablespoons liquid honey

4 tablespoons butter

½ teaspoon vanilla extract

1 cup toasted almonds

Butter and powdered sugar for pan

COMBINE sugar, corn syrup, and water in 2-quart saucepan. Blend with wooden spoon, place over low heat. Stir slowly but constantly until sugar begins to dissolve. Continue stirring until mixture boils, then insert the candy thermometer and let candy boil, without stirring, over moderate heat until thermometer registers 300 degrees F. (hard crack, or a little dropped in a cup of cold water instantly hardens and can be broken or cracked). Meanwhile beat egg whites until they stand in stiff peaks, add honey slowly, beating. Remove mixture from heat at the 300 degrees F. (hard crack in cold water) temperature. Remove and let stand until it stops bubbling. Then add hot syrup to egg whites and honey, beating continuously. Add butter, beat in well. When very thick, add vanilla and almonds. Pour into 8-×-11 pan lightly buttered and sprinkled with powdered sugar. Let stand overnight in cold place, not refrigerator. Cut with sharp knife. Wrap pieces in waxed paper, colored foils, or moisture-proof cellophane. Makes 80 pieces, about 2⅓ pounds.

★PULLED MINTS

2 cups sugar

⅔ cup water

1 tablespoon light corn syrup

Cornstarch

Flavoring and coloring

Confectioners' sugar

COMBINE sugar, water, and corn syrup in 2-quart saucepan; stir to blend well. Place over low heat, stir until sugar dissolves and mixture comes to boiling. Wipe away any crystals that form in pan while cooking, using either pastry brush or fork wrapped in muslin and dipped in hot water. After syrup boils, put candy thermometer into saucepan and cook without stirring until 265 degrees F. is reached (or a little dropped in a cup of cold water forms a hard ball). Remove pan from heat and pour candy onto buttered plates, dividing into portions to be colored separately. When candy is cool enough to handle, dip fingers in little cornstarch, fold edges into center. Add flavor and coloring to each plate of taffy as you start pulling. One teaspoon peppermint extract is enough for whole batch. Amount of coloring depends on tint desired; pink, green, and white are favorites, made with a drop or two of pure food colorings. The less color used, the more appetizing the candy. Pull candy, using corn-starch on fingers and hands to prevent sticking. When candy is hard to pull and has become quite cool, twist it out into long rope and cut with scissors in small pieces. Dust pieces generously with confectioners' sugar. Store in airtight container, with confectioners' sugar over and around all pieces. After a few days the candy becomes smooth and mellow. Makes about 90 pieces ½ inch long, about 1 pound.

The three recipes above from THE HOLIDAY CANDY BOOK, *by Virginia Pasley*

❦

Sugary popped corn or cereal balls are other favorites for kitchen parties in *Holiday Candies,* by Edna Beilenson.

★COCOPOP BALLS

4 cups sugar-coated popped
  corn, puffed rice, or wheat
½ cup sugar
½ cup light molasses
¼ cup light corn syrup

¼ cup light cream
⅛ teaspoon salt
1 tablespoon butter
1 cup shredded coconut

START oven at moderate (350 degrees F.). Spread popped corn or puffed cereal in pan and heat 10 minutes, or until lightly toasted. Combine sugar, molasses, syrup, cream, salt, and butter in 2½-quart saucepan. Cook over low heat, stirring until sugar dissolves. Bring to boiling and stir occasionally, insert candy thermometer and when mixture reaches 248 degrees F. (or a little dropped in a cup of cold water forms a firm ball), remove from heat. Quickly mix corn or cereal and coconut into syrup. Let cool only minute or two, use little butter on hands and shape into balls. Makes 2½ dozen, 2 inches in diameter.

★CHOCOLATE PECAN CRUNCH

1½ cups butter
2 cups sugar
1 cup coarsely-chopped pecans

¼ pound semisweet chocolate
¼ cup grated pecans

IN heavy iron pan or skillet cook butter and sugar together, slowly, until candy thermometer registers 260 degrees F. (firm ball in cold water). Add chopped pecans and continue cooking until thermometer registers 300 degrees F. (hard crack in cold water). Pour mixture out in well-buttered pan. When candy is almost firm, melt chocolate over hot water, brush bottom of candy with chocolate, lifting candy in pan, then replacing it to brush top with chocolate. Sprinkle ground nuts over chocolate while still soft. Let stand until cool and chocolate is firm. Break or cut in pieces. Makes about 30 pieces, slightly more than 1 pound.

The two recipes above from HOLIDAY CANDIES, *by Edna Beilenson*

Preserves and Relishes

These are favorites for sandwich tray, the dinner table, and to give as Christmas gifts, or to make for church bazaars and fairs.

★UNCOOKED CHERRY RELISH

1 cup dark cherry preserves
¼ cup sliced blanched almonds
  or chopped pecans
¼ cup grated orange peel

1 tablespoon finely-cut fresh
  mint leaves
Orange or pineapple juice

COMBINE preserves, nuts, peel, and mint. If necessary, thin with little orange or pineapple juice. Serve with cold cuts or hot roast duck, chicken, turkey, browned hash, barbecued meats. Makes about 1½ cups relish.

PICKLED APRICOTS

8 or more ripe apricots (2 pounds)
1 pound sugar
1 cup cider vinegar

1 cup water
2 (3-inch) sticks cinnamon
⅛ teaspoon ground cloves

SCALD apricots, let stand few minutes, pull skins off. Leave whole. Combine sugar, vinegar, water, and spices in agate or enamel saucepan. Bring to boiling, cover, and boil 5 minutes. Add 2 or 3 apricots at a time to hot syrup, keep syrup boiling gently until all fruit has been added; let cook 10 to 15 minutes after last apricots are added or until fruit is tender. Have two 1-pint glass jars washed and in a kettle of boiling water. When fruit is tender, remove jars one at a time with sterile lifter. Drain jar, spoon hot fruit into it, pour syrup over fruit to fill jar; seal at once. Let stand few weeks or longer before using. Makes 2 pints.

PICKLED GREENGAGE PLUMS

3 pounds small greengage plums
1 pound sugar
1 (3-inch) stick cinnamon,
  broken

6 whole cloves
1 cup cider vinegar
1 tablespoon finely-minced
  pickled watermelon rind

WASH plums, drain, prick each in several places with large needle. Place fruit in large agate or enamel kettle. Combine sugar, spices, vinegar, and watermelon pickle in another enamel saucepan and bring to boiling. Pour boiling hot over plums. Let stand 15 minutes. Drain off syrup, bring to boiling again, and pour over plums again. Let stand 15 minutes. Drain off, reheat to boiling, pour over plums, and boil 5 minutes. Have ready two 1-pint glass jars and one ½-pint jar, washed and in kettle of boiling water. As soon as fruit is ready, remove jars one at a time from boiling water with sterile jar lifter, drain jar. Spoon fruit into jar, fill with hot syrup. Seal at once. Repeat, filling remaining two jars. Let stand several weeks or longer before using. Makes 2½ pints.

SPICED CURRANTS

4 quarts fresh ripe red, white, or black currants
½ teaspoon whole cloves
1 (2-inch) piece cinnamon

2 pounds sugar
1 pint cider vinegar
¼ cup grated orange peel

WASH, drain, and stem currants. Tie spices in small cheesecloth bag; heat spices, sugar, vinegar, and orange peel in 4-quart agate or enamel kettle to a boil. Add currants, cook slowly, uncovered, about 20 minutes, or until fruit is bursting. Remove spice bag. Let fruit cook down a little and thicken. Stir occasionally. Have six 1-pint glass jars washed and in boiling water. When mixture is ready, remove jars one at a time with sterile jar lifter, drain jar, fill with hot mixture, and seal at once. Repeat until all jars are filled. Makes about 6 pints.

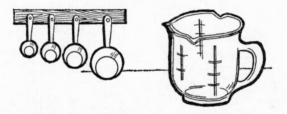

TOMATO FIGS

2 pounds small yellow egg-shaped tomatoes
1 lemon, thinly sliced
2½ cups sugar

¾ cup brown sugar, packed
1½ cups water
1 ounce green ginger root
½ teaspoon ground ginger

WASH and drain tomatoes. Do not scald and peel. Pierce each with needle in 2 or 3 places. Remove any seeds from sliced lemon. Combine sugars and water in 3-quart agate or enamel saucepan, stir until dissolved, add thinly sliced, mashed, or pounded ginger root, ground ginger, and lemon. Bring to a boil, stir, and boil 5 minutes longer. Add tomatoes. Cook slowly until tomatoes are transparent. Have two 1-pint glass jars and one ½-pint jar washed and in boiling water. When mixture is ready, remove jars one at a time with sterile jar lifter, drain jar. Spoon tomatoes in, pour syrup over tomatoes to overflowing. Seal at once. Let stand several weeks or longer before using. Makes about 2½ pints.

Sandwiches

In the large, colorful *Picture Cook Book,* by the editors of *Life* magazine, sandwiches are given the glamour treatment they deserve. Because, as that book makes dramatically clear in color photographs of many American parties, a sandwich today can be a full supper, a meal in itself. Various fillings are set out on buffet or table, and diners help themselves—fillings and breads, spreads, and condiments varied endlessly. Here are examples.

★CHICKEN ROLL SANDWICH

Toast hard rolls, cut slice off top, scoop contents out, fill shells with chicken salad. Garnish with sliced pimiento-stuffed olives. Have plenty of olives, pickles, seasoned cottage cheese, radishes, and fruit to go with these.

← ROAST TURKEY

1 turkey, 10 to 12 lbs., ready-to-cook
2 teaspoons Accent

1 to 2 teaspoons salt
Melted fat

Clean the turkey and cut off the neck, if not already removed. Leave on the neck skin. (If turkey is frozen, thaw according to package directions.) Rinse, drain, and pat dry with absorbent paper. Rub cavities of turkey with a mixture of salt and Accent. Lightly fill body and neck cavities with stuffing. (See stuffing recipes in Poultry and Game Bird chapter.) Close body cavity by sewing or by skewering and lacing with cord. Fasten neck skin to back with skewer. Tie drumsticks to tail. Bring wing tips onto back. Brush skin thoroughly with melted fat.

To roast turkey, place breast side up on rack in roasting pan. If meat thermometer is used, place it in center of inside thigh muscle. Place fat-moistened cheesecloth over top and sides of turkey. Keep cloth moist during roasting by brushing occasionally with fat from bottom of pan. Roast uncovered in moderate oven (325 degrees F.) for 4 to 4½ hours, or until turkey tests done. (The thickest part of drumstick feels soft when pressed with fingers protected with clean cloth or paper napkin. Or drumstick moves up and down or twists out of joint easily. Or meat thermometer registers 190 degrees F.) Remove turkey from oven, and put it in a warm place. Allow turkey to stand 30 to 40 minutes so that it will absorb its juices and become easier to carve. Remove cord and skewers. Serve turkey on a hot platter garnished with parsley. Makes about 16 servings.

Recipe and color photograph, from Culinary Arts Institute Cookbook © Book Production Industries, Inc.

★POOR-BOY SANDWICH

Derived from the hero-type sandwich of Italian laborers' lunch boxes, this teen party favorite calls for long thin French or Italian loaves. Cut thin flute loaves straight down from top to bottom, butter both pieces generously, arrange an array of good things on bottom slice such as thin rounds of salami, thin slices Swiss cheese and boiled ham. Have mustard pot at hand, other savory garnishes such as thin slices pickle, green pepper, and scallions. Cover bottom half with buttered top half, cut long sandwich crosswise in sections. Or, for big eaters, serve the whole thing, or slice across once, making 2 long poor-boys. Vary spreads and vary shape by using round Italian bread and other loaves. The loaf must be outsize in length or diameter, however, so sandwich is a whopper.

CROWN ROAST OF PORK WITH CORN STUFFING———→

5 to 6-pound crown roast from pork loin (12 ribs)
Salt and pepper
9½-ounce package corn crackers, rolled coarsely
¾ cup butter or margarine, melted
3 cups pared, diced cooking apples

1 cup cooked dried apricots, drained and chopped
1 cup minced peeled onions
¼ cup sugar
Chop frills
Spiced crab apples
Parsley

Have meat dealer shape and tie roast to form a circle with ends of rib bones exposed. Make sure backbone is removed for easy carving. Wrap exposed bones with aluminum foil to prevent charring. Rub surface of meat with salt and pepper. Combine cracker crumbs with melted butter or margarine. Add apples, apricots, onions, ⅛ teaspoon pepper, and the sugar. Mix well. Makes about 4 cups stuffing. Pack lightly into center of roast. Start oven at moderate (325 degrees F.). Roast 3 to 4 hours, or until roast-meat thermometer inserted into center or meaty part of one chop registers 185 degrees F. Remove roast to heated platter; discard bone coverings and decorate chop ends with paper frills. Garnish roast with spiced crab apples and parsley. Makes 6 or more servings.

Recipe for Crown Roast of Pork and color photograph, courtesy Nabisco

★PINK ONION AND LIEDERKRANZ SANDWICH

1 pink onion per person, sliced
Seasoned vinegar
1 to 3 slices softened Liederkranz cheese per person

Sour rye bread
Pumpernickel and other favorite
  breads
Softened butter

Buy large pink Italian onions, peel, slice into bowl, cover with seasoned vinegar, let marinate 1 hour. Remove cheese from refrigerator 2 hours before serving. To serve, drain onions, place in decorative bowl, slice cheese and stack neatly on cheese board. Slice breads, provide softened butter, salt, and pepper, and let everyone make his own. Fresh fruit and a cold or hot beverage complete this supper.

★RIVIERA SANDWICH

Largest round-loaf Italian bread, cut crosswise through loaf to give large round slices. Spread slices with butter. Arrange sliced tomatoes in ring around each slice, place sliced or pitted ripe olives and sardine fillets in center of slice. This, like some other large sandwiches, is eaten with knife and fork, and calls for vinegar and oil, or salt, pepper, and finely pulverized dried herbs or herb salt.

★CHEESE AND CHILI-BURGER SANDWICH

Traditional hamburger patty, seasoned with red wine and dressed with chili sauce or cheese sauce or both, sauces kept hot in casseroles over candleflame. Raw onion rings. Butter, toasted split hamburger buns go with these. So do long crisp leaves of romaine or endive.

The sandwich recipes from PICTURE COOK BOOK, *by the editors of* Life

See Index for Sandwich suggestions in Foreign Section.

THE "BEST-OF-ALL"

FOREIGN DISHES

THE "BEST-OF-ALL" FOREIGN DISHES

THE RECIPES THAT FOLLOW HAVE BEEN SELECTED FROM THESE DISTINGUISHED BOOKS:

Alexandre Dumas' Dictionary of Cuisine	*edited by Louis Colman*
Andre Simon's French Cook Book	*edited by Crosby Gaige*
Around the World in Eighty Dishes	*Lesley Blanch*
The Art of Caribbean Cookery	*Carmen Aboy Valldejuli*
The Art of Chinese Cooking	*The Benedictine Sisters of Peking*
The Art of Hungarian Cooking	*Paula Pogany Bennett*
The Art of Italian Cooking	*Maria Lo Pinto*
Colette's Best Recipes	*Marie Jacques*
Dinner at Omar Khayyam's	*George Mardikian*
Elena's Secrets of Mexican Cooking	*Elena Zelayeta*
The Escoffier Cook Book	*Auguste Escoffier*
European Cooking	*prepared in Wezäta Förlag, Sweden*
Favorite Recipes from the United Nations	*United States Committee for U.N.*
French Home Cooking	*Claire de Pratz*
The Gentle Art of Cookery	*Mrs. C. F. Leyel and Miss Olga Hartley*
German Cookery	*Elizabeth Schuler*
Good Food From Sweden	*Inga Norberg*

II.

FOREIGN COUNTRIES, U.S. POSSESSIONS AND NEW STATES

Books on cookery from other countries have been popular in America since settler days. Some of the very earliest of these have been newly published, their ancient recipes given modern-kitchen testing to make them usable in today's homes. For linguists, great encyclopedias of cuisine in French, German, and Swedish, still untranslated, head up the varied stimulating, and rewarding collection of foreign cook books now available to American cooks and homemakers. Along with these huge professional volumes, there are the hundreds of cook books written in English, by chefs and epicures of other countries for American publishers. And, the most useful and appreciated group, the cook books written by Americans who have lived in other parts of the globe long enough to understand and capture the essence of the cuisine of countries visited.

We have selected delectable, adaptable, practical recipes from these best-of-all books on foreign cookery. They are all excellent, no matter the flag under which they originated.

To keep our foreign cookery alphabetical, we start with recipes from Africa.

Africa

Twenty years ago it wasn't as easy to circle the earth as it is today. But Pearl V. Metzelthin, a gourmet and the wife of a diplomat, did go around the world five times. She lived in eleven different countries long enough to learn the housekeeping and cookery of those lands, and she collected recipes from her friends and the good cooks of a great many more places. She spoke eight languages, which may have helped in convincing native cooks they should share their culinary gifts with her, and she put these recipes, menus, and much good talk of food into her book, *The New World Wide Cook Book,* which Tony Sarg illustrated for her.

There are many Africas—the Belgian Congo, Nigeria, Abyssinia, Ethiopia, French Equatorial and West Africa, British East Africa, British West Africa, Federation of Central Africa, Senegal, Madagascar, Ghana, Union of South Africa. Native foods are interesting and varied on that continent, but not easily adapted to United States homes; the dishes more likely to satisfy us are those which French, German, Dutch, and British settlers in Africa lived upon, dishes made of locally-grown products but cooked in European recipes only slightly modified by their African locale. Such as this recipe from British Equatorial Africa, which is also popular in the Cape area:

ROAST TURKEY WITH ROAST POTATOES

12-pound turkey ready for cooking	2 quartered peeled onions
¼ cup flour	2 tablespoons butter
1 teaspoon each, sugar, salt, pepper, and ground cinnamon	12 or 14 potatoes
	Flour
½ teaspoon ground ginger	Fat
½ clove garlic, peeled and minced	Salt

RINSE and drain dressed, cleaned turkey; pat dry. Mix together flour, sugar, salt, pepper, cinnamon, ginger, and garlic; rub mixture over turkey inside and out. Place bird in large pan, cover with waxed paper, and let stand in refrigerator overnight. To cook, place turkey in large kettle, cover with cold water, add onions. Bring to boiling, lower heat and boil slowly until tender, about 4 hours. Drain boiled turkey, save stock for gravy and basting. Place bird in uncovered roasting pan, dot generously with butter.

Start oven at moderately hot (400 degrees F.). Place pan in oven, baste bird frequently with a little stock. While turkey roasts, prepare potatoes. Scrub, rinse, drain, and pare, cut into thick slices or quarters. Boil gently in salted water about 10 minutes; drain; pat dry. Roll semicooked potatoes in flour, place in shallow pan, dot with butter or fat, and bake in oven with turkey. Turn potatoes frequently, adding more fat if needed for good browning. Sprinkle lightly with salt. Turkey should roast until lightly browned all over, about 1 hour. Start potatoes in oven after first half hour; potatoes should be browned at end of turkey's roasting time. Makes 12 or more servings.

In North Africa, in the Egyptian area the cookery is similar to that of Near Eastern Europe and other Arabic peoples' cookery. Here is one of Madame Metzelthin's favorite Egyptian fish dishes:

SAYADIA
Fish with Lemon

2½ pounds sea bass or other
  fish fillets
⅓ cup olive oil
1½ cloves garlic, peeled and
  minced
Juice 4 lemons

4 cups water
1½ teaspoons salt
¼ teaspoon pepper
1 teaspoon curry powder
¼ cup chopped parsley

PLACE fillets in saucepan. Heat oil in another pan, sauté garlic about 5 minutes. Combine lemon juice, water, salt, pepper, curry powder, and parsley, pour over fish; add hot oil and garlic. Cover pan and cook over low heat 25 to 30 minutes. Let cool, then chill until set. Serve chilled with sections of lemon and garnished with sprigs of parsley or mint. Makes 4 to 6 servings.

This popular dish, another favorite in Cape homes, originates in South Africa.

BABOTJE
Casserole of Meat and Eggs

2 pounds ground meat, raw or
  cooked
1 thick slice bread
¼ cup milk
3 eggs
1½ teaspoons curry powder
1 tablespoon sugar
1 teaspoon salt
¼ teaspoon pepper
14 almonds, blanched and
  pounded

1½ tablespoons lemon juice or
  vinegar
2 medium-sized onions, peeled
  and chopped
2 tablespoons fat or butter
6 orange or lemon leaves,
  optional
1½ cups milk
¼ teaspoon salt

USE any preferred meat, raw or cooked. Soak bread in milk and beat until creamy. Beat in 1 egg, add curry powder, sugar, salt, pepper, almonds, and lemon juice or vinegar. Combine with meat, mix well. Cook onions in butter or fat until brown but not crisp. Add to mixture, stir well.

Start oven at moderate (350 degrees F.). Grease deep 2-quart or larger baking dish. Lay 2 or 3 orange or lemon leaves in bottom if you have them; they give a flavor much appreciated by Cape settlers. Spread meat mixture in dish, adding 2 or 3 additional orange leaves. Cover with buttered piece of waxed paper. Bake 30 to 35 minutes for raw meat, 20 to 25 minutes for cooked meat. When done, remove paper. Beat remaining 2 eggs and mix with milk and salt, pour over top of baked babotje. Reduce oven heat to 325 degrees F. and bake until this top custard is set. Serve with boiled potatoes or rice. Makes 6 or more servings.

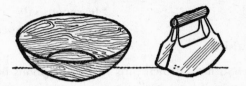

BOER FISH PUDDING WITH ANCHOVY SAUCE

This old Dutch-African dish is served as a fish course for dinner, or as a main dish for supper.

½ cup melted butter	2 tablespoons chopped capers
2¼ cups soft bread crumbs	1 tablespoon chopped parsley
3 cups flaked cooked fish	⅛ teaspoon ground nutmeg
¾ teaspoon salt	3 beaten eggs
¼ teaspoon pepper	½ cup light cream
1½ teaspoons anchovy essence or paste	

SAUCE

2 tablespoons butter	⅛ teaspoon pepper
2 tablespoons flour	⅛ teaspoon ground nutmeg
1¾ cups milk	1½ teaspoons anchovy essence or
¼ teaspoon salt	paste, optional

To prepare the pudding: Melt the butter, mix with crumbs and fish, add salt, pepper, anchovy, capers, parsley, nutmeg, eggs, and cream. Pour into buttered 2-quart mold. Cover top of mold with buttered waxed paper. Set mold in kettle, add hot water to kettle to not more than half way up mold; cover kettle; steam pudding by boiling water gently 1½ to 1¾ hours.

To prepare sauce: Melt butter in pan, add flour smoothly, and gradually stir in milk to make a white sauce; cook, stir until thickened. Add salt, pepper, and nutmeg. Add anchovy essence or paste if desired. When pudding is done, unmold it on warm serving dish, pour a little Anchovy Sauce over it, and serve rest of sauce in warmed sauceboat. Makes 6 servings.

★ROZZ DUMYAT
Chicken Giblet Rice

Also called Chicken Giblet Pilaf by some Middle-Eastern and Arabic cooks.

4 cooked sets chicken giblets	6 to 7 cups chicken broth, or
¼ pound pine nuts	use bouillon
½ pound butter	2 teaspoons salt
4 cups raw rice	¼ teaspoon pepper
1 cup seedless raisins	

DRAIN giblets; chop fine. Brown nuts in 2 tablespoons butter. Wash rice and drain. (If packaged, washed rice is used, omit washing.) Wash and drain raisins. Combine raisins in 3-quart saucepan with nuts and giblets, add rice, remaining butter, cover with chicken broth or bouillon. Cover pan and cook about 1 hour over moderate to low heat. Add salt and pepper if broth was not well seasoned. The mixture should be fluffy and nearly dry. Serve hot with peas. Makes 8 or more servings.

The five recipes above from THE NEW WORLD WIDE COOK BOOK, *by Pearl V. Metzelthin.*

Alaska

The wide-world traveler, Pearl V. Metzelthin, visited Alaska when it was a U.S. Territory, and she was enthusiastic about the fish dishes and game served in homes and restaurants. We listed this part of the northern world in her cookery right after Africa— and although we are happy now to claim these good dishes as U.S., we'll leave them in this section on far-away cookery. Here's an exceptionally good dish of salmon—famous Alaskan salmon— from *The New World Wide Cook Book,* by Pearl V. Metzelthin:

ALASKA CREAM SALMON

4 thick slices or steaks fresh	½ teaspoon dried or fresh savory
salmon (about 3 pounds)	1 cup light cream
¾ teaspoon salt	1 tablespoon butter
¼ teaspoon pepper	2 tablespoons flour
1 bay leaf	⅔ cup milk
3 peppercorns	1 small lemon, sliced
2 sprigs fresh thyme	2 sprigs parsley

START oven at moderately hot (400 degrees F.). Rinse and drain salmon steaks; pat dry. Lay side by side in well-greased shallow baking dish. Season with salt and pepper. Combine bay leaf, peppercorns, thyme, savory, and cream, and pour over salmon; use more cream if necessary to cover salmon. Bake in moderately hot oven 25 to 30 minutes. Baste fish from time to time with the cream sauce in its dish or with additional cream. After 15 minutes' baking, cover dish. When fish is done and flakes easily with fork, dot with butter and transfer to warmed serving platter. Stir flour smoothly into sauce in baking dish, add milk, and bring to a boil. Stir and boil 2 to 3 minutes. Pour over salmon and serve. Garnish with parsley and lemon slices. Makes 6 to 8 servings.

REINDEER OR VENISON CHOPS

6 large tender double-rack or loin reindeer chops (3½ pounds)
3 tablespoons olive oil
¼ teaspoon coarse black pepper
1 tablespoon chopped fresh fennel
½ teaspoon salt
¼ teaspoon paprika

1 teaspoon minced parsley
2 tablespoons red wine
3 tablespoons lemon juice
3 tablespoons olive oil or butter
6 slices half-cooked bacon, optional
1 glass currant jelly
¾ cup prepared horse-radish

RINSE chops, drain, pat dry. Combine oil, pepper, fennel, salt, paprika, parsley, wine, and lemon juice; rub each chop well with mixture. Place chops in wide shallow dish, pour remaining marinade over them, let stand covered in refrigerator 3 to 4 hours.

Drain chops, reserve remaining marinade; wipe chops with damp cloth, removing excess marinade; rub each chop with olive oil or butter on both sides. Broil 1½ to 2 minutes on each side under moderate broiler heat. Cut cooking parchment or heavy waxed paper in pieces just large enough to wrap each chop. Brush broiled chops again with oil or butter, sprinkle few drops marinade liquid over each, lay half bacon slice on each side of chop, wrap in parchment or waxed paper, tucking ends in. Lay wrapped chops in roasting pan and cover pan.

Start oven at hot (450 degrees F.). Bake wrapped chops 15 to 18 minutes, or longer if chops are extra thick. Heat serving platter, unwrap chops quickly, and place in center of platter, pouring juices from wrappers over chops. Serve with mixture of equal parts currant jelly and prepared horse-radish beaten together. Makes 6 servings.

The two recipes above from THE NEW WORLD WIDE COOK BOOK, *by Pearl V. Metzelthin*

Australia

As in Africa, cookery in Australia varies from primitive dishes of the ancient Maoris to sophisticated cookery in the hotels of the large cities and dishes which English, Scotch, Irish, and other settlers have created, using recipes from home but ingredients from their Australian markets and gardens.

These recipes for Australian sausage and the soup are similar to Scotch dishes. They are from Madame Metzelthin's *The New World Wide Cook Book.*

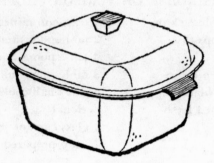

KOLENDO SAUSAGE

1 cup dry bread crumbs
1 teaspoon salt
¼ teaspoon pepper
2 teaspoons mixed poultry seasoning
1 teaspoon curry powder
1 tablespoon lemon juice
1½ tablespoons tomato paste or condensed canned tomato soup
2 tablespoons Worcestershire sauce

2 teaspoons prepared mustard
2 cups ground mutton or lamb (about 14 ounces)
2 sheep or lamb kidneys, cleaned and ground
1 small onion, peeled and ground
2 beaten eggs
Cold bouillon or milk
Extra bread crumbs
1 tablespoon butter

COMBINE in large mixing bowl the cup of bread crumbs, salt, pepper, poultry seasoning, curry powder, lemon juice, tomato paste or purée, Worcestershire, and mustard and mix well. Mix meat, kidneys, and onion, and combine with crumbs mixture. Beat eggs in; knead or work with fingers or beat with wooden spoon few minutes. Add little bouillon or milk gradually; mixture must not be too dry, and amount of liquid depends on dryness of crumbs. Fill greased billycan (a straight 1½-quart or 2-quart mold with tight cover) and steam in covered pot of boiling water about 4 to 4½ hours. To serve, turn out of mold onto warmed serving dish, cover with browned buttered crumbs. Serve hot with creamed potatoes and green salad. Or let sausage cool, then chill thoroughly and slice as a cold cut, or for sandwich filling. Makes 6 servings hot; more when sliced cold.

LEEK AND CARROT SOUP

10 medium leeks, cut in 1-inch pieces
1¼ cups chopped celery
¼ cup melted butter
5 cups milk
1 teaspoon salt

¼ teaspoon white pepper
2½ cups sliced cooked carrots
3 tablespoons butter
2½ tablespoons flour
Chopped parsley

SAUTÉ leeks and celery in butter in soup kettle 6 or 7 minutes. Add milk, salt, and pepper; cover and cook slowly until vegetables are soft, about 20 minutes. Add carrots, cook 8 to 10 minutes longer. Strain or press through sieve. Melt butter, add flour, and stir until smooth; then stir into strained soup and reheat. Boil only 2 to 3 minutes. Serve in warmed soup plates or bowls. Sprinkle parsley over top. Makes 4 to 5 servings.

For the American taste, the soup needs no flour thickening—use ¼ cup heavy cream instead, stir, bring to boiling but do not boil.

The two recipes above from THE NEW WORLD WIDE COOK BOOK, *by Pearl V. Metzelthin*

Austria

Enthusiastic travelers come home from a visit in Vienna declaring that everything the Austrians cook is superb–it looks better, tastes better, than food anywhere else. Just reading *The Viennese Cookbook,* by Irma Rhode, gives one the same sort of enthusiasm. Delicious reading. Then, if you go into the kitchen, the results can be another visit to Vienna. Let's begin with her recipe for strudel.

★APFEL STRUDEL
Apple Strudel

First, real strudel dough must be made. The author says that strudel dough is a sort of noodle dough and very thin. However, it is not rolled, but pulled as thin as thin can be. For a strudel dough, the iron rule in Viennese kitchens is "read the paper through it." Be sure to have filling for the strudel ready before pulling the dough. Follow recipe exactly.

2 cups all-purpose flour, sifted	⅔ cup water (scant), amount
¼ teaspoon salt	depends on flour
1 beaten egg	1 tablespoon melted butter

PUT flour on board. Make a well in center and add salt, egg, and water mixed with melted butter. Pull flour into well by stirring. The dough should be sticky in the beginning. Knead on lightly floured board, moving it to another spot on the board as soon as it begins to become elastic. Rub hands with flour to remove excess dough, continue kneading. Toss dough on the board, stretch it a little, and knead again. Cover with china or earthenware bowl which has been well heated through with boiling water. Let stand 30 to 50 minutes.

In this waiting period, prepare the filling.

APPLE FILLING

5 pounds tart apples, pared, cored, quartered	5 to 10 bitter almonds, blanched and chopped
1 cup seedless raisins	Grated peel ½ lemon
½ cup chopped blanched almonds or walnuts	1½ cups sugar
	1 cup melted butter for basting

Slice apple quarters into fine pieces, combine with all ingredients (except basting butter) and sprinkle over stretched, spread-out strudel dough.

Here are the stretching directions: As soon as dough is ready to stretch (after the 30- to 50-minute rest period) cover a table about 3 feet wide and 4 feet long with a clean cloth, and dust it heavily with flour. Place dough in the middle, dust it with flour, and roll out slightly. From this point on two people do a better job than one. Dust the back of the hands and palms with flour, and holding the thumbs inward, put hands under dough and begin to pull. Lift dough only slightly. If center part is pulled thin enough, let it drop to cloth and continue to pull slowly. Stretch dough until it covers the table. Let thick ends hang over edges. (Cut them off and let dry; then chop and use as noodles in soup.)

Spread the apple filling over thin dough, leaving an empty strip of about 1 inch along the edges. Spread some of the melted butter over apples. Lift the cloth and roll strudel like a jelly roll. Pinch edges together to seal in filling.

Start oven at moderately hot (400 degrees F.). Place strudel on baking sheet. Brush with melted butter. Bake 30 minutes; reduce heat to moderate (350 degrees F.) and bake an additional 30 to 35 minutes. Brush with melted butter every 10 minutes during baking. Serve warm or cold. Makes 10 to 16 servings.

CHOCOLADEN-TORTE
Chocolate Torte

⅓ cup butter	2½ (1-oz.) squares baking chocolate
⅔ cup sugar	
6 eggs	¾ cup grated almonds

START oven at moderate (350 degrees F.). Grease 9-inch spring-form pan. Cream butter, add sugar, cream together until light. Stir in 5 egg yolks and 1 whole egg, mix well. Melt chocolate, add almonds, and beat into egg mixture. Beat the 5 egg whites until stiff but not dry. Fold in carefully. Pour mixture into the prepared spring-form pan and bake in moderate oven about 1 hour. (Test for doneness as for layer cake.) Let cool in pan; remove, brush top with Apricot Sauce, and glaze with Cold Chocolate Frosting (below). Makes 6 or more servings.

APRICOT SAUCE

One-half cup apricot jam diluted to a consistency that can be easily applied with a brush. The purpose of brushing cake tops before they are frosted is to keep the frosting moist. If commercial apricot jam is used, it should be rubbed through a fine sieve, then diluted with enough water so that it can be applied with a pastry brush.

KALTE CHOCOLADEN GLASUR
Cold Chocolate Frosting

⅓ cup butter	¼ cup cocoa powder
1 egg yolk	1 teaspoon instant coffee dissolved in
3 cups sifted confectioners' sugar	⅓ cup boiling water

Cream butter, add egg yolk, and blend well. Sift together sugar and cocoa and add to butter-egg mixture gradually, alternating with the hot coffee. Stop adding liquid as soon as the frosting is smooth and right consistency for spreading. Spread on torte over Apricot Sauce. Makes enough for top and sides of one torte.

LINZER TORTE

1½ cups chopped, blanched almonds
1 cup (½ pound) butter, very
cold
1 cup sugar
2 eggs
2 cups all-purpose flour, sifted

1½ teaspoons ground cinnamon
⅛ teaspoon ground cloves
2 teaspoons cocoa powder
½ teaspoon baking powder
2 to 4 cups any red jam, especially raspberry, currant,
or cherry

COMBINE almonds and very hard butter in wooden bowl and chop until butter is cut into pieces the size of peas. Add sugar and eggs and beat well. Sift flour with spices, cocoa, and baking powder and work into butter mixture to make elastic dough. Remove dough from bowl, wrap in towel, and chill at least 1 hour.

Start oven at moderate (350 degrees F.). Grease 9-inch pie pan or spring-form mold. Divide chilled dough into two parts, one a little larger than the other. Roll out larger portion and fit it into the prepared pan. Fill with jam. Roll out other portion of pastry, cut into strips, and arrange in lattice top over jam. Bake in moderate oven 30 to 40 minutes. Let cool. Fill lattice openings with more jam. Makes 6 or more servings.

MOHN TORTE
Poppy Seed Torte

12 eggs
2¼ cups sugar
¾ cup seedless raisins, plumped
in wine
Grated peel ½ lemon

1 teaspoon ground cinnamon
½ teaspoon ground cloves
¾ pound poppy seed, ground
¾ cup fine bread crumbs
½ cup rum

BEAT egg yolks and sugar together until thick and lemon-colored with hand beater or an electric beater at low speed. Add raisins, lemon peel, cinnamon, cloves, and the poppy seed which has been put through a fine-blade meat grinder repeatedly with fine knife until it is very fine. Mix thoroughly.

Start oven at moderate (350 degrees F.). Grease two 9-inch layer-cake pans and dust with bread crumbs. Whip egg whites until stiff but not dry, fold into batter, pour into prepared pans. Bake 1 hour in moderate oven. Remove from pans, let cool. Sprinkle rum on bottom of one layer, and over top of the other. Put layers together with whipped cream or Apricot Sauce (above). Makes 6 or more servings.

POLSTERZIPFEL
Turnovers, Deep-Fat Fried

2 tablespoons dry white wine
⅔ cup sour cream
6 egg yolks
½ teaspoon salt
1¼ to 1½ cups all-purpose flour,
　sifted

2 egg whites beaten with 2
　tablespoons water
Jam or preserves
Fat for deep frying

COMBINE in mixing bowl wine, sour cream, egg yolks, and salt and beat until foamy. Gradually add flour, beating until soft dough is formed. turn dough out on lightly-floured board and knead until smooth. Roll out very thin, ⅛- to ¼-inch, and cut into squares of any desired size. Spoon jam or preserves in center, brush edges with egg white, and fold into triangle. Pinch edges together all around to seal. Fry in deep hot fat as for doughnuts (360 degrees to 365 degrees F.) . Makes 1½ to 2 dozen turnovers.

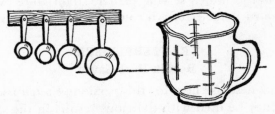

VIENNESE FISH AND MEAT DISHES

FISCH SCHNITZEL MIT SARDELLENSAUCE
Fish Steak with Anchovy Sauce

8 portions fish steak or 8 fillets
Salt and pepper
½ cup butter
1 tablespoon chopped parsley
2 tablespoons chopped shallots
　or scallions

¾ tablespoon flour
1 anchovy fillet, chopped
Juice 1 lemon
1 cup clam juice or water

RINSE fish, drain, pat dry. Rub lightly with salt and sprinkle with freshly ground pepper. Melt butter over medium heat, add parsley and shallots or scallions, and sauté 3 or 4 minutes. Increase heat, add fish, and fry quickly on both sides. Remove fish and keep it hot. Sprinkle flour over contents of pan, blend it in, but do not brown. Add chopped anchovy, lemon and clam juices. Cook, stirring well, until sauce is smooth and thickened. Reduce heat and cook 5 minutes longer; return fried fish to sauce, reheat. Serve fish in sauce. Makes 8 servings.

PAPRIKA FISH

The best-liked fish dish in Vienna.

8 fillets fish, or cleaned whole
   fish weighing about 4 pounds
   (bass, haddock, scrod, porgies)
¼ to ½ cup butter
2 large onions, peeled and sliced

1 cup heavy cream
2 tablespoons paprika
1 teaspoon salt
½ teaspoon pepper

START oven at moderate (375 degrees F.). Use roasting or baking pan, depending on size of fish. Melt butter, add onions, and sauté until light yellow. Place fish on top of onions. Whip cream lightly with paprika, salt, and pepper and pour over fish. Bake in moderate oven, basting frequently with juices in pan or with additional seasoned cream. For 4-pound fish, baking time is 30 to 35 minutes. For fish steaks, 25 minutes or a little more is sufficient. Fillets, fastened into rounds with wooden pick, require only 15 minutes baking.

Remove fish to heated serving platter; strain sauce over fish. Serve with plain boiled potatoes or with noodles. Makes 8 servings.

KRAUTERFLEISCH
Beef in Herb Sauce

The Viennese use beef for this version of a fricassee, but veal or chicken may be used with delicious results in the same recipe.

2 large onions, peeled and sliced
2 tablespoons lard or butter
2 pounds beef-stewing meat cut
   in ¾- to 1-inch squares
Salt and pepper
2 tablespoons finely-chopped
   parsley
2 teaspoons chopped chives, or

1 tablespoon chopped leeks or
   scallions
½ teaspoon chopped chervil
2 tablespoons butter
2 cups thick White Sauce or
   canned condensed mushroom
   soup
Juice 1 lemon

IN A Dutch oven or flameproof (metal-base) casserole with cover, sauté onions in lard or butter. When faintly yellow, sear meat lightly with them but do not brown. Add salt, pepper, and enough water to cover meat. Adjust casserole cover and cook over low heat about 45 minutes.

Combine herbs and butter and sauté 2 or 3 minutes in saucepan, add White Sauce or undiluted mushroom soup, stir and mix well. When meat is tender, strain off its cooking liquid and remove as much of the fat as possible. Return fat-free liquid to the meat, add herb sauce, blend and reheat. Stir in lemon juice, taste for seasoning. Serve hot with rice or noodles. Makes 8 servings.

LUNGENBRATEN IN BUTTERTEIG
Beef Tenderloin in Pastry Blanket

DOUGH

2 beaten eggs
3 cups melted butter or margarine

6 cups all-purpose flour, sifted
½ teaspoon salt
Dry white wine

*Combine beaten eggs with slightly cooled melted butter or marga-
rine; mix into flour sifted with the salt. Add enough wine to make
soft dough. Chill 1 hour. Roll out about ⅜-inch thick.*

3- to 4-pound beef tenderloin
½ cup finely chopped parsley
1 pound mushrooms, chopped
6 shallots, chopped
1 teaspoon salt

¾ teaspoon pepper
About ¼ cup goose-liver pâté or
any liver pâté
1 beaten egg

START oven at very hot (500 degrees F.). Rinse meat, pat dry. Place tenderloin in a roasting pan and sear in a very hot oven 10 minutes. Remove
from oven. Mix the parsley, mushrooms, shallots with salt and pepper and
spread on one side of tenderloin. Spread other side with liver paste. Wrap
tenderloin in the rolled-out dough, keeping side spread with liver paste
on top. The edges of dough should meet at the bottom, pinch together.
Place dough-wrapped tenderloin on baking sheet, brush with beaten egg.
Reduce oven heat to moderate (325 degrees F.). Bake about 45 minutes.
Makes 6 to 8 servings.

Most Americans like beef cooked more than the 10-minute searing
and the gentle 45-minute roasting through the pastry wrapping. If desired, cook the tenderloin longer before wrapping, then season and wrap
as described.

SCHNITZEL

The author of *The Viennese Cookbook* says that of all the popular Viennese dishes which are known internationally, the most
famous is schnitzel. What steak is to the American, schnitzel is to
the Austrian.

Although a schnitzel is cut from leg of veal, it is not veal steak.
For a true schnitzel the meat should be cut on a slant, half with
and half against the grain, the slices from ⅛- to ¼-inch thick. After
slices are cut and trimmed, they should be placed between several
thicknesses of waxed paper and pounded gently with a flat-faced
wooden mallet or with the flat side of a cleaver until they are ¹⁄₁₆-

to ⅛-inch thick. Some meat dealers do all this advance preparation for customers.

Schnitzels are fried in a large amount of butter so they will cook evenly, and should be turned only with pancake turner; a fork pierces and lets the delicate juice out.

PAPRIKA SCHNITZEL

2 pounds veal, cut and prepared
  for schnitzel
Lemon juice to cover
½ pound butter
1 cup chopped peeled onions
1 cup sour cream

½ cup meat stock, or use bouillon cube
2 tablespoons flour
Salt and pepper
1 tablespoon paprika

MARINATE the pounded veal in lemon juice to cover for 1 hour. When ready to cook, melt a little butter in frying pan and sauté onions until light yellow. In another pan brown drained schnitzels quickly in the remaining butter. Lay them on top of sautéed onions. Pour remaining pan butter over them, cover, and cook over low heat 5 minutes. Blend sour cream, meat stock or bouillon, flour, salt, pepper, and paprika. Pour this mixture over schnitzels and simmer 5 minutes longer. Serve immediately. Makes 8 servings.

WIENER SCHNITZEL

2 pounds veal, prepared for
  schnitzel
Lemon juice to cover meat
¾ pound butter
12 anchovy fillets, mashed
Paprika

2 eggs
2 tablespoons water
1 cup fine dry bread crumbs
  mixed with
¼ cup flour
Lemon quarters

MARINATE the pounded schnitzels in lemon juice to cover 1 hour. Just before sautéing them, prepare the sauce by melting ¼ pound butter and adding mashed anchovies and paprika. Keep this sauce hot.

Beat eggs lightly in bowl, add water. Dip drained schnitzels into egg mixture, then dredge with mixed bread crumbs and flour and let stand 15 to 20 minutes.

In a good-sized skillet melt remaining ½ pound butter and let it foam well. Reduce heat, add schnitzels, and sauté 1 to 1½ minutes for each side. The slices are done as soon as the coating turns golden brown. Sprinkle lightly with lemon juice at once and pour the hot anchovy butter over them. Serve immediately with lemon quarters on the side, as garnish. Makes 8 servings.

The thirteen recipes from THE VIENNESE COOKBOOK, *by Irma Rhode*

Belgium

Belgian cooking is similar, in some dishes, to Dutch cookery, and in others, to provincial French cookery. The sophisticated dishes of its large-city hotels are Continental, a blend of many European styles and flavors. Lesley Blanch (Mme. Romain Gary), the wife of a diplomat, has lived in many parts of the world. She collects recipes wherever she goes, one such collection being her book *Around The World In Eighty Dishes,* from which these recipes have been selected.

★FLEMISH ASPARAGUS

Mrs. Blanch says of this recipe: "The thrifty Belgian people I knew in Bruges used to serve asparagus this way."

2½ pounds asparagus   ¼ pound butter
3 yolks hard-cooked eggs   Salt and pepper

WASH asparagus thoroughly; cut off coarse ends. Rinse, drain. Tie in bundles, cook standing up in asparagus steamer. Add boiling water to steamer to cover lower part of stems, cover steamer tightly. Let water boil briskly 25 minutes for thick stalks, 20 minutes for slender stalks. While asparagus cooks, mash hard-cooked yolks fine. Melt butter, add gradually to mashed eggs, beating smoothly. Add little salt and pepper to this creamy yellow sauce; pour into warmed serving pot or jug. Serve with drained asparagus. Makes 4 or more servings.

★HOT DILL PICKLES AU GRATIN

4 medium-sized dill pickles   Grated Cheddar or Swiss cheese
1 cup medium White Sauce   Butter

SLICE pickles thickly into buttered 1-quart casserole. Start oven at moderate (350 degrees F.). Make White Sauce and pour over pickles, sprinkle generously with grated cheese and dabs of butter. Bake in moderate oven about 15 minutes, until top is bubbly and browning. Serve as hot appetizer, or with cold-cuts supper. Makes 4 servings.

The two recipes above from AROUND THE WORLD IN EIGHTY DISHES, *by*
   Lesley Blanch

We must go back to *The New World Wide Cook Book,* by Pearl V. Metzelthin, for the good veal recipe she found in Belgium.

TENDRONS DE VEAU AUX CHICOREES
Breast of Veal with Belgian Endives

4 pounds breast of veal	4 tablespoons butter
1 teaspoon salt	10 to 12 (2 pounds) Belgian
¼ teaspoon pepper	endives
⅓ cup flour	1 cup stock, or more

THE part of the breast of veal which has the most gristle is preferred. Have ribs removed from other parts. Rinse meat, pat dry. Cut meat into serving-size pieces. Mix salt and pepper and rub over meat, roll pieces in flour. Sauté in hot butter until light golden brown on all sides.

Start oven at moderately slow (300 degrees F.). Trim and wash endive bunches, loosening leaves. Add veal to 2-quart flameproof (metal-base) casserole, lay drained endive leaves around meat. Butter piece of waxed paper and lay over top of dish. Bake in moderately slow oven about 2 hours, basting meat and endives frequently with a little stock at a time, always replacing the paper, which keeps the dish from browning too quickly. When meat is done, there should not be too much gravy, but if too much has accumulated, set casserole on top of the stove and reduce the sauce quickly over high heat; the gravy should be light golden brown and not thick. Serve on hot platter, pile meat in center and endives at each end. Pour small amount of gravy over meat. Serve with boiled or mashed potatoes or hot rice. Makes 6 to 8 servings.

BARQUETTES DE RIS DE VEAU
Sweetbreads in Cases

Another Belgian delicacy, just right for an American luncheon dish:

2 pairs sweetbreads	½ cup heavy cream
3 cups water	⅛ teaspoon salt, or more
¾ teaspoon salt	¼ teaspoon celery salt
½ pound mushrooms	⅛ teaspoon black pepper
1½ cups water	⅛ teaspoon paprika
1 slice onion	2 tablespoons chopped capers
2 peppercorns	⅓ cup sliced toasted almonds
⅛ teaspoon salt	8 individual pastry tart shells or
4 tablespoons butter	8 hard rolls
⅓ cup flour	Parsley
1¼ cups milk	Lemon slices

RINSE and drain sweetbreads; cook in boiling salted water 15 to 20 minutes; drain, cover with cold water, and let stand 15 minutes; drain. Skin sweetbreads, cover, and set aside. Wash mushrooms, cut caps from stems, slice stems, combine with 1½ cups water, onion, peppercorns, and salt; simmer 20 minutes. Drain; there should be one cup of stock; if not, supplement with a little bouillon. Cut mushroom caps in half or quarters, melt 2 tablespoons butter in skillet, and sauté caps over low heat. Rub remaining 2 tablespoons butter with flour to a paste, stir mushroom liquor in slowly, and stir and cook until smooth. Add to mushrooms in pan, cook slowly, stirring; add milk gradually. Stir constantly and cook until thickened.

Cut sweetbreads in ¾-inch dice, add to sauce, and cook 3 to 5 minutes. Add cream, seasonings and capers and simmer over low heat. Add almonds. Fill pastry shells. Or slice top off rolls, scoop out centers, brush inside and out with melted butter; toast under moderate broiler heat 2 or 3 minutes. Fill with creamed sweetbreads. Garnish plates with sprigs of parsley and slice of lemon. Makes 8 servings.

The two recipes above from THE NEW WORLD WIDE COOK BOOK, *by Pearl V. Metzelthin*

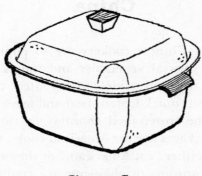

Canada

French home cooking and the more elaborate cookery of French hotels are found in French Canada, as they are in France, and are only slightly modified by being on the American continent. In the British areas of Canada, English-style cookery abounds; so does Scotch, Irish, and in some cases, Welsh. So do American dishes—as presented by the women's pages in Canadian newspapers and home magazines. In addition to a beefsteak pie (which is included elsewhere in this book), a berry pudding is the only dish selected by *Favorite Recipes from the United Nations,* as typical of Canada. Here is that recipe:

★BLUEBERRY CRISP PUDDING

4 cups fresh blueberries	⅓ cup brown sugar, packed
⅓ cup sugar	⅓ cup all-purpose flour, sifted
2 teaspoons lemon juice	¾ cup quick-cooking oats
4 tablespoons butter or mar- garine	Cream or whipped cream

START oven at moderate (375 degrees F.). Grease 1½-quart baking dish. Sprinkle washed and drained berries into dish, scatter sugar over them, add lemon juice. Cream butter or margarine, gradually add brown sugar. Blend in flour and oats with fork. Spread this over berries. Bake in moderate oven 35 to 40 minutes, until top is crisp and browned. Serve warm with cream or whipped cream. Makes 6 servings.

Recipe from FAVORITE RECIPES FROM THE UNITED NATIONS, *by the United States Committee for the U. N., edited and tested by the American Home Economics Association*

China

Certain kinds of Chinese cookery are so popular in America that many of the special vegetables and sauces for it are now canned commercially and widely distributed through general grocery stores, and quick-frozen heat-and-serve Chinese meals are available at the frozen-food counters in the same markets. These cans and packages are for American cooks. Chinese families living in America either "eat American," or they eat at restaurants in Chinese communities, or they prepare traditional dishes at home. They shop for their supplies for these in Chinese and Japanese grocery stores, which are numerous in West Coast cities, in New York City, and wherever Chinese-Americans live.

One of the most revealing discussions on the subject of their cookery is in the introduction to *The Joy of Chinese Cooking,* by Doreen Yen Hung Feng. Writing of old China, she says: "The joy of eating is given great importance in China; and cooking, through the decades, has been dreamed and fussed over, in times of want as well as times of plenty, until it has ceased to be plain cooking, but has grown and developed into an art.

"Food has been represented through other mediums of art, especially poetry, literature, and folklore; and these tales and food beliefs have been handed down, from generation to generation, with ever-increasing glamor. Every aspect of food is analyzed, from its palatableness and from its fragrance to its colorfulness; until, as in other works of art, proportion and balance are instilled in every dish. To possess the services of a good Chinese chef in one's home is like having a prima donna in close vicinity. He includes all the talents of a connoisseur with the knowledge of an herb doctor, the sensitiveness of a mother-in-law, and the benevolence of a clucking hen."

This charming and useful book is full of such talents, as well as Chinese recipes American homemakers can prepare with the help of products bought in Chinese grocery stores.

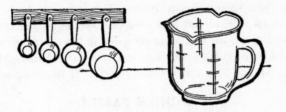

DOW SEE LOONG HAAH
Cantonese Lobster

1½ pounds live lobster
¼ pound minced loin of pork
1 teaspoon salt
¼ teaspoon pepper
1 teaspoon sugar
1 tablespoon cornstarch
2 tablespoons dow see (black
  fermented beans)

Cooking oil
1 clove garlic, peeled and
  mashed
2 cups hot broth
2 tablespoons cold water
2 beaten eggs

KILL lobster the spinal way. (Cut sharply and quickly through spinal cord, at base of head.) Chop off claws and legs. Split lobster lengthwise and discard stomach and intestinal canal. Chop lobster meat in shell into serving-size pieces. Chop legs and claws at joints and crack shells.

Mix pork with salt, pepper, sugar, ½ teaspoon cornstarch, and the dow see, add tablespoon oil. Heat a little oil in a large skillet, fry minced garlic few minutes, add pork mixture, fry 3 or 4 minutes, then drop in pieces of lobster in shell. Fry 1 or 2 minutes, pour in hot broth to almost reach level of lobster. Simmer 10 minutes, or until lobster is done.

Mix remaining cornstarch with 2 tablespoons cold water and slowly add to simmering gravy. Stir and let boil. When gravy is thick, take skillet off heat, stir eggs in, mixing well. Pour into serving dish and serve at once. Makes 8 servings.

★FOO YOONG DAAHN
Rich Egg Omelet

2 cups pea sprouts	½ cup finely-minced ham
Cooking oil	1 cup shredded roast or barbe-
1 slice ginger root, minced	cued pork, or crab meat, raw
6 scallions, chopped	shrimp, or cooked chicken
1 stalk celery, sliced thin	6 eggs
2 Chinese mushrooms, sliced	Parsley
1 teaspoon salt	Soy sauce
½ teaspoon pepper	

BREAK pea sprouts in half. Heat a little oil in pan and fry ginger, scallions, celery, pea sprouts, mushrooms, salt, pepper, ham, and pork or other meat until well mixed and cooked. Beat eggs, stir cooked mixture into eggs. Add more oil to frying pan, let it heat, and pour enough egg mixture in to form small omelet. Serve in warmed dish with pan sauce poured over. Makes 3 or more small omelets, 1 or more servings.

★CHOW FAAHN
Fried Rice

½ cup shredded Chinese roast pork	1 teaspoon salt
4 scallions	¼ teaspoon pepper
Cooking oil	3 beaten eggs
4 cups boiled rice, at least 1 day old	1 cup parsley leaves
	Soy sauce

DICE roast pork. Chop scallions. Heat little oil in frying pan, toss rice in. Fry rice until hot, stir, and gently press out all lumps. Add scallions, salt, pepper, pork, mix well. Make hollow well in center of mixture, pour in beaten eggs and scramble. When eggs are semicooked, stir into rice mixture until blended. Stir in parsley, sprinkle with soy, and serve at once. Makes 2 to 4 servings.

★BAW LAW GHUY
Pineapple Chicken

½ pound uncooked, boneless chicken meat	3 slices canned pineapple
1 tablespoon cornstarch	Juice from can of pineapple
⅛ teaspoon pepper	2 tablespoons water
Cooking oil	½ clove garlic, peeled and mashed
½ teaspoon salt	Parsley
1 tablespoon soy sauce	

SLICE chicken into thin, long strips, sprinkle with 1 teaspoon cornstarch, the pepper, about 1 tablespoon oil, the salt, and 1 teaspoon soy sauce. Drain pineapple, reserve juice. Cut pineapple into small wedges. Heat little oil in skillet and cook chicken until just barely done, add pineapple, cover skillet, and braise 3 minutes. Remove to warmed serving dish. Mix together remaining 2 teaspoons soy sauce, 2 tablespoons water, 4 tablespoons pineapple juice, and the remaining 2 teaspoons cornstarch. Heat a little oil and fry garlic, stir soy-and-pineapple sauce mixture in, and cook until thickened. Pour over pineapple and chicken. Garnish with parsley. Serve hot. Makes 2 servings.

The four recipes above from THE JOY OF CHINESE COOKING, *by Doreen Yen Hung Feng*

❧

Sou Chan, one of the most popular Chinese restaurateurs in America, has long served a great variety of Chinese dishes to New Yorkers and their friends. So many asked him for recipes that in self-defense he wrote a cook book. *The House of Chan Cookbook* sells in his restaurant as well as in book shops all over the country, and Sou Chan gives his royalties from it to a scholarship fund he established for Chinese students in America.

Here are five of his most popular dishes, always on the menu in his restaurant.

★BARBECUED SPARERIBS

1 clove garlic, peeled and mashed	¼ teaspoon pepper
½ cup soy sauce	1 tablespoon grated orange peel
⅓ cup sugar	2½- to 3-pound piece young spareribs (whole piece)
1 teaspoon salt	

MIX garlic, soy sauce, sugar, salt, pepper, and orange peel. Rinse meat, drain, pat dry; trim fat from spareribs; do not chop or break; use piece whole. Place meat in shallow dish, pour garlic sauce over, and spread on meat. Let stand in refrigerator from 30 minutes to 1 hour; turn meat 2 or 3 times during that period, spreading sauce over it thoroughly each time.

To barbecue in broiler, place meat, curved side down, on rack in baking pan. Preheat broiler 15 minutes at moderate, place baking pan 6 to 8 inches from heat, and broil ribs about 20 minutes. When meat is crusty and done on one side, turn it and continue cooking until second side is browned. Total cooking time is 40 to 50 minutes, depending on heat. Cut quickly with sharp knife, serve hot. Makes 4 servings.

BUTTERFLY SHRIMP

1½ pounds large fresh shrimp
2 egg whites
½ teaspoon salt
4 tablespoons flour

4 or 5 strips lean bacon cut
   crosswise in 1½-inch pieces
1 or 2 tablespoons cooking oil

WASH and shell shrimp, rinse and drain. With sharp knife cut gash down back of each, remove dark vein, then make few gashes crosswise on each shrimp. Mix egg whites, salt, flour, smoothly together. In the long cut of each shrimp spread a thin coat of this mixture. Then lay bacon strip on top of shrimp and press lightly. Heat oil in frying pan. Lay shrimp, bacon-side down, in hot oil and sauté on low heat until bacon is cooked and almost crisp. Turn each shrimp and bacon carefully with wide spatula; cook other side. When shrimp are pink and done, spear on wooden picks and serve as appetizer. Makes 4 or more servings.

To serve as main dish. After shrimp are cooked, add to the hot fat in the pan 2 small onions peeled and chopped fine, cook until golden, then add ½ cup ketchup and 1 cup hot water or chicken or shrimp stock. Stir and cook until steaming. Thicken if desired with 1 tablespoon cornstarch mixed with 3 tablespoons cold water. Stir and boil 2 or 3 minutes, until thickened. Pour over drained cooked shrimp. Serve with hot rice. Makes 4 servings.

CHICKEN EGG DROP SOUP

6 cups chicken stock
3 tablespoons cornstarch
4 tablespoons cold water
½ teaspoon sugar
1 teaspoon salt

¼ teaspoon pepper
2 beaten eggs
2 or 3 scallions, chopped green
   and white

HEAT stock to boiling point. Mix cornstarch and water smoothly together, add sugar, salt, and pepper, stir slowly into hot stock until blended and boiling. Reduce heat; add beaten eggs, stir slowly about 1 or 2 minutes, until eggs separate in shreds. Turn heat off. Add scallions, stir, and serve at once. Makes 4 servings.

CHINESE BEEF STEW

2-pound piece stewing beef
3 tablespoons cooking oil
1 cup soy sauce
3 cups water
1-inch piece stick cinnamon
1 or 2 anise seeds
1 tablespoon salt

1 tablespoon sugar
¾ cup sherry
1 pound celery, cut in 1-inch
   pieces
4 young white turnips, scraped
   and quartered

SAUTÉ beef in hot oil until golden on all sides. Mix soy sauce, water, cinnamon, anise seeds, salt, sugar, and sherry and pour over beef in stew kettle. Cover kettle, bring to a boil; lower heat and cook 45 minutes on just enough heat to keep barely boiling. Add celery and turnips. Add additional hot water if needed. Cover kettle, continue cooking 20 minutes, or until both meat and vegetables are tender. Makes 6 servings.

★SWEET AND PUNGENT PORK

1 pound pork shoulder, cut in cubes	½ cup vinegar
	¼ cup brown sugar, packed
Oil for deep frying	1 cup water
1 cup canned pineapple cubes	1 tablespoon molasses
1 green pepper, cut diagonally in 1-inch wide strips	1 tomato cut in 4 to 6 pieces
	2 tablespoons cornstarch

RINSE pork, drain, place in bowl. Mix batter.

BATTER

1 egg	½ teaspoon salt
½ cup all-purpose flour, sifted	3 or 4 tablespoons water

BEAT egg; mix flour, salt, and water with egg to form thin batter. Beat well, pour over pork, mix to coat pieces. Fry in deep hot oil, a few pieces at a time, until browned. Drain on thick paper towels.

Combine pineapple, green pepper, vinegar, sugar, ¾ cup water, and the molasses. Stir and heat until boiling; add tomato. Mix cornstarch with remaining ¼ cup water and stir into sauce. Cook until thickened, add fried pork, stir to mix well. Makes 4 servings.

The five recipes above from THE HOUSE OF CHAN COOKBOOK, *by Sou Chan*

❧

Another good book of Chinese cooking written for Americans is *The Art of Chinese Cooking,* by the Benedictine Sisters of Peking. Two American nuns who went to China in 1930 as missionaries at the Catholic University of Peking, and later in Kaifeng, Honan Province, learned the best of local cooking from their cook, Ta Shih Fu. War and invasion and other adventures swept them along until now, with one other Sister, in Tokyo, they teach Chinese cooking to a steadily growing school. Sister M. Francetta, one of the authors of this unique cook book says: "Our recipes have been selected with the availability of ingredients in mind, and you should be able to prepare them in any part of the Western world.

They are chiefly from northern China, and are the type used in good Chinese homes, not necessarily in restaurants."

Here are four of their best.

LI TZU CHI
Chestnut Chicken

This dish is best made in the winter months when freshly roasted chestnuts are sold on street corners and in nut stores. These shell easily, and boil to tenderness much more quickly than freshly gathered nuts.

If Chinese dried mushrooms are used, rinse well, cover with lukewarm water, let stand 15 to 20 minutes, until spongy. Squeeze water out and save this liquid. Remove stems, and simmer them for soup. If Chinese dried mushrooms are not available, use canned or fresh; 1 (3-oz.) can equals 6 dried.

1 pound uncooked chicken meat	1 tablespoon cornstarch
2 tablespoons cooking oil	2½ cups hot water
2 cups sliced peeled onions	1 tablespoon chopped fresh gin-
6 Chinese mushrooms, sliced	ger root or ⅛ teaspoon
4 tablespoons soy sauce	ground ginger (fresh)
1 teaspoon salt	30 chestnuts, shelled and boiled
1 tablespoon sugar	30 minutes
1 tablespoon sherry	

CUT chicken into 1-inch pieces. Heat large frying pan, add 1 tablespoon oil, sauté onions until light brown, and remove. Reheat pan, add remaining 1 tablespoon oil, and sauté chicken until light brown. Add sliced mushrooms and continue cooking for a few minutes.

Mix soy sauce, salt, sugar, sherry, and cornstarch; stir into chicken pan, cooking 2 or 3 minutes. Add sautéed onions, the hot water, ginger, and chestnuts. Cover and simmer until chicken is tender, 20 to 30 minutes longer. Or less! Test for doneness. Serve hot with rice. Makes 6 servings.

K'OU MO CHI TING
Mushroom Chicken

1 pound uncooked chicken meat	5 tablespoons cornstarch
½ cup soy sauce	2 (3-oz.) cans mushrooms
2 tablespoons sugar	2 cups soup stock or bouillon

CUT chicken in 1-inch pieces. Combine soy, sugar, and cornstarch, and mix with chicken to coat all pieces thoroughly. Heat mushrooms in their liquid in 1-quart saucepan over low heat. When boiling, add seasoned chicken. Gradually stir in stock or bouillon, cover, and cook until chicken is tender, 30 minutes, more or less. Test for doneness. Serve hot with rice. Makes 6 servings.

If mushroom juice is too salty, pour it off mushrooms and heat them in a little water; if fresh mushrooms are used, sauté in small amount of oil first, then cover with ½ cup water, heat to boiling, and complete recipe as described.

NIU JOU CH'AO HUNG LO PO
Beef with Radishes

½ pound tender beef, sliced thin
2 tablespoons soy sauce
Cornstarch
2 tablespoons cooking oil

3 tablespoons vinegar
⅜ cup water
½ cup sugar
8 radishes, peeled and sliced

CUT beef into narrow strips or small pieces. Combine soy sauce and 2 teaspoons cornstarch, mix with beef to coat it thoroughly. Combine oil, vinegar, water, sugar, and 1 tablespoon cornstarch in saucepan, stir, and cook about 1 minute. Add seasoned meat and cook slowly until meat is done, 3 to 5 minutes or a few more. Stir in radishes, mix and heat but do not cook. Serve at once, with hot rice. Makes 4 servings.

P'ANG T'ANG
Crab Soup

¼ cup cooking oil
3 slices fresh ginger root (about
   1 inch wide) or about ½ teaspoon ground ginger (spice)
½ cup finely chopped, peeled
   onions
½ cup cleaned crab meat
¼ teaspoon salt

1 tablespoon sherry
4 cups chicken stock or bouillon
2 egg whites
¼ cup light cream
2 teaspoons cornstarch mixed
   with
2 tablespoons cold water

HEAT oil in 2-quart saucepan, add ginger and onions, and sauté about 1 minute. Add crab meat, salt, sherry, stir lightly, and cook about 1 minute. Add stock or bouillon and bring to a boil. If ginger root is used, remove it at this time.

Beat egg whites until stiff, combine with cream and cornstarch which has been mixed with water. Stir gradually into hot crab mixture. Stir constantly and let soup simmer about 1 minute but not boil. Serve at once in warmed cream-soup cups or bowls. Makes 4 servings.

The four recipes above from THE ART OF CHINESE COOKING, *by the Benedictine Sisters of Peking*

Cuba

Cuba's population is a medley of settlers from the entire Caribbean area, Africa, Spain, and South America. Its cookery reflects the origins of the people, but certain of the dishes have been long established and are characteristic of all parts of Cuba.

In Cuban kitchens, says Pearl V. Metzelthin, in her *The New World Wide Cook Book,* there are collections of earthenware of all sizes and shapes, with or without matching lids, for Cuban cookery is casserole cookery. In many homes charcoal fire is still used for the cooking, although in modern houses of more affluent families gas and electric ranges and refrigerators appear. In these homes native cookery shares honors with dishes inspired by American food advertisements and those served in Havana hotels.

"But no matter what kind of kitchen stove is used, and no matter how well-to-do the family, soup is served at least once a day, even before a large meal, and a bowl of salad is brought to the table; rice and beans in many kinds of dishes are favorites in town and country, and at least one bean dish is present in every menu."

BLACK BEANS CUBAN STYLE

2 cups (1 pound) large black
  beans
4 to 5 cups cold water
1 teaspoon salt
4 cloves garlic
2 tablespoons oil
¼ teaspoon powdered sage

1 bay leaf
1 green pepper, seeded and
  chopped
1 onion, peeled and chopped
1 tablespoon cider vinegar
Salt and pepper

WASH and pick over beans, drain, soak overnight in cold water to cover. Drain, pour into 2-quart pot, cover with 4 or 5 cups water, enough to stand over beans 1½ inches deep. Add salt and 1 large clove garlic, peeled and cut in half. Cover pot, let cook slowly until beans are tender, about 2 hours or longer.

Prepare sauce: heat oil in saucepan, add remaining 3 cloves garlic peeled and mashed, sage, bay leaf, green pepper, and onion. Let simmer slowly, add the vinegar, and salt to taste. Let cook, stirring occasionally, until thickened. Pour over drained cooked beans. Sauce is pleasantly flavored with garlic; if more peppery flavor is desired, add a little freshly ground pepper. Makes 6 servings.

Comments and recipe from THE NEW WORLD WIDE COOK BOOK, *by Pearl V. Metzelthin*

In *The South American Cook Book,* by Cora, Rose, and Bob Brown, recipes are included for famous Cuban soups and many other dishes which can add flavor to our North American tables. This characteristic plantain dish is a good example. Plantains often appear in our city markets. This vegetable-fruit looks like an elongated green banana. For a flavor surprise at cocktail party or buffet supper, try this recipe.

CUBAN FRIED PLANTAINS

Peel plantains, cut in very thin diagonal slices. Drop into deep hot fat (390 degrees F.) and fry like potato chips. Drain on thick paper towels; sprinkle with salt while still hot. Should be crisp even when cold. One plantain makes 10 to 20 slices.

CUBAN GREEN SOUP

2 leeks
2 green onions
1 head lettuce
2 sprigs parsley
1 tablespoon lard, butter or
    cooking oil

1 quart boiling water
Salt and pepper
2 beaten egg yolks
Croutons

WASH greens and vegetables, drain, and grind together. Cook in hot fat in 2-quart kettle or flameproof marmite until soft; pour boiling water over them, add seasoning to taste, bring to boiling. Lower heat and let simmer 30 minutes. Stir in egg yolks and remove from heat. Pour into warmed soup cups or bowls. Serve with croutons freshly fried in lard. Makes 4 servings.

CUBAN HOT GAZPACHO

1 cup drained, cooked lima beans
½ cup peeled, blanched almonds
1 clove garlic, peeled
2 to 3 tablespoons cooking oil
1 quart cold water

Salt and pepper
Paprika
1 slice dry bread cut in 1½-inch
    squares

REMOVE skins from lima beans. Grind beans with almonds and garlic. Combine with oil in 2-quart saucepan or flameproof marmite, add water, salt and pepper to taste, light sprinkling of paprika, and the bread. Stir, bring to boiling, cover, lower heat and cook gently about 25 minutes or until well blended. Serve hot. Makes 4 or 5 servings.

THE COCIDO, OR STEW

The cocido, which means a stew cooked in an olla—the big round Cuban earthenware pot with a small opening at the top resembling the Boston bean pot—is a classic dish of all Spanish and Portuguese peoples. There is no one recipe for the cocido, olla, or stew. It is left more or less to the resources of the kitchen and the genius of the cook, so it varies from country to country. The Browns quote Don Quixote, who said of the *olla grande,* the great or especially large stew to which game birds are added: "It is eaten only by canons and bishops." You may not want to wait for a dinner of such distinguished guests, in which case the stew makes a wonderful one-dish meal for a winter buffet evening.

CUBAN COCIDO, OR OLLA

2 pounds beef or veal	4 tender carrots
1 pound fresh pork	1 young eggplant
6 slices bacon	½ cabbage
½ pound dried beef (tasajo, actually jerked beef)	2 cups cleaned string beans
½ pound salt pork (carne salada)	6 potatoes
1 pork sausage	2 onions
2 cups drained soaked chick peas (garbanzos)	1 young white turnip
Salt	4 tomatoes, quartered
2 plantains or bananas	3 garlic cloves
2 ears green corn, husked and cleaned	Chili powder
1 young summer squash	Ground cumin
	Ground coriander
	½ teaspoon saffron

Use 1½-gallon olla or kettle. Half fill it with cold water. Add meats and chick peas. Cover and set over moderate heat to cook slowly. Skim during first hour of cooking, then add salt if needed. At the end of 1½ hours' slow cooking, add plantains or bananas cut in small chunks in their skins, and the ears of corn also cut in 3 or 4 pieces each. Wash remaining vegetables, pare and quarter squash, scrape and slice carrots, peel and dice eggplant, pare and dice potatoes, peel onions, pare and dice turnip, add with all other vegetables to kettle. Peel and mash garlic cloves with a few grains chili powder, a few ground cumin and coriander seeds, and pound to a paste. Work in a little of the stew broth to thin the garlic mixture, then stir all into the kettle. Let cook until all vegetables are soft, 30 to 45 minutes. When ready to serve, dissolve saffron in a little broth from kettle and stir into stew, mixing until thoroughly blended.

The Cuban olla or cocido, is served with very little of its broth; the rich stock is reserved and used as the foundation of soups. Serve olla very hot, in soup plates. Makes 10 or more servings.

In Cuba several other vegetables, especially yuca and chayote, go into this great stew; and in place of beef or veal, game birds, or chicken.

Comments and four recipes above from THE SOUTH AMERICAN COOK BOOK, *by Cora, Rose, and Bob Brown*

Denmark

Travelers in the Scandinavian countries are tempted to forget all ideas of weight loosing; even those with the most will power succumb to the good food. The Danish cuisine, influenced by the best of French, German, and Austrian cookery, abounds in rich butter-and-cream dishes, light flaky pastries, inventive and wonderfully flavored fish and meat dishes. And the delicious smørrebrød:

SMORREBROD

The difference between the smørrebrød of Denmark and the smörgåsbord of Sweden is brought out in *Smörgåsbord and Scandinavian Cookery,* by Florence Brobeck and Monika Kjellberg, from which the comments and recipes which follow have been selected. Danish restaurants and housewives, say these authors, pride themselves on the variety and style of the famous open sandwiches which, on occasion, may alone make up the smørrebrød display. Lunch in Danish homes is often nothing more than one or more of these delicious concoctions and coffee or beer. In making them, the butter is creamed to spread smoothly; the breads are assorted dark and light rye and various combinations of rye-wheat loaves; the design is open-face, savory fillings heaped on large richly buttered slices with garnishes added; they are cut at the table with knife and fork, not eaten from the fingers.

One of the most popular is heaped with shrimp—*rejer dobbelt belagt*—shrimp doubly heaped. This is rye bread well buttered and piled with cooked cleaned shrimp. Salt and pepper, lemon juice, and perhaps a tart dressing are added to the shrimp.

Another favorite is thick slices of Swiss cheese and smoked eel on a big slice of buttered white bread. Very small sandwiches, called snitter, are cut in fancy shapes, covered with oysters, caviar, smoked salmon or sturgeon, and similar delicacies with plenty of lemon garnish.

Sometimes the sandwiches are served on the scrubbed bread-cutting board, with homemade *pâté* in the earthenware mold in which it was chilled. Or the smørrebrød table may be crowded with sumptuous dishes like those on the smörgåsbord tables in American Swedish restaurants. In the display may be cold sliced roast goose, turkey, duck, chicken and game, cold broiled chops, cold Wiener schnitzel, cooked eel in many forms, and countless salads, all smørrebrød favorites. As in other Scandinavian countries, this kind of appetizer display includes herring in many forms, salmon and other fish, caviar of various kinds, many smoked and pickled specialties, cheese, aspics, stuffed eggs, celery, and hot appetizers. Danish delicatessens, for which Copenhagen is famous, sell these ready to take home, but the old-fashioned penny-watching, careful Danish housekeeper wouldn't think of buying prepared food. Her recipes are traditional, handed down in her family and her neighborhood for generations.

Danish soups are just as famous as the smørrebrød, and they are good. For instance:

OLLEBROD
Beer and Bread Soup

This is served as a porridge on Saturday morning, or as a supper dish any night.

½ pound whole-wheat bread	¼ teaspoon salt
½ pound pumpernickel	1-inch cinnamon stick
4½ cups water	Grated peel ¼ lemon
4½ cups dark beer or ale	½ cup heavy cream
6 tablespoons sugar	

COMBINE breads in 3-quart enamel kettle, pour water over, cover kettle, and let stand overnight. When ready to make the soup, place kettle over low heat, cook uncovered, stirring frequently until mixture forms thick paste. Stir beer or ale, sugar, salt, cinnamon, and lemon peel into kettle. Let come to boiling; boil few minutes. Serve hot in warmed porridge or soup bowls with spoonful chilled cream or whipped cream on each serving. Makes 6 servings.

BRUN SUPPE MED PARMESANBOLLER
Brown Soup with Parmesan Balls

4 tablespoons butter	Salt
¼ cup all-purpose flour, sifted	⅛ teaspoon cayenne
2½ quarts meat stock or bouillon	2 tablespoons sherry

MELT butter in 3-quart soup kettle; stir flour in smoothly and let brown well. Add stock or bouillon, mix and stir, let boil 10 to 15 minutes. Add salt if stock is not highly seasoned; add cayenne. When boiling, remove from heat, stir in sherry, and pour onto warmed soup plates over cheese balls. Makes 8 servings.

PARMESAN BALLS

4 hard-cooked eggs	¼ teaspoon salt
1½ tablespoons melted butter	¼ teaspoon pepper
2 tablespoons grated Parmesan cheese	

Shell eggs, cut into halves from top to bottom. Mash yolks with butter, add cheese and seasoning. Mix well, shape into 16 balls. Place half egg white in each of 8 warmed soup plates, lay 2 cheese balls on the egg white. Pour hot soup into each dish and serve at once. Makes 8 servings.

FISK SALAT
Danish Fish Salad

2 cups cubed boiled cod, salmon, or halibut	1 cup cubed or sliced cooked or canned mushrooms
1 bunch celery, boiled, and cut in small pieces	Crisp lettuce

BONE and trim fish while it is warm, cut into 1-inch pieces. Cut celery into smaller pieces. Combine with fish, add mushrooms, mix and chill thoroughly. Make this special dressing:

DRESSING

4 tablespoons butter	1 tablespoon vinegar
¼ cup all-purpose flour, sifted	½ teaspoon sugar
1¼ cups fish stock	3 beaten egg yolks
1 teaspoon salt	1 tablespoon sherry
½ teaspoon pepper	1 tablespoon chopped parsley

Melt butter in saucepan, stir flour in smoothly, add stock gradually, stirring continually and cooking until thickened. If stock is not highly seasoned, add salt and pepper. Remove from heat and let cool a little; add vinegar and sugar and mix well; add egg yolks and stir; add sherry and parsley. Beat and combine with chilled salad. Serve at once on crisp salad leaves. Makes 6 or more servings.

KJOD SALAT
Meat Salad

2 cups chopped cooked lamb,
   veal, or beef
10 anchovy fillets

6 to 8 small pickled onions
Crisp lettuce leaves

MEAT should be cut into small cubes, not minced. Cut anchovy fillets into small pieces, chop onions, combine all with meat and chill.

DRESSING

¼ teaspoon dry mustard
½ teaspoon salt
¼ teaspoon pepper
1 tablespoon vinegar

3 tablespoons tomato paste, purée,
   or condensed canned tomato soup
3 tablespoons olive oil
1 teaspoon chopped parsley
Crisp lettuce

Mix dressing; *Combine dry ingredients, add vinegar and tomato paste, purée, or soup, stir well. Add about 1 tablespoon oil and beat with wheel egg beater 1 minute. Add remaining oil and parsley and beat again 1 minute. Combine with salad. Serve on crisp lettuce. Makes 4 or more servings.*

FISK GRATIN
Fish au Gratin

1 pound cod fillets
Boiling water
1 teaspoon salt
½ teaspoon pepper
1 bay leaf
3 tablespoons butter
2 tablespoons flour
2 cups fish stock

Salt and pepper
Juice ½ lemon
2 beaten egg yolks
¼ cup sherry
12 to 18 cooked or canned small
   mushrooms or 12 to 18 slices
   cooked large mushrooms

RINSE and drain fish fillets, place in strainer, cook in boiling water containing the salt, pepper, and bay leaf 25 minutes. Lift cod out and keep it hot.

Melt butter in saucepan, stir flour in smoothly, add stock, stirring continually. When slightly thickened, add ¼ teaspoon each salt and pepper, the lemon juice, and beaten yolks, stirring smoothly and slowly. Add sherry and remove pan from heat. Butter 6 scallop shells or 1 shallow baking dish. Arrange cut fillets in shells or leave whole and place in dish, cover with sauce, garnish with mushrooms. Set under broiler heat or in hot oven until delicately browned on top. Serve in shells or baking dish. Makes 4 to 6 servings.

SOUFFLE MED ANANAS
Pineapple Soufflé

2 cups drained, canned pineapple cubes
½ cup currant jelly
½ to 1 cup chopped almonds

8 eggs
¾ cup powdered sugar plus 2
  extra tablespoons
Whipped cream

START oven at slow (275 degrees F.). Combine drained pineapple with
jelly and spread in buttered straight-sided soufflé dish. Sprinkle almonds
on fruit. Beat egg yolks with 5 tablespoons of the sugar; whip egg whites
until stiff, beating in 5 tablespoons of remaining sugar. Combine egg
mixtures and heap on fruit in soufflé dish. Bake in slow oven about 30
minutes, or until delicately browned. Sprinkle top with the extra 2 tablespoons powdered sugar just before taking from oven. Serve at once with
whipped cream. Makes 6 servings.

Pineapple-Applesauce Soufflé. Use half pineapple, half applesauce for a delicious variation of above recipe.

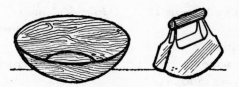

RODGROD MED FLODE
Red Pudding with Cream

1 cup red currants pulled from
  stems
1 cup red raspberries
⅛ teaspoon salt
1½ cups sugar

1½-inch cinnamon stick
1 quart water
6 tablespoons cornstarch
¾ cup heavy cream

COMBINE washed and drained fruit, salt, sugar, cinnamon, and water in
covered 2-quart saucepan. Bring to boiling and let boil 10 minutes. Remove from heat, let cool; then strain. Return strained juice to the heat.
Mix cornstarch with a little cold juice to a smooth paste, stir into hot
juice; cook and stir constantly until pudding is thickened and clear. Pour
into serving bowl or individual dessert dishes. Chill thoroughly. Serve
with sweetened thick cream. Makes 4 to 6 servings.

Comments and the eight recipes above from SMÖRGÅSBORD AND SCANDI-
NAVIAN COOKERY, *by Florence Brobeck and Monika Kjellberg*

England

Many young homemakers in England are as avidly interested in gourmet cookery and preparing interesting guest meals as their cousins across the Atlantic. They have a heritage of good cookery, too, in spite of the once-familiar tiresome complaint of travelers that they couldn't find a decent meal in the British Isles. Old out-of-print cook books by English housewives and present-day British cook books are full of delectable dishes, and the recipes in modern London homemaking magazines are as captivating and irresistible as those in our own home magazines.

One book filled with dishes popular in well-run English homes is *The Gentle Art of Cookery,* by Mrs. C. F. Leyel and Miss Olga Hartley. Even their inevitable sardine and turnip dishes can add good flavor and variety to our menus.

★BAKED SARDINES OR SMELTS

12 large boneless sardines or 12 smelts
4 tablespoons butter
½ cup dry white wine
½ teaspoon anchovy sauce, essence, or paste
Juice ½ lemon
Few grains nutmeg or mace
Cayenne
¼ cup bread crumbs

START oven at moderate (350 degrees F.). If smelts are used, split and clean, remove backbone with all attached small bones. Grease shallow baking dish, add 2 tablespoons butter to dish in small dabs, pour in wine, add anchovy paste or sauce and lemon juice. Arrange sardines or smelts in dish, sprinkle with nutmeg or mace, few grains cayenne, cover with crumbs, and add remaining 2 tablespoons butter in dabs over the crumbs. Bake 20 minutes, or until browned. Makes 6 servings. (Makes good hot dish for buffet service.)

★BAKED TURNIPS

6 small white turnips
¼ cup grated Parmesan cheese
Ground nutmeg
Salt and pepper
Cayenne
1 cup milk or thin White Sauce
3 tablespoons bread crumbs
1 tablespoon butter

START oven at moderate (350 degrees F.). Butter 1½-quart baking dish. Scrub turnips, rinse, drain, and pare. Slice thinly into greased dish in alternate layers with cheese; season each layer of turnips lightly with nutmeg, salt, and pepper. Add little cayenne to top layer, pour milk or White Sauce over contents of dish, sprinkle top with crumbs, dot with butter. Bake in moderate oven 35 minutes, or until turnips are done. Makes 4 to 6 servings.

These traditional English recipes for sauces to serve with game and beef tongue add tang and color to our menus.

CURRANT JELLY SAUCE FOR BEEF TONGUE

1 tablespoon red currant jelly
¼ cup port or claret
1 tablespoon chopped chutney
1 teaspoon Harvey sauce

1 teaspoon Worcestershire sauce
Juice 3 oranges and 1 lemon
1 or 2 tablespoons chopped candied cherries

HEAT all ingredients together in enamel saucepan; cook slowly until reduced almost half. Serve hot on hot or cold boiled smoked tongue. Makes about 1 cup sauce.

HOT ORANGE SAUCE FOR GAME OR MEAT

2 oranges
Boiling water
Juice 1 lemon

1 cup rich Brown Sauce or gravy
Salt and pepper

CUT peel of 1 orange into thin strips, pour boiling water over them, and boil 5 minutes; drain. Add juice of oranges and lemon and the Brown Sauce or gravy to orange peel, season as needed. Heat and stir until hot. Serve hot with game or turkey, sliced cold roast pork, lamb or veal. Makes about 2 cups.

★ONIONS AU GRATIN

3 or 4 large onions
Salt and pepper

1 cup medium White Sauce or Béchamel Sauce
¼ cup bread crumbs

START oven at moderate (350 degrees F.). Butter shallow baking dish. Wash, drain, peel onions; cut into quarters. Arrange onions in prepared baking dish, season with salt and pepper, pour sauce over, and top with crumbs. Bake in moderate oven about 30 minutes to 1 hour, or until onions are tender. If onions are very large, use only three, or increase amount of sauce to 1½ or 2 cups. Makes 4 or more servings.

OYSTERS WITH MUSHROOMS

12 large mushroom caps
3 tablespoons butter
12 oysters
Salt and pepper

1 cup or more medium White
   Sauce or Béchamel Sauce
Cayenne or paprika

START oven at hot (425 degrees F.). Butter shallow baking dish. Rinse mushroom caps, drain; sauté in about 1 tablespoon butter until lightly cooked. Place caps in prepared baking dish, set 1 oyster on each mushroom; season lightly with salt and pepper, add dabs of remaining 2 tablespoons butter. Pour sauce over, sprinkle lightly with cayenne, or little paprika. Bake in hot oven only until oysters are cooked and sauce is hot and bubbling, about 10 minutes. Makes 4 to 6 servings.

There are many good desserts in this English book, but these two old-time favorites are still important in every British home menu, and sure to be welcomed to tables in the U.S.A.

★BLACKBERRY FOOL

1 pound blackberries
Sugar

1 pint heavy cream

WASH and look over berries, hull them, drain, and pour into saucepan. Add only enough water to cover, add 1 or 2 tablespoons sugar unless berries are very ripe. Boil gently until berries are soft. Let cool, put through finest sieve. Chill. To serve, stir cream lightly through berry purée, do not stir to mix; pour into dessert dishes, and serve very cold, with shortbread cookies. Makes 6 or more servings.

PEAR CUSTARD

6 halves large, tender canned or
   cooked pears
½ cup raspberry or currant jam
¼ cup kirsch
½ cup heavy cream

2 egg whites
½ teaspoon vanilla extract
Chopped pistachio nuts or candied
   cherries

USE wide saucer-champagne glasses or dessert dishes. Cut core from pears, place drained pear-half in each glass, add 1 teaspoon jam to pear, pour about 1 dessert spoon of kirsch over each. Whip cream until stiff. Beat egg whites until stiff, combine with whipped cream, adding vanilla. Top each pear with spoonful of cream–egg-white mixture, sprinkle with chopped nuts or candied cherries. Makes 6 servings.

The eight recipes above from THE GENTLE ART OF COOKERY, *by Mrs. C. F. Leyel and Miss Olga Hartley*

One of the most popular and best-known dishes in English cookery is a steak-and-kidney pie. A very good recipe for this time-honored delicacy appears in Marian Tracy's *The Peasant Cookbook. Traditional* is a better name than *peasant* for the recipes in this volume, since in many countries the word *peasant* has no meaning. Certainly Britons of all classes, from farmer to gentleman in his club, relish this favorite meat pie.

★STEAK AND KIDNEY PIE

1 pound lean steak, round or   3 tablespoons cooking oil
  chuck, cubed   10 small white onions, peeled
1 beef kidney   Pastry for 1-crust pie
Flour   1 egg yolk
Salt and pepper

RINSE meat, drain; cut white away from kidney, rinse, drain and slice. Dredge both meats lavishly with flour, season with salt and freshly-ground black pepper. Start oven at moderate (325 degrees F.). Grease 1½-quart casserole. Sauté beef and kidney in oil until lightly browned on all sides. Turn into casserole, add onions, cover with hot water. Simmer uncovered in moderate oven about 1 hour, or until onions are tender and meats done. By this time the flour on the meat should have cooked with the water and reduced to a smooth, thick, lumpless gravy.

Prepare pastry for top crust. Remove casserole from oven, put crust on top of dish, pinch edge into decorative border, pierce top in several places with sharp fork tines. Brush top with egg yolk beaten with 2 tablespoons water. Turn oven up to hot (425 degrees F.). Set pastry-covered casserole back in oven and bake until top is browned and shiny, about 15 minutes. Makes 4 to 6 servings.

The recipe above from THE PEASANT COOKBOOK, *by Marian Tracy*

❦

André Simon's first cook books were concerned with French dishes and wines. But he has lived so many years in England as founder and president of The London Wine and Food Society that his later books contain menus and dishes English gourmets have enjoyed at their L. W. and F. Society dinners and in their guest luncheons and dinners at home. This great man is without a peer in the knowledge of wines and the foods with which they should be served. *The Wine and Food Menu Book,* by M. Simon is a source of some of the best-of-all dishes in the world's library of cook books. The recipes are not always detailed—many are mere suggestions—but they are easily followed by a home cook. Such as his words on these good dishes:

BLACK CURRANT PIE

Make like any other fruit pie. The washed and drained fruit is placed in a deep pie dish, sweetened with sugar, and covered with a rich pastry crust. Bake until crust is crisp and brown. Serve with thick fresh cream. "One of the best and most typically English fruit pies," said M. Simon.

BOMBE AFRICAINE

Fill ice-cream bombe mold with chocolate ice cream; make large center of apricot ice cream. Pack as usual in ice until time to unmold on chilled dessert platter.

BOMBE MARINETTE

Line fancy ice-cream mold with vanilla ice cream; fill center with raspberry mousse. Pack as usual in ice until time to unmold on chilled dessert platter.

FLAN OF CHERRIES

Use ripe black or dark red cherries, stones removed. Cover with brandy in glass bowl and let stand overnight. When ready to make the flan, cook the cherries a few minutes with very little water and sugar added. There should be practically no juice or syrup. Start oven at slow (275 degrees F.) . Butter shallow casserole pie dish, or fluted round tartlet dish. Make layer of cherries, cover with thick cream, another layer of cherries and another of cream. Cover with pastry, crimp edge, pierce with sharp tines of fork. Bake in slow oven so that pastry does not brown too quickly. Serve hot or cold. Better cold, said the illustrious author of this sublime dessert.

★MOUSSE OF RASPBERRIES
MOUSSE OF STRAWBERRIES

Fresh raspberries or strawberries   Whipped cream
Sugar

USE evenly-ripened berries. Wash, hull, and drain. Crush in bowl, add little sugar if needed. Combine with about the same amount of whipped cream. Pour into serving bowl, cover, and chill several hours. Suggested as dessert for a May dinner. Two cups berries and the same amount of whipped cream make about 6 servings.

★RASPBERRIES AND CHOCOLATE

2½ cups heavy cream
1 cup grated sweet chocolate
1 or 2 tablespoons sugar

1 quart raspberries, washed and hulled

WHIP cream until stiff, fold in chocolate and sugar. Fold drained berries into chocolate cream. Pour into serving dish. Chill. Serve very cold. Suggested as dessert for July party. Makes about 8 servings.

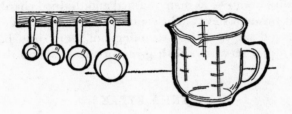

M. Simon's recipes are not confined to desserts. He suggests in one luncheon menu that the humble fish cake has been misunderstood. Here is his recipe for it.

FISH CAKES

2 cups leftover cooked fish
1 or 2 onions, peeled and
  minced
2 tablespoons butter
2 beaten egg yolks

Fish stock
Flour
Fat for deep frying or
  3 tablespoons cooking oil
Tomato Sauce

FLAKE cooked fish, shred any large pieces. Sauté onions lightly in butter until golden. Combine onions, beaten yolks, and fish; if necessary, moisten with stock or a little hot water. Shape into balls, flour lightly. Fry in deep hot fat (390 degrees F.) or sauté lightly in a little hot olive oil. Drain for a few seconds on thick paper towels. Serve piping hot with hot Tomato Sauce. Makes 6 servings.

RICE PANCAKES

M. Simon's rice pancakes are made with rice which has been boiled the day before and left in a colander, closely covered, overnight. To cook, combine rice with a little whipped cream and only enough flour to hold mixture together. Bake spoonfuls on greased griddle or in skillet, serve hot with sifted sugar and lemon juice. Sugar may be added to rice mixture for sweeter cakes.

SPINACH WITH NEW FLAVOR

M. Simon calls this Tarte Niçoise. It is a pleasant variation on the monotony of the eternal spinach.

2 pounds spinach	2 tablespoons butter
½ pound chard	2 beaten egg yolks
½ teaspoon salt	½ cup chopped stoned ripe olives
¼ teaspoon pepper	Baked pastry shell

WASH spinach thoroughly, let drain only a little, cook in own moisture until tender with about ¼ as many washed and drained chard leaves. Put cooked greens through sieve. Reheat purée with salt and pepper, butter, beaten yolks, and olives. When steaming hot, pour into baked pastry shell. Cut like pie, serve hot with game or meat. Makes 6 servings.

VIENNA STEAK

Vienna steak, according to this London epicure, is minced beef, shaped like a small steak, broiled with seasoned butter and served with braised onions and Brown Sauce.

VEAL REBOUX

This is veal at its best, according to M. Simon.

2-pound square piece best roasting veal	1 cup Béchamel Sauce
	1 cup Mushroom Sauce
Bacon fat or bacon strips	¾ cup bread crumbs
French mustard	

START oven at moderate (350 degrees F.). Lard veal with bacon fat, or cover with bacon strips; cover all sides with French mustard. Roast in open pan in moderate oven about 30 minutes per pound, or until veal is tender. Let stand until cool. Slice with very sharp knife in even slices. Dip each into mixture of the two sauces (canned condensed mushroom soup may be used as Mushroom Sauce). Put slices together again to look more or less the same as before the piece was carved. Place in baking pan, pour remaining sauce over it, cover thickly with crumbs. Reheat in oven until crumbs are browning. Makes 4 to 6 servings.

The eleven recipes above from THE WINE AND FOOD MENU BOOK, *by André Simon*

Englis dishes are included in *European Cooking*, that handsome color-illustrated cook book prepared in Swedish test kitchens and published in the U.S.A. Here are four more English favorites.

CORNISH PASTIES

These individual meat pies or dumplings are a stand-by of the diet in Cornwall.

1½ cups all-purpose flour, sifted	2 tablespoons chopped, peeled
¾ teaspoon salt	onion
½ cup lard	1 teaspoon salt
3 tablespoons water	¼ teaspoon pepper
1 cup minced raw beef	1 beaten egg or 3 tablespoons
1 cup diced, peeled raw potato	milk

MAKE pastry by combining flour and salt, sift together into mixing bowl, cut in lard with pastry blender. Add water by spoonful, mixing with fork to stiff dough. Place in refrigerator half hour. Make filling by combining remaining ingredients (except egg and milk) and mixing well.

Start oven at hot (450 degrees F.). Roll pastry out about ⅛ inch thick on lightly-floured board. Cut into four rounds about the size of a saucer. Divide filling on rounds, slash edges with knife, fold pastry over filling and press edges together. Cut small hole in top of each pasty. Brush with beaten egg or milk. Bake in hot oven 45 minutes. Makes 4 servings.

LANCASHIRE HOTPOT

1 tablespoon butter	3 onions, peeled and sliced
¼ cup cooking oil	¼ pound green beans, halved
6 lamb chops	6 potatoes, pared and sliced
½ pound lamb kidney, sliced	1½ tablespoons flour
2 teaspoons salt	1½ cups stock
½ teaspoon pepper	

START oven at moderate (350 degrees F.). Heat butter and oil in skillet, brown chops and sliced kidney, sprinkle with half of salt and pepper. Arrange meat, vegetables, and potatoes in layers in deep 2-quart casserole. Brown flour in drippings, stir in stock, mix, and boil 2 or 3 minutes, then pour over contents of casserole. Cover dish tightly. Bake in moderate oven about 2 hours, or until meat is done. Uncover and bake another half hour to brown potatoes on top. Makes 6 servings.

OLD ENGLISH PLUM PUDDING

Plum pudding is served in England at Christmastime, but it is usually made in September or early October to allow the pudding to ripen.

2 cups seeded raisins
1 cup seedless raisins
1 cup dried currants
¼ cup each finely-chopped candied lemon peel, orange peel, and citron
1¼ cups all-purpose flour, sifted
3 cups coarse soft bread crumbs

1 cup brown sugar, lightly packed
1 teaspoon each ground nutmeg, mace, salt
2 cups finely-chopped suet
6 beaten eggs
1 cup molasses
½ cup brandy

WASH and drain fruits; let dry. Combine fruits in large mixing bowl. Sift flour over and mix until all pieces are coated. Combine crumbs, sugar, spices, and salt; add suet and mix evenly. Stir in eggs with molasses and brandy. Add to floured fruit and combine well.

Turn mixture into 3 or 4 well-buttered pudding molds, filling each about ⅔ full. Cover molds with greased heavy waxed paper and tie paper into place. Place in steamer, steam over boiling water from 3 to 5 hours, depending on size of molds. Keep lower pan generously filled with boiling water.

Let puddings rest 2 or 3 days, then steam again 2 to 3 hours. Reheat pudding for serving by steaming 2 to 3 hours. Unmold, slice and serve with Vanilla Sauce, Hard Sauce, or Brandy Butter. Just before serving ½ cup good brandy or rum may be poured over pudding and a match set to it, so the pudding is brought flaming to the table. Makes 12 or more servings.

The three recipes above from EUROPEAN COOKING, *prepared in Wezäta Förlag, Sweden*

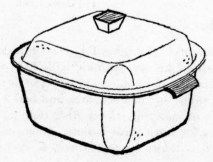

Finland

Travelers in Finland find the food in restaurants and homes similar to the cookery in the other Scandinavian countries; the appetizers, voileipäpöytä, are practically indistinguishable from the smörgåsbord of Swedish restaurants. Other dishes, although bearing Finnish names, are identical with those served in Sweden, Denmark, and Norway. Other cookery of this clean, beautiful country is Russian influenced. In the Karelian district of Finland open pies of vegetables or of cereal mixed with meat and vegetables are served as the main dish of the meal. Another section, Viipuri, has long been famous for its coffee rings; Savo, for fish pies; Turku, for sausages. Four-fifths of the population live in rural or fishing districts, which means that thousands are close to the source of their foods, and that good food is plentiful.

Here are six typical Finnish dishes easily adapted to American menus, from *Smörgåsbord and Scandinavian Cookery*, by Florence Brobeck and Monika Kjellberg.

LINDSTROMIN PIHVI
Chopped Beef and Potatoes

2 pounds ground cooked beef	2 tablespoons capers
3 large cooked beets	1 tablespoon salt
4 boiled potatoes	1 teaspoon white pepper
3 beaten eggs	3 to 4 tablespoons butter
1 tablespoon minced pickled onions	2 large onions, peeled and sliced

Sauce:

1½ tablespoons flour	Salt and pepper
1 tablespoon tomato juice	½ cup light cream
1 teaspoon prepared mustard	

PUT ground meat, beets, and potatoes through grinder together. Add eggs, pickled onions, capers, and seasonings and mix well. Shape into loaf, slice loaf, and brown slices on both sides in butter. When lightly browned, remove meat and keep warm on serving dish. Brown onions in same fat. Pour onions over meat. Make sauce in same pan, pour over meat, serve hot.

Sauce: Stir flour smoothly into pan, add tomato juice, mustard, salt, and pepper, stir, and mix well. Stir cream in slowly, let boil 2 or 3 minutes until thickened. Pour over meat and onions. Serve very hot. Makes 8 or more servings.

LINNIT
Finland Blini

½ cake or ½ ounce yeast
2 cups lukewarm milk
3 cups all-purpose flour, sifted
2 tablespoons sugar

3 eggs
6 tablespoons butter
¾ teaspoon salt
Butter for griddle

COMBINE yeast and milk in large bowl. Sift flour with sugar; stir 1½ cups flour-sugar mixture into yeast and milk, mix well. Cover bowl lightly with clean cloth, let stand in warm, not hot, place about 1½ hours, or until well risen. Beat egg yolks with butter, the remaining flour and the salt. Mix into risen sponge, cover again and let rise about 1½ hours. Beat egg whites until stiff, fold into batter, let stand 10 minutes while you prepare griddle.

If using a plättar pan (Swedish pancake pan), melt a little butter in each depression, heat slowly, spoon into each about 1½ tablespoons batter. Bake until brown on 1 side, turn blini and brown other side. If using griddle or skillet, rub hot surface with a little butter. When hot, pour blini like any other pancake mixture; bake until browned on 1 side, turn and brown other side. Serve hot with fresh caviar, or with sardine, anchovy, or salmon paste and sour cream, or with butter, sour cream, and thin slices smoked salmon. Makes 20 or more blini.

SILL A LA KAMP
Herring à la Kamp

Clean, skin, and bone washed salt herring which has soaked overnight. Cut into small pieces, place on platter, and garnish with sliced red onions, chopped chives, sliced or diced cooked beets, sliced hard-cooked eggs, and capers.

Thin mayonnaise with a little wine vinegar, add prepared mustard and little sugar, beat well. Serve with herring, as appetizer or with green salad.

SILAKKALAATIKKO
Baked Herring and Potatoes

1 pound salt herring
12 potatoes
2 onions
2 slices salt pork
White pepper

2 tablespoons flour
2 cups milk
2 tablespoons butter
2 tablespoons bread crumbs

SOAK herring overnight in cold water to cover. Drain, rinse, remove head, tail, skin, and bones. Cut fillets in 1-inch pieces. Wash potatoes, pare, cut into thin slices. Wash onions, skin, and slice. Cut salt pork into small cubes.

Start oven at moderate (325 degrees F.). Grease 2½- or 3-quart baking dish. Fill dish with alternate layers of potatoes, pork, herring, and onions. Season each layer with pepper; make bottom and top layer potatoes. Stir flour into little cold milk, then mix with rest of milk. Pour over potato mixture; it should just cover top. Add dabs of butter, sprinkle with crumbs. Bake in moderate oven 1½ hours. Makes 6 servings.

KESAKEITTO
Summer Vegetable Soup

This soup is served as a main dish in Finland during the brief summer season. Open-face sandwiches of cold meats are served with it, making the whole meal.

8 small carrots, scraped and diced
1½ cups small green peas
1 small cauliflower, diced
3 small new potatoes, pared and quartered
1 cup string beans, sliced
8 small radishes, peeled and cut in half
2 cups chopped spinach
Boiling water

1 tablespoon salt
1½ tablespoons sugar
3 tablespoons butter
1 tablespoon flour
2 quarts hot milk
1 egg yolk
⅜ cup light cream
1 cup cooked, cleaned shrimp or crawfish
2 tablespoons chopped parsley

Use young garden-fresh vegetables if possible. Wash all and prepare as directed. Cover all but spinach with boiling water to which salt and sugar have been added. Cook until tender. Add washed and drained spinach and cook 10 minutes longer. Melt butter in large soup kettle, stir flour in smoothly, stir in hot milk, mixing and cooking. Beat egg and cream together, stir into milk and mix. Add vegetables and their liquid, and the shrimp or crawfish. Stir until thoroughly hot. Serve at once. Sprinkle parsley on top of tureen or bowls. Should be thick porridgelike mixture. Makes 8 or more servings.

KIELI TALON TAPAAN
Tongue à la Maison

Sliced boiled beef tongue	1 cup fine cracker crumbs
Sautéed or boiled onions	Butter
Flour	1 lemon, sliced
1 or 2 eggs	Cooked vegetables

SPREAD each slice tongue thickly with either sautéed or mashed or puréed boiled onions. Lay 2 slices together sandwich fashion; dip in flour, covering both sides well, then dip into beaten egg thinned with a little cold water, then into cracker crumbs. Sauté in hot butter until golden brown on both sides. Serve on warmed round platter, garnished with cooked asparagus tips, cooked peas, and small fried potato balls. Pour any butter remaining in pan over tongue and add thin slice lemon to each serving. Allow 2 or 3 double slices per serving.

Comments and the six recipes above from SMÖRGÅSBORD AND SCANDINA-VIAN COOKERY, *by Florence Brobeck and Monika Kjellberg*

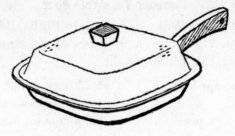

France

France and good cookery are synonymous terms to thousands of Americans who have lived in Paris or traveled through the French country, and to thousands more all over the world who know and use French cook books. There are so many kinds of cookery in France, and so many books written about the *cuisine de famille*—home cooking—as well as the great art of the epicurean chefs in hotels and restaurants, that the best-of-all French cooking would make a book in itself, or several of them.

One of the most useful on French home cooking for Americans is *Colette's Best Recipes,* by Marie Jacques. It is full of good advice and good recipes, as simply told as "a gossip in the kitchen," which is the way Marie Jacques described her summer afternoons in Colette's kitchen, gathering recipes from this woman who (unlike Gigi's Colette, who *wrote*) had spent her life cooking.

Here are some of the best dishes from that book.

OEUFS A L'ARDENNAISE
Eggs Ardennaise

5 eggs
½ teaspoon salt
¼ teaspoon pepper

¼ teaspoon mixed herbs such as
  tarragon, chives, parsley
5 tablespoons heavy cream

START oven at hot (425 degrees F.). Butter deep casserole. Whip egg whites until stiff, seasoning with salt, pepper, and herbs. Pile whipped whites roughly in dish, slip whole yolks in wherever they fit best, trickle cream over each yolk and the puffs of whites. Set dish in oven until yolks are set and whites barely golden on the peaks. Serve immediately in the dish in which they cooked. Makes 3 to 5 servings.

CHAMPIGNONS SAUTES AUX FINES HERBES
Mushrooms with Chopped Herbs

1 pound mushrooms
2 tablespoons vinegar
Boiling water
Salt and pepper

2 tablespoons olive oil
½ garlic bud, peeled and grated
2 tablespoons chopped parsley

WASH mushrooms, peel, tossing them as you peel into saucepan of cold water containing the vinegar. Drain, add to pan of lightly-salted boiling water, boil 5 minutes, drain well. Sauté in hot olive oil to which is added garlic, a little salt and pepper, and the parsley. Toss mushrooms until well buttered and very hot. Serve hot. Makes 4 or more servings.

HUITRES A LA CREME
Oysters in Anchovy Cream

2 tablespoons butter
1 teaspoon anchovy paste
Cayenne
5 eggs

½ teaspoon salt
12 oysters, cut in small dice
12 toast strips spread with anchovy paste

BLEND butter, anchovy paste, and dash cayenne. Beat eggs with salt. Melt anchovy butter in chafing dish over hot water, add eggs, and stir until mixture starts to thicken. Add oysters, stir until egg thickens around them, which it will do at the end of 1 or 2 minutes. Hand chafing dish pan around to your guests, offering anchovy toast strips with it. Makes 4 servings.

★PETITS POIS A LA FRANCAISE
Peas French Style

2 cups drained cooked peas, or
  canned small peas from France
¼ cup heavy cream
Salt and pepper

½ teaspoon powdered sugar
Large sprig fresh mint
1 tablespoon chopped parsley

COMBINE peas with cream in saucepan, add a little salt, pepper, powdered sugar, and sprig of mint. Stir carefully as mixture heats; it must not boil. When steaming and about to boil, pour into warmed serving dish, sprinkle with parsley, and serve. Makes 3 or 4 servings.

The four recipes above from COLETTE'S BEST RECIPES, *by Marie Jacques*

Another book which presents the simple, typical dishes of average French families, instead of the elaborate cookery of the famous restaurants, is *French Home Cooking,* by Claire De Pratz, newly edited for American homes by Georgia Lingafelt. This stand-by in many U.S. households, as the one French cook book the family understands and uses, is a joy to own. Here are some popular dishes from its pages.

BOEUF A LA MODE
Beef à la Mode

3-pound pot roast of beef
Salt pork
Drippings
2 cups hot water
1 tablespoon red wine
2 calf's feet, ready to cook, prepared by meat dealer
1 teaspoon salt

6 carrots, scraped and halved
6 onions, peeled and halved
1 stalk celery
1 sprig each parsley and thyme, or ½ teaspoon dried thyme
3 cloves
Flour

RINSE meat, pat dry. Lard with salt pork or lay salt pork over roast and tie with thread. Brown roast in drippings, add hot water, wine, washed and drained calf's feet, and salt. Bring to a boil, boil 5 minutes, reduce heat and add vegetables, herbs, and spice. Cover, let simmer about 4 hours.

Remove meat and vegetables (discard string). Remove calf bones. Arrange roast on hot platter with vegetables. Strain liquor, thicken with little flour, stirring smoothly, bring to a boil. Pour over meat or serve separately. Makes 6 to 8 servings.

If stock in which meat was cooked is not thickened, it becomes jelly-like when chilled. Left-over cold pot roast may be sliced thin, served with garnish of this jelly and crisp lettuce, water cress, and tomatoes.

TENDRONS DE VEAU BOURGEOISE
Breast of Veal Bourgeoise

1½ pounds breast of veal, cut into serving pieces
Salt and pepper
Flour
2 tablespoons butter
1½ cups Tomato Sauce
6 carrots, scraped and quartered
1 onion, peeled and sliced

RINSE meat, pat dry. Sprinkle with salt and pepper on all sides, dredge with flour. Brown in butter until golden. Start oven at moderate (325 degrees F.). Butter 2-quart casserole, pour in Tomato Sauce, add carrots and onion. Pour browned meat on top. Cover dish, cook in moderate oven about 45 minutes, or until meat is done. Makes 4 or more servings.

PIEDS DE VEAU A LA POULETTE
Calf's Feet Poulette

3 calf's feet, ready to cook, prepared by meat dealer
1 quart water
1 small onion, stuck with 2 cloves
Bouquet garni
½ cup canned or sautéed fresh mushrooms
½ tablespoon lemon juice
Toast points or pastry shells

WASH meat through several waters, drain, place in kettle, cover with 1 quart cold water. Add onion and herb bouquet, bring to a boil, let boil rapidly 4 or 5 minutes. Lower heat, let simmer 4 hours, or longer if meat is not completely tender. Let cool in stock. Remove calf's feet from stock, cut meat from bones, and dice into small pieces. Strain stock and use in making the Poulette sauce.

Poulette Sauce:

3 tablespoons butter
3 tablespoons flour
1 cup calf's feet stock
½ cup bouillon or mushroom stock
1 beaten egg yolk
1 teaspoon white wine
¼ cup light cream
Salt and pepper
Chopped parsley

MELT butter in saucepan, stir flour in smoothly and cook until blended. Stir in calf's feet stock and bouillon or mushroom stock, cook slowly, stirring continually until thickened, add seasoning. A few minutes before serving, stir in egg yolk, wine, and cream, heat gently, do not boil. Add seasoning if needed. Add diced calf's feet and mushrooms, heat, do not boil. Add lemon juice. Serve hot in pastry shells or on toast. Sprinkle with parsley. Makes 6 servings.

★OEUFS A LA TARTARE
Eggs Tartare

1 cup finely-chopped cooked beef	¼ cup sour cream
1 tablespoon softened butter	1 tablespoon finely-chopped spring onion cooked until golden in butter
Salt and paprika	
4 eggs	

START oven at moderately hot (400 degrees F.). Combine meat and butter, season with salt and few grains paprika. Spread in small shallow baking dish. Break 4 eggs, one at a time, in saucer and slip onto meat in baking dish. Pour sour cream over eggs, sprinkle with onion. Cook in moderately hot oven until eggs are set to desired doneness. Serve in baking dish. Makes 2 or 4 servings.

★OEUFS SAUCE MOUTARDE
Eggs with Mustard Sauce

4 tablespoons butter	6 eggs
1 tablespoon flour	Salt
1 tablespoon prepared mustard	Pepper

START oven at moderate (350 degrees F.). Melt butter, stir in flour smoothly, add mustard and blend well. Add about 2 teaspoons of this mustard sauce to each of 6 cocottes or individual custard cups, break each egg into saucer, slip into cocotte, season with salt and pepper. Set cocottes in shallow pan containing about ½ inch of hot water. Bake in moderate oven until eggs are set and cooked to desired doneness. Serve in baking dishes. Makes 6 servings.

POTAGE AUX HERBES
Herb Soup

1 small head lettuce	1½ quarts stock or hot water
1 bunch water cress	½ cup cream, warmed
1 bunch sorrel	1 beaten egg yolk
2 sprigs chervil	Salt and pepper
3 tablespoons butter	6 pieces French bread, toasted

WASH greens and herbs thoroughly, drain, shred lettuce, and cut cress and herbs into small pieces. Cook in melted butter in soup kettle for 10 minutes, stirring just enough to prevent browning. Add stock or hot water, mix, cover kettle, and let cook slowly half hour or longer. Remove from heat, stir in warmed cream and egg yolk, reheat slightly but do not boil. Add salt and pepper; pour over toast in warmed soup plates. Makes 6 or more servings.

COTELETTES DE PORC AUX MARRONS
Pork Chops with Chestnuts

3 cups shelled chestnuts	6 pork chops
6 small onions, peeled and sliced	Salt and pepper

GASH nuts with sharp knife, parboil 10 minutes, drain, remove shells. Slice large nuts, or cut into pieces. Brown onions in fat trimmed from chops; remove onions and sauté chops until well browned on both sides. Sprinkle with salt and pepper. Add chestnuts and onions, cover skillet, cook slowly about 1 hour, until chops are very tender. Add little stock or hot water if needed. Makes 6 servings.

The eight recipes above from FRENCH HOME COOKING, *by Claire De Pratz, revised by Georgia Lingafelt*

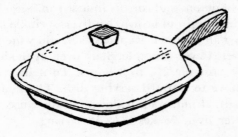

Louis Diat was chef at the Ritz-Carlton Hotel in New York for more than forty years. He came to the Ritz as one of the youngest chefs ever to fill so important a post. But he had behind him years of experience at both the London and Paris Ritz Hotels, as well as a tradition of cookery—his mother and grandmother were noted cooks of the Vichy region. At the time his book was published, M. Diat said the theme of his *French Cooking for Americans* was "my mother's kitchen, and my aim was to recapture its spirit, which was typical of a French home, and in doing so, to give Americans the recipes that have made French cooking famous. Then in order that it would be completely comprehensible to American housewives using American equipment in American kitchens, I worked for two years in the preparation of recipes in an American kitchen. My recipes, I feel, insure the same results with modern kitchen ranges, modern pots and pans, as with French coal or wood stoves and clay marmites and casseroles."

Every dish in M. Diat's book tastes good in the reading—the first test of a recipe—and here are some of his entrées.

FOIE DE VEAU BRAISE
Braised Calf's Liver

1 whole calf's liver
3 tablespoons butter or kidney
  suet
2 onions, peeled and sliced
2 carrots, scraped and sliced
Bouquet garni

1 clove garlic, peeled and halved
1 teaspoon salt
Pepper
2 tablespoons flour
1 pint red wine

ASK meat dealer to lard liver with strips of pork fat. Put 1 tablespoon butter or suet in flameproof (metal-base) casserole; when hot, add onions, carrots, herb bouquet, and garlic. Season liver with salt and pepper. Heat remaining 2 tablespoons butter or fat in another pan until very hot, add liver, and brown it, turning it so it will brown all over. Remove liver and place on top of onions and carrots in first pan. Set over low heat and cook until vegetables begin to brown, lift liver, sprinkle flour over onions and carrots, mixing all together. Replace liver, add wine and just enough water to cover liver. Cover casserole. Start oven at moderately hot (400 degrees F.). Cook casserole 2½ to 3 hours. Turn liver several times to cook evenly. Remove to warmed serving dish. The sauce should be reduced to about half. If not, cook it down. Strain sauce, skim off fat, reheat and serve over liver. Makes 8 to 10 servings.

COEUR DE VEAU SAUTE
Veal Heart Sautée

1 veal heart
Salt and pepper
2 to 3 tablespoons fat
2 tablespoons butter
3 or 4 mushrooms, washed,
  peeled, minced
1 onion, peeled and chopped

1 shallot, finely chopped
1½ tablespoons flour
½ cup chopped canned tomatoes
½ cup sherry
½ teaspoon chopped parsley
Hot cooked rice

WASH heart, drain, cut into thin slices. Remove arteries, rinse again, season with salt and pepper. Heat fat in skillet, sauté slices of heart a few minutes on each side, remove from pan. Drain off fat and add butter, mushrooms, and onion to same pan and cook until golden brown. Add shallot and flour, mix all together, and cook until light brown. Add tomatoes, boil few minutes, add sherry and parsley. Bring to boiling, add heart slices. Do not allow to boil after adding meat; make very hot and serve in rice ring. Makes 2 or 3 servings.

TORTE DE FROMAGE
Cheese and Potato Pie

"This is a very old-fashioned recipe," says M. Diat, "which both my mother and grandmother served often. Ours was a dairy section where milk was plentiful and cottage cheese was made so frequently that it was almost always on hand. So we used it in many ways. This cheese pie was a main dish with which we ate a cooked vegetable and, in season, a green salad. What was left, we ate cold the next day, usually after generous bowls of hot soup— and a good meal we thought it."

2 cups cottage cheese	½ teaspoon salt
½ cup sour cream	Pastry for 10-inch pie
2½ cups freshly cooked potatoes, diced	Milk
	1 tablespoon butter

BREAK up cheese with wire whip or a slotted spoon, then run it through a fine strainer or sieve so it is very smooth. Mix with sour cream, and add potatoes while they are still warm, add salt. Start oven at moderate (350 degrees F.). Line 10-inch pie pan with pastry, form decorative edge around rim. Fill with cheese-and-potato mixture, brush top with milk, dot with small pieces butter. Bake in moderate oven about 45 minutes, or until pastry is browned. Makes 6 servings.

CROQUETTES AU FROMAGE
Cheese Croquettes

2 tablespoons butter	½ teaspoon salt
3 tablespoons flour	Pepper
1½ cups boiling milk	¾ cup bread crumbs
¾ cup cubed Cheddar cheese	Fat for deep frying, or butter for sautéing
2 beaten egg yolks, or 1 whole egg	

MELT 2 tablespoons butter in saucepan, stir flour in smoothly, and cook until it begins to turn golden. Add milk slowly, stirring constantly until it is reduced to about 1 cup. Add cheese and mix, then egg yolks or whole egg, mixing and cooking over low heat until blended. Correct seasoning. Pour out on buttered flat dish or into buttered shallow pan and let cool. When cold, shape into croquettes. Dip in crumbs and sauté in butter in frying pan, or lower in frying basket into deep hot fat (390 degrees F.). Fry few minutes until browned, drain on thick paper towels. Serve hot with Tomato Sauce. Makes 4 servings.

QUICHE LORRAINE
Cheese and Bacon Torte

Rich pie pastry for 8- to 10-inch pan	1 tablespoon flour
6 slices lean bacon, not too thin	½ teaspoon salt
6 ounces Swiss cheese, thinly sliced	Ground nutmeg
3 beaten eggs plus 1 extra yolk	2 cups milk
	1 tablespoon butter

START oven at moderately hot (400 degrees F.). Line 8- to 10-inch pie plate with pastry, shape decorative edge around rim. Cut bacon slices in half and broil, drain. Overlap pieces of bacon and slices of cheese in the pastry-lined pan. Mix together eggs, flour, salt, few grains nutmeg, and combine with milk. Melt butter and cook until turning brown, then add to milk mixture. Pour all over bacon and cheese. Bake in moderately hot oven until filling is set and browned on top, about 35 to 40 minutes. Remove from oven, let cool slightly. Should be served warm. Makes 6 servings.

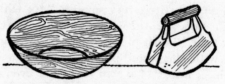

ECREVISSE A LA BORDELAISE
Crawfish à la Bordelaise

Crawfish look like tiny lobsters; the part eaten is the flesh in the tail and claws. They are always served in the shell, which the diner removes with his fingers. In preparing crawfish, the end of the intestinal tract lying under the tail must be pulled out before cooking. If this is left in, both fish and sauce have a bitter taste. Wine is important in cooking crawfish because the best flavor of the dish is lost without it, but if wine is unavailable, substitute lemon juice.

24 to 36 crawfish	Small bay leaf, pulverized
1 carrot, scraped and diced	3 tablespoons butter
1 onion, peeled and diced	1 teaspoon salt
2 shallots, chopped fine	1½ tablespoons cognac
1 sprig parsley	¼ cup white wine, or water-and-juice ½ lemon
1 clove garlic, peeled and crushed	1 teaspoon flour
¼ teaspoon dried thyme or small piece fresh thyme	1 teaspoon chopped parsley

CLEAN crawfish and remove end of intestinal tract under tail. Rinse, drain. Put carrot, onion, shallots, parsley, garlic, thyme, bay leaf, and 2 tablespoons butter in saucepan. Cook very slowly, until vegetables are soft, about 15 minutes. Add crawfish and salt. Cook over high heat, shaking pan all the time until fish turn red. Add cognac and wine, or water-and-lemon juice, cook over high heat 12 minutes. Remove crawfish to deep warmed serving dish. Continue cooking liquid until reduced to ½ original quantity. Then add remaining tablespoon butter creamed with flour, stir and cook but do not allow to boil after sauce thickens. Correct seasoning of sauce, pour over crawfish, sprinkle with parsley. Makes 4 or 5 servings.

The six recipes above from LOUIS DIAT'S FRENCH COOKING FOR AMERICANS

❦

Before World War I, André Simon, president of The London Wine and Food Society, published his *French Cook Book* for his epicurean friends in London. It was later revised for Americans, with the U.S. measures and weights in the recipes, and the menus confined to foods plentiful in our markets. It is a rich source of menu ideas for family and entertaining, and of superb recipes to vary the familiar dishes too often prepared in our kitchens. Here's that French specialty, a purée of chestnuts, to accompany the holiday bird, or any festive roast.

PUREE AU MARRONS
Chestnut Purée

1 quart chestnuts	4 tablespoons butter
Boiling water	Salt and white pepper
1 quart veal or chicken stock	

CUT into chestnuts and strip off as much smooth brown shell as possible, cover with boiling water, and let stand 5 minutes. Drain, plunge into cold water, let stand few minutes, drain. Use short paring knife and scrape off as much skin as possible, breaking up nuts into small pieces as you go. Drain, put cleaned, broken nuts into saucepan, add veal or chicken stock, cover pan and cook slowly 1 hour, or until nuts are tender. Then put through sieve. Pour purée back into saucepan, add butter and seasonings, stir and heat. If too stiff, add little hot broth. Heap on warmed serving dish, serve hot with roast fowl, game, or meat. Makes 4 or more servings.

CHOCOLATE MARQUISE

½ pound sweet chocolate
4 eggs
½ cup sugar

¼ pound butter (½ cup) softened
    almost to melting
½ teaspoon vanilla extract

BRUSH decorative 1½-quart mold lightly with olive oil. Melt chocolate in top of double boiler over hot water. Beat egg yolks lightly, add sugar to yolks, beating until mixture froths. Add chocolate and continue beating. Add softened butter slowly, still beating. Whip egg whites until stiff (till you can reverse the bowl and they stay in it, says the recipe). Fold them into chocolate mixture, add vanilla. Pour into prepared mold. Cover with waxed paper or the mold's tight-fitting cover. Chill overnight in refrigerator. Unmold on chilled serving platter. This is rich but worth it, according to M. Simon. Makes 4 or 6 servings.

LEMON ICE WITH RUM

1½ quarts lemon ice or sherbet   Dark rum

BUY or make Lemon Ice or Sherbet. Stir 3 tablespoons dark rum loosely through it. Pile into ice-cube tray, and let stiffen about 1 hour or longer. Serve in sherbet or dessert dishes, with small depression in center of each serving into which you pour 1 teaspoon or so of rum. Makes 6 to 8 or more servings.

PRUNE MERINGUE

½ pound prunes
White wine
½ cup sugar
2 tablespoons lemon juice
¼ teaspoon salt

4 egg whites
1 tablespoon grated orange peel
Juice ½ lemon
Sugar

COOK prunes until very tender in half-and-half mixture of white wine and water to cover. Drain, save liquid. Stone prunes and put fruit through sieve. Sweeten the purée with ½ cup sugar, add lemon juice and salt, beat to blend well.

Start oven at moderate (350 degrees F.). Butter 1½-quart deep soufflé or baking dish. Whip egg whites until stiff, fold into prune mixture, turn into prepared dish. Set dish in shallow pan of hot water, bake in moderate oven until firm, about half an hour. Serve warm in baking dish.

Make the sauce: Add orange peel and lemon juice to liquid in which prunes cooked. Sweeten with half its own quantity of sugar, boil gently until reduced to a light syrup. Strain syrup, reheat, and serve hot over meringue. Makes 4 servings.

The four recipes above from ANDRÉ SIMON'S FRENCH COOK BOOK

Before we journey on into some of the more serious chef specialties of French cooking, the novel, amusing *Dictionary of Cuisine*,
by Alexandre Dumas, makes an entertaining and enlightening
spot at which to pause. It is reported that Dumas often said he
should write a cook book to crown his life's work. He had prepared for it by his practical experience in cooking for his friends
as well as by his foreign travels and his reading of the great classics
of cuisine.

In his more luxurious days, fifteen of his friends were invited
to his house every Thursday evening for a supper in the great tradition of the eighteenth century. His salads were so famous that
when one of his guests could not attend one of these suppers, he
sent his servant to Dumas to bring back his portion of the evening's
salad. Here is the recipe for the salad Dumas prepared in his home
that evening:

A DUMAS SALAD

Slices of cooked beet, half-moons of celery, minced truffles,
rampion (European bellflower with edible tuberous root which
is served with its leaves in salad), and boiled potatoes. Dumas says,
"First I put the ingredients into the salad bowl, then overturn
them onto a platter. Into the empty bowl I put 1 hard-boiled egg
yolk for each two persons, 6 for a dozen guests. These I mash with
oil to form a paste, to which I add chervil, crushed tuna, macerated
anchovies, mustard, a large spoonful soy sauce, chopped gherkins,
and the chopped white of the eggs. I thin this mixture by stirring
in the finest vinegar obtainable. Finally I put the salad back into
the bowl, and my servant tosses it. On the tossed salad I sprinkle
a pinch of paprika."

HASH BY DUMAS

When veal, beef, chicken, game or other meats are left over
from the previous night's dinner, chop them all together finely
until completely mixed. Then go out and buy some sausage meat,
about 1/5 by weight of the hash mixture, and half-cook it. Mix hash
into sausage, add piece of fresh butter, and cook and stir until
meats are completely blended. Season with salt and pepper. As
hash dries in cooking, keep adding 1 tablespoonful at a time of
good bouillon. Add pinch cayenne pepper. Taste to determine
when to stop cooking.

The two recipes above from ALEXANDRE DUMAS' DICTIONARY OF CUISINE

What to select from *The Escoffier Cook Book,* the American edition of the great French master-chef's *Guide Culinaire?* This book has been reference, source, and inspiration for thousands of cooks and cookbook writers all over the world. Much of the cookery is too elaborate for homemakers and calls for ingredients not readily available to all kitchens. But much of it also adapts to more simple recipes. His meat recipes, for example. The recipe for leg of mutton should be a standby in every kitchen. Here it is:

GIGOT A LA BOULANGERE
Leg of Mutton Boulangère

Use either boned leg, seasoned inside and out, or the bone may be left in but shortened. Rinse meat, drain, place in open roasting pan or an oblong roasting casserole, which French chefs use for this dish. (Should be flameproof ware.) Start oven at very hot (550 degrees F.). Place seasoned roast in oven, brown well on all sides; reduce heat to moderate (350 degrees F.) and continue roasting. Allow 25 minutes per pound for roasts under 6 pounds, and 22 minutes per pound for roasts over 6 pounds. When last half hour of cooking arrives, place in pan around meat 8 peeled onions which have been lightly cooked in butter, and 8 large potatoes thickly sliced. Baste vegetables with juices from pan, continue roasting. Repeat basting every 10 minutes. When meat and vegetables are done, serve in casserole. Makes 8 or more servings.

LAMB AND VEGETABLE KEBABS

1½ pounds leg or shoulder of lamb cut in 2-inch cubes
1½ cups washed, cleaned, drained Brussels sprouts
12 small boiled onions
2 medium-size green peppers, quartered

⅓ cup French dressing
Switzerland Swiss cheese
Large pimiento-stuffed green olives

Arrange lamb, sprouts, onions, and green pepper on skewers. Brush vegetables with French dressing. Broil 4 to 5 inches from source of heat, in broiling pan, or cook on outdoor grill 12 to 15 minutes, or until lamb is desired degree of doneness. Brush vegetables once or twice with French dressing during cooking time. Turn kebabs frequently. When done, garnish skewers with chunks of cheese and olives. Makes 4 to 6 servings.

Recipe and color photograph, courtesy American Lamb Council

CANETON ROUENNAIS AU CHAMPAGNE
Rouennais Duckling in Champagne

For this dish use young, well-fleshed duckling, cleaned and ready for cooking. Leave whole or cut into halves. Cook over moderate heat in butter seasoned with paprika, salt, and pepper until browned on all sides and done. Turn frequently. Remove bird to warmed serving dish and keep it warm. Add 1 cup champagne to pan juices, stir, then add 1/3 cup thickened veal or chicken stock, and heat. Strain, serve with duckling. Makes 2 to 4 servings.

Escoffier's way with those small beef cuts known as tournedos is noteworthy and new to many American home cooks. Tournedos are small steaks; two are usually cut from one slice of the narrower part of the tenderloin. They are also called kernels, and noisettes. For Escoffier's recipes they should be about 1½ inches thick, trimmed round and small. Usually 2 tournedos (about 2½ ounces each) are served as a portion.

TOURNEDOS ARLESIENNE
Tournedos Arles Style

Season tournedos with salt and pepper, sauté in butter and oil in skillet. When about to serve, arrange cooked tournedos on hot serving dish, garnish with alternate slices of fried eggplant and fried tomatoes. Add slice fried onion to each tournedo. Serve hot.

SAUSAGE-STUFFED BAKED APPLES

4 large cooking apples	1 teaspoon salt
½ pound sausage meat	½ teaspoon pepper
1 small onion, peeled and chopped	1 beaten egg
30 saltine crackers, crumbled	

Wash apples, drain, core, and slice off tops. Scoop out pulp leaving a half-inch shell; save scooped-out pulp. Cook sausage meat, draining off fat as it accumulates. When sausage is nearly done add onion. Cook 3 or 4 minutes longer. Add to crumbled crackers and scooped-out apple, season with salt and pepper, mix, add egg, blend well. Stuff hollowed apples. Start oven at moderate (375 degrees F.). Place stuffed apples in buttered baking dish or pan. Bake, uncovered, 25 minutes or until apples are tender; time depends on kind of apple. Serve hot with baked stuffed sweet potatoes. Makes 4 servings. (Any extra stuffing can be baked in same pan and served with stuffed apples.)

Recipe and color photograph, courtesy Nabisco

TOURNEDOS FORESTIERE
Tournedos Forester Style

Season tournedos with salt and pepper. Sauté in butter and oil. To serve, set them on round slices of bread fried in butter, place on warmed serving platter, surround with alternate mounds of buttered noodles and diced potatoes fried in butter.

TOURNEDOS TIVOLI
Tournedos Tivoli Style

10 small mushroom caps
Butter and cooking oil
10 halves ripe tomatoes
Flour
Salt and pepper
10 tournedos

10 round slices of bread
8 medium-sized potatoes, pared,
    cut in ⅛-inch slices
Fat for deep frying
Béarnaise Sauce

IF mushrooms are old, peel caps. Sauté lightly in butter. Season tomato halves, dredge with flour, sauté in butter in dish with mushrooms until golden. Keep both vegetables warm. Let tournedos sauté slowly in butter or oil in another pan. Toast rounds of bread. Soak potatoes in ice water 4 minutes. Have two kettles of deep fat heating; the first should be at 225 degrees F.; the second, at 425 degrees F. Drain potato slices, pat dry, drop a few at a time into first kettle, fry 4 to 5 minutes. Lift partly fried slices into second (hotter) kettle, where they should start to puff immediately. When golden brown and puffed, drain on thick paper towels, sprinkle with salt. Arrange cooked tournedos on toast-rounds on warmed serving platter. Place mushroom on each tournedo, surround all with tomato slices, and just before serving, spoon the puffy light soufflé potatoes around platter. Serve Béarnaise Sauce separately. Makes 10 servings.

If the Soufflé Potatoes are too difficult to manage, use quick-frozen French fried potatoes made very crisp in hot oven.

Here are four Escoffier desserts American hostesses will welcome. Chosen from the many inventive, delicious offerings in the famous book, these are simple yet novel enough to please today's guests as they have pleased generations of the world's epicures.

MANDARINES A LA CREME
Tangerines with Cream

Select large, handsome tangerines, cut top slice off each, and reserve slices, remove contents of shell. (Use this cut-out fruit in fruit cups or salads.) Fill shells with mixture of ⅓ heavy cream, ⅓ cake crumbs, ⅓ cold custard. Replace slice on each tangerine. Set fruit in cracked ice and chill thoroughly until time to serve. One filled tangerine makes 1 serving.

BEIGNETS DE POMMES
Apple Fritters

Wash, pare, and core apples. Cut crosswise into thick slices. Cover with confectioners' sugar moistened with brandy or rum. A few minutes before serving, drain slices, dip in fritter batter, and fry in deep hot fat (375 degrees F.). Drain, place on fireproof serving dish, sprinkle with sugar, and set under high broiler heat few minutes to glaze. Two or more fritters make 1 serving.

BEIGNETS SUZON
Suzon Fritters

Spread cooked rice in thin layer to cool. Divide into 3½-inch rounds, add spoonful thick cooked or preserved fruit to each round. Shape rice thickly around it into a ball, dip in fritter batter, let stand few minutes. Use frying basket and lower into deep hot fat (375 degrees F.). Fry until golden. Serve warm, sprinkled with confectioners' sugar. One or more fritters makes 1 serving.

BEIGNETS SYLVANA
Sylvana Fritters

Cut tops from small round brioches, reserving tops. Hollow out brioches, dip in sweetened cream, coating each inside and out. Fill centers with cooked berries, cherries, other small fruits, drained and flavored with kirsch. Replace brioche tops; dip whole thing into batter. Lower in frying basket into deep hot fat (375 degrees F.), fry until golden. Lift carefully to serving dish, sprinkle with powdered sugar, and serve warm.

POMMES AU BEURRE
Apples in Butter

Start oven at moderate (350 degrees F.) . Wash, pare, and core apples. Cut crosswise into thick slices. Cover with water to which a little lemon juice is added, bring to a boil, and boil 5 minutes. Remove from liquid, place apples in shallow buttered casserole. Add little vanilla to the syrup in which they cooked, pour over apples, cover casserole, and let cook in moderate oven 20 minutes, or until tender. Cut small brioches in half crosswise, use bottom halves only. Toast lightly. Place cooked apple ring on each round of brioche, fill core hollow with butter combined with sugar and flavored generously with brandy. Thicken juice from casserole with little apricot jam or purée, spoon over apples on brioches. Glaze in hot oven few minutes or under moderate broiler heat. Serve warm. Two or more slices make 1 serving.

The ten recipes above from THE ESCOFFIER COOK BOOK, *by Auguste Escoffier, American edition*

Jean Anthelme Brillat-Savarin (1755–1826) was born at the right time to play a role in his country's Revolutionary rebirth, and to visit the young America at the time of its Revolutionary struggles. Savarin, a French gentleman, was thirty-eight years old when he visited New York in search of employment, a quest which resulted in his spending a year or more teaching French here and playing the violin in the orchestra of a small New York theater. He returned to France to serve in various positions in the changing governments of the period. Later in life he became known as an essayist of elegance and charm, as a wit, and as a musician. But his name came down through the centuries as an epicure, author of books on gastronomy, most famous of which are the *Physiologie du Goût,* Physiology of Taste, containing much talk of eating and a few recipes (contributed by his sister) and a recently translated and American-published volume, *Real French Cooking,* which is Savarin's collection of his favorite French dishes and recipes from other countries. It is a wonderful source of good cookery.

Great writers on culinary matters, stated Savarin, have usually divided sauces into four groups, with four mother sauces from which all others spring. These mother sauces are: Espagnole, basically a piquant brown sauce; Velouté, a thick gravy sauce; Allemande, basically of flour, butter, eggs, consommé and lemon, and Béchamel, basically a white cream sauce. All are familiar to American home cooks under these names or new names given them by inventive U.S. cooks.

BEURRE NOIR
Black Butter Sauce

Melt butter and cook to very dark brown. Use frying pan. It must be dark, but not burned. Add 2 or 3 sprigs parsley and cook quickly. Add about 1 teaspoon vinegar to pan, or for large amount, 1 tablespoon vinegar, swirl, and pour over broiled fish. Allow about 1½ tablespoons butter for each fish steak or beefsteak.

ROBERT SAUCE

1 small onion, peeled and
  shredded
2 tablespoons butter
1 tablespoon flour
1 cup stock

Salt and pepper
1 tablespoon vinegar
1 teaspoon prepared French
  mustard

Cook onion in butter until brown. Stir in flour smoothly and cook 1 or 2 minutes; add stock slowly, stirring. Add salt and pepper. Cook gently until thickened and smooth. At the moment of serving, stir in vinegar and mustard, pour into warmed sauce dish, and serve. Makes about 1¼ cups sauce.

Robert Sauce is also called Charcutière Sauce. Leftover meats, especially pork, goose, and turkey, are often warmed up in Robert or Charcutière Sauce. Garnish with gherkin strips.

REMOULADE SAUCE

2 hard-cooked egg yolks
1 uncooked egg yolk
1 tablespoon prepared French
  mustard

Olive oil
1 tablespoon vinegar

Mash hard-cooked yolks smoothly in bowl, beat raw yolk in with mustard, working to a paste. Add oil gradually while beating, as for mayonnaise. When fluffy and right consistency, add vinegar. Serve like Hollandaise. Makes about 1 cup sauce.

(Some French cooks make a Rémoulade Sauce starting with 1 pint mayonnaise, adding to it 1 tablespoon each prepared mustard, chopped gherkins, capers, and chopped parsley with little chervil, and tarragon, plus about 1 teaspoon anchovy essence.)

WINE MERCHANT'S ENTRECOTE

The entrecôte is the meat cut from between two bones in the rib section. The entrecôte should be trimmed; usually one makes 1 serving, but if very small, allow 2 per serving.

1 or 2 entrecôtes
Salt and pepper
Butter
2 tablespoons chopped shallot

1 cup red Burgundy
1 tablespoon heavy cream
½ tablespoon vinegar
1 tablespoon chopped parsley

RINSE meat, pat dry. Season with salt and pepper and cook gently in hot butter. As soon as cooked to desired doneness, remove meat to warmed serving dish. Add shallots to cooking pan, stir, and cook until yellowing, add wine and cream, stir and cook 1 or 2 minutes, add vinegar, stir and cook quickly to reduce sauce. Pour sauce over meat and sprinkle with parsley.

COQ AU VIN
Chicken in Wine

We've grown accustomed in America to *Coq au Vin* on menu cards and in various versions in American cook books. Here is what Savarin said about this dish:

"Coq au Vin is a chicken prepared in wine, any chicken, not necessarily a cockerel or cock. It is *Coq au Vin Alsacienne* when a Riesling wine is used in the cooking." Here it is prepared with a Chambertin wine.

1 roasting chicken, cut in serving pieces
Salt and pepper
Cooking oil
6 small onions, peeled
6 small mushrooms, quartered
2 tablespoons bacon fat or
  chopped bacon

1 or 2 tablespoons brandy
1 bottle red wine (Chambertin
  if possible)
3 garlic cloves, peeled and
  chopped

SEASON chicken, sauté in hot oil in flameproof casserole (metal-base) until nicely browned and almost done. Cook onions and mushrooms lightly in bacon fat until onions are yellow. Pour contents of pan into chicken casserole, stir in brandy, pour wine over, cover, and bring to boiling. When it boils, add garlic. Cover, cook 20 minutes longer. Serve at once. Makes 6 servings.

MIREPOIX SAUCE

As well as being a sauce in its own right, Mirepoix serves as basis for other sauces.

¼ pound lean bacon cut in small cubes

2 medium-sized carrots, scraped and sliced

1 onion, peeled and sliced

Bay leaf

Sprig fresh thyme, or ¼ teaspoon dried

COMBINE all ingredients in saucepan, cook over low heat 30 minutes, stir frequently. Press through sieve, reheat, and use as called for in recipes. Makes about ¾ to 1 cup sauce.

The six recipes above from REAL FRENCH COOKING, *by Savarin*

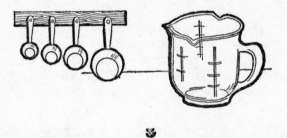

In London and Paris the name *Prunier* is identified with famous restaurants. Madame S. B. Prunier of that gastronomical family put together a book of fish cookery, *Mme. Prunier's Fish Cookery Book,* for her friends and clients, confessing that it was the inspiration of her father which made the book possible. He asked his chef and collaborator to help put all their famous fish recipes down on paper, but before the gigantic task could be finished, he died. The book was completed by the chef, then edited by Madame Prunier, and published in memory of her father.

Cook-book writers as well as cooks and chefs have long used it as a source of ideas, superb recipes, and inspiration for fish and sea food cookery.

Here are some of Madame Prunier's suggestions and recipes.

HOMARD THERMIDOR
Lobster Thermidor

Cut freshly-boiled lobster in half lengthways. Remove stomach and intestinal vein, cut meat into slices; crack claws, remove meat. Heap meat in bottom half of shell. Cover with combination of mustard-flavored Bercy and Béchamel Sauces. Brown lightly in hot oven or under low broiler heat. Lobster slices may be alternated with mushrooms sautéed in butter. One filled lobster shell makes 1 serving.

HOMARD ROTI AU WHISKEY
Roasted Lobster with Whisky

1 freshly-boiled lobster	2½ tablespoons browned bread
Salt and pepper	crumbs
¼ cup melted butter	¼ cup whisky
1 teaspoon dry mustard	Additional butter

START oven at moderate (325 degrees F.). Cut lobster in half lengthwise, remove stomach and intestinal vein. Place halves in shallow baking dish. Crack claws, remove meat, and add to meat in shells. Season lightly with salt and pepper. Pour 2 tablespoons melted butter mixed with about ½ teaspoon dry mustard on each half. Sprinkle with crumbs. Bake lobster in moderate oven about 15 minutes, basting well with butter. To serve, spoon all melted butter from bottom of dish, pour whisky over lobster, ignite and let flame. Baste with butter from dish and serve very hot. Makes 2 servings.

COQUILLES SAINT-JACQUES A LA BRETONNE
Scallops Bretonne

2 pounds (1 quart) small scallops	1 tablespoon chopped parsley
2 tablespoons butter	¼ cup browned bread crumbs
1 onion, peeled and chopped	2 tablespoons melted butter
1 shallot, peeled and chopped	6 or 8 scallop shells
White wine	

RINSE scallops, drain, slice, or cut into small dice. Cook lightly in butter in saucepan with onion and shallot. After 5 minutes moisten lightly with wine, add 1 tablespoon parsley and 2 tablespoons crumbs, mix well. Remove from heat, pour into 6 or 8 buttered scallop shells, sprinkle with remaining crumbs and melted butter. Brown quickly under moderate broiler heat. Makes 6 to 8 servings.

COQUILLES SAINT-JACQUES PROVENCALE
Scallops Provençale

2 pounds (1 quart) small scallops	1 garlic bud, peeled and mashed
Butter	3 tablespoons browned bread
Olive oil	crumbs
3 or 4 mushrooms, sliced	1 tablespoon chopped parsley
Salt and pepper	6 scallop shells
1 or 2 shallots, peeled and diced	

WASH scallops, drain, dice or slice. Cook in a little butter and olive oil about 5 minutes. Add mushrooms, seasoning, shallots, and garlic, stir and cook until scallops are done. Add crumbs and parsley and serve very hot in warmed decorative scallop-serving shells. Makes 6 servings.

SOLE ALSACIENNE
Sole Alsatian

2 pounds sole fillets	2 tablespoons butter
White wine	1 cup Mornay Sauce
Salt and pepper	3 tablespoons grated cheese
1½ cups sauerkraut	

RINSE fillets, drain, place in saucepan, and cover with mixture of equal parts of water and wine, with light seasoning of salt and pepper. Let cook slowly, 8 to 15 minutes, or until fish is just done. Cook sauerkraut about 5 minutes in butter, turning kraut so all of it is heated and buttered. Pour into baking dish and arrange in neat mound. Place poached fillets on sauerkraut, cover with Mornay Sauce, sprinkle with cheese. Brown quickly under high broiler heat. Makes 6 servings.

SOLE BERCY

2 pounds sole fillets	1 shallot, chopped
1½ cups white wine	4 tablespoons butter
½ cup liquor from cooked or canned mushrooms	

RINSE fish, drain, place in saucepan. Combine wine, mushroom liquor and half as much water, add shallot and 2 tablespoons butter, and pour over fish. Cover and poach 8 to 15 minutes, or until fish is just done. Lift fish from poaching liquor, place in buttered shallow baking dish. Reduce liquor a little, add remaining 2 tablespoons butter, stir and pour over fish. Brown quickly under high broiler heat. Makes 6 servings.

★SUPREME DE SOLE
Supreme of Sole

2 pounds sole fillets	2 tablespoons browned bread crumbs
2 cups fairly thick Mushroom Sauce	1 tablespoon butter
½ cup sliced raw mushrooms	Juice ½ lemon
6 sautéed mushroom caps	1 tablespoon chopped parsley

START oven at moderate (350 degrees F.). Pour enough Mushroom Sauce into shallow baking dish to cover bottom, lay fillets in sauce, surround with sliced raw mushrooms overlapping each other, lay cooked mushroom caps on sole, pour rest of Mushroom Sauce over, sprinkle with crumbs, dot with butter. Cook in oven about 20 minutes, or until fish is done. Add additional sauce and butter if needed. On taking from oven, squeeze lemon juice over, sprinkle with parsley, and serve at once. Makes 6 servings.

Some French chefs use an onion-flavored Mushroom Sauce for this dish, Cream Sauce containing minced mushrooms and truffles.

BOUILLABAISSE A LA MARSEILLAISE

Mme. Prunier's description of this dish, which has been made so many (wrong) ways outside that French port, states: "The bouillabaisse of Marseilles is not a fish dish, it is a soup in every accepted meaning of the word. The fishes which have been used in its preparation have left all their flavor in the stock. Those which should be used include rock fish, conger, bass, whiting, small crawfish and prawns." (Or use whatever is at the fish dealer's.) For 12 persons allow:

8 to 10 pounds fish	Small leaf fennel
5 pounds shellfish	1 bay leaf
2 medium-sized onions, peeled and chopped	1/8 teaspoon saffron
2 leeks, whites only, chopped	1/4 cup olive oil
4 tomatoes, skinned and chopped	Boiling water
1 garlic bud, peeled and crushed	Salt and pepper
1 dessert spoon of chopped parsley	Thick slices French bread
	Chopped parsley

CLEAN fish, remove scales, bones, tails, heads, cut across into pieces. Clean crawfish and prawns, cut into sections. Use very large kettle, add onions, leeks, tomatoes, garlic, parsley, fennel, bay leaf, saffron, and the pieces of fish and shellfish, and olive oil. Any fish with tender flesh, such as red mullet, bass, and whiting, can be put in later.

Cover with boiling water so liquid stands at least 2 inches above fish mixture. Add salt and pepper, bring quickly to boiling over high heat. Boil rapidly for 7 minutes, add any tender-fleshed fish which you may have held out, and continue boiling rapidly for another 8 minutes. Place bread in large (warmed) tureen, and pour liquor of the bouillabaisse over the bread. There should be enough bread so that soup is thick after it has been absorbed by the bread. (Do not toast or fry bread in advance.) Serve fish from kettle into warmed soup plates, sprinkle with parsley, surround with slices of prawns or crawfish. Serve soup from tureen over fish in soup plates. Or serve soup first into soup plates, then serve fish in large side dishes, a separate dish for each guest. The fish and soup are eaten together. Makes 12 servings.

GARNISHES FOR FISH

Slices of lobster tail, button mushrooms, Sauce Américaine (cooking liquor of lobster lightly bound with creamed butter, chopped chervil, and tarragon added) for any fish dish Américaine.

Glazed button mushrooms, button onions, crayfish cooked in court bouillon, Bercy sauce with cooking liquid of mussels added for broiled or poached fish.

Poached oysters, shelled shrimp or prawns and white sauce made with wine as part of liquid for broiled, poached, sautéed fish.

Thick rounds of hot boiled potato, arranged overlapping one another around broiled fish. Mornay Sauce.

Cucumbers cut olive-shape and stewed in butter, arranged around fish cooked à la meunière, or sautéed in browned butter.

Asparagus tips, truffle slices, Mornay Sauce, for broiled and sautéed fish.

Rice cooked with saffron; Curry Sauce for fish steaks or poached fish.

Peeled, pressed, and roughly-chopped tomatoes, cooked lightly in olive oil, with touch of garlic. Fillets of anchovy, little olives and capers, finish with chopped tarragon for poached, broiled, or sautéed fish.

The nine recipes above from MME. PRUNIER'S FISH COOKERY BOOK, *edited by Ambrose Heath*

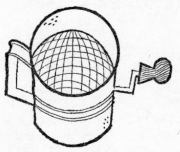

French-pastry making is not unknown in America, since many excellent French cook books have long been available to U.S. cooks and homemakers. But no one has done so much to encourage French-type pastry baking as Charlotte Turgeon in her simple, accurate, easy-to-follow book, *Tante Marie's French Pastry.*

Here is her simplified recipe for Flaky Pastry, and some recipes that use it.

PATE FEUILLETEE RAPIDE
Flaky Pastry (Quick method)

¾ cup unsalted butter   1 teaspoon salt
2¼ cups all-purpose flour, sifted   ¾ cup ice water

REMOVE butter from refrigerator and let stand at room temperature 20 to 30 minutes; butter should be workable but not too soft. Heap the flour on a cold marble slab, or enamel-top table or pastry board, or in a bowl. Make well in center and pour in the salt and a little ice water. Using fingertips of one hand, work flour toward center, adding water gradually with other hand until dough works into a well-blended ball. Put dough on lightly-floured plate and let it rest in cool place about 20 minutes.

Dust rolling pin and work surface lightly with flour. Roll dough out in ½-inch thick rectangle. Cut half the butter into thin slices over whole surface of rectangle. Roll it up lengthwise like a jelly roll. Turn roll so one end is near you. Roll out again, then roll dough up again like a jelly roll. Do this once more, and when it is rolled out flat, cut remaining butter over surface. Roll it up like a jelly roll again. Repeat turning and rolling process twice more. The dough is ready for use (*see* recipes).

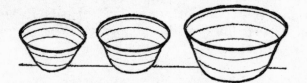

FEUILLETES A L'ABRICOT
Apricot Squares

Flaky Pastry   1 teaspoon water
Apricot jam   ¼ cup powdered sugar
1 egg yolk

START oven at hot (425 degrees F.). Give Flaky Pastry a fifth turn (*see* recipe). Divide dough in half and roll out two strips ⅓ inch thick, 3 inches wide, and 24 inches long. Trim to size with thin sharp knife. Cut each strip into 8 pieces, making 16 squares in all. Spread 8 of the squares with jam, leaving ½-inch margin on all sides. Moisten margin with cold water, cover each jam-filled square with another pastry square. Roll edges up to jam and press rolled borders with tines of fork. With point of knife trace a lattice pattern on surface of each square and brush with blend of egg yolk and water. Place squares on baking sheet which has been moistened with water. Bake 15 to 20 minutes in hot oven, or until pastry is golden. Sprinkle with powdered sugar and return to oven to glaze few minutes. Let cool on wire rack. Makes 8 squares.

CROISSANTS PATISSIERES

Flaky Pastry
2 egg yolks

2 teaspoons water
Confectioners' sugar

START oven at moderately hot (400 degrees F.). Give pastry dough a fifth turn (see recipe). Roll pastry out a sixth time into a large rectangle ⅛ inch thick. Trim edges evenly and save trimmings. Cut rectangle strips 4 inches wide. For smaller croissants, cut strips 3 inches wide. Take the strips one at a time and place with long sides parallel to edge of working surface. With thin knife cut each strip into triangles. Place triangles with wide side toward you. On each triangle place strip of trimmings along wide edge to give croissant fuller shape. Roll up triangle, pressing lightly with base of palm and stretching the dough a little as you press. Curve rolled-up triangle into crescent, ends turned in, and lay on unbuttered baking sheet. Brush croissants twice with blend of egg yolk and water. Bake 12 to 15 minutes in moderately hot oven. Just before croissants are finally removed from oven, take pan out, sprinkle croissants with confectioners' sugar, and return to oven for 1 or 2 minutes. Makes 24 croissants.

ALLUMETTES
Frosted Pastry Sticks

⅓ recipe Flaky Pastry
½ egg white

⅛ teaspoon lemon juice
1⅓ cups sifted confectioners' sugar

START oven at moderately hot (400 degrees F.). Before rolling out pastry dough for final two turns, combine egg white and lemon juice with sugar and beat 10 minutes with electric or rotary beater; this frosting should be thick and creamy.

Give pastry fifth turn (see recipe). Roll it out sixth time into a band 4 inches wide, ⅛ inch thick, and 24 inches long. Turn strip so that long sides are parallel to near edge of working surface. Spread pastry dough with frosting, smoothing frosting into place with knife dipped in hot water. Still using hot knife, cut strip into 1-inch sticks. Place on buttered baking sheet. Bake 15 minutes in moderately hot oven. Let cool on wire rack. Makes 24 sticks.

PATE BRISEE OR PATE A FONCER
Kneaded Pastry

This pastry dough is called broken pastry because of the way in which it is kneaded. It is very simple to make and roll, and serves as bottom crust for fruit and custard tarts, large and small, and as a foundation for many French pastries. If filling of tart is to be juicy, add egg yolk to dough to make a baked crust that is less absorbent. After mixing dough, it must rest at least 20 minutes. It is better if allowed to stand in refrigerator for 2 hours, and even better if left overnight. If dough becomes too stiff in refrigerator, let stand 20 minutes at room temperature before rolling. Pastry dough can be divided according to the requirements of recipes. Wrap unused dough in waxed paper; it will keep in refrigerator for several days.

2 cups all-purpose flour, sifted   1 teaspoon salt
¼ pound butter   ½ cup cold water, approximately
1 tablespoon sugar   1 egg yolk, optional

PILE flour on cold marble slab, pastry board, or enameled table top. Cut butter into slices over surface of flour, rub flour and butter between your hands for 2 minutes as though you were washing your hands. Mixture will become rough and pebbly. Pile mixture in small mound and make well in center. Put sugar, salt, egg yolk (if desired), and a little of the cold water in the well and work the mixture into the flour, adding more water gradually with other hand. Always work toward center. If you are not using egg yolk, you will need a little more cold water, but use only enough to form a slightly sticky ball. In true French fashion you will wipe up the working surface or the sides of the bowl with the dough, picking up stray bits of flour and butter and leaving the working surface spotless. Now comes the breaking process. Push off small pieces of pastry with the base of your palm, crushing each piece on the working surface. When all dough has been broken off and crushed, re-form the ball and repeat the process. Do this once more, wrap dough in waxed paper to rest. Then use as called for in recipes.

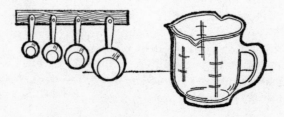

PALMIERS GLACES
Golden Palm Leaves

Flaky pastry   Powdered sugar

START oven at moderately hot (400 degrees F.). Give pastry dough fifth turn (see recipe), but before turning and refolding it, sprinkle strip generously with sugar. Before sixth turn, lift pastry and sprinkle working surface of table, slab, or board with sugar; this works more sugar into dough. Roll out dough into large rectangle. Turn it and roll rectangle into square. Pastry should be very thin. If making small palm leaves, cut square in half. Determine the center horizontal line of the pastry. Fold in the near and far edges toward the center, using 4-inch laps for large palms, 2-inch laps for small ones. When folds meet in center, fold them together as though you were closing a book. If a large fold for large palms, cut pastry into ½-inch slices, if smaller fold for small palms, cut into ¼-inch slices. Place palm leaves on unbuttered baking sheets. Bake 12 to 15 minutes in moderately hot oven. Turn them with spatula for last 3 minutes' baking so they caramelize a little on both sides. Makes 18 large palm leaves, or 36 small ones.

The six recipes above from TANTE MARIE'S FRENCH PASTRY, *by Charlotte Turgeon*

Germany

With so many German-Americans long established in the Middle Western part of the United States and in our large cities, German cookery is not unknown on this side of the Atlantic. If it were, the excellent translated edition of *Mein Kochbuch,* now called *German Cookery,* by Elizabeth Schuler, would soon make converts to the traditional delicious dishes. Edited by Joy Gary, it is one of a series of translated international cook books for which Charlotte Adams is general editor. It is a volume any cook can label "treasure" and count on for special, accurate recipes for dishes with which to change familiar home menus and to spotlight important guest dinners.

Remember Lebkuchen and Pfeffernusse? They are the Christmas cookies which German families and German bakeshops always made ready for old-time Christmas trees. Here they are.

COOKIES

HONIGLEBKUCHEN
Honey Spice Cookies

2 eggs

¾ cup sugar

1 teaspoon ground cinnamon

⅛ teaspoon ground cloves

¾ cup chopped candied orange or
lemon peel

2 tablespoons rum

4 cups all-purpose flour, sifted

¾ cup honey

1 cup chopped almonds

1 teaspoon baking powder

Egg-White Icing

STIR eggs and sugar together to a froth, add spices, candied peel, rum, and 1 cup sifted flour; mix well. Combine honey and almonds and stir in 1 cup sifted flour. Combine egg dough and honey dough and knead together on lightly-floured board. Sift baking powder with remaining flour and knead into dough. Roll out ½ inch thick and cut into desired shapes with cookie cutters.

Start oven at moderately hot (400 degrees F.). Grease baking sheets and place cookies on sheets, leaving ½ inch between cookies. Bake in moderately hot oven 10 to 12 minutes. Brush cookies while still hot with Egg-White Icing (below) or, when cool, with any other icing. Makes 5 to 7 dozen 2-inch cookies.

★PFEFFERNUSSE
Peppernuts

3 eggs

1 cup sugar

⅓ cup almonds, blanched and
ground

⅓ cup chopped candied lemon
and orange peels

1 teaspoon ground cinnamon

⅛ teaspoon ground cloves

⅛ teaspoon pepper

¼ teaspoon baking powder

3 cups all-purpose flour, sifted

Sugar, or Egg-White Icing

STIR eggs and sugar together until frothy. Combine with almonds and chopped peels, mixing well; add spice, pepper, and sifted baking powder and flour, mix, turn out on lightly-floured board and knead into dough. Grease baking sheets. Roll out dough, cut with biscuit cutter about size of half-dollar. Place cookies on buttered sheets. Let stand overnight to dry.

Next day start oven at moderately slow (300 degrees F.). Bake cookies about 20 to 30 minutes, or until browned. Frost while warm with Egg-White Icing. Makes about 4 to 5 dozen cookies.

EGG-WHITE ICING

Sift 1 cup confectioners' sugar; combine with 2 egg whites and 1 tea-spoon lemon juice or vanilla in electric beater; beat 5 minutes. Or beat 15 minutes by hand. Spread on warm cookies. Makes about 1½ cups icing.

The holiday season and all other seasons in German house-holds call, not only for cookies, but for certain other traditional sweets, such as these:

DESERTS

★KIRSCHPFANNKUCHEN
Cherry Pancakes

4 hard rolls, about 3½ inches
   long
¼ cup all-purpose flour, sifted
2 beaten eggs
1 cup milk

2 teaspoons sugar
1 pound sweet cherries, pitted
Butter or fat
Cinnamon and sugar, mixed

SOAK rolls in a little cold water; when thoroughly soft, squeeze dry and break up, mashing with fork. Mix rolls with flour, eggs, milk, and sugar. Drain cherries (fresh or canned) and fold into batter. Drop by spoonful into hot butter in frying pan, or into deep hot fat (375 degrees F.). Fry until lightly browned. Drain on thick paper towels, sprinkle with cinnamon and sugar. Makes 4 servings. (More fritter than pancake, but translated as a pancake. Also see Apple Pancake, in Lüchow section this chapter.)

REIS TRAUTMANNSDORFF
Fruit Rice

¾ cup long-grain rice
2 cups milk
½ teaspoon vanilla extract
3 tablespoons sugar
1 envelope, or 1 tablespoon,
   gelatin

2 tablespoons rum or cognac
1 cup heavy cream
1 cup sliced fresh or canned
   peaches, apricots, or cherries

COOK rice 20 minutes, drain well; cook again briefly in milk with vanilla added. Stir sugar and gelatin into rum or cognac until softened and dissolved over hot water, stir into hot rice, mix well. Whip cream until stiff, fold into rice mixture. Turn into lightly-buttered 1-quart ring mold. Chill. Turn out onto chilled platter, serve garnished with fruit. Makes 4 servings.

INGWERCREME
Ginger Cream

1 cup milk

2 beaten egg yolks

¼ cup sugar

⅛ teaspoon salt

½ envelope, or ½ tablespoon,
  gelatin softened in

¼ cup cold water

¼ cup preserved ginger, minced

3 tablespoons ginger juice

1 teaspoon vanilla extract

1 cup heavy cream

COMBINE milk, egg yolks, sugar, and salt in top of double boiler. Cook over hot water and let come to boiling. Remove at once from heat, add softened gelatin, and mix. Chill. When mixture begins to thicken, stir in ginger, ginger juice, and vanilla; whip cream until stiff and fold in. Chill until very cold. Makes 4 servings.

★HASELNUSSCREME
Hazelnut Cream

½ cup shelled hazelnuts

1 cup milk

2 beaten egg yolks

¼ cup sugar

1 teaspoon vanilla extract

½ envelope, or ½ tablespoon
  gelatin dissolved in

¼ cup water

½ cup heavy cream

HEAT nuts in oven until brown skins peel. Rub in towel to remove skins, grate nuts. Combine with milk, egg yolks, sugar, and vanilla in top of double boiler over hot water. Bring almost to a boil, remove from heat, stir in dissolved gelatin until mixture thickens. Whip cream until stiff, fold into nut mixture. Turn into glass serving bowl. Chill. Decorate with additional whirls of whipped cream to serve. Makes 3 or more servings.

★SCHOKOLADEPUDDING
Hot Chocolate Pudding

1½ (1-oz.) squares sweet chocolate

2 cups milk

3 tablespoons butter

½ teaspoon vanilla extract

1¼ cups all-purpose flour, sifted

⅜ cup sugar

4 eggs

MELT chocolate and stir into 1 cup milk. To second cup milk add butter and vanilla and heat almost to boiling. Combine with chocolate-and-milk and stir into flour, mix smoothly, let cool. Add sugar and egg yolks and beat 20 minutes. Whip egg whites until stiff, fold into chocolate mixture. Butter 1-quart pudding mold, pour chocolate mixture in to fill about ⅔ full. Cover tightly, set in kettle containing water to half the height of pudding mold. Cover kettle, bring water to boiling, steam 1 hour. Turn pudding out on warmed serving plate. Serve warm with Vanilla Sauce or any favorite sauce. Makes 4 to 6 servings.

German cooks are also famous for the dumplings they make to add to various soups and stews.

DUMPLINGS

GEKOCHTE KARTOFFELKLOSSE
Potato Dumplings

2 pounds potatoes	Ground nutmeg
2 cups all-purpose flour, sifted	2 slices bread
2 beaten eggs	1 tablespoon butter
Salt	Boiling water

COOK potatoes in their skins. Let cool and "rest" overnight. Next day peel and mash potatoes. Combine with flour, eggs, and seasoning; knead into firm dough. Cut bread into cubes, sauté lightly in butter. Shape dumplings, make hole in each, and put in several fried bread cubes. Close dumpling dough well over hole. Try 1 test dumpling in kettle of boiling water. If dumpling falls apart, work more flour into dough. Drop dumplings into rapidly boiling, lightly-salted water and cook 10 to 15 minutes. Makes 4 servings.

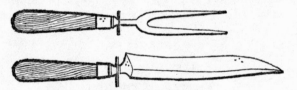

★SPATZLE
Noodle Dumplings

4 cups all-purpose flour, sifted	1 tablespoon salt
3 beaten eggs	Boiling water
1 cup water	

COMBINE flour, eggs, 1 cup water, and salt to make firm dough. Beat until it comes easily away from sides of bowl. Drop by spoonful into rapidly-boiling, lightly-salted water. Cook 10 to 15 minutes. Skim out dumplings, dip into cold water, drain, serve on hot platter with meat and vegetables. Spätzle also may be browned lightly in butter after cooking in boiling water. Makes 4 servings.

Cheese Spätzle. Prepare spätzle by above recipe, take from boiling water, drain, and tumble in grated cheese. Serve on hot platter with *Onion Butter:* 1 small onion peeled, chopped and sautéed in 4 tablespoons butter until golden. Makes 4 servings.

MEATS AND ENTREES

EINGEMACHTES KALBFLEISCH
Pickled Veal

3 pounds breast of veal cut in
    thin palm-size slices
Boiling water
2 or 3 tablespoons butter
1 small onion, peeled and
    chopped
Hot water
Salt and pepper
4 peppercorns

1 bay leaf
3 tablespoons flour
½ cup sauterne or any white
    wine
½ teaspoon lemon juice
1 beaten egg yolk
1 tablespoon diced mushrooms
Cooked noodles or buttered rice

SCALD meat by placing briefly in boiling water. Melt butter in deep skillet, cook drained meat and onion briefly in butter; do not brown. Add hot water to cover, add seasonings, cover skillet and cook slowly about 1½ hours. Mix little water with flour to smooth paste, stir into pan with wine and lemon juice. (Add more lemon juice if desired.) Cook and stir until boiling, reduce heat, add egg yolk, cook slowly until thickened; add mushrooms. Serve with hot noodles or buttered rice. Makes 4 servings.

SAUERBRATEN
Savory Beef Fricassee

½ cup vinegar
½ cup water
1 onion, peeled and sliced
Salt and pepper
1 bay leaf
1 clove

1½ pounds beef shoulder
1 marrow bone
2 tablespoons fat
1 onion, peeled
1 tomato, peeled, quartered

BOIL vinegar, water, sliced onion, seasoning, bay leaf, and clove together in enamel or glass saucepan 10 minutes. Pour this over beef in pottery or glass bowl; let stand, covered, in refrigerator 2 or 3 days. Spoon liquid over meat frequently during this marinating period. To prepare for table, remove meat from marinade and save marinade. Brown meat and marrow bone in hot fat in heavy kettle. Add onion, tomato, and ½ cup marinade, cover and simmer about 1 hour. When done, turn meat in liquid in kettle so it is coated on all sides. Slice onto warmed serving platter and keep it warm.

Sauce:

1 tablespoon flour	Salt
Vinegar or lemon juice	1 tablespoon butter
½ teaspoon sugar	1 or 2 tablespoons cream or wine

For sauce, mix flour with liquid in kettle, add rest of marinade, and stir and boil until smooth and thickened. Add, to taste, a little vinegar or lemon juice, the sugar, a little salt, 1 tablespoon butter and 1 or 2 tablespoons cream or wine. Stir, heat to a boil but do not boil again. Pour over sliced meat or serve separately. Makes 3 to 4 servings.

★SPINATPFANNKUCHEN
Spinach Pancakes

½ pound spinach	1 cup milk
2 beaten eggs	Salt
3 tablespoons flour	2 tablespoons butter

WASH spinach thoroughly, drain, and chop. Mix with eggs, flour, milk, and salt to form smooth batter. Melt butter in frying pan, pour pancakes and cook until nicely browned on both sides. Delicious with Tomato or Caper Sauce. Makes 2 servings.

★GEFULLTE KALBSBRUST
Stuffed Breast of Veal

5- or 6-pound breast of veal	2 onions, peeled and chopped
Salt and pepper	1 or 2 beaten eggs
Lemon juice	2 tablespoons chopped parsley
4 hard rolls, about 3½ inches long	1 cup, or more, beef stock
1 cup milk	1 tablespoon flour

HAVE meat dealer make deep pocket in meat. Rinse meat, pat dry. Rub inside of pocket with salt and lemon juice. Make stuffing: cut up rolls and simmer briefly in milk, let cool. Cook 1 chopped onion in little fat 2 or 3 minutes, add to bread mixture, add eggs, parsley, seasoning. Mix well and stuff into pocket. Sew up or skewer tightly.

Heat stock in Dutch oven or other heavy kettle, add remaining chopped onion, place stuffed veal in stock, cook 1¼ hours. Turn meat frequently and add liquid if necessary. Or roast stuffed veal in moderate (350 degrees F.) oven for 1½ hours. When done, remove meat from kettle or roasting pan, keep it warm, add flour and seasoning, stirring smoothly, and as much additional liquid stock or light cream as needed for gravy. Stir and boil 2 or 3 minutes until slightly thickened. Remove thread or skewers from roast, place meat on warmed serving platter, slice with very sharp, thin knife to prevent stuffing crumbling. Serve with hot gravy, and Spätzle, and a green salad. Makes 6 servings.

★GEFULLTE KAPSELBROT
Stuffed Dark Bread

1 square loaf dark bread
(pumpernickel)
2 hard-cooked eggs
½ cup mashed and puréed anchovies
6 to 8 tablespoons creamed butter
1 cup chopped boiled beef tongue or ham

½ cup grated Swiss cheese
1 tablespoon capers
1 tablespoon prepared mustard
Salt and pepper
Aspic for garnish
Sliced tomatoes for garnish
2 tablespoons chopped parsley

REMOVE crusts from bread, scoop out most of the inside. Chop eggs finely, combine with anchovies and creamed butter. Mix well, combine with tongue or ham, cheese, capers, mustard, and seasonings. Blend well, stuff hollowed loaf. Cover with waxed paper and chill thoroughly. To serve, cut into thick slices, garnish with aspic, tomato, and parsley. Add to cold-cut platter or serve as first-course appetizer. Makes 6 or more servings.

SOUP GARNISHES

★WECKKLOSSCHEN
Bread Dumplings

2 pieces day-old bread
1 tablespoon butter
Salt and ground nutmeg

Chopped parsley
1 beaten egg

GRATE bread or cut in small pieces, dampen with little hot soup. Cream butter, add seasoning, parsley, egg, and dampened bread. Blend well, form balls. Drop into boiling soup. Reduce heat, let balls cook 5 minutes. Makes enough for 4 soup servings.

★BUTTERKLOSSCHEN
Butter Balls

3 tablespoons butter
2 beaten egg yolks

¼ cup all-purpose flour
Salt and ground nutmeg

CREAM butter, add alternately small amounts of egg yolk and flour, stirring smoothly. Season to taste with salt and nutmeg. Let mixture stand 1 hour. Measure teaspoon-size lumps into simmering hot stock or soup, cook over slow heat until balls float to top. Makes enough for 4 soup servings.

★MARKKLOSSCHEN
Marrow Balls

3 ounces beef marrow
2 hard rolls, about 3½ inches
  long
¼ cup milk

2 beaten eggs
1 tablespoon flour
Salt, pepper, ground nutmeg

MELT marrow over low heat. Crumble rolls into milk and let soak, squeeze dry. Mix all ingredients and shape into dumplings. Place in boiling soup stock and let simmer until they float to the surface. Makes enough for 4 soup servings.

SOUPS

KALTSCHALE
Cold Fruit Soup

1 pound apples, or cherries,
  rhubarb, or gooseberries
2 quarts water
1 tablespoon cornstarch or 4
  tablespoons tapioca

½ cup water or fruit juice
2 tablespoons sugar
Juice and chopped peel ½ lemon
½ cup white wine, optional

PREPARE washed fruit for cooking: pare, core, and quarter apples; or pit cherries, or cut rhubarb into small pieces, or stem gooseberries. Cover with 2 quarts water in enamel kettle, cook until fruit is soft; drain, reserving liquid. Put fruit through fine strainer, replace puréed fruit in its cooking liquid and reheat. Dissolve cornstarch or tapioca in ½ cup water or fruit juice, stir into hot fruit mixture. If tapioca is used, cook until it is transparent. Add sugar as needed (more with gooseberries and rhubarb), add lemon juice, peel, and wine. Chill until very cold. Serve in cold soup dishes garnished with cut fruit or whole berries. Makes 4 to 6 servings.

WEINKALTSCHALE
Cold Wine Soup

4 cups water
5 tablespoons seedless raisins
5 tablespoons semolina
2 beaten egg yolks
2 tablespoons sugar

1 cup white wine
Juice ½ lemon
2 egg whites
5 tablespoons sugar
Ground cinnamon

BRING 3 cups water and the raisins to boiling in enamel saucepan. Mix semolina with 1 cup water, add to raisins and water and stir well, cooking

20 minutes. Blend egg yolks, sugar, wine, and lemon juice and stir into soup. Keep on low heat 4 minutes, do not boil. Let cool. Place in refrigerator to chill. When ready to serve, whip egg whites until stiff with 3 tablespoons sugar. Serve soup in chilled soup dishes, drop small floats of the meringue into each serving (like croutons). Add dash of sugar and cinnamon to each. Makes 4 or more servings.

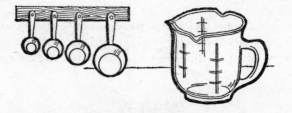

BUTTERMILCHSUPPE
Buttermilk Soup

1 pound potatoes
1 tablespoon flour
1 quart buttermilk

3 strips bacon
1 onion, peeled and chopped
Salt and pepper

SCRUB potatoes, rinse, drain. Pare and chop, cover with salted water and cook until tender; drain. Mix flour smoothly with a little buttermilk, stir into rest of buttermilk and bring to boiling. Chop bacon and cook with onion until browned. Combine potatoes, hot buttermilk-flour mixture, and bacon and onion, heat again, adding seasoning as needed. Bring to a boil but do not boil. Serve in warm soup bowls. Makes 4 servings.

These twenty-two recipes above from GERMAN COOKERY, *by Elizabeth Schuler, edited and translated by Joy Gary*

❧

Another German cook book which has pleased many Americans, especially New Yorkers, is *Lüchow's German Cookbook* by Leonard Jan Mitchell. Mr. Mitchell owns that famous old Fourteenth Street landmark, Lüchow's Restaurant, and he takes pride in maintaining its long-established standards of German cookery and hospitality. In addition to recipes for some of the most popular dishes served at Lüchow's, the book is amusingly illustrated by Ludwig Bemelmans, and the introduction by the same artist-writer whets the appetite for the hearty and time-honored dishes which are described (in modern American-recipe form) in the rest of the book. Travelers have been known to cross the sea just to have another of Lüchow's dishes.

CALF'S HEAD CHEESE VINAIGRETTE

1 calf's head	½ teaspoon dried sage
1 beef head	1 cup wine vinegar
2½ gallons water	¼ cup cooking oil
½ pound salt	½ teaspoon coarsely-ground
1 tablespoon saltpeter	black pepper
1 bay leaf	2 onions, peeled and chopped
6 cloves	2 tablespoons minced chives
6 peppercorns	

HAVE meat dealer clean and bone heads, remove eyes, brains, ears, snout, and most of fat. Soak heads in cold water to extract blood. Wash thoroughly, drain, place in large crock. Cover with 2½ gallons water; add salt and saltpeter. Let stand in cold place 10 days.

Drain, rinse, place meat in large kettle (discard bones), cover with cold water and bring to a boil. Lower heat, add bay leaf, cloves, peppercorns, and sage. Let cook slowly (simmer) 5 hours. Remove from heat. Pour meat and stock into large mold or pan. Let cool. When stock has jelled firmly, cut into narrow strips.

Mix vinegar, oil, pepper, and onions, and pour over these strips which are called head cheese. Garnish platter with chives. Serves 6 or more.

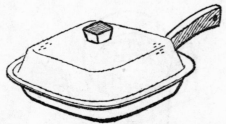

★CHICKEN LIVERS SAUTEED WITH APPLES AND ONION RINGS

12 chicken livers	½ Spanish onion, peeled and
½ teaspoon salt	sliced in rings
¼ teaspoon paprika	4 apple slices about ½-inch
2 tablespoons flour	thick
3 tablespoons butter	2 tablespoons sugar

RINSE and drain livers; if very large, cut in half. Season lightly with salt and paprika, sprinkle lightly with flour. Cook gently in 2 tablespoons butter until browned. In another small pan cook onion in a little butter. Sprinkle over cooked livers.

In a third pan brown apple slices in remaining butter. Sprinkle with sugar to give glaze and flavor. Top liver and onions. Makes 2 servings.

LUCHOW'S CHEESE CAKE

2 cups Graham-cracker crumbs
1½ teaspoons ground cinnamon
¾ cup melted butter
6 eggs
1½ cups sugar
¼ teaspoon salt
1 tablespoon grated lemon peel

3 tablespoons lemon juice
1 teaspoon vanilla extract
3 cups heavy cream
½ cup all-purpose flour, sifted
2¼ pounds (7 cups) smooth cottage cheese

Mix crumbs, cinnamon, and butter smoothly together. Measure 1 cup crumb mixture and set aside. Press remaining mixture in bottom and sides of 12-inch spring-form cake pan. Use hand or wooden spoon to make smooth, even lining. Cover with waxed paper and chill shell in refrigerator 1 hour or longer.

Start oven at moderate (350 degrees F.). Beat eggs until light. Sift sugar gradually into them, and beat until light and fluffy. Add salt, lemon peel, juice, and vanilla. Whip cream until stiff and fold in. Mix flour and cheese, put through sieve. Fold into egg-cream mixture. Fill chilled pie shell. Sprinkle remaining cup of crumbs evenly over top. Bake in moderate oven about 1 hour. When done, turn heat off, open oven door, and let cake remain in oven about ½ hour longer, or until cooled. Makes 12 servings.

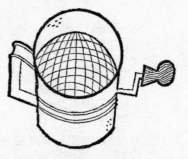

LUCHOW'S GERMAN PANCAKE

At Lüchow's an order of a German pancake dessert for two calls for a spectacular performance on the part of the chef and the waiter or captain who is in charge of your table. The pancake, when borne from the kitchen, measures about a foot-and-a-half in diameter. It is deliciously browned, hot, ready for the captain's ministrations.

Working swiftly at a serving table at your elbow, he sprinkles the top of the pancake thickly with sugar and powdered cinnamon from huge glass shakers. He quickly squeezes the juice of a lemon over this and then spreads the famous imported Preisselbeeren (lingonberries) or huckleberry jam, cooked apples, or chocolate sauce thickly over the sugared surface and rolls the cake like a jelly roll.

Next he cuts the roll into 2 pieces, sprinkles them with more sugar and cinnamon, and slips each onto a plate. If you like, he will sprinkle these rolls with Jamaica rum or kirsch, ignite it, and then place the succulent dessert before you while the sugary flames are dancing across its surface.

The chef's pan for this mammoth pancake is a large, long-handled thin iron frying pan. Each cake is made with 4 or more tablespoons or large cooking spoons of batter poured into the heated pan, which has been generously buttered. The batter must be spread quickly over the pan and up the sides to form a large thin pancake. As soon as it bubbles and the bottom is set, it is turned with a wide pancake turner and baked on the other side. Here is the recipe:

6 eggs	Sugar in shaker
1½ cups all-purpose flour, sifted	Juice 1 lemon
¼ teaspoon salt	Cooked or canned Preisselbeeren,
1 tablespoon sugar	huckleberry jam, cooked apple
1 pint milk	slices, or Chocolate Sauce
½ pound butter	Rum or kirsch, optional
Powdered cinnamon in shaker	

BEAT eggs lightly; beat in flour, salt, sugar, then add milk, a little at a time, beating well. Beat 5 minutes in all. The batter should be thin and smooth.

Melt enough butter in a wide frying pan to coat bottom and sides. When hot, pour in 4 or 5 generous tablespoons batter. Turn and slant pan to make batter spread to form large, thin flat pancake. Cook until batter bubbles, turn cake with wide pancake turner, and bake other side. Slip onto hot plate. See directions at beginning of this recipe. Dress pancake as described, roll and cut into 2 or more pieces to serve 2 or more people. Batter recipe makes 4 to 6 such pancakes.

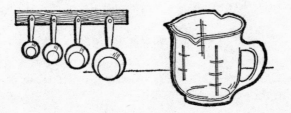

A planked fish dish at Lüchow's is almost as glamorous as the pancakes. In the spring many regulars at this restaurant make their luncheon or dinner on:

PLANKED BONED SHAD

4 fillets boned shad, about ½
   pound each
1 teaspoon salt
¼ teaspoon pepper
Olive oil
8 slices lean bacon
4 tablespoons butter, melted,
   mixed with
1 tablespoon lemon juice

1 large fish or steak plank
4 cups hot mashed potatoes
4 hot broiled tomato halves,
   seasoned
2 or 3 cups hot cooked string
   beans
16 hot cooked asparagus tips
Lemon slices

RINSE and drain shad, pat dry, season with salt and pepper. Brush lightly with oil and broil under moderate heat until golden on both sides, 15 to 20 minutes. At the same time broil bacon in another pan until crisp. Warm plank, place cooked fillets in center, pour a little mixed butter and lemon juice over them, then top with bacon curls. Use pastry tube or spoon and make border of hot mashed potatoes around plank. Place broiled tomato halves, string beans, and asparagus attractively around fish. Garnish with lemon slices. Serve at once. Or omit lemon, set plank under broiler heat until potatoes are delicately browned. Remove plank, garnish with lemon slices and serve at once. Makes 4 servings.

The five recipes above from LÜCHOW'S GERMAN COOK BOOK, *by Leonard Jan Mitchell*

Haiti

The cookery of Haiti is similar to that of Cuba and of the other island peoples of the Caribbean. In *Favorite Recipes from the United Nations* these three dishes from Haiti are given as Haitian favorites, recipes which were tested for American kitchens by the American Home Economics Association.

BANANAS IN RUM

6 large ripe bananas
½ cup olive oil
½ teaspoon vanilla extract

3 tablespoons rum
¼ cup powdered sugar

PEEL bananas, cut across into thin slices. Sauté in hot oil for a few minutes. When all are lightly browned, remove from fat, drain on thick paper towels, let cool. Place in shallow serving dish. Add vanilla to rum and sprinkle mixture over bananas. Sieve powdered sugar over top. Serve cold as dessert. Makes 6 servings.

NATIONAL PLATE

1 cup dried pinto or kidney
  beans
3 cups water
1¾ teaspoons salt
6 tablespoons bacon fat
1 clove garlic, peeled and
  minced

1 onion, peeled and chopped
1 tablespoon minced parsley
½ teaspoon pepper
¼ teaspoon ground cloves
1 cup rice

WASH beans, drain. Pour into 3-quart kettle, add 3 cups water; bring to boiling and boil 5 minutes. Remove from heat, add salt, and let soak 1 hour. At end of hour drain beans, reserving liquid. Heat bacon fat, sauté garlic, onion, and parsley; add pepper and cloves. Sauté beans in same fat 5 minutes.

Measure bean liquid and add sufficient water to make 5½ cups; add sautéed beans and garlic-onion mixture and cook 1 to 1½ hours over slow heat, or until beans begin to soften. Add 1 cup washed and drained rice and continue cooking until rice is done. If mixture becomes dry before rice is done, add a little hot water.

Start oven at slow (250 degrees F.). Pour bean-and-rice mixture into well-oiled 2-quart casserole. Bake in slow oven about 30 minutes. Makes 8 to 10 servings.

★SWEET POTATO CAKE

1 cup mashed cooked sweet
  potatoes
2 small bananas, peeled and
  mashed
1 cup milk

2 tablespoons sugar
½ teaspoon salt
2 beaten egg yolks
3 tablespoons finely-chopped
  raisins

START oven at moderately slow (300 degrees F.). Combine sweet potatoes and bananas, add milk, and blend thoroughly. Add sugar, salt, egg yolks, and raisins. Mix well, pour into well-oiled 1-quart shallow baking dish. Bake in moderately slow oven 45 minutes, or until cake is set and firm to touch; the top should be golden brown. Let cool slightly, or serve cold. Cut into pie-shaped pieces, serve on dessert plates. Makes 4 to 6 servings.

The three recipes above from FAVORITE RECIPES FROM THE UNITED NATIONS, *by the United States Committee for the U.N.*

In the introduction to *The Art of Caribbean Cookery,* by Carmen Aboy Valldejuli, the author points out that Caribbean cuisines have resulted from a blending of the foods and cooking methods that West Indies settlers—Spanish, British, French, Danish, and African—brought with them. In Haiti, where French is spoken and French culture enjoyed by Government officials and their families and many residents, varied culinary influences are found in dishes served at hotels as well as in native homes. Here are some popular dishes from this Caribbean authority's book.

CHICKEN IN SWEET WINE

3½-pound chicken, cleaned and
   ready for cooking
1 clove garlic, peeled
3 peppercorns
1 teaspoon orégano
2¼ teaspoons salt
1¼ teaspoons cooking oil
½ teaspoon vinegar
4 tablespoons butter
1 cup water

1 pound onions, peeled and sliced
1 teaspoon capers
10 green olives, pitted
3 bay leaves
10 prunes, pitted
2 tablespoons raisins
1½ pounds potatoes, pared and
   cut in pieces
1½ cups muscatel wine
½ cup sugar

RINSE and dry chicken. Mash garlic, peppercorns, and orégano together in mortar. Add salt, oil, and vinegar, mix smoothly together. Use this seasoning to rub inside and all over chicken. Melt butter in flameproof (metal-base) casserole, brown chicken over moderate heat 10 minutes. Add all ingredients except wine and sugar. Cover casserole and cook 15 minutes on moderate heat, add wine and sugar, cover, cook 15 minutes more. Uncover and let cook 25 minutes longer, or until sauce thickens slightly. Serve hot in dish in which it cooked. Makes 6 servings.

CODFISH SALAD

1 pound dried, salted codfish
   fillets, washed, drained, soaked
   4 hours in water to cover
1 pound onions, peeled and sliced
1 pound large tomatoes, peeled
   and sliced

1 cup olive oil
½ cup vinegar
½ teaspoon salt
¼ teaspoon pepper

DRAIN soaked codfish. Cover with water and boil 15 minutes. Drain, rinse in fresh water. Discard skin and bones, shred flesh, and chill. Arrange fish on chilled platter, garnish with chilled onions and tomatoes. Combine oil, vinegar, salt, and pepper and pour over fish. Serve very cold. Makes 4 to 6 servings.

GOLDEN FISH

4-pound fish, cleaned, left whole for baking
Juice 2 large limes
2 tablespoons salt
½ teaspoon pepper
2 medium-sized onions, peeled and sliced
2 bay leaves
12 green olives, pitted
1 tablespoon capers

1 tablespoon liquid from caper jar
½ cup water
½ cup olive oil
2 cloves garlic, peeled and mashed
1¼ pounds whole tomatoes or No. 2 can
2 canned pimientos

WASH fish inside and out, drain. Cut 2 slight gashes on both sides. Place fish in buttered baking dish, squeeze juice of limes over it, and sprinkle with salt and pepper. Start oven at very hot (550 degrees F.). Cover fish with sliced onions, bay leaves, and all ingredients except pimientos, surrounding fish well and covering completely. Bake in very hot oven 15 minutes, lower temperature to 425 degrees F. and bake 25 minutes longer. Drain pimientos, cut in strips, heat and use as garnish on top of fish. Serve hot in dish in which it cooked. Makes 8 servings.

POT OF FRESH HAM WITH WINE

5½ pounds fresh ham
1 large clove garlic, peeled
6 peppercorns
2 teaspoons orégano
2 tablespoons salt
2 tablespoons olive oil
5 cups water
½ pound onions, peeled and sliced

2 bay leaves
¾ cup muscatel wine
¾ cup sugar
2 pounds potatoes, pared and halved
2 teaspoons salt

RINSE meat, pat dry. Remove skin and excess fat. Reserve fat. Make superficial crisscross gashes on top of meat. Combine garlic, peppercorns, orégano, salt, and olive oil in mortar and mash and mix smoothly. Rub meat all over with this seasoning. Brown meat in a heavy kettle with little of reserved fat; use high heat and brown on all sides. Add water, onions, and bay leaves and bring to a boil. Cover, lower heat to moderate, and cook 2½ hours. Turn meat occasionally. Add wine, sugar, potatoes, and salt, cook uncovered 1 hour. Serve meat on hot platter surrounded by potatoes, with gravy from the kettle poured over. Makes 8 to 10 servings.

TURKEY IN SHERRY

6-pound turkey, cleaned and
   ready for cooking
3½ cups sweet sherry
½ cup butter
1 pound tiny onions, peeled

No. 2½ can whole tomatoes
2 bay leaves
5 teaspoons salt
3-ounce jar stuffed olives, drained

RINSE turkey, pat dry, cut into serving pieces. Place turkey in deep glass or pottery bowl, pour sherry over pieces, cover dish and place in refrigerator overnight.

Next day, drain turkey, reserving sherry. Melt half the butter in large frying pan over moderate heat. Brown turkey about 4 minutes on each side, turn heat low, and add remaining butter, onions, tomatoes and their juice, bay leaves, and 3 or 4 teaspoons salt (1 teaspoon for each pound turkey when ready to cook). Add reserved sherry, cover pan, and cook over low heat about 30 minutes. Uncover and continue cooking slowly 30 minutes longer. Add olives, and 1 teaspoon salt if needed. Increase heat to moderate and cook uncovered 1 hour. Serve hot in the pan sauce. Makes 6 to 8 servings.

The five recipes above from THE ART OF CARIBBEAN COOKERY, *by Carmen Aboy Valldejuli*

Hawaii

Besides bringing another star to our flag, Hawaii's joining state-side Americans as the "Aloha State" brings us wondrous gifts of good cookery. And we are fortunate in having an authoritative, carefully compiled, and home-economist edited cook book of the varied cookery of the islands. The book is *Hawaiian and Pacific Foods,* by Katherine Bazore Gruelle.

Her collection includes Samoan, Chinese, Japanese, Korean, Filipino, Portuguese, and Hawaiian recipes. And while many of them are not for state-side kitchens because we cannot get the fruits, leaves, fish, and other ingredients called for, there are interesting and delicious dishes of these island groups which can be prepared for our tables. Each given here is Hawaiian—that is, it is a native dish of some racial group living in those islands; but note its racial origin in the recipe's title.

See recipe for Spanish Soufflé Omelet on page 173, *see also recipes for Stuffed Eggs, Soft Cooked Eggs, and Poached Eggs.*

Color photograph, courtesy Tabasco, McIlhenny Company

YEH CHOY FA LUT TSIU NGAU YUK (CHINESE)
Cauliflower, Green Pepper, and Beef

3¾ cups sliced cauliflower
¼ cup sliced green pepper
¾ cup sliced lean beef
3 tablespoons soy sauce
1½ teaspoons salt
2 teaspoons sugar
3 tablespoons peanut oil

1 teaspoon fresh or dried ginger
root soaked in 1 tablespoon
water
½ teaspoon cornstarch
1 cup water
⅛ cup sliced green onions with
tops

WASH cauliflower, drain, cut into slices ½ inch thick. Wash green pepper, remove stem and seeds, cut pepper into pieces about 1 × ¾ inch. Slice beef into strips about ½ inch wide, ⅛ inch thick, and 1 inch long. Combine 1 tablespoon soy sauce, ½ teaspoon salt, 1 teaspoon sugar, add to beef and let stand 5 minutes. Make sauce of remaining salt, sugar, soy, and ginger juice. Heat ½ the oil until very hot, add beef, cook 1 minute. Stir, remove beef from pan. Add remaining oil and heat; add cauliflower and green pepper, stir and cook 2 minutes, add 1 cup water. Make smooth paste of cornstarch and water and combine with remaining ginger-soy sauce. When vegetables begin to boil, add onions and cornstarch paste. Boil 30 seconds, stirring constantly. Add beef, reheat. Serve very hot.

★FRILADANG MANOK (FILIPINO)
Chicken Friladang

1½-pound young chicken
1 teaspoon salt
3⅓ tablespoons fat
2 cloves garlic, peeled and
crushed

1 medium-size tomato, peeled
and sliced
¼ cup sliced peeled onions
½ cup water
1 (5-oz.) can pimientos

HAVE poultry dealer clean chicken ready for cooking. Rinse, drain, cut meat from bones in 1½-inch pieces. Sprinkle with salt and let stand 15 minutes or longer. Cover chicken and bones and steam 15 minutes over boiling water. Heat fat, brown garlic in it; remove and discard garlic. Add chicken (discard bones) to garlic fat, cover and cook slowly about 20 minutes. Add tomato, onions, and ½ cup water. Cover, simmer 1 hour. Drain pimientos, cut into eighths, add to chicken. Cook mixture about 5 minutes longer. Serve very hot. Makes 6 servings.

An American country dinner in the summer time features sweet corn, hot, and plentiful. Whipped, melted, or seasoned butter goes with the corn. Hot biscuits, roast fresh pork with tomato sauce, pickles, salad, fresh strawberries and pineapple, plenty of hot coffee make this a feast for hungry harvest hands and visiting city relatives.

Color photograph, courtesy National Pickle Packers Association

★FISH BAKED IN COCONUT CREAM (SAMOAN)

1¼ cups shredded packaged coconut

¾ cup light cream

1½ to 2 pounds mild-flavored fish

1 tablespoon salt

SOAK coconut in cream 30 minutes, simmer 10 minutes, let cool. Strain through several thicknesses of cheesecloth, squeezing out as much liquid as possible.

Start oven at moderate (350 degrees F.). Wash, scale, and clean fish, but do not remove head or tail. Rub fish inside and out with salt. Place in buttered baking dish, add coconut cream, and bake in moderate oven 1 to 1½ hours. Makes 4 to 6 servings.

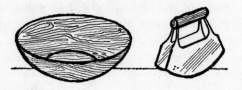

★KUN KOKI (KOREAN)
Broiled Meat

1½ pounds tenderloin or round steak, or 2 pounds short ribs

¼ cup soy sauce

3 tablespoons sesame or salad oil

3 tablespoons sesame seeds, browned and pulverized or ground

1 tablespoon sugar

⅓ cup finely-chopped peeled onions

4 tablespoons finely-chopped green onions with tops

⅓ teaspoon finely-chopped garlic

¼ teaspoon black pepper

IF short ribs are used, choose ribs having large amount of meat, trim, cut ribs apart. If steak is used, clean, trim, and cut into pieces about 3 × 4 inches and ⅓ inch thick; pound meat, score with sharp knife, slashing it lengthwise and crosswise. Combine remaining ingredients, pour over meat, and let stand 1 hour or longer. Or meat may be drained and broiled immediately. Broil under moderate heat in broiler, or over charcoal; or panbroil in skillet. Turn meat until cooked on both sides and done. Serve hot. Makes 6 servings.

DESERTS

★AVOCADO MILK SHERBET

1¼ cups sugar
1 cup skim milk
1 cup mashed avocado pulp
½ cup pineapple juice
½ cup orange juice

½ cup lemon juice
¼ teaspoon salt
Few drops pistachio flavoring if
  desired

DISSOLVE sugar in milk, add avocado pulp, mix thoroughly. Add fruit juices and salt. Freeze by either crank freezer or refrigerator-tray method. Makes 1½ quarts, 6 to 8 or more servings.

★GINGER ICE

½ cup sugar
¼ cup light corn syrup
½ cup water
¾ cup orange juice

⅓ cup lemon juice
2½ tablespoons to ¼ cup syrup
  from preserved ginger

COOK sugar, corn syrup, and water until sugar is dissolved. Let cool. Add fruit juices and ginger syrup. Pour into crank-freezer and freeze, using 8 parts salt to 1 part ice. Or use refrigerator-tray method. Makes 6 to 8 servings.

★GUAVA MILK SHERBET

No. 2 can (2¼ cups) unsweetened
  guava juice
1⅛ cups sugar
2 tablespoons lemon juice

1¼ cups light cream
2 egg whites
1⁄16 teaspoon salt

BOIL 1 cup guava juice and 1 cup sugar together 3 minutes. Let cool, add remaining guava and lemon juice. Pour mixture into freezing tray of automatic refrigerator and let freeze. Scrape mixture into chilled bowl, beat with egg beater until fluffy. Add cream and beat, fold in stiffly beaten egg whites to which the salt has been added. Pour sherbet back into refrigerator tray and freeze. Makes 1¼ quarts, 6 or more servings.

SHRIMP DISHES

★GUINISA SA MISUA (FILIPINO)
Noodles with Shrimp

½ pound fresh shrimp
Boiling water
4½-oz. package egg noodles
1 cucumber
1½ cloves garlic, peeled and
  crushed

½ cup sliced peeled onions
1½ tablespoons fat
2 teaspoons salt
Pepper
2½ cups hot water

POUR boiling water over shrimp and scald 3 minutes. Drain, remove shells and black vein. Break noodles into 1½-inch pieces, rinse, and drain. Wash, peel, and cut cucumber into ¼-inch slices. Fry garlic, onions, and shrimp in hot fat. When garlic is brown, remove it and discard. Add cucumber to shrimp mixture, stir and cook until lightly browned. Add noodles, salt, pepper, and 2½ cups hot water. Cover and cook until noodles are tender. Serve hot. Makes 6 servings.

POH LOH HA (CHINESE)
Pineapple and Shrimp

2 beaten eggs
1 teaspoon salt
2 tablespoons flour
1 pound fresh shrimp, shelled
  and cleaned
2 cups peanut or salad oil
¾ cup pickled vegetables, or
  mixed pickles, and preserved
  ginger

4 slices canned pineapple
⅓ cup vinegar
1 cup water or pineapple syrup
2 teaspoons soy sauce
2¼ tablespoons sugar
⅛ cup sliced green onions and
  tops
1 tablespoon cornstarch
2 tablespoons water

MAKE smooth batter of eggs, salt, and flour. Rinse and drain cleaned shrimp, pat dry. Dip into batter and fry in hot oil until lightly browned. Drain on thick paper towels. Cut each slice pineapple into 8 wedge-shaped pieces. Slice pickled vegetables and ginger fine. Heat 1 tablespoon oil, add pickled vegetables or mixed pickles and ginger, pineapple, vinegar, 1 cup water or pineapple syrup, soy sauce, and sugar. Heat to boiling, add onions and smooth paste made of cornstarch stirred with 2 tablespoons water. Bring mixture to boiling, stir, add shrimp, serve very hot. Makes 6 servings.

★HA CHOU CHOY (CHINESE)
Shrimp and Vegetables

1 pound fresh shrimp, shelled
  and cleaned
Salt
1 beaten egg
3 tablespoons peanut oil
¼ pound ham, diced
1 pound cauliflower, parboiled,
  cut in thin slices

2 pieces cooked celery, sliced diagonally in ¼-inch pieces
1 teaspoon cornstarch
3 tablespoons water
1 tablespoon soy sauce
2 tablespoons finely-chopped
  green onions and tops

COVER shrimp with slightly-salted water and let stand 15 minutes. Drain, combine with beaten egg. Heat oil to very hot, add shrimp and ham and cook 4 minutes. Add all vegetables except onions, and cook 2 minutes longer. Make smooth paste of cornstarch, water, and soy sauce. Stir this slowly into shrimp mixture, cook until it begins to thicken, stirring constantly. Add onions and a little salt, stir, and serve very hot. Makes 6 servings.

The ten recipes above from HAWAIIAN AND PACIFIC FOODS, *by Katherine Bazore Gruelle*

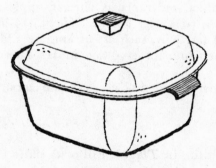

Holland

Some of the best of German, Scandinavian, and French cookery has been adapted by Dutch housewives and long since become native Dutch dishes with good variations the Netherlands cooks added. So have some of the exotic Indonesian dishes and others from Dutch-settled areas of Africa. Cook-book writers reporting on the Dutch kitchen for Americans seem to stress the vegetables, soups, and such delectable entrées or side dishes, as Marian Tracy has done in *The Peasant Cookbook.*

Here are two simple but delicious Dutch dishes from her book.

★DUTCH POPPY-SEED NOODLES

3 tablespoons butter

3 tablespoons poppy seeds

½ cup slivered roasted almonds

1 tablespoon lemon juice

8-ounce package broad egg noodles, cooked in salted boiling water, and drained

Salt

Cayenne pepper

MELT butter, add poppy seeds, almonds, and lemon juice. Pour over hot drained noodles, toss. Season and serve very hot. Makes 4 servings.

DUTCH RED CABBAGE AND APPLES

3 tablespoons butter

1 small red cabbage, washed, drained, shredded

2 tablespoons wine vinegar

3 apples, cored and diced

Salt and pepper

1 tablespoon sugar

HEAT butter in skillet, add cabbage, vinegar, apples, salt, pepper, and sugar. Cover tightly, cook over low heat about 1½ hours. Sometimes a few tablespoons of tart jelly, such as currant, are added to the mixture and allowed to melt into it. Serve hot. Makes 4 servings.

The two recipes above from THE PEASANT COOKBOOK, *by Marian Tracy*

❧

Pearl V. Metzelthin, in *The New World Wide Cook Book* gives us a few more glimpses of Dutch kitchens and cookery. The best of her Dutch recipes are:

★HOLLANDSE BIEFSTUK
Dutch Steak

2 pounds tender round steak cut 1½ inches thick

2 tablespoons vinegar

1 teaspoon salt

¼ teaspoon pepper

¾ to 1 cup butter

½ to 1 cup water

Parsley

RINSE steak, pat dry. Pound meat on both sides, score with sharp knife in deep gashes across the steak, and then from top to bottom. Mix vinegar, salt, and pepper together and rub on both sides of meat; let stand 30 minutes. Heat butter in heavy skillet until browning, place steak in hot butter, turn over after frying 1 minute. Cook 1 minute on other side. Continue to turn steak every minute throughout cooking period until desired doneness. Lift steak onto hot platter and keep it hot. Stir cold water into hot butter in pan, bring to boiling point quickly, serve in warmed gravy boat with steak. Garnish steak with parsley. Serve hot. Cut into wafer-thin slices slanting down across the grain. Usually served with hot boiled potatoes. Makes 2 to 4 servings.

SNEEUWBALLEN
Fried Cake Balls

½ cup cold water
⅛ teaspoon salt
½ cup butter
⅝ cup all-purpose flour, sifted
3 eggs
2 tablespoons dried currants or
  sultana raisins

2 tablespoons finely-chopped
  citron
1 tablespoon rose water or rum
Oil or fat for deep frying
Confectioners' sugar

COMBINE water, salt, and butter in saucepan and heat until boiling. Remove from heat, stir flour in smoothly with wooden spoon. Add eggs one at a time, beating well into the paste. Add currants, citron, and rose water or rum. Heat oil or fat to 360 to 375 degrees F. Use tablespoon, dip it in hot oil, cut off spoonfuls of batter and fry until golden brown on both sides. These will puff up and become light. Drain on thick paper towels. Sprinkle with confectioners' sugar. Makes 24 snowballs, or cake balls.

BOERENKOOL MET ROOKWORST
Kale and Sausage

3 pounds kale
2 pounds rookworst or smoked
  beef sausage, or frankfurters
Boiling water

3 pounds potatoes, boiled and
  mashed
3 tablespoons butter
Salt and pepper

REMOVE roots, coarse stems, and imperfect leaves of kale. Wash thoroughly, drain, cover with salted boiling water and boil about 30 minutes. Wash sausage or frankfurters, drain. Cook in boiling water to cover about 25 minutes. Drain, cut in quarters, keep hot. Drain kale, chop fine. Combine with mashed potatoes, butter, and salt and pepper to taste. Serve in warmed dish with quartered sausage or frankfurters on top. Makes 6 servings.

NIERBROODJES
Kidney Toast

1 large veal kidney	⅛ teaspoon pepper
⅓ cup chopped peeled onions	2 beaten eggs
4 tablespoons butter	6 slices day-old bread, crusts
¾ teaspoon salt	cut off
3 tablespoons flour	¼ cup dry bread crumbs
⅔ cup hot water or stock	Fat for deep frying
2 teaspoons soy sauce	Parsley
2 tablespoons sherry	Lemon wedges

SCALD and clean kidney, cut out core, discard fat and white. Slice kidney into ½-inch pieces. Sauté onions in 2 tablespoons butter, add kidney and salt and continue cooking until kidney is browned. Sprinkle flour over mixture and gradually add hot water or stock with soy sauce. Cover, let simmer very slowly 15 minutes. Add sherry and pepper, mix, set aside to cool. When mixture has cooled, add 1 beaten egg to it. Heat remaining 2 tablespoons butter, brown bread slices on 1 side only. Mound kidney mixture on fried side of bread. Brush with beaten egg, and coat with crumbs. Lower in frying basket, fry until golden brown. Serve on hot platter. Garnish with parsley and lemon. Makes 6 servings.

The four recipes above from THE NEW WORLD WIDE COOK BOOK, *by Pearl V. Metzelthin*

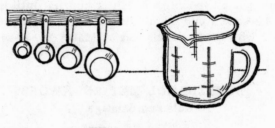

Hungary

In Paula Pogany Bennett's sound and inspiring book, *The Art of Hungarian Cooking,* the subtle, delicious foods of her native land are described, and their recipes kitchen-tested by an American home economist for our use. A brief selection, to which we are limited, does not do justice to the superb cuisine of her country. But here are recipes enough to give the flavor and quality of Hungarian home cooking. First, a famous punch always served in Hungary on New Year's Eve.

KRAMPAMPULI
Burnt Punch for New Year's Eve

1 cup chopped dried figs
1 cup chopped dried dates
1 cup chopped candied fruit
  peel
1 pound lump sugar
2 tablespoons grated orange peel
1 cup brandy or rum

4 cups wine
2 sticks cinnamon
2 or 3 strips lemon peel
2 cups hot tea
Juice 2 lemons
Juice 2 oranges

As midnight approaches, place a deep earthenware or glass baking dish in the center of the table. Into it put figs, dates, and candied peel. Place wide meshed grill over fruit and pile sugar on it. Sprinkle sugar with grated orange peel, then with brandy or rum. Let stand until all is absorbed by sugar and dripped over fruit. (Remove grill.) Put out lights and set brandy-sugar mixture ablaze. Heat wine, cinnamon, and lemon peel to boiling, remove cinnamon and peel. When brandy flame dies down, pour hot wine mixture, tea, and fruit juices over all. Stir, and serve in punch glasses with some of the fruit in each glass. Makes 25 to 30 servings.

CSOKOLADES PALACSINTA
Chocolate Pancake Dessert

¼ cup butter
¼ cup sugar
⅔ cup all-purpose flour, sifted
2 cups milk

½ teaspoon vanilla extract
8 eggs
2 ounces (2 squares) semisweet
  chocolate, grated

MELT butter in top of 2-quart double boiler over hot water, stir in sugar and flour, mix smoothly. Gradually blend in milk, stirring constantly until mixture becomes very thick and smooth. Remove from heat, let cool slightly, add vanilla, and blend in egg yolks.

Beat egg whites until they stand in peaks, then fold into batter. Start oven at moderate (325 degrees F.).

Pour batter for 6-inch cakes on hot griddle. They will be tender and require careful handling. When lightly browned on both sides, place first one in a buttered baking dish. Sprinkle with chocolate. Keep dish warm in oven, with door open. Continue adding pancakes as they come from the griddle, sprinkle each with chocolate. Continue until all are baked. Garnish with meringue topping. Brown lightly in closed oven. Serve warm, cut pie-fashion. Makes 8 servings.

MERINGUE TOPPING
Beat 3 egg whites until they stand in stiff peaks, fold in ½ teaspoon vanilla extract, and 3 tablespoons sugar. Use as described on top of pancakes before baking.

★GULYAS
Goulash

This is a favorite dish of most Hungarian hostesses. The goulash is served hot from a casserole. With it are served soft noodles, dill pickles, a green salad, dark bread, and good coffee. The meal is complete without dessert.

4 pounds beef chuck or rump cut in 2-inch pieces	6 medium-size onions, peeled and coarsely chopped
1 cup hot water	3 tablespoons paprika
2 strips bacon or salt pork, or 2 tablespoons bacon fat	1½ teaspoons salt
	2 green peppers, coarsely chopped

RINSE meat, drain. Brown half of meat in skillet in its own fat. Transfer to flameproof (metal-base) casserole and repeat with other half of meat. Rinse skillet with cup of hot water and add the liquid to the meat in the casserole. Cover and cook over low heat.

Chop bacon or salt pork and fry in skillet; add onions and brown lightly. Stir in paprika and salt, then stir all into simmering beef. Add uncooked green peppers. Cover, cook slowly 2 hours, or until meat is tender, not soft. Makes 8 to 10 servings.

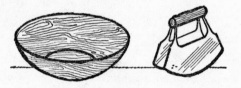

★RAKOTT SONKASPALACSINTA
Layer Ham Pancakes

Prepare your favorite pancake batter. Bake in large cakes. Have the ham filling ready:

1 pound boiled ham, finely chopped	1 cup sour cream
2 beaten egg yolks	1 tablespoon butter

COMBINE ham, egg yolks and cream. Start oven at moderate (350 degrees F.). Place freshly-baked pancake in buttered casserole, spread with 1 or 2 tablespoons ham filling. Repeat until dish is full. Add dabs of butter to top cake. Place dish in moderate oven and let heat and top brown lightly, about 20 minutes. Cut pie-fashion and serve. Makes 8 to 10 servings.

★PAPRIKASCSIRKE
Paprika Chicken

This is a favorite dish for dinner or supper. Its popularity in the United States is almost as great as in Hungary.

3-pound frying chicken, disjointed	1 tablespoon paprika
2 medium-size onions, peeled and finely chopped	1 teaspoon salt
	1 cup sour cream
3 tablespoons fat	Hot noodles

WASH chicken, drain. Brown onions lightly in fat, add paprika, mix, and add chicken. Sprinkle with salt, cover and cook slowly about 1 hour, or until tender and done. Pour cream over chicken, heat 1 minute only. Serve with hot noodles. Makes 6 servings.

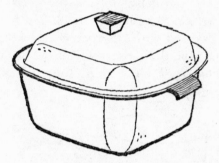

★BORJUBECSINALT
Veal Fricassee

3 pounds breast of veal, cut in 2-inch pieces	½ cauliflower, broken into flowerettes
3 tablespoons butter	¼ pound mushrooms, sliced
1 teaspoon salt	2 tablespoons flour
⅛ teaspoon pepper	1 tablespoon lemon juice
2 carrots, scraped and sliced	½ cup hot water

RINSE meat, drain. Brown veal lightly in butter. Sprinkle with salt and pepper, cover, and cook slowly 30 minutes. Add few tablespoons water if meat becomes dry. Add vegetables and mushrooms and continue cooking until all are tender. Sprinkle with the flour and stir it in well. When flour begins to brown, stir in lemon juice and ½ cup hot water. Stir mixture until it boils. Serve hot. Makes 6 servings.

The six recipes above from THE ART OF HUNGARIAN COOKING, *by Paula Pogany Bennett*

India

While a number of books on Indian cooking have been published in English, the most information about the cookery of India is still to be found in that unusual *The New World Wide Cook Book,* written by Pearl V. Metzelthin. Madame Metzelthin says: "Menus in India are definitely affected by the limitations of the Hindu and Mohammedan dietary laws. The Moslems eat lamb, beef, fowl, and fish, but no pork; and the Hindu eats no meat at all but is a vegetarian." Menus and cookery vary widely from the simple rice of the very poor to elaborate banquets of the well-to-do families.

Besides the curries, the typical Indian dish which is well known in America, eggplant, hot spicy vegetable combinations, pigeons cooked with rice, sweet chutneys, lentils with onion, and various desserts flavored with rose petals and rosewater are popular. Here are a salad and a dessert which the author of *The New World Wide Cook Book* enjoyed in India.

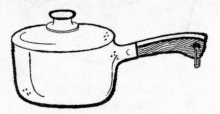

★MAIWA KACHUMAR
Nut Salad

2 cups chopped nuts
3 dried figs, quartered
6 dates, stoned and quartered
¼ cup fresh shredded coconut
2 tablespoons washed raisins
1 tablespoon melted butter
1 head crisp lettuce
2 large tomatoes, peeled and sliced
1 large apple, pared, cored, chopped
¼ cup French dressing
4 sprays water cress

COMBINE nuts, figs, dates, coconut, and raisins, mix with melted butter. Arrange leaves of washed and drained lettuce on 4 salad plates. Put 2 or 3 slices tomato on each plate, a spoonful of apple, and pour salad dressing over; mound dried-fruit mixture in center. Garnish with water cress. Makes 4 servings.

★SHARBATEE GULAB
Rose Petal Pineapple Crush

4 or 5 large full-blooming roses	2 cups finely-cracked or crushed
2 quarts cold but not iced water	ice
¼ cup lemon juice	Few rose petals
1⅓ cups sugar	
3 cups crushed fresh or canned	
pineapple	

WASH roses in cold water, shake excess water from them. Pluck off petals and place in large jar or bowl. Pour cold water over them, cover and let stand in dark, cool place (not refrigerator) 4 hours. Strain water off petals. To it add lemon juice and sugar mixed until sugar dissolves. Stir, add pineapple, mix. Add large spoonful crushed ice to 6 to 8 glasses, pour pineapple mixture in. Place fresh rose petal on top. Makes 6 to 8 servings.

The two recipes above from THE NEW WORLD WIDE COOK BOOK, *by Pearl V. Metzelthin*

Ireland

According to *European Cooking,* that handsome small picture cook book prepared in Sweden but published in America, Ireland "has gained citizenship in the international culinary field primarily through Irish Stew, a superb dish based upon the excellence of its mutton. Comparable in quality is Irish beef and pork."

Bacon is a favorite in simple cottage homes as well as in the great houses of the well-to-do. But potatoes, cabbage, and kale are crops on which lower-income families depend for the mainstay of their diet. Puddings similar to English desserts are popular, so are puddings of the gelatin type, made with a seaweed moss (for its jellying ingredient) available along the northern coastline. In the homes of families who have traveled abroad and who can shop in the larger centers, the cookery is more likely to be Continental, a mixture of favorite meat, fish, poultry, and vegetable dishes from various parts of Europe, England, and the United States, including pastries of Austria and France. But Irish scones remain a favorite with all Irish as well as U.S. cooks. Here are the scone and stew recipes from *European Cooking.*

BOLOGA BEAGA
Irish Scones

1½ cups all-purpose flour, sifted
1½ teaspoons baking powder
½ teaspoon soda
½ tablespoon sugar

½ teaspoon salt
3 tablespoons shortening
½ cup buttermilk

START oven at hot (450 degrees F.). Sift flour, baking powder, soda, sugar, and salt together. Mix shortening in with pastry cutter. Pour all buttermilk over at once. Stir with fork until mixture is smooth and takes the shape of a ball in center of bowl. Knead lightly 5 to 8 times on lightly floured board. Divide dough in half, roll lightly and quickly or pat out into 2 round cakes about ½ inch thick. Cut each round pastry into pie-shaped pieces. Bake on ungreased baking sheet in hot oven 10 to 12 minutes, until risen, baked, and lightly browned. Makes 12 scones. Serve warm or, when cold, split and toast, butter lightly, and serve with jam.

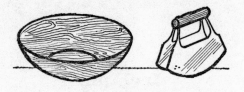

★BEIRBHIUCHAN EIREANNACH
Irish Stew

Originally Irish stew consisted only of mutton, potatoes, and onions. Gradually it developed into this more lavish stew.

2½ pounds boned lamb shoulder
    cut in 2-inch cubes
4½ cups water
1 onion, peeled and sliced
4 carrots, scraped and diced
2½ cups cubed pared potatoes

1 turnip, pared and diced
2 teaspoons salt
½ teaspoon pepper
1 bay leaf
⅛ teaspoon dried thyme
Sprigs of parsley

RINSE meat, drain, place in heavy kettle. Add water and bring to a boil. Reduce heat, cover, and let simmer about 1 hour. Add remaining ingredients and cook slowly until vegetables are tender. For a thickened stew, mix ¼ cup flour with ⅓ cup cold water, stir slowly into stew. Turn heat high and bring to boiling. Boil and stir 2 or 3 minutes. Makes 6 servings.

The two recipes above from EUROPEAN COOKING, *recipes prepared in Wezëta Förlag, Sweden*

Italy

A small but flavorsome book of Italian cooking for Americans, *The Art of Italian Cooking,* by Maria Lo Pinto, is a sure guide to those dishes Americans have enjoyed in Italian restaurants—home dishes which look like chef specialties, which taste better, if that is possible, and which, surprisingly, are easy to prepare. Many spaghetti and macaroni dishes and others made with pastas have long since become American, their Italian origin forgotten. Here are a few dishes which are just as welcome in our menus. First the antipasto, Italian appetizers or first course, on which one can make a meal with good Italian bread and butter and hot coffee.

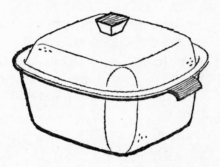

ANTIPASTO LO PINTO

Make a selection of five or more of the good things listed below, serve on chilled plate with crisp lettuce or romaine. Oil and vinegar may be added if desired. Anchovy fillets. Capocollo, which is delicately-smoked pork sliced very thin, as is salami. Carciofini, artichoke hearts canned or cooked and dressed with vinegar and oil. Finocchio, anise-flavored species of celery cut and served like celery. Funghi Con Aceto E Olio, sautéed mushrooms, chilled, and marinated in vinegar and oil. Olives, the special black olives cured in oil instead of brine. Peperoni, very peppery dry sausage served in wafer-thin slices. Peperoncini All'aceto, small green peppers pickled in vinegar. Pimientos, canned sweet red peppers. Prosciutto, slightly pungent smoky-flavored Italian ham cut wafer-thin. Radishes. Salami, highly-seasoned Italian sausage served in wafer-thin slices. Celery hearts. Herring roe. Tuna-fish roe.

POLLO ALLA CACCIATORA
Chicken, Hunter's Style

4-pound roasting chicken,
cleaned and disjointed
2 tablespoons butter
3 tablespoons olive oil
1 stalk celery, chopped
1 carrot, scraped and chopped

1 medium onion, peeled and
chopped
1 teaspoon chopped parsley
Salt and pepper
¾ cup dry sherry
1 tablespoon tomato paste

RINSE chicken, pat dry. Heat butter and oil in skillet, brown chicken on all sides, about 5 minutes. Add all chopped vegetables and salt and pepper to taste. Cover, cook on low heat about 10 minutes, or until vegetables are partially tender. Add sherry blended with tomato paste, stir and mix. Cover and cook about 30 minutes. Stir frequently to prevent sticking and scorching. Add small amount of hot water from time to time if needed. Serve very hot. Makes 4 to 6 servings.

★CARCIOFI FRITTI
Fried Artichoke Hearts

12 boiled artichoke hearts, fresh
or canned
Salt and pepper
1 tablespoon chopped parsley

1 cup bread crumbs
2 eggs
⅜ cup olive oil

SPRINKLE drained artichoke hearts with salt and pepper. Mix parsley and crumbs. Beat eggs lightly. Dip artichoke hearts in egg, roll in crumbs, fry in hot oil about 3 minutes on each side or until golden brown. Serve very hot. Makes 6 servings.

LASAGNE IMBOTTITE
Stuffed Noodles

SAUCE

½ (6½-oz.) can tomato paste
½ cup hot water
2 cloves garlic, peeled and sliced
¼ cup olive oil

1 stalk celery, diced
1 large can plum tomatoes
Salt and pepper

STUFFING

¾ pound bulk sausage
1½ pounds broad noodles or
lasagne
Boiling water

1½ cups grated Parmesan cheese
1½ cups cubed mozzarella cheese
1½ pounds ricotta (Italian cottage
cheese)

MAKE sauce: Blend tomato paste and hot water. Brown garlic in hot oil 3 minutes; add celery, blend tomato paste and plum tomatoes. Boil over high heat about 3 minutes; lower heat, cover, and simmer 1 hour. Add pepper and salt to taste.

Broil sausage under high heat about 15 minutes, or until brown on both sides; cut into small pieces.

Cook noodles in rapidly-boiling salted water about 15 minutes, or until tender but not too soft. Drain. Start oven at moderate (350 degrees F.). Butter or oil baking pan. Pour ½ cup sauce into pan; over this place layer of drained noodles, then layer of grated Parmesan, layer of sauce, layer of mozzarella, then sausage, and tablespoon of ricotta here and there. Repeat layers until all ingredients and almost all sauce are used. Top layer should be sauce and grated cheese. Bake in moderate oven 15 minutes, or until firm. When done, this lasagne is cut into serving portions and served on dinner plates, with topping of sauce and grated cheese. Makes 8 to 10 servings.

MANICOTTI

PASTA

1 pound all-purpose flour, sifted	½ teaspoon salt
1 tablespoon butter	1 cup lukewarm water
3 beaten eggs	

STUFFING

1 pound ricotta (Italian cottage cheese)	¼ pound chopped ham
	Salt and pepper
2 beaten eggs	½ cup grated Romano cheese

Also prepare or buy 1½ cups well-seasoned Tomato Sauce.

MIX pasta: Combine flour, butter, eggs, and salt, mixing well with fork. Gradually add enough lukewarm water to make medium-soft dough. Knead into smooth ball, cut in half. Roll each half out on lightly-floured board until thin (usual noodle thickness). Cut into rectangles 5 × 6 inches.

STUFFING: Mix ricotta, eggs, and ham; add very little salt and pepper, keep mixing until smoothly blended. Spread 1½ tablespoons mixture on each piece dough; roll and close; moisten edges and press tightly to keep filling in. These are the manicotti, "little muffs." Cook manicotti about 10 minutes in extra-large pot rapidly boiling salted water (about 8 quarts). When dough is tender, lift manicotti out carefully with wide pancake turner or flat skimmer. Drain. Serve hot with Tomato Sauce and grated Romano cheese. (Or place in shallow baking dish, cover with sauce and cheese and brown under low broiler heat.) Makes 6 to 8 servings.

The five recipes above from THE ART OF ITALIAN COOKING, *by Maria Lo Pinto*

There is a great Italian cook book, *Il Talismano,* which, according to the publishers of the American edition, *The Talisman Italian Cook Book,* has been the one outstanding cook book of Italy for more than twenty years. "It contains in simple and clear form, and for home quantities and usage, the right recipes for all the notable delicious foods and dishes that make up the best Italian cuisine. Included are authentic recipes for all the various styles of Italian cooking: Milanese, Bolognese, Venetian, Neapolitan, Sicilian, Roman, Genoese, Sienese, Veronese, Florentine," and the cookery of many other provincial areas.

Madame Ada Boni, editor of Italy's leading woman's magazine, is the editor of this superb cook book, which has sold throughout the world in hundreds of thousands of copies. The edition which American homemakers can use with pleasure and assurance that recipes are right for U.S. measures, ingredients, and appetites has been translated and augmented by Matilde La Rosa. Each recipe seems better, more interesting, and "tastes better" in the reading than the last one.

Here is a sampling of what the authors call General Antipasto, those various savory dishes served first at Italian meals. They can make fine one-dish cold luncheons or suppers for many diet-conscious Americans.

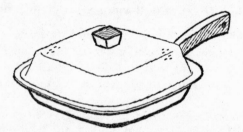

✸FRIED BREAD WITH ANCHOVIES

½ pound mozzarella cheese, sliced thin
8 anchovy fillets
16 slices bread ½-inch thick from long French loaf

½ teaspoon pepper
½ cup all-purpose flour, sifted
2 beaten eggs
1 cup olive oil

PLACE slice of cheese and 1 anchovy fillet on each of 8 slices bread, sprinkle with pepper, cover with another slice of bread. Dip sandwich into cold water, then into flour, then into beaten eggs. Fry in hot oil until golden brown on each side. Serve immediately. Makes 4 to 8 servings.

★ITALIAN ANTIPASTO TALISMANO

1 (7-oz.) can tuna fish

1 small jar imported Italian
   antipasto, optional

4 thin slices Italian salami

4 thin slices prosciutto

4 anchovy fillets

2 celery hearts, cut in halves
   lengthwise

8 large green olives

2 teaspoons capers

4 canned artichoke hearts in oil

1 (4-oz.) jar pimientos

4 slices tomato

4 small pickled peppers

8 black ripe olives

USE large chilled oval platter. Place drained tuna fish and imported antipasto in center of dish. Arrange all other ingredients around, making as pretty a pattern as you can. Serve with crusty Italian bread and butter. Makes 4 servings.

MUSSELS IN PIQUANT SAUCE

2 pounds fresh mussels in shells

Salt

1 clove garlic, peeled and sliced

2 tablespoons olive oil

5 anchovy fillets, chopped

1½ cups dry white wine

1½ cups vinegar

1 tablespoon chopped parsley

Cayenne pepper

WASH and drain mussels in shells, open, remove mussels, reserve shells.

Wash mussels in salt water, drain. Brown garlic in oil, remove garlic and discard it. Add mussels and anchovies to oil, cook over low heat, adding wine and vinegar. Simmer until liquid is half original quantity. Add parsley and cayenne. Pour mussels and sauce into pottery or china bowl, cover, chill in marinade 3 days. Serve cold in chilled shells. Makes 4 servings.

★STUFFED TOMATOES

4 large firm tomatoes

2 hard-cooked eggs, diced fine

1 (7-oz.) can tuna fish, drained
   and flaked

¼ teaspoon pepper

1 teaspoon drained capers

1 teaspoon chopped parsley

2 tablespoons mayonnaise

CUT tops off tomatoes, remove seeds and liquid. Mix eggs, tuna, pepper, capers, parsley, and mayonnaise. Fill tomatoes with mixture, chill and serve. Makes 4 servings.

DESSERTS

★PEACHES PIEDMONT STYLE

7 ripe peaches

2 tablespoons sugar

1¼ tablespoons butter

5 macaroons, crushed

1 egg yolk

START oven at moderate (375 degrees F.). Wash and drain fruit. Cut 6 peaches in half, remove pits, scoop out a little of the pulp from each half. Remove all pulp from the remaining peach and mash together with pulp removed from peach halves. Add sugar, butter, macaroon crumbs, and egg yolk and mix well. Fill each peach half with pulp mixture, place in well-buttered baking dish. Bake 1 hour in moderate oven. Serve warm or cold. Makes 6 servings.

RUM BABA

1¾ cups pastry flour, sifted

1 cake yeast

Lukewarm water

3 beaten eggs

¾ cup butter at room temperature

¼ teaspoon salt

1 tablespoon sugar

2 tablespoons seedless raisins

PLACE 1¼ cups flour in bowl, crumble yeast in a little lukewarm water, add to bowl, mix well; add more lukewarm water as needed to bring mixture to the consistency of paste. Cover bowl, set in warm place. In about 15 minutes dough should be double in size. Place remaining ½ cup flour in large bowl, add yeast dough, eggs, butter, and salt and work well with hands, slapping dough on floured pastry board with force and working until dough is smooth, velvety, and elastic. Work in sugar and raisins.

Butter well a 1½-quart tubular cake pan and place dough in it. (Dough must not take up more than ⅓ of pan.) Set dough in warm place, let rise 1½ hours, or until dough reaches top of pan. Start oven at hot (425 degrees F.) and bake 25 minutes, or until cake tester or wooden pick inserted comes out clean.

While cake is baking, make syrup:

½ cup water

3 tablespoons sugar

3 jiggers rum (½ cup plus 1 tablespoon)

Combine water and sugar in small saucepan, bring to a boil, boil 3 minutes, remove from heat, add rum and mix.

Remove cake from oven, turn out in deep dish, remove pan. Pour rum syrup over cake. Baste occasionally with syrup while baba is cooling. Makes 8 servings.

STRUFOLI NEAPOLITAN STYLE

2½ cups pastry flour, sifted

4 beaten eggs

1 egg yolk

¼ cup leaf lard

½ tablespoon sugar

⅛ teaspoon salt

½ teaspoon grated lemon peel

2 cups shortening for deep frying

1½ cups honey

1 teaspoon grated orange peel

PLACE flour on mixing board, make well in center, and place in the well the eggs, egg yolk, lard, sugar, salt, and lemon peel. Mix well, working dough with hands as in making noodles. When evenly and well mixed, shape into small balls the size of marbles. Fry in deep hot fat (375 degrees F.), a few at a time, until golden brown. Drain on thick paper towels.

Warm honey in saucepan, add orange peel. As soon as balls are fried and drained a few seconds, drop them into the honey mixture. Remove them with a strainer, place on serving dish, piling them into conical mounds. Let cool. Makes 6 servings.

EGGS

★ANCHOVY OMELET

4 eggs

2 tablespoons grated Parmesan cheese

¼ teaspoon pepper

4 tablespoons butter

2 teaspoons Anchovy Butter

BEAT eggs lightly with fork, add cheese and pepper. Cook egg mixture in butter in 4 parts, making 4 small omelets. Spread each little omelet with ¼ of the Anchovy Butter, fold quickly and serve immediately. Makes 4 servings.

★COUNTRY STYLE OMELET

4 tablespoons olive oil

1 zucchini, diced

1 celery heart, diced

2 tomatoes, skinned and cut in pieces

¼ teaspoon salt

⅛ teaspoon pepper

4 slightly-beaten eggs

2 tablespoons grated Parmesan cheese

1 teaspoon minced fresh basil or ½ teaspoon dried

PLACE 2 tablespoons oil with zucchini and celery in frying pan and brown vegetables well. Add tomatoes, salt and pepper, and cook over moderate heat 15 minutes. Mix eggs with cheese and basil and pour over vegetables. Lower heat, cook slowly, adding remaining 2 tablespoons oil. Cook omelet 12 minutes on each side. Makes 4 servings.

EGGS SPRING STYLE

4 hard-cooked eggs
1½ tablespoons butter
1 tablespoon flour
½ cup milk
¼ teaspoon salt
¼ teaspoon pepper
⅛ teaspoon ground nutmeg
½ pound spinach, boiled, chopped, and strained

1 tablespoon grated Romano cheese
1 cup all-purpose flour, sifted
1 slightly-beaten egg
2 cups bread crumbs
1 cup olive oil

CUT hard-cooked eggs in half from top to bottom. Melt butter in saucepan, blend flour in smoothly, add milk slowly, stirring. Cook over moderate heat, stirring continually until thick. Add salt, pepper, nutmeg, spinach, and minced egg yolks to sauce and blend. Add cheese, pour into dish and let cool. When mixture is cool and firm, fill egg whites with it. Roll in flour, then in beaten egg, then in crumbs. Fry in hot oil until golden color. Makes 4 servings.

EGGS WITH CHICKEN LIVERS

4 chicken livers, diced fine
3 tablespoons butter
1 tablespoon Marsala or sherry
3 tablespoons warm water

4 eggs
½ teaspoon salt
½ teaspoon pepper
8 cooked asparagus tips

START oven at moderately hot (400 degrees F.). Brown chicken livers lightly in 2 tablespoons butter, add wine, and cook 5 minutes. Add warm water and cook 2 minutes longer. Break eggs into saucer, one at a time, and slip into greased shallow baking dish. Sprinkle with small bits of remaining 1 tablespoon butter, add salt and pepper. Cook in moderately hot oven 10 minutes. Pour chicken livers over eggs, garnish with asparagus tips, return dish to oven for 5 minutes' more cooking. Makes 4 servings.

FISH

★FRESH SARDINE CROQUETTES

1½ pounds fresh sardines, heads removed, cleaned, boned, and chopped
4 tablespoons butter
2 slices white bread, soaked in water and squeezed dry
½ teaspoon salt

½ teaspoon pepper
⅛ teaspoon ground nutmeg
1 teaspoon minced parsley
1 tablespoon seedless raisins
½ cup flour
1 cup olive oil
2 cups Tomato Sauce

COMBINE chopped sardines, butter, bread, salt, pepper, nutmeg, parsley, and raisins. Shape into small croquettes. Roll in flour, fry in hot oil 4 minutes on each side. Heat Tomato Sauce, place croquettes in sauce and heat gently 5 minutes. Makes 4 servings.

FRESH SARDINES PALERMO STYLE

16 fresh sardines, heads removed, and cleaned
½ cup olive oil
¼ cup fine bread crumbs
2 tablespoons white raisins
1 tablespoon shelled pine nuts
½ teaspoon sugar
½ teaspoon salt

½ teaspoon pepper
⅛ teaspoon ground nutmeg
1 tablespoon chopped parsley
10 anchovy fillets, chopped
3 bay leaves
3 tablespoons olive oil
Juice 1 lemon

SLIT sardines down one side and bone. Mix together the ½-cup olive oil, crumbs, raisins, nuts, sugar, salt, pepper, nutmeg, parsley, and anchovies. Stuff sardines with this mixture and close with small skewers or pull edges together and place fish, stuffed side down, in well-buttered baking dish. Start oven at moderately hot (400 degrees F.). Dot stuffed fish with crumbled bay leaves, sprinkle with 3 tablespoons olive oil, and if any stuffing is left, sprinkle it over fish. Bake in moderately hot oven 20 minutes. Remove from oven, sprinkle with lemon juice, and serve at once. Makes 4 servings.

MEATS

BEEFSTEAK CACCIATORA

1 tablespoon olive oil
Porterhouse steak cut 1½ inches thick
½ teaspoon salt
½ teaspoon pepper
2 tablespoons Marsala or sherry

½ cup dry red wine
½ clove garlic, peeled and minced
½ teaspoon fennel seeds
1 tablespoon tomato paste or thick sauce

HEAT oil in skillet, add steak, cook on both sides until done to your taste. Add salt and pepper, remove from pan to warmed platter and keep it warm. Add Marsala or sherry to pan gravy and cook slowly, scraping bottom of pan with wooden spoon; slowly add red wine, cook and stir until well blended, slightly reduced, and very hot. Add garlic, fennel seeds, and tomato paste or Tomato Sauce, mix into pan gravy, stir and cook 1 minute longer. Pour over steak and serve. Makes 2 servings.

BRAISED BEEF GENOESE STYLE

2 tablespoons dried mushrooms
1 slice bacon
1 small onion, peeled
1 stalk celery
1 small carrot, scraped
1 teaspoon chopped parsley

4 pounds eye of the round of
beef
1 tablespoon lard
1 cup dry red wine
Salt and pepper
2 cups stock or water

SOAK mushrooms in cold water to cover for 30 minutes. Chop bacon and
all vegetables and parsley fine. Rinse meat, drain, place in heavy kettle
with lard, mushrooms, vegetables, parsley and ¾ cup wine. Cook slowly
until wine has evaporated. Add rest of wine and salt and pepper to taste,
cover kettle, and continue cooking slowly until meat is browned. Add
stock or water, cover kettle tightly, cook 2 hours, or until meat is tender
to the fork. Slice meat onto hot platter, serve with gravy from the kettle.
Makes 8 or more servings.

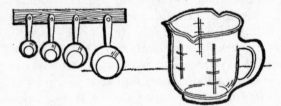

LARGE MEATBALL HOME STYLE

1¼ pounds chopped beef
1 slice prosciutto or lean bacon,
chopped
4 slices bread, soaked in water
and squeezed dry
1 beaten egg
2 tablespoons grated Parmesan
cheese

2 teaspoons chopped parsley
1 teaspoon chopped sweet basil
½ teaspoon salt
8 cups water
1 onion, peeled and quartered
1 stalk celery, diced
1 carrot, scraped
1 fresh tomato, quartered

MIX chopped beef, bacon or prosciutto, bread, egg, cheese, 1 teaspoon
parsley, basil, and ¼ teaspoon salt thoroughly together, shape into large
meatball. Combine water in 3-quart kettle with onion, celery, carrot,
tomato, 1 teaspoon parsley, and ¼ teaspoon salt and bring to a boil.
Immerse meatball in boiling water, lower heat to a simmer, and cook for
2 hours. Do not boil at high speed because the meat ball will come apart.

After simmering 2 hours, remove meatball from liquid, place on
platter, cover with plate and press down a little. When cold, slice and
serve with mayonnaise or any favorite cold-meat sauce. Save liquid from
kettle to add to soup. Makes 4 or more servings.

★PIZZA

Biscuit or roll ready-mix
3 tablespoons olive oil
4-oz. can anchovy fillets
No. 2 can tomatoes
¾ pound mozzarella cheese,
  sliced thin

¼ teaspoon salt
⅛ teaspoon freshly-ground pepper
½ teaspoon orégano

MIX dough, pull out with hands until about ½ inch thick and the size to cover 18-inch round baking pan or two 12-inch pans. Sprinkle dough with oil. Place drained anchovies, chopped, drained tomatoes, and cheese all over dough. Sprinkle with salt, pepper, orégano, and little more oil. Start oven at moderately hot (400 degrees F.). Bake pizzas about 20 minutes, or until dough is done and mixture is browning. Makes 4 servings.

The seventeen recipes above from THE TALISMAN ITALIAN COOK BOOK, *by Ada Boni, translated by Matilde La Rosa*

Japan

From *Hawaiian and Pacific Foods,* by Katherine Bazore Gruelle, some of the best Japanese dishes may be enjoyed in our menus.

★TORI NO SUKIYAKI
Chicken Sukiyaki

2¾ pounds tender chicken
1 bunch green onions, with tops
½ bunch (½ pound) water cress
2½ cups thinly-sliced canned or
  soaked dried mushrooms
2 tablespoons fat or salad oil

¾ cup sugar
1½ cups soy sauce
4 cups thinly-sliced canned
  bamboo shoots
½ cup sake or dry white wine

RINSE cleaned chicken, pat dry. Without removing bones, use sharp knife and cut meat into 1-inch cubes. Wash and cut green onions and water cress into 2-inch lengths. Wash and soak dried mushrooms or drain canned mushrooms; reserve soaking liquor or can liquor. Heat fat in heavy iron frying pan (preferably on table heater), add ⅓ of the chicken and fry 15 minutes, turning pieces to brown well. Add some liquid if necessary from time to time to keep meat from burning. Add ⅓ of the sugar and ½ cup soy sauce, stirring. Cook 3 minutes, add ⅓ of the mushrooms and bamboo shoots. After 5 minutes add ⅓ of the onions, water cress, and sake or wine. Cook 5 minutes. Serve hot with rice. Add remaining ingredients to pan in same order, cook and serve. Makes 8 servings.

TEMPURA

12 fresh shrimp

1¾ cups string beans cut in 3-inch
  lengths

1 beaten egg

⅞ cup all-purpose flour, sifted

1 teaspoon baking powder

½ teaspoon salt

½ cup water

2 pounds fat or salad oil for
  deep frying

WASH shrimp, remove shell, clean by slitting center back ⅛ inch deep and removing black vein. Rinse shrimp, dry thoroughly with towel. Wash and string beans, cut, and dry on towel. Combine egg and sifted dry ingredients and stir well. Add water, a tablespoon at a time, until smooth batter is obtained. Heat fat or oil to 350 to 360 degrees F. Dip shrimp, one at a time, into batter, fry 3 to 4 minutes, or until fritter turns golden brown. Fry only few at a time. Remove fritters from fat, drain on thick paper towels.

Dip string beans in batter and fry in hot fat, holding two beans together with forks for about 5 seconds after they have been placed in hot fat. Drain on thick paper towels. Serve with fried shrimp with Tempura Sauce. Other foods such as sweet potato, carrot, eggplant, crab, fish with firm flesh may be cut into thin slices and fried in this manner and served together with the Tempura Sauce. Makes 6 servings.

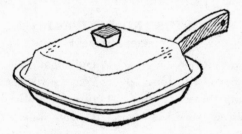

TEMPURA SAUCE

1 tablespoon flaked, dried
  bonito (fish)

1 cup water

⅓ cup soy sauce

½ teaspoon sugar

1 cup grated daikon
  (white radish or turnip)

BOIL bonito in water 10 minutes. Add soy sauce and sugar, boil 3 minutes longer. Drain, let liquid cool, add to grated radish. Tempura or fritters are dipped into this sauce to be eaten. Bonito may be omitted and the soy sauce, sugar, and water combined, boiled 5 minutes, cooled, then mixed with radish. Makes sauce for 6 servings.

★SUKIYAKI

2 tablespoons peanut or salad
  oil
1½ pounds round steak sliced diagonally very thin
½ cup sugar
1⅛ cups soy sauce
1 bunch green onions, cut in
  1½-inch lengths, with tops
1 cup diagonally-sliced celery,
  1½-inch pieces
8-ounce can mushrooms, sliced

10½-ounce can bamboo shoots,
  sliced thin
1 cup water or mushroom stock
2 large tomatoes cut in eighths
2 medium onions, peeled and
  sliced
½ pound water cress or spinach
  cut in 1½-inch lengths
1 block tufu (soy-bean curd) cut
  in inch cubes

HEAT oil in heavy skillet, fry about ⅓ of meat 2 or 3 minutes, add 2 tablespoons sugar, 3 minutes later add ½ cup soy sauce, cook 3 minutes, then
add ⅓ of the green onions. When onions are soft, add ⅓ of celery, mushrooms, bamboo shoots, ½ cup water or mushroom stock, and cook 3 minutes. Add ⅓ of the tomatoes, onions, and bean sprouts. Add ⅓ cup more
soy sauce, more sugar and water, let cook 3 minutes; add tufu, stir it
around skillet, and serve immediately with rice.

As guests are served, add remaining ingredients to skillet in the
order described, cook, and serve. Serve very hot with rice. Makes 6
servings.

Japanese hosts cooking this dish at the table for their guests use
chopsticks to pick up ingredients and place them into skillet, to stir
mixture gently when necessary, and to serve plates of guests.

The four recipes above from HAWAIIAN AND PACIFIC FOODS, *by Katherine
Bazore Gruelle*

A number of delicious Japanese dishes are given in Irma Walker Ross's little cook book, *Recipes from The East.* Here are some of the best:

KAMO-NANBAN
Barbarian Duck

3 cups chicken stock, or 1½ (10½-oz.) cans chicken soup
½ cup soy sauce
5 tablespoons sake or sherry
2 tablespoons sugar
1 pinch Aji-no-moto

10½-ounce can bamboo shoots, sliced thin
1 pound cooked duck or chicken meat, sliced thin
3 long green onions, cut in 1-inch lengths

HEAT stock or soup to boiling with soy sauce, sake, sugar, and Aji-no-moto added. Add bamboo shoots and duck and cook 5 minutes, add onions, cook 5 minutes longer. Serve very hot over cooked noodles. Makes 6 servings.

★TERIYAKI
Grilled Savory Salmon

2 pounds fresh salmon
1 tablespoon finely-chopped fresh ginger root
2 cloves garlic, peeled and chopped fine

1 onion, peeled and sliced
2 tablespoons sugar
½ cup soy sauce
¼ cup water

HAVE fish dealer clean salmon, remove head, tail, fins. Slice fish in serving pieces. Make sauce by combining ginger root, garlic, onion, sugar, soy sauce, and water. Heat to boiling, let cool, pour over fish. Cover bowl, let stand in refrigerator 1 to 2 hours. Spread drained fish in shallow pan, broil under moderate heat 3 to 5 minutes on each side. Serve hot. Makes 6 servings.

NIHON EGG ROLES

2 cups cooked rice
7-ounce can tuna, drained and flaked
2 beaten eggs
½ small onion, peeled and chopped fine

Salt and pepper
½ teaspoon curry powder or paste
Fat for deep frying

COMBINE rice, fish, eggs, and onion; mix well. Add salt and pepper to taste and curry powder or paste. Form into balls or rolls and fry in hot fat (375 degrees F.). Makes 10 balls or 4 to 6 rolls.

The three recipes above from RECIPES FROM THE EAST, *by Irma Walker Ross*

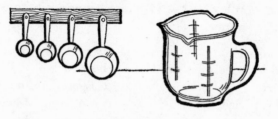

Mexico

For many years cooks on both sides of the Rio Grande were made happy in their kitchens because they owned a little paper-bound spiral-back cook book by Elena Zelayeta. Elena is blind, and a group of San Francisco home economists, knowing her good recipes and her need to earn money for the support of a young family, edited her Mexican cookery for North American kitchens and put the recipes into that first paper edition. Now her book, much enlarged, many completely new recipes added, is handsomely published as *Elena's Secrets of Mexican Cooking.* A wonderful source of ideas for Mexican dinners for dozens of home meals. Today Elena is in business with her sons, preparing, freezing, and marketing some of her recipes. Here are five favorites from the new book.

★ARROZ DE VIGILIA CON JAIBA
Lenten Crab and Rice

3 tablespoons butter or margarine

2 cups uncooked rice

1 bunch green onions, chopped

2 tomatoes, peeled and chopped

1 clove garlic, mashed or pressed

2 tablespoons minced parsley

2 peeled green chiles, chopped

¼ cup finely-cut celery

1 pound crab legs, cleaned shrimp, or lobster meat

4½ cups water

Salt and pepper

FRY rice lightly in butter in large kettle. Add all other ingredients and simmer 30 minutes, or until all liquid has been absorbed. Makes 6 to 8 servings.

TAMAL DE POLLO Y ELOTE
Chicken and Fresh Corn Tamale Pie

Elena says, "It is a little trouble to prepare the corn in this manner but the texture of the dough will reward your efforts. I prefer to use choice pieces of chicken rather than a whole one. This is a superb casserole dish." And what a conversation piece for a dinner or buffet supper!

3 tablespoons oil
1 frying chicken, disjointed, or chicken parts
2 cloves garlic, peeled and minced
2 medium-sized onions, peeled and chopped
2 medium-sized tomatoes, peeled and chopped, or 1½ cups solid-pack tomatoes

1 can peeled green chiles, chopped
½ teaspoon orégano, rubbed between palms of hands
¼ teaspoon comino
Salsa Jalapeña, or your favorite chile relish, to taste
Salt

FRY chicken in oil in large kettle, but do not brown. Add garlic, onions, tomatoes, chiles, orégano, comino, salsa, and a little salt. Cover and cook slowly 15 minutes. While it cooks, prepare topping:

3 ears fresh corn
2 tablespoons butter or margarine, melted

2 eggs
Salt

Grate corn slightly just to break skin of each grain, then with table knife scrape all pulp from the cob. Add butter or margarine to it and slightly-beaten egg yolks. Whip egg whites stiff but not dry, fold into corn mixture. Start oven at moderate (350 degrees F.). Pour semicooked chicken into buttered 2-quart casserole. Pour corn mixture on top and bake in moderate oven 1 hour and 15 minutes. Makes 4 or more servings. (Elena says this can be frozen.)

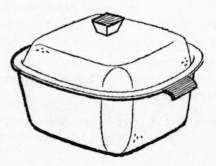

★SOPA SECA DE TORTILLA
Dry Tortilla Soup

This *sopa seca* makes a good casserole to serve with charcoal-broiled meats.

6 tortillas (can be bought in
   cans)
½ cup oil
1 onion, peeled and minced
2 cups tomato purée (canned,
   condensed tomato soup, or
   thick tomato sauce)

1 bay leaf
1 teaspoon orégano
Salt and pepper
Grated cheese
6 hard-cooked eggs, sliced

CUT tortillas into strips like macaroni. Fry in oil until crisp. Set aside to drain on thick paper towels. Fry minced onion in oil in which tortillas were fried. Add tomato purée, bay leaf, orégano, salt and pepper. Cook, covered, 30 minutes. Start oven at moderate (350 degrees F.). Butter a 2-quart shallow casserole, place in layers: tortilla strips, sauce, grated cheese, and hard-cooked egg slices. Follow same procedure until all ingredients are used, having egg slices for top layer. Cover with remaining sauce. Bake in moderate oven 30 minutes. Makes 6 servings. (This dish can also be frozen.)

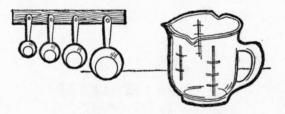

★HUEVOS A LA NAVARRA
Eggs Navarra Style

1 tablespoon butter
3 medium-sized tomatoes, peeled
   and chopped
2 tablespoons chopped parsley
Salt and pepper

8 eggs
¼ pound longaniza sausage
1 tablespoon grated Parmesan or
   Romano cheese

START oven at moderate (375 degrees F.). Generously butter shallow baking dish. Mix tomatoes, parsley, and salt and pepper to taste and put a layer of this mixture in dish. Break eggs, one at a time into a saucer, then slip into dish on top of tomatoes. Place rounds of sausage around yolks. Sprinkle with grated cheese. Bake until eggs are set about 10 to 15 minutes. Makes 4 to 8 servings.

GUAJOLOTE RELLENO A LA MEXICANA
Stuffed Turkey Mexican Style

16-pound turkey

10 apples, pared and quartered

2 cups sherry

½ pound butter

½ pound prunes, soaked and
  pitted

½ cup blanched almonds

½ of a pound-cake or butter
  cake, crumbled

Salt, pepper, nutmeg to taste

START oven at slow (250 degrees F.) to moderate (325 degrees F.). Have poultry dealer clean and prepare turkey for cookery. Rinse bird, drain. Cook apples slightly in sherry in large kettle. Melt butter, add to apples with remaining ingredients. Season to taste. Rub turkey inside with salt. Stuff turkey with apple mixture, skewer or sew vent, truss and roast.

For 10- to 16-pound bird, average cooking time is 3½ to 4½ hours, allowing 18 to 20 minutes per pound. Place bird in open roasting pan, roast uncovered in slow to moderate oven. Baste at 30-minute intervals with mixture of melted fat and hot water. When breast and legs become light brown, cover them with cloth dipped into melted fat. Baste over cloth; it holds fat and keeps otherwise exposed surfaces from browning too quickly. Makes 12 or more servings.

The five recipes above from ELENA'S SECRETS OF MEXICAN COOKING, *by Elena Zelayeta*

Near East

Much of the delicious cookery of Near Eastern countries and the Middle East was introduced to America by George Mardikian. Hundreds of thousands of visitors to San Francisco have lunched and dined at his restaurant, The Omar Khayyam. Many thousands have bought his cook book, *Dinner at Omar Khayyam's* and prepared the simple, flavorful, unusual dishes which he included in that book. Since it was first published in 1944, shish kebab and lamb and other foods cooked on skewers have become favorites not only in the many Near Eastern restaurants of American cities, but in thousands of American back yards where barbecue cookery is now the favorite outdoor pastime for summer entertaining. Other favorites from the Mardikian book are less well known, but equally delicious.

ARMENIAN BAKED STEAK

2 pounds rump steak, ½ inch
    thick, cut in 6 serving pieces
Salt and pepper
Flour
Butter or oil
1 large onion, peeled and
    chopped

1 large green pepper, seeds re-
    moved, and chopped
½ cup chopped celery
½ cup sherry
½ cup Tomato Sauce or juice
½ teaspoon paprika
1 cup hot water

START oven at moderate (375 degrees F.). Rinse steak, drain, season
with salt and pepper. Dip into flour, fry in butter or oil 1 minute on
each side. Place in baking pan or casserole. In same frying pan sauté onion, pepper, and celery 3 minutes, stirring. Add wine, Tomato Sauce
or juice, and paprika. Pour over steaks in casserole, and pour the hot
water over all. Bake uncovered in moderate oven 30 minutes. Turn steaks
over and bake another 30 minutes. Cover pan if sauce is cooking down too
much. Makes 6 servings.

★HAIGAGAN OMELET
Armenian Omelet

"This is a perfect dish," says Mr. Mardikian, "for large parties
or Sunday suppers."

1 green pepper, seeds removed,
    chopped fine
½ onion, peeled and chopped
Butter or oil
2 large fresh tomatoes, peeled
    and cut up

¼ pound salami, chopped fine
½ teaspoon salt
6 eggs

START oven at hot (425 degrees F.). Cook green pepper and onion in
saucepan in little butter or oil 3 minutes, add tomatoes and cook 5 minutes, mixing. Add salami and salt, mix, and heat thoroughly. Butter a
square cake pan. Beat eggs, mix well with tomato mixture. Pour into
prepared pan, bake 5 to 10 minutes in hot oven, or until eggs are set
and slightly browned on top. Cut into squares and serve immediately
onto hot plates. Makes 4 servings.

★KHOROVADZ SEMPOOG AGHTZAN
Eggplant Appetizer

1 medium-sized eggplant	3 tablespoons vinegar
2 tablespoons chopped peeled onion	Salt and pepper
	Crisp lettuce
2 tablespoons chopped parsley	Ripe olives
3 tablespoons olive oil	3 tomatoes, peeled and sliced

WASH eggplant, bake or broil whole until soft, about 30 minutes. If broiled under gas, the eggplant skin burns slightly, which gives a delicious smoked flavor to mixture. Let broiled eggplant cool. Then peel off browned or burned skin. Chop eggplant moderately fine, add onion and parsley. Season with oil, vinegar, salt and pepper, mix well. Heap on lettuce leaf and garnish with ripe olives and sliced tomatoes. Makes 6 or more servings.

GREGORIAN COCKTAIL

"This mixed-vegetable cocktail is named for the Armenian Gregorian Christian Church. The recipe is so called because it is eaten during the meatless Lenten season. In the interior of Armenia this dish, and bread, were the only foods eaten in Lent."

1 cup chopped broiled mixed green peppers, peeled onions, and tomatoes	¼ teaspoon pepper
	1½ teaspoons salt
	½ teaspoon finely-chopped fresh or dry mint
1 to 2 cups ketchup	
¼ cup pickle relish	½ cup juice of pickled grape leaves, or seasoned vinegar
½ teaspoon Tabasco sauce	
1 teaspoon Worcestershire	1 cup chopped walnuts

WASH 1 green pepper, onion, and tomato, broil few minutes under moderate broiler heat. Peel, chop very fine to make 1 cup mixed. Combine with remaining ingredients, except nuts. Chill. Serve in bowl, sprinkled with nuts. Makes 4 to 8 servings.

★IZMIR KUFTE

"Kuftés were served in Armenia as a basic quick meal. All were made with ground meats, the most popular being Izmir Kufté, which means meat ball of Smyrna. It is glorified hamburger given a Near Eastern touch by the addition of cummin and a good bit of parsley and onion. Kuftés can be made with any kind of ground meat or a mixture of several kinds."

1 pound ground meat
1 beaten egg
½ cup finely-chopped peeled onions
¼ cup finely-chopped parsley

1 cup soaked plain or toasted
bread crumbs
½ teaspoon ground cummin
Salt and pepper
Butter for frying

COMBINE and mix all ingredients except butter together. Shape in thumb-shaped patties. Fry in butter if you are in a hurry, but they are more delicious baked about 20 minutes in a well-buttered pan in a very hot oven. Serve with pilaff. Makes 6 or more servings.

★GARDEN DOLMA

1 pound ground shoulder of
lamb
½ cup rice
2 onions, peeled and chopped
1 large tomato, peeled and
chopped, or ½ small can
tomato sauce
1 tablespoon chopped parsley

1½ teaspoons salt
¼ teaspoon pepper
2 or 3 chopped fresh mint or
tarragon leaves
6 or more green peppers, or
6 large tomatoes, or 6 large
zucchini

COMBINE lamb, rice, onions, chopped tomato or tomato sauce, parsley, salt, pepper, and mint or tarragon leaves, mix well with fork. Cut tops off peppers or tomatoes, and spoon out contents. If zucchini is used, scrub, rinse, drain, cut off smaller end, and hollow out remaining larger end. Stuff vegetables with lamb mixture.

Start oven at moderate (325 degrees F.) . Place stuffed vegetables in baking pan or casserole. Add hot water almost to cover. Bake, uncovered, 1 hour. No gravy or extra sauce needed, the pan juice is enough. Makes 6 or more servings.

★AJEM PILAFF
Persian Pilaff

1 pound boneless shoulder of
lamb cut in 1-inch cubes
4 tablespoons butter
⅔ cup chopped peeled onions

½ cup chopped peeled tomatoes
2 cups rice
1 cup broth or hot water
Salt and pepper

START oven at moderate (325 degrees F.) . Use flameproof (metal-base) casserole. Cook meat in little butter until lightly browned on all sides. Add onions, stir and cook until browned. Add tomatoes, stir, cook 15 minutes. Wash rice in heavily salted hot water, drain, rinse in cold water, drain. Put rice carefully on top of meat in casserole. Place large piece butter in center of rice. Pour broth or hot water around edges of meat, cover casserole. Bake 1 hour in moderate oven. Makes 6 servings.

★SHISH KEBAB
Roast Lamb on Skewers

"The history of shashlik or shish kebab dates far back in the lives of mountain folk of the Caucasus, who during their migrations would kill game, stick it on their swords and roast it over the fire. Shish kebab means barbecue or skewer. Today roasted or broiled lamb on skewers is a popular dish all over America. The lamb should be seasoned with sherry, onion, and orégano, an herb that grows in all Mediterranean countries. The combination of these three gives a flavor similar to garlic but with none of the aftertaste. Always serve shish kebab with pilaff."

1 leg lamb (5 or 6 pounds)
½ pound onions, peeled and
    sliced
1 tablespoon salt

½ teaspoon pepper
⅓ cup sherry
2 tablespoons olive oil
1 teaspoon orégano

REMOVE all fat and gristle from leg of lamb. Bone it and cut meat into 1-inch cubes. Combine remaining ingredients, mix with meat in covered bowl. Let marinate at least 1 hour, preferably overnight. Put meat on skewers and broil over charcoal fire or under broiler heat until crisply browned on all sides; for lamb evenly cooked through, use lower heat and longer cooking. Makes 8 or more skewers, each skewer, 1 serving.

★PATLIJAN KARNI YARIK
Stuffed Eggplant

2 eggplants
Salt
Butter
1 pound ground lamb shoulder
1 large onion, chopped

¼ cup parsley
2 tomatoes, peeled and sliced
½ cup Tomato Sauce
Hot water

WASH eggplants, drain. Cut into quarters lengthwise, salt generously, and let stand ½ hour. Slit each quarter in the middle, down to the rind, but do not break the rind. Cook quarters in little butter for 5 minutes. Start oven at moderate (325 degrees F.) . Cook lamb, onion, and parsley in same pan in which eggplant cooked. Stir and cook 5 minutes. Place semicooked eggplant quarters in baking pan, spoon lamb mixture onto eggplant. Pour Tomato Sauce and hot water over and around stuffed eggplant. Cover and bake in moderate oven 30 minutes. Uncover and continue baking 10 minutes, or until top is browned. Makes 8 servings.

The nine recipes and comments above from DINNER AT OMAR KHAYYAM'S, *by George Mardikian*

New Zealand

T*he New World Wide Cook Book* reminds us that New Zealand menus read much like those of Australia, and of course are full of English, Scotch, various European, and even American dishes. Indian curries are also popular, and mutton cooked in many ways, since the sheep industry there and in Australia dominates most areas.

★INDIA CURRY, NEW ZEALAND STYLE

2 tablespoons butter or fat
⅔ cup chopped peeled onions
1 large apple, pared, cored, diced
2 tablespoons raisins
1½ tablespoons shredded coconut
4 teaspoons curry powder
1 teaspoon salt
¼ teaspoon pepper
1⅓ cups water, or coconut water
2 cups diced cooked meat or chicken
1 large firm banana, sliced
Hot cooked rice to serve 4 to 6 persons

MELT butter or fat in deep flameproof (metal-base) casserole or heavy kettle. Fry onion until golden. Add apple and stir. Add raisins and coconut and mix well. Add curry powder, salt and pepper. Cook all for 5 minutes, stirring until well blended. Add water or coconut water and meat. Cover pan tightly and cook about 1½ hours on lowest heat, or in slow oven (250 degrees F.). Uncover, add more water if curry seems dry. Should have the consistency of thin stew. Add banana, stir, cover, cook ½ hour or longer. Serve hot with rice. Makes 4 to 6 servings.

★NEW ZEALAND BROWN SPICE MUFFINS

½ cup shortening
¾ cup sugar
2 beaten eggs
½ cup molasses
2 cups all-purpose flour, sifted
1 teaspoon baking soda
1 teaspoon baking powder
1 teaspoon ground cinnamon
1 teaspoon ground nutmeg
¼ teaspoon salt

START oven at moderately hot (400 to 425 degrees F.). Butter 18 muffin tins. Cream shortening, beat sugar in until fluffy, add eggs and molasses and mix well. In another bowl sift flour, soda, baking powder, spices, and salt. Combine with butter mixture, blend well. Spoon into muffin tins. Bake 15 to 20 minutes, until risen and lightly browned. Makes 18 large muffins.

The two recipes above from THE NEW WORLD WIDE COOK BOOK, *by Pearl V. Metzelthin*

Norway

Norwegian cookery today is similar to that of the other Scandinavian countries. But old-time national favorites are still the first choice in country, village, and town homes and local restaurants. These traditionl dishes, according to *Smörgåsbord and Scandinavian Cookery for Americans,* by Florence Brobeck and Monika Kjellberg, include fish, game, and meats usually served with sharp or mellow sauces, vegetables in cream sauce, boiled potatoes and potatoes in many other forms, rich puddings filled with fruits, berries, and nuts served with clear fruit sauce or cream, hot or cold fruit soups, luxurious cakes and cookies, and coffee cakes and breads containing cardamom, almonds, and fruit.

Here are some favorites, easily prepared in any American kitchen.

LABSKAUS
Beef and Vegetable Pot Hash

2 pounds boneless beef	4 parsnips
2 pounds potatoes	1 small head cabbage
4 to 6 carrots	2 tablespoons minced parsley
1 or 2 stalks celery	Black pepper

RINSE meat, drain, cut, or chop into small pieces; do not grind it. Wash vegetables, pare potatoes, scrape carrots, celery, parsnips (pare any thick parsnip rind), and cut all vegetables into small pieces or chop them. Place meat in Dutch oven or heavy kettle, cover with lightly salted water, bring to boiling and boil about 1 hour or until tender. Skim top; add vegetables but not parsley. Add more boiling water if needed, but there should be only enough to cook the vegetables and to be absorbed by the time meat and vegetables are done. Cover kettle and cook on low heat 2 hours. Stir occasionally. When vegetables are falling to pieces, the cooking liquid should be absorbed and the mixture like hash. Stir in parsley, sprinkle top with freshly-ground black pepper, and serve. Makes 8 servings.

KIRSEBAER KOLDSKAAL
Cold Cherry Punch or Soup

2¾ pounds ripe cherries	Cinnamon stick
1 pound (3½ cups) powdered sugar	½ lemon peel, chopped
2½ quarts water	1 pint sherry

WASH cherries, remove seeds but do not discard them. Combine cherries, sugar, and water in glass or enamel saucepan and heat to boiling. Stir few minutes; with slotted spoon, lift out cherries to a deep tureen or punch bowl. Crush cherry seeds, add to hot juice with cinnamon and lemon peel. Let boil 3 or 4 minutes. Strain, pour over cherries. Chill thoroughly. Add sherry just before serving. Serve as fruit soup, or as a beverage. Makes 6 or more servings as soup; 12 or more as beverage.

EPLER A LA PINNSVIN
Porcupine Apples

3 very large apples
2 cups white wine
½ cup sugar
¼ cup water

1 cup sliced toasted almonds
Citron, sliced paper-thin
Whipped cream

WASH apples, drain, pare. Cut in halves and cut out cores. Heat wine, sugar, and water together in saucepan until boiling. Lay apples carefully in mixture and cook until tender but not too soft. Remove apples to serving dish, laying them on their cut surface. Stick almonds in them like porcupine quills. Cook wine sauce down a little and pour over apples. Let cool. Garnish dish with thin slivers of citron and serve with whipped cream. Makes 6 servings.

ROKET AAL I EGGERAND
Smoked Eel in Egg Ring

5 eggs
¾ cup milk
½ teaspoon salt

1 smoked eel
2 tablespoons butter
2 ripe peeled tomatoes

BEAT egg yolks with milk and salt in top of double boiler. Whip egg whites until stiff, fold into yolk mixture. Cook slowly over hot water until thickened and custard-like. Pour into buttered ring mold. Let cool.

Cut eel meat in small pieces, sauté few minutes in butter. When custard is cold and firm, turn it out on serving platter, fill center with sautéed eel. Garnish with thin slices tomatoes. Makes 6 or more servings.

DRONNING SUPPE
Queen Soup

4 beaten egg yolks
⅜ cup light cream
¼ cup sherry

2½ quarts boiling hot chicken
    broth
Chicken forcemeat balls

STIR yolks, cream, and sherry together in a warmed soup tureen. Pour the seasoned hot broth in slowly, stirring continually. Add small chicken forcemeat balls (ground cooked chicken, seasoning). Serve at once. Makes 6 to 8 servings.

★NORWAY'S KOLDT BORD

Many of the dishes served on the Swedish smörgåsbord are favorites on the Norwegian koldt bord, plus an array of open-face sandwiches. Smaller than the Danish sandwiches, there are usually 6 to 10 varieties on the koldt bord, gay in color, savory, delicious, and filling. Here are the general directions for making these sandwiches, which of course also are favorites for afternoon or late-evening coffee parties and with tea.

Cut bread as thin as possible and butter it well. Spread the slice completely to its edges with filling, cut off crusts, cut bread into 2 or 3 narrow pieces slantwise.

Garnish meat sandwiches with aspic, thinly-sliced cucumber, shredded horse-radish, finely-mixed salad combinations.

Garnish game sandwiches with a cooked prune and decorate with a rosette of whipped flavored butter such as Lemon Butter.

Garnish fish sandwiches with whole cooked shrimp, or finely minced shrimp and mayonnaise, or capers.

Garnish caviar sandwiches with whipped butter mixed with lemon juice, or with grated lemon peel or small pieces of sliced lemon. Other favorites: smoked herring and hard-cooked egg, tomato and cheese, tomato and egg, butter and chives, carrots and peas with mayonnaise, celery and radishes combined on buttered bread with mayonnaise, anchovies, goat cheese, other cheeses, herring in wine or dill sauce, mackerel in Tomato Sauce, sardines in oil or Tomato Sauce.

The six recipes above from SMÖRGÅSBORD AND SCANDINAVIAN COOKERY, *by Florence Brobeck and Monika Kjellberg*

Poland

In the old days in Poland," according to the introductory material of the *Old Warsaw Cook Book*, by Rysia, "there were cooks who cooked on a scale we do not hear of today, and people understood the art of gathering at a table with friendliness, relaxation, and generous hospitality and the ability to share the common table with humor and warmth." Rysia grew up in Poland, and lived in such a household as a child. She has lived in America for several years, but her memory of meals in Poland and her love for the art of cooking led to the compiling of her unusual cook book. Here are nine favorites from that book, beginning with one of the famous Polish soups:

DILL PICKLE SOUP

4 medium-size dill pickles	4 cups meat stock or bouillon
2 tablespoons flour	Salt and pepper
2 tablespoons butter	1 cup sour cream

DICE pickles. Sprinkle with the flour and mix, then sauté in soup kettle in butter 5 minutes. Add stock or bouillon and seasoning. Reduce heat, let simmer ½ hour. Turn heat high, add sour cream, stir and serve. Makes 4 or 5 servings.

BOILED PIKE WITH HORSE-RADISH SAUCE

2 pounds pike fillets	3 small onions, peeled and
Salt	quartered
1 tablespoon chopped parsley	Horse-Radish Sauce
4 carrots, scraped and sliced	

RINSE fillets, drain, and season with salt. Place in kettle with just enough water to cover. Add parsley, carrots, and onions and cook on slow heat until fish is tender, about 20 to 25 minutes. Drain, serve hot, with Horse-Radish Sauce. Makes 4 or more servings.

OYSTER "CAKES"

12 oysters in shells	3 or 4 tomatoes
¾ cup sliced mushrooms	3 tablespoons grated Parmesan
4 tablespoons butter	cheese
Pepper	½ cup bread crumbs

SCRUB oysters, rinse, drain. Open shells, remove oysters to saucepan. Rinse shells, drain, and reserve. Cook oysters 2 or 3 minutes in ½ cup lightly salted water; drain, saving liquor. Chop oysters fine. Cook mushrooms in 1 tablespoon butter until lightly browned. Combine with oysters, add pepper, and spoon mixture into shells. Place filled shells in large lightly-buttered baking dish. Wash tomatoes, drain, scald, and peel. Chop coarsely and cook with 2 tablespoons butter and reserved oyster liquor, about 8 minutes, stirring. Add cheese, mix, put through sieve. Pour over oysters. Start oven at hot (450 degrees F.). Sprinkle crumbs over sauce on oysters, add dabs of butter. Bake in hot oven 10 minutes. Serve immediately. Makes 4 to 6 servings.

COLD HAM A LA IMPERIAL

1 medium-size cooked boneless
  ham
½ pound chicken livers
3 mushrooms, chopped
2 tablespoons butter
1 teaspoon Worcestershire sauce

½ cup Madeira or red wine
2 cups heavy cream, whipped
2 envelopes (2 tablespoons) plain
  gelatin
2 cups ham broth or bouillon

THE Polish author says that the ham should be cooked in water to cover, seasoned with ½ teaspoon rosemary, ½ teaspoon basil, 1 onion, peeled and chopped. When tender, drain ham and let cool. Reserve liquid.

American hostesses can buy a canned, boned Polish ham for this recipe or a small boneless American ham. Place cooked or canned ham on large platter, slice thin. Drain chicken livers, press through sieve, cook with mushrooms in butter with Worcestershire and wine, 5 minutes, stirring well. Remove from heat, let cool slightly. Fold whipped cream into liver mixture. Coat each slice of ham well with mixture and reconstruct ham shape. Add gelatin to ham broth or bouillon, heat gently 2 or 3 minutes until gelatin dissolves, remove from heat, let stand until slightly jelled. Then pour slowly over ham, covering top, sides and ends. Chill until coating is set. To serve, garnish platter with greens. Serve mayonnaise separately. Count on about ¼ to ⅓ pound ham per serving.

PACZKI

1 cup light cream
12 beaten egg yolks
5 tablespoons butter, melted
⅜ cup sugar
2 cakes yeast, mashed in 2 tablespoons warm water

1 pound rice flour
3 tablespoons apricot brandy
Flour
Cherry preserve
Fat for deep frying

WARM cream slightly. Beat in egg yolks, butter, sugar, crushed yeast and water, and mix well. Fold in rice flour, mixing well. Add brandy. Work batter with spoon 10 minutes, and when it starts to bubble, set bowl aside in warm place, cover lightly with towel, and let rise about 1 hour, or until double in bulk. Then place on lightly-floured kneading board, sprinkle lightly with flour, roll dough out to 1 inch thickness. Cut out round patties. Place spoonful cherry preserve on half the number of patties, cover with remaining patties. Let rise again for about 1 hour. Fry in deep hot fat (370 degrees F.) until evenly browned, 5 to 7 minutes. Drain on thick paper towels. Sprinkle with powdered sugar. Serve warm. Makes 10 to 18 paczki.

★NALESNIKI WITH JAM

4 eggs
2 cups all-purpose flour, sifted
⅛ teaspoon salt
1 cup milk
1 cup water

1 tablespoon butter, melted and
  cooled
Fruit jam
Powdered sugar

BEAT egg yolks until light, sift flour in gradually, beating, add salt. Beat constantly, adding milk, water, and melted butter. Heat griddle with light coating of fat. Whip egg whites until stiff, fold into batter. Pour like pancakes, but cook on bottom only. Do not turn cakes. When baked through to top, lift cakes from griddle to bread board, spread each lightly with any favorite fruit jam, and roll into trumpet or cornucopia shape. Serve warm, sprinkled with powdered sugar. Makes 10 or more cakes.

★WARSAW SALAD

2 cups cooked or canned beets
2 cups cooked or canned kidney
  beans
2 cups cooked or canned peas
3 dill pickles, diced
3 scallions, chopped

¾ cup cooked or canned crab
  meat, bones removed
1 cup mayonnaise
1 tablespoon prepared mustard
½ cup sour cream
1 hard-cooked egg, carrots,
  radishes for garnish

DRAIN cooked or canned vegetables, dice beets, combine all with pickles, scallions, and crab meat. Mix mayonnaise with mustard and sour cream. Pour over salad, mix. Serve garnished with strips of hard-cooked egg and carrot, and radish roses. Makes 8 or more servings.

ZRAZY

2-pound piece veal or beef
Salt and pepper
4 onions, peeled and grated
¼ cup bread crumbs
½ cup chopped fresh dill

Beef or veal fat for frying
½ cup white wine
1 tablespoon Worcestershire
  sauce
1 cup bouillon

HAVE meat dealer cut veal or beef into very thin slices. Pound well, season on both sides with salt and pepper. Combine onions, crumbs, dill, and light dash of pepper; mix. Roll meat in mixture to coat slices well. Fry in hot fat until lightly browned on both sides. Pour in wine, Worcestershire, and bouillon, cover pan, bring to boiling on high heat, lower heat and cook 30 minutes, or until tender. Add more bouillon if needed. Makes 6 or more servings.

MUSHROOM PATTIES

1 pound mushrooms	2 egg yolks
2 onions, peeled and chopped	Flour
1 tablespoon chopped parsley	2 beaten eggs
Salt and pepper	2 tablespoons water
4 tablespoons butter	¾ cup bread crumbs
2 tablespoons flour	Fat for deep frying
½ cup light cream	Fruit jam

CLEAN and wash mushrooms, chop or slice fine. Sauté with onions and parsley, lightly seasoned in 2 tablespoons butter. Stir and mix, cook about 5 minutes, or until onions are yellow. Melt remaining 2 tablespoons butter in saucepan, stir flour in smoothly, add cream and cook 2 or 3 minutes, or until slightly thickened. Combine with mushroom mixture and cook 2 or 3 minutes over low heat. Let cool. Beat 2 egg yolks in one at a time, blend. With tablespoon, scoop out mixture, roll each spoonful lightly in flour, then roll in beaten eggs mixed with 2 tablespoons water. Roll in crumbs until well coated. Let stand 15 minutes. Fry in deep hot fat (375 to 385 degrees F.) 2 to 4 minutes, or until lightly browned on all sides. Drain on thick paper towels. Serve hot. Makes 6 or more servings.

The nine recipes above from OLD WARSAW COOK BOOK, *by Rysia*

Portugal

In Portugal fish is the basis not only of the national economy but also of the daily diet, according to that authentic little book *European Cooking,* prepared in the test kitchens of Wezäta Förlag, Sweden. And eggs, cheese, and fruits are almost as important as sea food in Portuguese cookery. Here is a delicious shrimp soup from that specialty cook book:

SOPA DE CAMARAO
Shrimp Soup

3 tablespoons olive oil	1 quart water
2 large onions, peeled and sliced	½ cup rice
2 tomatoes, peeled and quartered	1 tablespoon butter
1½ cups dry white wine	1 teaspoon salt
2 tablespoons port	¼ teaspoon pepper
1 pound fresh shrimp in shells	Bread croutons

HEAT oil in soup kettle, sauté onions and tomatoes 5 minutes. Add wines and washed, drained shrimp. When hot, add water, bring to a boil, remove shrimp. Add rice and cook until rice is done. Shell and devein shrimp, reserving a few for garnish in soup. Pound or grind rest of shrimp and return to soup. When hot, strain, add butter and seasonings, and reheat. Serve hot in warmed bowls, garnished with whole shrimp and croutons. Makes 4 servings.

The recipe above from EUROPEAN COOKING, *recipes prepared in Wezäta Förlag, Sweden*

❦

Along Cape Cod, in some parts of Florida, and in the Hawaiian Islands Portuguese settlers have given Americans a flavorful introduction to their native cookery. In *Hawaiian and Pacific Foods*, that inclusive, interesting cook book of the Islands, Katherine Bazore Gruelle recommends these Portuguese dishes.

★FEIJAO COM MOLHO DE TOMATE
Beans with Tomato Sauce

1½ cups dried Mexican brown or red kidney beans
3 cups water
2 teaspoons salt
½ cup finely-chopped parsley
1¾ cups sliced peeled onions
1 tablespoon bacon or ham fat
1 cup Tomato Sauce

WASH beans, drain, cover with fresh water and soak overnight. Drain, cover with 3 cups water, add salt, and bring to boiling. Reduce heat, cook slowly until tender, 2 hours or more. Fry parsley and onions in fat until onions are tender, add Tomato Sauce. When beans are tender, add tomato mixture, reheat, and simmer 5 minutes, or until excess liquid has evaporated. Serve hot. Makes 6 servings.

★OMELETTA DE ABADEJO
Codfish Omelet

½ cup shredded salted codfish
3 cups water
5 eggs
1 tablespoon finely-chopped parsley
½ teaspoon butter or olive oil

COVER fish with water, let soak several hours. Drain. Start oven at moderate (350 degrees F.). Separate drained codfish into small flakes. Beat eggs until light and frothy, add codfish and parsley. Heat butter or oil in frying pan, pour egg mixture in, and cook over low heat until bottom of omelet is light brown. Set frying pan in moderate oven until top of omelet is dry and lightly browned. Fold omelet and serve immediately. Makes 4 to 6 servings.

★ABADEJO COM VINAGRE E CEBOLAS
Codfish with Vinegar and Onions

1¼ pounds salted codfish in brine   5 tablespoons olive oil
Water to cover   5 tablespoons vinegar

DRAIN fish, cover with cold water, and let stand 18 to 24 hours. Drain, cover with water, boil 30 minutes. Drain. Fry drained fish slowly in hot oil 5 minutes. Remove from heat, pour vinegar over fish, cover, let stand on warm burner 5 minutes. Place fish in serving dish, and pour Onion Dressing over it. Serve warm or cold.

ONION DRESSING

3 large onions   3½ tablespoons vinegar
7 tablespoons olive oil   ½ teaspoon salt

Peel onion, cut into ⅛-inch slices. Combine olive oil, vinegar, and salt and beat with fork until thoroughly blended. Add onions to dressing. Pour over fish. Makes 6 servings.

MILHO FRITO COM AGRIOES
Fried Mush with Water Cress

½ bunch water cress   1 cup yellow corn meal
¾ teaspoon salt   Butter or oil
5 cups boiling water

REMOVE tough stems from water cress, wash and chop leaves fine. Add salt to boiling water in top of 2-quart double boiler, slowly add corn meal, stirring vigorously and pressing out all lumps. Cook over boiling water. After mush boils, reduce heat and cook about 1 hour. Add cress and continue cooking ½ hour longer. When mush is thick enough to mold and hold its shape, pour into loaf pan or dish. Let cool. When cold, cut in slices. Fry in little butter or oil. Makes 6 or more servings. Portuguese cooks serve hot mush for breakfast with codfish stew.

★FILOSES OR MALASSADAS
Sweet Doughnuts

2 sticks cinnamon   4 tablespoons butter, melted
½ cup milk   2¾ cups all-purpose flour, sifted
1 cake compressed yeast   3 beaten eggs
2 tablespoons lukewarm water   Fat for deep frying
½ teaspoon salt   ½ cup strained honey
1¼ cups sugar   Extra sugar

ADD cinnamon to milk and heat to boiling point, remove at once from heat, and let cool to lukewarm. Remove cinnamon. Moisten yeast with lukewarm water. Add yeast, salt, sugar, and melted butter to warm milk in mixing bowl. Stir in part of flour, beating vigorously to prevent lumps from forming. Add eggs and remaining flour to form soft dough. Cover bowl, set in warm place for 2 to 3 hours, or until dough has doubled in bulk. Drop by tablespoonful into deep hot fat at 350 degrees F. Fry until pieces are evenly browned. Remove, let drain on thick paper toweling. Roll pieces in honey, then in sugar. Makes 24 doughnuts.

The six recipes above from HAWAIIAN AND PACIFIC FOODS, *by Katherine Bazore Gruelle*

Russia

Alexandra Kropotkin, author of *How To Cook and Eat in Russian,* has lived many years in America, long enough to know that American cooks like definite measurements and exact directions when they go into their kitchens to try a new recipe. And she has been careful to give just such detailed information in her unique and informative book of the dishes served in well-to-do homes of old Russia, in the candle-lit restaurants and cafés of the large cities, and (many of the dishes) in Russian restaurants of our American cities. Borsch and bliniki are the only dishes most Americans can order in these restaurants and know what they are going to be served. There is such a rich array of good dishes in the old Russian cuisine that we can be grateful to Princess Kropotkin for introducing them and supplying us with the recipes for them.

ZAKOOSKAS

Russian appetizers are called zakooskas, and like similar foods in other countries, we can make a meal on them. Or feeling capable of a big Russian luncheon or dinner, we can do as Russians do and enjoy a variety of zakooskas, then go to the table. Each menu of old Russian families includes five cold zakooskas and one hot dish. "According to Russian practice this is adequate," says Princess Kropotkin. "But not lavish for a small informal party; we feel truer to our traditions of Slavic hospitality when we serve six or seven cold zakooskas, including caviar, and one hot zakooska."

Any of the following can be served as zakooska snacks: Fresh gray caviar, pressed black caviar, red caviar. Pickled herring, herring marinated in wine, herring in Mustard Sauce, herring in sour cream, chopped herring with eggs, herring salad with beets or other vegetable. Smoked salmon, whitefish, whiting, eel, sturgeon.

Jellied eel. Anchovies, sardines, pickled smelts, raw oysters, shrimp in mayonnaise, and lobster in mayonnaise.

Meats in small slices, especially spicy sausage, ham, smoked reindeer meat, smoked tongue, head cheese, liver loaf, meat *pâtés*, smoked turkey. Radishes in sour cream, cucumbers in sour cream. Pickled vegetables such as mushrooms, globe artichokes, beets, red cabbage, small onions. A variety of salads of smoked salmon, vegetables, duck, calf's brains.

The hot zakooska might be any one of these: chicken livers in Madeira, frankfurters in Tomato Sauce, mushrooms in Sour Cream Sauce, well-spiced meat balls in Tomato Sauce. Piroshki, little pastry rolls stuffed with meat, also are usually included. (How similar to the same kind of table in Finland, Denmark, Norway and Sweden!)

POJARSKIYA CUTLETS OF CHICKEN

3½- to 4-pound roasting chicken	1 tablespoon vodka or gin
2 cups crumbled bread from day-old French loaf	7 tablespoons butter
½ cup light cream	1 egg yolk
½ teaspoon salt	Flour

HAVE chicken ready for cooking. Remove skin and cut all meat from bones. Discard bones and gristle or use for soup. Put chicken meat through grinder twice, using fine knife. Soak crumbs in cream a few minutes, then squeeze dry. Combine bread, chicken, salt, vodka or gin, and 2 tablespoons butter, creamed. Mix thoroughly, add egg yolk, blend thoroughly. Turn mixture out onto wet wooden board. Divide into 12 parts. Form each into small thick oval cake. Sprinkle lightly with flour and fry immediately in hot butter until golden brown. Makes 6 to 12 servings.

★SIRNIKI
Cottage Cheese Cakes

3 pounds cottage cheese	Flour
4 egg yolks	Butter
1 egg	Sour cream
Salt	Sugar
1 cup all-purpose flour, sifted	

WRAP cheese in several thicknesses of cheese cloth, hang it up to drip over a bowl or place in colander with weighted plate on top to squeeze liquid out. Let drip either way 4 hours. When cheese is dry, rub through sieve. Mix in egg yolks, beat whole egg and add. Season to taste with salt.

Sift in one cup flour and beat mixture until thoroughly blended. Shape into rolls about 2 inches in diameter and 3 to 4 inches long. Chill 1 hour. Cut into slices about 1 inch thick. Dust these with flour. Fry in hot butter until browned on both sides. Drain on paper towels. Serve hot with sour cream and sugar. Makes 6 or more servings.

BORSCH

6 cups consommé	1 tablespoon vinegar
6 medium-size beets	1 tablespoon flour
3 tablespoons water	½ cup sour cream
2 tablespoons butter	

If using canned consommé, the best flavor is obtained by mixing 2 cans consommé with 2 cans bouillon and 2 cups water. Boil 30 minutes with 1 large cabbage leaf cut into pieces, 1 chopped peeled onion, and 6 peppercorns. Strain, keep hot.

Scrub beets, rinse, and drain. Peel and cut into matchstick strips or thin slices or shred on coarse grater. Set aside 1 heaping tablespoon raw beets mixed with 3 tablespoons water, this is for coloring. It gives that rich ruby glow, the fine red color essential to good Borsch.

Heat butter in 2-quart kettle, add beets (except the 1 tablespoonful), stir 3 minutes, add 1 cup consommé and vinegar and cook on low heat 3 minutes. Sift in flour, stirring well to avoid lumps. Let cook few minutes, then add 3 or 4 tablespoons warm consommé. Let boil up once. When beets are tender, add remainder of consommé. Exact timing depends on age of beets. Thin the sour cream with a little of the hot soup, then stir cream into soup, add reserve tablespoon raw beets and water, stir, and serve immediately. Makes 6 servings.

★PORGIES BAKED IN SAFFRON CREAM

6 porgies, ½ pound each cleaned, ready to cook	1½ cups sour cream
	½ teaspoon saffron soaked 1 hour in 1 tablespoon water
Flour	
3 tablespoons butter	Dry bread crumbs
½ cup milk	Salt and pepper

Wash fish, dry on towel. Roll in flour and fry quickly in 2 tablespoons butter, 3 minutes for each side of fish. Melt remaining 1 tablespoon butter, stir 2 tablespoons flour in smoothly, add milk, stirring, and cook until smooth; stir in sour cream and the saffron water and blend. Lay browned fish in buttered shallow baking dish. Start oven at hot (425 degrees F.). Pour sauce over fish, sprinkle with crumbs. Brown in hot oven 15 minutes. Serve sizzling hot in dish in which they browned. Makes 6 servings.

PIROSHKI

Piroshki, small stuffed pastry rolls, should be about 3 or 3½ inches long and about 2½ inches thick through the middle. The ends taper off like finger rolls. For these delicious rolls to serve with soup or to eat as appetizer or as luncheon dish, make rich pastry or puff pastry or sour-cream dough. For each pirojok, pinch off piece of pastry about the size of an egg, flatten it, then roll into an oval shape about ¼ inch thick. Place 1 to 1½ tablespoons filling in the center, leaving ½ inch or wider border free from filling all the the way around. Fold pastry over to meet on top, pinch together in neat ridge along top center of pirojok, crimp edges together with fingers. Let piroshki stand 15 minutes. Brush with beaten egg yolk mixed with 1 tablespoon water. Place on greased and lightly floured baking sheet. Start oven at moderately hot (400 degrees F.), and bake 15 minutes; then lower heat to moderate (350 degrees F.) and bake 20 minutes longer. Serve hot or cold.

Make smaller piroshki to serve as hors d'oeuvres. For filling of large or small piroshki, use chopped cooked chicken, meats, hard-cooked eggs, mushrooms, fish, or the savory mixture below.

COOKED MEAT AND ANCHOVY FILLING

3 cups ground cooked beef	¼ cup gravy or thickened
2 onions, peeled and chopped	consommé
3 tablespoons butter	1 tablespoon minced parsley
4 anchovy fillets, minced	2 hard-cooked eggs, chopped

Beef should be ground fine. Sauté onions in butter until yellow, add meat, stir and cook 5 minutes. Add anchovies and gravy or consommé and parsley. Mix, heat 2 minutes. Let cool. Add chopped eggs and mix. Use as filling for piroshki made with sour-cream pastry, puff pastry, or rich pie dough. Makes about 4 cups filling, enough for 64 small piroshki, or 30 to 50 larger ones.

BAKED ONION DUMPLINGS

The author added a note to this recipe in her book: "I consider this one of our finest Russian contributions to vegetable cookery. Try these dumplings with roast lamb."

6 large onions	2 cups consommé
Salt	Pepper
1 tablespoon butter	Puff pastry for 6 dumplings

PEEL onions. With thin skewer pierce each onion in 3 or 4 places. Cover with cold salted water and bring to boiling. Drain onions, add butter and consommé. Bring to a boil, then lower heat and simmer until onions are tender (onions must remain whole). Time depends on kind and size of onion, should be about 30 minutes. When tender, drain and let onions stand in colander 1 hour. Pat dry with paper towel. Dust with salt and pepper, then wrap in rounds of Puff Pastry which have been rolled about ¼ inch thick. Pinch pastry cover together at top. Chill 30 minutes. Start oven at hot (450 degrees F.). Place onions in buttered baking pan, bake in hot oven 20 minutes, or until pastry is golden. Serve very hot. Makes 6 servings.

BROILED SALMON STEAKS WITH CAVIAR SAUCE

2 thick salmon steaks (3 pounds)   1 teaspoon lemon juice
Salt and pepper   2 tablespoons Anchovy Butter
Olive oil   2 tablespoons fresh caviar
1½ cups thick Cream Sauce   1 tablespoon butter
2 beaten egg yolks

HAVE salmon steaks cut about 1½ inches thick. Rub with little salt and plenty of pepper. Brush with oil. Broil under moderate heat about 10 minutes on each side.

To Cream Sauce add egg yolks and lemon juice, mix, keep warm. When fish steaks are done, place on warmed serving platter, spread top of each with Anchovy Butter. Stir caviar and butter into Cream Sauce until smooth. Pour over steaks. Serve at once. Makes 4 or more servings.

★SMETTANICK
Jam and Cream Pie

Puff pastry for 2-crust 9-inch pie   ¼ teaspoon almond extract
1½ cups cherry or raspberry jam   3 tablespoons sour cream
1½ cups ground blanched almonds   1 egg yolk
  or pecans   ½ teaspoon ground cinnamon
¼ cup light cream   Sugar

START oven at moderately hot (400 degrees F.). Line pie plate with pastry. Spread jam on pastry in pan in even layer. Mix nuts with cream, adding almond extract. Combine sour cream, egg yolk, and cinnamon, mix with nut-and-cream mixture. Spread over jam. Cover with top crust. Trim pastry edge, press top pastry to bottom pastry with fork or crimp with fingers in even rim. Sprinkle with sugar. Bake in moderately hot oven about 25 minutes, or until pastry is golden. Let cool. Makes 6 servings.

★GOLUBTSI
Meat Wrapped in Cabbage Leaves

12 cabbage leaves

1 pound ground round steak

½ pound ground pork

1 cup cooked rice

2 tablespoons minced parsley

1 egg

1 large onion, peeled and
chopped

4 tablespoons butter

Salt and pepper

2 tablespoons flour

1 cup tomato juice

1 cup water

½ cup sour cream

SEPARATE leaves of large head of cabbage and select 12 perfect ones. Cut away hard part at bottom of each leaf. Scald leaves in salt water 10 minutes, drain, spread on towel, let dry while preparing stuffing.

Combine meats with rice, parsley, unbeaten egg, and onion which has simmered a few minutes in butter. Add salt and pepper to taste, stir mixture well. Divide into 12 portions. Make little rolls of meat and wrap each in a leaf, folding leaf all around meat to make neat, secure package. Tie with thin thread. Fry in hot butter until browned, cover pan and cook gently 30 minutes. Remove thread carefully, keep packets warm on serving platter. Add flour to pan in which they fried, stir and cook 5 minutes, add tomato juice and water, stirring. Bring to a boil, stir in sour cream, add salt if needed. Let come to a boil again. Pour over hot packets, or serve separately. Makes 6 servings.

The ten recipes and comments above from HOW TO COOK AND EAT IN RUSSIAN, *by Alexandra Kropotkin*

Scotland

In Scotland, as in Ireland, gourmets who have traveled in Middle and Southern Europe, and to North and South America, who may own historic beautiful homes in Scotland, and who may spend part of each year in London or some other large city, serve Continental meals and the dishes of the international menus known throughout the Western world. They may serve traditional Scots dishes, too, on their home table. But their neighbors, who may be less well-to-do, and the people of Scotland as a whole, cling to traditional favorites. Many of these old Scots dishes are well known in America, or they are on the list of dishes homemakers would like to know and prepare for their families. They are featured in *Recipes from Scotland*, by the Scots writer, F. Marian McNeill.

COCK-A-LEEKIE

Plump stewing chicken
2 quarts beef or veal stock, or
water
Salt and pepper
2 or 3 bunches leeks, blanched
and cut in 1-inch lengths

12 prunes, pitted
If water is used in place of stock
add 1 clove, blade of mace,
sprig of parsley, and 6 peppercorns tied in muslin

HAVE fowl cleaned and trussed, place in large kettle with stock or water, seasonings, and 3 or 4 chopped leeks. Bring to a boil, cook gently 2 hours, or until fowl is tender. Remove fowl, cut off enough meat to make ½ cup finely chopped. Reserve rest of chicken for salads or other recipes. Skim broth in kettle, removing all surface fat. Add remaining leeks and salt and pepper if needed. Simmer gently until leeks are tender. Half an hour before serving, add prunes. Continue slow simmering. Add the ½ cup minced chicken. Serve very hot. Makes 6 servings.

CREAMED FINNAN HADDIE

1 smoked haddock
1 cup (or more) medium White
Sauce
¼ cup grated cheese

Salt and pepper if needed
½ teaspoon dry mustard
2 tablespoons butter

RINSE haddock, drain, cook in just enough water to cover, about 20 min-utes, or until tender. Drain; reserve some of liquid. Remove skin and bones and cut fish into small pieces. Pour into buttered shallow flame-proof dish. Make White Sauce, 1 cup or more, depending on size of fish; use some of the liquor from cooked fish as part of liquid in White Sauce. When sauce is smooth and thickened, remove from heat, add half of grated cheese, stir, add salt if needed, pepper, and the mustard, stir until cheese is melted. Pour sauce over fish. Sprinkle with remaining cheese, add dabs of butter. Brown under moderate broiler heat few minutes. Serve hot. Makes 2 to 4 servings.

SCOTCH WOODCOCK

2 egg yolks
2 tablespoons butter
¼ cup light cream
1 teaspoon finely-chopped
parsley

Salt and pepper
2 slices hot toast spread with
Anchovy Butter

COMBINE egg yolks, butter, cream, and parsley in top of double boiler, stir, add seasoning. Cook gently over hot water until thickened. Pour over toast, serve at once. Makes 2 servings.

★BARLEY BROTH, OR SCOTS BROTH

½ cup dried peas
1½ pounds neck of mutton
2 quarts water
¼ cup barley
1½ teaspoons salt
1 leek, white part only, sliced
1 onion, peeled and sliced
⅔ cup diced pared white turnip

⅔ cup diced scraped carrot
½ small white heart of cabbage
1 carrot scraped and grated
1 tablespoon chopped parsley
Pepper
Additional slices pared turnip and
  carrot

WASH peas, cover with cold water, let soak overnight. Or use fresh peas if available, which require no soaking. Rinse meat, trim, put into soup kettle, cover with the cold water. Add barley, salt, peas, bring to a boil; skim. Add leek, onion, diced turnip and carrot. Simmer slowly 3 to 4 hours. Add shredded cabbage, grated carrot, and parsley as well as turnip and carrot slices and continue slow cooking 30 minutes longer. Remove meat, turnip and carrot slices, keep hot. Season broth with little pepper, and serve it in warmed soup bowls. Place meat on warmed platter, garnish with slices of turnip and carrot. Usually a hot Caper Sauce is served with the mutton. Makes 6 broth and meat servings.

FISHERMAN'S PIE

1 boiled salt cod
2 cups hot mashed potatoes
1 hard-cooked egg
1 shallot, peeled and chopped,
  or 2 tablespoons finely-cut
  chives

1 tablespoon chopped parsley
2 tablespoons butter
¼ cup hot milk
Black pepper
½ teaspoon prepared mustard
Salt if needed

SKIN and bone fish, flake fillets, mix with hot mashed potatoes. Dice egg fine and add with shallot or chives to fish mixture. Add parsley, dabs of 1 tablespoon butter, and just enough hot milk to moisten. Mix well, season with a little black pepper and the mustard, and add salt if needed. Turn into a buttered pie dish, dot with remaining 1 tablespoon butter. Brown under low broiler heat, or in moderate oven (350 degrees F.) few minutes. Serve hot. Makes 4 or more servings.

MUSSELBURGH PIE

1 pound steak
1 dozen bulk oysters
Suet or bacon fat
2 tablespoons flour
1 teaspoon salt

½ teaspoon pepper
Cayenne
1¾ cups water or stock
Pastry for 1-crust pie
Milk or beaten egg

START oven at hot (450 degrees F.). Pound steak well, cut into thin strips about 2 inches wide and 3 inches long. Drain oysters, cut in half, place half oyster on each piece steak with bit of suet or bacon fat. Roll meat around oyster. Season flour with salt, pepper, and cayenne. Dip meat rolls into seasoned flour, place in buttered pie dish. (Scots cooks use funnel pie dish or place china funnel in regular pie dish.) Add just enough water or stock to cover rolls. Cover with pastry, trim, make decorative edge. Brush pastry with milk or beaten egg thinned with milk. Bake in hot oven 10 minutes, then reduce heat to moderate (325 degrees F.) and continue baking another 50 minutes, or longer. If steak was cut very thin, 1 hour's baking is sufficient; if meat is thicker, bake 1½ hours. Makes 6 servings.

★RICH CREAM SCONES

2 cups all-purpose flour, sifted	2 tablespoons butter
1 teaspoon baking powder	1 beaten egg
½ teaspoon salt	1 cup sour cream

START oven at hot (450 degrees F.). Sift flour, baking powder, and salt together into mixing bowl. Work in butter with fingers. When well mixed, make hollow in center, pour in egg and cream and work together into soft dough. Turn out on lightly-floured board. Roll out lightly, or pat out to half-inch thickness. Prick all over with fork. Cut in rounds. Bake on lightly-floured or buttered baking sheet in hot oven 12 to 15 minutes. Split open while warm and spread with butter or jam. Makes 12 to 16 scones.

★SCOTS SHORTBREAD

½ pound butter	2¼ cups pastry flour, sifted
½ cup plus 1 tablespoon sugar	1⅛ cups rice flour

START oven at hot (425 degrees F.). Cream butter and sugar thoroughly together. Sift the two flours together several times. Gradually work flour into butter-and-sugar mixture until dough is like rich pie pastry. Do not roll out, but press with hand into two round cakes, either in oiled and floured wooden shortbread molds, or on baking sheet covered with parchment paper. Best thickness for shortbread is ¾ inch for cake 8 inches in diameter. Pinch edges with finger and thumb, prick all over with fork. Bake in hot oven 10 minutes, reduce oven to moderate (325 degrees F.) and continue baking 15 to 20 minutes, or until shortbread is crisp and pale golden brown. Makes 12 servings.

Shortbread may be cut with cookie cutter after patting out, and baked in moderate oven about 20 minutes. Makes 2 dozen small cookies.

The eight recipes above from RECIPES FROM SCOTLAND, *by F. Marian McNeill*

South America

The Spanish and Portuguese influences which flavor the cookery of South America are in plentiful evidence in the one cook book which generously covers the whole continent, *The South American Cook Book,* by Cora, Rose, and Bob Brown. Outstanding among the many unusual yet simply prepared dishes in this book are these four, from four different South American countries.

★ARROLLADO DE MATAMBRE
Argentine Meat Roll

4 peppercorns, crushed
½ teaspoon salt
2 garlic cloves, peeled and mashed or grated
¼ cup vinegar
2 pounds round steak, cut about 1-inch thick

1 pound veal cut in thin, narrow strips
½ pound salt pork, sliced very thin
Boiling water
1 onion, peeled
1 bay leaf

COMBINE crushed peppercorns, salt, garlic, and vinegar. Rub into both sides of steak, place in covered dish and keep in refrigerator overnight. When ready to cook, spread steak flat, place layers of veal and salt pork over it, roll up like jelly roll, secure with small skewers and string. Place in heavy kettle, barely cover with boiling water, add onion and bay leaf. Cook, covered, over low heat about 2 hours, or until meat is easily pierced with fork. Remove from liquid, put on plate, with another plate over it and heavy weight on it to press firm, or place in meat press overnight and chill it. Discard skewers and string. Next day serve sliced. Broth from kettle can be used in soup or beans. Roll makes 8 servings.

★ALBONDIGON DE HUEVOS
Bolivian Egg Meat Balls

1 pound lean beef
½ pound lean pork
3 beaten eggs
¼ cup dry crumbs
1½ teaspoons salt

½ teaspoon pepper
⅛ teaspoon ground nutmeg
4 hard-cooked eggs, shelled
1 cup broth

CHOP beef and pork very fine and mix thoroughly with beaten eggs, crumbs, and seasonings. Spread mixture on waxed paper or bread board, cut into 4 squares. Put 1 hard-cooked egg in center of each square, roll meat around egg. Place in deep flameproof casserole, add broth. Cover and cook over slow heat about 1 hour. Makes 4 servings.

POLLO EN SALSA DE MOSTAZA
Columbian Chicken in Mustard Sauce

Plump frying chicken, cleaned and
   disjointed
Salt and pepper
Butter
1 cup water
1 cup wine

2 beaten eggs
2 tablespoons vinegar
1 tablespoon water
1 teaspoon dry mustard
1 teaspoon sugar
Salt

RINSE chicken, drain, rub well with salt and pepper. Fry until light brown in butter in deep flameproof (metal-base) casserole. Add water and wine, cover tightly, cook slowly about 45 minutes, or until tender.

Prepare sauce by mixing eggs with vinegar, 1 tablespoon water, and dry mustard. Cook in top part of enamel or glass double boiler over boiling water, stirring continually until smooth and thick. When done, strain broth from chicken and stir into egg sauce, add sugar and salt to taste. Return casserole of chicken to low heat, spoon sauce over chicken, and as sauce runs off chicken, baste again with it; continue until all pieces are richly glazed. Makes 4 to 6 servings.

★PATO COM AZEITUNHAS
Brazilian Duck with Olives

1 plump duckling, cleaned and.
   disjointed
2 tablespoons butter
2 slices bacon
1 small onion, peeled and sliced
Salt
6 to 8 peppercorns

2 cups boiling water
1 bay leaf
2 sprigs parsley
1 sprig celery leaves
1 cup small green olives
Flour
2 tablespoons water

SAUTÉ duck in butter with bacon in deep flameproof (metal-base) casserole, and as it browns, add onion, continue frying and turning pieces until all are evenly browned. Add salt, peppercorns, boiling water, and herbs. Cover tightly, cook at simmer about 1 hour, or until duck is tender. Turn pieces frequently. With sharp knife cut flesh from each olive in unbroken spiral. When duck is done, strain gravy into saucepan, thicken with little flour worked smooth with 2 tablespoons water, stir into sauce, bring to a boil, stir until slightly thickened. Scald olive spirals 2 minutes in boiling water, drain, add to gravy. Pour over duck and serve, or serve gravy separately. Makes 4 to 6 servings.

The four recipes above from THE SOUTH AMERICAN COOK BOOK, *by Cora, Rose, and Bob Brown*

Spain

The cookery of Spain, which influenced the cookery of the New World in South America and later in Mexico, is varied, interesting, and practical for North American homes and guest meals. In *The Home Book of Spanish Cookery,* by Marina Pereyra de Aznar and Nina Froud, the recipes are tested for U.S. kitchens and call for ingredients which are found in our grocery stores and markets.

Appetizers before a meal are favorites in Spain, as in so many other countries. They can make a summer's day luncheon for some American appetites, or they can be special attractions for a Sunday buffet supper. Here are five appetizers from this Spanish book.

★REMOLACHA
Beet Salad

4 medium-size beets	4 sprigs parsley
2 or 3 cold boiled potatoes	French dressing or salt, pepper,
4 or 8 spring onions	oil and vinegar

SCRUB beets, rinse, drain. Bake in moderate oven (350 degrees F.) until tender. Let cool, then chill. To serve, peel, cut into thin slices. Slice potatoes, season lightly. Arrange sliced beets and potatoes on salad plate, garnish with onions and parsley, dress lightly with French Dressing or with salt, pepper, oil, and vinegar. Makes 4 servings.

★HUEVOS EN GELATINA
Eggs in Aspic

Hard-cooked eggs	Aspic made with beef stock or
Mayonnaise	bouillon
	Crisp lettuce

SHELL eggs, cut lengthwise into 6 or 8 sections. Cover with mayonnaise mixed with equal amount of diced aspic. Chill. Serve on lettuce leaves. One or 2 eggs make 1 serving.

★PASTELITOS DE HOJALDRE RELLENOS
Giblet and Mushroom Puffs

6 small puff-pastry shells	2 tablespoons thick White Sauce
½ to ¾ cup finely-chopped	
cooked giblets and mushrooms	

BAKE shells and let cool. Combine giblet-and-mushroom mixture with White Sauce, fill shells. Place on baking sheet and heat for a few minutes before serving. For very small shells, as finger foods, allow 2 per serving.

★PASTELES DE ATUN
Tuna Pies

Puff pastry for eight 2-crust tarts
1 large onion, peeled and
   chopped
1 or 2 tomatoes, peeled and
   chopped

2 green peppers, seeds removed
   and chopped
1 tablespoon butter
1 or 2 small cans tuna in oil
½ teaspoon salt
¼ teaspoon pepper

PREPARE pastry, roll out very thin, about $\frac{1}{10}$ inch thick. Cut into circles, fit into greased tartlet tins. Start oven at hot (450 degrees F.). Combine onion, tomatoes, and green peppers and cook 6 minutes in the butter. Add drained and flaked tuna, stir and cook 3 minutes, season. Fill pastry-lined tins, cover each with second round of pastry, crimp edge of top and bottom pastry together. Bake in hot oven 10 to 15 minutes, until pastry is golden. Serve either hot or cold. Makes 8 servings.

★RABANOS
White Radishes

Select small hard radishes. Scrub, rinse, and drain. Peel, but leave small stalk at top. Make incisions crossways in radishes, press little butter into each. Sprinkle with cayenne. Serve with raw appetizers and as garnish for salads.

★FILETES RELLENOS DE JAMON
Fillets Stuffed with Ham

6 thin fillets of beef, about
   5 inches square
6 thin slices boiled ham, same
   size as beef
2 tablespoons bread crumbs
1 tablespoon oil

3 cloves garlic, peeled and
   finely chopped
2 tablespoons finely-chopped
   parsley
Salt and pepper

POUND fillets, lay slice of ham on each piece of beef, roll up, secure with wooden pick. Combine crumbs, oil, garlic, and parsley. Dip rolled fillets into garlic mixture, pressing well to make coating and crumbs stick. Broil under moderate heat about 20 minutes, turning rolls to cook all sides. Or place in shallow pan and cook in hot oven (450 degrees F.) 35 minutes, or until browned on all sides. If meat seems dry, add small amount of oil when broiling or little oil and hot water for oven cooking. Season just before serving. Makes 6 servings.

★ALMEJAS A LA MARINERA
Mussels à la Marinera

3 to 4 pounds fresh mussels
¼ cup oil
1 onion, peeled and chopped
2 cloves garlic, peeled and chopped
1 tablespoon vinegar

1 tablespoon bread crumbs
¼ cup finely-chopped parsley
½ teaspoon pepper
1¼ cups stock or bouillon, optional
Slices fried bread

WASH mussels thoroughly, drain. Brown onion in oil in large kettle. Add mussels, garlic, and vinegar. Cover and cook on high heat until mussels open, lower heat and let them simmer 5 minutes. Add crumbs, parsley, and pepper. Shake kettle, and if too dry, add stock or bouillon. Cover, let simmer 10 minutes. Serve very hot with fried bread. Makes 6 to 8 servings.

PAELLA A LA VALENCIANA
Paella

There are many versions of paella in South America, Mexico, and Spain. According to the authors, paella is the most typical Spanish dish, and a la Valenciana, the queen of paellas.

3 tablespoons oil
1 jointed chicken, flesh on pieces cut ½ inch deep in tiny squares or dice, or
1 pound pork, cut in ½-inch dice
1 onion, peeled and finely chopped
3 tomatoes, peeled and chopped
1½ pounds rice, washed and drained
½ pound dried kidney beans, soaked overnight
½ pound shelled peas

1 dozen fresh or canned artichoke hearts (optional)
3 canned pimientos, drained and chopped
¾ pound cleaned hake, whiting, or cod
1 pint mussels, washed and drained
1 crayfish, cleaned, or meat of 1 lobster
1 cup cleaned prawns or shrimp
1 teaspoon salt
½ teaspoon pepper
½ teaspoon saffron
4½ cups water

HEAT oil in very large deep frying pan or kettle, add chicken or pork and brown lightly. Add onion and cook until golden. Add tomatoes, cook few minutes. Add rice, cover and let simmer 10 minutes. Add beans, peas, and artichoke hearts, cover and let cook few minutes. Add pimientos and 12 small pieces hake or other fish, the mussels in their shells, pieces of crayfish or lobster, the prawns or shrimp. Season to taste, turn heat up and boil fast for 8 minutes. Reduce heat and cook slowly 8 minutes. Add saffron and 4½ cups water, cover kettle, cook until all water is absorbed and rice is cooked. Start oven at hot (450 degrees F.) and set kettle uncovered in oven few minutes, until top is golden. Remove from oven, pick out most of mussel shells. Let paella settle about 2 minutes, then serve. Makes 6 to 8 servings as one-dish meal.

★PATATAS CON QUESO
Potatoes with Cheese

Select small, round potatoes. Boil, drain, and peel. Hollow out some of the center of each potato, fill with grated cheese. Dip in beaten egg, roll in flour, fry in butter until brown. Serve hot with chicken or meat.

★PATATAS RELLENAS
Spanish Stuffed Potatoes

6 large potatoes
¼ cup chopped boiled or baked ham
1 onion, peeled and chopped
1 tablespoon chopped parsley
½ pound mushrooms, washed and chopped

3 hard-cooked eggs, chopped
5 tablespoons butter
Seasoning
½ pound shallots or small onions, peeled
1¼ cups stock

SCRUB, rinse, and pare potatoes. Cut slice off and reserve this "lid." Scoop out potatoes carefully, leaving ½-inch shell all around. Combine chopped ham, onion, parsley, mushrooms, and eggs (or chop all these together). Mix with 3 tablespoons butter, season, and fill potatoes with mixture. Start oven at moderate (350 degrees F.). Place stuffed potatoes in greased baking pan or dish, cover each potato with lid previously cut off. Arrange shallots or onions around and between potatoes. Add stock. Top all with dabs of butter. Bake in moderate oven about 45 minutes, or until potatoes are done. Before serving, remove lids from potatoes. Makes 6 servings.

The ten recipes above from THE HOME BOOK OF SPANISH COOKERY, *by Marina Pereyra de Aznar and Nina Froud*

Sweden

Swedish cookery and Swedish restaurants are so popular in America that many useful cook books by Swedish home economists have long been available to U.S. cooks. One of the earliest to please homemakers is *The Princesses Cook Book,* by Jenny Åkerström. Of course, this book contains many smörgåsbord dishes—the salads, cold meats, cheese, canapés, stuffed celery and other delectables which appeal to our appetites—as well as those small hot dishes such as scrambled eggs with kidney or mushrooms, old-fashioned scalloped potatoes, sautée of kidneys in sherry, and similar tasty combinations which invariably add flavor and good eating to the appetizer table in Scandinavian restaurants. Here are the Swedish book's typical appetizers for such a table.

CANAPES
Canapés à la Riga

4 or 5 sprigs parsley or tarragon, or 2 sprigs each
Boiling water
1 tablespoon finely-chopped peeled onion
½ cup butter
½ tablespoon wine vinegar
¾ teaspoon French mustard
Salt and pepper
12 slices white bread cut in squares, crusts cut off
6 small smoked herring, boned, skinned, cut in narrow strips
1 small jar or can caviar

RINSE and drain parsley and tarragon, cover with a little boiling water, and boil 1 or 2 minutes, combine with onion. Put through sieve. Cream this purée with butter, vinegar, and mustard, add salt and pepper if needed, but usually the mustard is enough seasoning.

Spread mixture on bread squares, lay narrow strips of herring in parallel rows diagonally across bread. Add caviar between herring strips. Makes 36 to 48 small canapés, or 24 large open-face sandwiches.

These sandwiches or canapés should be made just before serving, and if they must stand a few minutes, cover tray and place in refrigerator.

SMOKED HERRING CANAPES

8 lightly-smoked herring
⅓ cup butter
3 or 4 tablespoons heavy cream or sour cream
Salt and pepper
12 slices white bread cut into rounds
2 or 3 tablespoons thinly-sliced stuffed olives
12 small crisp radish roses

FREE herring from skin and bones, mash fish with butter, beating well to form paste. Force paste through sieve and gradually add enough cream or sour cream to paste to give smooth consistency. Add seasonings to taste. Spread on bread rounds and garnish with ring of thinly-sliced olives. Just before serving, place a small crisp radish rose in center of each canapé. Makes 12 canapés.

★SMOKED SALMON CANAPES

7 ounces thinly-sliced smoked
  salmon
1 tablespoon heavy cream or
  sour cream
3 tablespoons butter

12 slices white bread, cut into
  rounds and buttered
3 hard-cooked eggs, thinly sliced
Small sprigs fresh dill

MASH salmon, cream or sour cream, and butter together in mortar to form paste. Force through sieve. Vary amount of cream, adding only enough to give good consistency. Lay slice hard-cooked egg in center of each buttered round of bread. With small fluted pastry tube, form rosettes of salmon paste around egg. Garnish canapés with small sprigs dill. Makes 12 to 24 canapés.

HANNA'S APPLE CAKE

7 tablespoons butter
½ cup sugar
½ cup (4½ ounces) ground
  almonds
Juice 1 lemon

Grated peel ⅓ lemon
2 egg yolks
3 egg whites
1½ cups thick applesauce

START oven at moderate (350 degrees F.). Butter 1½-quart baking dish. Cream butter and sugar until light and porous, add almonds, lemon juice, and peel, beat. Add egg yolks one at a time, beating well. Whip egg whites until stiff, fold into yolk mixture. Pour applesauce into prepared baking dish, pour egg mixture on top. Bake in moderate oven about 20 minutes, or until top is delicately browned. Serve warm or cold in baking dish, with cream or Vanilla Sauce. Makes 6 servings.

★PRUNE CUSTARD

½ cup sugar
3 eggs
1⅝ cups chilled light cream
1 teaspoon vanilla extract

½ pound prunes, cooked and
pitted
25 blanched almonds, chopped
Whipped cream

START oven at moderate (350 degrees F.). Butter 1½-quart baking dish. Beat sugar and yolks until light and creamy; add chilled cream gradually, and vanilla. Whip egg whites until stiff. Fold into yolk mixture. Pour prunes into prepared baking dish, cover with almonds, pour egg mixture over all. Set dish in shallow pan of warm water. Bake in moderate oven 30 to 40 minutes, or until meringue is golden. Serve warm in baking dish, with whipped cream. Makes 6 servings.

BRAISED PORK WITH MUSTARD

2¾ pounds boneless pork loin
1½ tablespoons each salt and sugar
4 teaspoons dry mustard
2 tablespoons butter

Stock, bouillon or hot water
1 to 2 teaspoons potato flour, or
flour

RINSE meat, drain, pat dry. Rub entire surface with mixture of salt, sugar, and mustard. Place in crock or bowl, cover, let stand in refrigerator 3 days. Turn meat frequently in that period and baste with juice which forms in bowl. After 3 days sear meat in hot butter in heavy kettle, then baste, using about ¾ cup stock, bouillon, or hot water. Cover pot, let meat cook about 1½ hours, or until tender. Baste frequently, turn meat several times during cooking period. When done, remove meat to hot platter and keep hot. Skim fat from cooking liquid, thicken with flour or potato flour mixed with little cold water. Stir and bring to a boil, slice meat on platter, leaving slices in place. Garnish with lettuce or mounds of cooked Brussels sprouts or small glazed carrots. Serve gravy with meat. Makes 6 servings.

PORK LOIN LARDED WITH PRUNES

2¾ pounds pork loin
6 to 8 prunes, partially cooked,
pitted, sliced in halves
½ teaspoon pepper
¼ teaspoon ground ginger
1¼ tablespoons salt
2 tablespoons butter

Prune juice, boiling water
1 stalk celery, sliced
1 small carrot, scraped and
cubed
1 yellow onion, peeled and
sliced
¾ tablespoon flour

RINSE meat, drain, and pat dry. Remove any excess fat. Make deep gashes in pork and insert prune halves in rows in the meat. Rub meat with mixture of seasonings, sear on all sides in hot butter in heavy kettle, baste with little prune juice or boiling water or mixture of these, add celery, carrot, and onion. Cover and cook about 2 hours. Baste several times during cooking period. When done, cut meat away from bone in 1 piece, slice, and place slices back onto bone. Skim fat from pan juice, strain, reheat in kettle, thicken with flour mixed with little cold water. Bring to a boil, boil and stir until slightly thickened. Serve with hot roast. Browned roast potatoes, peas, and applesauce are served with this dish in Swedish homes. Makes 6 servings.

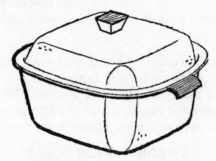

ROYAL POT ROAST

3½ pounds round or rump of beef	1 bay leaf
2 tablespoons butter	15 allspice
½ tablespoon salt	1½ tablespoons light corn syrup
6 peppercorns	2 tablespoons cognac
½ yellow onion, peeled and chopped	2 cups rich milk, stock, or boiling water
3 anchovy fillets, chopped	3 tablespoons flour
¼ cup vinegar	Additional milk

RINSE meat, pat dry. If meat dealer has not rolled it, pound beef with meat hammer, roll into shape, and tie with string. Sear well on all sides in hot butter in heavy kettle, add all seasonings, onion, anchovies, vinegar, bay leaf, syrup, brandy, and part of the milk, stock, or boiling water. Cover kettle, let braise slowly about 3 hours, or until roast is tender. Baste frequently with milk, stock, or boiling water during cooking period. When done, remove from kettle, cut and discard string. Keep meat warm on platter. Stir flour into little cold water, then into hot kettle juices, stir, mix, bring to boiling. Boil and stir until slightly thickened, season if needed. Pour over pot roast, or serve separately. Makes 6 or more servings.

The eight recipes above from THE PRINCESSES COOK BOOK, *by Jenny Åkerström*

Good Food From Sweden by Inga Norberg, is another popular cook book in America. Good flavor and great variety make this one of the best of all foreign cook books for the American home. Here is one of the famous Swedish beef dishes from this book:

BEEF A LA LINDSTROM

1 pound chuck steak	½ cup butter
1 beaten egg yolk	3 cups diced cooked potatoes
1½ cups milk	⅔ cup diced pickled beets
2 teaspoons salt	3 tablespoons pickled beet juice
2 tablespoons chopped peeled onion	½ teaspoon white pepper

CHOP meat very fine, or grind. Mix well with yolk, milk and salt. Brown onion lightly in about ½ tablespoon butter, add to meat mixture, work well with hands to make smooth. Mix potatoes, beets, and beet juice with meat. Shape into flat rounds about 2½ inches across. Fry in butter until well browned on both sides. Makes 6 servings.

SWEDISH MEAT BALLS

These meat balls are sometimes served cold on the smörgåsbord, and are delicious hors d'oeuvres at all times. Or they are served as a hot dish on the smörgåsbord, or as main dish of meal.

1½ pounds chuck beef	½ cup bread crumbs
½ pound lean pork	1 teaspoon pepper
2 tablespoons chopped peeled onion	2 tablespoons salt
	2 tablespoons flour
Butter	Hot water
2 or 3 beaten eggs	½ cup heavy cream

HAVE beef and pork ground together. Brown onion lightly in butter; combine with meat, adding eggs, crumbs, seasoning. Mix thoroughly with hand until smooth. Shape into small balls with spoon dipped in hot water. Brown balls evenly in butter in frying pan. When brown, remove meat balls with slotted spoon to kettle. Make gravy in frying pan using the pan liquid, add about 1 tablespoon butter, 2 tablespoons flour, and stir smoothly. When well blended, add enough hot water to make good gravy consistency, stir and bring to a boil. Pour over meat balls in kettle, let simmer 30 minutes. Add cream a few minutes before serving. Stir gravy around meat balls until cream is hot. Do not boil. Serve hot. Makes 6 servings.

To serve cold, as suggested above, omit gravy, simply brown meat balls, let cool, serve as described.

FISH CROQUETTES

4 tablespoons butter
5 tablespoons flour
1 cup fish stock
¾ cup light cream or milk
1 or 2 beaten egg yolks

1 cup minced cooked fish
½ tablespoon gelatin softened in
   2 tablespoons cold water
Salt, white pepper

MELT butter in saucepan, stir flour in smoothly, and cook 2 minutes; add stock and cream or milk gradually, stirring, cook and stir 5 minutes. Mix yolks in, add fish and softened gelatin. Season. Spread on large buttered platter, cover with waxed paper, let stand until cold. Then divide into 6 to 12 equal portions and form into cork-shaped croquettes.

COATING

1 beaten egg
1 teaspoon olive oil
¼ teaspoon salt

¼ cup bread crumbs
Fat for deep frying
Hot Lobster or Mushroom Sauce

Mix beaten egg with oil and salt. Brush croquettes with egg mixture, then roll in crumbs. Let stand 1 hour. Fry 2 to 4 minutes or to golden brown in deep hot fat (375 to 385 degrees F.). Drain on thick paper towels. Serve hot with hot Lobster or Mushroom Sauce. Makes 6 or more servings.

MOCK OYSTER PUDDING

4 or 5 medium-size salt soft
   herring roes, or fresh roes
⅔ cup bread crumbs
2 cups light cream or milk
6 tablespoons melted butter
5 beaten eggs

½ teaspoon salt
1 teaspoon sugar
Ground nutmeg
Extra ½ tablespoon butter and
   2 tablespoons crumbs for
   casserole

RINSE roes, soak salt roes 3 hours; drain, and chop fine. If fresh roes are used, no need to soak them. Start oven at moderate (350 degrees F.). Mix chopped roes with ⅔ cup crumbs, the milk or cream, melted butter, and eggs. Add salt, sugar, and little nutmeg. Rub 1½-quart baking dish with butter and sprinkle with the 2 tablespoons of crumbs. Pour roe mixture into prepared dish. Bake in moderate oven about 30 to 40 minutes, or until top is golden brown. Serve with hot melted butter. Makes 6 servings.

SWEDISH APPLE SOUP

6 fairly sour apples
1½ cups dried apples, soaked
7 cups boiling water
Peel ¼ lemon
1-inch cinnamon stick
⅔ cup sugar

1½ to 2 tablespoons flour, or
   potato flour
½ cup cold water
3 tablespoons lemon juice, or
   dry white wine, or Madeira

WASH and dry apples, core, cut into sections. Combine with chopped drained apples in large kettle, add boiling water, lemon peel, and cinnamon. Cook 30 minutes, or until apples are tender. Pass through sieve. Reheat soup with sugar added. When boiling, stir flour or potato flour with ½ cup cold water, then into hot soup, stir and boil 10 minutes. Add lemon juice or wine and more sugar if desired. Chill. Serve in chilled bowls with whipped cream and rusks. Makes 6 servings.

SWEDISH POTATO SALAD

1 cup cold sliced cooked
   potatoes
2 cooked beets cut in 1-inch
   strips
1 head lettuce
2 tablespoons drained capers
2 beaten egg yolks

½ teaspoon salt
½ teaspoon dry mustard
1 teaspoon sugar
3 tablespoons oil
1 to 2 tablespoons vinegar
1 tablespoon caper liquid
¼ cup heavy cream

HAVE all ingredients chilled. Combine potatoes, beets, lettuce cut in shreds or strips, and capers in salad bowl. Mix egg yolks with salt, mustard, and sugar. Add oil, vinegar, and caper liquid gradually and mix well. Add cream, stirring. Pour over salad, mix and serve. Makes 6 servings.

The six recipes above from GOOD FOOD FROM SWEDEN, *by Inga Norberg*

Switzerland

The cookery of France, Germany, and Italy is enjoyed in Switzerland in various modifications which the Swiss have long since made their very own. Other Swiss dishes, created with the famed abundant local dairy products, are so well known they have become international favorites. Lesley Blanch, in her refreshing book *Around The World In Eighty Dishes,* describes the customs of Swiss villagers who "at night, sit around the big white-tiled stoves in their scrubbed, polished clean kitchens, and someone sings and someone plays the accordion. And if it is a celebration they will probably eat a special cheese dish, a fondue."

Here is the famous fondue from her book:

★SWISS FONDUE

2 tablespoons butter	1 pound Swiss cheese, coarsely
3 tablespoons flour	grated or shredded
2 cups milk	Salt and pepper
	½ teaspoon grated nutmeg

To make this dish properly, says Miss Blanch, you need a chafing dish or some other table-cooking device. The fondue is made at the table over slow heat. It must be stirred every moment. If you use a flameproof casserole, warm it first by filling it with hot water, let stand, drain, wipe dry. Place over low heat, resting on chafing dish base or on some other cookery device.

Melt butter in dish. Stir in flour smoothly, round and round, with a wooden spoon. Add milk bit by bit, always stirring. When milk-and-flour mixture begins to thicken a little, add cheese. Stir continually. Never leave it alone. When cheese is melted, add salt, pepper, and nutmeg.

In Swiss tradition, the dish is in the middle of the table; guests around the table—each supplied with a plateful of bread cut in 2-inch cubes—spear their bread on a fork and dunk the pieces in the fondue. The first person who loses a chunk of bread, letting it fall into the fondue, has to stand the rest of the table a bottle of wine, the traditional drink with this dish.

This recipe for fondue is enough for 4 to 6 persons.

At American fondue parties coffee and green salad are usually served after the hot fondue.

The recipe above from AROUND THE WORLD IN EIGHTY DISHES, *by Lesley Blanch.*

Many versions of fondue are found in European cook books; the most popular in (untranslated) Swiss-French books calls for ¾ cup dry white wine and 2 tablespoons brandy or kirsch in the recipe. The procedure: slice 1 pound cheese finely into chafing dish or casserole, cover with the wine, let stand several hours. Then place over low heat until cheese melts. Add brandy or kirsch, continue heating few minutes, and serve with pieces of French bread as described. Soft Emmenthaler cheese is used in many Swiss homes for this dish.

Marian Tracy, in *The Peasant Cookbook,* reports on various kinds of Swiss cookery, all dishes of such good flavor that they will be welcomed in American kitchens.

★CHEESE SOUP

1 large onion, peeled and chopped fine	1 cup beef stock or bouillon
2 tablespoons butter	2 cups milk
2 tablespoons flour	1 cup freshly-grated Switzerland Swiss cheese or good Cheddar

SAUTÉ onion in butter in 2-quart kettle, until yellow and tender. Sprinkle with flour, stirring to blend well with butter and onion. Add stock or bouillon slowly, stirring; cook until smooth and thick, stirring continually. Add milk slowly, stirring; let simmer, but do not boil. After 15 minutes' simmering, remove from heat, stir in cheese, letting it melt in the soup. Stir until smooth; serve immediately. Makes 4 servings; or enough for 2 skiers.

★GREEN BEANS WITH POTATOES, SWISS FASHION

2 slices bacon, chopped	¼ pound salt pork, diced and scalded
1 medium-size onion, peeled and chopped	10 small new potatoes, scraped, or 5 larger ones, pared and quartered
1 clove garlic, peeled and chopped	4 garlic-flavored frankfurters, optional
1 pound green beans, slivered or broken in pieces	
1 cup water or bouillon	

SAUTÉ bacon in heavy kettle, pour off most of fat, leaving thin film in kettle. Cook onion and garlic in this, add beans and 1 cup water or bouillon. Bury pieces salt pork in beans, add potatoes, cover, and cook about 1 hour. If frankfurters are added, skin them first, cut into halves, add to kettle when potatoes are added. Makes 4 servings.

★SWISS CHEESE TART

Pastry for 1-crust 9-inch pie	1 cup milk or light cream
½ pound Switzerland Swiss cheese, grated	3 beaten eggs
1 tablespoon flour	Salt and pepper

START oven at moderately hot (400 degrees F.). Line pie dish with pastry, shape decorative edge around plate. Sprinkle cheese with flour, then pour into pie dish. Mix milk or cream with eggs and seasonings. Pour over cheese. Bake 15 minutes in moderately hot oven, reduce heat to moderately slow (300 degrees F.), and bake 30 minutes longer, or until silver knife inserted comes out clean. Serve hot. Makes 4 servings.

★SWISS ONION PIE

This is served as main dish for Sunday supper or a buffet, or for lunch, with salad and coffee. Many variations have been worked out by American home economists. This is a favorite Swiss version.

Pastry for 1-crust 9-inch pie
8 to 10 large onions, peeled and
    thinly sliced
¼ cup butter
¼ cup all-purpose flour, sifted

1 cup sour cream
2 beaten eggs
Salt
1 tablespoon caraway seeds

START oven at hot (450 degrees F.). Line pie dish with pastry and make decorative edge around dish. Sauté onions in butter until tender and glossy but not brown, remove from heat. In a bowl, mix flour slowly with sour cream, eggs, salt, and caraway seeds. Add onions, stir well. Turn into pastry-lined dish. Bake in hot oven 10 minutes. Reduce heat to moderately slow (300 degrees F.) and bake ½ hour longer, or until crust is golden. Makes 4 servings.

SWISS SAUERKRAUT

3 onions, peeled, sliced thin,
    boiled 5 minutes
2 tablespoons bacon drippings or
    other fat
½ pound salt pork in 1 piece,
    boiled 15 minutes
¼ pound bacon in 1 piece,
    boiled 15 minutes
2 pounds sauerkraut

1 cup white wine
Salt
7 or 8 peppercorns
1 bay leaf
1 dozen juniper berries
Boiled potatoes
6 cooked fat garlic frankfurters
3 or 4 cooked knackwurst

SAUTÉ onions in bacon drippings in deep heavy kettle such as Dutch oven. Add salt pork and brown it, add cooked bacon. Rinse sauerkraut, drain, squeeze out with fingers, then pull apart so it is not lumpy. Add sauerkraut to meats and onions. Add wine, a little salt, peppercorns, bay leaf, juniper berries. Cover and simmer 2 or 3 hours. It can't be over-cooked. Serve in warmed casserole with cooked potatoes, frankfurters, and knackwurst on top. Makes 6 to 8 servings.

The five recipes above from THE PEASANT COOKBOOK, *by Marian Tracy*

Yugoslavia

Delicate strudel and other puff-pastry desserts are famous in the Yugoslav cuisine. Balkan favorites such as lamb and mutton dishes, eggplant, rich fried cakes, casserole-cooked fish, and many meat and vegetable mixtures are in the daily menus of the well-to-do Yugoslavs. Lard is used in pastries and casseroles, and its richness is only partly offset by the abundance of fruit and fruit drinks included in the national menu. Prunes, raisins, and prune jam are served with fresh fruits. White cheese, a Balkan variety made with sheep's milk and another prepared in brine, is usually served as an appetizer with small hot pickled peppers, radishes, and scallions. From that abundant source of menus and cookery of seventy-two countries, *The New World Wide Cook Book*, by Pearl V. Metzelthin, here are two favorite Yugoslav dishes.

★DJUVECE
Dish of Meat and Vegetables

4 large onions, peeled and sliced
2 tablespoons lard
4 large potatoes, pared and sliced
4 tomatoes, peeled and sliced
2 large green peppers, seeded and sliced

1 cup rice
3 cups tomato juice
4 lamb or pork chops
1 teaspoon salt
¼ teaspoon pepper
Paprika, optional

BROWN onions in lard, pour ½ of them into greased 3-quart casserole. Place potatoes over onions, add ½ tomatoes. Place green peppers on top of tomatoes. Add remaining onions. Wash rice 3 or 4 times in cold water, drain, pour over vegetables. Add remaining tomato slices and pour tomato juice over all. Sauté chops in pan where onions browned. Turn chops after 2 minutes, giving them only the lightest surface cookery. Sprinkle salt and pepper over both sides of chops, place on top of vegetables and cover casserole.

Start oven at moderate (325 to 350 degrees F.). Bake mixture 30 minutes. Uncover, baste contents with juices in bottom of casserole, cover again and bake 15 minutes. Baste again, leave dish uncovered, and continue baking until chops are slightly browned on top and tender. Sprinkle little paprika over top. Serve very hot with green salad or with lentils in olive oil. Makes 4 servings.

★SOCIVO SALATA
Lentil Salad

2 cups (1 pound) lentils
1 large clove garlic, peeled and
   minced
½ teaspoon salt
½ teaspoon paprika

¾ cup vinegar
¾ cup olive oil
Lettuce leaves, or scooped out
   head of lettuce

WASH lentils, look over, drain. Cover with cold water, let soak 2 or 3 hours. Drain, add water to cover and stand 2 inches above lentils. Bring to a boil, reduce heat to moderate, and let lentils cook covered 2 hours, or until tender. Drain, let cool. Mix dressing of garlic, salt, and paprika, add to vinegar, mix and stir with the oil. Lentils should be dry, each one separate. Toss lightly in dressing, do not stir or mash. Let chill in refrigerator. Serve in lettuce leaves or in large scooped-out head of lettuce, filling the center with the lentil salad. Makes 6 servings.

The two recipes above from THE NEW WORLD WIDE COOK BOOK, *by Pearl V. Metzelthin*

INDEX

Note: This index is alphabetized in word-by-word style, up to the comma; for example,

Cup, champagne
Cup, claret
Cup custard
Cupcakes.

Unfamiliar foreign names of dishes will be found under the countries where they originated, while the better known ones are located in their usual alphabetical sequence.

THE
"Best-of-All"
COOK BOOK

The best recipes from
over 100 world-famous
cook books